# The Photoshop® 7 All-in-One Desk Reference For Dummies®

Cheat Sheet

P9-DBW-999

## Toolbox Shortcuts

| | | |
|---|---|---|
| M | | V |
| Shift + M | | W |
| None | | K |
| None | | Shift + K |
| L | | B |
| Shift + L | | Shift + B |
| Shift + L | | Y |
| C | | Shift + Y |
| J | | G |
| Shift + J | | Shift + G |
| S | | O |
| Shift + S | | Shift + O |
| E | | Shift + O |
| Shift + E | | T |
| Shift + E | | Shift + T |
| R | | Shift + T |
| Shift + R | | Shift + T |

| | | |
|---|---|---|
| Shift + R | | U |
| A | | Shift + U |
| Shift + A | | Shift + U |
| P | | Shift + U |
| Shift + P | | Shift + U |
| None | | Shift + U |
| None | | I |
| None | | Shift + I |
| N | | Shift + I |
| Shift + N | | Z |
| H | | |
| D | | X |
| | | Q |
| | | F |
| Ctrl + Shift + M (⌘ + Shift + M) | | |

## Painting and Editing Tricks

| | PC | Mac |
|---|---|---|
| Increase brush size | ] | ] |
| Decrease brush size | [ | [ |
| Change opacity or flow of tool in 10% increments | 1,…, 9, 0 | 1,…, 9, 0 |
| Paint or edit in straight lines | Click, Shift+click | Click, Shift+click |
| Erase to History | Alt+drag | Option+drag |

*For Dummies®: Bestselling Book Series for Beginners*

## Palette Shortcuts

|  | PC | Mac |
|---|---|---|
| Brushes palette | F5 | F5 |
| Color palette | F6 | F6 |
| Layers palette | F7 | F7 |
| Info palette | F8 | F8 |
| Actions palette | F9 | F9 |

## Navigation Tricks

|  | PC | Mac |
|---|---|---|
| Scroll image | spacebar+drag | spacebar+drag |
| Zoom in | Ctrl+spacebar+click | ⌘+spacebar+click |
| Zoom in and change window size | Ctrl+plus | ⌘+plus |
| Zoom out | Alt+spacebar+click | Option+spacebar+click |
| Zoom out and change window size | Ctrl+minus | ⌘+minus |
| Zoom to 100% | Double-click Zoom tool | Double-click Zoom tool |
| Fit on Screen | Ctrl+0 | ⌘+0 |
| Cycle through all open image windows | Ctrl+Tab | |
| Switch between Photoshop and Finder or other open programs (OS 9) | | ⌘+Tab |

## Selection Tricks

|  | PC | Mac |
|---|---|---|
| Draw straight lines | Alt+click with Lasso tool | Option+click with Lasso tool |
| Add to selection outline | Shift+drag | Shift+drag |
| Deselect specific area | Alt+drag | Option+drag |
| Deselect all but intersected area | Shift+Alt+drag | Shift+Option+drag |
| Deselect entire image | Ctrl+D | ⌘+D |
| Reselect last selection | Ctrl+Shift+D | ⌘+Shift+D |
| Select everything | Ctrl+A | ⌘+A |
| Hide extras | Ctrl+H | ⌘+H |
| Fill selection with foreground color | Alt+Backspace | Option+delete |
| Fill selection with background color | Ctrl+Backspace | ⌘+delete |
| Cut selection | Ctrl+X | ⌘+X |
| Copy selection | Ctrl+C | ⌘+C |
| Paste image last cut or copied | Ctrl+V | ⌘+V |
| Reapply last filter | Ctrl+F | ⌘+F |
| Adjust levels | Ctrl+L | ⌘+L |
| Free Transform | Ctrl+T | ⌘+T |

# Photoshop® 7
## ALL-IN-ONE DESK REFERENCE
# FOR
# DUMMIES®

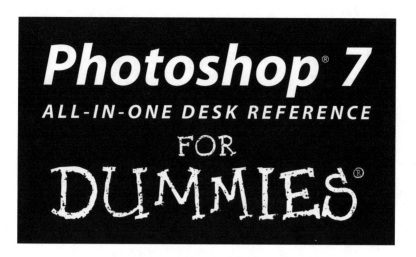

# Photoshop® 7
## ALL-IN-ONE DESK REFERENCE
# FOR
# DUMMIES®

by Barbara Obermeier

with David D. Busch

Wiley Publishing, Inc.

**Photoshop® 7 All-in-One Desk Reference For Dummies®**

Published by
**Wiley Publishing, Inc.**
909 Third Avenue
New York, NY 10022
www.wiley.com

Copyright © 2003 by Wiley Publishing, Inc., Indianapolis, Indiana

Published by Wiley Publishing, Inc., Indianapolis, Indiana

Published simultaneously in Canada

For general information on our other products and services or to obtain technical support, please contact our Customer Care Department within the U.S. at 800-762-2974, outside the U.S. at 317-572-3993, or fax 317-572-4002.

Wiley also publishes its books in a variety of electronic formats. Some content that appears in print may not be available in electronic books.

Library of Congress Control Number: 2002110268

ISBN: 0-7645-1667-1

Manufactured in the United States of America

10 9 8 7 6 5 4 3 2

1B/RS/RS/QS/IN

Wiley Publishing, Inc. is a trademark of Wiley Publishing, Inc.

# About the Author

**Barbara Obermeier** is principal of Obermeier Design, a graphic design studio in Ventura, California. She's coauthor of *Adobe Master Class: Illustrator Illuminated, Photoshop 7 For Dummies,* and *Illustrator 10 For Dummies*. She has contributed as coauthor, technical editor, or layout designer for 16 books. Barb also teaches computer graphics at the University of California, Santa Barbara, and at Ventura College. She hopes to win the California Lottery soon and retire to a remote tropical island without phones or e-mail.

# *About the Contributor*

**David D. Busch** is a two-time Computer Press Association winner and has been demystifying arcane computer and imaging technology since the early 1980s. As a writer, professional photographer, and contributing editor for 10 leading computer magazines, he has more than 70 books and 2,500 articles on computers, image editing, and photography to his credit.

# Dedications

I would like to dedicate this book to Gary, Kylie, and Lucky, who constantly remind me of what's really important in life.

David dedicates this book, as always, to Cathy.

# Authors' Acknowledgments

**Barbara:** I would like to thank my exceptional project editor, Nicole Haims, who has shown unheralded professionalism and patience with this project; Bob Woerner, for politely reminding me of the importance of those nagging little things like deadlines and production schedules; Andy Cummings, who was kind enough to bestow the project to me; David Busch, my contributing author — great writer, great photographer, great guy; David Herman, Technical Editor Extraordinaire; Kim Darosett, Rebecca Senninger, and Nicole Sholly, who made everything I wrote sound better; and all of the hard-working, dedicated production folks at Wiley. A special thanks to Ted Padova, colleague, fellow author, and friend, for always being there to let me vent and whine about being in book hell.

**David:** Nothing's more satisfying than working with someone you can learn from. Thanks, Barb, for showing this Photoshop veteran a few new tricks. And thanks, too, to the multitudes at Wiley who kept this mammoth project on track and on schedule.

## Publisher's Acknowledgments

We're proud of this book; please send us your comments through our online registration form located at www.dummies.com/register/.

Some of the people who helped bring this book to market include the following:

*Acquisitions, Editorial, and Media Development*

**Senior Project Editor:** Nicole Haims

**Acquisitions Editor:** Bob Woerner

**Senior Copy Editor:** Kim Darosett

**Copy Editors:** Rebecca Senninger, Nicole Sholly

**Technical Editor:** David Herman

**Editorial Manager:** Leah Cameron

**Senior Permissions Editor:** Carmen Krikorian

**Media Development Manager:** Laura VanWinkle

**Media Development Supervisor:** Richard Graves

**Editorial Assistant:** Amanda Foxworth

**Cartoons: Rich Tennant,** www.the5thwave.com

*Production*

**Project Coordinator:** Nancee Reeves

**Layout and Graphics:** Melissa Auciello-Brogan, Beth Brooks, Joyce Haughey, Gabriele McCann, Marie Kristine Parial-Leonardo, Jacque Schneider, Mary J. Virgin

**Proofreaders:** Laura Albert, Andy Hollandbeck, Susan Moritz, Sossity R. Smith, Charles Spencer

**Indexer:** Sharon Hilgenberg

*Special Help:* Daniela Richardson, Art Direction Manager, Wiley Publishing, Inc.

*Publishing and Editorial for Technology Dummies*

**Richard Swadley,** Vice President and Executive Group Publisher

**Andy Cummings,** Vice President and Publisher

**Mary C. Corder,** Editorial Director

*Publishing for Consumer Dummies*

**Diane Graves Steele,** Vice President and Publisher

**Joyce Pepple,** Acquisitions Director

*Composition Services*

**Gerry Fahey,** Vice President of Production Services

**Debbie Stailey,** Director of Composition Services

# Contents at a Glance

# Table of Contents

# *Book VI: Channels and Masks*.................................**435**

# Introduction

There's a reason why Photoshop is the world's industry standard in image-editing software. The depth and breadth of the program is unheralded. Photoshop immediately sucks you in with its easy-to-use interface and powerful tools and commands. It is so feature rich that you soon begin to lose track of time and start blowing off your commitments just to try one more thing. And just when you think you've finally explored every nook and cranny and mastered the program, you suddenly read a tip in a book or magazine that enlightens you about something you didn't know. Or even more likely, you stumble upon some great effect while working on a late-night project. That's the beauty of Photoshop. It's the program that just keeps giving.

The depth and breadth of Photoshop has downsides, too, of course. You must make a major time commitment and invest much effort to master it — hence the large number of books written on the program. Walk into your neighborhood bookstore or type *Photoshop* in the Search field at any online bookseller's site, and you'll see a barrage of choices. Some books are general reference books, some are targeted toward the novice user, and others focus on a specific mission, such as color management or restoration and retouching.

## About This Book

This book is written for the person who has a good grasp of using a computer and navigating the operating system and at least a cursory knowledge of Photoshop. It is intended to be a comprehensive reference book that you can read cover to cover or reach for when you're looking for specific information about a particular task.

Wherever I can, I sneak in a useful tip or an interesting technique to help you put Photoshop to work for your project needs.

## Numbered steps

When you see a sequence of triangles just before a section heading, you know that the section you're about to read contains a numbered sequence that shows you how to complete a specific task. Steps appear in an easy-to-follow, two-column format, along with plenty of images to help you out.

If you see a black box around a step number, it indicates that there is an accompanying figure for that step. For example, if the 2 in Step 2 has a black box around it, there is a figure that corresponds with that step. The figure itself will have a numbered callout referencing the step number.

## Putting It Together

Sometimes, knowing *how* to use a tool doesn't necessarily mean that you know *what* to do with it. That's why this book contains several exercises that help you make a connection between the multiple Photoshop tools at your disposal and the very specific task you need to accomplish. Want to get the red out of a subject's eyes or create a collage? Just check out the Putting-It-Together sections in Books III through X. These sections present info in easy-to-follow numbered steps, in a hands-on style, building on what's presented in the chapter so that you can go to the next level, put concepts to work, and move on to the next task.

# What's in This Book

This book is broken down into minibooks, each covering a general topic. Each minibook contains several chapters, each covering a more specific topic under the general one. Each chapter is then divided into sections, and some of those sections have subsections. I'm sure you get the picture.

You can read the book from front to back, or you can dive right into the minibook or chapter of your choice. Either way works just fine. Anytime a concept is mentioned that isn't covered in depth in that chapter, you'll find a cross-reference to another book and chapter where you'll find all the details. If you're looking for something specific, check out either the Table of Contents or the index.

The Cheat Sheet at the beginning of the book helps you remember all the shortcuts you'll use most often. Tear it out, tape it to your monitor, and don't forget to say "Thanks." You're welcome.

And finally, I've got pictures. Lots of them. And many of these pictures have callouts that point to specific steps or identify important concepts, buttons, tools, or options. With a program like Photoshop, an image often speaks louder than words.

This book contains ten minibooks. The following sections offer a quick synopsis of what each book contains.

## Book I: Photoshop Fundamentals

Ready to get your feet wet with the basics of Photoshop? Head to Book I. Here's where you get familiar with the Photoshop environment — the desktop, the menus, and the palettes. I also briefly introduce the tools and explain what each one does.

In this book, I cover how to get started on Photoshop and how to view and navigate your image window. Here's where I give you all the important details of the new File Browser palette and also how to customize your workspace and preference settings.

Finally, I go into the bare basics of printing, and then how to save files and close Photoshop.

## Book II: Image Essentials

This book covers all those nitpicky — but critical — details about images, such as size, resolution, pixel dimension, image mode, and file format. Turn to this book to find out how to safely resize your image without causing undue damage.

You can also find out how to crop images and increase their canvas size. In addition, I breeze through basic color theory and get you started using and managing color.

But wait, there's more. I give you the lowdown on the History palette and brushing and erasing to history. And, if that's not enough, I throw in a chapter on applying annotations and notes to your image and using and creating actions for enhanced productivity.

## Book III: Selections

This important book gives you all the juicy details and techniques on creating and modifying selections and paths. You find out about each of the selection tools and also the powerful — albeit sometimes unruly — Pen tool and its accompanying Paths palette.

## Book IV: Painting, Drawing, and Typing

If you want to know about the drawing and painting tools, this is the book for you. Here I cover the Brush and Pencil tools, along with the revamped and enhanced Brushes palette. I also show you how to create vector shapes by using the shape tools, and how to fill and stroke selections.

Head to this book to find out how to create both gradients and patterns and, last but not least, become familiar with the type tools and how to use them to create and edit both standard type and type with special effects.

## Book V: Working with Layers

Layers are an integral component in a Photoshop image, and Book V is where I explain them. In this book, you discover how to create and edit layers and how to use multiple images to create a multilayered composite image. I also introduce you to the various ways that you can manage layers for maximum efficiency. Finally, I show you how to enhance your layers by applying different blend modes, opacity settings, layer styles, styles, and clipping groups.

## Book VI: Channels and Masks

This book gives you all the how-tos you need to work with channels and masks. I show you how to save and edit selections as alpha channels so that you can reload them later. And I show you how to work with the various kinds of masks — quick masks, layer masks, and channel masks — and how you can use each to select difficult elements. I also cover other masking techniques, such as erasing and using the Color Range command.

## Book VII: Filters and Distortions

I filled this book with tons of handy tips and techniques on using filters to correct your images to make them sharper, blurrier, cleaner, and smoother — whatever fits your fancy. You also find out how to use filters to give your image a certain special effect, such as a deckled edge or water droplets. Then I introduce the Liquify command so that you can see the wonder of its distortion tools — and how they can turn your image into digital taffy.

## Book VIII: Retouching and Restoration

Everything you need to know about color correction or color enhancement can be found in Book VIII — getting rid of colorcasts, improving contrast and saturation, remapping, and replacing colors.

In addition, I've included a chapter on using the focus and toning tools to manually lighten, darken, smooth, soften, and sharpen areas of your image. And you get to see how you can use the Clone Stamp tool and the new Healing Brush and Patch tools to fix flaws and imperfections in your images, making them good as new.

## Book IX: Photoshop and the Web

This book gives you the lowdown on preparing your images for the Web. Find out how to optimize your images for maximum quality and quick download times. You also find information on slicing your images and creating a photo gallery that you can easily post on the Web. I show you where Photoshop comes to an end with its Web-friendly tools and where ImageReady then picks up the ball.

## Book X: Photoshop and Print

If you need to get the scoop on how to prep your images for print, this is the book you need to check out. Here you find the details on how to get the right resolution, image mode, and file format for various applications. You also discover how to set up both process and spot color separations. If you also work with other programs, I provide a chapter on how Photoshop plays nicely with other programs. And, for good measure, I throw in a chapter on how to create contact sheets and picture packages from your digital masterpieces.

## Appendix A: Working with Digital Cameras and Scanners

If you own either a digital camera or a scanner, be sure to take a gander at Appendix A. You'll find lots of juicy tidbits on prepping your images for scanning and then cleaning them up afterward. I've also included some useful information on getting images from your camera into Photoshop.

### Appendix B: A Visual Reference of Photoshop Tools

If you're like me, you're probably reeling from all the tools and options. Which one does what? How do you know which to choose? Check out Appendix B for a visual reference that shows you each of the tools — as well as what the tools do. How's that for handy?

### Color Insert

Trying to illustrate the powers of Photoshop without showing some images in full, living color would be about as useful as if I handed you a broken umbrella on a rainy day. The 16-page color insert does just that, so don't miss it.

## Conventions Used in This Book

You'll find that this book is cross-platform. Windows commands are given first, followed by Mac commands in parentheses, like this:

> Press Enter (or Return on the Mac) to begin a new line.

And occasionally, text will be specific to one platform or another. You'll find that figures are divided into both platforms as well.

Often the commands given involve using the keyboard along with the mouse. For example, "Press Shift while dragging with the Rectangular Marquee tool to create a square," or "Alt+click (Option+click) on the eyeball to redisplay all layers."

When you see a command arrow (⇨) in the text, it indicates that you should select a command from the menu bar. For example, "choose Edit⇨Define Custom Shape" means to click the Edit menu and then choose the Define Custom Shape option.

While this book has been written using Photoshop 7, you can still glean valuable info if you're using Version 5 or 6 . You may just have to poke around a little more to find a tool or option that's moved, and, of course, the topics covering new features won't be applicable. But hey, when you see the cool Version 7 features, you may get the impetus you need to go out and upgrade!

## Icons Used in This Book

While perusing this book, you'll notice some icons beckoning you for your attention. Don't ignore them; embrace them! These icons point out fun, useful, and memorable tidbits about Photoshop, plus facts you'd be unwise to ignore.

 This icon indicates information that will make your Photoshop experience easier. It also gives you an icebreaker at your next cocktail party. Whipping out, "Did you know that pressing the bracket keys will enlarge or shrink your brush tip?" is bound to make you the center of conversation.

This icon is a reminder of things that I've already mentioned and want to *gently* re-emphasize. Or I might be pointing out things that I want you to take note of in your future Photoshop excursions.

 The little bomb icon is a red flag. Heed these warnings, or else Photoshop may show its ugly side.

## Where to Go from Here

If you want your voice to be heard, you can contact the publisher or authors of the *For Dummies* books by visiting the publisher's Web site at www.dummies.com, sending an e-mail to customer@wiley.com, or sending snail mail to Wiley Publishing, Inc., 10475 Crosspoint Boulevard, Indianapolis, IN 46256.

And, of course, the very next place to go is to the section of this book that covers your favorite topic. Go ahead and dive right in.

# Book I

# Photoshop Fundamentals

The 5th Wave          By Rich Tennant

Okay, enlarge the chicken bone by 900 percent and attach it to an e-mail to the museum saying, "Getting close...send more money."

# Examining the Photoshop Environment

1

As environments go, Photoshop's working space is pretty cool: as inviting as a landscaped backyard and not nearly as likely to work you into a sweat. Each of Photoshop's many tools is custom-designed for a specific chore and chock full of more options than a Swiss Army knife. When you're familiar with your surroundings, you'll be eager to make like Monet in his garden, surrounded by palettes, brushes, buckets of paint, and swatches of color, ready to tackle the canvas in front of you.

## Dissecting Dialog Box Jargon

In many respects, the Photoshop dialog boxes are very much like the dialog boxes you find in all other Windows and Mac applications. You'll find text boxes with space to type in information (such as the name of a new layer, or the new width or height you want to apply to a resized document), *pop-up menus* of parameters you can choose from (such as whether you want the width and height expressed in pixels, inches, millimeters, picas, or some other unit of measurement), and controls like *sliders* that can be used to specify amounts (in percentages, pixels, or degrees) over a continuous range.

 Some dialog boxes are very complex and perform multiple tasks. However, even though Photoshop's dialog boxes perform a variety of functions, the controls in them are standardized and familiar enough that once you know how to use a few dialog boxes, you can use them all.

Photoshop dialog boxes, particularly filter dialog boxes, include preview windows so that you can check out the effects of your settings before clicking the OK button. The Photoshop Variations dialog box is one of the most complex of these. It includes a whole clutch of thumbnail images that show you the current image, plus several different renditions.

Dialog boxes generally appear when you choose a menu item followed by an ellipsis, such as Load Selection . . . . The ellipsis is your tip-off that the menu selection needs additional information to complete the operation. Dialog boxes can also pop up at other times, such as when you double-click the Quick Mask icon in the Tool palette to produce the Quick Mask Options dialog box, or double-click the Adobe Online icon at the top of the Tool palette.

If you know how to work with other applications, you already know how to use most of the controls you'll find in Photoshop dialog boxes. These include

- ✔ **Pop-up menus:** Drop-down lists of choices that have been preselected for you.

- ✔ **Spin buttons:** These are up-/down-arrow buttons that let you increase or decrease values quickly by clicking them.

- ✔ **Text boxes:** Areas in which you can type values of your own choosing.

- ✔ **Radio buttons:** A set of mutually-exclusive buttons; you can select only one of them, such as the Inside, Center, or Outside buttons, which tell the Stroke dialog box where to apply the stroke.

- ✔ **Check boxes:** Boxes that can be selected or deselected to turn a feature on or off, independently of other features.

- ✔ **Slider controls:** Used to specify any one of a continuous range of values.

- ✔ **Nested dialog boxes:** Some dialog boxes include a button with text followed by an ellipsis, indicating that when you click the button, a new, sub-dialog box will appear.

- ✔ **Action buttons:** Marked with text like OK or Cancel, you click these buttons to activate or cancel an operation.

## Playing with Palettes

Many image-oriented programs use palettes of a sort, and Photoshop itself has had palettes since version 1.0, released in January of 1990. However, since Photoshop 3.0, the program has used a novel way of working with palettes. Instead of stand-alone windows, Photoshop uses grouped, tabbed palettes, which overlap each other in groups of two or three (or more, if you rearrange them yourself). To access a palette that falls behind the one that's displayed on top, click the palette's tab.

Palettes operate a little like dialog boxes and may contain sliders, buttons, pop-up menus, options menus (as shown in Figure 1-1), and other controls. You'll also find icons at the bottom of many palettes. For example, at the base of the Layers palette are icons that let you create a new layer, add a layer style, or trash a layer that you no longer want.

Some palettes can change like chameleons. The Actions palette can be displayed in Button mode, in which you see only the name of each set of procedures you might want to invoke. Or you can flip the Actions palette to Normal mode, in which each of the procedures in the action is listed separately for you to view or edit.

**Figure 1-1**

Most palettes include options for defining sets of parameters (called *presets*) that you can store for reuse at any time.

Here's how to open, close, and otherwise manipulate a palette group from the Window menu:

- ✔ **To bring a palette to the front of its group:** Select the palette group from the Window menu to bring it to the front of its group. When the palette group is open, the palette that's visible is the palette that has a check mark next to it in the Window menu. In this mode, you can only select one palette in any group because only one tab in a group can be on top at one time.

- ✔ **To move a palette out of its group:** Grab the palette's tab and drag to its new location, such as another group, the Palette Well, or the desktop. If you move the palettes out of their groups or drag them onto the desktop so they stand alone, any of them so positioned can be check marked.

- ✔ **To hide a palette:** Click a check-marked palette in the Window menu.

- ✔ **To access a palette from the desktop:** Find its group and click the palette's tab to bring it to the front.

Here are some palette-manipulation tips:

- ✔ **Save space by keeping palettes in groups.** You can drag all the palettes in a group by dragging the group's title bar. Access an individual palette by clicking its tab to bring it to the front. As a result, several palettes occupy only the screen space required by one.

- ✔ **Use the Window menu if you can't find a palette.** If you can't find a palette or suspect that it's been hidden, access the View menu and click the palette's name to make it visible or to bring it to the top of its group.

✔ **Rearrange groups by dragging.** If you'd like to move a palette to another group or to display it in your workspace as a stand-alone palette, grab its tab and drag. Release the mouse button where you'd like the palette to reside in the workspace, or in the destination palette group.

✔ **Customize, customize, customize.** After you've used Photoshop for a while, creating your own custom palette groups based on the palettes you use can be a real time saver. For example, if you don't use the Paths palette constantly, but can't live without the Actions palette, you can drag the Paths palette to another group or the Palette Well and put the Actions palette in the same group as the mission-critical Layers and Channels palettes.

✔ **Minimize palettes to save even more space, but beware.** You can double-click a palette's title bar (or tab if you're using the Mac OS) to shrink the palette or palette group down to its title bar and tabs alone. If you use the Mac OS, double-clicking the title bar invokes Window Shade mode and hides the tabs, leaving only the title bar. (Because the palette contains no title, it is a bit difficult to differentiate from other tab-less palettes you might have shrunk — not a good idea in most cases.)

✔ **Restore default palette locations whenever you need a change.** If you decide you don't like the way you've arranged your palettes, you can choose Window⇨Workspace⇨ Reset Palette Locations to return them to the default configuration they had when Photoshop was installed.

# Launching Photoshop and Customizing the Desktop

You start Photoshop just as you launch any other program under Windows or the Mac OS. As with other programs, you can choose the method you find the easiest and most convenient. Here's a quick summary of your options.

✔ **Launch from the Windows Start menu or Macintosh Apple menu.** Windows PCs and Macs using Mac OS 9 or earlier have handy pop-up (or drop-down) menus that include your most frequently used applications. Just locate the program in the menu and click it.

✔ **Launch from the Windows taskbar or Macintosh OS X Dock.** You may have inserted icons for your *really* mission-critical programs in these readily accessible launching bars, usually found at the bottom of your screen. Click the Photoshop icon to start.

✔ **Launch Photoshop by double-clicking a shortcut or alias icon placed on your desktop.**

✔ **Double-click an image file associated with Photoshop.** When you installed Photoshop, the setup program lets you specify which type of common image file types (.TIF, .PSD, .PCX, and so forth) you wanted to be associated with (or linked to, for launching purposes) Photoshop, ImageReady, or neither. Double-clicking an icon, shortcut, or alias representing the file type you chose launches Photoshop.

When you launch Photoshop, the desktop workspace, shown in Figure 1-2, appears. Like the real-world desktop where your keyboard and display reside, the Photoshop desktop is a place for you to put all the documents you're working with.

**Figure 1-2**

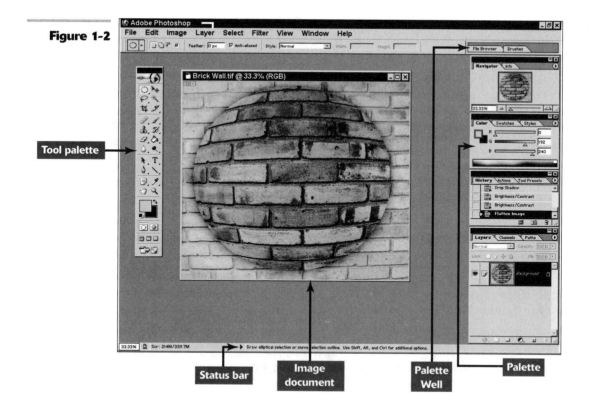

The desktop consists of a main window, called the *application window* if you're using Windows (and called the *document window* if you're using the Mac OS), which takes up the majority of your screen by default. Within the main window, you see a variety of other windows and boxes. For example, there's a window called the *image document window,* which enables you to view and edit images.

The main window contains the stuff you're probably used to seeing in other programs — a title bar at the top of the window, a status bar at the bottom (unless you have it turned off), and menus to help you arrange your tools and get important information about your image files. But the arrangement of tools may be a little unfamiliar to you. Photoshop arranges tools into groups called *palettes.*

 In Windows, gray borders mark the left and right edges of the Photoshop window — even if the main application window's contents fill up more than your screen can show.

Your virtual desktop can become as cluttered as the real thing, but Adobe has built in some special features (located in the Windows menu, which I discuss later in this chapter) that let you keep stuff close at hand but tuck things away so they're not constantly underfoot (or undermouse, so to speak). When you've arranged your desktop just as you like it for a specific project, you can even save the desktop so you can reuse it whenever you begin work on that project.

## Using Photoshop with two monitors

If you're serious about your graphics work, you may consider purchasing a second monitor (and video card if you don't own a *two head* video card that can operate a second display) to attach to your main computer system. A second monitor gives you additional monitor space to display multiple large image files and palettes of Photoshop tools. I often move stuff from screen to screen to maximize the area on my main screen for an image I'm working on.

If you have a dual-monitor setup, you can even move components from one display screen to another. Whether you're using Mac or Windows machines, whenever you want to use a tool that appears on your secondary screen, you just slide the mouse over to the alternate display and click.

In order to use a second monitor, your computer must have Windows 2000 or later installed. Or you should be running any recent Mac OS.

Every document you ever work on appears within the confines of this window and can't leave its borders. You can move around some other components, such as the various palettes and the Options bar, both inside and outside the Photoshop application window.

 Just as you can with most windows in other programs, you can close, minimize, and restore the main Photoshop window.

 The Photoshop window hides one cool secret for Windows users: If you double-click anywhere in the gray empty area, the Open dialog box pops up so you can navigate to a file you want to work on without wandering up to the File menu or using the Ctrl+O (⌘+O on the Mac) keyboard shortcut.

The following sections show you how to customize the main working area so that you can get to work.

### Setting display settings with the Window menu

The Window menu, shown in Figure 1-3, controls the display of palettes and some other elements of the Photoshop working area. It shows a list of palette groups, with each palette group divided from the others by a separator line. (Find out more about maneuvering palettes earlier in this chapter.)

The top two entries in the Window menu enable you to control image display, as well as help you manage your workspaces. In Window⇨Documents, you can choose any of the open documents or tell Photoshop to overlap (cascade), tile (butt them edge to edge), or close all open documents.

In the Window⇨Workspace menu, you can save your current desktop arrangement, load a stored arrangement, or reset your palette locations. For step-by-step instructions, see Chapter 6 in this book.

**Figure 1-3**

## Setting up the status bar

By default, the status bar appears at the bottom of the Photoshop working area in Windows. (Refer to Figure 1-2.) If you're using the Mac OS, each document window has its own status bar.

You can turn the status bar on or off by selecting it or deselecting it in the Windows menu.

Many people tend to associate status with wealth, so I don't really think there's a reason not to accept the free wealth of information that the status bar offers:

✔ At the far left is a box that displays an active image's current zoom level (such as 66.67 percent). The zoom level is also shown in the title bar of the document itself.

 If you installed Photoshop to a networked computer and you've activated the workgroup features, which enable file sharing and other perks, you see the icon for the Workgroup Services pop-up menu just to the right of the zoom info box.

✔ Next is the file and image information display area, which, by default, shows the document size information. You can customize this area to display other information.

✔ Because the good people at Adobe know just how complex a program Photoshop is, on the far right side of the status bar you see a description of the currently selected tool's functions, as well as information on how to select additional options for that tool.

 Although each Macintosh document includes its own status bar, all the bars for all the open documents show the same category of information. That is, if you change the status bar of one image to display scratch sizes, all the status bars of the other document images switch to display scratch sizes, as well.

Because Photoshop files can get pretty hefty in size, your status bar shows the file size of the active image by default. To display other types of information, click the right-pointing arrow in the status bar and select one of the following options from the menu that pops up:

✔ **Document Size:** When you select this option, Photoshop displays two numbers to approximate the size of the image. The first number shows you the size of the file if you were to combine all the layers into one and save it to your hard drive. The number on the right shows the full size of the image — including all the components of the image. You'll want this option active when you need to keep track of how large your image is.

✔ **Document Profile:** When you select this option, the status bar displays the name of the color profile used by the image. You probably won't use this option unless you have a need to know the profiles of all the open documents while making complex color corrections. You can find more information about profiles in Book II, Chapter 3.

✔ **Document Dimensions:** When you select this option, the status bar shows you the size of the image by using the default measurement increment you've set in Photoshop's preferences (pixels, inches, picas, and so on). You might need this for instant reference to the physical dimensions of your open files. For information on Photoshop's preferences, see Chapter 6 in this book.

✔ **Scratch Sizes:** *Scratch space* is the virtual memory that's been set aside on your hard drive to simulate RAM and make editing large files easier. Enabling this option shows two measurements for an active image. The amount of real memory and virtual memory used by all open images appears on the left. On the right, you see the total amount of RAM available for working with images. Photoshop needs a lot more memory and disk space to work on an image while it's open, and that's what's shown by the Scratch Sizes display, as opposed to the Document Size display that shows only the file size of the document itself.

✔ **Efficiency:** This indicator helps you gauge whether you really have enough RAM to perform a task. It shows the percentage of time Photoshop spends actually working on an operation, compared to the time it must spend reading or writing image information to or from your hard disk. If the value dips below 100% most of the time, you need to allocate more memory to Photoshop. For more information on parceling out RAM, see Chapter 6 in this book.

✔ **Current Tool:** This option shows you the name of the tool that's currently being used.

# Working with Your First Photoshop File

So many menus, so little time! The second you begin working with Photoshop, you may be convinced that Adobe's flagship image editor has somewhere on the order of 8,192 different menu selections for you to choose from. In truth, there are only about 530 separate menu items, including some that are duplicated. That figure doesn't count the 100 or so entries for filter plug-ins (which can expand alarmingly as you add third-party goodies). However, even 500-plus menu items are considerably more than you'll find in the most ambitious restaurants. Basically, if you want to do something in Photoshop, you need to use the menu bar. The menu bar consists of nine main entries, each of which holds a dozen or more nested sub-entries and sub-sub-entries that cascade into view as you drag the mouse down the list. If you're using the Mac OS, the Photoshop menu bar may share space with Finder components, such as the Apple menu or the Clock.

You'll find pop-up menus everywhere, next to icons on the Options bar, on menus that fly out from palettes, in the status bar, and especially in the menu bar. You can find detailed descriptions of the menus and how to use them elsewhere in this book, but here's a summary of what you can find and where you can find it.

 Photoshop also helps you by providing context sensitive menus, which change their listings depending on what you're doing. You don't see options you don't need and do see options appropriate to what you're working on.

## Opening and saving files

The File menu offers a cornucopia of file options, from opening new images and opening saved files to browsing existing files, closing files, and saving files. The first layer of file options is shown in Figure 1-4.

You can save a file optimized for the Web, import and export special file types, grab an image from your scanner or digital camera, and apply automated tasks to certain files or batches of files. There's an entry for retrieving specialized information you've stored about a file.

 If you installed Photoshop on a network and have workgroups features on, you can check files in and out of a workgroup server.

You'll find the page setup, preview, and printing commands in the File menu, and you can jump to ImageReady from here. There's even an entry for leaving Photoshop entirely. To open a file, choose File⇨Open and navigate to the folder containing the file you want to open. Select the file and click OK to open it.

For detailed instructions on all the many different ways you can open files, see Chapter 3 in this book.

**Figure 1-4**

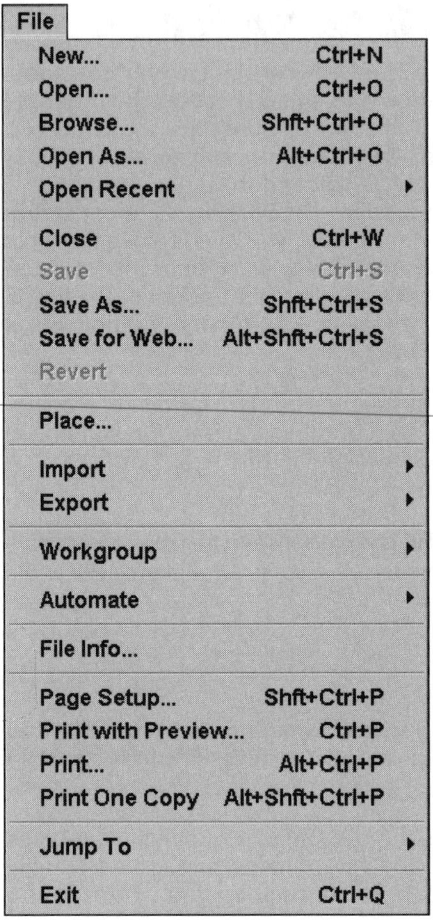

| File | |
|---|---|
| New... | Ctrl+N |
| Open... | Ctrl+O |
| Browse... | Shft+Ctrl+O |
| Open As... | Alt+Ctrl+O |
| Open Recent | ▶ |
| Close | Ctrl+W |
| Save | Ctrl+S |
| Save As... | Shft+Ctrl+S |
| Save for Web... | Alt+Shft+Ctrl+S |
| Revert | |
| Place... | |
| Import | ▶ |
| Export | ▶ |
| Workgroup | ▶ |
| Automate | ▶ |
| File Info... | |
| Page Setup... | Shft+Ctrl+P |
| Print with Preview... | Ctrl+P |
| Print... | Alt+Ctrl+P |
| Print One Copy | Alt+Shft+Ctrl+P |
| Jump To | ▶ |
| Exit | Ctrl+Q |

## Making selections

Selections let you work with only part of an image. You can choose all of a layer or only portions of a layer that you select with one of the selection tools, such as the Marquee or Magic Wand. The Select menu (shown in Figure 1-5) is short and sweet, but the capability and control the menu unleashes are nothing short of an image-editing miracle.

Understanding selections is such an important cornerstone to your Photoshop knowledge that I devote an entire book (Book III) to showing you how to use them.

**Figure 1-5**

I describe the four Selection menu options in Table 1-1.

**TABLE 1-1: SELECTION MENU OPTIONS**

| Menu Option | What It Lets You Do | Windows Keyboard Shortcut | Mac Keyboard Shortcut |
|---|---|---|---|
| All | Select a layer (and everything in the layer). | Ctrl+A | ⌘+A |
| Deselect | Undo (or *deselect*) a selection. | Ctrl+D | ⌘+D |
| Inverse | Reverse a selection so that everything that wasn't selected is now selected (and vice versa). | Shift+Ctrl+I | Shift+⌘+I |
| Reselect | Re-create your most recent selection. | Shift+Ctrl+D | Shift+⌘+D |
| Grow | Expand or contract a selection. | None | None |
| Feather | Blend a selection's edges into the surrounding area. | Alt+Ctrl+D | Option+⌘+D |
| Select Similar | Select similar pixels that aren't adjacent to those you've already selected. | None | None |
| Color Range | Select areas based only on a range of pixel colors (rather than on both brightness and color range). | None | None |
| Transform Selection | Resize and reshape a selection by dragging handles. | None | None |

Another important capability is the option of saving selections and loading them later for reuse. As you find out in Book VI, not only can you load a selection you've already made, but you can also subtract the saved selection from another selection or add it to another new or saved selection.

To save a selection, choose Select⇨Save Selection. In the Save Selection dialog box that appears, type a name for the selection and click OK.

### Making simple image edits

The Edit menu, shown in Figure 1-6, contains tools that enable you to cut, copy, or paste image selections in several different ways. You can fill selections or *stroke* their outlines (create a line along their edges); and you can use this menu to rotate, resize, distort, or perform other *transformations* (changes in size or shape) on your selections. You can undo the change you made in Photoshop, fade a filter, check your spelling, or find and replace text.

**Figure 1-6**

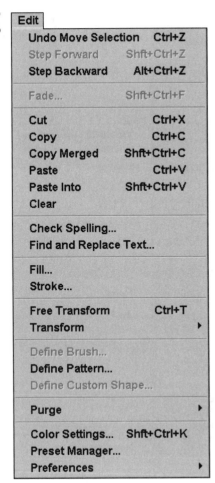

The Edit menu also offers some choices that may not logically belong here but which don't fit anywhere else. For example, you can define brushes, patterns, and shapes. You can clear the Photoshop clipboard, dump Photoshop's list of the changes you've made, and manage your color settings and tool presets. You also access Photoshop's preferences (your personal settings for things like memory, how cursors look, and so on) from the Edit menu. You find out more about preferences in Chapter 6 in this book.

### Making changes by using the Image menu

You'd think the Image menu (shown in Figure 1-7) might have something to do with making changes to an image document as a whole, wouldn't you? In practice, some of the entries you'll find here do apply to the whole document, but others apply only to particular layers or selections.

**Figure 1-7**

For example, the Mode menu item allows you to change an entire image from grayscale to color. The Duplicate, Image Size, Canvas Size, Rotate Canvas, Crop, and Trim selections all change the whole document in some way. (Their functions are obvious from their names, except for Trim, which removes pixels from the edge of an image.)

On the other hand, the changes wrought from the Adjustments submenu *can't* be applied to an entire image if the document has more than one layer. Adjustments such as Color Balance, Hue/Saturation, or Brightness/Contrast work only with a single layer or a selection on that layer.

One menu option, Histogram, doesn't do anything at all, other than present some information about the image. Even so, you'll find yourself turning to the Image menu more often than many of the other menus, partially because it's so useful, and partially because, for some reason, many of the options don't have keyboard shortcuts that let you bypass the menu.

### Creating layers

Layers give you a way of stacking portions of an image — overlay style — on top of one another so that you can work on individual pieces separately. Then, when you're satisfied with your changes, you can combine the changes into a final image.

Photoshop's layers feature, which gets an entire book of its own (Book V), is so useful it's hard to imagine that it hasn't always been present in Photoshop. (Thank your lucky stars if you didn't have to use versions of Photoshop that preceded version 3.0.) Those of us who worked with Photoshop 2.5 and earlier still wake up from nightmares in which a floating selection (the predecessor to the layer feature) permanently merged with the background because of an ill-timed sneeze.

The Layer menu in Photoshop 7 (shown in Figure 1-8) is the latest refinement of the layers concept. You'll find choices that let you create new and duplicate layers, delete one or several layers, change layer properties (such as a layer's name), or add special features such as drop shadows or beveled edges to objects in a layer. You can also create special kinds of layers that are used to make adjustments or mask out portions of an image. The menu has selections for changing the order of the layers (moving a specific layer to the front or top of the stack, and so on) and grouping layers together so that you can treat them as a set.

Layers can also be merged down, combined with all other visible layers, or flattened into one single-layer image. Although merging your layers makes the file smaller, after you close the file, flattening is irreversible. It's always a good idea to store an unflattened version of a file in case you want to make more changes later on.

Photoshop has *two* key layer facilities, the Layer menu and the Layers palette. Some of their functions are duplicated, but some are not, so make sure you're using both of them. You find out the distinctions in Book V.

### Applying filters

A *filter* is an effect that changes an entire layer, channel, or selection. Some common filters include the Blur and Sharpen filters as well as distortion filters like Spherize. The Filter menu, shown in Figure 1-9, consists almost entirely of cascading categories of image-transmogrifying plug-ins that you can wade through to find that the perfect effect to apply to an image or selection. Book VII has everything you need to know about filters.

After you apply a filter, Photoshop moves the filter to the top of the Filter menu for easy accessibility in case you want to reapply the filter by using the exact same settings.

To choose the last filter you used, use the Ctrl+F (⌘+F on the Mac) keyboard shortcut.

The Extract, Liquify, and Pattern Maker facilities are more like miniprograms than filters. The rest of the Filter menu consists of 13 different filter categories, each containing four to a dozen or more options:

✔ Single-step filters are pretty basic to use but can make a huge impact on an image. These include simple filters like the Blur, Facet, and Clouds filters. Just click the filter to apply it; there are no options to choose.

✔ Dialog box-based filters let you choose options galore. These filters come complete with preview windows, buttons, slider controls, and menus. You can distort, pixelate, sharpen, blur, apply textures, and perform other functions with these filters.

 If you've installed additional filters from third parties, Photoshop lists them at the very bottom of the Filter menu. You can find third-party filters at Web sites like `www.alienskin.com`, `www.andromeda.com`, and `www.autofx.com`.

**Figure 1-8**

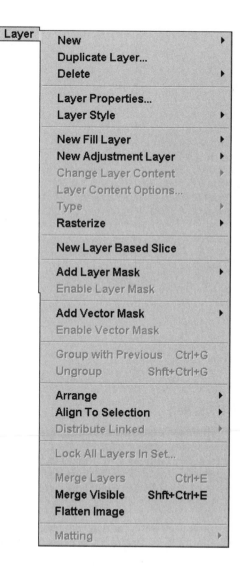

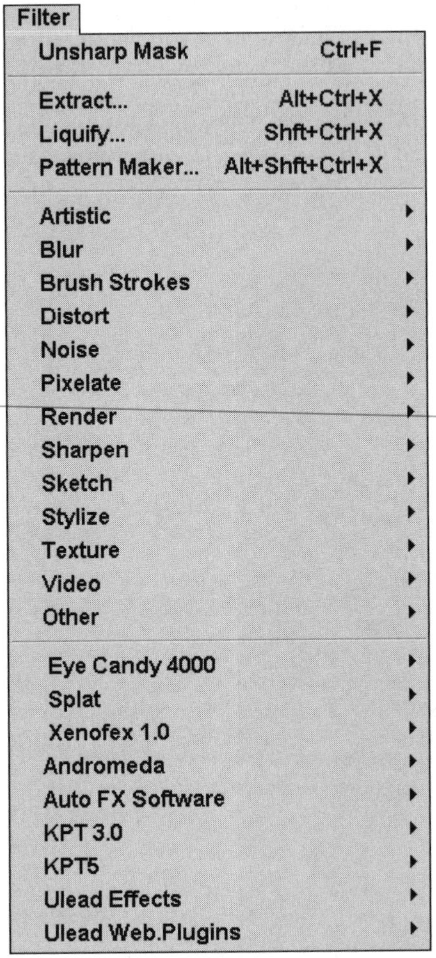

**Figure 1-9**

| Filter | |
|---|---|
| Unsharp Mask | Ctrl+F |
| Extract... | Alt+Ctrl+X |
| Liquify... | Shft+Ctrl+X |
| Pattern Maker... | Alt+Shft+Ctrl+X |
| Artistic | ▶ |
| Blur | ▶ |
| Brush Strokes | ▶ |
| Distort | ▶ |
| Noise | ▶ |
| Pixelate | ▶ |
| Render | ▶ |
| Sharpen | ▶ |
| Sketch | ▶ |
| Stylize | ▶ |
| Texture | ▶ |
| Video | ▶ |
| Other | ▶ |
| Eye Candy 4000 | ▶ |
| Splat | ▶ |
| Xenofex 1.0 | ▶ |
| Andromeda | ▶ |
| Auto FX Software | ▶ |
| KPT 3.0 | ▶ |
| KPT5 | ▶ |
| Ulead Effects | ▶ |
| Ulead Web.Plugins | ▶ |

### Simplifying your edits with the Options bar

The Options bar, shown in Figure 1-10, was a welcomed addition to Photoshop 6.0 because it eliminated the need to access a separate options palette for each tool. The bar remains available at all times, docked beneath the menu bar (unless you decide to hide it for some bizarre reason), and the options change as you switch tools. The Options bar even made the Tool palette cleaner by eliminating an entire tool, the old Airbrush tool, which is now an option for the Brush and other painting tools.

Because the Options bar changes its appearance with each active tool, it's difficult to explain all the components you might find there; but every Options bar does have some characteristics in common:

✔ **Gripper bar:** Grab this bar and drag to undock or dock the Options bar at the top or bottom of the Photoshop window. You can also let the Options bar float anywhere in the working space.

✓ **Tool options:** This box displays the icon of the currently active tool and may include some options for that tool.

✓ **Options pop-up menu:** The Options bar may include a pop-up menu that includes things like a selection of brush tips (for painting and erasing tools) plus a flyout-type options menu that lets you select presets (saved settings) for various tools, plus additional options, such as the size of the icons used to represent brush tips. You may also reset a particular tool or all tools to their Photoshop default values.

✓ **Bar options:** Additional options, such as brush mode, opacity, type styles, and fonts are arrayed on the rest of the Options bar.

✓ **Palette Well:** If your monitor has a screen resolution higher than 800 x 600 pixels, the Palette Well appears at the right side of the Options bar. You can drag palettes from their groups into the Palette Well, where only their tabs appear. Click the tab, and the palette appears, ready for use. When you click again in your document, the palette shrinks down to its tab. The Palette Well is a great tool for keeping your frequently used palettes accessible. I like to keep some palettes, particularly the Layers and Channels palettes, open in the workspace at all times, but some others (such as the Swatches or Styles palettes) don't need to be visible on-screen at all times.

**Figure 1-10**

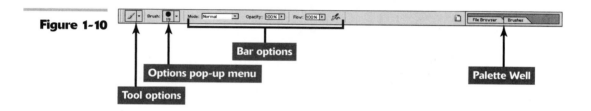

## Proofing and finalizing the image

A hodgepodge of functions are sprinkled throughout the View menu, shown in Figure 1-11. Some of them, like Proof Setup, Proof Colors, and Gamut Warning, won't trouble you until you've become a fairly advanced Photoshop user.

From the View menu, you can select which extras Photoshop displays. You can choose to see (or hide) the following:

✓ Selection edges (which are very useful, for obvious reasons)

✓ Grids and guides (which are useful when you're aligning selections, objects, or other components, and potentially distracting when you're not)

✓ Annotations (which sometimes can be confusing, unless you're already confused; then annotations can help you sort out what's what)

The View menu holds the controls for turning on and off Photoshop's *snap* feature. (The snap feature makes objects magnetically attracted to grids and guides.) You can also create new guides, lock and clear *slices* (see Book IX, Chapter 3, for slice-and-dice information), and turn rulers on or off.

**Figure 1-11**

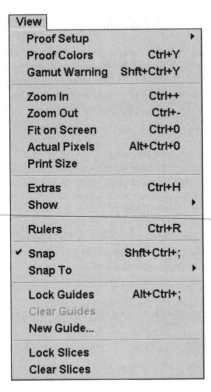

 Some functions, especially the zoom features, are better accessed through tools or keyboard shortcuts. Trust me, when you've learned to zoom in and out by pressing Ctrl++ (plus sign) (⌘++[plus sign] on the Mac) and Ctrl+- (⌘+-[minus sign] on the Mac), you won't be spending a lot of time in this menu searching for those functions.

## Accessing Help When You Need It

To access Photoshop's Help system, plus some other useful information, look no further than the handy-dandy Help menu on the Photoshop desktop, as shown in Figure 1-12.

 If you're using the Mac OS, the Help menu also lets you turn Balloon Help on and off.

Because you can view the Help screens (they pop up in a Web browser window) simply by pressing F1 (or ⌘+? on the Mac), you may not visit the Help menu very often, but if you ever want to find all your help resources in one location, this is the place to be. You can access the following information:

✔ The About Photoshop splash screen, which displays the version number of your Photoshop program. You will find this information important if you've installed updates to Photoshop 7 and are thus running Photoshop 7.*x.*

✔ The About Plug-In entry displays a list of all the plug-ins you've installed for Photoshop; clicking an item on the list shows an About screen of version information for that plug-in.

✔ The Export Transparent Image and Resize Image choices launch a wizard that leads you step by step through all the decisions you need to make to create an image that includes transparency. For example, you might want to create some text in Photoshop and then have it appear to "float" above your Web page's background. The Resize Image Wizard leads you through adjusting the image size so the document will print at the size you want.

✔ The System Info entry displays information about your computer, its operating system, and available memory, plus Photoshop-specific data such as the location you set for your Plug-Ins folder in the Preferences menu. If you like, you can click the Copy button to copy this information to the clipboard, and then paste it in a text document and print it out.

✔ The Updates, Support, Registration, and Adobe Online choices access Internet resources for Photoshop.

**Figure 1-12**

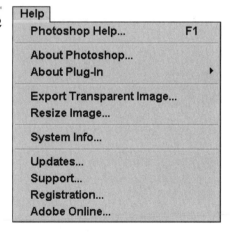

# Getting to Know the Tool Palette

2

After you have a good grasp of the overall Photoshop environment (described in Chapter 1 in this book), you're ready to dive into the cache of gadgets that, along with the menus and palettes and dialog boxes, make it all happen. Just as you can use a saw, hammer, and nails to transform a pile of 2 x 4s into a garden gazebo, you can use the Lasso tool, Healing Brush, and Smudge tool to convert a mediocre photo into a masterpiece fit to be framed. But remember, behind every garden gazebo is a carpenter who knew how to use the tools required to build it.

## Turning on the Toolbox

You can access the Tool palette — or Toolbox as it is often affectionately called — by choosing Window➪Tools. Here are a few tips for using the Toolbox:

✔ To quickly hide and show the Toolbox (along with the other palettes), press the Tab key.

✔ To collapse the palette, double-click the title bar above the eye icon at the top of the Toolbox.

✔ To move the Toolbox anywhere within the Photoshop window, drag the title bar above the eye icon.

### Selecting tools

To select a tool, simply click it in the Toolbox. A small black triangle in the bottom-right corner of a tool slot indicates that more tools are hidden behind that tool on a *flyout menu*. To display the flyout menu and reveal the hidden tools, press and hold the mouse button on the tool. Then drag to the right and down the column of tools, highlight the tool you want, and release your mouse button.

You can also access tools by using keyboard shortcuts (which are listed in Figure 2-1):

✔ **Selecting visible tools:** You can access the visible tools by pressing a single key on the keyboard. For example, to select the Move tool, press the V key; to select the Brush tool, press the B key.

✔ **Selecting hidden tools:** For the most part, you can access a hidden tool by pressing the Shift key along with the keyboard letter of the visible tool. For example, to select the Pencil tool, which shares the flyout menu with the Brush tool, press Shift+B.

There are a couple of exceptions, however. You can press Shift+M to switch between the Rectangular and Elliptical Marquee tools, but you can't access the Single Column and Single Row marquee tools. Press Shift+P to cycle through the Pen and the Freeform Pen; however, the remaining tools — the Add Anchor Point tool, Delete Anchor Point tool, and Convert Point tool — do not have keyboard shortcuts.

 You can adjust your preferences if you decide that you don't like having to press the Shift key to access a hidden tool. Choose Edit⇨Preferences⇨General (Photoshop⇨Preferences⇨ General in Mac OS X) and uncheck the option Use Shift Key for Tool Switch. You can then rotate through the tools by pressing the same letter repeatedly.

**Figure 2-1**

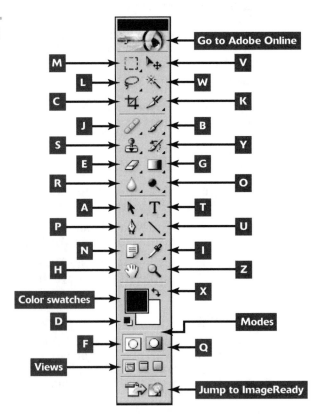

You can also press Alt+click (Option+click on the Mac) on a tool to cycle through all the tools hidden beneath it. The only exceptions are the Marquee tools and the Pen tools; some of the tools on their flyout menus aren't accessible this way.

When you hover your mouse over a tool, color control, or icon, you see a *tool tip*. The tool tip tells you the name of the tool or icon and its keyboard shortcut, if any. This feature is helpful when you first start working in Photoshop, but if it gets annoying after a while, feel free to turn it off. Choose Edit➪Preferences (Photoshop➪Preferences in Mac OS X) and uncheck the option in the General Preferences panel.

If you try to use a tool and all you see is the Cancel or No (the circle with a diagonal line) icon, click the image. Photoshop politely informs you why it isn't allowing you to use the tool. For example, if you try to apply color with the Brush tool on a shape layer, you get a message that you can't use the Brush because the content of the layer isn't directly editable.

## Getting to know your tools

The Toolbox is divided into three basic sections: tools, color swatches, and icons for masking modes and viewing options. The next several sections introduce you to the tools. The other residents of the Toolbox, shown in Figure 2-2, are detailed in the following list:

- ✔ **Foreground Color and Background Color:** *Color swatches* represent the current foreground and background colors. When using some of the tools, such as the Brush or Pencil, you may apply either of these colors. The small black and white swatches represent the default colors of a black foreground and white background. Click the Default Colors icon to reset the colors to the default. Click the curved arrow icon to switch the foreground and background colors. For everything you need to know on color, see Book II, Chapter 3.

- ✔ **Standard Mode and Quick Mask Mode:** The first set of icons allows you to work in either Standard mode or Quick Mask mode. For now leave the mode set to Standard. Quick Masks, which offer a way to view, make, and edit a selection, are covered in detail in Book IV, Chapter 2.

- ✔ **Standard Screen Mode:** The default setting, this mode enables you to see your entire Photoshop desktop.

- ✔ **Full Screen Mode with Menu Bar:** This mode hides your desktop background and other open images.

- ✔ **Full Screen Mode:** Use this mode to hide your desktop background, any open images, and the menu bar. In addition, the Photoshop window turns to black.

- ✔ **Jump to ImageReady:** When you click the bottom-most icon, you launch Photoshop's sister program, ImageReady, a Web graphics program. Check out Book IX, Chapter 5, for more on ImageReady.

- ✔ **Go to Adobe Online:** If you click the eye icon at the top of the Toolbox (refer to Figure 2-1), you open the Adobe Online dialog box. Click the Go Online button to launch your Internet browser and then go to Adobe.com (assuming you're connected to the Internet). If you select the Do Not Show This Again option, clicking the eye icon bypasses the dialog box and takes you directly to Adobe.com. This site is loaded with tons of great info, such as tips, tech support, upgrades, and news on products and events.

**Figure 2-2**

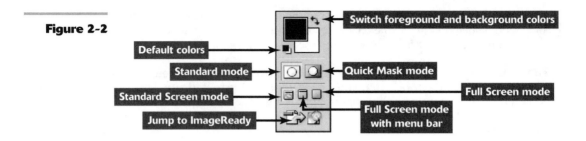

# Introducing the Photoshop Tools

I'm just giving you a very brief description of what each tool does. You'll be more thoroughly initiated with the use of each of the tools as you go through the book. Don't want to go page by page through the book? Okay. Well, you're in luck; I also give you the exact spot where you will find more on each of the tools. For what it's worth, I have organized the tools into logical groupings, although some can cross over into other groups and some are unique enough that they don't really fit well in any group. Check out Appendix B for even more information about Photoshop tools.

## Using selection tools

The selection tools, shown in Table 2-1, are the workhorses of Photoshop. They allow you to capture and isolate pixels so that you can edit or manipulate just a portion of an image. Marquee tools are used to capture rectangular, elliptical (see the results of the Elliptical Marquee tool in Figure 2-3), or single rows or columns of pixels. Whereas the Lasso tools are used for freeform selections, the Magic Wand tool creates selections by picking up pixels of similar colors. And the Move and Crop tools do just what their names describe — move and crop images. (The results of the Move tool are shown in Figure 2-4.)

**Figure 2-3**

**Figure 2-4**

### TABLE 2-1: Selection Tools

| Button | Tool | Does | See |
|---|---|---|---|
| | Rectangular Marquee tool | Makes a rectangular selection | Book III, Chapter 1 |
| | Elliptical Marquee tool | Makes an elliptical selection | Book III, Chapter 1 |
| | Single Row Marquee tool | Makes a selection of a single row of pixels | Book III, Chapter 1 |
| | Single Column Marquee tool | Makes a selection of a single column of pixels | Book III, Chapter 1 |
| | Lasso tool | Makes a freeform selection | Book III, Chapter 1 |
| | Polygon Lasso tool | Makes a straight-sided selection | Book III, Chapter 1 |
| | Magnetic Lasso tool | Makes a selection by magnetically snapping to the edge of an element | Book III, Chapter 1 |
| | Magic Wand tool | Makes a selection by selecting similarly colored pixels within a specified range | Book III, Chapter 1 |

*continued*

**TABLE 2-1:** *(CONTINUED)*

| Button | Tool | Does | See |
|---|---|---|---|
| | Move tool | Moves selections, layers, and guides | Book III, Chapter 3 (selections); Book V, Chapter 1 (layers); Chapter 5 in this book |
| | Crop tool | Trims images | Book II, Chapter 1 |

## Creating and modifying paths

The path tools, shown in Table 2-2, create and modify *paths,* which are elements comprised of straight and curved segments and anchor points. These paths can then be used as a basis for a selection. Because of their precision, using path tools to ultimately create a difficult selection usually yields better results than can be achieved with the selection tools. Figures 2-5 and 2-6 show examples of using the Pen tool and Direct Selection tool, respectively.

**TABLE 2-2:** **PATH TOOLS**

| Button | Tool | Does | See |
|---|---|---|---|
| | Pen tool | Makes a path consisting of anchor points and curved and straight segments | Book III, Chapter 2 |
| | Freeform Pen tool | Makes a path consisting of anchor points and curved and straight segments. It's more automated than the Pen tool | Book III, Chapter 2 |
| | Add Anchor Point tool | Adds anchor points to a path | Book III, Chapter 2 |
| | Delete Anchor Point tool | Deletes anchor points from a path | Book III, Chapter 2 |
| | Convert Point tool | Converts a smooth point to a corner point and vice versa | Book III, Chapter 2 |
| | Path Selection tool | Selects paths, including those comprising shapes | Book III, Chapter 2 (paths); Book IV, Chapter 2 (shapes) |
| | Direct Selection tool | Selects the various components of paths, including those comprising shapes | Book III, Chapter 2 (paths); Book IV, Chapter 2 (shapes) |

**Figure 2-5**

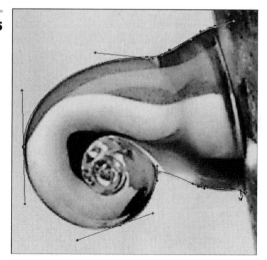

**Figure 2-6**

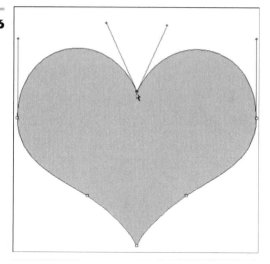

## Using painting tools

The painting tools, in general, allow you to apply color or erase pixels. In the case of the Gradient tool, you can apply multiple colors simultaneously. And with the Art History Brush you paint on a stylized effect rather than color. All the painting tools rely on the Brushes palette for the size, shape, texture, and angle for the tip of the tool. See Table 2-3 for a list of the painting tools.

Figure 2-7 shows examples of what you can do with the Brush tool. An example of the effects of using the Eraser tool is shown in Figure 2-8.

**Figure 2-7**

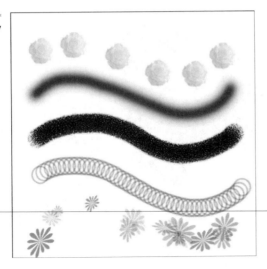

**Figure 2-8**

 If you're a veteran Photoshop user, you may have panicked when you noticed the Airbrush tool was missing from the Toolbox. I know I did. I was relieved to discover that it wasn't eliminated; instead, it was transformed into an option (in the Options bar) and is now available to all the painting and editing tools. Check out Book IV for more on the Airbrush option.

**TABLE 2-3: PAINTING TOOLS**

| Button | Tool | Does | See |
|--------|------|------|-----|
| | Brush tool | Paints with strokes by using a variety of attributes | Book IV, Chapter 1 |
| | Pencil tool | Paints with a hard-edged stroke | Book IV, Chapter 1 |
| | Gradient tool | Creates a blend between two or more colors in a linear, radial, angled, reflected, or diamond pattern | Book IV, Chapter 3 |
| | Paint Bucket tool | Fills similarly colored pixels with color | Book IV, Chapter 3 |
| | Art History Brush tool | Paints with artistic strokes that create a watercolor-like effect, using a selected state or snapshot from the History palette | Book II, Chapter 4 |
| | Eraser tool | Erases pixels, or with the Erase to History option selected, restores the image to a source state in the History palette | Book VI, Chapter 2 (eraser); Book II, Chapter 4 (history) |
| | Magic Eraser tool | Erases similarly colored pixels | Book VI, Chapter 2 |
| | Background Eraser tool | Erases the background pixels by detecting the edge between the foreground element and the background | Book VI, Chapter 2 |

## Using tools for cloning and retouching

The cloning and retouching tools, shown in Table 2-4, are the powerhouse tools to break out when you need to do some image repair work. These tools allow you to duplicate portions of your image, paint with a pattern, or seamlessly fix scratches, wrinkles, and other blemishes. The unique History Brush lets you actually paint a previous version of your image back into your current image — perfect for undoing mistakes or repairing edits that went awry. Figures 2-9 and 2-10 show examples of using the Clone tool and Pattern Stamp tool, respectively.

**Figure 2-9**

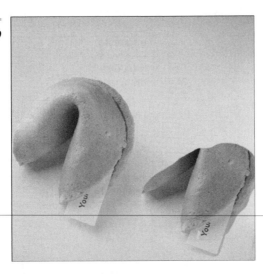

**Figure 2-10**

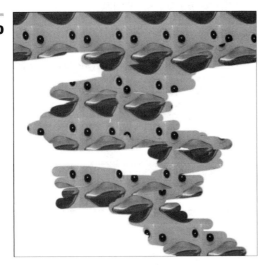

TABLE 2-4: CLONING AND RETOUCHING TOOLS

| Button | Tool | Does | See |
|---|---|---|---|
| | Clone Stamp tool | Paints with sampled pixels | Book VIII, Chapter 3 |
| | Pattern Stamp tool | Paints with a preset or custom pattern | Book IV, Chapter 3 |

| Button | Tool | Does | See |
|--------|------|------|-----|
| | History Brush tool | Allows you to restore the image to a source state in the History palette by painting with a brush | Book II, Chapter 4 |
| | Healing Brush tool | Paints with sampled pixels to repair flaws in an image | Book VIII, Chapter 3 |
| | Patch tool | Repairs flaws on a selected portion of an image by covering the area with sampled pixels | Book VIII, Chapter 3 |

## Creating effects with typographical tools

The type tools, shown in Table 2-5, pretty much do as their moniker suggests — create type of varying sorts. The Horizontal Type tool (shown in Figure 2-11) and Vertical Type tool create regular old type, whereas the Mask Type tools create selections in the shape of letters, which can then be filled with images. An example of using the Horizontal Type Mask tool is shown in Figure 2-12.

**TABLE 2-5: TYPE TOOLS**

| Button | Tool | Does | See |
|--------|------|------|-----|
| T | Horizontal Type tool | Creates type horizontally across the canvas | Book IV, Chapters 4 and 5 |
| T | Vertical Type tool | Creates type vertically down the canvas | Book IV, Chapters 4 and 5 |
| T | Horizontal Type Mask tool | Creates a horizontal selection marquee from type | Book IV, Chapter 5 |
| T | Vertical Type Mask tool | Creates a vertical selection marquee from type | Book IV, Chapter 5 |

**Figure 2-11**

**Figure 2-12**

### Using focus and toning tools

The focus and toning tools, shown in Table 2-6, allow you to enhance your image by altering the pixels in various ways. You can lighten, darken, blur, smudge (see Figure 2-13), sharpen, saturate, or desaturate color in selective portions of your image. These tools work best for touching up smaller areas rather than the entire image. For example, in Figure 2-14 the Burn tool was used to darken the pixels in the groom's face.

**Figure 2-13**

**Figure 2-14**

**TABLE 2-6: FOCUS AND TONING TOOLS**

| Button | Tool | Does | See |
|---|---|---|---|
| | Blur tool | Blurs pixels by decreasing the contrast between pixels | Book VIII, Chapter 2 |
| | Sharpen tool | Sharpens pixels by increasing the contrast between pixels | Book VIII, Chapter 2 |

*continued*

**TABLE 2-6:** *(CONTINUED)*

| Button | Tool | Does | See |
|---|---|---|---|
|  | Smudge tool | Smudges (smears) pixels in an image | Book VIII, Chapter 2 |
| | Dodge tool | Lightens pixels in an image | Book VIII, Chapter 2 |
| | Burn tool | Darkens pixels in an image | Book VIII, Chapter 2 |
| | Sponge tool | Saturates or desaturates color in an image | Book VIII, Chapter 2 |

## Creating shapes

The Shape tools, shown in Table 2-7, allow you to create vector-, rather than pixel-, based elements in your image. The beauty of vector-based elements is that they are resolution independent, meaning that they will always print at the resolution of the output device rather than the resolution of the image. Vector-based shapes created with the Shape tools can also be resized and transformed without any quality degradation, unlike raster images. For more on resolution, see Book II, Chapter 1. Figures 2-15 and 2-16 show the Polygon and Custom Shape tools, respectively, in action.

**Figure 2-15**

**Figure 2-16**

## TABLE 2-7: SHAPE TOOLS

| Button | Tool | Does | See |
|--------|------|------|-----|
|        | Rectangle tool | Creates a vector rectangle filled with the foreground color | Book IV, Chapter 2 |
|        | Rounded Rectangle tool | Creates a rounded vector rectangle filled with the foreground color | Book IV, Chapter 2 |
|        | Ellipse tool | Creates a vector ellipse filled with the foreground color | Book IV, Chapter 2 |
|        | Polygon tool | Creates a vector polygon filled with the foreground color | Book IV, Chapter 2 |
|        | Line tool | Creates a foreground-colored line of specified thickness | Book IV, Chapter 2 |
|        | Custom Shape tool | Creates a vector shape selected from a custom shape library and fills it with the foreground color | Book IV, Chapter 2 |

### Viewing, navigating, sampling, and annotating tools

Photoshop has an abundance of tools to help you view and navigate your image window. These tools allow you to zoom in (as shown in Figure 2-17) and out, move your image within the window, and measure distances and angles. The Eyedropper and Color Sampler tools let you pick up and sample color respectively — handy for grabbing or evaluating color in an image. The Notes tool (shown in Figure 2-18) and Audio Annotation tool create written and audio notes that you can leave in an image window — useful for collaboration purposes or simply for reminders to yourself. See Table 2-8.

**Figure 2-17**

**Figure 2-18**

**TABLE 2-8: TOOLS FOR VIEWING, EDITING, AND SAMPLING FILES**

| Button | Tool | Does | See |
|--------|------|------|-----|
| | Eyedropper tool | Samples a color in your image and makes it the foreground or background color | Book II, Chapter 3 |
| | Color Sampler tool | Samples and evaluates up to four colors in your image | Book II, Chapter 3 |
| | Measure tool | Measures distances and angles on your canvas | Chapter 5 in this book |
| | Zoom tool | Zooms into or out of your image | Chapter 5 in this book |
| | Hand tool | Moves your image within the window | Chapter 5 in this book |
| | Notes tool | Creates a digital Post It note that can be attached to your canvas | Book II, Chapter 5 |
| | Audio Annotation tool | Creates an audio annotation that is attached to your canvas and can be played back | Book II, Chapter 5 |

## Using tools for the Web

Photoshop doesn't have a whole lot of tools dedicated to the preparation of Web images (though it does have quite a few commands). That's mainly because its companion program, ImageReady, takes up the slack in that department. You will find the Slice tool and Slice Select tool (shown in Figure 2-19), which allow you to create and select *slices,* or rectangular sections, from an image. You can then optimize those slices separately for the best viewing experience on your Web page. See Table 2-9.

**TABLE 2-9: WEB TOOLS**

| Button | Tool | Does | See |
|--------|------|------|-----|
| | Slice tool | Creates *slices* (rectangular sections of an image used for display on the Web) | Book IX, Chapter 3 |
| | Slice Select tool | Selects slices | Book IX, Chapter 3 |

**Figure 2-19**

# Saving Time with Tool Presets

*Tool presets* enable you to create tool settings that you can save and use again. This feature is a real timesaver if you use specific tool settings on a frequent basis. For example, I make numerous 2-x-2-inch and 2-x-3-inch rectangular selections on images I use in a newsletter. I saved the settings as presets so that I don't have to redefine them each time I want to select an image for my project.

▼ ▼ ▼ ▼ ▼ ▼ ▼ ▼ ▼ ▼ ▼ ▼ ▼ ▼ ▼ ▼ ▼ ▼ ▼ ▼ ▼ ▼ ▼ ▼ ▼ ▼ ▼ ▼ ▼ ▼ ▼ ▼ ▼ ▼ ▼ ▼

## Creating custom tool presets

Here are the short and simple steps for creating your own custom tool preset:

**1.** **Choose a tool.**

Most tools are fair game. If a tool doesn't allow for presets, such as the Measure tool for example, the Tool Preset picker button (described in Step 3) is grayed out.

**2.** **Select the option you want for the tool in the Options bar.**

**3.** **Click the Tool Preset picker button in the Options bar, as shown in Figure 2-20.**

You can also choose Window⇨Tool Presets to bring up the Tool Presets palette. The Tool Presets palette offers an additional handy icon at the bottom

of the palette: the trash icon. This icon lets you delete a preset quickly. Select the preset and click the trash icon or simply drag the preset to the trash.

You can't create a new preset from the Preset Manager, which is accessible from the Tool Preset picker pop-up menu or by choosing Edit⇨Preset Manager. You can only load presets, as described in Step 6.

**4.** **Click the Create New Tool Preset picker button (the dog-eared page icon), or if you're using the Tool Presets palette, select New Tool Preset from the palette menu.**

**5.** **Name the preset and click OK.**

Your new preset is now saved and ready for reuse.

**6.** **To select the tool preset, you can do one of three things:**

✔ Click the Tool Preset picker button and select a preset from the pop-up tool preset picker.

✔ Select a preset from the Tool Presets palette.

✔ Select a preset from the Preset Manager. Choose Tools from the pop-up menu and select your preset.

**Figure 2-20**

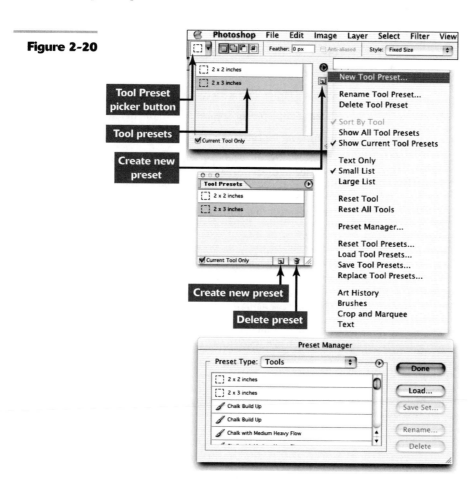

## Managing your presets

You can manage your presets by choosing options from the tool preset picker pop-up menu. These options are described in Table 2-10.

**TABLE 2-10: THE TOOL PRESET PICKER POP-UP MENU**

| Option | What It Does |
|---|---|
| Rename Tool Preset | Renames the preset. (Select the preset from the list and then choose this option.) |
| Delete Tool Preset | Deletes a preset. (Select the preset from the list and then choose this option.) |
| Sort by Tool | Groups your presets by tool. |
| Show All Tool Presets | Shows the presets for all your tools. |
| Show Current Tool Presets | Shows the presets for the active tool only. |
| Text Only | Gives you the name of the preset without the icon. |
| Small List | Shows a small icon, along with the preset name. |
| Large List | Shows a larger icon with the preset name. |
| Reset Tool | Closes active preset and returns to the default tool setting. |
| Reset All Tools | Returns all tools to their defaults. |
| Preset Manager | Opens the Preset Manager, which manages all the various libraries of preset brushes, swatches, gradients, styles, patterns, contours, custom shapes, and tools. You can also load other libraries and the custom preset libraries you have created. In addition, you can rename or delete a preset library. |
| Reset Tool Presets | Deletes all of your tool presets at once. If you want to add the defaults back with your custom tool presets, choose Append. |
| Load Tool Presets | Loads tool presets that have been previously saved or acquired elsewhere. |
| Save Tool Presets | Saves a custom set of tool presets for later retrieval. A .tpl extension is added to the saved file. |
| Replace Tool Presets | Replaces your current tool presets. Allows you to load a .tpl file that will replace your current tool presets. |
| Art History, Brushes, Crop and Marquee, and Text options | Allow you to either append or replace your current tool presets with the tool presets from each of those individual libraries. |

# Getting Started and Finishing Up

3

Although you can create some interesting images from scratch in Photoshop, most of the time you'll be working with digital pictures that already exist. These may be images captured by your scanner, photos you've grabbed with your digital camera, or snapshots stored on a Photo CD.

Photoshop offers you lots of different options for opening existing images, creating new images, and saving changes to your hard drive. This chapter takes you through the steps you need to know to begin working with your images.

If you want to capture an image with your scanner or import a photograph from your digital camera, opening such a digital image may involve a little more than just using the file navigation tools built into Windows Explorer or the Mac OS Finder. Check out Appendix A for a complete discussion.

## Browsing for Files

If you don't know the exact filename of the image you want to open or can't remember its location, you can use Photoshop's File Browser to search for and open files. (Check out Chapter 5 in this book for a complete description of the File Browser.)

Finding a file is about as easy as you might expect: Choose File⇨Browse, or press Shift+Ctrl+O (Shift+⌘+O on the Mac). Guess what! The File Browser window opens.

 You can also click the File Browser's tab in the Palette Well (if it resides there) or in a Palette group to bring it to the front.

To navigate to a folder you'd like to search, use the folder tree in the upper-left corner of the window. You may have to choose Expanded View from the File Browser's Option menu to reveal this pane. Click an image to see it in the Preview window (which shows up on the left side of the File Browser). Photoshop graciously provides information about the file in the pane below the preview.

When you find a file you're sure you want to open, double-click it, as shown in Figure 3-1.

**Figure 3-1**

▼ ▼ ▼ ▼ ▼ ▼ ▼ ▼ ▼ ▼ ▼ ▼ ▼ ▼ ▼ ▼ ▼ ▼ ▼ ▼ ▼ ▼ ▼ ▼ ▼ ▼ ▼ ▼ ▼ ▼ ▼ ▼ ▼ ▼ ▼

# Opening an Image

If you know exactly where an image file is stored, you can open the file in a similar way to opening a word processing, spreadsheet, or other file; the default Open dialog boxes resemble those that you find in most other applications. (I discuss other file-opening options in the following sections.)

The dialog boxes you use to navigate files differ slightly in Mac OS 9.*x* and higher and Mac OS X 10.1.3 and higher. Mac OS X uses a browser-style window that lets you see all the contents of your desktop in a single view, with a horizontal hierarchy.

Follow these steps to open a file:

**1. Choose File⇨Open, or press Ctrl+O (⌘+O on the Mac).**

The standard Open dialog box for Windows or the Mac OS appears. The layout of the dialog box differs slightly between the two operating systems, as

you can see in the Windows version in Figure 3-2, and the Mac versions in Figures 3-3 and 3-4.

**2. Navigate to the folder that contains your file.**

OS X has a Favorites folder like the Windows taskbar where you can add frequently used folders. It also sports a Find button in the Open dialog box for those hard-to-locate files.

From the Files of Type list (Windows) or Show list (Mac OS), you can choose which types of files you want displayed.

 To view all image files, choose All Formats (Windows) or All Readable Documents (Mac OS).

**3.** **Click the name of the image file you want to open.**

To select multiple files, click the first file and then Ctrl+click (Shift+click on Mac OS 9; ⌘+click on Mac OS X) each additional file.

You may see a preview of the image in the dialog box's Preview window. The

Mac Open dialog box has a Show/Hide Preview button that you can click to toggle the preview display on and off.

 Mac OS X doesn't have a Show/Hide Preview option.

**4.** **After you select the file you want, click the Open button.**

The file opens in Photoshop.

A menu of the last files you worked on appears. Click a filename to open it or simply type the number next to the filename. The number of files that appear on this menu is defined in Preferences. For the lowdown on how to specify this value, jump ahead to Chapter 6 of this book.

 You can open any recently used files by choosing File⇨Open Recent.

**Figure 3-2**

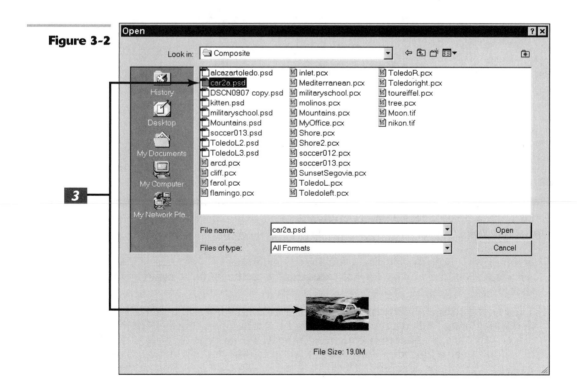

**Figure 3-3**

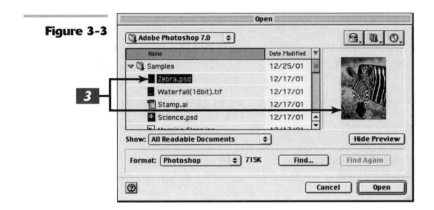

**Figure 3-4**

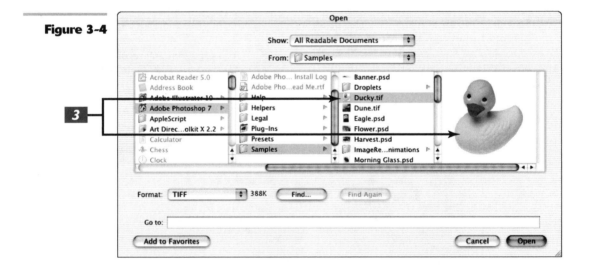

## Opening special files

Photoshop needs to know the image format of a file (that is, whether it's a TIFF, PCX, PSD, or JPEG file, for example) before it can open the file. Photoshop uses different methods in Windows and Mac OS to determine the format of an image file:

✔ In Windows, Photoshop looks at the file extension (.tif, .pcx, .psd, and so forth), and if it finds a standard image format extension, it assumes that the file was saved using that format.

✔ The Mac OS uses a slightly different (and more intelligent) system. Each file is embedded with a code (called a *creator code*) that tells the operating system which application created that file, and another code that indicates what type of file it is. Therefore, Mac files don't need a file extension for Photoshop to determine which kind of format was used for that file or which application created it. The file provides all the information needed.

For compatibility reasons, Macintosh applications like Photoshop usually use the Windows file extension. However, when you move files from one platform to the other, they can easily be misidentified. With Photoshop's Open As feature, you can specify the format you think (or know) that a given file uses. This facility works slightly differently in Windows than in the Mac OS.

▼▼▼▼▼▼▼▼▼▼▼▼▼▼▼▼▼▼▼▼▼▼▼▼▼▼▼▼▼▼▼▼▼▼▼▼▼▼▼

### Opening special files using the Windows OS

In Windows, follow these steps:

**1.** **Choose File⇨Open As.**

The Open As dialog box appears, as shown in Figure 3-5.

**2.** **Navigate to the file you want to open.**

**3.** **From the Open As drop-down list, choose the file format you want to use.**

**4.** **Double-click the file's icon.**

If you've chosen the right format, the file opens in Photoshop.

 If the file doesn't open, you may have chosen the wrong format. Choose another and try again.

**Figure 3-5**

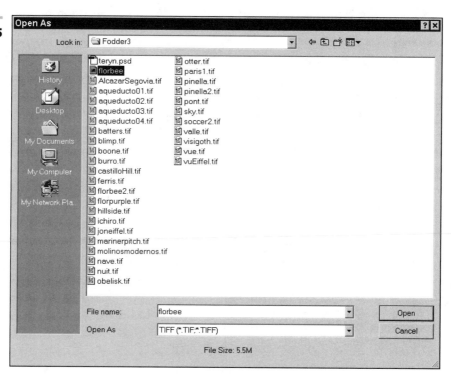

### Opening special files using the Mac OS

The standard Open dialog box includes a Format list at the bottom. Make sure that All Readable Documents is displayed on the Show list. Then you can choose the file format you'd like to try directly from the Format list. (I'm not a snooty Mac purist, but creator codes and features like this are a few of the things that the Mac OS has done more simply and logically than Windows . . . for almost two decades.)

▼ ▼ ▼ ▼ ▼ ▼ ▼ ▼ ▼ ▼ ▼ ▼ ▼ ▼ ▼ ▼ ▼ ▼ ▼ ▼ ▼ ▼ ▼ ▼ ▼ ▼ ▼ ▼ ▼ ▼ ▼ ▼ ▼ ▼ ▼ ▼

### Opening a Photo CD image

The Photo CD format was originally developed by Eastman Kodak Company more than a decade ago. It has become a popular image format option because of its flexibility and high quality. Photo CDs store each image in multiple versions as Image Pacs, so you can open the version that has the resolution you need. Professional versions of this format provide copy protection and other features that professional photographers need. Your photofinisher can save your images to a CD in Photo CD format for you; Photoshop can't save in this format, however.

Follow these steps to open a Photo CD image:

**1.** **Choose File➪Open and navigate to the folder containing the Photo CD image you want to open.**

**2.** **Double-click the file's icon.**

The Kodak PCD Format dialog box appears, as shown in Figure 3-6, containing the preview image and several other options.

**3.** **Choose the desired resolution from the Pixel Size drop-down list.**

Versions from 64 x 96 to 2048 x 3072 pixels are available.

You can select a color profile tailored to a specific type of image from the Profile drop-down list. (Generally, only advanced users will want to change the default value.)

**4.** **Under Source, choose the film type for the original image, such as color negative, Ektachrome, Kodachrome, and so forth.**

**5.** **In the Destination Image area, choose a resolution and indicate whether you want the image to open in landscape (wide) or portrait (tall) orientation.**

Only advanced users will want to change the Color Space definition.

The ProCD version of Photo CD has one additional higher resolution than is available in the consumer version: 4096 x 6144 pixels, a whopping 72MB per image! The top resolution of 2048 x 3072 (18MB) in the consumer version should be plenty for all but the most demanding applications.

**6.** **Click OK to open the image.**

In the Image Info area of the dialog box, you can see what type of equipment was used to scan the original as well as the original image type (color negative, transparency, and so forth).

**Figure 3-6**

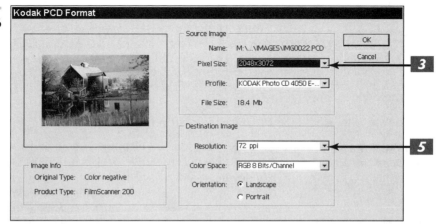

---

# Placing Files

In Photoshop, you use the File⇨Place command to put PDF (Portable Document Format), Adobe Illustrator (AI), or EPS (Encapsulated PostScript) files into a layer of their own. These files are often created by programs other than Photoshop, such as Adobe Acrobat, Adobe Illustrator, or CorelDraw. Although Photoshop can open these files independently, you must use the Place feature if you want to combine them with an existing image.

Follow these steps to place a PDF, Adobe Illustrator, or EPS file:

**1.** **Open an existing document into which you want to place a file.**

**2.** **Choose File⇨Place.**

The Place dialog box opens.

**3.** **Navigate to the file you want to insert and then double-click the file.**

For some types of files, such as PDF files, you may see a dialog box like the

one shown in Figure 3-7, which lets you specify how the placed image should be handled.

**4.** **Choose your options, which vary according to the type of file you're opening, and click OK to place the file in your image.**

**Figure 3-7**

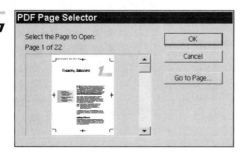

▼▼▼▼▼▼▼▼▼▼▼▼▼▼▼▼▼▼▼▼▼▼▼▼▼▼▼▼▼▼▼▼▼▼▼▼▼▼

## Creating a New Image

At some point, you'll want to create a new image from scratch. You may want an empty canvas to paint on or need a blank image as scratch space. Or you may want to paste a copied selection into a new document.

Follow these steps to use the New feature to create a new image:

**1.** **Choose File⇨New or press Ctrl+N (⌘+N on the Mac).**

The New dialog box appears, as shown in Figure 3-8.

**2.** **Type in a name for the new file.**

If you specify no name, Photoshop creates one for you, such as Untitled-1, Untitled-2, and so forth.

**3.** **Enter the width and height of your image by using one of the following methods:**

✔ **Enter the width and height manually.** Select Custom from the Preset Sizes drop-down list and then type the width and height of your choice in the boxes below it.

✔ **Choose from a list of document sizes.** The document sizes include Default Photoshop Size (which you set in Preferences, as described in Chapter 6 of this book); common printing sizes such as 4 x 6, 5 x 7, or 8 x 10 inches; display screen sizes such as 640 x 480 pixels or 800 x 600 pixels; plus an array of other popular sizes.

 As with other Photoshop dialog boxes, you may change from the default increment to some other measurement.

**4.** **Enter the resolution for the new document.**

For example, you may want to choose 72 pixels/inch for images that will be

displayed on-screen and 300 pixels/inch for images that will be printed.

 It's important to choose the right resolution at this point in the creation process because if you need to change the resolution later, you can lose sharpness. For more information on selecting an appropriate resolution, see Book II, Chapter 1.

**5.** **From the Mode drop-down list, select a color mode.**

Your choices include Grayscale, RGB Color, CMYK, and so on.

**6.** **In the Contents area, select an option for how you want the background layer to be filled.**

You choices are white, the current background color, or transparent.

**7.** **Click OK when you're finished entering your options.**

The new image is created.

 If you choose the Custom Preset Size, copy a selection to the Clipboard, and then choose File⇨New, Photoshop automatically selects the dimensions of the copied selection as the width and height of the new document. You can create the new, empty document and then paste the copied selection into it by pressing Ctrl+V (⌘+V on the Mac).

**Figure 3-8**

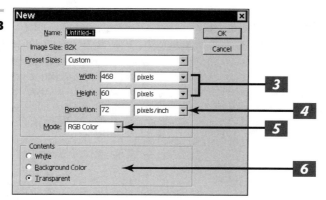

▼▼▼▼▼▼▼▼▼▼▼▼▼▼▼▼▼▼▼▼▼▼▼▼▼▼▼▼▼▼▼▼▼▼▼▼▼

# Saving a File

Before you exit Photoshop, you'll want to save your file on your hard disk or other media. Don't worry if you forget to do this; Photoshop won't let you exit without first asking you if you'd like to save any files that you've changed or newly created. However, it's a good idea to save files from time to time as you work on them so that you always have a recent copy safely stored on your drive.

Follow these steps to save a file:

***1.*** **Choose File⇨Save As.**

Choose File⇨Save to store the current file under its present name. Choose File⇨Save As to store a new file that's never been saved or a file that has already been saved under a different name.

The Save As dialog box appears, as shown in Figure 3-9.

***2.*** **Navigate to the folder where you'd like to store the file.**

***3.*** **Type a name in the File Name box.**

***4.*** **Choose a format from the Format drop-down list.**

Some file formats have special capabilities and requirements. For example, if your document has layers, you can save it in TIFF or PSD or PDF formats. JPEG files must be stored in 24-bit

format. Your options appear in the Save As dialog box when you select a format. For more information on file formats, see Book II, Chapter 2.

***5.*** **In the Save Options area, select or deselect the following check boxes as desired:**

⮑ **As a Copy:** Save the file as a copy.

⮑ **Annotations:** Include or delete annotations in the saved copy. (See Book II, Chapter 5, for more on annotations.)

⮑ **Alpha Channels:** Include or ignore alpha channels (stored selections). (See Book VI, Chapter 1, for a discussion of channels.)

⮑ **Spot Colors:** Enable spot colors in the saved file. (For more information on spot colors, see Book X, Chapter 2.)

CONTINUED
▼ ▼ ▼ ▼ ▼

✔ **Layers:** Photoshop should include layers or simply flatten the image to one layer. (See Book V, Chapter 1, for the lowdown on layers.)

✔ **Use Proof Setup:** Enable proof setup, which includes an on-screen preview of how the image will look when printed or viewed on a specific device. (See Book II, Chapter 3, for more information.)

✔ **ICC Profile:** Embed a color profile, which places a color profile in the file based on the settings established in your Color Settings dialog box. Leave this value at the default setting, but check out Book II,

Chapter 3, for information on the specialized situations when you might want to change it.

✔ **Thumbnail:** Embed a thumbnail image in the file if you've defined thumbnails as optional in Photoshop's Preferences. (You can find more on Preferences in Book I, Chapter 6.)

✔ **Use Lower Case Extension:** Use lowercase extensions (that is, .tif instead of .TIF) regardless of how you type the filename.

**6.** **Click Save to store the image.**

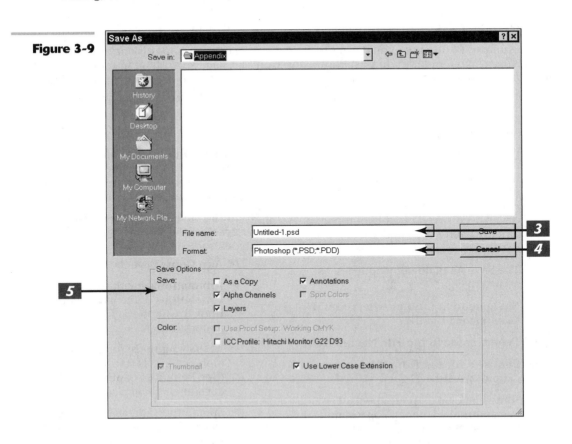

**Figure 3-9**

## Saving a backup copy

You'll usually want to have a backup copy of an image safe on your hard disk any time you make changes to a file and, often, periodically throughout a work session. If you change your mind about the modifications you've made to an image, you can always return to the backup copy. Photoshop offers several ways to create such copies:

✔ **Choose File⇨Save As and enter a new name to the file.** It's also a good idea to specify a new location, such as another hard disk drive or, perhaps, some removable storage destination, such as a Zip disk or a CD-R/RW disc.

✔ **Choose File⇨Save As and select the As a Copy check box.** Photoshop simply adds "copy" to the current filename (for example, `myfile.psd` becomes `myfile copy.psd`) and saves the file under that new name.

Photoshop also enables you to create backup snapshots of your images at any time (or even a snapshot of a previous time by using the History palette). However, these snapshots are not saved when you close an image and are best used as backups during a particular working session. For more information on snapshots and the History palette, see Book II, Chapter 4.

▼▼▼▼▼▼▼▼▼▼▼▼▼▼▼▼▼▼▼▼▼▼▼▼▼▼▼▼▼▼▼▼▼▼▼▼▼▼

# Applying Digital Copyrights

You may want to protect your work from unauthorized reuse by embedding digital copyright information in the file by using Photoshop's watermark capabilities provided by Digimarc technology. You should apply a watermark to a finished image. If you change an image later, you have to apply the watermark to a new copy of the image; you cannot add a watermark to an image that has previously been marked. Although watermarking isn't bulletproof, it can help preserve your rights.

Follow these steps to apply a digital copyright to an image:

*1.* **If your image has more than one layer, choose Layer⇨Flatten Image to combine all the visible layers into one.**

*2.* **If the image is an indexed-color image (for example, a GIF file), convert it to RGB mode.**

You can always reconvert it to GIF after the watermark is applied.

*3.* **Choose Filter⇨Digimarc⇨Embed Watermark.**

The Embed Watermark dialog box opens, as shown in Figure 3-10.

*4.* **If this is the first time you've applied a watermark, click the Personalize button and follow the instructions to register with Digimarc Corporation over the Web or by telephone. Enter your PIN and ID number as instructed.**

*5.* **Enter a copyright year for the image.**

*6.* **Choose from the following options:**

✔ **Restricted Use** to limit the use of the image.

✔ **Adult Content** to mark the image suitable for adults only.

CONTINUED
▼ ▼ ▼ ▼ ▼

↙ **Do Not Copy** to specify that the image should not be copied.

**7.** In the Target Output area, choose whether the image is intended for monitor, Web, or print display.

**8.** In the Watermark Durability area, drag the slider or enter a value.

Durability in this case is a compromise between visibility (very durable) and unobtrusiveness (not very visible.) If you make the watermark less visible, it can be accidentally (or intentionally) damaged or made less effective by

some image-processing operations. The more durable a watermark becomes, the more likely it will be visible to the eye, but the image will remain protected even if the image is scanned, modified with filters, or printed.

**9.** Select the Verify check box to tell Photoshop to double-check the image after the watermark is applied, to make sure it was successfully embedded.

**10.** Click OK to apply the watermark.

**Figure 3-10**

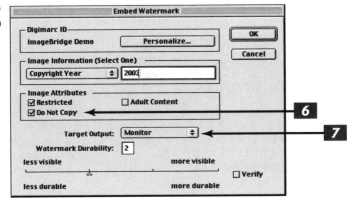

## Closing and Quitting

When your session is finished, you'll want to close up shop and close down Photoshop. In addition to using the traditional File⇨Exit option, you can close Photoshop in any of the following ways:

↙ Choose Close from the Windows Control menu in the upper-left corner of the Photoshop title bar.

↙ Click the Close box in the upper-right corner of the Photoshop title bar under Windows.

 In Windows, press Ctrl+Q or Alt+F4. Press ⌘+Q if you're using a Mac.

With any of these methods, Photoshop asks you, in turn, if you'd like to save any open file that has not been saved or has not been saved since it was modified in this session. Click the Yes button to close and save the files.

 You can also close any open files without exiting Photoshop by pressing Shift+Ctrl+W (Shift+⌘+W on the Mac).

# Getting It on Paper

## In This Chapter

✔ Looking at printers

✔ Printing from the Windows and Mac operating systems

✔ Choosing print options

Hard-copy prints have become a hugely popular output option, thanks largely to the swarm of sub-$200 photo-quality inkjet printers that are vying for your discretionary dollars. Today, anyone can afford a printer capable of producing sparkling prints from digital images. The chief problem is restraining the urge to print everything in sight before your ink tank (and wallet) runs dry.

Actually making the prints is only a minor puzzle, and one addressed in this chapter. Happily, you can print most images with just a few clicks. Most of the advanced options discussed in this chapter are needed only for special situations or specialized applications and are not discussed in detail; this chapter covers only the basics. If you need more detailed or advanced information on printing, see Book X, Chapter 2.

## Taking a Look at Printers

You can print Photoshop images on any kind of printer, but, aside from the occasional 200-copy print run of black-and-white "Have You Seen This Kitty?" posters, monochrome laser printers are not high on the list of favored Photoshop output hardware.

More often, you'll be choosing a full-color printer, probably an inkjet model, but also possibly a dye-sublimation, thermal-wax, or even color laser printer model. Although all of these printers produce roughly similar results, there are some differences, as detailed in the following list:

✔ **Inkjet printers:** These printers paint the page by spraying a jet of ink one dot at a time, under precision computer control. The ink can be water-based or solid ink that is melted just before application. Liquid inks tend to spread by soaking or wicking into the fibers of the paper, can smear when wet, and produce better results when used with photo paper designed especially for inkjets.

Most inkjet printers use four ink tanks for black, cyan, magenta, and yellow. A few use six tanks, adding "weak" cyan and magenta hues to the strong colors and black to provide more colors. Regardless of configuration, inkjet printers generally provide excellent full-color output, but the cost of consumables (ink and paper) can add up fast.

✔ **Dye-sublimation printers:** These printers potentially offer better-looking prints, but require even more expensive materials than inkjet printers. Most models cost more than the least-expensive inkjet models. Many consumer-oriented dye-sub printers you see are models capable of producing only snapshot-sized (roughly 4-x-6-inch) prints. They use a continuous *ribbon* of color panels in a roll that is the same width as the print, with each panel used only once. The print head's tiny heating elements can melt dots of dye over a range of 256 values to generate up to 16.8 million colors. Professional dye-sub printers are accurate enough to be used for color proofing.

✔ **Thermal-wax printers and solid-ink printers:** These printers use blocks of wax or resin that is melted and sprayed directly onto a page. Some apply ink to a drum that rolls against a piece of paper, like an offset printing press. Significantly more expensive to own and operate than inkjet printers, these devices are generally used for advanced-amateur or professional applications.

## Printing an Image

The process of printing an image in Photoshop is similar in the Windows and Mac OS 9 operating systems. (Things are a little different in Mac OS X.) The chief differences are in the Page Setup step, in which you select a printer and choose orientation, paper size, and other parameters. The next few sections take a closer look at Page Setup in the two operating systems.

### Page Setup in Micosoft Windows

With Windows applications like Photoshop, you open the Page Setup dialog box by choosing File⇨Page Setup or by pressing Shift+Ctrl+P. In this dialog box, shown in Figure 4-1, you can select the paper size, orientation (Portrait or Landscape), and other things, such as which paper tray to use. If you click the Printer button, a second Page Setup dialog box appears. Here, you can choose a specific printer from those attached to your computer or network. Clicking the Properties button takes you to specific options customized for your printer, such as print quality or special effects available with that printer. These vary from printer to printer, so consult your printer's instruction manual.

## Using professional printing services

Even if you own a photo-quality printer, you may want to take advantage of professional services from time to time. For example, you may own a dye-sublimation printer that cranks out snapshots with aplomb, but can't give you a 5-x-7-inch or 8-x-10-inch print.

Hop in the car and jaunt over to a retailer in your area equipped with one of those stand-alone kiosks, such as the Kodak Picture Maker. These devices accept images in many formats. You can use your digital camera's memory cards, Photo CDs, or diskettes to supply fodder for the kiosk. Most include scanners that can capture your original prints, slides, and negatives. They even offer Photoshop-like picture-fixing capabilities. You can adjust color, repair red-eye problems, crop or enlarge your images, and add text.

Many photofinishers or service bureaus can make prints from your Photoshop-edited images if you burn them to a CD, save them to a Zip disk, or upload them over the Internet to a Web-based service. You can often purchase greeting cards, T-shirts, souvenir mugs, and other printed output that is difficult to duplicate at home. Large-format prints, posters, and murals are other cool options.

**Figure 4-1**

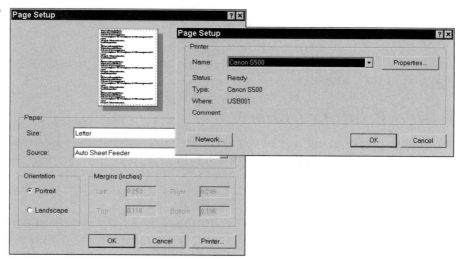

## Page Setup in the Mac OS

To choose which printer is active in the Mac OS, use the Chooser, which is generally available in the Apple Menu (in Mac OS 9) or in Print Center (in Mac OS X). To access the Page Setup dialog box, shown in Figures 4-2 and 4-3, choose File➪Page Setup, or press Shift+⌘+P. You can set the page size and orientation, scaling, and additional parameters, depending on your printer.

In Mac OS X, you can also choose a printer directly from the Print dialog box like in Windows. Also in Mac OS X, if you're connected directly to a printer via the USB port, the system automatically detects the printer, so you don't need to use the Chooser. If you're on a network, you can use Print Center and select a printer from the Printer list or from the Print dialog box.

**Figure 4-2**

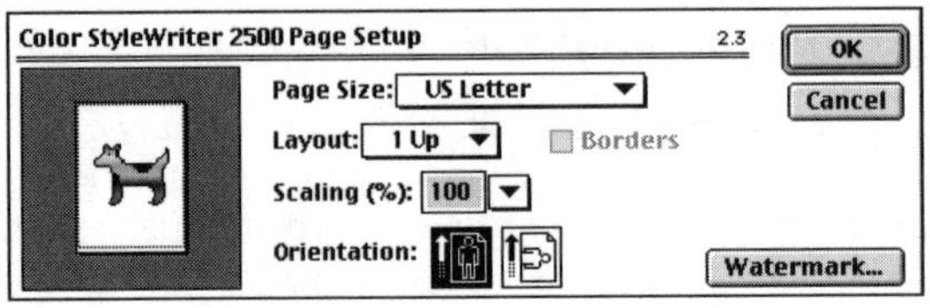

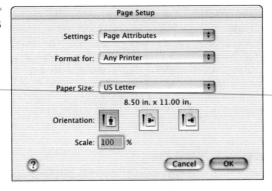

**Figure 4-3**

▼▼▼▼▼▼▼▼▼▼▼▼▼▼▼▼▼▼▼▼▼▼▼▼▼▼▼▼▼▼▼▼▼▼▼▼▼▼▼▼▼▼▼▼

# Setting Printing Options

Photoshop has several printing modes to choose from, depending on how much control you need and how much of a hurry you're in. Here are your options:

✔ **Print One Copy** (Alt+Shift+Ctrl+P, or Option+Shift+⌘+P on the Mac) is a quick way to print a hard copy using the default settings.

✔ **Print** (Alt+Ctrl+P, or Option+⌘+P on the Mac) pops up the standard Windows (or Mac) Print dialog box, with options to choose a new printer, select which pages to print, select the number of copies, and indicate whether to collate the output.

✔ **Print with Preview** (Ctrl+P or ⌘+P on the Mac) opens an expanded Print dialog box that includes a preview window and many more options to choose from. You can even access the Page Setup dialog box from this dialog box if you want to change the orientation, paper size, or switch to a different printer. This dialog box is almost identical under the Windows and Mac operating systems, as you can see in Figures 4-4, 4-5, and 4-6.

**Figure 4-4**

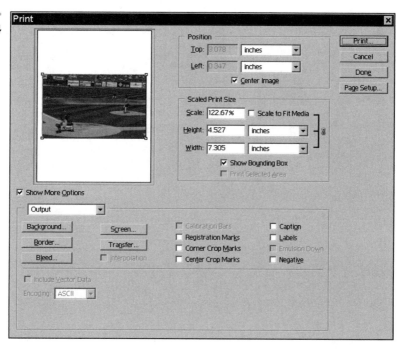

**Figure 4-5**

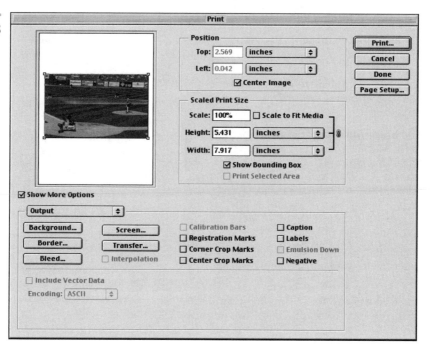

**Figure 4-6**

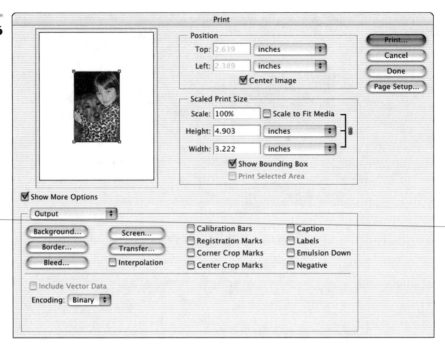

To set your print options, follow these steps:

**1.** **Choose File➪Print with Preview.**

The Print dialog box opens.

**2.** **Select the Show More Options check box and choose Output from the pop-up menu.**

The other option on the pop-up menu, Color Management, is used for advanced proofing and color profile tasks. Check out Book X, Chapter 2, for information on printing using color management, as well as Book II, Chapter 3, for more detail on general color-management topics.

 Note that any options that don't apply to your selected printer are grayed out.

**3.** **Use the Top and Left boxes in the Position area to indicate where you want the image to appear on the page.**

**4.** **To center the image, select the Center Image check box.**

**5.** **If you want to scale the image up or down, choose the scale percentage and/or enter height and width values in the Scaled Print Size area.**

(This doesn't change the physical dimensions of the image; just the print size.) Additional options include

✔ **Show Bounding Box:** Places the handles around the image area and allows for visual sizing.

✔ **Print Selected Area:** A useful option when printing only part of a large image.

✔ **Scale to Fit Media:** Sizes your image to fit on a particular paper size.

**6.** **Choose the printing options you want to apply:**

✔ **Background:** The area surrounding the printed image is called the background, not to be confused with the background color on the Colors palette or the background layer of an image. You can change this color from the default (white) to any other color. Clicking the Background button brings up the Color Picker tool. Black is often the best background choice if you are printing slides on a film recorder and want the area outside the image to remain dark.

✔ **Border:** The dialog box that pops up lets you specify a black border to be printed around an image in any width from 0 to 10 points, 0 to 3.5 millimeters, or 0 to 1.5 inches.

✔ **Bleed:** A bleed is an image that extends right up to the edge of the paper size on one or more edges. In effect, you're cropping *inside* the image area. In practice, most printers don't actually print right to the edge, so to bleed, say, a 5-x-7-inch image, you need to print it on a larger sheet of paper, such as 8 x 10. Clicking the Bleed button opens a dialog box in which you enter a width in inches, millimeters, or points inside the edge of the image.

✔ **Screen:** When you click the Screen button, you see the Halftone Screens dialog box, shown in Figure 4-7, which lets you create halftones for color separation. See Book X, Chapter 2, for more information on color separations and halftones.

✔ **Transfer:** This is an advanced function used for prepress operations to compensate for the change in dot sizes when halftoned images are printed on a press.

✔ **Interpolation:** This option is available only with some printers, particularly PostScript Level 2 (or higher models), to even out the jagged appearance of diagonal lines in low-resolution images.

**7.** **Select options for marking the area outside the print area. These include several items that appear only when the print area is smaller than the paper size:**

✔ **Calibration bars:** This option adds an 11-step grayscale bar outside the image area when printing to a paper size that is larger than the image area. Calibration bars can be used to gauge how accurately the gray tones of an image are being reproduced.

✔ **Corner crop marks:** Clicking this box prints crop marks at the corners of the image, which indicate where trimming should take place. You can see these and other marks in Figure 4-8.

✔ **Center crop marks:** These crop marks show where the page will be trimmed at the top, bottom, and each side.

✔ **Registration marks:** Registration marks are used when you're printing with multiple plates, such as those used in four-color or duotone processes. These marks help keep the plates aligned so the image is printed properly.

✔ **Caption:** To include a caption on a printout, choose File➪File Info and enter the text you want to appear. Then click the Caption button in this dialog box.

✔ **Labels:** Clicking this box prints the document name and channel name on the image.

CONTINUED
▼ ▼ ▼ ▼

**8.** Finally, set the options that apply when you're printing to film for color separations, if that's the case.

Here are your choices:

✔ **Negative:** When you're printing an image on paper, you will usually want a positive image, in which case you should not select the Negative check box. However, if you're printing the image on film (as is the case if you're printing color separations), your printer will probably request a negative. To print a film positive, do not select this check box.

✔ **Emulsion Down:** The side of a film or photographic print paper that is light sensitive is called the *emulsion* side. You must specify whether you want the emulsion side up or side down for film output. Emulsion Down is the most common film output choice, although some publications may request Emulsion Up. The default is Emulsion Up (the check box is not selected). This option is not available with all printers.

**Figure 4-7**

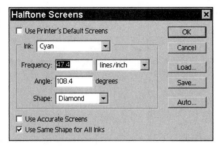

**Figure 4-8**

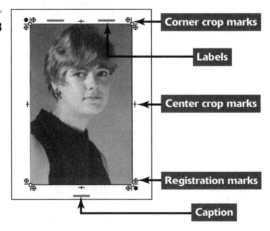

# Viewing and Navigating Images

**P**hotoshop offers a variety of ways to view your image documents as you work with them. You can pull back to look at the big picture or zoom in to work on a tiny portion of the image in minute detail. There's a useful Navigator at hand to show you exactly where you are in an image and help you move to a specific spot with a click of the mouse. Should you want to align objects precisely on the screen, Photoshop offers grids and guides with some "magnetic" properties. And, if you're having trouble finding the image you want, the latest version of Photoshop even includes a browser to help you search visually.

This chapter introduces you to all these viewing and navigating aids, each designed to help you spend less time cruising around the images and more time working with them.

## Looking at the Image Window

Each Photoshop image document resides in its own window, which provides multiple views of the same document. You can drag the window anywhere in the Photoshop working space, but you can't drag it to a second display screen if you're using Photoshop with more than one monitor under Windows.

 You can move palettes and dialog boxes out of the main working space (and onto a second monitor), but documents must stay put in the original display if you're using Windows.

The image window comes in handy because sometimes you'll want to look at an image from two perspectives. For example, you may want to get up close and personal with an image to edit pixels, but you still want to view the full image in a fairly large size. Or, you might want to zoom in on two different portions of an image, but find that simply enlarging the entire image on your screen doesn't show both parts at once.

In either case, all you need to do is create a new image window for the same image. Each window can be sized separately, and you can center the window on any portion of the image you like, as shown in Figure 5-1. For example, you can have one window zoomed in on the upper-right corner of an image and a second window zoomed in on the lower-right corner, and have both visible on the screen at once.

**Figure 5-1**

Here's a quick list of what you can do with multiple windows:

- ✔ **Keep different parts of an image straight by creating multiple windows.** Select the document window you want to duplicate and then choose Window⇨Documents⇨New Window from the menu bar. You can size and position the new window and zoom in or out without affecting the view of the original window. I describe some shortcuts for zooming later in this chapter.

- ✔ **Keep windows organized by cascading them.** If you find that you've created so many windows that you can't view them all easily, Photoshop can automatically arrange them for you in its working space. Choose Window⇨Documents⇨Cascade to create an overlapping stack of windows arranged from the upper-left to the lower-right side of your display.

- ✔ **Keep from losing important windows by tiling them.** Choose Window⇨Documents⇨Tile to arrange the windows side by side without overlapping. Photoshop changes the size of the document windows so they all fit on the screen, but doesn't change the zoom amount. In many cases, the reduced-size windows have scroll bars to let you view the hidden portion of the window.

✔ **Tidy up by closing windows you don't need anymore.** To close a specific window, click its Close box in the upper-right corner of its title bar under Windows (at the top left under the Mac OS).

✔ **Close all windows in one fell swoop.** To close all windows, choose Window⊏>Documents⊏>Close All (or press Shift+Ctrl+W) under Windows. If you're using Mac OS, choose File⊏>Close All instead. On the Mac, you can also hold down the Option key and click the Close box (Close button under Mac OS X) to close all open documents.

# Zooming In and Out of Image Windows

Photoshop offers several ways to zoom in or out of an image, but you'll probably find yourself using one method, such as the keyboard shortcuts, almost instinctively.

Each method has advantages of its own. Here's a quick discussion of each:

✔ **Keyboard shortcuts:** While using any tool, hold down the Shift key. Then press the Alt key (or the spacebar+Option on the Mac) and click to zoom out from a point centered on where you click. Press the Ctrl key instead (or the spacebar+⌘ key on the Mac) and click to zoom in to a point centered on where you click the mouse. Photoshop zooms in or out by one of its preset increments (such as 100 percent, 200 percent, or 50 percent, 33 percent, 25 percent, and so forth). This method is the best way to change magnifications on the fly.

The maximum magnification Photoshop allows is 1,600 percent; the minimum magnification is 0.1 percent.

✔ **Zoom tool:** Click the Zoom tool in the Tool palette or press Z to activate it. Click anywhere in the image to magnify the image by one of the preset magnifications mentioned in the preceding bullet. Hold down the Alt key (or the Option key on the Mac) and click with the Zoom tool to zoom out. In either case, the zoom will center on the point you click. The Zoom tool's big advantage is its zoom selection facility. With the Zoom tool, drag in your image to create a temporary selection. When you release the button, Photoshop zooms in to fill the image window at the highest magnification that includes the selected area.

✔ **Option bar zoom buttons:** When the Zoom tool is active, plus (+) and minus (–) zoom buttons appear in the option bar, as shown in Figure 5-2. You can click the buttons to enlarge or reduce the image to the next preset percentage, centering the zoom on the center of the image.

**Figure 5-2**
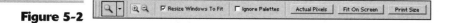

As you zoom in and out, Photoshop does not alter the size of the document window, so your image may become too large for its window (in which case scroll bars appear so you can view the rest of the image) or too small (in which case a gray border appears around the image).

Choose the Resize Windows to Fit option in the Option bar, and Photoshop automatically changes the size of the document window to show the full document in view, up to the size of the Photoshop working area.

✔ **Menu zoom:** Choose View⇨Zoom In or View⇨Zoom Out to enlarge or reduce the image from the menu bar. You can also choose from these options on the View menu:

   ▶ Actual Pixels (which shows your image on the screen at 1:1 pixel ratio)

   ▶ Fit on Screen (which enlarges the image to the maximum size it will fit on the screen)

   ▶ Print Size (which shows the image at the size it will print)

✔ **Magnification Box:** The Magnification box in the Status bar at the bottom of the Photoshop working area (under Windows) or the bottom of each document (under Mac OS) shows the current magnification ratio. Many Photoshop users don't realize you can also type in an exact magnification ratio in this box to produce a custom zoom level. This is handy if you need a specific amount of enlargement or reduction.

Another Magnification box appears in the Navigator palette, along with some other options for zooming. I describe them later in this chapter.

## Zooming tricks

After you've absorbed the basic features of the various zoom alternatives in Photoshop, you'll want to find out about some of the special tricks built into them. Here's a list of the most useful options:

✔ **Press Shift to freeze a selection's border, move the selection, and zoom in.** If you're using the Zoom tool to zoom in on a selection, hold down the Shift key (or the Spacebar under the Mac OS) after you've defined your selection. The selection border freezes; now you can drag the selection anywhere in the document. When you release the mouse button, Photoshop zooms in on the area you've selected.

✔ **Double-click the Zoom tool to display the image at 100 percent magnification.** You can also choose View⇨Actual Pixels from the menu bar or, if the Zoom tool is active, click the Actual Pixels button on the Option bar.

✔ **Choose View⇨Fit on Screen to make an image the largest possible size that will fit on the screen.** You also can click the Fit on Screen button in the Option bar if the Zoom tool is active or (the fastest way) just double-click the Hand tool. (You can find more on the Hand tool later in this chapter.)

To resize windows to fit on the screen when you're not using the Zoom tool, choose Edit⇨Preferences⇨General (or Photoshop⇨Preferences⇨General under Mac OS X) and select the Keyboard Zoom Resizes Windows option.

## Handling the Hand tool

The Hand tool helps you to quickly move around in an image document. The Hand tool works similarly to a scroll bar, but you'll probably find the scroll bar to be more efficient.

The Hand tool is more of a function than an actual tool because you rarely need to click the Hand tool to use it. Simply press the space bar while using any other tool, and the cursor changes into the Hand icon, enabling you to move the image around in its window by dragging.

Here are some tips for using this tool:

✔ **Press H to activate the tool:** To activate the Hand tool without clicking its icon on the Tool palette, just press the H key.

✔ **Use the Options bar to change the size of a window:** When the Hand tool is active, the Actual Pixels, Fit on Screen, and Print Size buttons appear in the Option bar. Click these buttons to enlarge/reduce the image window so the whole image fits in the window; make the document as large as it can be in your working space; or make the document appear in the size it will be when printed.

✔ **Use the Hand tool as a spacebar lock:** When the Hand tool is active, you can hold down the Alt key (Option key on the Mac) and click in the image to zoom out, or hold down the Ctrl key (⌘ on the Mac) and click to zoom in — without needing to hold down the space bar as you would with the normal keyboard shortcut.

 Double-clicking the Hand tool resizes the document image so its longest dimension expands to fill the screen in that direction. A tall, portrait-oriented image balloons up until the document is as tall as possible in the Photoshop working area. A wide, landscape-oriented image expands its width to fit within the left and right borders of the screen.

✔ **Press the Page Up or Page Down buttons to change the view.** These buttons move the view up or down by a windowful.

## Cruising with the Navigator Palette

Many Photoshop users don't use the Navigator palette, which is a roadmap to your image document, nearly as often as they could, and there's a simple reason for that: In its default size, the Navigator palette is just too darned small to be of use.

Most new Photoshop users see the tiny Navigator window and decide that working with such a small thumbnail image isn't worth the bother. There's a quick fix, and after you've seen exactly what the Navigator can do for you, it may become one of your favorite tools.

 If you enlarge the Navigator palette to provide a generous thumbnail image and use the tool in conjunction with a few simple zoom tools, you'll find that the Navigator can be a very fast way to move around within an image.

Here are the keys to using the Navigator:

✔ **Resize the Navigator:** Before you begin working with the Navigator, grab the size box at the lower-right corner of the Navigator palette and drag it down and to the right to create a jumbo version with a much larger, more viewable thumbnail, as shown in Figure 5-3.

**Figure 5-3**

 The Navigator Palette is one palette that you probably won't want to relegate to the Palette Well. It's most useful when it is visible at all times. Position the Navigator to one side of your image so it's ready for instant use.

✔ **View the thumbnail:** The entire Navigator window shows the full document image, with an outline called a *View box* showing the amount of image visible in the document window at the current zoom level.

✔ **Change the view:** Click anywhere in the thumbnail *outside* the View box to center the box at that position. The comparable view in your main document window changes to match.

✔ **Move the view:** Click anywhere in the thumbnail *inside* the View box and then drag to move the box to a new position. The main document window changes to match the new view.

✔ **Zoom in or out:** Click the Zoom In button (which has an icon of two large pyramids) or Zoom Out button (which has an icon of two smaller pyramids) to zoom in or out. Or drag the Zoom slider that resides between the two icons. The View box changes sizes as you zoom in or out, and the view in the original document window is magnified or reduced to match, as well.

✔ **Specify an exact magnification:** The lower-left corner of the Navigator palette has a Magnification box just like the one in the status bar. It shows the current magnification, and you can type in a new value to zoom to the exact magnification level you need.

 If the View box color is too similar to a dominant color in your image, you can choose a new color for its outline by selecting Palette Options from the Navigator palette's Options menu.

# *Choosing a Screen Mode*

Photoshop's working area can become horribly cluttered. And here's a secret: The more adept you become, the more cluttered the desktop becomes. Just when you begin to appreciate a neatly docked Option bar and the convenience of storing palettes in the Palette Well, you realize that you've gobbled up all your free working space.

 **Even if you do as I do and use a dual monitor setup (a 19-inch monitor set at 1920 x 1440 pixels and a 17-inch monitor set at a 1024 x 768 resolution), you may still find that your screens fill up faster than Yankee Stadium on Bat Day. (Mine do.)**

Photoshop has three different screen modes (or, maybe five, depending on what you consider to be a screen mode). Each mode shows or hides some of the elements on the screen at the press of a key or click of the mouse. Three screen modes are shown on the Tool palette; two more are hidden but easily accessible. Table 5-1 shows you how to unclutter your screen quickly.

**TABLE 5-1: CLEANING UP WORKING SPACE CLUTTER**

| Do This . . . | . . . To Change to This Screen Mode | What's Happening |
|---|---|---|
| Press Shift+Tab | Hide all palettes | All the palettes in your working space — except for the Tool palette and any palettes stowed in the Palette Well — vanish. When you need to access them again, press Shift+Tab again. |
| Press the Tab key | Hide all palettes and the Option bar | All the palettes (including the Tool palette) and the Option bar vanish, leaving you with a clean workspace showing only the menu bar, application title bar, and any open documents. |
| Click the Full Screen with Menu Bar icon in the second row from the bottom of the Tool palette | Full Screen mode with menu bar | Only the active document window is visible, along with the palettes, menu bar, and Option bar. The document window is maximized, and the other documents are hidden. (See Figure 5-4.) |
| Click the Full Screen button to view the image alone, with the menu bar and other components hidden | Full Screen mode | Press Shift+Tab and the Tab key to hide the palettes and/or Option bar. |
| Click the Normal Screen button | Standard Screen mode | The default Photoshop screen appears, displaying all menus and palettes. |

In the Full Screen mode, Standard Screen mode, or Full Screen mode with menu bar, you can still press Shift+Tab and the Tab key to hide the palettes and/or Option bar.

 If you hide the Tool palette when in either Full Screen mode, you won't be able to click the icons to return. Press Tab or Shift+Tab to reveal the Tool palette, or simply press F to cycle among the screen modes.

**Figure 5-4**

## Getting Precise Layout Results

Photoshop includes numerous useful features that help you lay out your images precisely. There are dozens of reasons to make a selection in a particular place, position an object at an exact location, or align several objects along the same imaginary line. Here are a few examples:

- ✔ You want to draw parallel lines exactly 50 pixels apart to create a "window blind" effect.

- ✔ You're creating a set of thumbnails that need to be aligned so they line up in neat rows and columns.

- ✔ You want to create an object that is the exact same size (in one or more dimensions) as another object already in your image.

You have several tools to help you do this, and more.

▼ ▼ ▼ ▼ ▼ ▼ ▼ ▼ ▼ ▼ ▼ ▼ ▼ ▼ ▼ ▼ ▼ ▼ ▼ ▼ ▼ ▼ ▼ ▼ ▼ ▼ ▼ ▼ ▼ ▼ ▼ ▼ ▼ ▼ ▼ ▼ ▼ ▼

## Creating guides

Guides are nonprintable horizontal and vertical lines you can position anywhere you like within a document window. Normally, they are displayed as solid blue lines, but you can change guides to another color and/or to a dashed line.

To use guides, choose Edit⇨Preferences⇨Grids, Guides, & Slices (or Photoshop⇨Preferences⇨ Grids, Guides, & Slices under Mac OS X), as discussed in Chapter 6 in this book. Guides would be useful even if they were only, well, guides. However, they have another cool feature: Objects and tools dragged to within 8 screen pixels of a guide are magnetically attracted to the guide and snap to it. That makes it ridiculously easy to align objects precisely. Because the objects snap to the guides, you can be confident that the objects are placed exactly on the guide and not just near it. You can turn off the "snap to" feature if you want a little less precision in your arrangements.

To place guides, follow these steps:

*1.* **Make sure that rulers are visible in your image. Choose View⇨Rulers to display them, if necessary.**

Anytime you create a guide by dragging from the ruler, the Show Guides option is automatically switched on. At other times, you can show or hide guides by choosing View⇨Show⇨Guides, or by pressing Ctrl+semicolon (⌘+semicolon on the Mac).

**2.** **Click in the horizontal ruler and drag down to create a new horizontal guide. Release the mouse button when the guide is in the location you want.**

**3.** **Click in the vertical ruler and drag to the right to create a new vertical guide.**

When you release the mouse button, your new guide stops.

You can also create a horizontal guide by Alt+clicking in the *vertical* ruler (Option+clicking on the Mac), or a vertical guide by Alt+clicking in the *horizontal* ruler (Option+clicking on the Mac). Use whichever method is faster for you.

*4.* **Use the Move tool (press V to activate it) to reposition your guides.**

Guides are shown in Figure 5-5.

## Using guides

After the guides are in place, here are a few of the things you can do with them:

✔ **Turn the Snap to Guides feature on or off:** Choose View⇨Snap To⇨Guides from the menu bar.

✔ **Lock all guides so they can't be accidentally moved:** Choose View⇨Lock Guides. You can also select Alt+Ctrl+semicolon (Option+⌘+semicolon on the Mac).

✔ **Remove all guides and start from scratch:** Choose View⇨Clear Guides from the menu bar.

✔ **Change a horizontal guide to a vertical guide (or vice versa):** Hold down the Alt key (Option key on the Mac) as you drag the guide.

✔ **Align a guide at a precise location on the ruler:** Hold down the Shift key as you drag a guide to force it to snap to the ruler ticks.

✔ **Create a new guide in a precise location:** Choose View⇨New Guide, click the Horizontal or Vertical options and type in a distance from the ruler where you want the new guide to reside.

**Figure 5-5**

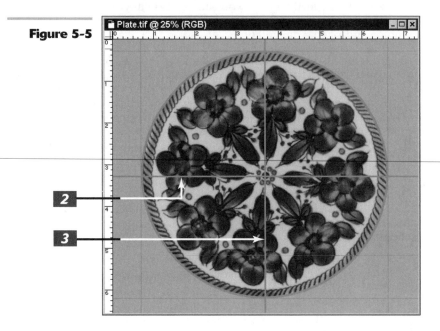

## Using grids

Photoshop's grid feature offers a convenient canned set of guidelines already nicely arranged for you at preset intervals. You can use a grid for any application where you want to align objects in a pleasing geometrically precise arrangement.

Grids share some features in common with guides but boast a few differences, too:

✔ Like guides, grids don't print with your image. They are transparent artifacts used only as reference lines in your image, as shown in Figure 5-6.

✔ Objects and tools can optionally snap to the lines on a grid, depending on whether you have View⇨Snap To⇨Grid turned on or off.

✔ Grids can be shown or hidden by choosing View⇨Show (Hide)⇨Grid.

✔ You can change the color of the grid and choose solid lines, dashed lines, or dots for the grid by choosing Edit⇨Preferences⇨Guides, Grids, & Slices.

✔ You can specify the distance between grid lines and the number of subdivisions between grid lines in Preferences. For more information on setting grid and guide preferences, see Chapter 6 in this book.

**Figure 5-6**

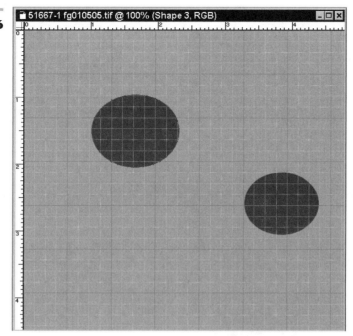

# *Measuring On-Screen*

You can measure distances and objects within Photoshop many different ways. The rulers, used in combination with guides, are a good way to mark distances precisely so you can create objects of a particular size. You can change the increments used for these measurements in Photoshop's Preferences, as detailed in Chapter 6 in this book.

However, Photoshop also has a handy Measure tool you can use to lay measurement outlines in any direction (not just vertically or horizontally as with grids and guides). These lines tell you a great deal more than just the size of the object you're measuring. You can also measure angles and determine the exact coordinates of an object.

When you use the Measure tool, the Option bar offers a readout of information that includes the following values:

- ✔ **X, Y — the X and Y coordinates of the start of the line:** For example, if you start at the 1-inch position on the horizontal ruler and the 3-inch position on the vertical ruler, the X and Y values in the Option bar are 1.0 and 3.0, respectively. (The X and Y values are shown in the increments you've selected for the ruler in your Photoshop Preferences.)

- ✔ **W, H — the horizontal (W) and vertical (H) distances traveled from the X and Y points:** A 1-inch long perfectly horizontal line drawn from the X,1 and Y,3 position would show a W value of 1.0 and an H value of 0.0.

- ✔ **A:** The angle of the line.

- ✔ **D1:** The total length of the line.

▼▼▼▼▼▼▼▼▼▼▼▼▼▼▼▼▼▼▼▼▼▼▼▼▼▼▼▼▼▼▼▼▼▼▼▼▼▼▼▼▼▼▼

## Measuring an object

To measure an object, follow these steps:

**1.** **Choose the Measure tool.**

It's tucked away in the Tool palette with the Eyedropper. Press I to cycle among the Eyedropper, Color Eyedropper, and Measure tool until it appears.

**2.** **Click at a starting location for the measuring line and then drag to the end location.**

Hold down the Shift key to constrain the line to multiples of 45 degrees.

**3.** **Release the mouse button to create the measurement line, as shown in Figure 5-7.**

**Figure 5-7**

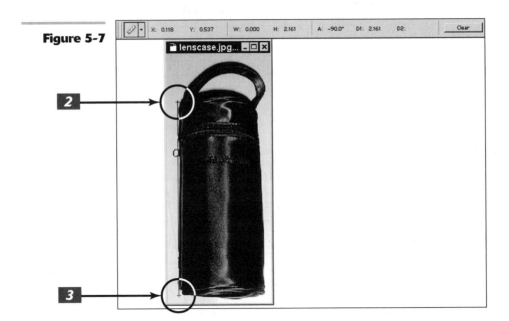

▼▼▼▼▼▼▼▼▼▼▼▼▼▼▼▼▼▼▼▼▼▼▼▼▼▼▼▼▼▼▼▼▼▼▼▼▼▼▼▼▼▼▼

## Measuring an angle

You can measure an angle by drawing two lines and reading the angle between them from the option bar. Just follow these steps:

**1.** **Choose the Measure tool.**

**2.** **Click at a starting location for the first line and drag to the end location.**

You can hold down the Shift key to constrain the line to multiples of 45 degrees.

**3.** **Release the mouse button to create the first line.**

**4.** Hold down the Alt key (or the Option key on the Mac) and click in the end point of the first line where you want to measure the angle.

**5.** Drag the second line and release the mouse button when it is finished.

**6.** In the Option bar, read the angle between the two lines (A).

You can also see the length of each of the lines as D1 and D2, as shown in Figure 5-8.

**Figure 5-8**

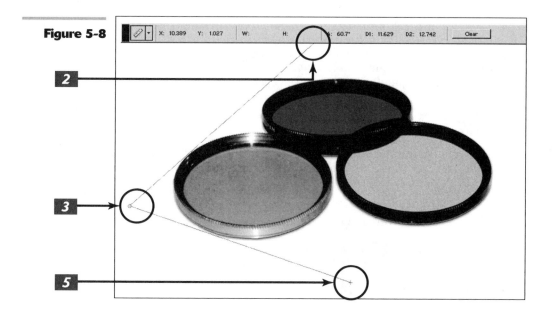

## Using the Info Palette

The Info palette, shown in Figure 5-9, displays a variety of information, depending on what tool you're using. For example, if you're using the Measure tool, the information in the Info palette duplicates the measurements shown in the Option bar. Choosing other tools modifies the Info palette's display to reflect the functions of that tool. Here is some of the information you can find out by keeping the Info Palette visible on your desktop:

✔ When using most tools, the Info palette displays the X and Y coordinates of the cursor as well as the color values of the pixel directly beneath the cursor.

✔ When the Marquee or Lasso tools are active, the Info palette shows both the X and Y coordinates of the cursor as well as the width and height of the selection.

✔ When using the Crop or Zoom tools, the Info palette shows the width and height of the marquee used to define the cropping or zoom borders. The Crop tool's current angle of rotation is also displayed.

✔ With the Line, Pen, and Gradient tools, the Info palette shows the X and Y coordinates of the starting position for the line, pen line, or gradient you are defining, as well as the distance (D) of the line you've dragged, the change in X and Y directions (DX and DY), and the angle (A).

**Figure 5-9**

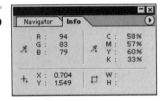

The Info palette's Options dialog box lets you define a second color readout in addition to the default readout, using a different color model if you want (that is, both CMYK and RGB). You can also define a measurement increment for the mouse cursor (in inches, pixels, millimeters, and so forth) independently of the increment you've selected in Preferences. (For more information on setting increments in Preferences, see Chapter 6 in this book.)

## Working with Extras

Extras are the optional items displayed on your screen, such as grids, guides, selection edges, annotations, slices, and the *target path* (a line drawn with the Pen tool). Although you can turn on and off the display of each of these options independently, the Extras function helps you to create a set of extras that you want to see or hide. You can then turn them all on or off at once.

The following list explains how to show or hide these extras:

✔ To turn one extra on or off, choose View↪Show and then choose the extra you wish to show or hide in the Show Extras Options dialog box, shown in Figure 5-10.

✔ To show or hide extras in a group, choose View↪Show↪Show Extras Options. Mark each extra you want to show in the dialog box that appears.

✔ To show or hide all the extras you've marked in Extras Options, choose View↪Extras, or press Ctrl+H (⌘+H on the Mac).

**Figure 5-10**

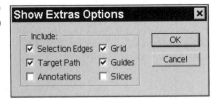

## Managing Images with the File Browser

The File Browser, shown in Figure 5-11, is a new feature that first appeared in Adobe Photoshop Elements and then burst forth in its full glory in Photoshop 7. It's a powerful tool that lets you visually explore your hard disk to find the exact image you need. It has sorting features that let you list the images in various ways.

**Figure 5-11**

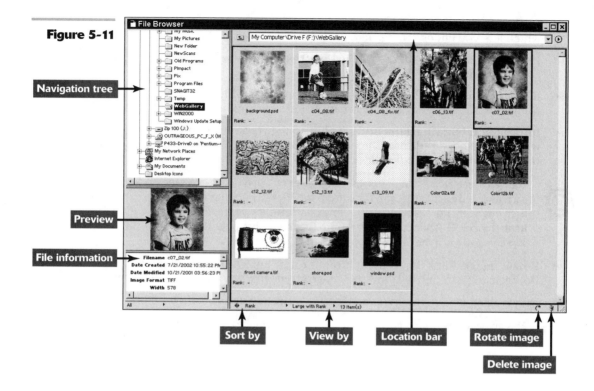

When you've found an image you want to work with, just double-click it to open it. (You can also choose Open from the palette options menu or drag the thumbnail onto the desktop.)

Like any browser, the Photoshop File Browser can be used with very little practice. Many of its functions are similar to browsing functions you already know. Although it's tucked away in the Palette Well, you can drag the File Browser into the main Photoshop desktop to use it, if you like.

 You can add file information for images by using the File Browser. You must choose File⇨File Info within Photoshop to add this information.

Here's a description of the key components of the File Browser window:

- ✔ **Navigation tree:** Located in the upper-left corner of the File Browser is a navigation tree of your computer. If there's an image file available to your computer, the File Browser lets you use this navigation tree to find it.

- ✔ **Location bar:** Across the top right edge of the File Browser is a location bar that lists the current location (such as a folder on your hard disk) on display.

- ✔ **Main browser window:** Beneath the Location bar is a scrollable browsing window that shows thumbnail images of all the image documents in the currently selected folder. In addition, any folders located within the current folder are shown with a folder icon.

✔ **Options menu:** To the right of the Location bar is the File Browser's options menu, which lets you choose things like the size of the thumbnails.

✔ **Preview image:** Beneath the Navigation tree is a preview image of the currently selected image.

✔ **File information:** Underneath the Preview image is a file information box that shows things like the filename, date of creation, date last modified, image format, and so on.

✔ **Information bar:** Along the bottom of the File Browser window is an information bar with several pop-up menus (such as View By and Sort By) that you can use to change the way thumbnails are displayed.

You can create your own custom sorting order by applying a *rank* ranging from A to E for each image. Select Large with Rank from the View By pop-up menu. Then apply a rank to each image by right-clicking the thumbnail (Ctrl+click on the Mac) and choosing Rank A, Rank B, Rank C, Rank D, or Rank E from the menu that pops up. Then select Rank as the sort criterion from the Sort By pop-up menu.

✔ **Rotate image:** Click the rotate button to rotate selected images in the browser window. Double-click a thumbnail, and the image opens in Photoshop already rotated.

✔ **Delete image:** Click the trash can icon to delete selected images.

This actually deletes the file from your hard drive, not just from Photoshop's file browser view!

# Customizing Your Workspace and Preferences

**6**

To a certain extent, Photoshop lets you have it your way without having to make a trip down to the local burger shack. You can easily customize the look of your workspace, specifying everything from the location of palettes to the arrangement of dialog boxes when you begin a session. Starting with Photoshop 7, you can even store these physical layouts and recall them anytime you like.

Photoshop also makes it easy to choose how certain tools and features operate. You can choose how the cursors for tools like brushes are displayed, tell Photoshop your preferred way of storing files, and specify just how much memory you'd like to set aside for image editing. You can set all these preferences once and then forget them, or you can change them from time to time as your needs change. This chapter shows you how to customize your workspace and preferences so Photoshop works your way.

## Creating Workspace Presets

Photoshop is a complicated program; the more you learn, the more complicated (and routine) your activities become. For one project, you may find yourself using the Styles palette repeatedly to add special effects to layers. For your next project, you may never use the Styles palette but require frequent access to the Paths palette to create curves that will be used to make selections. And so it goes. Use custom presets to save time and effort, or to instantly clean up a messy desktop.

Custom workspaces come in handy if you share a computer with students, family members, or coworkers. Those who prepare images for both Web and print have different needs that may call for special workspaces, too.

You can create customized workspace presets that handle all of these needs and a great deal more. Here are some of the ways you can tailor your workspace:

✔ **Combine palettes to group the ones you use most often together.** (For more information on arranging palettes, see Chapter 1 in this book.) Drag a palette's tab into another palette group to add it to that group. If the Layers, Channels, and History palettes are the ones you use most often, you might want to group them together. You can also hide palettes that you rarely use for a particular project, tuck them away in the Palette Well, or minimize them to their title bars.

 Move a palette out of the way quickly by Shift+clicking its title bar. The bar snaps to the nearest screen edge.

Before saving your workspace preset, show or hide the palettes as you prefer them and move them to the locations you want on your screen.

✔ **Position dialog boxes.** Photoshop's menu bar dialog boxes pop up in the same location they appeared the last time you used them. You may want to drag them to a specific place on your screen and store that location when you save your workspace preset. When I'm working with a large image, I sometimes position dialog boxes on the screen of my second monitor to maximize the area for the image on my main display.

✔ **Customize the Options bar.** You can grab the gripper bar at the left edge of the Options bar and drag it to another location. For example, you can dock the bar at the bottom edge of your screen or have it float in a specific place on your Photoshop desktop. You can also double-click the title bar of the floating Options bar to collapse it so only the active tool's icon is showing. Photoshop stores these settings with your workspace preset.

## Saving and Deleting Presets

After you've set up your workspace, you can save it by choosing Window➪Workspace➪Save Workspace. In the Save Workspace dialog box that appears, type a name for your saved workspace and click the Save button. Your saved workspace now appears as a listing on the Workspace submenu.

To delete a saved workspace, choose Window➪Workspace➪Delete Workspace. In the Delete Workspace dialog box that appears, choose the name of the workspace you want to remove from the drop-down list. Click the Delete button, and your preset is gone, gone, gone.

# *Setting Your Preferences*

Photoshop stores settings for many different options in a Preferences file on your hard disk. The first time you run Photoshop after a new installation, you'll probably want to go through the Preferences and customize them to suit your own needs.

You can access the Preferences dialog box by choosing Edit⇨Preferences (in Windows or Mac OS 9) or Photoshop⇨Preferences (in Mac OS X). You can also press Ctrl+K (⌘+K on the Mac). The General Preferences dialog box (shown in Figure 6-1) pops up by default, but you can choose any of the other Preferences dialog boxes from the drop-down list. You can also move between the dialog boxes by clicking the Prev or Next buttons that appear in each of the Preferences dialog boxes. The next several sections give you a rundown of what you can do with the settings in the different Preferences dialog boxes.

**Figure 6-1**

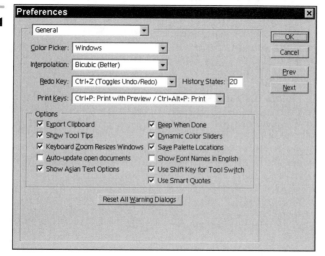

---

### *The ghost in your machine*

From time to time, you may discover that Photoshop has inexplicably trashed your preferences and reset all your settings to their default values. Your first clue that this has happened may be when you open the program and find the palettes arrayed neatly on the right side of the workspace in an arrangement you'd never use.

Surprise! An impossible-to-trace, tiny fault (think *bug*) or unexpected behavior (either in Photoshop or your operating system) has confused Photoshop to the extent that the program has wisely decided to reset your preferences rather than continue with (possibly) corrupted settings.

When the General Preferences dialog box is visible, you can switch to the other Preferences dialog boxes by pressing Ctrl+1, Ctrl+2 (⌘+1, ⌘+2 on the Mac), and so forth. These short-cuts can be useful if you need to frequently access particular dialog boxes.

## Setting general preferences

The General Preferences dialog box is where you select some options that are, well, general in nature. You can select some choices from drop-down lists, and others are check boxes you can select or deselect to activate or disable that option. Here's a rundown of options in the upper part of the dialog box:

- ✔ **Color Picker:** Choose the familiar Adobe Color Picker to select precise colors or work with the Windows or Macintosh system color pickers, as desired. You might want to use the Windows color picker, for example, if you've previously defined some custom colors outside of Photoshop and now want to make them available for a Photoshop project.

- ✔ **Interpolation:** When Photoshop resizes an image, it must either create new pixels (when making the image larger) or combine existing pixels (to make the image smaller). To do this, the program examines neighboring pixels and uses the information to derive the new or replacement pixels. You can select the type of mathematical algorithm Photoshop uses. The Interpolation drop-down list offers these options:

    - ▶ **Nearest Neighbor:** This is the fastest (and lowest quality) interpolation method, under which Photoshop examines only one pixel to perform its calculations. Use this method only if your work is not critical and your computer is relatively slow.

    - ▶ **Bilinear:** This choice provides better quality and is almost as fast as Nearest Neighbor. With this method, Photoshop looks at pixels on either side of the pixel being processed.

    - ▶ **Bicubic:** Most users stick with this option, which is the default setting. Photoshop takes a little longer to perform its calculations but generates an optimized pixel after looking at pixels next to, above, and below the pixel being processed.

    For more on interpolation, see Book II, Chapter 1.

- ✔ **Redo Key:** You can change the key shortcut used to undo/redo an operation from the default Ctrl+Z (⌘+Z on the Mac) to Ctrl+Y (⌘+Y on the Mac). In previous versions of Photoshop, Ctrl+Y was used to preview an image in CMYK, but it's now available as an alternate redo key if you want to move it from next to the oft-used X, C, and V keys — also known as the cut, copy, and paste keys.

- ✔ **Print Keys:** By default, when you press Ctrl+P (⌘+P on the Mac), Photoshop opens a Print dialog box that includes a preview window (as described in Chapter 4 in this book). If you want to bypass the Print dialog box, you can press Ctrl+Alt+P (⌘+Option+P on the Mac) to print the image. The Print Keys setting lets you reverse the two shortcut keys, which you might want to do if you have lots of images to print and don't want to bother with the full Print dialog box (or the Alt/Option key).

- ✔ **History States:** Photoshop remembers how your document looks at various stages of editing, storing all the image information on your hard disk and listing the individual *states* in the History palette. (For more information on using the History palette, see Book II, Chapter 4.) Keeping track of every change you make requires lots of memory and hard disk space, so you can specify how many resources to use by typing a value into this box. The default is 20. If you have resources to burn and frequently find yourself stepping way back in time to modify or delete a step, you can type a larger number. If your resources are skimpy and you don't anticipate making many changes to earlier steps (or are willing to take frequent snapshots or save interim images), you can enter a smaller number.

In the Options section of the dialog box, you find nearly a dozen check boxes that you can select or deselect, as described in the following list:

✔ **Export Clipboard:** When this feature is active, Photoshop transfers its private clipboard (used only within Photoshop) to the general Windows or Macintosh Clipboard so you can paste information into other applications. If you activate this option, switching from Photoshop to other applications takes a little longer, and Photoshop's clipboard contents replace whatever was in your system clipboard when you switched.

The clipboard is generally a poor vehicle for moving image data between applications because the transferred information may not be of the best quality. Instead, save your file and open it in the other application. If you do this, you can turn off the Export Clipboard option, saving you some time when switching between applications.

✔ **Show Tool Tips:** Photoshop can display little pop-up reminders about tools and other objects on your screen. If you find them distracting, deselect this check box to turn Tool Tips off.

✔ **Keyboard Zoom Resizes Windows:** Select this check box if you want your document windows to grow and shrink to fit your document as you zoom in and out. Deselect this check box if you want the document's window to always remain the same size; you might want to do this if you frequently work with several documents side by side and don't want them to change relative size as you zoom in and out.

✔ **Auto-update Open Documents:** When you're working on an image and move to another application (such as ImageReady) to work on the same image, you'll probably want the changes made in the other application to be reflected in the document still open in Photoshop. Select this check box so Photoshop will monitor the document and update its version whenever the document is changed in the other application.

✔ **Show Asian Text Options:** Although Photoshop supports Chinese, Japanese, and Korean text, this option is switched off by default. You can activate it here so that Asian text options become available as you work.

✔ **Beep When Done:** I remember the bad old days when Photoshop would take a minute or two to apply the Gaussian Blur filter or perform calculations when merging even moderate-sized image layers. Photoshop wasn't inefficient; computers a decade ago were really slow compared to those available today. The Beep When Done signal was my cue to stop watching television and resume working with Photoshop. Although most operations are a lot faster today, if you're working with very large images or simply like to be notified when a step is finished, the beep option can be useful (or incredibly annoying to your coworkers).

✔ **Dynamic Color Sliders:** The sliders in the Color palette change colors to match the settings you make. If your computer is on the slow side, you can turn off this feature to improve performance.

✔ **Save Palette Locations:** Select this check box if you want Photoshop to restore your most recent palette locations the next time you start up. Deselect this check box if you always want your palettes in the same location each time you begin working.

✔ **Show Font Names in English:** If you've selected the Show Asian Text Options check box, font names can be displayed in Chinese, Japanese, or Korean by turning this option off. Activate this option if you want font names displayed only in English, regardless of the other Asian text options you're using.

✔ **Use Shift Key for Tool Switch:** When this feature is active, you can change from one tool in the Tool palette to another in the same group (say, to change from the Gradient Tool to the Paint Bucket) by pressing the Shift key and the keyboard shortcut for that tool.

✔ **Use Smart Quotes:** Love 'em or hate 'em, you can instruct Photoshop whether to use *smart* (curly) quotes or *plain* (straight) quotes with this option.

✔ **Reset All Warning Dialogs:** If you've turned off the display of certain warnings by selecting the Don't Show Me This Dialog Box Again check box, you can reactivate all the warnings by clicking this button.

## Deciding how you want files handled

The options in the File Handling Preferences dialog box, shown in Figure 6-2, control how Photoshop handles files as they are opened and closed. Here's the lowdown on these options:

**Figure 6-2**

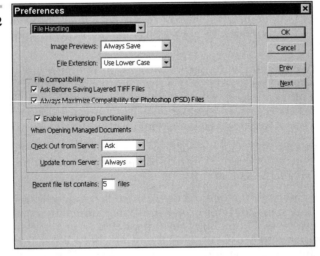

✔ **Image Previews:** Storing a preview thumbnail with an image can speed up browsing for the image you want. You can tell Photoshop to save a preview by default or to ask you first (in case you want to create images that are a little smaller in size, especially for the Web).

✔ **File Extension:** You can select whether the file extensions appended to filenames (such as .psd, .tif, and so forth) are consistently uppercase or lowercase, as you prefer. (On Macs, you can choose whether to add extensions Always, Never, or to Ask When Saving.)

✔ **Ask Before Saving Layered TIFF Files:** Photoshop can save an advanced type of TIFF file that includes layers, exactly as with its own native PSD files. However, many applications cannot read these files. If you always open TIFF files in Photoshop and don't mind creating larger TIFF files in the process, you can disable this option. Otherwise, Photoshop will ask you for confirmation each time you want to save a TIFF file that contains layers.

✔ **Always Maximize Compatibility for Photoshop (PSD) Files:** Not all applications (even earlier versions of Photoshop) can handle the more sophisticated features that may be stored in a PSD file (such as fancy layer effects). If you frequently open PSD files in applications other than Photoshop 7, you may want to activate this option. Keep in mind that you may lose some features when you do this.

When you maximize compatibility, Photoshop saves a *composite* (flattened) version along with the layered file to ensure that older applications (like Version 2) can read the files. However, this option also makes your file size balloon enormously. In addition, when you save in this mode, you get an annoying warning that your file may not be read by future versions of Photoshop. This silly warning appears every time you save a layered PSD file.

 If you plan on using your PSD files in InDesign or Illustrator, you need to have the maximize compatibility feature turned on because those programs need to have a composite along with the layers.

✔ **Enable Workgroup Functionality:** Select this check box if your computer is located on a network and you need to share your files with others in your workgroup by using a WEBDAV server. Then when you open a managed document, Photoshop can do the following:

  ▶ **Check Out from Server:** Automatically "check out" a document from the server when you request it, display a dialog box when you open a file not already checked out, or never open a local copy of a file without first showing a dialog box and checking the document out.

  ▶ **Update from Server:** Automatically download the latest version of the file, ask you whether you want to download the latest version, or never open a file without showing you the dialog box and downloading the latest version.

✔ **Recent File List Contains:** Type a value from 0 to 30 to specify the number of recently used files you want displayed in the Recent File list under the File menu.

## Adjusting your display and cursors

This Display & Cursors Preferences dialog box, shown in Figure 6-3, lets you set several options that control how cursors are displayed on-screen and three display parameters that may affect how quickly your computer completes an operation. These options are described in the following list:

**Figure 6-3**

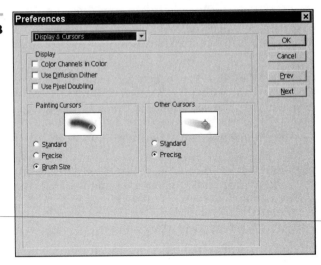

✔ **Color Channels in Color:** When selected, this option tells Photoshop to show each of the color channels (for example, red, green, blue or cyan, magenta, yellow, and black) in their respective colors in the Channels palette. In most cases, you won't want to use this feature. You need to be able to see the channels in their grayscale form to perform image-editing tasks such as converting from color to grayscale, channel masking, or for selective sharpening on certain channels.

✔ **Use Diffusion Dither:** This option is a holdover from the days when those working with images sometimes used graphics cards and displays that could show only 256 different colors. When this feature is activated, Photoshop simulates all the colors in an image by creating mixtures of the 256 available colors in a pattern that the human eye automatically merges together. You can use this option to work with full-color, 24-bit images in 256-color viewing mode. However, any computer that meets the specs needed to run Photoshop 7 should be able to operate in full-color display mode.

✔ **Use Pixel Doubling:** Many dialog boxes and tools have preview windows that show the effect of the settings you're working with. With this feature active, Photoshop doubles the size of the pixels in the preview only, reducing the resolution of the preview but speeding display.

✔ **Painting Cursors:** Choose Standard to show a tool's cursor as an icon representing the tool itself (although I don't know why you'd want to do this). Use Precise to switch to a cursor that has crosshairs useful for positioning the center of a tool's operational area in a particular place. Brush Size (available for painting tools only) tells Photoshop to show the cursor in the same size as the brush itself. Most users prefer to set the painting cursors to Brush Size and the other cursors to Precise. Some folks do complain that precise cursors are hard to see against some backgrounds, but you can always press the Caps Lock key to toggle precise cursors on or off.

## Adjusting transparency and gamut

Photoshop uses colors and patterns to represent information about an image that is normally invisible, such as areas that are transparent, or parts of an image that contain colors that cannot be represented by your current display or printing system. The Transparency & Gamut Preferences dialog box, shown in Figure 6-4, lets you tailor these displays to your own preferences.

**Figure 6-4**

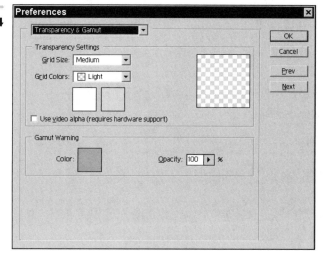

For example, transparency is typically shown on the screen by using a gray-and-white checkerboard pattern. You can change the pattern and colors if you prefer another type of display.

Here is a rundown of the options you find in this dialog box:

- ✔ **Grid Size:** You can choose small, medium, large, or no grid at all. You may want to switch from the default medium-sized grid to a large grid if you're using a very high-resolution setting (such as the 1920 x 1440 pixel setting I use on my monitor) so the grid is a little easier to see. (I don't bother with this, myself.) Or you can switch to a smaller grid if you're working at a 640 x 480 or an 800 x 600 resolution.

- ✔ **Grid Colors:** The default light grid is least obtrusive, but you can switch to a medium or dark grid if you want. Also, you are not limited to gray-and-white checkerboard squares. To choose custom colors, double-click the white and gray squares below the Grid Colors list.

- ✔ **Gamut Warning:** You can adjust the color used to represent out-of-gamut colors and to specify the transparency for the warning color. Double-click the Color box to set the hue and choose the transparency with the Opacity slider. The gamut warning is generally used before converting RGB images to CMYK to see which colors will be lost. For more information on color gamuts, see Book II, Chapter 2.

A *gamut* is the range of colors that can be displayed or printed. In Photoshop talk, out-of-gamut colors generally are those that can't be represented by cyan, magenta, yellow, and black and, therefore, can't be printed. To turn gamut warnings on or off, choose View➪Gamut Warning.

### Setting measurement preferences

In the Units & Rules Preferences dialog box, shown in Figure 6-5, you can set the units used to measure things on-screen (inches, pixels, millimeters, and so forth) and define a default column size when typing text in multiple columns. In addition, you can define the resolution of the image when you choose File➪New and select Default Photoshop Size from the Preset Sizes list. (See Chapter 3 in this book for more on preset sizes.)

**Figure 6-5**

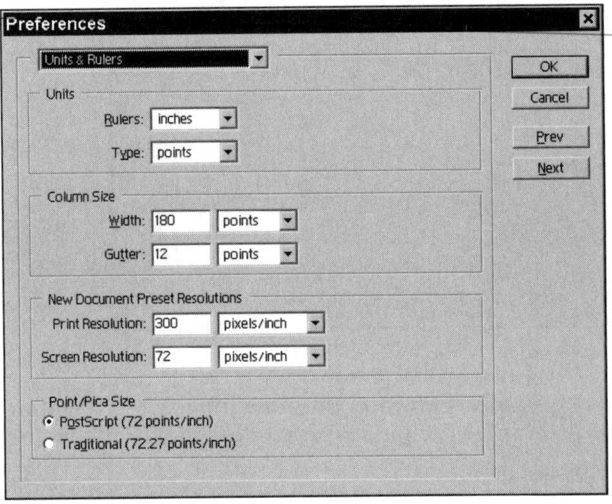

In the Units area of the dialog box, you find these options:

✔ **Rulers:** Select the measurement units Photoshop uses for rulers. Your choices are inches, centimeters, millimeters, points, picas, or percent. The most popular sizes are inches and millimeters, but if you're working with publications and specifying in picas, you might prefer that increment instead. If you're building a Web page, you may prefer to have your rulers incremented in pixels.

✔ **Type:** Choose the measurement used to represent the dimensions of type. Point size is almost universally used, but pixels and millimeters are also available. You may want to use pixels if you're trying to fit type into a specific-sized area of an image.

In the Column Size area, you can specify the following:

✔ **Width:** The width of the column in inches, centimeters, millimeters, points, and picas.

✔ **Gutter:** The width of the area separating columns, also in inches, centimeters, millimeters, points, and picas.

In the New Document Preset Resolutions area, you can set the following:

- ✔ **Print Resolution:** (Most commonly, 300 pixels per inch.) You can change to another value and use pixels per centimeter as a measurement if you want.

- ✔ **Screen Resolution:** Generally, 72 pixels per inch works with most documents. You can select another resolution and use pixels per centimeter if you like.

 Changing the resolution of an image after it's been created can impact the sharpness of your image. It's best to choose the final resolution you want when a document is created, whether you specify the resolution manually or use these presets.

In the Point/Pica Size area, you can choose whether you want to use a measurement of 72 points per inch (which first became relevant in the Macintosh realm and spread as desktop publishing became widespread) or the traditional 72.27 points per inch definition used in the precomputer era. Unless you have a special reason to choose otherwise, use the Postscript (72 points per inch) option.

## Setting up guides, grids, and slices

Guides are nonprinting lines you can create on your screen to make it easier to align objects. Grids are vertical and horizontal lines in the background that make lining up objects even easier. Slices are sections of an image you can create for Web page graphics so that each slice can be loaded and treated separately (usually in a table or similar arrangement). For more information on using grids and guides, see Chapter 5 in this book. For a full explanation of slices, check out Book IX, Chapter 3. The Guides, Grid & Slices dialog box is shown in Figure 6-6.

**Figure 6-6**

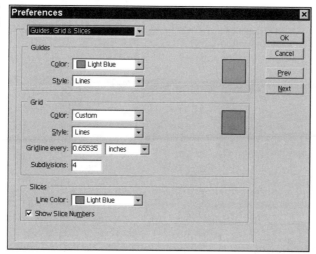

In the Guides area, you can set these options:

✔ **Color:** Either select a color from the drop-down list or double-click the color sample patch to choose your own color. You may want to change the default color if that color is too similar to a dominant color in your image.

✔ **Style:** Select from lines or dashed lines. If you work with images that contain many horizontal and vertical lines that extend across most of an image, dashed lines may be more visible.

In the Grid area, these are your options:

✔ **Color:** Select a color from the drop-down list or double-click the color sample patch to define a specific hue.

✔ **Gridline Every:** Choose the distance between gridlines.

✔ **Subdivision:** Select the number of subdivisions for each gridline.

In the Slices area, these are your choices:

✔ **Line Color:** From the drop-down list, choose a color for the lines that surround each slice.

✔ **Show Slice Numbers:** If you select this check box, Photoshop adds a slice number to the display of slices, which makes it easier to keep track of individual slices.

## Plug-Ins and Scratch Disks

Plug-ins and scratch disks are a couple of unrelated options combined in a single dialog box. The Windows version of this dialog box is shown in Figure 6-7. The Mac version is shown in Figure 6-8.

**Figure 6-7**

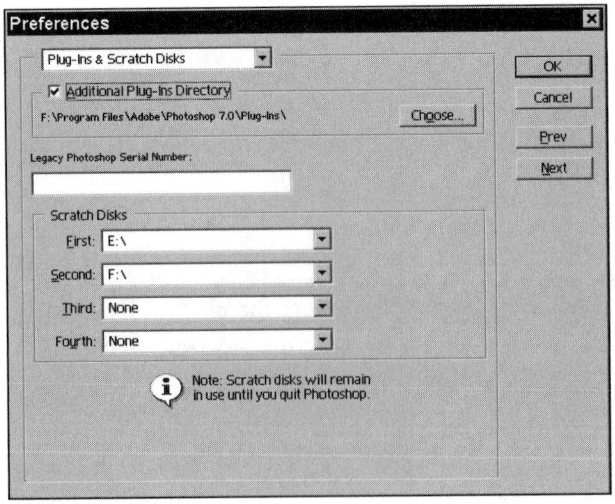

**Figure 6-8**

```
┌─────────────────── Preferences ──────────────────┐
│  ┌─────────────────────────┐                      │
│  │ Plug-Ins & Scratch Disks │ ▲▼                  │    ┌──────────┐
│  └─────────────────────────┘                      │    │    OK    │
│  ┌─ ☐ Additional Plug-Ins Folder ───────────────┐ │    ├──────────┤
│  │  <None>                          [ Choose... ]│ │    │  Cancel  │
│  └───────────────────────────────────────────────┘ │    ├──────────┤
│  Legacy Photoshop Serial Number:                  │    │   Prev   │
│  ┌─────────────────────────────────┐              │    ├──────────┤
│  │                                 │              │    │   Next   │
│  └─────────────────────────────────┘              │    └──────────┘
│  ┌─ Scratch Disks ─────────────────────────────┐  │
│  │   First: │ FWB 2 GB        │ ▲▼             │  │
│  │  Second: │ None            │ ▲▼             │  │
│  │   Third: │ None            │ ▲▼             │  │
│  │  Fourth: │ None            │ ▲▼             │  │
│  └──────────────────────────────────────────────┘ │
│         ┌──┐ Note: Scratch disks will remain       │
│         │▓▓│ in use until you quit Photoshop.       │
│         └──┘                                        │
└───────────────────────────────────────────────────┘
```

## Plug-ins

The Plug-Ins folder is where Photoshop stores all your filters and other plug-in add-ons. A default folder is created when you install Photoshop.

Photoshop allows you to specify an additional folder to search other than its own Plug-Ins folder. This additional folder may come in handy if you want to keep your third-party add-ons separate from Photoshop's native plug-ins. An auxiliary plug-ins directory (not nested within Photoshop's own Plug-Ins folder) can simplify managing those extra filters, and you can turn off their use (potentially speeding up Photoshop's load time) by deselecting the Additional Plug-Ins Directory check box in this dialog box. You can also use this option when you have some plug-ins installed for another application and want to share them with Photoshop without having to make extra copies in your Photoshop Plug-Ins directory.

To activate a new plug-ins directory, select the Additional Plug-Ins Directory check box and then click the Choose button. Navigate to the folder you want to use and select it. Click OK. You then need to exit Photoshop and restart the program to activate the new directory.

 If you have a plug-in or folder you'd like to deactivate, use a tilde (~) as the first character of the plug-in or folder name. Photoshop will ignore the plug-in(s) specified. Just remove the tilde from the name to activate the plug-in or folder.

## Scratch disks

Scratch disks are areas on your hard disk that Photoshop uses to substitute for physical RAM when you don't have enough RAM to work with the images you have opened. Scratch disks are no replacement for physical memory, but there are many times when Photoshop will need them, even if you have huge amounts of memory.

Photoshop uses your startup disk (the disk used to boot your operating system) as its first scratch disk by default. That may not be the best choice because your startup disk is usually pretty busy handling requests of your operating system and, if you're running Windows, for

Windows' own virtual memory scheme (your so-called *swap file* or *paging file*). Ideally, your scratch disk(s) should be a different hard disk and, preferably, the fastest one you have available.

If you have more than one hard disk, choose one other than your startup disk as your first scratch disk. Select your fastest drive; for example, select a FireWire (IEEE1394) or USB 2.0 drive over one using the original, slow, USB 1.1 connection. If you have an Ultra-DMA EIDE drive or, better yet, a SCSI drive, use that. Although Ultra-DMA disks have transfer rates that rival even the speediest SCSI models, SCSI can be better because the SCSI bus is designed for multitasking. You'll often get better performance than with an EIDE disk that shares one of the two EIDE channels with other devices.

 If you don't have a second hard drive, you can improve scratch disk performance by creating a partition on an existing drive for use as a scratch disk. Remember to keep the scratch disk defragmented (that is, with the files all organized together on your hard disk) by using your favorite defragmentation utility. See Chapter 1 in this book for information on how you can monitor how much scratch disk space you have available and how it is being used.

 Adobe changed the format for serial numbers with Photoshop 7, and if you have old plug-ins that require a valid Photoshop serial number, you can enter the serial number from an older version into the space provided in this dialog box.

## Changing Memory and Cache Settings

The perennial question: How much memory does Photoshop require? The perennial answer: As much as you can cram into your computer! Memory is so inexpensive right now there's no excuse for not having at least 512MB of RAM, and more is even better if you're using an operating system that can handle extra memory efficiently, such as Windows 2000, Windows XP, Mac OS 9, or Mac OS X.

When you've crammed your RAM, you'll want to make sure Photoshop can use as much as you can spare. You can use the Memory & Image Cache Preferences dialog box (in Windows) to allocate your memory. You follow slightly different procedures for Mac OS. The Windows version of this dialog box is shown in Figure 6-9.

▼▼▼▼▼▼▼▼▼▼▼▼▼▼▼▼▼▼▼▼▼▼▼▼▼▼▼▼▼▼▼▼▼▼▼▼▼▼▼▼▼▼

### Managing Windows memory

Here's how to allocate RAM in Windows:

**1.** **Choose Edit⇨Preferences⇨Memory & Image Cache.**

The Memory & Image Cache Preferences dialog box opens.

**2.** **In the Physical Memory Usage area, change the Maximum Used By Photoshop parameter.**

Use a value of 50 to 80 percent, depending on how much memory you

have to waste. Allocating more to Photoshop reduces the RAM for other applications, so if you have other programs that need lots of memory, choose a prudent value.

**3.** **Click OK to apply the option.**

**4.** **Exit Photoshop and relaunch the program to activate the new setting.**

**Figure 6-9**

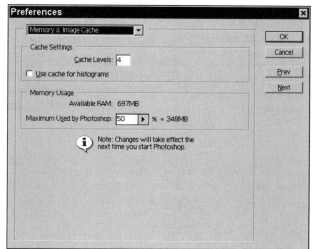

▼ ▼ ▼ ▼ ▼ ▼ ▼ ▼ ▼ ▼ ▼ ▼ ▼ ▼ ▼ ▼ ▼ ▼ ▼ ▼ ▼ ▼ ▼ ▼ ▼ ▼ ▼ ▼ ▼ ▼ ▼ ▼ ▼ ▼ ▼ ▼ ▼ ▼ ▼ ▼ ▼ ▼ ▼

## Managing Macintosh 9 memory

Mac OS X automatically manages memory used by applications like Photoshop, so you don't need to make a special allocation for your image editor. Mac OS 9 and earlier versions of the Mac OS let you specify how much memory each application should use. Just follow these steps for those versions:

1. **If you're using the Simple Finder in Mac OS 9, change to the regular Finder. Choose Edit⟹Preferences and deselect the Simple Finder check box on the General tab to turn it off.**

2. **Exit Photoshop.**

   The Mac OS can't set memory preferences for an open program.

3. **Locate the Photoshop application icon.**

    If you can't find your Photoshop folder, Sherlock 2 in Mac OS 9 can find it for you quickly. Choose Edit⟹Find to open the Sherlock dialog box, type **Photoshop** into the Search box, and select Applications from the drop-down specifications list. Then click the magnifying glass icon to see Photoshop's location.

4. **Select the Photoshop icon and choose File⟹Get Info⟹Memory.**

You can also press ⌘+I and choose Memory from the drop-down list in the General Info dialog box.

Three different memory values are shown:

✔ **Suggested Size** is the value recommended by the software vendor and cannot be changed by the user. Sometimes this value will be lower than is actually practical for running the program because the vendor doesn't want buyers to know what an actual memory hog the application really is.

✔ **Minimum Size** is the amount of memory that's the bare minimum for the application to run. While some programs do set a minimum that is more than they actually need, Photoshop is not one of them. Leave this setting alone.

CONTINUED
▼ ▼ ▼ ▼ ▼

↙ **Preferred Size** is the amount of memory a program can use if it needs to. Under Mac OS 9, it will never use more than this and will instead use something between the minimum and this size, depending on how much memory is available. You should set this to a large enough value that Photoshop has plenty of RAM to work with, while leaving enough for other applications.

**5.** To monitor how much memory Photoshop is actually using, select About this Computer from the Finder, and view the dialog box shown in Figure 6-10.

**Figure 6-10**

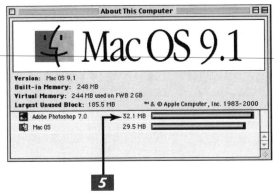

## Adobe Online Preferences

Adobe Online Preferences is a separate setting not grouped with the Preferences dialog boxes. Select it by choosing Edit⇨Preferences⇨Adobe Online. The Adobe Online Preferences dialog box, shown in Figure 6-11, includes buttons you can use to find out about Adobe Online and to check for updates to the application. A drop-down list lets you specify whether Photoshop should automatically check for updates never, once a day, once a week, or once a month. If your computer is always online (say, through a cable modem or DSL connection), you may want to let Photoshop check for its own updates frequently.

### Setting aside memory for storing screen images

You can also set aside the amount of memory for storing screen images in the Image Cache dialog box (Mac), or Memory & Image Cache dialog box (Windows), to speed up redraws of a reduced-view image on your screen as you make changes. You have two options. You can specify the number of copies of your image stored in memory, from the default value of 4 up to 8 levels. You can also set aside cache memory for drawing histograms (brightness graphs produced by the Levels command) if you use histograms frequently.

**Figure 6-11**

# Using the Preset Manager

Many of the palettes and tools Photoshop works with can use settings that you store on your hard disk as presets. For example, you can create custom colors and brush tips, build your own gradients, create a library of shapes, or compile a set of styles to apply to layers.

You'll want to become familiar with the Preset Manager, which provides a central management tool for all the options that are individually available from the palettes and tools themselves. Just as with the tools, you can create, edit, and delete presets. The only thing you can't do with the Preset Manager is actually create a preset. You must do this with the Tool Presets or Tool Presets palettes. Here are some tips on using the Preset Manager, shown in Figure 6-12:

**Figure 6-12**

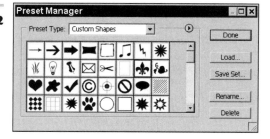

- ✔ To show the Preset Manager, choose Edit⇨Preset Manager. To hide it, click Done.

- ✔ To select a specific type of preset to work with, choose it from the Preset Type drop-down list.

- ✔ To modify a preset, choose the option from the flyout Option menu available in each preset's dialog box.

- ✔ To load an existing set of presets from your hard disk, click the Load button and navigate to the presets you want to access.

- ✔ To store a new or modified group of settings, click the Save Set button and type a name.

- ✔ To give a particular preset a new name, select the setting, click the Rename button, and type the new name.

You can rename multiple settings consecutively by clicking and Shift+clicking the items to be renamed and then clicking the Rename button. Photoshop asks you to supply a new name for each in turn.

- ✔ To quickly load the default preset library for any tool or palette, choose Reset *[name]* Preset from the palette menu.

- ✔ The one thing you can't do with the Preset Manager is actually create a preset. You'll need to use the individual tool palettes for that.

# Book II

# Image Essentials

# Specifying Size and Resolution

1

P hotoshop 7 has evolved into a Swiss Army knife. Once only a pixel-based (or *raster*) application designed primarily for print, it has been transformed into a program capable of both vector- and pixel-based output with added features aimed at producing Web content as well.

You need to be aware of important issues when you produce both pixel-based and vector-based graphics. I give you a bit of background in that department in this chapter. Also, I show you the components that make up the physical aspect of your pixel-based image — the dimensions, the file size, and the resolution — and how they relate to one another.

 Even though Photoshop can now produce vector graphics, its primary mission is to create awe-inspiring raster images. And because the issue of resolution is so critical to raster images, this chapter primarily discusses methods for sizing and resizing raster images. I cover producing vector art in more detail in Book IV, Chapter 2.

You find out how to change any of the three components without harming your image. Yes, you can harm your image. Not intentionally, of course. But it can happen quicker than you can close a dialog box. But with a firm understanding of how pixels live and breathe, you can ensure that your images are safe from any undue damage.

## Putting Images Under the Microscope

Digital images fall into two camps, *vector* images, which are created based on mathematical formulas, and *raster* images, which are made up of pixels. Photoshop allows you to produce both types of images and even to combine both types within a single file.

Table 1-1 gives you the skinny on vector and raster images. For the details, keep reading.

**TABLE 1-1: CHARACTERISTICS OF VECTOR AND RASTER GRAPHICS**

| Graphic Type | How It Works | File Size | Image Degradation Possible? | Resolution Dependent? |
|---|---|---|---|---|
| Vector | Uses mathematical formulas to precisely locate and connect geometric objects and segments | Usually smaller | No | No |
| Raster | Breaks pieces of an image into a grid made up of pixels | Usually larger | Yes | Yes |

## Vector images

One cool thing about vector images, also called object-oriented images, is that when you zoom in on them, they don't look blocky. That's because vector images are comprised of *segments* — curved or straight — and *anchor points* — elements that indicate the endpoints of the segments — that are defined by mathematical objects called *vectors*. Vectors use a unique mathematical formula to define the specific location of an object as well as its geometric shape.

Vector images are usually the product of drawing programs, such as Adobe Illustrator, but Photoshop is now also capable of producing a vector or two. And not to be outdone, its cousin Illustrator can also *rasterize* (or convert into pixels) vector artwork, thereby providing you with raster images to work with.

Here is some additional information about vector graphics:

- ✔ **A curve is still a curve, even at 20,000 feet.** Because they are mathematically defined, vector graphics can be sized and otherwise transformed without an inkling of quality loss. Take that little 2-inch spot illustration and size it up to mural size, and it will appear identical. A perfect true curve remains a perfect true curve, whether it's 2 inches or 20 feet long.

- ✔ **You can get pretty pictures in small packages.** Vector images can be small in file size because the file size depends on the complexity of the vector objects, not the size of the illustration.

 Graphics that need clean lines such as logos, typographic illustrations, and line art work great in vector format, such as my logo, shown in Figure 1-1.

- ✔ **Vector images are independent — resolution independent, that is.** Not only can they be transformed and printed without a degradation in quality, but they also have no built-in resolution — they take on the resolution of the output device. For example, print my logo in Figure 1-1 to an *imagesetter* (a high-end printing device used for color separations) at 2400 dots per inch (dpi), and the image will come out at 2400 dpi. Print it to a 300 dpi laser printer and what do you get? A 300 dpi image. (If all this technical lingo like imagesetter and dpi is confusing, it might help to skim over Book X, Chapter 2.)

 Because your monitor can only display images on a grid, vector images display on-screen as pixels. This accounts for the jagged appearance you see when you zoom into a curved vector object. But don't worry; it will print just fine.

**Figure 1-1**

## Raster images

Raster images are usually the result of the digitizing of *continuous-tone* images, such as photographs or original painted or drawn artwork. Raster images are comprised of a grid of squares, which are called pixels. If you've ever looked at a bathroom wall made up of those small square tiles reminiscent of the '40s, you're familiar with what a grid of pixels looks like: Each pixel lives in a specific location on that grid and contains a single color. When you edit a bitmap image, you are editing one or more pixels rather than an object-oriented shape.

Although it doesn't seem like it when you're viewing an image that fits inside your computer screen, your entire image can be broken down into a grid of square pixels. That means the elliptical shapes of my beanie, shown in Figure 1-2, also have to fit within this system of squares. But how do you fit a round peg in a square hole? By faking it. Unlike the true mathematical curve possible when drawing vector shapes, raster images must try to approximate a curve by mimicking the overall shape with square pixels.

**Figure 1-2**

Fortunately, the mimicry the pixels have to do is indecipherable with high-resolution images viewed at a reasonable distance. But when you zoom in, you can see that a curve in an image (like the curve of my beanie) is indeed comprised of square pixels. Raster graphics work great for photorealistic or painterly images where subtle gradations of color are necessary. On the downside, because they contain a fixed number of pixels, raster graphics can suffer a degradation of quality when they're enlarged or otherwise transformed. They are also large in file size.

Bitmap images are resolution dependent. Because they contain a fixed number of pixels, the resolution of the device they are being printed to is only one of two factors that influence the quality of the image. The quality of the output also depends heavily on the resolution of the image. For example, an image with 72 dots per inch (dpi) doesn't look any better printed on a 600 dpi printer than it does on a 1200 dpi printer. Likewise, a 300 dpi image won't look as good printed on an old 72 dpi dot matrix printer as it would on a 1200 dpi printer.

# *Viewing Raster Images On-Screen*

Resolution really doesn't play a role in how you view images on-screen. The display of images on-screen is based on 1 image pixel per 1 screen pixel.

The most important issue, then, is making sure that your image fits inside your (or your audience's) monitor when viewed at 100%. This is where pixel dimensions come into play — especially if you're putting images on the Web.

 When you view an image on-screen, the display size is determined by the pixel dimension, plus the size and setting of the monitor. You therefore need to determine the demographics of your audience and then size your graphics accordingly.

✔ A 17-inch monitor probably displays 1024 by 788 pixels. An 800 x 600 pixel image fills part of the screen. Change the monitor setting to 800 x 600, and the image fills the screen, with each pixel appearing larger.

✔ On a 15-inch monitor, an 800 x 600 pixel image fills the screen. But a 1024 x 768 image can't be viewed in its entirety.

 Resolution is measured in pixels per inch, or ppi. You may also run across the term samples per inch (spi). Another term you will see often is dots per inch (dpi). Dots per inch is always used in reference to printers, scanners, imagesetters, and other paper outputting devices.

You'll see recommended resolution settings somewhere between 72 ppi and 96 ppi even though resolution isn't really a factor in preparing screen images. That's just because monitors display somewhere in the 72 to 96 ppi range. So if you change the physical dimensions of an image, then it will always be at a one to one ratio with the monitor. If you view an image whose resolution is higher than that of the monitor, the image appears larger on-screen than in its printed state. For example, try opening (or dragging and dropping) a 300 pixel-per-inch (ppi) jpeg file into a browser window. It explodes on your screen. Because the monitor can only display 72 to 96 ppi, it needs a ton of space to show all the pixels in the image.

▼ ▼ ▼ ▼ ▼ ▼ ▼ ▼ ▼ ▼ ▼ ▼ ▼ ▼ ▼ ▼ ▼ ▼ ▼ ▼ ▼ ▼ ▼ ▼ ▼ ▼ ▼ ▼ ▼ ▼ ▼ ▼ ▼ ▼ ▼ ▼ ▼ ▼ ▼

# *Using the Image Size Command*

A time will come when you need to mess with the resolution or dimensions of an image. You may want to change the file size, or you may simply need to make sure that the resolution is appropriate for printing or some other paper output. Or you need to adjust the dimensions so that they're just right for viewing on-screen. And sometimes — only sometimes — you may need to add or delete pixels.

Or you need to change the width, height, and/or resolution of your image for printing or some other paper output. Photoshop, being the powerhouse that it is, certainly allows you to do so with the Image Size command found on the Image menu.

### Resolution, dimension, and size in raster images

Every raster image has these physical attributes — resolution, dimension, and size. Size takes on two personalities. You have the file size, which is a result of the pixel dimensions, and you have print size, which is the width and height of an image. These attributes are interrelated. Change any one and at least one of the other attributes is affected also.

The file size of a raster image is determined by the *pixel dimensions* — the number of pixels along the height and width of the image. The following figure shows a Photoshop dialog box that lists all the vital statistics of an image that takes up 176K of space and is 200 pixels wide and 300 pixels high. Just multiply these values:

$200 \times 300 = 60,000$ pixels contained in the image

How does 60,000 pixels lend a file size of 176K?

$60,000 \times 3 = 180,000$

$180,000 \div 1024 = 176$

There are 3 bytes in a 24-bit color image. Multiply 3 bytes by 60,000 pixels, and the result is 180,000 pixels. Divide 180,000 pixels by 1024

bytes per kilobyte, and you get the file size value of 176K.

**Remember:** These are the basics that affect file size, but other factors contribute to size as well, such as layers and channels. For more on layers, see Book V, and for details on channels, see Book VI.

Resolution is usually measured in pixels per linear inch (ppi), although it can also be measured in pixels per millimeter. The image in my example has a resolution of 120 pixels per inch (ppi), or 14,400 pixels, which just happens to be $120 \times 120$, or $120^2$.

The dimensions of an image are its width and height when it is printed. To calculate these dimensions, all you have to do is divide the number of pixels by the image's resolution:

$200 \div 120$ ppi = 1.667 inches (image width in print)

$300 \div 120$ ppi = 2.5 inches (image height in print)

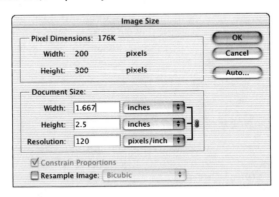

Follow these steps to resize your image:

**1. Open the image and then choose Image⇨Image Size.**

The Image Size dialog box opens, as shown in Figure 1-3. This is where the magic happens.

**2. Note the current pixel dimensions of your image and the resulting file size.**

Mine shows 1536 pixels in width and 1024 pixels in height for a file size of 4.5M.

**3.** **Also note your current document size.**

This is the size of your image when it prints on paper. Mine shows a width of 21.333 inches and a height of 14.222 inches with a resolution of 72 ppi. A resolution of 72 ppi isn't adequate for printing purposes. I will be able to see some *pixelation* (visible little squares) on my printout. Therefore, I need to reduce the size of the image so that my total pixels are spread out over a smaller area, making them more densely packed.

**4.** **Make sure that the Resample Image check box is deselected and then enter a new value for the width.**

Don't worry about the definition of *resample;* I explain it in the next section. I entered a value of 5.12 inches. Note how my height value automatically changed to 3.413, as shown in Figure 1-4. That's because the Constrain Proportions check box is selected, as indicated by the chain and bracket icon. Notice that the check box is also grayed out. If the Resample

Image option is deselected, the Constrain Proportions option is unavailable. Nine times out of ten, you're probably going to want your image to stay proportional. You can also change your units of measurement by choosing from the pop-up menu.

**5.** **Note how the resolution automatically changed based on what you entered in Steps 3 and 4.**

In my example, my resolution went from 72 ppi to 300 ppi. When you do not have Resample Image selected, your pixel dimensions remain unchangeable (note how there is no text box for you to enter new pixel dimension values). Therefore, when you enter a smaller width or height value, the resolution must increase in order to accommodate all the pixels in the image. Similarly, if you enter a new resolution value (rather than a width value as I did), Photoshop then adjusts the width and height values in order to accomplish the same thing.

**Figure 1-3**

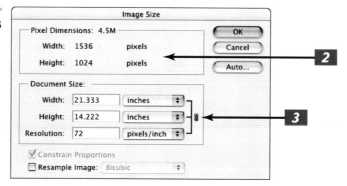

CONTINUED
▼ ▼ ▼ ▼ ▼

Before you close out of this dialog box, I would be remiss in not telling you about the Auto button. This is Photoshop's way of giving you a suggested resolution setting based on your screen frequency. Don't worry about it for now. But if you feel the burning need to know about screen frequencies, check out Book X, Chapter 2.

6. **Click OK.**

 You won't notice any difference in the way your image appears on-screen because you haven't added or deleted any pixels; you've merely compacted them into a smaller space.

Congratulations! You have just safely resized your image. You can proudly say "No pixels were harmed in the making of this image."

**Figure 1-4**

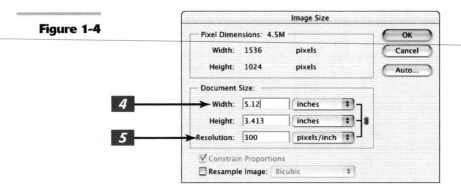

## Resampling Images

Resampling means you are changing the pixel dimensions of an image. When you *downsample* (or resample down), you are eliminating pixels and therefore deleting information and detail from your image. When you resample up, you are adding pixels. Photoshop adds these pixels by using *interpolation*. Interpolation means Photoshop analyzes the colors of the original pixels and "manufactures" new ones, which are then added to the existing ones.

You can specify the interpolation method in the Image Size dialog box. The default that appears in the dialog box is based on the interpolation method you specified in your General Preferences. Here are your three choices:

- **Nearest Neighbor:** This method is fast and provides for the smallest file size, but it is less precise and therefore of the lowest quality. This method works by copying the color of the nearest pixel. It can result in jagged edges, so use it only for images with non-anti-aliased edges (hard edges).

- **Bilinear:** Considered a medium-quality method, it works by averaging the color of the pixel above, below, and to the right and left of each pixel.

- **Bicubic:** This method is the slowest but most precise. It averages the color of the pixel above and below and the two on the right and left of each pixel. It provides a smoother transition between pixels but also increases the contrast between pixels to reduce blurriness.

If you really must resample, I recommend leaving it set to Bicubic. Notice I said if you *really* must. Here are some reasons why you might choose to add or delete pixels:

- ✔ You no longer have access to the original artwork, which you could rescan at the proper resolution and size.

- ✔ You no longer have access to the original high-resolution version of the file.

- ✔ You absolutely cannot substitute the low-resolution image with another of higher resolution.

 Resampling isn't a recommended activity. I mean as smart as Photoshop is, having to manu-facture pixels out of the blue is not an exact science. Your image tends to lose detail and sharpness and get blurry and mushy. The bottom line is your resampled image will never look as good as the original.

▼ ▼ ▼ ▼ ▼ ▼ ▼ ▼ ▼ ▼ ▼ ▼ ▼ ▼ ▼ ▼ ▼ ▼ ▼ ▼ ▼ ▼ ▼ ▼ ▼ ▼ ▼ ▼ ▼ ▼ ▼ ▼ ▼ ▼ ▼ ▼ ▼ ▼

## Adding pixels to an image

To add pixels to an image, follow these steps:

**1.** **With your desired image open, first choose Image➪Duplicate to make a copy of your original. With the dupli-cate active, choose Image➪Image Size.**

See Figure 1-5.

 This is where the havoc happens. Be careful!

**2.** **Make sure that the Resample Image option is selected and then enter a higher value for the resolution.**

I entered a resolution of 300 ppi and a width of 8 inches.

**3.** **If desired, enter a higher value for the width or height.**

I entered a width of 8 inches.

**Figure 1-5**

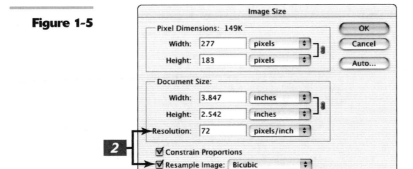

CONTINUED
▼ ▼ ▼ ▼

Note how the pixel dimensions increased dramatically as did the file size (from a mere 149K to 10.9M), as shown in Figure 1-6.

The Width and Height under Pixel Dimensions are now text boxes into which you can enter values as well. They are no longer fixed values as they were when Resample Image was deselected.

Leave your Interpolation method set to Bicubic.

 If you get all discombobulated when working in the dialog box, press Alt (Option on the Mac). The Cancel

button will change to a Reset button. Click it, and you're back to where you started.

**4. Click OK.**

Photoshop now goes through its interpolation ritual and churns out a newly resampled image. Do a side-by-side comparison to the original, looking at both at 100% view. Your original should look better than the resampled image. Notice the overall blurriness and goopy edges that are an unfortunate side effect of interpolation, as shown in Figure 1-7.

**Figure 1-6**

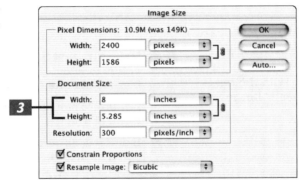

**Figure 1-7**

## Taking pixels out of an image

As I mention earlier, when you *downsample* you eliminate pixels and therefore delete information and detail from your image. Although I have emphasized the pitfalls of resampling up, you can sometimes damage your image by downsampling, as well.

Granted, downsampling is sometimes necessary when converting high-resolution print graphics into Web graphics. For example, you may be forced to take images used for a corporate brochure and repurpose them into content for the company's Web site. You probably won't notice much degradation in image quality because the images are just being viewed on-screen. In addition, downsampling can occasionally camouflage the moiré patterns caused by scanning halftones (for more on halftones, check out Book VII, Chapter 1). However, you can downsample to the extreme where the images look horrid even on-screen, as shown in Figure 1-8. But just remember, there should never be a need for you to make an image smaller than 72 ppi.

 If you have to significantly downsample your image, for example to 25% of its original size, you will get better results if you do several successive 50% downsamples, applying a Unsharp Mask filter on the image in between each image sizing. For more on the Unsharp Mask filter, see Book VII, Chapter 1.

To remove pixels from an image, follow the steps in the preceding section and change the image settings accordingly.

**Figure 1-8**

4 x 3.75 inches at 72 ppi    4 x 3.75 inches at 36 ppi

### A potpourri of image size do's and don'ts

Here are some tips and tricks to keep in mind when you're messing around with image size and resolution settings:

- ✔ **Use the Unsharp Mask filter when you resample.** If you resample your image, either up or down, it is sometimes helpful to apply an Unsharp Mask filter (choose Filter⇨Sharpen⇨Unsharp Mask). This filter heightens the contrast between pixels to give the illusion of sharpening or forcing the image more in focus.

- ✔ **You can always look without touching.** If you don't want to change the resolution or size of your image, but just get its vital statistics, use the file information box at the bottom of the application window (document window on the Mac). Press Alt (Option on the Mac) and click your mouse over the file information box. You can see the width, height, channels (see Book VI, Chapter 1), and resolution of the document.

- ✔ **Don't change your settings — just use Print with Preview.** If you want to leave the size and resolution settings unmolested, but need to print your image at a different size, use the Print with Preview command. For details on Print with Preview, see Book I, Chapter 4.

- ✔ **Try starting out with the proper dimensions.** It goes without saying, but I'll say it anyway. You want to try and enter the proper dimensions and resolution when creating a *new* document. You don't want to find yourself in the unfortunate situation of creating your file at 72 ppi, spending hours getting it just perfect and then remembering that you were supposed to prep it for print and really needed it to be 300 ppi. Resampling your image from 72 ppi to 300 ppi is going to make it go from perfect to, well, far less than that. And when scanning an image, make sure that you scan it at a high enough resolution that if you need to enlarge the dimensions, you can do so without changing the pixel dimensions. See Book X, Chapter 2, for more details on prepping an image for print.

- ✔ **Don't use a higher resolution than you need.** All you'll do is create an unnecessarily huge file with a slower print time. In addition, the output device may not be able to reproduce all the detail in the image. In some cases, it may actually make your printout look darker and muddier.

- ✔ **Look no further than this book.** Use the handy, dandy table of recommended resolution settings for a variety of output devices in Book X, Chapter 2.

## Resizing Images with the Resize Image Wizard

You find the Resize Image Wizard (Resize Image Assistant on the Mac) under the Help menu on the Photoshop menu bar. When selected, the Wizard/Assistant dialog box, shown in Figure 1-9, appears and asks you questions about your intended use for the image. The wizard/assistant then guides you through the image-sizing process. If you happen to choose options that the wizard doesn't like, you get a warning that your changes are likely to lower your image quality. You can then go back and try another setting.

The Resize Image Wizard is more for beginners and doesn't offer quite the control that the Image Size dialog box does. In addition, you are unable to see all of your options on one screen and must continually go back and forth between screens when entering different values.

**Figure 1-9**

When you're done changing settings and choosing options, the wizard/assistant creates a new file called Resize Wizard_1 (Resize Assistant 1 on the Mac), leaving your original unharmed. Like any kind of wizard, this one is pretty savvy, but I recommend having a firm understanding of proper output resolution (see the beginning of this chapter for info on that topic) before you use the wizard/assistant. And actually with that firm understanding, you can do manually everything the wizard/assistant can do and more. Remember the old adage, knowledge is power.

While using the Resize Image Wizard is fine, try to avoid using the File⇨Automate⇨Fit Image command. When I see a dialog box having to do with image sizing that only contains two text boxes, it's an immediate red flag! This command resizes your file as close to your entered dimensions as possible, while maintaining the same proportions. But in order to do so, Photoshop enlarges or decreases your image while leaving the resolution the same. And if you've read earlier sections of this chapter, you know this is also called resampling — not a nice thing in image-editing circles.

## Changing the Canvas Size

I've probably harped on you to the point that you're slightly paranoid, or at least ultraconscious, of using the Image Size command. Well, you can relax now because the Canvas Size command is as safe as can be. Unlike the Image Size command, which enlarges or reduces the dimensions or resolution of your image, the Canvas Size command merely changes the size of the *canvas,* or page, on which the image sits.

When you increase the size of the canvas, Photoshop fills the expanded area outside the image with your background color. Increasing your canvas size can come in handy if you are trying to add a frame or border around your image. If you make the canvas smaller, Photoshop *crops* (cuts away) the image.

Here are the quick and easy steps to changing your canvas size:

**1. Choose Image⇨Canvas Size.**

The Canvas Size dialog box, shown in Figure 1-10, appears. The current size of your canvas appears at the top of the dialog box.

**2. Enter new values in the Width and Height text boxes.**

You can also change the unit of measurement by using the pop-up menus. Select the Relative check box to specify an amount of space for Photoshop to add around your image. This feature is handy when adding equal amounts of canvas around images with fractional measurements.

**3. Specify your desired anchor placement and click OK.**

The anchor shows how the image sits inside the canvas. By default, the image is centered, and the canvas will be added equally around the image. Click any of the other eight squares

to have the canvas added asymmetrically around the image, as shown in Figure 1-11.

If you reduce either the Width or Height value and click OK, an alert box appears asking if you really want to proceed because you will be clipping the image. This is actually another way of cropping an image, albeit not one you will use everyday. There are more exact ways of cropping an image (see the next section). However, this method can occasionally come in handy when you want to crop your image on one or more sides by a certain number of pixels. For example, sometimes it's difficult to crop (using the Crop tool described in the next section) a one- or two-pixel-wide row or column along the edge of an image. In this case, use the Canvas Size command and specify a value for the Width and/or Height that is a couple of pixels smaller than your original. Pesky problem solved.

**Figure 1-10**

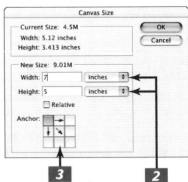

## Cropping an Image

Even a novice photographer knows that cropping an image can make for a stronger composition. *Cropping* entails cutting away background clutter or endless expanses of empty space in order to focus in on your desired subject.

**Figure 1-11**

This simple process can transform a ho-hum photograph into a visually exciting one. Take a look at my example in Figure 1-12. I mean, it doesn't take an Ansel Adams to figure out which image is stronger. (It would be even better if the fence wasn't in the background, but hey, that's nothing that a little Photoshop retouching can't take care of. Check out Book VIII; it's all about retouching and restoration techniques.)

▼ ▼ ▼ ▼ ▼ ▼ ▼ ▼ ▼ ▼ ▼ ▼ ▼ ▼ ▼ ▼ ▼ ▼ ▼ ▼ ▼ ▼ ▼ ▼ ▼ ▼ ▼ ▼ ▼ ▼ ▼ ▼ ▼ ▼ ▼ ▼ ▼

## Using the Crop tool

The most popular way to crop an image is by using the Crop tool. This simple tool is as easy and effective to use as a T square and X-ACTO knife, and without the possibility of bodily injury. Select the Crop tool or press C on the keyboard and then follow these steps:

**1.** **With the Crop tool, drag around the part of the image you want to keep and then release your mouse.**

As you drag, a *marquee* (a dotted outline) appears displaying the cropping boundaries. Don't worry if your cropping marquee isn't exactly correct. You can adjust it in the next step.

Notice how the area outside the cropping marquee appears darker than the inside, in order to better frame your image. Adobe calls this a *shield.* You control the color and opacity (the amount of transparency) of the shield by adjusting the settings in the Options bar. If, for some strange reason, you don't want the shield, deselect the

CONTINUED
▼ ▼ ▼ ▼ ▼

check box. Figure 1-13 shows a great example of way too much background clutter. I dragged around the only thing I want to retain — my daughter.

**2.** **Adjust the cropping marquee by dragging the handles.**

The small squares on the sides and corners of the cropping marquee are called *handles*. When you hover your mouse over any handle or the marquee itself, your cursor changes to a double-headed arrow, indicating that you can drag.

If you drag the handles outside the image boundary, Photoshop adds a canvas around the image when you crop.

To move the entire marquee, position your mouse inside until you see a black arrowhead cursor and then drag. Adjust the marquee until you're satisfied.

You can also drag the origin point to change the axis of rotation.

 If you move your mouse outside the marquee, the cursor changes to a curved, double-headed arrow. Dragging with this cursor rotates the marquee. This feature can be extremely useful when you need to rotate and crop a crooked image. By using the Crop tool, you can perform both commands in one step and often more quickly and accurately. Just be aware that rotation, unless it's in 90-degree increments, resamples your image, which, if done repeatedly, can damage your image (see the beginning of this chapter for more on resampling). So it's best to try and get the rotation right the first time around.

**3.** **Double-click inside the cropping marquee.**

You can also just press Enter (return on the Mac) or click the Commit (check mark icon) button on the Options bar. Photoshop discards the area outside the marquee, as shown in Figure 1-14. If you want to cancel the crop, just press Esc or click Cancel (the slashed circle icon) in the Options bar.

**Figure 1-12**

**Figure 1-13**

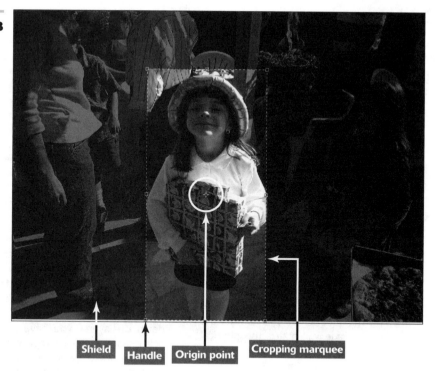

Shield    Handle    Origin point    Cropping marquee

**Figure 1-14**

---

### Sure-fire cropping tips

Even though cropping is about as simple an image-editing maneuver as you can get, there are a few other options you need to know about:

✔ If you need a nonrectangular cropping marquee, select the **Perspective** check box in the Options bar. This allows the corner handles to move independently. Cropping with Perspective selected can help to rectify images that have keystone distortion, which occurs when you photograph an image from an angle rather than straight on.

✔ If you want to crop an image to an exact measurement, enter a value in the **Width**, **Height**, and **Resolution** text boxes in the Options bar. Note that these options are only available when the Crop tool is active and you haven't yet dragged a cropping marquee. You can still freely drag and adjust the cropping marquee. Once you commit the crop, your image will match the physical dimensions you specified. You can enter values in just one, two, or all three options. But again, be careful about the value you use for the Resolution setting. Remember, resampling is not a good thing. To remove the entered settings, click the Clear button in the Options bar.

✔ The **Front Image** option enables you to crop one image so that it's the exact same size as another image. Open two images and crop the first one. Click Front Image. Photoshop enters the width, height, and resolution values from the first image in the Options bar. Drag the Crop tool on your second image and adjust the marquee as desired. Double-click inside the marquee. Photoshop automatically crops your second image to match your first. The Front Image command is also only available in the Options bar *before* you drag your cropping marquee.

✔ If your image doesn't contain any layers — that is, it only consists of a background — any cropped areas are permanently deleted from your file. However, if your image consists of one or more layers (see Book V for the lowdown on layers), you have the choice of deleting or hiding your cropped area. **Delete** eliminates the cropped areas, whereas **Hide** just hides the cropped area. You can see the cropped area if you move the layer with the Move tool. Another way to see the hidden area is to choose Image⇨Reveal All. Photoshop expands the canvas to show all areas in all layers. These options are only available while the crop marquee is active.

## Cropping with the Marquee tool

If you get bored using the Crop tool, you can also crop a selected area by choosing Image⇨Crop. Simply make a selection with any of the tools and then choose this command. Although it makes the most sense to use the Rectangular Marquee tool for your selection, you don't have to.

You can use the Image⇨Crop command with any selection — circular, polygonal, kidney bean, even feathered. Photoshop can't crop to those odd shapes, but it gets as close to the outline as it can, as shown in Figure 1-15.

**Figure 1-15**

## Using the Trim command

The fabulous Trim command trims away transparent or solid-colored areas around your image. Choose Image⇨Trim, and a dialog box appears. Select Transparent Pixels (for layered images), Top Left Pixel Color, or Bottom Right Pixel Color as a basis for the trim. Next, instruct Photoshop to trim away the Top, Bottom, Left, or Right side(s) from the image. This command works great for quickly eliminating black-and-white borders around images, as shown in Figures 1-16 and 1-17.

**Figure 1-16**

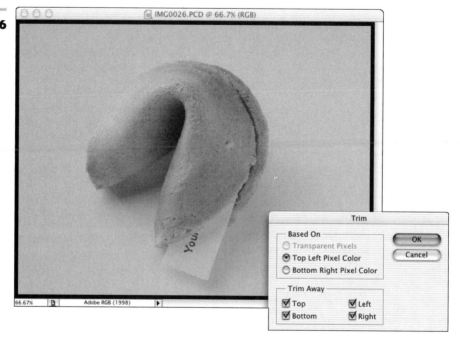

**Figure 1-17**

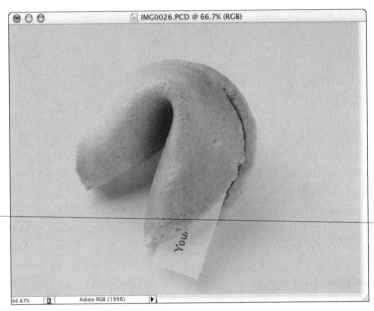

# Choosing Color Modes and File Formats

**2**

In addition to choosing a size and resolution (discussed in the previous chapter), you need to decide on an image mode and file format for your image. This decision is usually based on the final use for the image. Will it be imported into a page layout program and then offset printed? Will it be posted on a Web page? Will it be used for a newspaper article?

When you know an image's final destination, you can make intelligent choices of which color mode and file format is best. This chapter gives you some background to help you make those choices so that you don't end up having to do extra work, spend extra time, or waste extra money.

## Understanding Color Theory

There are many books, most of them detailed and lengthy, devoted to a single subject — color. They're written by bona-fide color experts who spend their days analyzing complex color algorithms for fun. I recommend owning at least one heavy-duty tome on color, even if its main function is to act as a paperweight. Even as an occasional reference, a book on color theory is essential if you're serious about using Photoshop in your daily activities. In this chapter, I provide you with the minimalist's take on color theory.

### Knowing RGB basics

When you view an RGB image, you are looking at an image comprised of three colors — red, green, and blue. These colors are

✔ The primary colors of light

✔ The colors that correspond to the three types of cones inside your eyes

✔ The colors that comprise white light from the sun

✔ The colors your monitor uses when displaying images

Mixing these three primary colors can yield up to 16.7 million colors. In Photoshop, each of these colors resides in a *color channel* in the image. Photoshop looks at a color image in terms of its channels — individual bands of 8-bit grayscale images. When you view the channels individually in Photoshop, you can visually see that each channel appears as a grayscale image made up of light-, medium-, and dark-colored pixels (assuming the Color Channels in the Color check box is deselected). RGB images have three bands, and CMYK images have four bands. Each one of these bands, or grayscale images, is a channel, or more specifically a color channel. For the lowdown on channels, check out Book VI, Chapter 1.

Each pixel is assigned a value ranging from 0 (black) to 255 (white). These grayscale pixels from each channel mix together to form colors, which in turn provide you with a composite color image.

Here are some color channel examples to help you see how the RGB system works to create so many different color variations:

✔ A light-colored pixel from the green channel, a dark-colored pixel from the red channel, and a dark-colored pixel from the blue channel combine to give you a green pixel.

✔ A value of 255 from all three channels produces white.

Because RGB colors combined at 255 create white, they are known as *additive colors*. When you view this white on your computer monitor, for example, all visible wavelengths are transmitted back to your eyes.

✔ A value of 0 from all three channels produces black.

✔ If all three values are equal, a neutral gray is produced.

✔ A medium-dark pixel from the red channel, a black pixel from the green channel, and a light-colored pixel from the blue channel combine to produce purple.

✔ Mixing colors in RGB produces lighter colors. Try playing with the RGB color sliders in your Color palette and mix your own colors to see this concept in action. Remember that the right side of the slider (the higher numbers) represents light, and the left side of the slider (the lower numbers) represents dark. For more on working with the color sliders and Color palette, see Chapter 3 of this book.

### Knowing CMYK basics

The CMYK color scheme is based on the light-absorbing quality of ink on paper. In theory, a white light hits these inks. Visible wavelengths are absorbed, while others are reflected back to your eyes. CMYK images are comprised of various percentages of only four colors of ink — cyan, magenta, yellow, and black. These colors correspond to the inks used in the offset printing process.

Cyan, magenta, and yellow are called *subtractive colors*. Technically if you combine these three colors of ink, you produce black. But because of ink impurities, you actually end up with a nasty brown color. (That's why K, or black, is added to produce black.)

CMYK colors are also known as process colors. Mixing colors in CMYK produces darker colors. When all four inks are set to 0%, pure white is produced.

 Subtractive and additive colors are complementary. This means that each pair of subtractive colors creates an additive color and each pair of additive colors creates a subtractive color.

# Selecting a Color Mode in Photoshop

Every file has a color mode, also called an *image mode* or just plain *mode*. To determine the color mode of an image, look in the title bar of the image window or choose Image⇨Mode. Color modes define the color values used to display the image. Photoshop offers eight different modes and allows you to convert images from one mode to another. The color mode you choose for a particular image depends on a couple of factors:

- ✔ **What file format you plan to save it in.** Some modes call for specific file formats. You may find that a certain format is unavailable because your file isn't in the appropriate color mode.

- ✔ **The end use for the image.** Do you plan to post the image on the Web? Or are you putting it in a brochure that will be offset printed? For more on prepping images for print, see Book X, Chapter 2.

The next few sections provide a brief description of each mode and any file format or usage connections. For examples of some modes, in full, living color, be sure to check out the color insert.

 Color modes affect the number of colors that will be displayed, as well as the size of the file and the number of channels. Each mode is also represented by one or more channels, where the color data is stored. Grayscale images have one channel — black. CMYK images have four channels — cyan, magenta, yellow, and black. For the lowdown on channels, see Book VI, Chapter 1.

## RGB Color

**Uses:** RGB is the gold standard for most scanners, all monitors, and some desktop inkjet printers. And it's the primary color mode (with Indexed Color being secondary) to be used with any images to be viewed on-screen (whether on the Web or in any kind of multimedia presentation).

**File formats:** RGB can handle just about every format except GIF.

RGB can be considered the default color mode of Photoshop. RGB images contain values of 0–255 for each of three colors — red, green, and blue. With RGB images, you can reproduce up to 16.7 million colors on-screen. Most scanners also scan images in RGB, all monitors display in RGB, and some desktop inkjet printers prefer to print RGB (rather than CMYK) images.

## CMYK Color

**Uses:** CMYK is the standard for images that will be color separated for offset printing.

**File formats:** CMYK can handle just about every format except GIF.

CMYK images contain a percentage of one or more of four-process color inks — cyan, magenta, yellow, and black. CMYK is the required mode for images that will be color separated for offset printing. Darker colors have higher percentages, whereas lighter colors have lower percentages. Many other composite printing devices also require images to be in CMYK mode.

Make sure that you do all of your image editing in RGB mode, where you have access to the full range of filters. When your editing is complete, convert the image from RGB to CMYK. (For details, see "Converting from RGB to CMYK," later in this chapter.)

## Grayscale

**Uses:** Grayscale images are used when you need black-and-white images.

**File formats:** All of the most commonly used file formats accept Grayscale mode.

Grayscale images contain up to 256 levels of gray. Each pixel has a brightness value ranging from 0 (black) to 255 (white). You can scan an image in Grayscale mode, or you can convert color images to grayscale. If you convert a color image to grayscale, Photoshop discards all the color information, and the remaining gray levels represent the luminosity of the pixels. (Check out the "Converting to Grayscale" section, later in this chapter.) You can also convert a grayscale image to a color image, which, while it doesn't convert your grayscale image to color, it allows you to apply color on top of the grayscale image.

## Monotone, Duotone, Tritone, and Quadtone

**Uses:** Because printing presses can only print about 50 gray levels per ink color, duotones, which use two to four inks, are used to increase the range of tones of grayscale images. Duotones are often created by using black and spot colors (premixed inks), although process colors can also be used. For more on spot colors, see Book X, Chapter 2.

**File formats:** The only file formats that can save duotones, tritones, and quadtones are native Photoshop, EPS, PDF, or Raw.

These modes create one-color, (monotone), two-color (duotone), three-color (tritone), and four-color (quadtone) images. Note that all the various "tone" modes are lumped under duotone. You will find a pop-up menu in the Duotone options dialog box where you can select the various options. Unlike RGB and CMYK images where the components of the image display with different colors, monotones, duotones, tritones, and quadtones have the colors mixed throughout the image. The colored inks are used to reproduce tinted grays, not the different colors you find in RGB and CMYK images.

To access the Duotone mode, you must first convert the color image to grayscale by choosing Image⇨Mode⇨Grayscale. Then choose Image⇨Mode⇨Duotone. In the dialog box that appears, choose Monotone, Duotone, Tritone, or Quadtone from the pop-up menu. Next, select ink colors — either spot or process — by clicking the swatches. Finally, you can adjust the curves settings and tell Photoshop how to distribute the ink(s) among the various tones.

Note that you do not have access to the individual color channels in Duotone mode. The only manipulation that you do is with the curves settings.

If you are new to these modes, Photoshop offers numerous preset duotones, tritones, and quadtones. To access these presets, click the Load button and go to the Duotones folder (which is located in the Presets folder in the Photoshop folder).

## Indexed Color

**Uses:** Indexed Color mode is used primarily for Web graphics and multimedia displays.

**File formats:** Indexed Color mode supports only the GIF format.

Indexed Color mode uses 256 colors or less, what graphics aficionados call 8-bit color. When you convert an image to indexed color, a Color Lookup Table (CLUT) is built, which stores and indexes the color. (Note the Color Table option in the Mode menu.) If a color in the original image isn't in the table, Photoshop chooses the closest match or makes a new one from the available colors. The small amount of colors reduces the file size, which is why this mode is used for the GIF file format used for Web graphics. (See the "GIF" section, later in this chapter.)

 The Indexed Color mode does not support layers, and editing capabilities are limited. For more on indexed color, see Book IX, Chapters 1 and 2.

## Lab Color

**Uses:** Lab Color mode is used to provide a consistent color display, which is ideal for high end retouching of images.

**File formats:** You can save an image in Lab Color mode in native Photoshop, EPS, TIFF, PDF, or Raw formats.

Lab Color mode is usually thought of as the internal color mode Photoshop uses when converting from one color mode to another — for example, when going from RGB to CMYK. It is also the mode preferred by color-retouching experts because it is considered to be *device independent* (it appears consistent on various devices).

Lab Color mode consists of a lightness channel and two additional channels, *a* and *b,* which contain the range of color from green to red (a) and blue to yellow (b).

## Bitmap

**Uses:** This mode is best for scanned line art and signatures (your John Hancock).

**File formats:** EPS, TIFF, Photoshop, Photoshop PDF, BMP, PNG, GIF, PCX, and PICT.

Bitmap images contain pixels that are either black or white, exclusively. You must convert color images to grayscale before you can access Bitmap mode. Upon choosing Image➪Mode➪Bitmap, a dialog box appears, offering options for resolution and method. The various methods give different appearances, as shown in Figure 2-1, so try each one to see which you prefer.

If you save a file in Bitmap mode as an EPS (see "EPS," later in this chapter), you can convert the white areas in the image to transparent areas. This allows you to overlay the file over a background containing color or an image, and only the dark pixels will show.

Figure 2-1

## Multichannel

**Uses:** Multichannel mode is used for special printing needs or as an intermediate mode when converting between different color modes.

**File formats:** The only file formats available for multichannel images are native Photoshop, Photoshop DCS 2.0, or Raw formats.

The Multichannel mode is comprised of multiple grayscale channels, each containing 256 levels of gray. Whenever you delete or mix channels, you end up with a multichannel image. You can also convert any image with more than one channel to this mode. In a multichannel image, each channel becomes a spot channel, with 256 levels of gray.

You cannot print a composite image in this mode to your desktop printer.

For more on channels, see Book VI, Chapter 1.

# Converting to a Different Color Mode

Sometimes, you'll start out in one color mode and then find you need to convert to another. Maybe you need to strip the color out of an image you're submitting to the local newspaper. Or maybe you need to convert your RGB image to CMYK to get it ready for an offset print job.

 When you convert modes, you are permanently changing the color values in your image, so save a backup image just in case.

The next few sections offer pointers for the most common conversions you'll make.

## Converting from RGB to CMYK

As I mention several times in this book, CMYK is the image mode necessary for high-end composite printing and offset printing. You will first want to perform all of your necessary image-editing tasks in RGB mode for the following reasons:

- ✔ The image size is smaller because RGB mode only has three channels.
- ✔ The RGB color space provides more device independence because it isn't reliant on inks.
- ✔ You have full accessibility to filters.
- ✔ RGB mode provides a large color gamut, so more colors will be preserved after image adjustments are made.

When you're finished editing the image in RGB mode, you can convert the image from RGB to CMYK (you can perform any fine-tuning in CMYK mode if necessary). If you're new to this procedure, you may be surprised at what can result. Because the color gamut (range of colors) of the RGB model (16.7 million) is much larger than that of CMYK (approximately 55,000), you may see a color shift, which may range from slight to major.

The extent of the shift depends on the colors in the RGB image and how many of them are *out of gamut*. RGB colors that are out of gamut are replaced with the closest match available within the CMYK gamut. The electric blues, fiery reds, and sunny yellows are often replaced by duller, muddier CMYK equivalents. Unfortunately, you can't do anything to prevent this. It is just the way of the world of color. However, if you can select colors (rather than acquiring them from a scan), be sure that you don't select any colors that are out of gamut to begin with. Check out Chapter 3 of this book for all you need to know about working with and managing color in Photoshop.

 If you want to see what the effects of your CMYK conversion will be without actually converting, choose View➪Proof Setup➪Working CMYK. This view is referred to as a *soft proof* — previewing on-screen how your image will look on various output devices or various modes. For more on soft proofs, see Chapter 3 of this book.

## Converting to Grayscale

You can convert a color image to grayscale a multitude of ways. The next few sections cover a few that you may want to try out.

You can also use the Channel Mixer to create custom grayscale images. For more on the Channel Mixer, see Book VI, Chapter 1.

### Quick and dirty method

Choose Image➪Mode➪Grayscale. Photoshop then asks you whether you want to discard color information. Click OK. The RGB or CMYK channels are merged into one black channel, and you now have a grayscale image. You may find that although this method does the job in stripping color from your image, you may be left with an image that is flat and lacking contrast. You can apply a Levels adjustment (choose Image➪Adjustments➪Levels) to boost the contrast, or you can try one of the other conversion methods. If your image contains multiple layers, Photoshop asks whether you want to merge your layers. If you want to keep your layers, click the Don't Merge button.

Be aware that you can no longer apply color to your image. If you choose a color in the Color palette, the color appears gray in the foreground and background color icons. If you *want* to apply color to your grayscale image, you must convert it back to RGB or CMYK mode.

### Lab Color mode method

Choose Image➪Mode➪Lab Color. As mentioned earlier, converting to Lab Color mode converts the channels into a lightness channel and *a* and *b* channels containing ranges of color. Delete the *a* channel. The *b* channel then changes its name to Alpha 2. Delete the Alpha 2 channel. That leaves you with the lightness channel, which is now named Alpha 1. Choose Image➪Mode➪Grayscale. Your color image is now a grayscale one. Note that if your image contains multiple layers, the layers are flattened when you convert to grayscale. Make sure that you've finished all your edits requiring layers before you convert to grayscale. This method will most likely provide a better grayscale image than the quick and dirty method.

### Best channel method

If you look at the individual channels in the image, one often stands out as being a very good grayscale image by itself. (If channels are a mystery to you, check out Book VI, Chapter 1, for details.) You may find that the red channel provides a good grayscale image when the subject is people, because humans have a lot of red in their skin. Or you may find the green channel looks good in a scenic shot. Rarely will the blue channel yield a nice image, though. Most of the crud picked up from scanners finds its way into the blue channel.

In the Channels palette, select each channel and view its contents. Find the channel that looks the best and then choose Image➪Mode➪Grayscale. Photoshop asks you if you want to discard all the other channels. Click OK. Like with the lab method, if your image contains multiple layers, the layers are flattened when you convert to grayscale.

## Converting to Indexed Color

You may need to convert your RGB or CMYK images to Indexed Color to save them as GIFs and prepare them for posting on the Web. The main issue to be aware of is that the Indexed Color mode contains only 256 colors (or even less). That is a far cry from the thousands or millions offered by CMYK and RGB images. If color is critical, you may want to reconsider making the conversion and instead leave or convert your image to RGB mode.

The Indexed Color mode cannot support layers, so again, be sure to perform all necessary editing functions before making the conversion. When converting to indexed color, you have options for specific palettes, numbers of colors, dithering, and so on, as shown in Figure 2-2. These options affect the appearance of the image. For more on the Indexed Color mode and these options, see Book IX, Chapters 1 and 2.

**Figure 2-2**

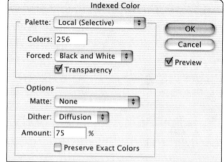

# Picking the Right File Format

A critical component in saving a file is choosing the file format. The file format is the way the file's data is represented and saved. Photoshop generously offers numerous file formats to choose from. Some you'll use frequently, and others you'll never set eyes on.

I provide quite a bit of detail on the formats you'll use most frequently, and throw in a brief description of those you'll encounter only once in a blue moon (if at all).

Be sure to check out the handy table in Book X, Chapter 2. It offers a list of what file formats work for various applications and uses.

## TIFF

TIFF, Tagged Image File Format, is by far one of the best and most useful formats. One of the great qualities of TIFFs is that they are and have always been totally cross-platform. In addition, almost every program on the planet can import TIFFs. Okay, so that's a slight exaggeration. Almost every word processing, presentation, page layout, drawing, painting, and image-editing program can import TIFFs. This file format works especially well for images that will be printed or color separated.

Photoshop allows you to save layers and transparency and also use various methods of compression. You have the option of having Photoshop warn you that including layers will increase your file size. To enable this option, select the Ask Before Saving Layered TIFF Files check box in the Preferences dialog box. Photoshop saves the layers along with a flattened version of the image. Be aware that some applications may display only the flattened version.

It should come as no surprise that the most commonly used format offers a variety of options — all of which are available in the TIFF Options dialog box (shown in Figure 2-3). The following sections give you everything you need to know about your various options so that you can make an informed decision based on your intended uses for the image.

**Figure 2-3**

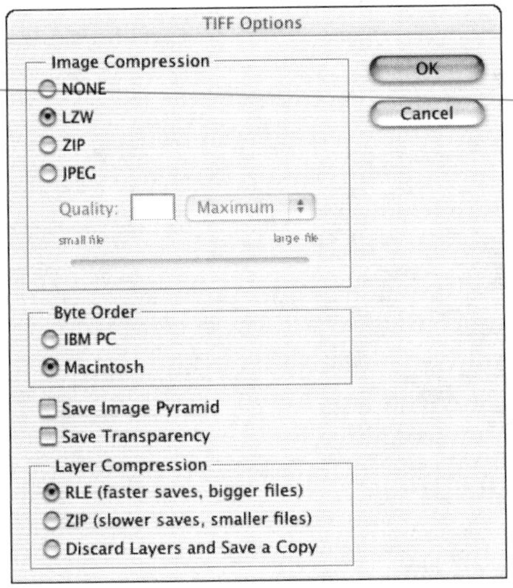

TIFF Options

Image Compression
- ○ NONE
- ⦿ LZW
- ○ ZIP
- ○ JPEG

Quality: [   ] Maximum ▴▾

small file        large file

[ OK ]
[ Cancel ]

Byte Order
- ○ IBM PC
- ⦿ Macintosh

☐ Save Image Pyramid
☐ Save Transparency

Layer Compression
- ⦿ RLE (faster saves, bigger files)
- ○ ZIP (slower saves, smaller files)
- ○ Discard Layers and Save a Copy

## Image Compression

Photoshop offers three methods of compression:

- ✔ **LZW:** This method has been around for eons and is a *lossless* compression scheme. This means that data is not deleted to make your file smaller. LZW does an especially good job when you use it to compress images with large areas of a single color. Most programs that support TIFF also support LZW compression, so you can use this method without much hesitation.

 If your files are unusually large, compressing them will make your file save and open more slowly.

- ✔ **Zip:** Zip compression is also a lossless method and is popular in the Windows arena. Like LZW, it works well with images that have large areas of a single color.

- ✔ **JPEG:** This method, while popular and very effective, is a *lossy* compression process. When compressing, data is deleted in order to reduce the file size. (That's where the *loss* in lossy comes from.) When you open the file again, that deleted data is remanufactured by the program. Over time, this repetitive deleting and remanufacturing can degrade image quality. I recommend that you stick with LZW compression.

Lossy compression can eat away at the quality of your image. Photoshop recompresses a JPEG image *every* time you save it. During a single edit session, this compression won't hurt because JPEG works from the on-screen version. But if you close, reopen, and resave the image in JPEG format, degradation occurs. You may not see the results right away, but you will over time. Leave your image in either TIFF or native Photoshop file formats while editing. Then when you're completely done editing and you need to compress the image, save the file as a JPEG at a high to maximum quality setting.

## Byte Order

Specify whether you want to save the TIFF for a Mac or a PC. If you want to be able to use the image on both platforms, select IBM PC. Macs are much more forgiving when it comes to exchanging files.

## Save Image Pyramid

This option allows you to save multiple resolutions of an image. The top of the pyramid is the lowest resolution, and the bottom of the pyramid is the highest resolution. If the program supports them, you can choose to open any of the resolutions.

Currently, only Adobe InDesign supports image pyramids. Photoshop can only open the image at the highest resolution within the file. I recommend leaving this option deselected.

## Save Transparency

Check this option to preserve transparent areas when the TIFF is opened in other applications. Of course, those applications must also support transparency. If you open a TIFF with transparency in Photoshop, the transparent areas are *always* preserved whether or not you check the option.

## Layer Compression

If you want to save the layers in your file, Photoshop saves a flattened version along with your layered version to ensure compatibility with programs that don't recognize layers. If you retain the layers, you have the choice of RLE (Run Length Encoding) or Zip compression. Because RLE compression is also lossless, you have the choice of faster saves (RLE) or smaller files (Zip). The last choice is for Photoshop to discard the layers, thereby flattening the image and then saving it as a copy. Your original layered file will also remain intact.

# JPEG

JPEG, the acronym for Joint Photographic Experts Group, is a file format that uses *lossy* compression (explained in the "Image Compression" section). The JPEG file format offers 13 compression settings — the higher the quality, the less the compression, and vice versa.

JPEG compression is very effective. It can squeeze your file size to practically nothing. JPEG compression works best with continuous-tone images, such as photographs. But because the compression is lossy, I don't recommend this format for high-end printing and color separations. JPEG supports RGB, CMYK, and Grayscale image modes. It doesn't support alpha channels.

If you want to post your image on the Web, you have to save it as a JPEG, GIF, or PNG. JPEG works great with photographic images where there are a wide range of colors. Check out Book IX, Chapters 1 and 2, for the lowdown on all the JPEG options and settings.

## GIF

GIF is another file format used for Web graphics. GIFs must be saved in the Indexed Color mode, which is comprised of 256 colors or less. Although this is great for making tiny files, it's not so great for continuous-tone images where the number of colors displayed is critical. Therefore, the GIF format is usually reserved for illustrations (spot illustrations, buttons, logos, and so on) and type with large areas of flat colors and sharp details. For the whole story on GIFs, see Book IX, Chapters 1 and 2.

## EPS

EPS is short for Encapsulated PostScript. PostScript is a page-description language developed by Adobe and used by many printers. The EPS format can contain both vector and raster graphics. (For details on vector and raster graphics, see Chapter 1 of this book.) EPSs tend to create larger file sizes and do not have a built-in compression scheme like JPEGs or TIFFs. EPS is the recommended file format for creating color separations for high-end, four-color print jobs. This is also the file format to use for images with clipping paths and those with a Duotone color mode. In addition to duotones, EPS supports Lab, CMYK, RGB, Indexed Color, Grayscale, DCS, and Bitmap modes. It does not support alpha channels. Finally, EPS is the format of choice for importing to and from drawing programs such as Illustrator, FreeHand, and CorelDraw.

Here are the options when saving in the EPS format, as shown in Figure 2-4:

**Figure 2-4**

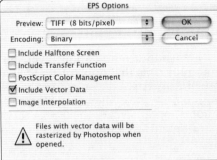

- ✔ **Preview:** If you import your EPS into another application, this option provides a low-resolution image for you to view. I recommend choosing 8-bit TIFF, which works on both PC and Mac.

- ✔ **Encoding:** This option specifies the way an image is sent to the PostScript printer. Choose Binary if you can; it produces smaller files and keeps all original data. If you're having printing problems, choose ASCII. JPEG compresses the file, but discards data and may cause color-separation problems. Avoid it if possible.

✔ **Include Halftone Screen and Include Transfer Function:** These options are used for offset print jobs. Leave these options to the service-bureau or commercial-printing experts.

✔ **Transparent Whites:** If your image is in Bitmap color mode, this option allows white areas to appear transparent.

✔ **PostScript Color Management:** This option converts the file's color data to the printer's color space. I do not recommend selecting this option if you are importing your image into a document that is color managed. For more on color management, see Chapter 3 of this book.

✔ **Include Vector Data:** When selected, this option preserves any vector graphics, such as type and shapes. However, it is only preserved when you import the file into another program. If you reopen the EPS in Photoshop, however, your vector data is rasterized.

✔ **Image Interpolation:** This option anti-aliases (softens the edges) of low-resolution images when printed.

## PDF: The Universal Donor

PDF is the acronym for Portable Document Format, which is the native format of Adobe Acrobat. This format, developed by Adobe, can contain editable text, vector, and raster data. PDF files are often used for electronic documentation that will be downloaded from the Web. You've probably noticed that every Adobe Help document is in PDF format, and if you're a Web user, you've probably downloaded more than a few PDFs. The government, notoriously slow to catch on to new technology, has even embraced PDF. The military uses PDFs for technical documentation. And all of your tax forms are available as downloadable PDFs.

You might be thinking, "So what. I'm into images, not documents." Well, hold on a second. PDFs can be extremely useful in the imaging world as well. Anyone with a computer running Windows, Mac OS, or Unix can read a PDF. All you need to view a PDF file is Adobe Acrobat Reader, which is available as a free download from Adobe's Web site. If you save your image as a PDF and e-mail it (or post it on the Web as a downloadable file) to a colleague, manager, client, or friend, that person can see your image — colors, fonts, and all — exactly like you see it. The other nice thing about PDFs is that they have an automatic compression process that makes the files small and manageable for mail transfer or loading on the Web.

When you save a file as a Photoshop PDF, you have all the same save options of the native Photoshop format. PDF supports layers and annotations, so check these options if you have either one. It also supports the same image modes as the native Photoshop format. Here is a description of the other options found in the PDF Options dialog box, shown in Figure 2-5:

✔ **Compression:** Choose Zip compression if optimum print quality is an issue. Otherwise, select JPEG at the maximum setting.

✔ **Save Transparency:** When selected, this option preserves any transparent areas in your file.

✔ **Image Interpolation:** This option anti-aliases, or slightly softens the edges, of low-resolution images when they are printed. Keep this option selected.

✔ **Downgrade Color Profile:** If you selected ICC Profile (Windows) or Embed Color Profile (Mac) in the Save dialog box in Photoshop Version 4, checking this option downgrades the profile to Version 2. Select this option if you need to open the file in a program that doesn't support Photoshop Version 4 profiles.

✔ **PDF Security:** Click the Security Settings button to access the PDF Security dialog box, also shown in Figure 2-5. You can assign a password for opening the file in Acrobat Reader. You can also assign a master password that is required to open the file in Photoshop, which then allows for full access, enabling you to make changes to the image and to the passwords themselves. Choose a level of encryption — 40-bit encryption is fine if you just want to prevent opening the file. Finally, choose whether you want your user to be able to print or change the document, copy it or extract content, or add or change comments and form fields. Choose 128-bit encryption if you want more specific options regarding accessibility (for disabled persons), level of content changes allowed, and allowable printing resolutions.

✔ **Include Vector Data:** Select this option to preserve vector paths. If you have text in your file, select the Embed Fonts option, which ensures that your fonts will display correctly on any computer, even if those fonts aren't installed. But be sure not to use any faux styles or warped text. Embedding fonts increases file size, but it is well worth it. If you select the Use Outlines for Text option, Photoshop converts all of your text to paths. This can be helpful if your fonts aren't displaying or printing properly, but you won't be able to select the text or use the Search command in Acrobat. Your text does remain editable in Photoshop, however.

**Figure 2-5**

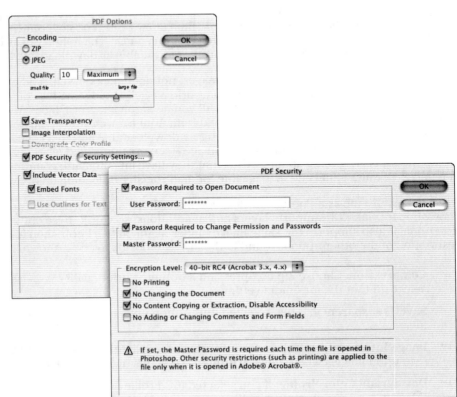

## Photoshop

Of course, I can't forget the native Photoshop format (.psd). This format offers a lot of benefits. First of all, along with TIFF and PDF, Photoshop allows you to save layers in your image. The other formats flatten the layers into a single background. This format works well if you are going to spend a considerable length of time working on your image. The Photoshop format also supports all image modes, is the fastest format for opening and saving, and offers all the various save options.

Like TIFF, the Photoshop format uses a lossless compression process, although it's invisible to you. If you need to open a file in an older version of Photoshop, be sure to save it as a native Photoshop file. Finally, almost all drawing and layout programs now support the importing of Photoshop files.

## PICT

PICT, for Macintosh Picture, is a format that was developed by Apple as its main format for Mac graphics. It is based on the QuickDraw screen language. And although many Mac programs support PICT, I don't recommend using it for any images that you plan to print. PICTs are notorious for being absurdly slow in the printing department. Today, PICT images are usually used for graphics to be incorporated into slides, screen presentations (like PowerPoint), multimedia projects, and digital video. PICT supports RGB (with a single alpha channel), Indexed Color, Grayscale, and Bitmap (without alpha channels) image modes.

Make sure that QuickTime is running if you want to save a file as a PICT. Here are the options that appear in the PICT File Options dialog box, shown in Figure 2-6:

**Figure 2-6**

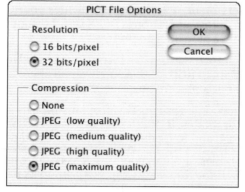

✔ **Resolution:** Options for grayscale images are 2, 4, and 8 bits per pixel. Options for color images are 16 and 32 bits per pixel. Under no circumstances should you change the default option. If you do, you will delete colors from your image, and you will not be able to access the compression settings.

✔ **Compression:** The compression settings for PICT are more limited than those for the regular JPEG format. Be aware that the compression scheme used for PICTs causes even more degradation to your image than with JPEGs. To minimize the damage, always select the maximum quality setting.

## BMP

BMP is a standard Windows file format commonly used for saving images that you want to make part of your computer's resources, such as the wallpaper that you see on your Windows desktop. It is also a format used by computer programmers. BMP supports RGB, Indexed Color, Grayscale, and Bitmap image modes.

Here are your options when saving a BMP file:

- ✔ **File Format:** Choose between Windows and OS/2.

- ✔ **Depth:** Although you can select a bit depth, I recommend leaving the default setting Photoshop has selected for you.

- ✔ **Compress (RLE):** The compression scheme used is lossless, which is great, but don't select this option if you are creating wallpaper. Windows won't recognize it.

- ✔ **Flip Row Order:** This option enables Windows to recognize the file by reading the first row of pixels first and the last row last. It is for programmers who are coding for Windows applications. Leave it deselected unless you're one of them.

Don't worry about the Advanced Modes option. It is even more egg heady than the other options and strictly programming territory.

## The others

The formats I describe in previous sections are ones you'll use 99 percent of the time, but here's a brief description of some of the others, just in case you're curious:

- ✔ **Photoshop DCS 1.0 and 2.0:** A version of EPS, this format divides your CMYK or Multichannel image into Desktop Color Separations (DCS). DCS 2.0 supports spot and alpha channels. It requires a PostScript printer to print.

- ✔ **PICT Resource:** This format, Macintosh Picture Resource, is used for Mac start-up screens. You can use images that are in RGB (with a single alpha channel), Indexed Color, Grayscale, or Bitmap (without alpha channels) modes.

- ✔ **PCX:** This is the native format for PC Paintbrush. This format supports RGB, Indexed Color, Grayscale, and Bitmap color modes. It doesn't support alpha channels. Images can have a bit depth of 1, 4, 8, or 24, and RLE compression is supported.

- ✔ **PNG:** A newer format for Web graphics. It offers good lossless compression, transparency, and 24-bit color. PNG (Portable Network Graphics) supports RGB, Indexed Color, Grayscale, and Bitmap image modes. See Book IX, Chapters 1 and 2.

- ✔ **Pixar:** This is the format used for Pixar workstations, which are high-end, 3-D-modeling computers. You can use RGB or grayscale images with a single alpha channel.

- ✔ **Filmstrip:** This format is used for animation and digital video. For more information, see Book X, Chapter 1.

- ✔ **WBMP:** This format, Wireless Bitmap, is used for images that will appear on mobile devices such as cell phones and PDAs. It only supports 1-bit color (black or white).

- ✔ **Scitex CT:** This format, Scitex Continuous Tone, is designed for Scitex prepress software and hardware.

- ✔ **Targa:** Developed by TrueVision for its video boards. It's used to capture still frames from video on PCs. This format supports RGB, Indexed Color, and Grayscale images, the latter two without alpha channels.

- ✔ **Raw:** The format used to exchange files between PCs and Macs and mainframe computers. It is often used to save images created by scientific applications. Be aware that this format sacrifices colors and other image data.

- ✔ **Alias PIX, Wavefront RLA, Electric Image, and Soft Image:** These are extremely high-end formats used for 3-D, animation, and special-effect graphics.

- ✔ **Photoshop 2.0:** Use this format if you know someone living in an ice cave in Siberia who is still using Photoshop 2. Mac only.

# Using and Managing Color

Color in Photoshop takes on two personalities. On one hand, choosing colors and applying them is easy, fun, and stress free. On the other hand, managing color — that is, making what you see on-screen match what comes out on paper (or in your browser) — can be difficult, frustrating, and chock full of stress.

Unfortunately, you have to be well versed in both picking great colors and managing colors for print. (What's the use of creating the next *Mona Lisa* in Photoshop only to find it looks like a fifth-generation color Xerox copy?) In this chapter, I start out by showing you how to define and apply color; then I ease you into the world of color management.

If you haven't already read the section in Chapter 2 of this book on color theory, you might want to give it a gander before you dive into this chapter. Knowing a little color theory might make this chapter a little more, er, *palette-able*.

## Dealing with Foreground and Background Colors

Photoshop has two categories of color — a *foreground color* and a *background color*. You apply the foreground color when you use the type tools, the painting tools, or the shape tools. It is also the beginning color of a default gradient applied by the Gradient tool. The background color is the color you apply with the Eraser tool and is the ending color of the default gradient. When you increase the size of your canvas, you will fill the additional canvas with the background color (assuming you don't have layers). You find the swatches that represent the two color categories in the lower part of the Toolbox, as shown in Figure 3-1.

**Figure 3-1**

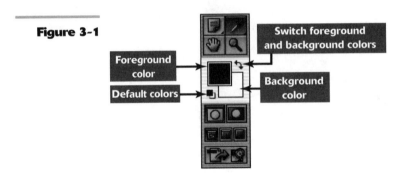

 The default color for the foreground is black; the background is white. Click the small icon labeled in Figure 3-1 to return the colors to the defaults or simply press the D key. That's easy to remember. To switch the foreground and background colors, click the curved arrow in the Toolbox or press X.

Here are a few tips about using tools with foreground and background colors:

✔ **Use the Brush or the Pencil with the foreground color.** These tools always apply the foreground color.

✔ **Blend the foreground and background with the Gradient tool.** When you drag with the Gradient tool across the canvas and the gradient is set to the default, you get a blending of the foreground and background colors.

✔ **Fill selected areas with the foreground color.** Just click your canvas with the Paint Bucket tool to fill selected areas with the foreground color.

✔ **Apply the background color by erasing.** Use the Eraser tool to apply the background color. Some people prefer to say you are erasing to the background or canvas color.

If you use the Eraser on a layer, you'll erase to transparency. See Book V for the scoop on layers.

✔ **Use the Shape tools to create shapes that are filled with the foreground color.** Simply create the shape, and voilà.

✔ **Add more background to your canvas and fill it with the background color.** When you enlarge your canvas size, the added canvas is automatically filled with the background color.

If you enlarge a layer, the extra canvas is transparent. See Chapter 1 of this book if the word *canvas* seems foreign to you.

# Defining Color

Like most everything else in Photoshop, there are several ways to choose color. I explain each of the following color definition options in upcoming sections:

- Click a color in the Color Picker.
- Move the sliders in the Color palette.
- Lift color from your image (or elsewhere) with the Eyedropper tool.
- Grab a color from the Swatches palette.

▼ ▼ ▼ ▼ ▼ ▼ ▼ ▼ ▼ ▼ ▼ ▼ ▼ ▼ ▼ ▼ ▼ ▼ ▼ ▼ ▼ ▼ ▼ ▼ ▼ ▼ ▼ ▼ ▼ ▼ ▼ ▼ ▼ ▼ ▼ ▼ ▼ ▼ ▼

## Poking around the Color Picker

When you click either the Foreground or Background color swatches in the Toolbox, you're transported magically to the Color Picker. This huge dialog box, shown in Figure 3-2, allows you to select a color from the color spectrum (called a color slider) or to define your color numerically.

Choosing a color visually is fine for Web or multimedia work, but not recommended for print work, of course. Among other reasons, your monitor uses an RGB (red, green, blue) color model, while printers use a CMYK (cyan, magenta, yellow, and black) model. For more on this and other color management issues, see "Color Management Essentials," later in this chapter. For the basics of color theory, see Chapter 2 of this book.

To choose a color visually with the Color Picker, follow these steps:

**1.** **Click on either the foreground or background color swatch in the Toolbox.**

The Color Picker dialog box appears, as shown in Figure 3-2.

**2.** **Click in the narrow color slider to get in the ballpark for the color you want.**

You can also move the slider.

**3.** **To fine-tune your choice, click in the large square on the left.**

This square area is called a *color field*. The circular icon targets your selected shade. The dialog box displays your new chosen color as well as the original foreground or background color.

The numeric values also change accordingly to represent the exact shade you've chosen.

Alternatively, if you know the numeric values of the color you want to use, you can plug in the values in the text boxes on the right side of the Color Picker.

You can do pretty much the same thing in the Color palette that you can do with the Color Picker. I prefer the Color palette, so I go into more detail about it in the next section.

CONTINUED
▼ ▼ ▼

**Figure 3-2**

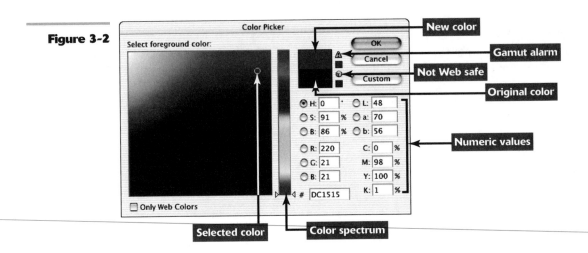

## Mixing with the Color palette

To open the Color palette, shown in Figure 3-3, choose Window⇨Color. A couple of swatches in this palette may look vaguely familiar. That's because they represent the foreground and background colors, just like the swatches in the Toolbox. And just like the Toolbox swatches, if you click the swatches in the Color palette, the infamous Color Picker appears. But forget the Color Picker; you don't need to go there. Everything you need is right here in this tiny palette.

Before you use the Color Picker to define your colors, you should know which color model you want to use. Here is a short description of each:

- ✔ **RGB (Red-Green-Blue)** is the color model used for anything that will be viewed on-screen — from multimedia and slide presentations to content for the Web. Occasionally, you can use it if you plan to print on certain desktop inkjet printers.

- ✔ **CMYK (Cyan-Magenta-Yellow-Black)** is the color model used in printing.

- ✔ The **Web Color** model is strictly used for the Web. If you choose this model, make sure that you also choose Make Ramp Web Safe from the Color palette options menu.

- ✔ **HSB (Hue-Saturation-Brightness)**, which I don't cover in Book II, Chapter 2, is based on percentages of saturation and brightness and an angle (0 to 360 degrees), which corresponds to a location on the color wheel.

- ✔ **Lab (Lightness, a, b)** color model contains three channels, one for lightness; one (a), which contains colors from green to red; and one (b), which contains colors from blue to red. It is more complex to understand and work with than the others and is the color model of choice for high-end color experts.

- ✔ **Grayscale** is the color model if you want to work strictly in black and white. You'll get one slider, K, which represents black. Move the slider to get shades of gray, including complete white and black.

## *If you're monkeying around with print media*

One thing that you do find in the Color Picker that is absent from the Color Palette is the ability to select custom colors, which are also known as *spot colors*. Spot colors are premixed inks, manufactured by various companies such as Pantone or Trumatch, that are used in printing. Spot colors can be used in addition to or in lieu of CMYK colors in the printing process. To pick a custom color, follow these steps:

*1.* **Click the Custom button in the Color Picker dialog box.**

The Custom Colors dialog box opens, as shown in the following figure.

*2.* **Choose your desired custom color book from the pop-up menu and then select your color from the scrolling list of swatches.**

*3.* **Click OK to accept the color as your new foreground or background color or click the Picker button to return to the Color Picker.**

Do not choose spot colors visually; choose them from a printed swatch book published by the ink manufacturer. The books, which provide the numeric values for each spot color, provide a true representation of how the color will appear when printed.

During the RIP (raster image processing) — the process your image goes through to create color separations for printing — Photoshop converts custom colors to CMYK for every image mode (except Duotone), unless you create spot color channels. For more on this technique, see Book X, Chapter 2. For more on image modes, see Book II, Chapter 2.

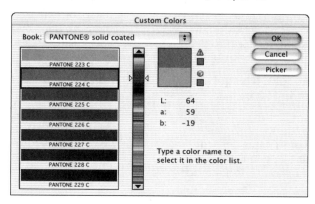

Here are the quick and easy steps to define a color by using the Color palette:

**1.** **Choose either the foreground or background color swatch in the Color palette.**

You can only change one swatch at a time. If the one you want is already selected, do nothing. A double outline appears around the swatch indicating that it's selected.

If you accidentally click the swatch that is already selected, the Color Picker dialog box appears. Just click Cancel and start over.

**2.** **Select your desired color model from the Color palette options menu.**

CONTINUED

Your options are RGB, CMYK, Lab, Web Safe, HSB, and Grayscale. You'll probably be using RGB, CMYK, or Web Safe the majority of the time. If you're not sure what these color models represent, check out the previous list and review Book II, Chapter 2. (See Figure 3-3.)

**3.** **Move the sliders for each component of the color model or enter a numeric value.**

RGB values are based on brightness levels, from 0 to 255, with 0 being black and 255 being the pure color or white. CMYK values are based on percentages (1–100) of the four process colors Cyan, Magenta, Yellow, and Black. The Web Color model gives you only the 216 colors used by Web browsers.

You can also select a color by clicking inside the color ramp at the bottom of the Color palette. And to quickly return to the default colors, click the small black and white swatches at the end of the color ramp.

**4.** **Keep an eye open for a triangular alert icon, shown in Figure 3-3.**

This icon is known as the *gamut alarm*. Its appearance is Photoshop's way of saying, "Hey, you! That color you mixed won't print like you think it will because it's out of gamut." Remember *gamut* is the range of colors a system can either display or print.

Because the RGB color model has a much wider gamut than the CMYK color model, some of the colors can only be viewed on-screen and not reproduced on paper.

Photoshop offers you a substitution. Inside a little square to the right of the gamut alarm icon, the closest printable color to the one you chose appears.

**5.** **Click either the icon or the square if you want to use the printable color instead of your original choice.**

The gamut alarm is not available if you choose Web Color Sliders.

If you want to use the RGB color model but also want to ensure that any color you choose is printable, select CMYK Spectrum from the Color palette options menu. By default, all the colors in the ramp are printable. Just be sure to choose your colors by clicking in the ramp.

**6.** **Be on the lookout for a small cube icon. Click either the icon or the square to use the Web-safe color.**

The cube indicates that the color you mixed is not a Web safe color. Clicking the cube tells Photoshop that you want to use its Web-safe alternative instead.

**Figure 3-3**

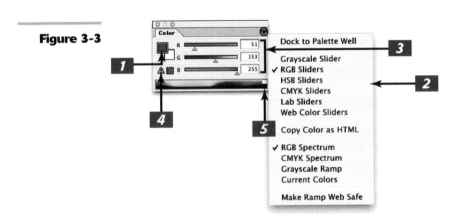

## Grabbing color from the Swatches palette

One way to define a foreground or background color is by clicking a color in the Swatches palette, shown in Figure 3-4.

**Figure 3-4**

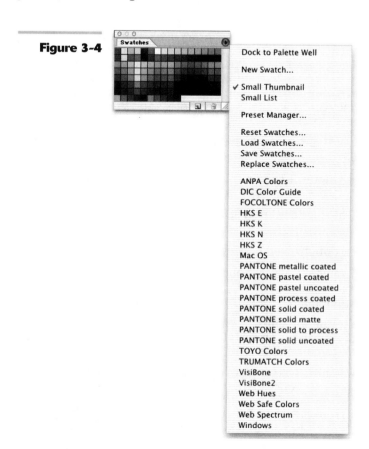

Any tool can be active when you use the Swatches palette to define a color because as soon as you move the tool over the Swatches palette, it changes to an eyedropper icon that sucks up the color.

 Besides being a way to select your foreground and background colors, the Swatches palette acts like a traditional artist's paint palette in digital form by letting you store as many colors as you want in the palette for later use.

To change the background color, either select the background swatch icon in the Color palette or simply Ctrl+click (⌘+click on the Mac) a swatch.

Here are some of the things you can do with the Swatches palette:

✔ **Customize the Swatches palette's display.** You can choose how to display the Swatches palette by choosing Small Thumbnail (swatch thumbnails) or Small List (swatch thumbnails along with a name) from the options menu.

✔ **Use preset colors.** To load a particular preset swatch library, choose it from the list in the options menu and click Append to add it to the existing swatches or OK to replace the existing swatches. You will find libraries specific for Web graphics and for implementing spot colors such as those created by Pantone, Toyo, and Focoltone. You can also select Load Swatches from the options menu. In the Load dialog box, navigate to the Color Swatches folder by following this path: Adobe Photoshop➪Presets➪Color Swatches; and select your desired library.

You can also work with swatches by using the Preset Manager. For more on the Preset Manager, see Book I, Chapter 6.

✔ **Customize your own Swatches palette.** To add a color to the Swatches palette, do one of the following:

  ▶ Click the New Swatch icon (the dog-eared page icon) at the bottom of the Swatches palette.

  ▶ Choose New Swatch from the options menu. Name your swatch and click OK.

  ▶ Click an empty spot in the Swatches palette (your cursor will change to a Paint Bucket icon). Name your swatch and click OK. Or Alt+click (Option+click on the Mac) on an empty spot to add the color and bypass the name dialog box.

✔ **Delete swatches that you don't want anymore.** To delete a swatch, drag it to the Trash icon at the bottom of the Swatches palette. Or Alt+click (Option+click on the Mac) over a swatch. Your cursor changes to a pair of scissors.

✔ **Create your own library of swatches.** To save a set of swatches as a library, choose Save Swatches from the options menu. Navigate to the folder you want to save it in.

 I recommend saving libraries in a subfolder of the Presets folder. Follow this path: Adobe Photoshop➪Presets➪Swatches; then create your own folder, name the file, and click Save.

✔ **Restore your default swatch libraries.** To return to the default library of swatches, choose Reset Swatches from the options menu. You can choose to either replace or append to the current library.

▼▼▼▼▼▼▼▼▼▼▼▼▼▼▼▼▼▼▼▼▼▼▼▼▼▼▼▼▼▼▼▼▼▼▼▼▼▼▼

## Lifting and sampling color

Photoshop lets you change foreground or background colors by lifting them from the image with the Eyedropper tool. Using the Eyedropper tool comes in handy when you want to sample an existing color in an image for use in another element. For example, if I want my text to be the same color as the flower in my image, I would click a petal with my Eyedropper tool, which would then lift the color and make it my new foreground color. I would then create my type, which would use that foreground color. Voilà — color coordination at its finest.

Here are some handy tips for when you use the Eyedropper to suck up color from one place and use it elsewhere in your image:

✔ **Choose any color you want from any image that's open.** If you have multiple images open, you can also click inside an image that you're not working on. In fact, if that doesn't knock your socks off, you can lift any color you see on-screen, even from a file in another application such as Illustrator or from your desktop. Just drag your Eyedropper from the image window onto the color you want to sample.

✔ **Choose your sampling area.** You only have one option (found in the Options bar) to worry about when using the Eyedropper tool. You have the option of selecting the color of just the single pixel you click (Point Sample). Or Photoshop will average the colors of the pixels in a 3-x-3 or 5-x-5 pixel radius.

✔ **Make colors Web safe with a right-click of your mouse.** For you Webbies out there, if you right-click (Ctrl+click on the Mac) on your image to bring up the context menu, you have one more option — Copy Color as HTML. This option converts the sampled color to Hexadecimal code and copies the code to the Clipboard so you can paste the code into an HTML file.

✔ **Toggle between the Eyedropper and other tools.** For your productive painting pleasure, when you're using the Brush, Pencil, Gradient, Paint Bucket, or Shape tools, pressing Alt (Option on the Mac) allows you to temporarily access the Eyedropper tool. Release the key and return to your original tool.

✔ **Toggle between the background and the foreground.** If the foreground color swatch is active, press Alt+click (Option+click on the Mac) with the Eyedropper tool to lift a new background color. If the background color swatch is active, pressing Alt+click (Option+click on the Mac) lifts a new foreground color.

To use the Eyedropper tool, you first need to decide whether you want to change the foreground or background color. Then follow these steps:

*1.* **Select the foreground (or the background).**

*2.* **Select the Eyedropper tool (or press the I key).**

Fortunately, the Eyedropper looks exactly like a real eyedropper.

*3.* **Click the color in your image that you want to use.**

That color becomes your new foreground (or background) color.

▼▼▼▼▼▼▼▼▼▼▼▼▼▼▼▼▼▼▼▼▼▼▼▼▼▼▼▼▼▼▼▼▼▼▼

## Using the Color Sampler tool to measure color

The Eyedropper's cousin, the Color Sampler tool, looks like an eyedropper with a small target next to the icon. It also shares the Eyedropper's flyout menu.

The moniker of "Sampler" is kind of misleading because this tool only *measures* the colors you click. Aside from merely obtaining the numeric value of a color, another use of the Color Sampler tool is to monitor changes to your image after you apply color-correction techniques and filters.

Follow these steps to use the Color Sampler tool:

**1.** **Click the color you want to measure.**

Note the target icon that appears on your image. It is labeled as #1.

Photoshop automatically opens the Info palette and shows you the numeric values for that color, as shown in Figure 3-5.

**2.** **Repeat Step 1 three more times for a total of four targeted colors.**

Target icons appear for your second, third, and fourth samples.

**3.** **With the Color Sampler tool, drag the targets to sample new areas of your image if you want. Delete a target by Alt+clicking (Option+clicking) it.**

You can actually measure a fifth color by just moving the Color Sampler cursor around the image. The numeric value will display in the upper portion of the Info palette.

**Figure 3-5**

# *Color Management Essentials*

Grab some Tylenol. You're about to delve into the rather confusing and sometimes cantankerous world (or as some users would call it — underworld) of color management. It is, by far, the biggest headache of every graphics professional's day-to-day experience. And I'm sure there are also quite a few home users who scratch their heads wondering why their digital photo looked so great on-screen and turned into a muddy mess on paper.

 Reproducing color is not an exact science. In fact, sometimes you would think it takes an act of voodoo magic to get the output you want. Don't throw up your hands and live with whatever output comes out the other end; if you can't change the color, you can at least change your attitude toward color. Getting a handle on color management requires four things — some knowledge, some patience, a significant amount of time to experiment and test, and, most importantly, acceptance. Acceptance of the unfortunate fact that we don't live in a WYSIWYG world. What you get in one medium is sometimes merely an approximation of what you see in another.

Why? Well, I'll start with the basic gripe of many users as they look disapprovingly at their printout — "But it didn't look like that on the screen!" As detailed in Chapter 2 of this book, there are two major color models — RGB (Red-Green-Blue) and CMYK (Cyan-Magenta-Yellow-Black). The RGB color model (16.7 million colors), which all monitors use, has a significantly wider range of color (called a *gamut* in computer lingo) than the CMYK color model (approximately 55,000 colors) that is used by printers. The result is that many of the colors you see on-screen fall outside of the CMYK gamut and therefore cannot be reproduced on paper. And in some cases, some CMYK colors fall outside of the RGB gamut. Programs like Photoshop try to do their best by providing colors that are the closest match. But those bright and vibrant colors that are out of gamut are matched with duller, darker versions at best.

And if that difference alone isn't enough to complicate matters, hardware devices that share the same color model can possess different gamuts within the same color model. For example, the RGB color space of a monitor can differ from the RGB color space of a scanner. Not only that, but you can also have different color spaces within the same type of device. A 15-inch generic monitor won't display color equal to a 21-inch Sony Trinitron monitor. Likewise, an Epson printer may not share the same color space as a Hewlett-Packard or Lexmark printer. So when you take into account the differences that can occur between platforms, monitors, printers, browsers, scanners, applications, paper and other substrates, or any of the almost infinite number of possible permutations, it makes you want to return to the days of quill and parchment. Techies often call this mind-numbingly large number of possible inconsistencies *device-dependent* color. In other words, the color is dependent upon the hardware device. And device dependent-color varies. That's just the cold, harsh reality, and nothing's changing that.

But Adobe, being the kind and benevolent software mega giant that it is, has developed (first introduced in Version 5.0) a color management system that is designed to be *device independent*. The five-cent explanation of this system is that you first identify your working color spaces. Photoshop then *tags* your files with that color space by embedding a color profile (also known as an ICC profile) with your files. The program then analyzes any color space in which you either view or output a file and makes adjustments on the fly so that the color is viewed and printed reasonably accurately and consistently, in theory, independent of the device. Photoshop also reads the embedded color profile (or lack thereof) any file you open and addresses how you wish to deal with that profile if it doesn't match your working color space.

In the upcoming sections, I give you the 25-cent explanation — which I hope is enough to get you managing color. If color management is an extremely critical workflow issue to you, I would recommend buying a book or two strictly devoted to nothing but managing color. It would be well worth the dollars.

### Setting up your work environment

One aspect of color management that people often overlook is setting up a good working environment for digital image editing. You may wave your hand impatiently and say, "Yeah, yeah, I just want to get to the important stuff." This is the important stuff.

Don't worry. Setting up a good work environment won't cost you anything. Just do these things:

- ✔ **Do** always keep your computer desktop a neutral gray. I know it is tempting to have dancing bears and family photos in the background, but these elements don't contribute to a good viewing environment. Colors and patterns behind your images influence the way that you view those images. Creating a neutral, gray desktop is the closest you can get to mounting your work on gray, black, or white mat board (and not neon green or paisley) the way professional graphic designers and photographers do.

- ✔ **Do** keep your lighting as consistent as possible. Avoid working on or viewing images in full, bright afternoon sun and then again under a single desk lamp late at night. Keep the level and intensity as consistent as possible, and be sure to look at your source material, along with the images you're working on, under the same intensity of light. Likewise, view images on-screen and your printed output under the same lighting. And please, no disco balls.

- ✔ **Do** keep the walls of your work environment as neutral as your monitor desktop. You don't have to paint your office gray, but try to avoid lots of colorful posters and artwork in your direct line of vision (around and behind your monitor).

- ✔ For print work, **do** keep a swatch book (or two) handy, such as those from Pantone or Trumatch, to choose your colors. Don't make a decision based on what you see on-screen. These books give you a true representation of how color will look when printed on paper.

 I recommend getting a swatch book that shows both spot (premixed inks of a single color) and process colors (colors made by mixing the four process colors — Cyan, Magenta, Yellow, and Black [CMYK]).

 But be prepared for a healthy monetary investment when you buy a swatch book. These little buggers can cost anywhere from $75 to $200 and need to be replaced over time as the colors can fade. Keep them in a dark location to extend their life span. You can purchase swatch books from some larger art supply stores or order them online. You can purchase Pantone books from www.pantone.com. Do a search for others such as Trumatch, Focoltone, and Toyo.

- ✔ If you buy imaging or printing services, **do** spend some time finding the best service bureau and printer in your area and develop a good working relationship. Most likely, you'll run into a digital color expert or two hanging around.

✔ **Do** take some time to test your *workflow* (production methods) and your computer system. Scan images using multiple settings, print images using multiple settings, and view your images using different browsers on different monitors and different platforms.

Get to know the strengths and limitations and quirks of every piece of your equipment. Experiment with Photoshop. I know, I know, you have a life. But trust me, it will be an investment with great returns.

## Calibrating your monitor

*Calibrating* your monitor and creating an ICC profile of your monitor ensures that your monitor doesn't display any red, green, or blue *color casts* and that it provides as neutral a gray screen as possible. Calibration is incredibly important if you want to standardize your image display.

If you really want to do a great calibration job, consider investing in a combination hardware/software calibration package. These products used to be really pricey, but you can get a decent package for around $300. You can choose from several manufacturers. ColorVision (www.colorcal.com), for example, offers more than one program. The package includes a photoelectric device that attaches to your monitor with a suction cup and measures the actual output.

If more software isn't within your budget, you can use the simple calibration tool that comes with Photoshop.

Turn on your monitor and let it warm up at least an hour. Then, if you're a Windows or Mac OS 9 user, you can use Photoshop's Adobe Gamma utility. (Look for it in the Control Panels.) You can either use the Gamma utility's Wizard, which walks you through the calibration process by asking you a series of questions, or manually calibrate your monitor by using sliders in the Adobe Gamma control panel.

If you're a Mac OS X user, you can use the Display Calibrator Assistant. Choose Apple⇨System Preferences⇨Displays⇨Color. Click the Color tab and then click the Calibrate button. Answer the questions in the Display Calibrator Assistant. (See Figure 3-6.)

Both utilities, Adobe Gamma and the Display Calibrator Assistant, help you remove any color casts and get as neutral a gray background as you can. They also create a profile of your monitor for Photoshop, Illustrator, and other programs so that those applications know how your monitor displays color.

 When you calibrate your monitor, display an image for which you already know the color values. For example, use an image that you've worked with and for which you have a good print and then use that image each and every time you calibrate. Your goal is to match the digital image on your screen to the printed image. You should calibrate every so often because monitors can drift.

**Figure 3-6**

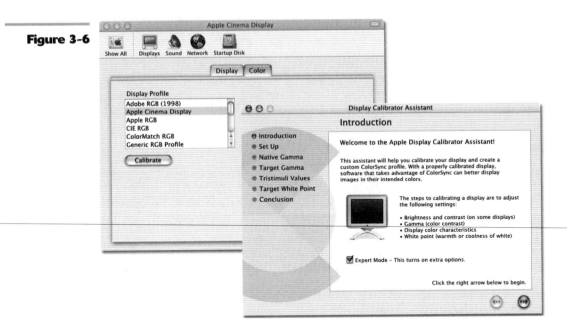

## Establishing your settings

When your monitor is calibrated (see the preceding section), and you have adequately arranged your work environment, you need to nail down the color settings and make sure that they're the right match for your intended output.

Choose Edit⇨Color Settings (Preferences⇨Color Settings on Mac OS X). The intimidating Color Settings dialog box rears its ugly head, as shown in Figure 3-7.

 As you're perusing the dialog box, hover your mouse over any item, and a great description of that item appears at the bottom of the dialog box.

In the Color Settings dialog box, you can choose from predefined settings established for specific types of output, or you can customize your own settings to fit your individual needs. And there's no law that says that you can't have multiple groups of settings — one for each type of project. Maybe you create both Web and print graphics. In that case, you may want to have a set of options for each workflow.

### Handling Photoshop's predefined settings

Photoshop allows you to take the easy route and choose from a long list of predefined color settings based on your desired output.

After you've set up the predefined settings, Photoshop provides all the appropriate working color spaces and color management policies you need to get good color results. Being the smart program that it is, Photoshop won't steer you down the wrong path with its predefined settings. The only way you can mess up the predefined settings is if your output doesn't match the setting. Say you choose the Web Graphics Defaults setting for your high-end, four-color print job; you'll be in for a surprise. (**Hint:** You may want to change those settings.)

**Figure 3-7**

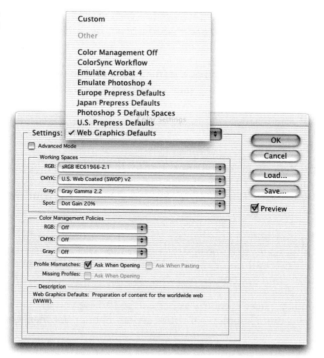

Here is a brief description of the predefined color settings in the Color Settings dialog box:

✔ **Custom:** Allows you to manually assign your own settings. When you define a custom configuration, save your settings so you can reload them later if necessary.

✔ **Color Management Off:** Deactivates Photoshop's color management system. I recommend it for video output but not for anything else, unless you're a color guru and know what you're doing.

✔ **ColorSync Workflow (Mac only):** Uses ColorSync 3.0 Color Management System and ColorSync profiles. It's not recognized by the Windows platform.

✔ **Emulate Acrobat 4:** Emulates Acrobat 4 and earlier versions.

✔ **Emulate Photoshop 4:** Turns color management off and emulates Photoshop 4's display. Photoshop 4 didn't employ color management.

✔ **Europe Prepress Defaults:** Provides settings to be used for printing in Europe.

✔ **Japan Prepress Defaults:** Provides settings to be used for printing in Japan.

✔ **Photoshop 5 Default Spaces:** Uses the default color settings found in Photoshop 5, the first version to use color management.

✔ **US Prepress Defaults:** Provides the settings for printing in the United States. This is a good overall selection if you use Photoshop mainly for print work.

✔ **Web Graphics Defaults:** Provides the settings for Web graphics. If you use Photoshop primarily for Web content, this setting is a good option because it reflects the average PC monitor.

> You can always use a predefined setting as a starting point and adjust whatever individual settings you need to. Note that if you do, your predefined setting name automatically changes to Custom.

### Indicating your working spaces

If you choose one of the predefined color settings, Photoshop plugs in all of the necessary remaining options in the dialog box. (If you choose Custom, Photoshop leaves whatever settings were there previously because it knows you are going to choose your own settings anyway.)

When you chose one of the predefined color settings, the first group of settings Photoshop plugged in were your working spaces. *Working spaces* are the color profiles associated with the RGB, CMYK, Grayscale, and Spot color modes. If you choose the Custom color setting, you need to choose your own working spaces.

> Each of the four working spaces is equally important, so I advise you to read all of the following sections — and read them in order — if you're serious about color management.

### RGB working spaces

Table 3-1 gives you a quick view of your RGB working space options.

**TABLE 3-1: RGB WORKING SPACE OPTIONS**

| Working Space | What It Does | Recommendation |
|---|---|---|
| Monitor RGB | The default setting for the predefined setting of Color Management Off and Emulate Acrobat 4. Sets the working space to your current monitor space (which it gets from the monitor profile you established during calibration). Forces Photoshop to turn off color management. | I don't recommend this setting unless you have a specific need to use it. |
| ColorSync RGB | Sets the working space to the profile specified in the Apple Color Sync control panel. The default setting for the ColorSync Workflow predefined setting. | For Macintosh only. |

| Working Space | What It Does | Recommendation |
|---|---|---|
| Adobe RGB (1998) | The default setting for all of the Prepress predefined settings. It is the best color profile to use for viewing 24-bit images and for converting RGB files to CMYK. Provides a large gamut of RGB colors. | I recommend this setting for all print work and as an overall setting if you're unsure what to choose. |
| Apple RGB | The default setting for the Emulate Photoshop 4 predefined setting. Can also be used for older Mac OS scanners and monitors. | Adobe also says it can be used with other older desktop publishing applications, but unless you're the proud owner of a 13-inch Apple monitor, I'd avoid it. |
| Color Match RGB | Use this working space only with Radius Pressview monitors. | I don't think I need to give you a recommendation on this one! You Radius Pressview users know who you are. |
| sRGB | The default setting for Web Graphics Defaults. This color profile, developed by Microsoft, HP, and Kodak, represents a standard, Trinitron PC monitor — the viewing platform of choice for many of the world's Web surfers. Can also be used with Windows scanners. Avoid it for print work due to its limited RGB color gamut. | If your goal is to ensure your Web graphics look relatively the same in Los Angeles as they do in Bangladesh, sRGB is a good profile to use. |

 After you set RGB working spaces, don't forget that you also have to configure the other three working spaces, as described in the following sections.

## CMYK working spaces

CMYK working spaces are a little more involved than RGB options, listed in the preceding section. They serve a threefold purpose:

✔ CMYK is the color space to which your RGB file will be converted when you choose Image➪Mode➪ CMYK.

✔ CMYK is the color space you will view your RGB image in when you choose View➪Proof Setup➪Working CMYK (see the upcoming section on Soft proofing colors).

✔ The CMYK color space determines how a CMYK file will be displayed on an RGB monitor.

 There are specific color profiles for printing in Europe, Japan, and the United States. Those four CMYK options are divided between those for coated and uncoated paper, and sheet-fed or Web printing presses. The latter two have different percentages of ink coverage and paper stock. I would leave it at U.S. Web Coated (SWOP)v2 unless your commercial printer tells you otherwise.

 Don't forget to keep reading to find out how to configure the other working space settings.

### Grayscale working spaces

Grayscale working spaces have to do with two parameters — *viewing* and *dot gain* of grayscale images (Image⇨Mode⇨Grayscale). You can choose Gray Gamma 1.8 for a Macintosh monitor or Gray Gamma 2.2 for a PC monitor. You can also view an image according to how it will print, based on typical dot gain.

Dot gain is how much ink the paper will absorb, thereby increasing the size of every halftone dot. When continuous-tone images are digitized, they are converted into a series of dots known as a *halftone.*

If you're preparing graphics for the Web, you may want to set your working space to Gray Gamma 2.2 — whether you're using a Mac or not — because most of the Web surfers world-wide are PC users.

 For print work, leave the setting at Dot Gain 20% unless your commercial printer tells you otherwise.

 Don't forget — you still have to adjust another working space.

### Spot working spaces

Spot working spaces have to do with spot colors. Spot colors are premixed inks that are printed in addition to, or in lieu of, the four process colors — cyan, magenta, yellow, and black. Unless your commercial printer tells you otherwise, stick with a setting of Dot Gain 20%.

## After You Define Your Settings

Your specified working space acts as the default color profile for any new images you create. That means that every file you create on your computer will now use the colors within the gamut of your color profiles (either RGB or CMYK depending on your document color mode).

 Any images that are untagged — that don't already have an embedded profile (for example, Photoshop files created before Version 5) — will also use your working spaces.

In addition, your working spaces also define how your images will be converted. For example, say your CMYK working space is U.S. Web Coated (SWOP) v2. When you convert an RGB image to CMYK (Image⇨Mode⇨CMYK) prior to sending it off to the printer, the image will automatically be tagged with the U.S. Web Coated (SWOP) v2 color profile. (If this looks like a whole lot of letters jumbled together, read the sections devoted to RGB and CMYK working spaces.)

 When you save your file, make sure that you select the Embed Color Profile option in the Save dialog box, if it's available. (Some file formats don't support color profiles.) This ensures that the file will be tagged with the specified color profile and that its origins will always be known.

# Setting Color Management Policies

After you've established working color spaces, the next step is to establish the default color management policy for each color mode. In other words, you need to tell Photoshop how to interpret and manage the color profiles of files it opens.

Photoshop looks at the color profile of an opened or imported file, compares it to your working spaces, and then employs the default policies you have established. If the files it opens have been embedded with the same color profile as yours, there isn't an issue. You're good to go. But sometimes this isn't the case:

✔ **You may open files that have no profile.** These can be older files, files that were created with color management turned off, or files created in other applications that do not employ color management.

✔ **You may open a file that has a color profile that doesn't match your working space.** Say that you have a Web designer friend and his settings are based on the Web Graphics Defaults. He gives you a file, and you open it on your computer. You do mostly print work, so your settings are set to the U.S. Prepress Defaults. He gives you a file, which you open in Photoshop on your computer. Photoshop then displays an alert that says the file has an embedded color profile that doesn't match your current RGB working space — his working space is sRGB and yours is Adobe RGB (1998). The alert then goes on to describe the default policy that will be invoked on the file, as shown in Figure 3-8.

**Figure 3-8**

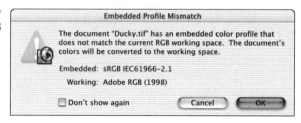

Embedded Profile Mismatch

The document "Ducky.tif" has an embedded color profile that does not match the current RGB working space. The document's colors will be converted to the working space.

Embedded: sRGB IEC61966-2.1

Working: Adobe RGB (1998)

☐ Don't show again          Cancel          OK

Again, if you have selected a predefined setting, the policies have already been established for you, and those should work fine. I do recommend however, that you change the policies of one of the predefined settings. If you choose Web Graphics Defaults, the Color Management Policies options are all set to Off. Unless you have a good reason not to, I would change these to Convert to Working RGB. Remember color management is a good thing.

Here are the three policy options:

✔ **Off:** This option turns color management off for any new files you create, import, or open. However, if the opened or imported file's color profile matches your current working space, the profile is preserved.

✔ **Preserve Embedded Profiles:** This option displays the files in their original embedded color space. No color conversion occurs. Untagged files remain untagged but use the current working space for display.

✔ **Convert to Working RGB (or CMYK or Grayscale, depending on your image mode):** This option converts any files with missing or mismatched embedded profiles to your working RGB space. Untagged files remain untagged but use the current working space for display.

The next decision you have to make is whether you want Photoshop to automatically invoke your default management policies or you want to be able to evaluate them on a file-by-file basis. If you do not check the Ask When Opening option for Profile Mismatches and Missing Profiles, Photoshop will display the Embedded Profile Mismatch alert message (refer to Figure 3-8), describing what default policy will occur. You can then select the Don't Show Again check box, and from that point forward, Photoshop will execute the policy without displaying an alert. For files with missing profiles, Photoshop will simply invoke the default policy without an alert.

If you select the Ask When Opening option for Profile Mismatches, Photoshop will not only display an Embedded Profile Mismatch alert, but also provide you with options for handling the color of that file, thereby overriding the default policy, as shown in Figure 3-9.

**Figure 3-9**

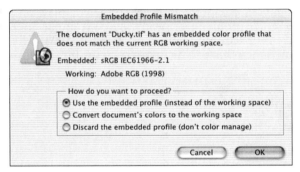

The options are similar to the default policies of the Color Settings dialog box:

✔ **Use the Embedded Profile (Instead of the Working Space):** Photoshop displays the file in its original embedded color space and does not perform any color conversions.

✔ **Convert Document's Colors to the Working Space:** Photoshop converts the file from its embedded color space to your working color space.

✔ **Discard the Embedded Profile (Don't Color Manage):** Photoshop doesn't utilize any color management when opening files but displays the file in your working space.

Be cautious about making any CMYK conversions. If you encounter a Profile Mismatch with a CMYK image, you will probably want to preserve the image's embedded profile unless you're absolutely sure it should be converted to another CMYK working space. But, if the image doesn't have a profile, then by all means convert it to your CMYK working space.

If you select the Ask When Pasting option for Profile Mismatches, Photoshop prompts you when you drag and drop layers or selections that have the same color mode (see Chapter 2 of this book for more on modes) but different color profiles. In the Paste Profile Mismatch alert dialog box, you have two options:

✔ **Convert (Preserve Color Appearance):** Photoshop converts and matches the appearance of the color rather than the RGB numerical values. For example, the RGB color of R 152, G 122, B 250 may be a different shade of purple in one RGB working space versus another. If you preserve the numerical values, the shades won't match. If you preserve the appearance, Photoshop will attempt to maintain the two shades.

✔ **Don't convert (preserve color number):** Photoshop does not convert the appearance of the color but instead matches the RGB numerical values.

If you don't select the Ask When Pasting check box, Photoshop pastes the color appearance between RGB images and pastes the numerical values between CMYK images.

If you select the Ask When Opening option for Missing Profiles, Photoshop displays a Missing Profile alert and also provides you with the following options, as shown in Figure 3-10:

**Figure 3-10**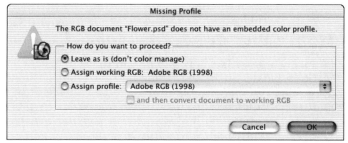

✔ **Leave As Is (Don't Color Manage):** This leaves the image untagged and without a color profile, but displays the image in your working space.

✔ **Assign Working RGB (or CMYK or Grayscale, depending on your image mode):** *your working space*: Photoshop tags the image with your working space and displays it in that working space. If you change your working space, the image retains the old working space.

✔ **Assign profile:** This option allows you to assign any color profile contained within the pop-up menu. (You can then also choose and then convert the document to working RGB — or CMYK or Grayscale.) You can use this option if you know where the untagged image originated. For example if you scanned your image and your scanner doesn't embed profiles, you can assign the scanner profile.

Unless you have a specific reason not to, I recommend that you assign your working RGB space to those orphan files.

I recommend selecting the Ask When Opening and Ask When Pasting check boxes. That way you know when there is a profile mismatch and you have the choice of picking your course of action, which includes overriding the defaults you set in the policy settings. This allows you to evaluate whether you want to preserve or convert on a file-by-file basis.

For example, if you're a print designer (like I am), and a Web designer gives you a file, you get a profile mismatch alerting you that the file has the sRGB color space and that it doesn't match your working space of Adobe RGB (1998). If you're going to use the image as-is for Web content, you tell Photoshop to preserve the embedded profile and not to make any conversion. But if you want to repurpose the image (for, say, a logo), you have to instruct Photoshop to convert the file to your working RGB space. (Of course, ultimately, you would have to also convert the image mode to CMYK for printing purpose.)

 To find out the color profile of an image, choose Document Profile from the pop-up menu at the bottom of the image window (described in detail in Book I, Chapter 1). Also if an image has a color profile that differs from your working space, an asterisk appears in the title bar. An untagged image displays a pound sign.

By the way, when you select the Advanced Mode option, you have a few additional options regarding color conversion engines and rendering intents, which are methods of color translation. I recommend putting your trust in Photoshop and leaving these options at their defaults, unless you're a bona-fide color expert.

## Getting Consistent Color between Adobe Applications

If you have a complete Adobe workflow like I do, you'll want to use the same Color Settings for all of your Adobe applications. Illustrator, InDesign, and Acrobat share a similar Color Settings dialog box. There are a few minor differences, but nothing major. If there is an element that doesn't exist in one application's Color Settings dialog box, Adobe merely plugs in the default setting. You can save your Color Settings in Photoshop by clicking the Save button in the Color Settings dialog box. To ensure that all of your Adobe applications can access the settings file, save it to a default location:

- ✓ For Microsoft Windows, that's the Program Files/Common Files/Adobe/Color/Settings folder.

- ✓ If you're using Mac OS 9, the default location is the System Folder/Application Support/Adobe/Color/Settings folder.

- ✓ For Mac OS X users, the default folder is User/CurrentUser/Library/ApplicationSupport/Adobe/Color/Settings.

Launch your other applications, open the Color Settings dialog box, and click the Load button. Navigate to the saved settings file and select it. You should be all set for color consistency between applications.

## Reassigning, Removing, or Converting Color Profiles

Before you read this section, let me gently note that the operations described are really for advanced users. Although these aren't overly difficult, you should know why you're doing a particular operation and have a good reason for doing it. That said, once in a great while, you may want to either assign a different color profile to an image without converting the color, convert an image's color profile, or on a very rare occasion, eliminate the color profile of your image altogether. For example, say you're a photographer and you need to take a folder of photos and hand them off to a Web design firm. In that case, you might want to change the Adobe RGB (1998) color profile of those images to sRGB.

To reassign or eliminate a color profile, choose Image➪Mode➪Assign Profile and select one of the following three options, shown in Figure 3-11:

- **Don't Color Manage This Document:** Strips the color profile and doesn't employ color management.

- **Working RGB (or CMYK or Grayscale, depending on your color mode):** *your working space*: Assigns your current working space to a file that either is untagged or has a different color profile than your working space.

- **Profile:** Choose the color profile you want from the pop-up menu. Photoshop assigns that profile to the file but doesn't convert the colors to that profile. Be aware that this option may drastically change the appearance of the colors because the color numbers are retained (the numeric value of the color) in the new color profile.

**Figure 3-11**

| Assign Profile |
| --- |
| Assign Profile: |
| ○ Don't Color Manage This Document |
| ○ Working RGB: Adobe RGB (1998) |
| ◉ Profile: sRGB IEC61966-2.1 |
| OK |
| Cancel |
| ☑ Preview |

Make sure that the Preview check box is selected so you can see the result of your action.

To convert to another color profile, choose Image➪Mode➪Convert to Profile. Choose your desired color profile for conversion from the Profile pop-up menu, shown in Figure 3-12. Your file is now converted and tagged with this color profile. You can also specify the color management engine (specifies the color matching method), rendering intent (the method used for color translation), and whether to use black point compensation (when selected, the full dynamic range is mapped to the destination space), and dithering options (colors are mixed to simulate a missing color in the destination space). Again, unless you are a real color guru, I recommend taking Adobe's word for it and leaving the default settings for whatever destination profile you choose. Even if you don't, I recommend that you select the Use Black Point Compensation and Use Dither check boxes (unless the size of your Web graphics is critical). If you have layers, you can choose to flatten all the layers into a single one. I recommend this because it makes the preview more accurate. Keep the Preview check box selected to view your conversion.

**Figure 3-12**

| Convert to Profile |
| --- |
| Source Space |
| Profile: Adobe RGB (1998) |
| Destination Space |
| Profile: Working CMYK – U.S. Web Coated (SWOP) v2 |
| Conversion Options |
| Engine: Adobe (ACE) |
| Intent: Relative Colorimetric |
| ☑ Use Black Point Compensation |
| ☑ Use Dither |
| ☐ Flatten Image |
| OK |
| Cancel |
| ☑ Preview |

# Soft Proofing Colors

Photoshop allows you to preview on-screen how your image will look on a variety of output device. First, choose View⇨Proof Setup and select your desired setup. The Working options are based on the working spaces you specified in the Color Settings dialog box.

- ✔ Macintosh RGB and Windows RGB display your image as it will appear on a standard Macintosh or Windows monitor. This can come in handy when you want to see how your Web graphic will generally look on another platform.

- ✔ Monitor RGB allows you to view the image by using your current monitor's color space. This essentially turns off your RGB working space and lets you see the image without any color management.

- ✔ Custom allows you to choose a specific device. For example, choosing U.S. Web Coated (SWOP)v2 lets you to see how your RGB image will look when they're converted to CMYK for printing.

After you have chosen your setup, choose View⇨ Proof Colors to view the image in your chosen working space. For the most reliable results, use a good quality monitor. And don't forget about the importance of setting up a good viewing environment as well.

# Time Travel — Undoing in Photoshop

When Tom Wolfe said "You can't go home again," he wasn't talking about Photoshop. If you change your mind about something you've done and want to return to your starting place (or any point in between), Photoshop is very forgiving. Our favorite image editor offers many different ways to reverse actions, undo what you did, reapply effects you've cancelled, and, generally, change your mind as often as a new apartment owner deciding where to put the couch.

Photoshop is the ultimate time machine. Not only can you reverse actions, but you can also go back to the future to restore them. This flexibility enables you to work on your image as you please, without worrying that a particular action will be locked in stone. Confident in your ability to retrace or repeat your steps as necessary, you can experiment, try different effects, and be much more creative.

This chapter helps you master Photoshop's powerful time-traveling features, including the Undo command, the History palette, and tools like the Art History Brush.

## Undoing What's Done

Photoshop gives you two simple ways to undo your efforts: the Undo/Redo command and the Revert command. Both are easy to master, as described in the next few sections.

### Using the Undo command

Your first stop in your journey through time is the Undo/Redo command. This command simply reverses the last action you took or reapplies it if you just undid something. For example, if you apply a brush stroke you don't like, use Undo to remove that stroke. Then if you immediately change your mind, you can redo it.

To undo your last action, choose Edit➪Undo or simply press Ctrl+Z (⌘+Z on the Mac).

If you want the shortcut key for Redo to be different from the one for Undo (Ctrl+Z, or ⌘+Z on the Mac), choose Edit➪Preferences➪General (Photoshop➪Preferences➪General on Mac OS X) and select one of the alternates: Ctrl+Y (⌘+Y on the Mac) or Shift+Ctrl+Z (Shift+⌘+Z on the Mac). After you set up a separate shortcut for each command, you can no longer toggle back and forth between the two with a single shortcut.

Use Undo/Redo to toggle an effect on and off to compare the before and after effects quickly. For example, you can apply a filter, examine the results, and then flip back and forth between the filtered and unfiltered version by pressing the Undo/Redo shortcut keys rapidly. When you decide which way to go, stop. This procedure works best if you've chosen to press Ctrl+Z (⌘+Z on the Mac) to apply both Undo and Redo.

Remember that Undo/Redo works only for a single command. If you do anything else after applying a command and then change your mind, you have to resort to one of the other time-travel techniques described later in this chapter.

If an action can't be undone or redone, Undo/Redo is grayed out and unavailable. For example, if you apply a brush stroke and then save the file to your hard disk, you can no longer undo the brush stroke. (However, you can use the History palette to remove the brush stroke. See "Working with the Almighty History Palette," later in this chapter.)

### Reverting to what's saved

*Revert* replaces your current file with the last saved file, effectively wiping out everything you've done since the file was last saved. You can revert to the last version of the file by choosing File➪Revert (or by pressing F12). All the changes in your current file are lost when the last saved version replaces it on the screen.

On the surface, Revert seems like an all or nothing proposition to be resorted to only when you've given up all hope of salvaging the current file. However, that's not necessarily the case.

For example, you may find it beneficial to use Revert to produce two versions of an image. Perhaps you've done some work on an image and now want to compare this version of the image with a version of the image that you apply an entirely different set of commands to. Just duplicate the current version (choose Image➪Duplicate) and revert back to its pristine state to apply the other effects. Then you can compare versions to see which you like best. (This tactic only works if you haven't saved the file along the way, of course.) You can use revert in this manner as many times as you like to create two, three, or more versions all based on one original image.

The Revert command is stored on the History palette, so in many cases, you can remove the Revert command to restore the file to its manipulated state once again. You find out how to do this in the next section.

Revert only restores the last saved version of your image. If you open an image, make some changes, and then save it, Revert backtracks to that *saved* version, not to the original. That's why it's a good idea to work with a copy of an image in case at some point you really do want to go back to the original version.

# Working with the Almighty History Palette

Undoing and redoing commands are kid's stuff next to the power of the almighty History palette. Think of this tool as a recipe listing all the steps you took to cook up your image in its present state. Using the History palette, you can browse through the recipe and return to any step in the list to begin work anew from that point. In this mode, the History palette operates like a multistep undo process.

 You can customize the keyboard shortcuts for stepping backward and forward in the General Preferences. You also can find these commands on the History palette options menu.

## Understanding states and snapshots

You can't go too far in your use of the History palette without understanding two important concepts, as well as how the concepts are different:

- **States:** States are just another way of saying steps. At any given point in your image-editing activities, Photoshop saves your individual edits into states. By default, Photoshop remembers 20 states for an image.

- **Snapshots:** You can save temporary copies of an image, each containing all its various states. For example, say you make six edits to an image before you take a snapshot. The snapshot shows the image, but it also contains a complete history of the six states. Make a few more changes, and take another snapshot: The new snapshot contains the six states you made previously, as well as any new ones. See "Taking Snapshots," later in this chapter, to find out how to use snapshots.

When you have these concepts down, you can get to the business of understanding how the individual tools in the History palette use states and snapshots to help you go back in time (and back to the future again) to undo, redo, and modify each miniscule edit you make to your images.

## Changing the default number of steps that the History palette displays

The History palette displays a list of each change you make to your image — every brush stroke you dab, every deletion you make, every layer you create — up to a default limit of 20 steps, or *states*. The list begins at the top of the History palette, and each new step is tacked on at the bottom. When you reach the limit of 20 steps, the oldest step (at the top of the list) is dropped off to make room for the latest one at the bottom.

 If you move something repeatedly and don't choose another tool, all the moves are considered a single step, until you do select another tool.

If your computer has lots of memory and you want to be able to move back and forth more than 20 steps, you can increase the number of steps to as many as 1,000 in the General Preferences dialog box. Choose Edit➪Preferences➪General (or Photoshop➪Preferences➪ General under Mac OS X) and enter a new value in the History States box. Keep in mind that boosting this number can eat up your available memory quite quickly, because after you've activated a higher number of states, Photoshop will *always* store up to that number every time you edit an image (even images with which you don't contemplate needing access to more than 20 steps). A better choice may be to leave the states set to 20 and instead save snapshots of your image, as described in the following sections.

## Introducing History palette options and tools

The History palette has several components you should know about, as shown in Figure 4-1:

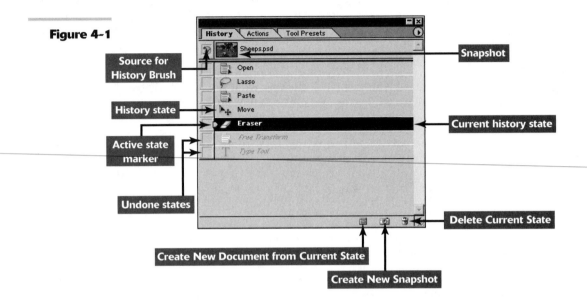

**Figure 4-1**

- Source for History Brush
- Snapshot
- History state
- Current history state
- Active state marker
- Undone states
- Delete Current State
- Create New Document from Current State
- Create New Snapshot

✔ **Snapshot thumbnail.** This is a miniature image of the most recently saved *snapshot* image, which is a copy of your document with all the current states included. (For more on snapshots, see "Taking Snapshots," later in this chapter.)

✔ **Source for History Brush column.** Click in this column next to a particular snapshot or state, and when you begin painting with the History Brush or when erasing with the Erase to History option, Photoshop uses the snapshot or state you select as the source.

✔ **History state.** This is a particular step or edit in your document's list of steps. An icon appears in this column showing what kind of action occurred in that state.

✔ **Active state marker.** This slider points to the currently active state. You can drag it up or down to change the current state.

✔ **Create New Document from Current State.** Click this icon to create a duplicate copy of your image at the currently selected state. Your new document starts out with a clean slate and an empty history list.

✔ **Create New Snapshot.** Click this icon to store an image of your document, preserving all the states listed.

✔ **Delete Current State.** Click this icon to remove a selected state.

✔ **Undone states.** These are the grayed-out states that are undone when you select an earlier state in the list.

✔ **Opened state.** This is the original document when first opened.

✔ **Current history state.** This is the active state you've selected in the history list.

# Viewing an Image's Various States

You can move back to any state listed in the History palette, remove a state to cancel a step, or perform other time-travel stunts with the History palette. The following sections outline some basic time-shifting techniques you should know.

## Going back to a particular state

To go back in time and resume editing at a particular point, just click the state you want to return to. All subsequent states appear grayed out, or what Adobe calls *undone*. Then begin editing your image as usual. As soon as you perform a new step, all the states that follow your reentry point vanish. It's like applying the Undo command to a group of steps with one click.

 If you intentionally (or accidentally) begin editing while a previous state is highlighted, and you change your mind, immediately undo your first action — press Ctrl+Z (⌘+Z on the Mac). The subsequent steps that were removed will reappear.

## Reviewing your image at different states

To review how your image looked at various previous states, just click the state you want to take a look at. (You can also drag the history slider up and down the list.) The document image immediately changes to reflect that earlier state. You can move back and forth between any points in the history list if you like. As long as you don't make any editing changes during your time-traveling jaunt, your current history list is preserved.

## Removing a state

To remove a state and all the steps that follow it, select the state and then do one of the following:

- ✔ Press the Delete key.
- ✔ Click the trash can icon.
- ✔ Drag the state's icon to the trash can icon.
- ✔ Right-click the state (or Control+click on the Mac) and choose Delete from the menu that pops up.
- ✔ Choose Delete from the History palette options menu.

## Clearing all states

You can clear all the states from the palette by choosing Clear History from the palette options menu. To delete all the states except the last one in the history list, as well as keep the snapshots you've saved, choose Edit⟹Purge⟹Histories. You can clear or purge your history list when you don't need the states that are included anymore, to save memory or to return to the original state of your document. Just be sure you're really, seriously, not interested in going back again later to make changes.

### Navigating the history list

You can move up and down the history list even if the list isn't visible on your screen. The Edit⇨Step Forward and Edit⇨Step Backward commands move forward and back in the history list. The best way to access these commands is to use the keyboard shortcuts:

- ✔ Press Alt+Ctrl+Z (Option+⌘+Z on the Mac) to move backward in time (upward in the history list).

- ✔ Press Shift+Ctrl+Z (Shift+⌘+Z on the Mac) to move forward in time (down the history list).

## *Looking at the History Options Dialog Box*

The History palette has four options that change its behavior. To access these options, choose History Options from the History options palette menu to open the History Options dialog box, shown in Figure 4-2. The dialog box offers these options:

**Figure 4-2**

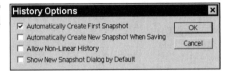

- ✔ **Automatically Create First Snapshot:** This option, selected by default, tells Photoshop to create a snapshot of the image when it is first opened, before any changes are made. You can return to this snapshot at any time by clicking its name in the History palette. Keep this option selected. That way, you can always return to your original image if necessary.

- ✔ **Automatically Create New Snapshot When Saving:** This option tells Photoshop to create a new snapshot each time you save the image. If you're like me and save every couple of minutes, you probably won't want to select this option; otherwise, you'll end up with a palette full of unwanted snapshots.

- ✔ **Allow Non-Linear History:** This option makes it possible to edit or delete a state without removing all the states that follow it.

    When the Non-Linear History capability is active, you can make an editing change to an intermediate state in the history list, perhaps save the edited state as a snapshot, or even delete the state, leaving the other steps below it unchanged. (When you delete a state you've edited, the edit you made is added to the end of the history list.)

 Use this option with caution because steps are interdependent. A change you've removed may form the basis for another edit later on, so deleting it can cause weird results.

- ✔ **Show New Snapshot Dialog by Default:** This option ensures that Photoshop will ask you for a name for any new snapshot you create. Applying names to snapshots makes it easier to remind yourself of the state of the image when you saved the snapshot.

### Keeping the New Snapshot dialog box close at hand

If you want the New Snapshot dialog box to open when you click the New Snapshot button, select the Show New Snapshot Dialog by Default option described in the preceding section.

Hold down the Alt key (Option key on the Mac) when you click the New Snapshot button to access the dialog box even when the Show New Snapshot Dialog by Default option is deselected. If you remember this technique, you can alternate between creating generic snapshots and using the dialog box.

▼▼▼▼▼▼▼▼▼▼▼▼▼▼▼▼▼▼▼▼▼▼▼▼▼▼▼▼▼▼▼▼▼▼▼▼▼▼▼

## Taking Snapshots

*Snapshots* are duplicates of your image at a particular point in time, similar to saving a document under an alternate name. (The snapshots are automatically named something generic like Snapshot 1 or Snapshot 2.) However, snapshots are temporary copies, available only during your current work session. When you save your image and close it, all the snapshots are lost. So it's best to think of snapshots as a way of saving your history lists at various points in time while you're working.

Snapshots are a handy way to alternate between versions of an image when you're making major changes. For example, if you plan to apply several filters that will drastically modify your image, you may want to save a snapshot before you use the filters and save another one after you've applied them. You can then click either snapshot to switch from one version to the other quickly.

 The second you close a file, the snapshots you've taken disappear forever.

To take a snapshot, follow these steps:

**1.** **Select the state at which you want to take a snapshot.**

The state can be the most recent one with all your latest editing changes, or an earlier state.

**2.** **Choose New Snapshot from the palette options menu.**

Or right-click (Control+click on the Mac) the state and choose New Snapshot from the pop-up menu.

The New Snapshot dialog box opens, as shown in Figure 4-3.

If you want to bypass this dialog box, just click the New Snapshot button to create a snapshot. Your first snapshot is called Snapshot 1.

**3.** **In the Name box, enter a name for the snapshot, preferably one that will help you remember the contents of that particular snapshot.**

You can add or change the name of the snapshot later by double-clicking the snapshot name in the history list.

**4.** **Choose one of the subtypes of snapshots in the From menu (as shown in Figure 4-3):**

CONTINUED
▼ ▼ ▼ ▼ ▼

✔ **Full Document** creates a snapshot of all the layers in the image at the currently selected state. (This is the default.)

✔ **Merged Layers** creates a snapshot with a single layer, merging all the layers in the image at the currently selected state. Use this option to create a flattened version with the visible layers combined.

✔ **Current Layer** creates a snapshot of only the active layer of the current state.

**5.** **Click OK to create the snapshot.**

 If you no longer need a snapshot, select the snapshot and press the Delete key. You can also click the trash icon, or drag the snapshot to the trash icon, or choose Delete from the palette options menu.

**Figure 4-3**

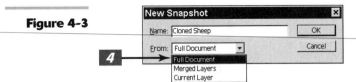

# Restoring Part of an Image

Although the concept may seem like quantum physics, you can erase and brush on an image by using previously saved states or snapshots.

What? Okay, let me try this again. You can erase portions of an image to a history state, as well as paint on an image from a history state. This means that traveling through time doesn't have to be an all or nothing thing; you can erase or paint portions of a different state onto your currently active state.

For example, suppose you've applied a blur filter to a face and decide later you want to make the eyes sharp again. You can use the Eraser with the Erase to History option, or the History Brush tool, to paint over the eyes with information from an earlier state before you blurred them, as shown in Figure 4-4.

▼▼▼▼▼▼▼▼▼▼▼▼▼▼▼▼▼▼▼▼▼▼▼▼▼▼▼▼▼▼▼▼▼▼▼▼▼▼

## Using the Eraser in Erase to History mode

You'd want to use the Eraser in Erase to History mode when a portion of an earlier state or snapshot contains information that you want to include in an image that has otherwise been extensively edited. To erase and restore to a portion of an earlier state or snapshot, just follow these steps:

**1.** **In the History palette, click in the far-left column of the state or snapshot you want to use as the source for the Eraser with the Erase to History option.**

An icon appears, indicating that this state will be used as the source for the Eraser with the Erase to History option.

**2.** Select the Eraser tool.

**3.** Choose the Erase to History option in the Options bar.

**4.** Choose any other Eraser options you want to use, such as Brush, Mode, Opacity, Airbrush, or Flow.

**5.** **Select the layer and state you want to erase.**

**6.** **Begin to erase.**

The image in the layer is removed and replaced with the image in the state you've specified as the origin for the Eraser in Erase to History mode.

 You can convert the Eraser temporarily to Erase to History mode by holding down the Alt key (Option key on the Mac) when you erase or paint. Using Alt with the Eraser (or any other brush) gives you the Eyedropper tool.

**Figure 4-4**

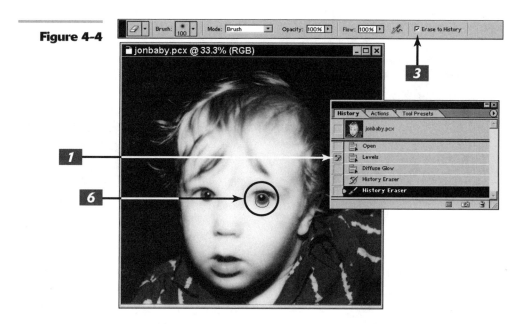

## Using the History Brush tool

You can also use the History Brush tool to apply an image area from a different state or snapshot to your current state. You'd want to use this tool to restore a portion of an image to an earlier state, while leaving the rest of the heavily modified image alone. Just follow these steps:

**1.** **In the History palette, click in the far-left column of the state or snapshot you want to use as the source for the History Brush, as shown in Figure 4-5.**

An icon appears, indicating that this state will be used as the source for the History Brush.

In my example, I chose my original image just after cropping it.

**2.** **Select the History Brush tool in the Tool palette.**

You can also press Y or Shift+Y to select it.

CONTINUED

**3.** **On the Options bar, choose any other brush options you want to use, such as Brush, Mode, Opacity, Airbrush, or Flow.**

Allowing access to blend modes is one advantage the History Brush has over the Eraser and the Erase to History option.

**4.** **Select the layer and state you want to paint on.**

**5.** **Begin to paint.**

The image in the layer is painted over with the image from the state you've specified as the origin for the History Brush.

I painted my original over my filtered image. (I used the Graphic Pen filter.)

**Figure 4-5**

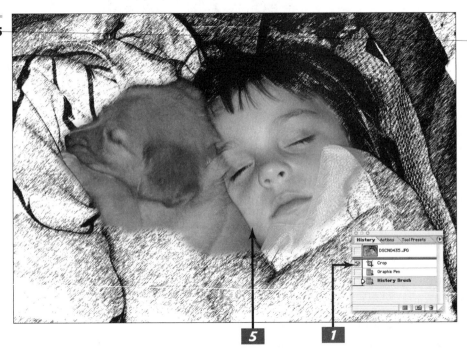

## When Photoshop won't let you go back

Sometimes you may see a No symbol when trying to use the Eraser and Erase to History option, the History Brush, or the Fill with History command. You must be sure that your current image is the same file size (same number of pixels) as the state you are trying to go back to. Actions such as cropping, trimming, using the Image Size or Canvas Size commands, or rotating any amount other that 180 degrees can prevent you from going back to a previous state.

▼▼▼▼▼▼▼▼▼▼▼▼▼▼▼▼▼▼▼▼▼▼▼▼▼▼▼▼▼▼▼▼▼▼▼▼▼

## Using the Fill to History feature

If you can easily select the area you want to replace with a specific state, you can use the Fill to History feature. Suppose you didn't like the sky in a particular image. You selected the sky area and then added clouds by using the Clouds filter. Now you want to put the original sky back, but don't want to reverse any of the other edits you performed in the meantime. Just follow these steps to replace an area by using the Fill to History feature:

**1.** Select a state as the source for the Fill to History function in the History palette.

For example, select the state that has the original sky.

**2.** Choose the current state and use your favorite selection tools to select the area you want to replace.

For example, if you remembered to save your original sky selection when you originally added clouds, you can choose Select⇨Load Selection and retrieve that selection.

**3.** Choose Edit⇨Fill and then select History from the Use pop-up menu.

**4.** Click OK to fill your selection with the image area from the selected state.

▼▼▼▼▼▼▼▼▼▼▼▼▼▼▼▼▼▼▼▼▼▼▼▼▼▼▼▼▼▼▼▼▼▼▼▼▼

## Using the Art History Brush tool

The Art History Brush is an interesting variation on the plain old History Brush. Both paint over an image by using information from a previous state. The Art History Brush, however, includes several choices in the Options bar that let you apply brush-stroke effects to your image as you paint:

✔ **Style.** The Style menu contains various-shaped brush stroke styles, such as Tight Short, Loose Medium, Dab, or Loose Curl. Although their names describe the look of the strokes fairly well, you'll want to experiment with them to see exactly what they look like.

✔ **Area.** This controls the area covered by the paint stroke independently of the brush size you select. The larger the size, the more area that's covered, and the more brush strokes that are applied per movement.

✔ **Tolerance.** This adjusts the amount of the change applied to your image. A low tolerance value lets you apply strokes anywhere in the image, regardless of color values. A high tolerance limits Art History strokes only to areas that are very different from the source state or snapshot, thereby making your image not quite as dramatically different from the original.

The result of using these options is an interesting painting effect that you can control quite easily after you've had some practice.

The Art History Brush often works best when you use a state that is quite different from the state you're painting over. For example, you can apply a heavy filter that makes the image almost unrecognizable and then use that filtered image to paint with the Art History Brush. You can even completely fill an image with color or texture and work with that.

To paint with the Art History Brush tool, follow these steps:

**1.** **Apply any effects you want to use to a state.**

**2.** **Click in the far-left column in the History palette to select the state you want to use as the source for the Art History Brush, as shown in Figure 4-6.**

**3.** **Select the Art History Brush from the Tool palette.**

You can also press Y or Shift+Y to select it.

**4.** **Select from the choices in the Options bar.**

Several of the options, such as Brush, Mode, or Opacity, are similar to the options available with the ordinary Brush tool. The new options are Style, Area, and Tolerance.

**5.** **Paint with the brush to get the effect you want.**

Don't forget that you can use the History palette to reverse Art History strokes that you change your mind about!

**Figure 4-6**

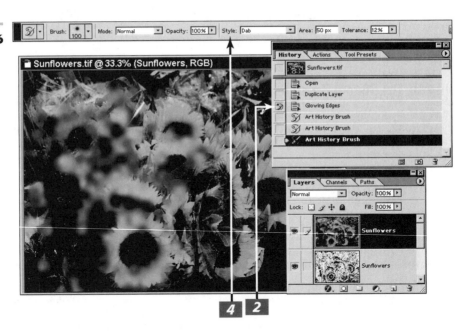

# Applying Annotations and Notes

Everybody's a critic! That's especially true when you're using Photoshop in a work environment — or in any scenario that involves anything but 100 percent freedom to perform your Photoshop magic as you want.

Sometimes, you'll want to collect comments from your colleagues, approvals from your supervisors, ideas from your friends, or nit-picks from your clients. Photoshop lets everyone have his or her say by using annotations, notes, or audio comments. You can use these clever feedback tools without worrying about physically modifying the work that you've carefully done. Imagine sticky notes you can move around your screen, and you'll see what Photoshop's annotations feature can do for you.

Text documents often are distributed for approval in a Portable Document Format (PDF) format by using Adobe Acrobat Reader, and comments are added by using the full Acrobat application. Photoshop is compatible with Acrobat, too, so you can save your Photoshop files in the PDF format. For more information on the PDF format, see *Adobe Acrobat 5 PDF For Dummies*, by Greg Harvey (Wiley Publishing, Inc.).

This chapter provides a quick introduction to Photoshop's annotation and voice notes features.

## Having Your Say with Notes and Audio Annotations

Text annotations (which Photoshop calls *notes*) are text comments that appear as icons within an image document when you choose to make them visible.

If you're reviewing someone else's notes, you simply double-click the note to view it or to modify the text it contains.

You can do lots of things with notes:

- ✓ **Show or hide all the notes:** Choose View⇨Show⇨Annotations.

- ✓ **Expand any note from its icon:** Double-click the icon.

- ✓ **Edit a note:** Expand the note and revise the text by using standard editing commands.

- ✓ **Delete a note:** Select the note and press Delete.

- ✓ **Remove all closed notes:** Right-click any note (Ctrl+click on the Mac) and choose Delete All Annotations from the context menu that pops up. You can also select a note and click Clear All in the Options bar. This removes all closed notes but doesn't remove notes that are open.

- ✓ **Move a note's icon:** Drag the icon. (The note still pops up in its original location, however.)

- ✓ **Relocate a note's window:** Open the note and drag its title bar to the new location. It then pops up in the new location.

▼ ▼ ▼ ▼ ▼ ▼ ▼ ▼ ▼ ▼ ▼ ▼ ▼ ▼ ▼ ▼ ▼ ▼ ▼ ▼ ▼ ▼ ▼ ▼ ▼ ▼ ▼ ▼ ▼ ▼ ▼ ▼ ▼ ▼ ▼ ▼ ▼ ▼ ▼ ▼ ▼

## Creating a text annotation

To create a text annotation, follow these steps:

**1.** **Select the Notes tool in the Tool palette (or just press N).**

**2.** **If necessary, change the name in the Author text box in the Options bar.**

Just double-click inside the Author text box, shown at the top of Figure 5-1, and start typing.

By default, when you create a note, the name you entered when you installed Photoshop appears as the author of the note. However, you may be working on an image with someone else's computer, or you may be on the lam and using an assumed name.

 Be sure that everyone looking at the file uses a unique name so that you can sort out the various notes and, perhaps, give all of them their proper weight (that is, always do what the boss says, but take Seymour the intern's comments with a grain of salt).

**3.** **From the Font and Size drop-down lists in the Options bar, choose a font and font size for the text.**

Selecting a particular font and size for each author may just be a matter of preference or readability or can be used to further differentiate between authors' comments. You choose font sizes in relative sizes from Smallest to Medium to Largest so Photoshop can adjust the notes to be readable on monitors set for different resolutions.

**4.** **Click the Color box on the Options bar and select a color for the title bar of each note and the color of its icon when the note is minimized.**

Color-coding is a good way to differentiate authors, as well as priorities. For example, you can use Red, Yellow, and Green to indicate relative status of a particular suggestion, or select a color to represent a particular author.

**5.** Finally, click in the note's window and type the text you want to enter, as shown in Figure 5-1.

You can use traditional editing commands, such as the Backspace key, Ctrl+X, Ctrl+C, and Ctrl+V (⌘+X, ⌘+C, and ⌘+V on the Mac) to edit the text.

**6.** When you're finished entering a note, click the note's Close box on the right end of the title bar (Windows) or the left end of the title bar (Mac OS).

The note is minimized to an icon. You can see a minimized icon in the upper-left corner of Figure 5-2.

Book
**II**
Chapter
**5**

**Figure 5-1**

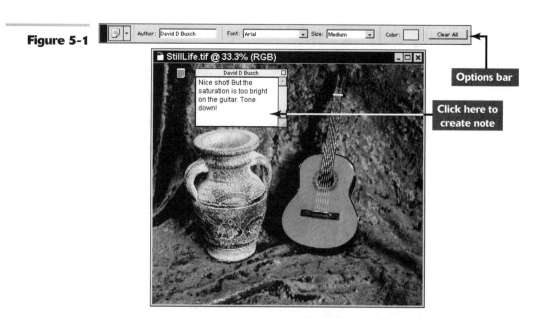

**Figure 5-2**

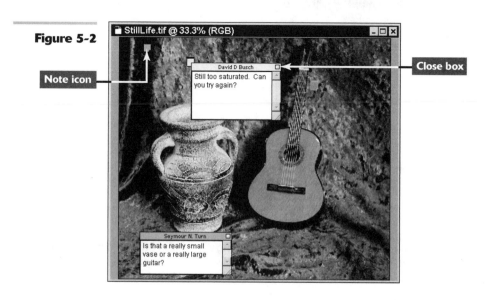

▼▼▼▼▼▼▼▼▼▼▼▼▼▼▼▼▼▼▼▼▼▼▼▼▼▼▼▼▼▼▼▼▼▼▼▼▼▼▼

### Creating an audio note

If you have a microphone connected to your computer, you can add audio notes to your image files. Audio notes are great for adding annotations that would take a long time to type or that are better explained through audio.

 Audio annotations can bloat your file size, so unless it's really more advantageous to use audio annotations, stick with notes.

To add an audio message to your file, just follow these steps:

*1.* **Select the Audio Annotation tool.**

Press N to activate the Notes tool and then Shift+N to choose the Audio Annotation tool.

*2.* **If necessary, change the author name or note color in the Options bar.**

Figure 5-3 shows the Options bar with the Audio Annotation tool activated.

*3.* **Click in the image where you'd like to include the audio annotation.**

The Audio Annotation dialog box, shown in Figure 5-4, pops up.

*4.* **Click the Start button (Windows) or Record button (Mac OS) and begin speaking into the microphone.**

*5.* **Click Stop when you're finished talking.**

To play the audio annotation, double-click its icon.

**Figure 5-3**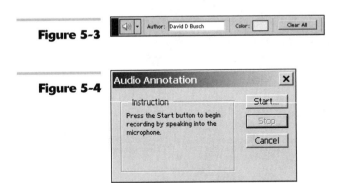

**Figure 5-4**

▼▼▼▼▼▼▼▼▼▼▼▼▼▼▼▼▼▼▼▼▼▼▼▼▼▼▼▼▼▼▼▼▼▼▼▼▼▼▼

## Importing and Exporting PDF Files with Annotations

You can view PDF or FDF (Forms Data Format) documents that contain annotations, review the annotations, and make new notes of your own.

 If you want to send an image file to a friend or colleague who doesn't have Photoshop, you can still get input. You can even include notes of your own. To export your file (and its annotations) for review in Adobe Acrobat, just save the document and choose PDF as the format.

Then when your Acrobat-using friend sends the file back to you, just follow these steps to access his or her input:

*1.* **Choose File⇨Import⇨Annotations.**

*2.* **Navigate to the PDF or FDF file you want to open.**

*3.* **Click the Load button.**

The file is imported into Photoshop with the annotations intact.

Book
**II**
Chapter
**5**

# Creating Actions for Productivity and Fun

**6**

P ractice makes perfect, but when it comes to repeating the same steps in Photoshop over and over, the result is often tedium and impatience. You wouldn't want to have to re-invent the wheel each time you wanted to go for a spin around the block, so why repeat the labor needed to carry out specific tasks if you don't have to? Photoshop lets you record steps by using a fast and fun feature called *Actions*. Photoshop actions are similar to the macro recording features found in your word processing or spreadsheet program, but they're usually easier to create and have capabilities custom-tailored for image editing and customization.

For example, Photoshop has preset actions to create a wood frame, simulate water reflections, or provide a molten lead look. You can also use preset actions to create filterlike effects.

And then there are the chores you can automate on your own. This chapter shows you how to do a few of them and how to take advantage of Photoshop's macro recording and editing capabilities.

## Using the Actions Palette

Not surprisingly, there's a palette dedicated to the automation of various chores. To view the Actions palette, choose Window⇨Actions, or click the Actions tab in its palette group or the Palette Well. You can view the Actions palette in two different modes, each of which is useful in its own way. Here's a short description of each mode:

✔ **List mode:** List mode, shown in Figure 6-1, is the default display in which each action is shown as a folderlike heading. You can open the heading to reveal all the steps within the action or collapse the heading to hide them.

You operate in List mode when you record an action and when you edit individual steps. List mode also lets you perform only some of the steps in a macro.

✔ **Button mode:** Button mode, shown in Figure 6-2, is a convenient, compact mode that hides all the inner workings of the actions, presenting only a button face that you can click to trigger a particular macro. Button mode is fast and easy; just click and go.

**Figure 6-1**

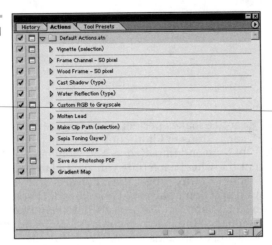

**Figure 6-2**

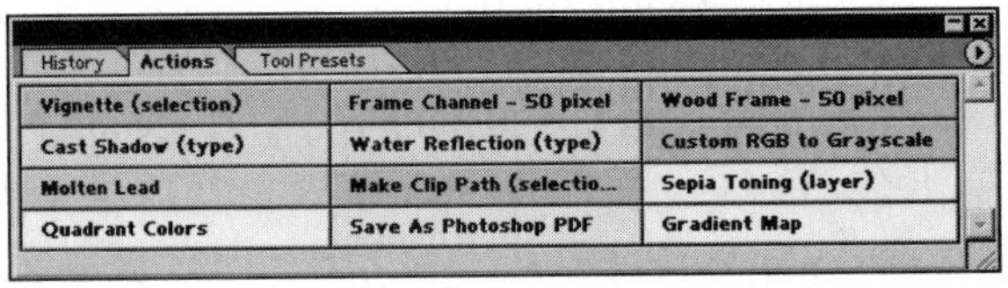

## Getting to know List mode

When you're working in List mode, the Actions palette has these three columns:

✔ **The leftmost column contains check boxes that you can select or deselect to control what actions are available in Button mode.** You can use this column to ensure that your most commonly used actions are available for use in Button mode, while hiding those that you don't use very often.

✔ **The second column toggles on or off the display of dialog boxes in actions.** Some actions include options you can select while running the macro. For example, the Vignette (Selection) action, which creates a faded frame around a selection, includes a dialog box that lets you specify the width of the fading. This dialog box is shown only when the dialog box column is selected; if you deselect that option, the action uses a default value of 5 pixels as the width for the feathered effect.

Book
**II**
Chapter
**6**

✔ **The third and widest column shows the name of the action.** Click the right-pointing arrow to the left of the action's name to reveal the individual steps of the action. Many (but not necessarily all) steps have their own arrows, which can be expanded or collapsed to show or hide the options used to carry out that step. In case you're curious, the good folks at Adobe call these twisty-turny arrows *disclosure triangles.*

At the bottom of the Actions palette in List mode, you find six icons, not all of which are available at all times. The icons are described in the following list from left to right:

✔ **Stop Recording/Playing:** This icon is active when you're recording a macro. Click it to stop recording (or to stop playing back an action).

✔ **Begin Recording:** Click this icon to begin recording a macro (as described in more detail later in this chapter).

✔ **Play Selection:** Click this icon to begin playing a selected action. Playback begins at the step selected; you can choose the action's name to start the macro at the beginning, or expand the macro and select any step to begin playback at that point.

✔ **New Set:** Click this icon to create a new action set (as described later in this chapter).

✔ **New Action:** Click this icon to begin a new action.

✔ **Delete:** Click this icon to remove a selection action or step.

▼▼▼▼▼▼▼▼▼▼▼▼▼▼▼▼▼▼▼▼▼▼▼▼▼▼▼▼▼▼▼▼▼▼▼▼▼▼

## Creating an action in List mode

Try this quick practice run to see exactly how the Actions palette works:

**1.** **Display the Actions palette in List mode.**

If you're in Button mode, click the palette options arrow and select List mode. You need to be in List mode to create an action.

**2.** **Under the Default Actions folder, click the right-pointing arrow next to the name of the action.**

The steps for the Vignette (Selection) action are displayed in Figure 6-3.

**3.** **Click the right-pointing arrow next to the step you want to change.**

The step expands to show the parameters used for that step. For the Vignette (Selection), the parameters are filled by using white at an opacity of 100 percent and by using the Normal fill mode.

You can click in the dialog box column for several of the steps (Make Snapshot, Feather, Make Layer, and Fill). You can select or deselect this column for a specific step to control whether the dialog box for that step is displayed. For example, with the Vignette (Selection) action, if you deselect all the boxes in the dialog box column except for the one next to Fill, the action proceeds without input from you until it reaches the Fill step. Then the Fill dialog box pops up, and you can change settings such as the fill color, opacity, and fill mode. You can also click in the dialog box column next to the action's name to turn on or off all the marked dialog box steps in the macro.

CONTINUED
▼ ▼ ▼ ▼ ▼

**Figure 6-3**

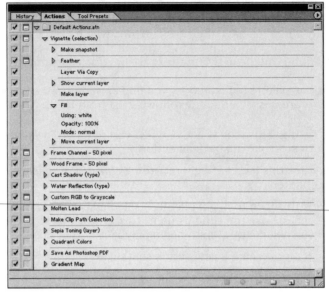

# Introducing Preset Actions

Photoshop's preset actions are located in a series of files in the Actions folder. The default actions are opened by, um, default, when you first open Photoshop. However, other preset actions are available for you to open and use. They include Frames (for putting frames around your images), Text Effects (for enhancing your text), and Textures, for adding textures to your selections.

## Preset action options

Here are some other options for loading actions sets:

- ✔ If you've saved actions of your own (as described later in this chapter) somewhere other than the Photoshop Actions folder, you can navigate to that folder by using the usual file navigation commands.

- ✔ To remove the existing actions and replace them with the set you are loading, choose Replace Actions from the palette options menu.

- ✔ To reset the Actions palette to the Default Actions set (removing all other sets you might have loaded), choose Reset Actions from the palette options menu.

- ✔ To clear all actions from the Actions palette, choose Clear Actions from the palette options menu. (You might want to do this when creating your own set of actions from scratch.)

▼ ▼ ▼ ▼ ▼ ▼ ▼ ▼ ▼ ▼ ▼ ▼ ▼ ▼ ▼ ▼ ▼ ▼ ▼ ▼ ▼ ▼ ▼ ▼ ▼ ▼ ▼ ▼ ▼ ▼ ▼ ▼ ▼ ▼ ▼ ▼ ▼ ▼ ▼ ▼ ▼ ▼ ▼ ▼

## Opening preset actions

Follow these steps to open preset actions.

**1.** **In the Actions palette, click the palette options menu arrow and choose Load Actions.**

Photoshop opens the Photoshop Actions folder in the Load dialog box, as shown in Figure 6-4. This folder contains several sets of actions presets.

**2.** **Select one of the actions sets.**

**3.** **Click the Load button.**

 Photoshop's additional actions presets also appear at the bottom of the palette options menu. You can add any of them to your current set by clicking the set's name. Any action sets that you create

yourself (as described later in this chapter) also appear in the options menu if you save them in the Photoshop Actions folder.

The new actions presets appear in the Actions palette, appended after the default actions that were already there. You can show or hide the actions in the Default Actions or Image Effects sets by clicking the expand/collapse arrow in the third column.

 You can also make actions available or unavailable for an entire set by clicking the first column in the Actions palette next to the action set's folder icon.

**Figure 6-4**

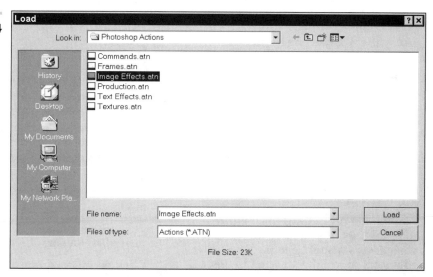

## Playing a preset action

To play a preset action, just open the file you want to apply the action to and then do one of the following:

✔ In List mode, select the action you want to play, or expand the action and select the step you want to begin with. Then click the Play Action button at the bottom of the Action palette. You can also choose Play from the palette options menu.

✔ In Button mode, click the action you want to play. There are no other options.

> If you want to play back just one step of an action, say, for testing purposes, select the step you want to play in List mode and then Ctrl+click (⌘+click on the Mac) the Play button in the Actions palette. You can also simply double-click the step in the list while holding down the Ctrl key (the ⌘ key on the Mac).

▼▼▼▼▼▼▼▼▼▼▼▼▼▼▼▼▼▼▼▼▼▼▼▼▼▼▼▼▼▼▼▼▼▼▼▼▼▼▼▼▼

## Creating a New Action

The hardest part about creating a new action is figuring out what functions you want to automate. Think about steps that you carry out over and over, and whether you could be more productive if you had an action that could do them for you. Then, examine the actual steps you want to automate so you can record them. After that, creating a new action involves little more than starting Photoshop's macro recorder and carrying out the steps you want to include in the action. You might want to create your own action to reduce images to a constant 500 pixels wide for display in an eBay auction, for example. Or you might want to save a bunch of files in a particular format or convert them from RGB color to grayscale.

Here are the steps to follow to create a new action:

*1.* **Open an image.**

*2.* **Display the Actions palette in List mode.**

*3.* **Click the New Action button at the bottom of the Actions palette.**

You can also choose New Action from the palette options menu.

The New Action dialog box opens, as shown in Figure 6-5.

*4.* **In the Name text box, enter a name for the action.**

*5.* **From the Set drop-down list, choose the actions set. If you have more than one actions set open, choose the actions set in which you want to place the new action.**

You may want to associate the action with a button on the keyboard. Function keys like F2, F3, and so on are very useful for actions you perform all the time.

*6.* **To associate the action with a function key shortcut, choose the name of** the function key from the Function Key drop-down list.

Select the Shift or Control (⌘ on the Mac) check boxes to use either of these keys along with the function key.

 Any keyboard shortcut you assign to an action will override the default function that was already assigned to the keyboard shortcut. You can revert to the original shortcut by choosing File➪Revert.

*7.* **From the Color drop-down list, select a color to mark your action in Button mode.**

This option enables you to group related actions by color.

*8.* **Click the Record button to begin recording.**

*9.* **Carry out all the steps you want to record.**

*10.* **Click the Stop Recording button to finish the action.**

Your new action appears in the Actions palette in both List and Button modes.

**Figure 6-5**

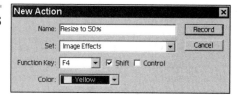

# Editing and Managing Actions

The first thing you need to do after you've created a new action is to try it out by opening an image and clicking the Play button in the Actions palette. If the action doesn't perform as you expect, you may need to edit your action to fine-tune it. You also may need to edit an action to add features or change the action's behavior in some way. For example, you might decide that you want your resizing action to change the size to 45 percent rather than 50 percent. Photoshop enables you to edit your actions fairly easily.

You have a lot of editing options; you can change the action's name, keyboard shortcut, or color-coding of an action. That's easy enough: Just double-click the action name in the Actions palette to enter a new name, or select the action and choose Action Options from the palette options menu and change the information as desired. You can also hold down the Alt key (Option key on the Mac) and click the action's name in the Actions palette to open the Actions Options dialog box.

## Rerecording an action

As easy as editing an action is, often your best option is to simply rerecord the action from scratch. If the action is not long or complex, you can often rerecord it in less time that it would take to edit the existing action.

You can rerecord an action two ways:

✔ **Create a new action from scratch:** Perform all the steps again to replace the old action with a new one, saving the action under the same (or a different) filename.

✔ **Use the clever Record Again facility:** Photoshop runs through the steps you already recorded, opening the appropriate dialog boxes used the first time around so you can enter new values.

  This method is very handy if you just want to change some of the parameters but keep the steps the same and in the same order. You don't even have to remember what steps you used. Photoshop runs through them for you as you record the macro again.

To rerecord a macro with the Record Again option, select the name of the macro you want to rerecord and choose Record Again from the palette options menu. As the different dialog boxes appear, enter the values you want and click OK until the macro is finished.

### Slowing down action playback

When you play back an action to test it, the action may run too quickly for you to see exactly what is going on. To slow things down, choose Playback Options from the palette options menu, as shown in the following figure, and choose a playback speed in the Playback Options dialog box.

Select *Accelerated* to zip through an action at normal speed; *Step by Step* to command Photoshop to stop between actions so you can examine what has happened, or *Pause For* to create a short pause before moving on. If you want to get really fancy, you can select the Pause for Audio Annotation check box and use your microphone to describe what each step does.

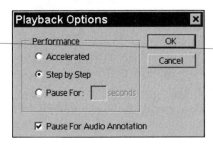

## Editing an action

You can also edit individual steps of an action. Here are some of the editing changes you can make:

- **Move a step:** To move a step from one place in the action to another, click the action you want to relocate and drag it to its new place in the action list.

- **Add a step in the middle:** To add a new step in the middle of an existing action, select the step that you want to precede the new step. Click the Record button and perform the steps you want to add. Click the Stop Recording button when you're finished.

- **Add a step to the end:** To add a new step at the end of an existing action, select the name of the action, click the Record button, and perform the steps you want to add. Click the Stop Recording button when you're finished.

- **Remove a step:** Click the step you want to delete and either drag the step to the trash icon, or click the trash icon and click OK in the dialog box that pops up. (Hold down the Alt key [Option key on the Mac] to bypass the dialog box and delete the step without confirmation.) You can also select a step and choose Delete from the palette options menu.

- **Duplicate a step:** Hold down the Alt key (Option key on the Mac) and drag the step you want to duplicate to another location in the Actions palette. Photoshop then creates a copy of the step, leaving the original step where it was. You can also select a step and choose Duplicate from the palette options menu or click the New Step button in the Actions palette. Photoshop then creates a duplicate step immediately after the one being copied. You can then drag the duplicate to the position where you want it to appear. You can also drag a step onto the Create New Action button to duplicate the step.

You can remove or duplicate an entire action by using the procedures described in the preceding list for removing a step and duplicating a step.

### Saving actions

If you create your own sets of actions, you may want to include them in custom sets that you can load or remove as needed. Just follow these steps:

**1.** Display the Actions palette in List mode.

**2.** Click the Create New Set button in the Actions palette or choose New Set from the palette options menu.

The New Set dialog box appears.

**3.** Enter a name for your actions set.

**4.** Drag any existing actions you want to include from their locations in the Actions palette to a new location within your new set folder.

**5.** Create any new actions you want to include within the new set.

**6.** Select the name of the set and choose Save Actions from the palette options menu.

**7.** Save the set in the Photoshop Actions folder or another folder of your choice.

## Batch Processing Actions

Photoshop's batch mode lets you apply an action to a group of files. Suppose you want to make changes to a series of files. You could open each file in Photoshop, play the desired macro, and then save the file. But that might take a few minutes, or much longer if you have a lot of files to process. If you want to keep your original file, too, you have to remember to save each file in a new folder. Batch processing can automate tedious chores like this for you.

To check out this useful tool, copy some files (at least five or six) to a new folder and follow these steps:

**1.** Make sure that the files are in a separate folder of their own.

Photoshop by default works on all the files in a folder. You have to use the File Browser if you want to choose only some of them in Batch mode. You can find out more about the File Browser in Book I, Chapter 5.

**2.** Choose File⇨Automate⇨Batch.

The Batch dialog box opens, as shown in Figure 6-6.

**3.** From the Set drop-down list, choose the set that contains the action you want to apply.

If you have only one set of Actions loaded, it appears by default.

**4.** Choose the action you want to apply.

**5.** From the Source drop-down list, choose Folder.

CONTINUED

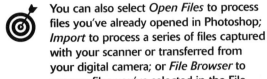 You can also select *Open Files* to process files you've already opened in Photoshop; *Import* to process a series of files captured with your scanner or transferred from your digital camera; or *File Browser* to process files you've selected in the File Browser. File Browser is a good method for processing files that do not appear in the same folder.

**6.** Click the Choose button and navigate to the folder you want to use and click OK (under Windows) or Choose (under Mac OS).

**7.** Select other options in the Source area, as desired. Here's a description of your choices:

✔ **Override Action "Open" Commands:** Normally, Photoshop automatically opens each of the files in the selected folder and processes them, so your action doesn't need to contain an Open command. However, if the macro does contain an Open command, you'll want to select this option to tell Photoshop to substitute files in the selected folder rather than those that might be specified in your action's own Open command.

 Don't select the Override Action "Open" Commands option if you do want Photoshop to use files specified by the action. For example, your action might open a file and copy its contents to the file being batch processed. In that case, you would not want to override the macro's Open commands.

✔ **Include All Subfolders:** Select this option to process files in subfolders within the folder specified.

✔ **Suppress Color Profile Warnings:** When Photoshop opens a file that contains its own color profile, it asks whether you want to use that profile or Photoshop's default profile. Selecting this check box suppresses that choice; Photoshop always uses its own default color profile.

**8.** In the Destination area, tell Photoshop what to do with each file after it has been processed with the macro. Choose one of the following options from the drop-down list:

✔ **None:** Leaves the file open on your Photoshop desktop without saving it (unless the action itself contains a Save command).

✔ **Save and Close:** Closes the files in the same folder where Photoshop found them. Your original file will be overwritten, so use this option only when you don't want to save the original or have another copy.

✔ **Folder:** Saves the document in a folder.

**9.** If you chose Folder in Step 8, click the Choose button and navigate to a destination folder for your files.

**10.** Select the Override Action "Save As" Commands check box to ignore any Save As parameters in the action and use the filenames of the files as specified in the File Naming section described in Step 11.

**11.** In the File Naming section, specify how you want Photoshop to create the filenames for the new, processed files by choosing from the drop-down lists.

You can choose options from six drop-down lists, depending on how long and complicated you want the filenames to be. Here are a few suggestions:

✔ You'll usually want to choose Document Name from the first drop-down list. If you do that, Photoshop retains the document name of the original file. If your documents are named `Sunset.tif`, `Sunrise.tif`, and `Winter.tif`, for example, the processed versions are given exactly the same names.

There are other choices in the drop-down list, such as consecutive serial numbers or mm/dd/yy choices, which you can apply if you want.

The serial numbers choices will create consecutive numbers, either 1-, 2-, 3-, or 4-digit numbers, as well as serial letters, such as a, b, c or A, B, C, for each file created.

✔ You'll usually stick with the file's extension in the second drop-down list. Choose *extension* to apply a lowercase version of the file's original extension, or *EXTENSION* to apply an uppercase version.

✔ Use the four additional boxes if you want to create longer and more complicated filenames.

For example, if you choose Document Name in the first box, 4 Digit Serial Number in the second box, ddmmyy in the third box, and extension in the fourth box (as shown in Figure 6-6), the Sunset.tif, Sunrise.tif, and Winter.tif files will be renamed Sunset0001120302.tif, Sunrise0002120302.tif, and Winter0003120302.tif if they're saved on December 3, 2002.

 When processing large numbers of files, these naming tools can help you keep track of when and how the files were created.

**12.** Select the Windows, Mac OS 9, or Unix check boxes to specify what operating system you want the saved filenames to be most compatible with.

**13.** From the Errors drop-down list, choose whether you want Photoshop to stop processing a batch when it encounters an error or whether you want it to simply continue and list the errors in a file. If you choose the latter option, click the Save As button to specify a log file and location for the log.

If you want to apply several different actions to a single set of files, or to apply the same action to multiple folders of files, just create an action that includes multiple batch-processing directives. To process multiple folders, you can also deposit shortcuts (under Windows) or aliases (under Mac OS) to each of the additional folders in the main source folder, and then select the Include All Subfolders check box in the Source area.

Book **II** Chapter **6**

**Figure 6-6**

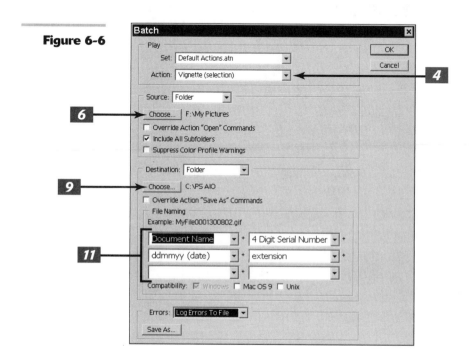

▼▼▼▼▼▼▼▼▼▼▼▼▼▼▼▼▼▼▼▼▼▼▼▼▼▼▼▼▼▼▼▼▼▼▼▼▼▼▼

## Creating Droplets

*Droplets* are drag-and-drop miniapplications, or applets, in macro form that can exist outside of Photoshop on your desktop, in your taskbar, or within a folder. They're always available so that you can apply them to any files you want. Think of them as batches waiting to happen.

 Even though you don't have to be running Photoshop to use droplets, you do need to have Photoshop installed on your computer. If you move the droplet to another computer that doesn't have Photoshop on it, all the droplet will do is sit there and look pretty.

All you need to do is drag the file or files you want to process onto the droplet. Photoshop doesn't even have to be open at the time. When the file or files are dropped, the droplet opens Photoshop and carries out the steps in the action embedded in the droplet's instructions. You must use an existing action as the core of the droplet.

To create a droplet, follow these steps:

**1.** **Choose File➪Automate➪ Create Droplet.**

The Create Droplet dialog box opens, as shown in Figure 6-7.

**2.** **In the Save Droplet In area, click the Choose button and enter a name and** **location on your hard disk for the droplet application.**

The location isn't of overriding importance because after the droplet is created, you can drag it to your desktop, a toolbar, or wherever you like.

**Figure 6-7**

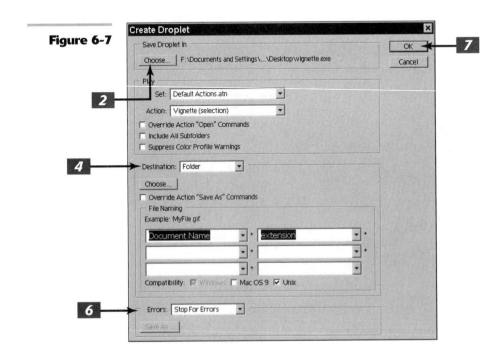

The rest of the Create Droplet dialog box is the same as the Batch Processing dialog box (described in the steps in the preceding section), except that you don't have to specify a Source. Droplets use the files dropped on them as their source files.

**3.** In the Play area, choose the actions set, action, and options.

**4.** Select a destination from the Destination drop-down list.

**5.** Specify any filenaming options you want.

**6.** Specify how Photoshop should process errors.

**7.** When you're finished, click OK to create the droplet.

To use the droplet, just select the file, files, or folders you want to process and drag them to the droplet applet.

Book
**II**
Chapter
**6**

# Book III

# Selections

The 5th Wave     By Rich Tennant

"Well, well! Guess who just lost 9 pixels?"

# Creating Selections

No matter how much you learn about Photoshop, if you can't make a good selection, your work will look like it belongs with the creatively, but poorly, composed images from one of those weekly tabloid rags. You know what I'm talking about — those pictures that go alongside headlines like "Bat Boy Wins Bake-Off" and "Woman with 16 Fingers Wins Typing Contest." Those pictures could look better, don't you think? It seems like some artists intentionally make their composite photos look like they were constructed with a dull pair of scissors and some Elmer's glue.

Making accurate selections is the key to creating and editing images effectively so that the end result looks flawless. Fortunately, Photoshop offers a bevy of tools and techniques for creating selections, from the simple to the complex. Photoshop offers three methods of creating a selection: using a selection tool or method, using the Pen tool, or creating a mask.

 No matter which technique you use, creating selections is one of the most important skills you can acquire. Trust me when I say that every minute you spend perfecting your selection techniques will pay off tenfold.

In this chapter, I give you the foundation you need to use the selection and pen tools. In fact, the rest of Book III covers these tools in detail. I cover the more complex method of masking in Book VI.

## Defining Selections

The tools I discuss in this chapter require you to take a little piece of a larger image so that you can dig in and make some serious edits. Defining a selection means that you specify which part of the image you want to work with.

Everything within a selection is fair game for manipulation and is considered *selected*. Everything outside the selection is protected, or *unselected*. Simple enough, right? Well, you can also have partially selected pixels. Confused yet? A *partially selected* pixel has usually been anti-aliased, feathered, or masked. (I cover anti-aliasing and feathering later in this chapter. You can find out about masking in Book VI.)

 When you use a selection tool to define a selection, a moving dotted outline called a *selection marquee* appears.

# Marqueeing When You Can

Photoshop geeks call the selection marquee by a variety of names. Sometimes it's referred to as a marquee, other times as a selection, and you might even hear people call it a selection outline, an outline, selection edges, or just plain old edges. A favorite name for these dotted lines is marching ants. Throughout the book, I usually call them *selection marquees*. Boring? Maybe. Accurate? Yup. Whatever you want to call the selection marquee, how you create one depends on the particular marquee tool you use.

The marquee tools are the easiest selection tools to use — so I suggest that you use them when you can.

 In the Photoshop repertoire of tools, you'll find four types of marquee tools: Rectangular Marquee, Elliptical Marquee, Single Row Marquee, and Single Column Marquee.

▼▼▼▼▼▼▼▼▼▼▼▼▼▼▼▼▼▼▼▼▼▼▼▼▼▼▼▼▼▼▼▼▼▼▼▼▼▼▼▼

## Using the Rectangular Marquee tool

The first tool on the Marquee tools flyout menu is the Rectangular Marquee tool. (If you skipped Book I, Chapter 2, a flyout menu describes the hidden tools that appear when you click any tool that has a small triangle in the bottom-right corner.) Use this tool to create rectangular or square selections.

 The Rectangular Marquee tool is a good tool to use when you want to zero in on an image, plucking it out of a larger background to provide a better focal point.

Here's how to make a selection with the Rectangular Marquee tool:

1. **Select the Rectangular Marquee tool from the Toolbox.**

   You can also use the keyboard shortcut — press the M key.

2. **Drag from one corner of the area you want to select to the opposite corner.**

   As you drag, the selection marquee appears. The marquee follows the movement of your mouse cursor.

For example, in Figure 1-1, I dragged from the lower-left corner to the upper-right corner.

 If you want to drag your selection from the center outward instead of corner to corner, press the Alt key (Option on the Mac) after you begin dragging. When you have your desired selection, release your mouse button and then release the Alt (Option) key.

**3.** Release your mouse button.

**4.** If you want to create a perfect square, press the Shift key after you begin dragging.

When you have your desired selection, release the mouse button and then the Shift key.

You now have a full-fledged rectangular selection.

**Figure 1-1**

## Using the Elliptical Marquee tool

The Elliptical Marquee tool is designed for elliptical or circular selections. You can easily select objects such as clocks, balls, and full moons with this tool.

The Elliptical Marquee tool works almost exactly like the Rectangular Marquee tool (described in the preceding section). The only difference is that you don't drag from corner to corner; you drag from a given point on the ellipse, which makes the process a little tougher. Here are the steps:

**1.** Select the Elliptical Marquee tool from the Marquee flyout menu in the Toolbox.

You can also use the keyboard short-cut. If the Elliptical Marquee tool is visible, press the M key. If the Rectangular Marquee is visible, you must press Shift+M.

**2.** Position the crosshair (the plus sign icon of the cursor) near the area you want to select and then drag around your desired element.

As you drag, the selection marquee appears.

CONTINUED

You may find it easier to create an elliptical selection by pressing the Alt (Option) key and dragging from the center outward. First press the mouse button, and then before you move the mouse, press the Alt (Option on the Mac) and finally the Shift key. Then drag. When you have your desired selection, release your mouse button and then the Shift+Alt (Shift+Option) keys. This technique works for creating circles or squares.

 To create a perfect circle, press the Shift key after you begin dragging. When you have your desired selection, release your mouse button and then your Shift key.

**3.** **When you're satisfied with your selection, release your mouse button.**

Your elliptical selection is alive and well, as shown in Figure 1-2. If you need to move the selection marquee to better center your selection, drag inside the marquee.

 You can also move a selection with any of the marquee tools, by pressing the spacebar while you're drawing.

If the selection isn't quite the right shape and size, jump to Chapter 2 to find out how to make perfect selections.

**Figure 1-2**

## Using the Single Column and Single Row Marquee tools

You probably won't find a lot of uses for the Single Row and Single Column Marquee tools. These tools select a single row or single column of pixels. If you select a row, the selection can only be 1 pixel long. Likewise, if you select a column, it can only be 1 pixel wide.

If you don't go blind using them, these tools can occasionally come in handy for selecting and repairing a thin scratch or fold line on an image or for getting rid of an artifact such as a colored line that has somehow appeared on a scanned image. (You can find out more about making repairs in Book VIII.)

To use either of these tools, simply choose a row or column of pixels on your image and click it. You don't have to do any dragging, but it does help to zoom into your image so that you can better position the tool on the offending row or column.

For more on zooming, see Book I, Chapter 5. Check out Figure 1-3 to get familiar with a single row selection.

 The Single Row and Single Column Marquee tools don't have keyboard shortcuts, so you're stuck with having to click the tools to select them.

**Figure 1-3**

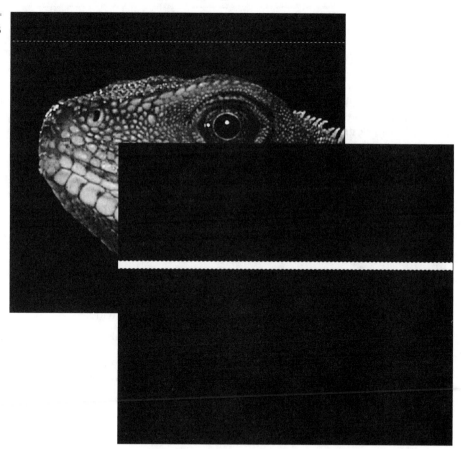

## Using the marquee options

If drawing from the center outward or creating a perfect circle or square doesn't give you enough control, you may want to take a look at the marquee settings provided by the Options bar. These options allow you to make even more precise selections by specifying exact measurements.

You must select the options in the Options bar *before* you make your selection with the marquee tools.

For now, you can ignore the first five icons on the left of the Options bar, as shown in Figure 1-4. The first icon has to do with tool presets, which I cover in Book I, Chapter 2. The next four icons are the selection state icons, which I discuss in Chapter 3 in this book.

**Figure 1-4**

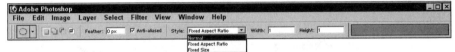

Here's the lowdown on each of the remaining options:

✔ **Feather:** Feathering blurs or feathers the edges of a selection. The amount of blur depends on the pixel value that you enter for the radius — the higher the radius, the blurrier the edge. For example, in Figure 1-5 you see that a higher Feather radius means a blurrier edge. The *radius* measures how far in all directions the feather effect extends. For example, a radius of 4 means that the feather extends 4 pixels to the right, left, up, and down from the selection outline.

You can use feathers to create a subtle and natural transition between selections or to create a special effect where an image slowly fades out to the background or to transparency. If you want to apply a feather *as you are selecting,* select the Feather option in the Options bar before using the marquee tools. However, if you have already made your selection, you can feather it after the fact by using the Select menu. Check out Chapter 2 in this book for more feathering details.

✔ **Anti-aliased:** Whereas feathering completely blurs edges, anti-aliasing just slightly softens the edge of an elliptical selection so that very hard, jagged edges aren't quite so prominent, as shown in Figure 1-6. You don't have an option for entering a pixel value for anti-aliasing. An anti-aliased edge is always 1 pixel wide.

You can use the anti-aliasing option only with the Elliptical Marquee tool. It isn't available for the other marquee tools because the selections you make with the other tools always have straight edges — there aren't any jagged edges to soften. I recommend keeping this option checked, especially if you plan to create composite images. Anti-aliasing helps in creating natural-looking blends between multiple selections.

✔ **Style:** The Style pop-up menu contains three settings:

  ▶ The *Normal* setting enables you to freely drag a selection to any desired dimension.

  ▶ The *Fixed Aspect Ratio* option allows you to specify a ratio of height to width in a selection. For example, if you enter 1 for height and 2 for width, you *always* get a marquee selection that's twice as wide as it is high, no matter what the size. A selection that's 2 inches high is automatically 4 inches wide. You aren't limited to whole numbers, by the way; decimals are acceptable as well. This option is frequently used to create vertically oriented images from horizontal multimedia screen captures and photos taken with digital cameras.

▶ And finally, select *Fixed Size* to specify exact values for the Width and Height. This option comes in handy when several images need to be the same exact size, as in a row of head shots of executives in a corporate brochure.

✔ **Width and Height:** When you select a Fixed Size from the Style pop-up menu, the Width and Height text boxes are available for you to enter values.

Even though the default unit of measurement in the Width and Height text boxes is pixels (px for short), you can enter any unit of measurement that Photoshop recognizes — pixels, inches, centimeters, millimeters, points, picas, and percents. Simply type in the word or abbreviation of your desired unit of measurement after the number. Photoshop even lets you enter mixed units of measurements, so if you want a selection 100 pixels by 1.25 inches, you can do so.

Why would you do this? Who knows, but Photoshop allows you to. You'll only use this option if a selection must be a certain number of pixels wide, and even though you're not sure of the exact pixel measurement of the height, you're guessing that it's, say, 1.25 inches.

Book
***III***
Chapter
**1**

**Figure 1-5**

Feather radius
4 pixels

Feather radius
20 pixels

**Figure 1-6**

Anti-aliasing off

Anti-aliasing on

▼ ▼ ▼ ▼ ▼ ▼ ▼ ▼ ▼ ▼ ▼ ▼ ▼ ▼ ▼ ▼ ▼ ▼ ▼ ▼ ▼ ▼ ▼ ▼ ▼ ▼ ▼ ▼ ▼ ▼ ▼ ▼ ▼

## Lassoing When You Can't

Unfortunately, not much in life is rectangular or elliptical in shape. Most of the time, you'll have to deal with irregular shapes with *extrusions* and *protrusions* (outside the graphics world, these are called bumps or bulges) of some sort or another. That's where the lasso tools come in handy. This group of tools allows you to make free-form selections.

Photoshop offers three lasso tools: the Lasso tool (which I call the regular Lasso to distinguish it from the others), the Polygon Lasso tool, and the Magnetic Lasso tool. Each of the lasso tools has its own special purpose in the realm of free-form selections. But in the category of simplicity, they're all almost as easy to use as the marquee tools. If you can drag with your mouse, you're qualified to handle any lasso tool. Just don't indulge in too much caffeine. A steady lasso hand is a good lasso hand.

To make a selection with the regular Lasso tool, all you have to do is drag around the part of the image you want to select. The selection you make is only as good as how accurately you can trace around your desired element. You need a steady hand — and a lot of practice — to become a good Lasso tool user. But don't fret; if you don't make an exact selection the first time around, you can always go back and make corrections (which I cover in Chapter 3 of this book).

Book
**III**
Chapter
**1**

 The Lasso and the Polygon Lasso tools both have only two choices in the Options bar to worry about — Feather and Anti-aliased. These options work exactly like they do with the marquee tools. To find out more, check out the earlier section "Using the marquee options."

To make a selection by using the Lasso tool, here's what you do:

**1.** **Select the Lasso tool from the Toolbox.**

It's the tool that looks like a rope. You can also use the keyboard shortcut; press the L key.

**2.** **Position the cursor somewhere on the edge of the element that you want to select.**

The hot spot of the lasso cursor is the end of the rope.

Where you start doesn't really matter. You may need to zoom in on the image a bit if there isn't a lot of contrast between the element and the background.

In my example, I started at the top of the pitcher, as shown in Figure 1-7.

**3.** **Trace around the element, trying to capture only what you want to retain in your selection.**

As you trace, a line forms that follows the movement of your mouse.

Don't release your mouse button until you've completed the selection by closing the loop or returning to the starting point.

When you release your mouse button, Photoshop thinks you're done and closes the selection from where you released the mouse button to your starting point, as shown in Figure 1-8.

**4.** **Continue tracing until you return to your starting point; release the mouse button.**

Recognizing that you're now done, Photoshop presents you with a selection marquee that matches your lasso line (see Figure 1-9).

CONTINUED
▼ ▼ ▼ ▼ ▼

**Figure 1-7**

**Figure 1-8**

**Figure 1-9**

## Selecting straight sides with the Polygon Lasso

Whereas the regular Lasso tool is great for selecting undulating, curvy elements, the Polygon Lasso tool shines when it comes to the more regimented, straight-sided subjects, such as city skylines, buildings, and stairways.

 Unlike the regular Lasso tool, the Polygon Lasso tool has rubber-band-like qualities, and instead of dragging, you click and release the mouse at the corners of the object you're selecting. It's like a digital connect the dots. Bonus: less manual dexterity required.

The following steps show you how to select with the Polygon Lasso tool:

*1.* **Select the Polygon Lasso tool from the Toolbox.**

You can also use the keyboard shortcut. Press the L key and then press Shift+L until you get the Polygon Lasso tool. It looks like the regular Lasso tool, but it has straight sides.

*2.* **With the Polygon Lasso tool selected, click to establish the beginning of the first line of your selection.**

 A corner is always a good place to start.

*3.* **Move the mouse and click at the next corner of the object.**

The line stretches out from your cursor like a rubber band.

*4.* **Continue clicking at the various corners of your object.**

*5.* **To close your selection, return to the first point you clicked and click one last time.**

CONTINUED

When you place your cursor over the starting point, a small circle appears next to your cursor, a sure sign that you're at the right place for closing the selection.

You can also double-click your mouse, and Photoshop automatically closes

the selection from the point you double-clicked to your starting point.

A selection marquee that matches your Polygon Lasso line appears, as shown in Figure 1-10.

**Figure 1-10**

## Attracting with the Magnetic Lasso tool

The newest member of the lasso tool trio is the Magnetic Lasso, which I admit can be kind of tricky to use and sometimes even downright obstinate. The Magnetic Lasso tool works by analyzing the colors of the pixels between the elements in the foreground and the elements in the background. Then it snaps to the edge between the elements, as if the edge had a magnetic pull.

 The Magnetic Lasso tool performs best when your image has a lot of contrast between the foreground and background elements — for example, a dark mountain range against a light sky or a shadow against a stucco wall.

The Magnetic Lasso also has some unique settings, which you can adjust in the Options bar, to tame its behavior. I cover those settings in the next section, "Adjusting the Magnetic Lasso options." For now, follow these steps to use the tool:

*1.* **Select the Magnetic Lasso tool from the Toolbox.**

You can also use the keyboard shortcut: Press the L key and then press Shift+L until you get the Magnetic Lasso tool. The tool looks like a straight-sided lasso with a little magnet on it.

 **Click on the edge of the object you want to select.**

You can start anywhere; just be sure to click on the edge between the element you want and the background you don't want.

**3.** Move your cursor around the object, without clicking.

The Magnetic Lasso creates a selection line similar to the other Lasso tools. It also adds little squares called *points* along that selection line, as shown in Figure 1-11. These points pin down the selection line the way you might section off an area of your yard with ropes and stakes.

✔ If the Magnetic Lasso starts veering off the edge of your object, back your mouse up and click it to force a point down on the line.

✔ If the Magnetic Lasso adds a point where you don't want one, simply press your Backspace (Delete on a Mac) key to delete it.

**4.** Continue moving your mouse around the object; return to your starting point and release the mouse button to close the selection.

As with the Polygon Lasso tool, you see a small circle next to your cursor indicating that you're at the correct place to close the selection. If you double-click, Photoshop closes the selection from where you double-clicked to your starting point. The selection marquee appears when the selection is closed.

**Figure 1-11**

## Adjusting the Magnetic Lasso options

The Magnetic Lasso tool comes equipped with a few settings in the Options bar that control the sensitivity of the tool (see Figure 1-12).

**Figure 1-12**

I recommend starting out by messing around with the Magnetic Lasso using its default settings. If the tool isn't cooperating, then play with the options.

The first icon has to do with Tool Presets, and the next four icons are the selection state icons (check out Chapter 2 in this book). The Feather and Anti-aliased options work like they do with the marquee tools (see the earlier section "Using the marquee options"). The remaining options are explained in the following list:

- **Width:** This option, measured in pixels from 1 to 256, determines how close to the edge you have to move your mouse before the Magnetic Lasso recognizes the object you're selecting.

  Decrease the value if

  - ▶ The object's edge has a lot of indentations and protrusions.
  - ▶ The image is of lower contrast.

  Increase the value if

  - ▶ The image is of higher contrast.
  - ▶ The image has smoother edges.

  When using the Magnetic Lasso tool, you can change the Width value from the keyboard by pressing the open bracket ( [ ) key to lower the value and the close bracket ( ] ) key to increase the value.

- **Edge Contrast:** Measured in percentages from 1 to 100, this option specifies the required contrast between the object you're selecting and its background before the Magnetic Lasso hugs the edge between them. If your image has good contrast between the foreground and background, use a higher percentage.

- **Frequency:** This setting, measured in percentages from 1 to 100, specifies how many points to place on the selection line. The higher the percentage, the greater number of points.

  - ▶ If the object you want to select has a fairly smooth edge, keep the percentage low.
  - ▶ If the edge is jagged or has a lot of detail, a higher percentage may be more effective in getting an accurate selection line.

 ### *Having it both ways with the lasso tools*

Which tool do you use if you have an object with both curves and straight sides? You can have two, two, two tools in one! Press the Alt (Option on the Mac) key to have the Polygon Lasso tool temporarily transform into the regular Lasso tool. Then drag to select the curves. Release the Alt (Option) key to return to the Polygon Lasso. And this trick works with the regular Lasso tool as well. Press Alt (Option) to temporarily access the Polygon Lasso. When you want the regular Lasso tool back again, just drag your mouse. In this case, you can hold down the Alt (Option) key;

it makes no difference. If you want to release the Alt (Option) key, just make sure that you're pressing down the mouse button; otherwise, Photoshop will close the selection.

To temporarily change the Magnetic Lasso tool into the Polygon Lasso tool, press the Alt (Option on the Mac) key and click. As you hold down the Alt (Option) key, drag to get the regular Lasso tool. When you want the Magnetic Lasso tool back again, release the Alt (Option) key and move your mouse without clicking.

# Performing Wand Wizardry

The Magic Wand. The name is intriguing, isn't it? Any tool that has the audacity to call itself the Magic Wand must be so powerful that it can grant your every selection wish with a mere swoosh. Unfortunately, it's not quite so awe-inspiring. A better name for this tool would be the Click-'n-Select tool. You click your image, and the Magic Wand makes a selection, which contains areas of similar color, based on the color of the pixel you clicked.

Simple enough. What's not quite so simple is how to determine how *similar* the color has to be to get the Magic Wand to select it. That's where the important Tolerance setting comes in. Before you tackle tolerance (and find out how it affects the Magic Wand's performance), you first need to get the hang of using the Magic Wand.

## Selecting with the Magic Wand

As with the Magnetic Lasso tool, the Magic Wand works best when you have high-contrast images or images with a limited number of colors. As shown in Figure 1-13, a black-and-white checkered flag is a perfect example of something that the Magic Wand effectively selects. I click once on the top of a black square, and the Magic Wand picks up all the other surrounding black pixels. I can now easily change the color of my black squares to red or yellow in one fell swoop.

As you can see, Figure 1-14 is a poor candidate. This image contains a ton of colors and no real definitive contrast between the scale and the background. Although it only takes one click to select the black squares on the flag, other high-contrast candidates may take a few clicks. And some images may need a tweak or two of the Tolerance setting, described in the next section.

**Figure 1-13**

**Figure 1-14**

## Setting your Tolerance

Sometimes an image may contain a few shades of a similar color. Consider a cloudless sky for example. A few shades of blue make up the bright blue yonder. With the Magic Wand tool, if you click a darker shade of blue in the sky, all similar shades of blue are selected, but the lighter shades remain unselected. This is usually a sure sign that you need to increase your Tolerance level. The *Tolerance* setting determines the range of color that the Magic Wand selects.

Tolerance is selected based on brightness levels that range from 0 to 255:

✔ Setting the Tolerance to 0 selects one color only.

✔ Setting the Tolerance to 255 selects all colors — the entire image.

To use the Magic Wand and adjust Tolerance settings, follow these steps:

**1.** **Select the Magic Wand tool from the Toolbox.**

The Magic Wand tool looks like the weapon of choice for many Disney characters. You can also use the keyboard shortcut; press the W key.

**2.** **Click the portion of the image that you want to select; use the default Tolerance setting of 32.**

The pixel that you click determines the base color. The default value of 32 means that the Magic Wand selects all colors that are 32 levels lighter and 32 levels darker than the base color.

If you selected everything you wanted the first time you used the Magic Wand, stretch your arm and give yourself a pat on the back. If you didn't (which is probably the case), go to Step 3.

**3.** **Enter a new Tolerance setting in the Options bar.**

If the Magic Wand selected more than you wanted it to, lower the Tolerance setting. If it didn't select enough, raise the setting.

**4.** **Click again on the portion of the image that you want to select.**

 Changing the tolerance doesn't adjust your current selection.

The Magic Wand deselects the current selection and makes a new selection based on your new Tolerance setting, as shown in Figure 1-15. If it still isn't right, you can adjust the Tolerance setting again. I regret that I can't give you a magic formula that you can use to determine the right value. It's all about trial and error.

**Figure 1-15**

Tolerance of 32

Tolerance of 64

## Using the Magic Wand Options bar

If you get a selection close to what you want, stop there and then use the selection-refining techniques discussed in Chapter 2 in this book. But before you do that, you need to know about the other Magic Wand settings in the Options bar. The three remaining options are as follows:

✔ **Contiguous:** When you check this option, the Magic Wand selects *only* pixels that are adjacent to each other. If you leave the option unchecked, the Magic Wand looks throughout the image and selects all pixels within the range of Tolerance, whether or not they're adjacent to each other.

✔ **Use All Layers:** This option is valid only when you have multiple layers in your image. (For more on layers, see Book V.) If you have multiple layers and this option is checked, the Magic Wand selects color from all visible layers. If you uncheck this option, the Magic Wand selects colors from the active layer only.

✔ **Sample Size:** Although this option affects the Magic Wand, it appears in the Options bar *only* when you've selected the Eyedropper tool. (For more on the Eyedropper, see Book II, Chapter 3.) Select the Eyedropper tool and, in the Sample Size pop-up menu that appears, choose from the following:

▶ **Point Sample:** Samples just the color of the pixel you clicked

▶ **3 by 3 Average:** Averages the color of the pixel you clicked and the surrounding 8 pixels

▶ **5 by 5 Average:** Averages the color of the pixel you clicked and the surrounding 24 pixels

# Creating and Working with Paths

**2**

Although the Marquee, Lasso, and Magic Wand tools are fun, friendly, and pretty easy to wield, sometimes they don't quite have the horsepower to make that really precise selection. So either you spend a lot of time cleaning up what you've selected (see Chapter 3 in this book for more on that topic), or you live with a ho-hum selection. That's where the Pen tool and its related cronies come to the rescue. The Pen tool creates paths, which can then be converted into selections.

Because the Pen tool (along with its related path-editing tools) offers control and precision, it is very capable when it comes to nailing that accurate selection. The only problem is that the Pen tool is a far cry from fun, friendly, and easy. Getting the hang of it can be tricky. Many new users try the Pen a few times, but end up muttering in disgust and returning gratefully to the Lasso tool. However, I guarantee that if you obligate a good chunk of time to mastering the Pen tool, you'll soon turn your elite little nose up at the simple Lasso tool.

 Another added benefit of knowing how to use the Pen tool is that it's also the main drawing tool of Adobe Illustrator. And similar tools exist in layout programs such as Adobe InDesign and QuarkXPress.

## Introducing Paths

Unlike the other selection tools, the Pen tool doesn't initially produce a selection marquee. When you select the Pen tool and start clicking and dragging around your image, you create a path. *Paths* are comprised of three components — anchor points, straight segments, and curved segments.

These paths are called *Bézier paths* (after Pierre Bézier who, in the 1970s, invented the equation used for CAD/CAM programs), which means that they are based on a mathematical cubic equation where the path is controlled by direction lines that end in direction points (often referred to as *handles*), as shown in Figure 2-1. The length and angle of direction lines control the pitch and angle of the Bézier curve.

Figure 2-1 and the following list introduce all the different kinds of anchor points Photoshop puts at your disposal, and show you exactly what they do. You can use some or all of these anchor points in a single path:

- ✔ A true corner point has no direction lines. Use corner points when selecting objects with straight sides, such as stairs or barns.

- ✔ A smooth point has two direction lines pointing in opposite directions but dependent on one another. Use smooth points when selecting objects that have alternating curves, such as a sea of rolling waves.

- ✔ A cusp point has two direction lines that are independent of one another. Use cusp points when selecting an object with curves going the same direction, such as the petals on a daisy.

- ✔ A point between a straight segment and a curve is a corner point with only one direction line.

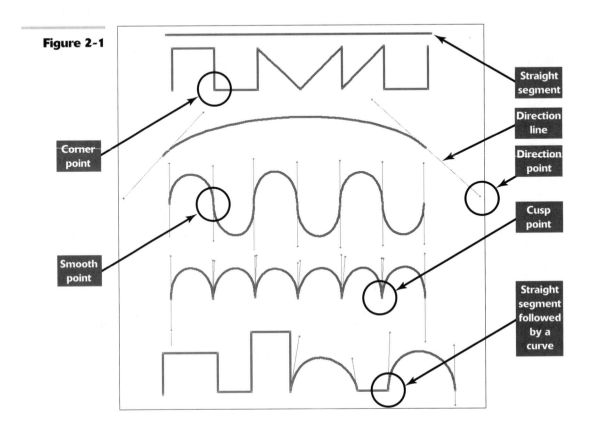

**Figure 2-1**

After you create a Bézier path, you can then edit the path by moving, adding, deleting, or converting anchor points and by manipulating the direction lines. You can also transform paths by choosing Edit⇨Transform Paths (see Chapter 3 of this book for details).

The path hovers over the image in its own space, and is controlled via the Paths palette where you can save it, duplicate it, stroke it with color (apply color to the edge only), fill it with color or a pattern, and most importantly load it as a selection. I say "most importantly" because nine times out of ten, you are going to painstakingly create a path as a means to an accurate selection marquee. The one other time you may use the path as a clipping path to hide a part of a layer or part of an entire image. I cover clipping paths in the last section of this chapter.

# Creating a Path with the Pen Tool

The best way to get the hang of the Pen tool is to dive right in and work with it. You'll want to start with straight lines, which are very easy, and then move on to the more difficult curves. The more you practice with the Pen, the more comfortable and proficient you'll become. It definitely is an example of the old adage "you get out what you put into it."

## Knowing your Pen tool options

Although every path consists of three basic components — segments, points, and direction lines — the Pen tool enables you to use these components to create a few different types of paths. See Book IV, Chapter 2, for more information on the following options, accessible from the Pen tool's Options bar. You must choose one of the following:

✔ **Shape Layers:** This option creates a shape on a new layer that's called, not surprisingly, a shape layer. After you create the path that defines the shape, the shape is filled with the foreground color, and the path is also stored as a vector mask in the Paths palette. A shape layer is a unique entity.

✔ **Fill Pixels:** This option is available only when you're using the Shape tools. It allows you to create a shape and fill it with the foreground color, but it does not create a shape layer nor does it retain the path.

✔ **Paths:** This option enables you to create a traditional path that hovers over the image. The path you create will be a *work path,* which is temporary, appears in the Paths palette, and is unsaved. If you're creating a path that will eventually be loaded as a selection, this is your option.

▼ ▼ ▼ ▼ ▼ ▼ ▼ ▼ ▼ ▼ ▼ ▼ ▼ ▼ ▼ ▼ ▼ ▼ ▼ ▼ ▼ ▼ ▼ ▼ ▼ ▼ ▼ ▼ ▼ ▼ ▼ ▼ ▼ ▼ ▼ ▼ ▼ ▼

## Creating your first work path

Making a work path is the easiest of the three options, and you'll use it frequently when you've gotten the hang of using the Pen tool. The following steps show you how to create a simple, straight path:

 Rarely (if ever) will you create a work path that's a single, straight line. Please keep reading the other sections in this chapter.

**1. Open an image you want to practice on.**

I suggest choosing an image that has an element with both straight edges and curves, if you want to also practice creating curved paths later.

**2. Select the Pen tool from the Toolbox.**

Or you can just press the P key.

**3. In the Options bar, click the Paths button.**

This button is shown in Figure 2-2.

**4. To create a straight line, click and release your mouse button at the points where you want the line to begin and to end, leaving anchor points at those positions.**

 You don't need to do any dragging to create straight segments.

As you click and add your anchor points, Photoshop creates straight segments that connect the anchor points, as shown in Figure 2-3.

**5. To draw a constrained line — horizontal, vertical, or 45° angle — hold the Shift key down as you click.**

**6. To end the path, click the Pen tool to deselect it.**

Or use this very handy shortcut: Hold down the Ctrl key (⌘ on the Mac), which gives you the Direct Selection tool (the white arrow), and then click away from the line. Release the Ctrl key (⌘ on the Mac), and the Pen tool reappears.

When you've deselected the path, you're free to start another, unconnected path, if you need to.

Continue on to the following sections if you want to add other kinds of segments to the path. Otherwise, skip to "Closing a path," later in this chapter.

**Figure 2-2**

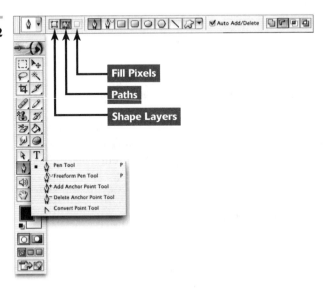

**Figure 2-3**

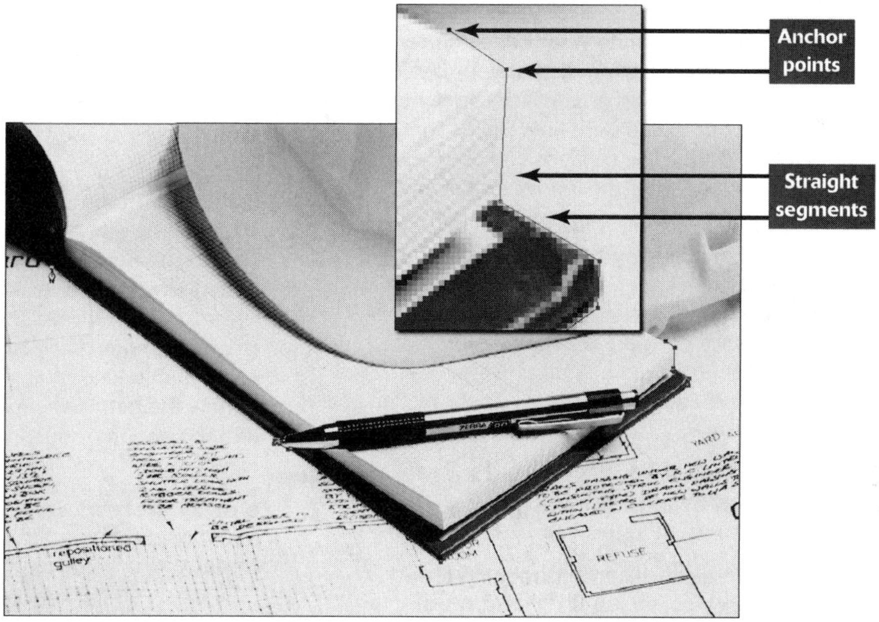

Anchor points

Straight segments

## Drawing curves

You're probably never going to create a simple work path that doesn't have curves as well as straight lines. I mean not much in life is perfectly linear. Most things have undulations here and there. Picking up from the preceding section, here's how to create curved paths:

***1.*** **If you are adding onto a previously created open path, make sure that you position your cursor on the last anchor point you created on that open path to continue.**

You will see the appearance of a slash mark or small square next to your cursor. If you are starting a new path, position the cursor where you want the curve to begin.

In both cases, drag toward the direction that you want the bump of the

curve to go. Release the mouse button when you're done.

If you are creating a new path, an anchor point along with two direction lines, which have direction points at their ends, appear. If you are adding a curve to your straight segment, an anchor point along with one direction line along with one direction point appears. The direction lines and direction points control the angle and pitch of the curve.

CONTINUED

How do you know how far you should you drag? You can do what I do and use the rule of thirds. Imagine that your curve is a piece of string that you have stretched and laid out in a straight line. Divide that line into thirds. The distance you drag your mouse is one-third the length of that line.

 How do you establish the angle? Drag the mouse straight from the anchor point for a steeper curve and at an angle from the anchor point for a flatter curve. The element in my example is a flatter curve; therefore I dragged up and to the right at an angle of about 4.5 degrees, as shown in Figure 2-4.

2. **Move the cursor to the end of the curve and drag in the opposite direction, away from the bump.**

   You now see another anchor point and a set of two direction lines and points.

Photoshop creates the curve segment between the anchor points, as shown in Figure 2-5.

 If you drag both direction lines in the same direction, you create a curve shaped like an *S*.

 In the Options bar, click the down-pointing arrow at the end of the row of tools and choose the Rubber Band option. With this option selected, Photoshop draws a segment between the last anchor point you create and wherever your cursor is located, giving you a kind of animated preview of how the path will appear. I personally find the option distracting, but some users love it.

3. **To draw more alternating curves, just repeat these steps, dragging in an opposite direction each time.**

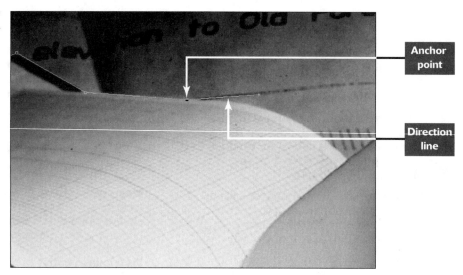

**Figure 2-4**

**Figure 2-5**

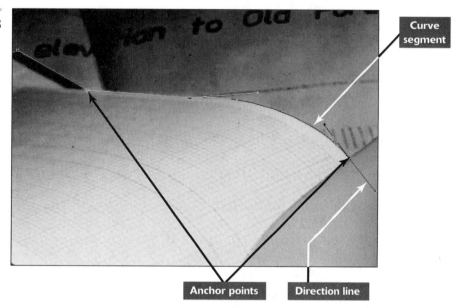

Curve segment

Anchor points

Direction line

## Connecting a straight segment to a curve segment

If you need to create a straight segment after creating a curve (or vice versa), you need to convert the point where the path changes from curved to straight. To convert a point, follow these steps:

*1.* **Position your cursor over the second anchor point in the existing curve and press the Alt key (Option on the Mac).**

You see a caret (which looks like an upside down *V*) next to the pen cursor. Click and release your mouse button over the anchor point.

The bottom direction line disappears. You have converted a smooth point into a corner point with one direction line. This action will now allow you to create a straight segment.

It's no coincidence that the tool icon for the Convert Point tool is also a caret. Whenever you see a caret symbol in Photoshop, it's an indication that you are converting an anchor point, from smooth to corner or vice versa.

*2.* **Move your mouse to the end of the straight edge you want to select and click and release.**

You can press the Shift key if you want the line to be constrained horizontally, vertically, or at an angle with a multiple of 45 degrees.

Photoshop connects the two anchor points with a straight segment, as shown in Figure 2-6.

CONTINUED

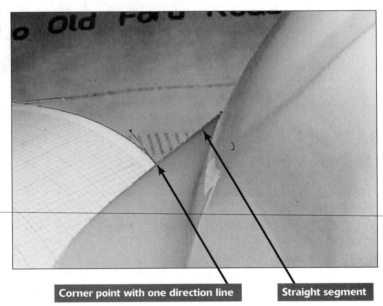

Figure 2-6

Corner point with one direction line    Straight segment

## Connecting curve segments with cusp points

If you need to create a curve that goes in the same direction as a curve that is adjacent to it, a couple additional steps are involved:

1. **Convert the point — this time from smooth to cusp — position your cursor over the second anchor point in the existing curve, and press the Alt key (Option on the Mac).**

2. **Drag toward the bump of the curve. Release the mouse button and then release the Alt (Option on the Mac) key.**

   Essentially, your actions are pulling the direction line out from the anchor point. Both direction lines move to the same side of the anchor point, yet are independent of each other, creating the cusp point, shown in Figure 2-7.

3. **Move your cursor to where you want the curve to end and drag away from the bump to create your second curve.**

 Try to keep anchor points on either side of the curve, not along the top. It is also good to try to use the fewest number of anchor points possible to create your path. That way, the path will result in a much smoother curve. It will also create a smaller file size and reduce the possibility of printing problems.

 To draw a curve after a straight segment, first position your cursor directly on the last anchor point of the straight segment. Drag your mouse toward the bump of the curve you need to draw. A direction line appears. Position your cursor where you want the curve to end and drag away from the bump.

**Figure 2-7**

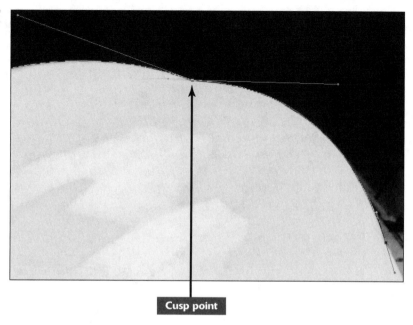

Cusp point

## Closing a path

To close the path, return to your first anchor point and click. You see a small circle next to your pen cursor, indicating that you will close the path when you click.

Congratulations! You are now the proud owner of a work path (see Figure 2-8). Don't worry if the path isn't perfect, you find out how to edit paths in an upcoming section. If your path is perfect and you want to save it now, skip ahead to the section "Working with the Paths Palette."

 If your path is incomplete and you need to continue drawing it, either click or drag on the endpoint with the Pen tool. You will see the appearance of a slash mark or small square next to the pen cursor.

### *Leaving your path open*

If you want to leave the path open — for example, to create a stroke rather than a selection — end the path by clicking the Pen tool. You can also use the shortcut I mentioned earlier. Hold down the Ctrl key (⌘ on the Mac), which gives you the Direct Selection tool (white arrow), and then click away from the curve. Or just press Enter (Return on the Mac) to deselect the path and also hide it from view. You haven't lost it. You can load it again via the Paths palette (more info on that coming up next).

**Figure 2-8**

## Creating subpaths

You can also create a series of lines or curves. For example, you may want to create a border consisting of some decorative curve shapes, which you could later stroke with color. These *subpaths* can then be saved under a single path name. To create a series of subpaths, simply end one path before starting another. Make sure that the paths are not hidden when you do so; otherwise, Photoshop will eliminate the previous path when you start another.

If working with the Pen tool feels awkward, difficult, and frustrating, don't worry. Those are all perfectly natural emotions to feel when you first use it. It took me months of grappling with it before I could get to the point where I could use the tool without uttering several unmentionable words. All I can say is keep practicing. Open up any images you have laying around on your hard drive and select something. Before you know it, no image will be safe from the prowess of your Pen.

# Working with the Paths Palette

Working hand in hand with the Pen tool is the Paths palette. You can think of it as a kind of Command and Control Center for your paths. Although it isn't mandatory, it's a good idea to open up your Paths palette, shown in Figure 2-9, before you create a path so you can stay apprised as to what is happening with your image. To open the palette, choose Window⇨Paths.

The icons at the bottom of the Paths palette from left to right, as shown in Figure 2-9, are

- Fill Path
- Stroke Path
- Load Path as Selection
- Make Work Path from Selection
- Create New Path
- Delete Current Path

The following sections highlight some of the stuff you can do with the Paths palette.

**Figure 2-9**

## Creating a path

When you create a path, it automatically appears in the Paths palette as a work path.

 Remember a work path is temporary and unsaved, and you can only have one work path in the Paths palette at a time.

If the work path is selected when you begin another path, it's added to the current work path. But if the existing work path is hidden and you begin drawing another path, that new work path replaces the existing one. Remember you can only have one work path in the Paths palette at any given time.

## Creating a new path

You can save yourself a lot of grief if you make sure that your path will be saved before you start. If you select New Path from the Paths palette options menu *before* you create the path, the work path is automatically saved and becomes a saved path or named path. You can also just click the Create New Path icon (the dog-eared page icon) at the bottom of the Paths palette.

### Saving a work path

To save a work path, double-click the path in the Paths palette. Or choose Save Path from the Paths palette options menu. Then provide a name in the Save Path dialog box and click OK.

After you save your path, you can reload it at any time. Unlike layers, paths take up very little storage space, so don't hesitate to save them. Plus, you don't want to go through all that work again if you don't have to. Unlike work paths, you can have as many saved paths as your heart desires.

### Deleting, duplicating, and renaming a path

To delete a path, drag the path to the trash icon at the bottom of the palette. Or choose Delete Path from the Paths palette options menu.

You can duplicate a saved path by choosing the path in the Paths palette and selecting Duplicate Path from the Paths palette options menu.

 You can also drag the saved path on top of the Create New Path icon at the bottom of the palette.

To rename a path, double-click the path name in the Paths palette. Then enter the new name directly within the palette.

▼ ▼ ▼ ▼ ▼ ▼ ▼ ▼ ▼ ▼ ▼ ▼ ▼ ▼ ▼ ▼ ▼ ▼ ▼ ▼ ▼ ▼ ▼ ▼ ▼ ▼ ▼ ▼ ▼ ▼ ▼ ▼ ▼ ▼ ▼ ▼ ▼ ▼ ▼ ▼

### Stroking a path

You can use the Stroke path command to paint a stroke along the path. You can choose which painting or editing tool to use to stroke the path. Follow these steps:

*1.* **Select the path in the Paths palette. Then choose Stroke Path from the Paths palette options menu.**

Or press the Alt key (Option on the Mac) and click the Stroke path with the brush icon (an outlined circle) at the bottom of the palette. Note that this option bypasses the dialog box in Step 2 and just strokes your path with whatever setting was used previously.

*2.* **In the dialog box that opens, choose one of the 15 painting or editing tools you want to use to apply color to the stroke. Click OK.**

 Make sure that you check your chosen tool's settings in the Options bar because Photoshop uses those settings to stroke your path. Photoshop will also apply your current foreground color to the stroke.

If you're using a pressure-sensitive drawing tablet, you can select the Simulate Pressure check box to create strokes with varying widths. If everything has gone well, you should end up with a stroked path (see Figure 2-10).

 If you select one or more paths with the Direct Selection tool, the Stroke Path command changes to Stroke Subpath(s), enabling you to stroke only the selected paths.

**Figure 2-10**

## Filling a path

You can fill the interior of a path with color by choosing the Fill Path command. Follow these steps:

**1.** **Select the path in the Paths palette and choose Fill Path from the Paths palette options menu.**

A dialog box gives options for Contents, Opacity, Blending, and Rendering. (For more on the Contents and Opacity options, see Book IV, Chapter 3.)

Or you can press the Alt key (Option on the Mac) and click the Fill Path with Foreground Color icon (a solid circle) at the bottom of the palette. This option will bypass the dialog box and just fill your path with whatever setting was used previously.

**2.** **In the dialog box, leave the Blending Mode option set to Normal.**

It's better to use the Layers palette to apply your blend modes because you

have more flexibility (see Book V for more on layers). Here is the scoop on the remaining options.

✔ The feathering option gradually blurs the edges of the fill into the background.

✔ The anti-aliased option just slightly softens the very edge of the fill so it doesn't appear as ragged.

 If you select one or more paths with the Direct Selection tool, the Fill Path command changes to Fill Subpath(s), enabling you to fill only the selected paths.

**3.** **After you set your options, click OK.**

Your path should now be filled like mine, as shown in Figure 2-11.

Book
***III***
Chapter
**2**

CONTINUED

**Figure 2-11**

## Loading Paths as Selections

Creating a path is usually the means to an end — an accurate selection. Therefore, most likely, you will frequently be using the Paths palette to load your path as a selection.

Follow these steps to get the lowdown on how to do just that. Open an image, make a selection by using the Pen tool, and get started:

1. **Choose Make Selection from the Paths palette options menu.**

   Alternatively, you can also press Alt (Option on the Mac) and click the Load Path as a Selection icon in the Paths palette.

2. **In the Make Selection dialog box, shown in Figure 2-12, you can**

   ✔ Feather your selection by entering a pixel value in the Feather Radius box. (For more on feathering, see Chapter 3 of this book.)

   ✔ Leave the feather radius at 0 for a hard-edged selection.

   ✔ Select the Anti-aliased option. This option slightly softens the edge of the selection so that it doesn't appear so jagged. (It's my personal recommendation.)

If you happen to have another selection active when you load your current path as a selection, you can choose to add, subtract, or intersect with that other selection.

After the path is made into a selection, it acts like any other selection.

If you need a selection refresher, see Chapter 1 of this book. If you want to save your selection, jump ahead to Book VI, Chapter 1.

 Here's one of my favorite shortcuts. To quickly load the path as a selection, select the path and then press Ctrl+Enter (⌘+Return on the Mac). You can also Ctrl+click (⌘+click on the Mac) on your path name in the Paths palette to do the same. Just be aware that you bypass the dialog box and its options when you use the shortcuts.

**Figure 2-12**

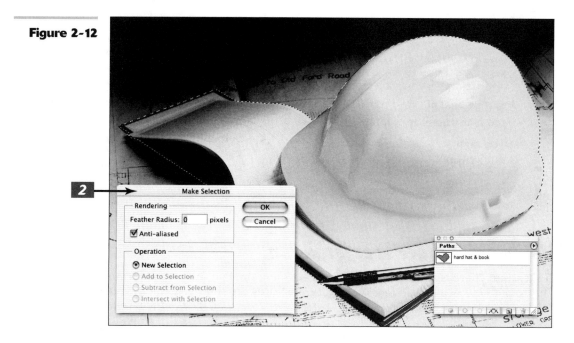

# Making a Selection into a Path

Although you probably won't use this option nearly as often as you use the option to turn a path into a selection, the option is, indeed, available: You can create paths from existing selections.

Creating a path from a selection can come in handy if you need to save a path as a clipping path (described in the last section of this chapter).

**1.** If you've been reading from the beginning of this chapter, you probably have a selection on-screen ready and raring to go. If you are just jumping in, go ahead and select the desired element in your image.

**2.** With the selection marquee active, select Make Work Path from the Paths palette options menu.

**3.** In the dialog box that appears, enter a Tolerance value.

 You can also create a path from a selection by clicking the Make Work Path from Selection icon in the Paths palette, but you bypass the dialog box.

This number controls how sensitive Photoshop is to the nooks and crannies

CONTINUED
▼ ▼ ▼ ▼

in the selection marquee when it creates the path:

✔ The lower the value, the more sensitive it is, and the better it approximates your selection.

✔ Too low a value, like 0.5, may create too many anchor points.

✔ Too high a value, like 10, will round out your path too much. Start with the default setting of 2.0.

 You can always tweak the path later (check out "Editing Paths").

**4.** **If the path is still showing after you load your selection marquee, simply click in the gray area below the path names in the Paths palette.**

This action deselects the path and leaves you with just the selection marquee.

**5.** **Select the work path in the Paths palette and choose Save Path from the Paths palette options menu. Name the path and click OK.**

## Using the Kinder Freeform Pen

Confession: There is a more amicable incarnation of the Pen tool — the Freeform Pen tool. This tool is kind of a hybrid Lasso/Pen tool. Just drag around the element you want to select, and the tool creates an outline that follows your cursor, exactly like the Lasso, as shown in Figure 2-13.

**Figure 2-13**

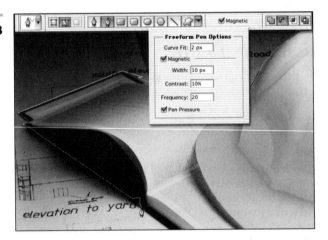

After you release your mouse button, Photoshop provides the anchor points, lines, and curves for that path, exactly like the Pen.

In my humble opinion, the Freeform Pen rates just an okay. The downside is that you are back to having to have a really steady hand in order to get an accurate selection. The tool is probably one notch better than the Lasso tool because you do get a path that you can refine before you load it as a selection. But I'd rather pay my dues and get skilled with the regular Pen.

Here are some Freeform Pen tips:

✔ To create straight segments with the Freeform Pen, press Alt (Option on the Mac) while the mouse button is pressed down and then click to create the anchor point.

✔ Pressing Alt (Option on the Mac) temporarily turns the Freeform Pen into the regular Pen. When you want to return to drawing curves, release Alt (Option on the Mac), keeping the mouse button pressed down.

 **Be careful:** If you release Alt (Option on the Mac) while the mouse button is not pressed down, Photoshop ends your path, and there's nothing you can do about it.

The following sections give you the scoop on the options that go hand in hand with the Freeform Pen tool.

## Curve Fit

The Curve Fit option lets you adjust the amount of error Photoshop allows when trying to fit your cursor movement to a path. You can enter a value from 0.5 to 10 pixels; the default setting is 2 pixels.

At the default setting, Photoshop doesn't register any movement of your cursor that is 2 pixels or less. Setting the value to 0.5 pixels makes the Freeform Pen very sensitive to your movement and forces the tool to very closely follow the edge.

The disadvantage of this option is that using it also causes a lot of unnecessary anchor points. On the other hand, a value of 10 pixels makes it less sensitive, but your path may not be as accurate.

 I recommend trying the Freeform Pen at each of these settings and then getting a feel for the kind of path it makes.

## Magnetic

When selected, the Magnetic option makes the Freeform Pen act much like the Magnetic Lasso tool. Click anywhere on the edge of the element you want to select. Release your mouse button and then move the cursor around the edge. The tool snaps to the edge of your element, creating anchor points and segments. You can

✔ **Manually control the magnetism:** If the Freeform Pen tool starts to veer off course, you can manually force down an anchor point by clicking your mouse.

✔ **Create straight segments:** To create straight segments, again press Alt (Option on the Mac) and click (you temporarily get the regular Pen). Alt+drag (Option+drag on the Mac) to temporarily access the regular Freeform Pen. To return to the magnetic Freeform Pen tool, release Alt (Option on the Mac), click again, and continue moving the cursor.

To close a path with the magnetic Freeform Pen, you must double-click your mouse.

### Width, Contrast, Frequency, and Pen Pressure

The Width, Contrast, and Frequency settings are specifically for the Magnetic option and work just like the Magnetic Lasso options. Width specifies how close to the edge (1–256) the tool must be before it detects an edge. Contrast (1–100) specifies how much contrast there must be between pixels for the tool to see the edge. And Frequency (5–40) specifies the rate at which the tool lays down anchor points. For more details, see Chapter 1 of this book.

The Pen Pressure option is only available if you're using a pressure-sensitive drawing tablet and allows you to adjust how sensitive the tool is based on how hard you press on the stylus.

▼▼▼▼▼▼▼▼▼▼▼▼▼▼▼▼▼▼▼▼▼▼▼▼▼▼▼▼▼▼▼▼▼▼▼▼▼▼▼▼▼▼

## Creating Paths without the Pen

I want to let you in on a fun way to create paths. Yes, I said fun. You have to assume by fun I mean there is no Pen tool involved in the method.

You can grab any of the shape tools and create a work path. Before you do, however, be sure to click the Paths icon in the Options bar. It's the icon that looks like a pen cursor with a square path around it. Drag the shape tool of choice on your canvas and presto, an instant path.

 Of course, you're stuck with only the shapes that are available, but once in awhile you might have a need for one of them. They can come in handy for creating small spot illustrations, logos, and Web buttons.

Follow these steps:

1. **Open an existing image and select a shape tool.**

   In the example shown in Figure 2-14, I used the Custom Shape tool.

2. **Choose a shape from the shape preset library and open an image.**

   I chose a fish shape.

3. **Using the Shape tool, drag a path in your image window.**

   You can then use the Paths palette to load the path as a selection. See "Loading Paths as Selections," earlier in this chapter.

4. **Choose Layer⇨New⇨Layer via Copy.**

   You've just put the selection on its own layer.

5. **If you want, add some type with the Type tool.**

   If you want to give your type some motion, click the Create Warped Text button in the Options bar. You can also apply drop shadows, bevels, and other effects by choosing Layer⇨Layer Style.

   I chose the Flag style warp in the Warp Text dialog box.

   I also applied a Bevel and Emboss and Drop Shadow Layer Style to both the selection and the type. (For more on type, see Book IV, Chapter 4.)

6. **Delete the original image.**

   When I was done, the image in Figure 2-15 was what I ended up with — fun and very easy.

**Figure 2-14**

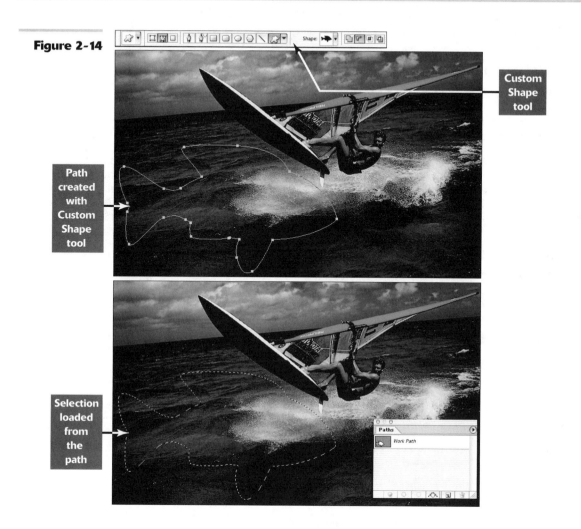

Custom Shape tool

Path created with Custom Shape tool

Selection loaded from the path

**Figure 2-15**

▼▼▼▼▼▼▼▼▼▼▼▼▼▼▼▼▼▼▼▼▼▼▼▼▼▼▼▼▼▼▼▼▼▼▼▼▼▼

# Editing Paths

Often, it is easier and less time consuming to try and get a reasonably decent, but not perfect path with the Pen tool. Then after you've got that, go back and edit your path for more accuracy. And while following the Eyeball-It-Then-Fix-It strategy is valuable any time in your Photoshop career, it is especially true when you're first learning to use the Pen tool.

Photoshop offers you a bevy of editing tools that can make your path repair a snap. These tools even share the same flyout menu as the Pen tool. In addition, the arrow tools, which Adobe calls the Path Selection and Direct Selection tools, are also extremely helpful when it comes to fine-tuning your path. In fact, you may find, like I do, that the Direct Selection tool, is one of your favorite tools — so simple to use, yet so functional. Both sets of tools are shown in Figure 2-16.

**Figure 2-16**

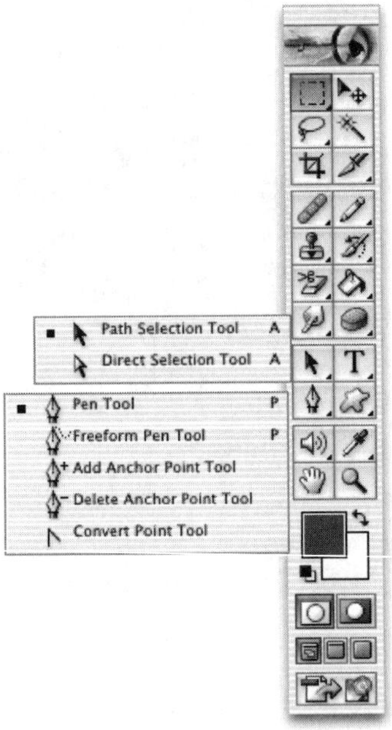

To edit a path follow these steps:

1. **If you can't see the path you want to edit, select the path in the Paths palette.**

   This activates the path.

2. **To see the individual anchor points so you can edit them, select the Direct Selection tool (remember, it's the white arrow). Click anywhere along the path.**

   You should now see the individual anchor points and segments that comprise the path. Most of the anchor points, if not all, will be hollow because they are unselected, as shown in Figure 2-17.

3. **If you need to move an anchor point, click it with the Direct Selection tool. Once selected, the point then becomes solid, also shown in Figure 2-17. Drag to move the anchor point. If you need to, you can move a curved or straight segment in the same fashion.**

**4.** **If you're in need of some major repair and need to move an entire path, use the Path Selection tool (the black arrow).**

You can also select multiple paths by pressing the Shift key while clicking the paths.

 If you move any part of the path beyond the boundary of the image canvas, it is still available just not visible. Use the Zoom tool to zoom out until you see the hidden portion of the path.

**5.** **Manipulate the direction lines to change the shape of the curve. First, click the anchor point of the curve to select it. Then click and drag the direction point going the same direction as the bump.**

By lengthening or shortening the direction line, you can control how steep or flat the curve is. By rotating the direction line, you change the slope of the curve, as shown in Figure 2-18.

🖝 To add an anchor point in your path, use the Add Anchor Point tool. Click in the path where you need an anchor point. This tool always adds a smooth point, no matter where you click.

🖝 To delete an anchor point, select the Delete Anchor Point tool, position the cursor over the anchor point you no longer need, and click it. The anchor point disappears while keeping your path intact.

🖝 To convert an anchor point from smooth to corner or vice versa, select the Convert Point tool. Position your cursor on your desired anchor point. If the anchor point is a corner point, drag away from the anchor point to create the direction lines that create a smooth point. If the point is a smooth point, simply click and release on the anchor point to convert it into a corner point. To convert a smooth point to a cusp point, make sure the direction lines are showing and then drag a direction line to break it into independent direction lines. And finally to convert a cusp point back to a smooth point, just drag out from the anchor point.

🖝 To copy a path, first select it with the Path Selection tool. Then press Alt (Option on the Mac) and drag away from the path. As you drag, you will carry a copied path with you, while leaving the original path intact. Note that you can drag a copied path onto another image window as well as within the same image.

🖝 To delete a path, select the path with the Path Selection tool and press the Backspace key (Delete key on the Mac). You can also select a point on the path with the Direct Selection tool and press Backspace (Delete on the Mac) twice.

Book
**III**
Chapter
**2**

**Figure 2-17**

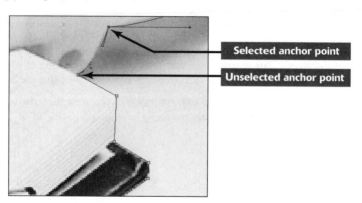

Selected anchor point

Unselected anchor point

CONTINUED
▼ ▼ ▼ ▼ ▼

**Figure 2-18**

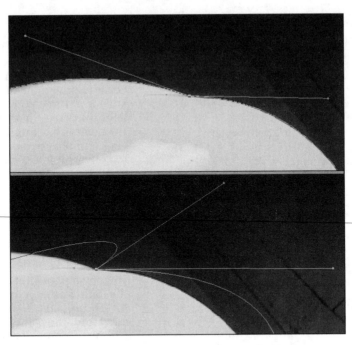

## Using the Options Bar

Quite a few options appear in the Options bar when the Pen tools or Path Selection/Direct Selection tools are active. Here is the scoop on those options:

- ✔ The **Auto Add/Delete option** enables you to add or delete an anchor point with the regular Pen tool.

- ✔ **Show Bounding Box** places a box around the path, allowing you to transform the path. It isn't a path or part of your image. It is merely a visual guide to assist you in transformations. You can scale it by dragging the handles or rotate it by dragging just outside the box. Press Ctrl (⌘ on the Mac) and drag a handle or side to distort or skew the path. For more on transformations, see Chapter 3 of this book.

- ✔ The **path state buttons** (add, subtract, intersect, and exclude) combine all visible paths by adding, subtracting, intersecting, or excluding paths. Click your desired button to direct Photoshop on how to control the overlapping portions of the path(s) when you convert it to a selection. For example, clicking the Add button selects all areas whether they overlap or not. Clicking Intersect only selects the overlapping areas.

- ✔ The **align and distribute buttons** align two or more paths and distribute three or more paths. The icons give you a good visual cue as to how the alignment or distribution will appear.

## Using the Export Transparent Image Wizard

Being the ever helpful program that it is, Photoshop gives you another way to export an image with transparent areas. Found under the Help menu, the Export Transparent Image Wizard (called an Assistant on the Mac) guides you through exporting an image with transparency to print or display on the Web. To use the wizard/assistant, you must have an active selection marquee, or your element must be on a transparent layer. From there, just answer the questions the wizard/assistant poses, as shown in the following figure, and you're set.

# *Clipping Out the Unwanted*

A *clipping path* hides areas that fall outside your path and displays the area inside your path. For example, without a clipping path, if you were to import a silhouetted image into Microsoft Word or an older page layout program or illustration program that doesn't support transparency, and place it against a colored background, it would appear against a rectangular white background, as shown in Figure 2-19. This occurs whether the background was transparent in Photoshop or not. This is because the image must be flattened before it can be imported and therefore loses any transparency. (For more on flattening, see Book V.)

With the advent of more sophisticated page layout and illustration programs, such as InDesign 2.0, PageMaker 7.0, QuarkXPress 5.0, and Illustrator 10, the need for clipping paths has pretty much lost its urgency. That's because these programs all support TIFFs with transparency. (For more on working with Photoshop and other programs, see Book X.) But just in case you're using older or less sophisticated software and you need to use a clipping path, here's what you need to do:

 Because an overabundance of complex clipping paths can cause printing problems, I recommend using clipping paths as a last resort. Even if your illustration or page layout program doesn't support transparency, you can always composite your elements in Photoshop. For more on layers and creating composites, see Book V.

**Figure 2-19**

Image imported with clipping path

Image imported without clipping path

**1.** **Create your path by using the Pen tool.**

A work path appears in the Paths palette.

**2.** **Save the path by choosing Save Path from the Paths palette options menu.**

Enter a name and click OK.

**3.** **Immediately return to the options menu on the Paths palette and choose Clipping Path.**

In the dialog box, choose the path name from the Path pop-up menu.

**4.** **Leave the flatness value blank. If it is blank, the default value of the output device will be used. And usually the default value is a good number for the particular printer used.**

Briefly, flatness represents how closely your curves approximate a true mathematical curve. A higher value causes more of a polygon shape (albeit often not noticeable by the eye), but results in easier printing.

**5.** **Choose File⇨Save and choose a file format from the Format pop-up menu.**

I like the Photoshop EPS format, personally.

Some programs, such as the latest versions of InDesign, PageMaker, and QuarkXPress, will also accept TIFFs with clipping paths. In addition, you can save the file as a JPEG, PDF, DCS, and in the native Photoshop format from Windows. And the Mac will let you save the file in any available format. Because most of my page layout files are ultimately offset printed, I stick with EPS. EPS is the preferred file format for color separations (see Book X, Chapter 2) necessary for offset print jobs.

**6.** **Set the Preview at Tiff (8 bits/pixel) and encoding as ASCII (Macintosh [8 bits/pixel] and encoding as Binary on the Mac) and click OK.**

Your clipping path is now in place, and the silhouetted image can be imported into the desired program.

Occasionally when you import an image with a clipping path into certain page layout programs on the PC, the screen preview may not display the image correctly. The clipped, or hidden portion, of the image may appear opaque (solid white or black) on-screen. But it should print okay on a PostScript printer. You may not be so lucky if you use a non-PostScript printer.

# Modifying and Transforming Selections and Paths

I f you're like me, you may find it tough to get the perfect selection the first time around. I mean all it takes is one too many cups of coffee, and that Lasso tool seems to take on a mind of its own. That's okay. Photoshop is way too benevolent to leave you hanging with a mediocre selection. A multitude of techniques are available to modify and transform your selections. You can select or remove pixels from your selection, scale your selection outline, smooth out jagged edges, or switch what is selected for what isn't. Knowing how to clean up and modify your selections helps you to nail your desired element with precision.

If you haven't already thumbed through the first two chapters of this book and gotten a good grasp of how to create selections by using the mighty Photoshop Toolbox, go ahead and browse those chapters now.

## Achieving Selection Perfection

Although the selection tools, such as the Lasso and Magic Wand, usually do a pretty fair job at capturing the bulk of your selection, making a really accurate selection often requires another sort of tool — concentration. Give your selections a little extra attention, and you'll be amazed by the results. By adding and subtracting from the outline here and there, you can refine a selection and ensure that you capture only what you really want — and nothing that you don't.

The following few sections show you how to use keyboard shortcuts, along with your mouse, to make perfect selections. If you're not one for keyboard shortcuts, you can use the four selection option buttons in the Options bar, shown in Figure 3-1, to create a new selection, add to a selection, subtract from a selection, or intersect one selection with another. All you need to do is grab the selection tool of your choice, click the selection option button you want, and drag (or click if you're using the Magic Wand or Polygon Lasso tools).

 When adding to a selection, a small plus sign appears next to your cursor. When subtracting from a selection, a small minus sign appears. When intersecting two selections, a small multiplication sign appears.

**Figure 3-1**

## Adding to a selection

To add to a current selection, simply press the Shift key and drag around the pixels you want to include with the regular Lasso or the Rectangular or Elliptical Marquee tool. You can also press the Shift key and click the area you want with the Magic Wand tool.

To include an area with straight sides in your selection, you can press the Shift key and click around the area with the Polygon Lasso. And although you may not have much need to do it, you can also press the Shift key and click with the Single Column or Single Row Marquee tool. I wouldn't use the Magnetic Lasso to add to a selection; it is way too cumbersome.

 You don't have to use the same tool to add to your selection that you used to create the original selection. Feel free to use whatever selection tool you think will get the job done.

Here are the steps to use for adding to a circular selection:

1. **First make your initial elliptical selection. Select the larger circle with the Elliptical Marquee tool. Then press the Alt key (Option on the Mac) to draw from the center out.**

   See the left image in Figure 3-2.

2. **To add the smaller image, first press the Shift key and then press the Alt** key (Option on the Mac) to draw from the center out.

3. **Drag around the smaller selection ball with the Elliptical Marquee tool.**

   The resulting selection is shown in the example on the right in Figure 3-2.

**Figure 3-2**

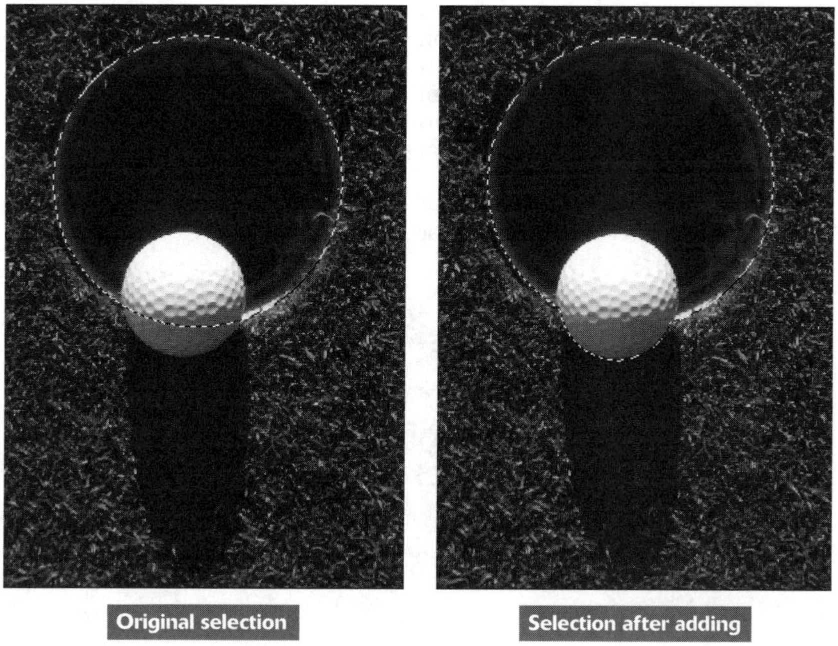

Original selection | Selection after adding

## Subtracting from a selection

Just as you can add to a selection marquee, you can also subtract, or deselect, from the selection. To subtract from a current selection, press the Alt key (Option on the Mac) and drag around the pixels you want to subtract with the regular Lasso or the Rectangular or Elliptical Marquee tool.

Press the Alt key (Option on the Mac) and click the area you want to remove with the Magic Wand tool.

To subtract a straight-sided area, press the Alt key (Option on the Mac) and click around the area with the Polygon Lasso.

You can press the Alt key (Option on the Mac) and click with the Single Column or Single Row Marquee tool. The Single Column and Row Marquee tools come in handy when you want to get rid of just the very edge of a selection.

In the top example of Figure 3-3, I first selected the frame with the Polygon Lasso tool. I didn't use the obvious tool of choice — the Rectangular Marquee tool — because the frame was not completely straight. To deselect the inside of the frame from the selection, I pressed the Alt key (Option on the Mac) and clicked at each corner of the inside of the frame with the Polygon Lasso tool, resulting in the selection shown in the bottom example of Figure 3-3.

**Figure 3-3**

## Intersecting two selections

What happens when you press the Shift and Alt (Option on the Mac) keys together? Not a collision, but an intersection. Pressing both keys while dragging with a Lasso or Marquee tool or clicking with the Magic Wand creates the intersection of the original selection with the second selection.

 To retain only the part of an image where two selections overlap, press Shift and Alt (or Shift and Option on the Mac) and then drag.

You can select a portion of an image with a tool like the Polygon Lasso. (In Figure 3-4, I selected the top-right portion of the framed photo.) Then press the Shift and Alt (Option on the Mac) keys at the same time and drag with the Rectangular Marquee. (I selected the bottom-left portion of the image.) The resulting intersection of the two selections appears in the bottom example of Figure 3-4.

**Figure 3-4**

Original selection

Second selection

Intersected selection

# Getting the Keys to Behave

There's a little glitch in Photoshop's way of doing things. Well, not so much of a glitch as a conflict. With so many ways of doing things with Photoshop, it's no wonder that somewhere along the line you have to jigger with Photoshop to get it to do what you want. For example, how does Photoshop know whether you want to create a perfect square or add to a selection when you press the Shift key?

Let me lay this out for you:

✔ When you make an initial selection with the Rectangular or Elliptical Marquee tool, pressing the Shift key constrains the proportions of the selection, thereby allowing you to create a perfect square or a perfect circle.

✔ If you press Alt (Option on the Mac) with either of these tools, you can draw from the center out.

✔ If you press Alt (Option on the Mac) with the Lasso tool, the Lasso temporarily becomes the Polygon Lasso tool.

Unfortunately, despite numerous requests, the ability to read users' minds wasn't a Version 7 upgrade feature. The following sections show you what you have to do to get Photoshop to recognize your wishes.

## Adding a perfectly square or circular selection

To add a perfectly square or round selection to an existing selection, follow these steps:

**1.** Press Shift and drag with the Rectangular or Elliptical Marquee tool.

   Your selection is unconstrained.

**2.** As you drag, keeping your mouse button pressed down, release the Shift key for just a moment, and then press it down again.

Your unconstrained selection suddenly snaps into a constrained square or circle.

**3.** Release the mouse button before you release the Shift key.

 If you don't release the mouse button before you release the Shift key, the selection shape will revert back to its unconstrained form.

## Deleting from an existing selection while drawing from the center out

To delete part of a selection while drawing from the center out, follow these steps:

**1.** Press Alt (Option on the Mac) and drag with the Rectangular or Elliptical Marquee tool.

**2.** As you drag, keeping your mouse button pressed down, release the Alt (Option on the Mac) key for just a moment and then press it down again.

   You are now drawing from the center outward.

**3.** Release the mouse button before you release the Alt (Option on the Mac) key.

   See Figure 3-5.

 Use this technique when you're selecting a doughnut, tire, inflatable swim ring, and other circular items with holes in the middle.

**Figure 3-5**

## Using the Select Menu

Although you can add, subtract, and intersect selections with the Shift and Alt (Option on the Mac) keys and the selection option buttons in the Options bar, you can do much more with the commands found on the Select menu, shown in Figure 3-6. Here you'll find ways to expand, contract, smooth, fuzz, and turn your selection inside out. You can also use this menu to automatically select similar colors and create selection borders. And I show you how to do this in the next few sections. With this kind of knowledge, imperfect selections will soon be a thing of the past.

**Figure 3-6**

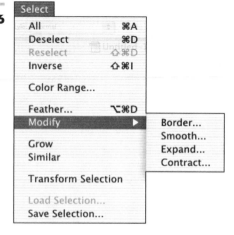

### Deleting a straight-sided selection

If you have an existing selection, pressing Alt (Option on the Mac) with the Lasso tool subtracts from the selection. If you want to subtract a straight-sided selection from an existing selection, you can press Alt (Option on the Mac) and begin to drag. Then quickly release Alt (Option on the Mac) and then select the Polygon Lasso with your mouse. But this can be tricky and is really unnecessary. I recommend just grabbing the Polygon Lasso tool itself to delete your straight-sided selection. Ditto for adding and getting intersections with straight-sided selections.

## Selecting all or nothing

The Select All and Select Nothing commands are pretty self-explanatory. To select everything in your image, choose Select⇨All. To deselect everything, choose Select⇨Deselect. The key commands Ctrl+A (⌘+A on the Mac) and Ctrl+D (⌘+D on the Mac), respectively, come in very handy and are easy to remember.

In most cases, you don't have to select everything in your image. If you don't have an active selection marquee, Photoshop naturally assumes that whatever command you execute should be applied to the entire image.

## Reselecting a selection

If you have taken 20 minutes to carefully lasso a spiny sea anemone from its ocean home, the last thing you want to have happen is to lose your coveted selection marquee. But that is exactly what happens if you accidentally click your mouse on the canvas when you have an active selection tool in hand. The selection marquee disappears.

Sure, you can choose Edit⇨Undo if you catch your mistake right away. And technically, you could access the History palette to recover your selection (see Book II, Chapter 4, for more on History). A much easier solution is to choose Select⇨Reselect. This command retrieves your last selection.

Besides immediately bringing back a selection that was accidentally deselected, the Reselect command can come in handy if you decide to select an element again for a second time. For example, if you do such a great job retouching your spiny anemone that you decide to add, by cloning, another anemone to your image, go ahead. It's all up to you. By using the Reselect command, you can easily load the selection again rather than start the selection from scratch.

The Reselect command only works for the last selection you made, so don't go planning to reselect a selection you made last week — or even ten minutes ago — if you've selected something else in the meantime.

## Swapping a selection

Sometimes it's easier for you to select what you don't want than it is to select what you do. For example, if you're trying to select your pet dog, photographed against a neutral background, why spend valuable time meticulously selecting him with the Pen or Lasso when you can just click the background with the Magic Wand? (Don't forget to use the Shift key to select bits of background you might have missed the first time.)

After you've selected the background, just choose Select➪Inverse. Presto, Fido the Retriever is now selected and obediently awaiting your next command, as shown in Figure 3-7.

**Figure 3-7**

## Feathering a selection

In Chapter 1 of this book, I described how to *feather* (blur the edges) a selection when using the Lasso and Marquee tools by entering a value in the Feather box in the Options bar. This method of feathering requires that you set your Feather radius *before* you create your selection.

Unfortunately, using this method, a problem arises if you want to modify the initial selection. When you make a selection with a feather, the marquee outline of the selection adjusts to take into account the amount of the feather. That means that the resulting marquee outline doesn't resemble your precise mouse movement. As a result, modifying, adding, or subtracting from your original selection is pretty tough.

A much better way to feather a selection is to make your initial selection without a feather, as shown in top image of Figure 3-8. Clean up your selection as you need to, and then apply your feather by choosing Select⇨Feather. Enter a Feather Radius value and click OK. The resulting selection appears in the bottom image of Figure 3-8.

 The radius is how far out in all directions the feather will extend. A radius of 8 means the feather will extend 8 pixels to the right, left, up, and down from the selection outline. A large feather radius will make the image appear to fade out.

**Figure 3-8**

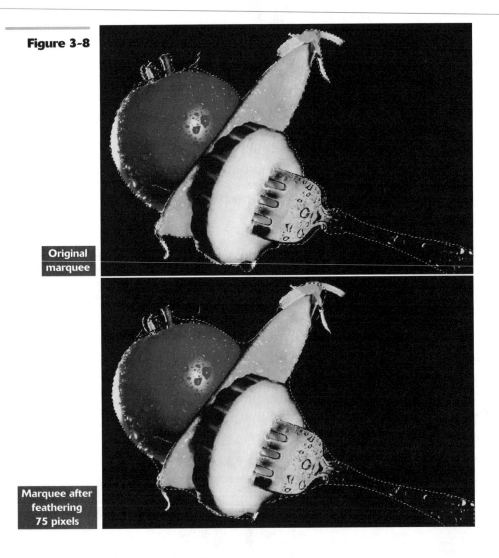

Original marquee

Marquee after feathering 75 pixels

## Using the Modify commands

The Select Modify menu contains a group of modification commands that are lumped categorically. With the exception of the Contract command, you probably won't use these options everyday. But when you do use them, you'll find that they prove useful. Here is the lowdown on each command:

- ✔ **Border:** This command selects the area around the edge of the selection marquee. You specify the width of the area, from 1 to 200 pixels, and you get a border marquee, like the one shown in the example on the left in Figure 3-9. Choose a foreground color, choose Edit➪Fill, pick Foreground Color from the Use pop-up menu, and then click OK to fill your border with color, as shown in the example on the right in Figure 3-9. By the way, you can also achieve a similar look by using the Edit➪Stroke command.

 As you can see in Figure 3-9, the Border command creates an anti-aliased (or soft-edged) selection. On the other hand, the Stroke command, on the Edit menu, creates a hard-edged selection.

- ✔ **Smooth:** If your selection marquee seems a big ragged around the edges, try selecting the Smooth command to round off the nooks and crannies. Enter a sample radius value from 1 to 100 pixels. Photoshop examines each selected pixel and then includes or deselects pixels in your selection based on the range specified by the radius amount. If most of the pixels are selected, Photoshop includes the strays; if most of the pixels are unselected, Photoshop removes the pixels. Start with 2 pixels and, if that doesn't seem like enough, increase it by a few more pixels or so.

 Use this command with great caution and a steady hand. The results can be mushy, ill-defined selections.

**Figure 3-9**

✔ **Expand:** This command allows you to increase the size of your selection by a specified number of pixels, from 1 to 100. This can come in handy if you just missed the edge of a circular selection and want to enlarge it, as shown in Figure 3-10.

✔ **Contract:** To shrink your selection by 1 to 100 pixels, choose Contract. I use this command a lot, in conjunction with the Feather command, when compositing multiple images.

After you make a selection, contract it and then feather it before you drag it onto the canvas. This technique helps to create a nice, natural-looking transition between the various images in your composite. The amount you decide to contract and feather varies according to the resolution of your images. For example, if you're using low-resolution (72 dpi) images, you may want to use 1 pixel for the Contract amount and 0.5 pixels for the Feather amount; higher resolution images may warrant 2 to 3 pixels for the Contract amount and 1 to 2 pixels for the Feather amount. (For more on compositing images, see Book V on layers.)

**Figure 3-10**

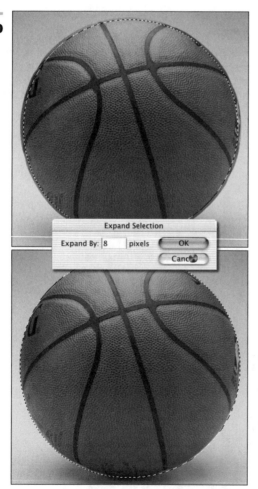

## Applying the Grow and Similar commands

The Grow and Similar commands are close cousins to the Magic Wand tool. (For more on the Wand and Tolerance, check out Chapter 1 of this book.) If you're familiar with the modus operandi of the Magic Wand, you know that you rarely get the perfect selection on the first click. That's because you are making an intelligent guess as to what Tolerance setting will pick up the pixels you want.

The Grow command compensates a little for the Magic Wand's inaccuracy. For example, if you need to include more in your selection, you can increase the Tolerance setting and try again — press Shift and click the area you need to include. Or you can choose Select⇨Grow. The Grow command increases the size of the selection by including adjacent pixels that fall within the range of Tolerance.

Book
*III*
Chapter
*3*

The Similar command is like Grow, only the pixels don't have to be adjacent to be selected. The command searches throughout the image and picks up pixels within the Tolerance range, wherever they may fall.

Both commands use the Tolerance value that is displayed in the Options bar when the Magic Wand is selected. Adjust the Tolerance setting to include more or fewer colors by increasing or decreasing the setting respectively.

# Moving and Cloning Selections

When you have your selection refined to the ultimate in perfection, you may then want to move it or clone it. To move a selection, simply grab the Move tool (the four-headed arrow) at the top right of the Tool palette, and drag the selection.

Sounds easy enough, right? When you move the selection, however, be warned that the area where the selection used to reside is now filled with the background color, as shown in Figure 3-11. (Note that if you are moving a selection on a layer you'll be left with transparent pixels.) When you use the Move tool, your cursor icon changes to a pair of scissors, letting you know that you are cutting out the selection.

### Drag 'n' drop 'til you can't stop

You can move and clone selections within a single image or between multiple images. To move a selection from one image to another, choose Edit⇨Cut, activate the second image, and choose Edit⇨Paste. To clone a selection, simply drag the selection with the Move tool from one image window and drop it onto another image window. The original image stays intact. To clone a selection marquee, drag the marquee with any selection tool from one image window to another.

For more on dragging and dropping selections, see the Putting-It-Together sections on creating a digital collage, which run throughout Book V.

**Figure 3-11**

## Cloning

If the idea of leaving a big hole in your image doesn't appeal to you, you can copy and move the selection, leaving the original image intact. Just press Alt (Option on the Mac) with the Move tool and drag. This action is often referred to as *cloning* because you're essentially making a duplicate of a selected area and then moving that duplicate elsewhere.

When cloning, your cursor icon changes to a double-headed arrow, notifying you that you are duplicating the selection. If you want to move your selection in small increments (1 pixel), press your arrow keys while the Move tool is selected. Press Shift along with an arrow key to move 10 pixels. And of course, adding the Alt (Option on the Mac) key to the key commands will allow you to clone a selection while you move it.

 You can temporarily access the Move tool by pressing the Ctrl (⌘ on the Mac) key when you have any tool, except for the Hand tool, Pen tools, Slice tools, Path Selection tool, Direct Selection tool, and Shape tools. Likewise, press Alt along with Ctrl with any of these tools to clone and move a selection.

## Moving the selection outline, but not the pixels

If all you want to do is move the selection marquee without moving the pixels underneath, you want to avoid using the Move tool. Instead, grab any selection tool — the marquee tools, the lasso tools, or the Magic Wand — and just drag the marquee. That way you move only the outline of the element, not the element itself. You can also use the arrow keys to nudge a selection marquee.

# Transforming Pixels

Although the distortions that fall under the Transform menu may be considered somewhat mundane when compared to the fun and flashy Liquify command (described in Book VII, Chapter 3), I'm sure you'll find them a lot more practical and useful in your daily digital-imaging chores.

Here's how to transform a selection:

**1. Create your selection.**

I'll leave this task up to you; just use your now well-honed selection expertise.

 You can also apply transformations to a layer or to multiple layers (for more on this topic, see Book V).

**2. Choose Edit➪Transform.**

If all that you want is a single transformation, this command is adequate. However, if you want multiple transformations, you're wise to stick with the Free Transform command, which I cover later in this section.

**3. Choose a transformation type from the submenu, as shown in Figure 3-12:**

- ✔ **Scale:** Increases or decreases the size of your selection

- ✔ **Rotate:** Rotates your selection in either direction

- ✔ **Skew:** Distorts your selection on a given axis

- ✔ **Distort:** Distorts your selection with no restrictions on an axis

- ✔ **Perspective:** Applies a one-point perspective to your selection

- ✔ **Rotate 180°, 90° CW, or 90° CCW:** Rotates the selection by specified amounts

- ✔ **Flip Horizontal or Vertical:** Flips your selection along the vertical and horizontal axes respectively

As soon as you select your desired distortion and release the mouse button, a box called the *bounding box,* or *transform box,* surrounds your selection, complete with handles on the sides and corners.

**4. Depending on which transformation type you chose in Step 3, drag a handle.**

- ✔ **Scale:** Drag a handle, corners work best. Press Shift to scale proportionately. Press Alt (Option on the Mac) to scale from the center.

- ✔ **Rotate:** Move your cursor outside the bounding box. When the cursor becomes a curved arrow, drag CW or CCW. Press Shift to rotate in 15-degree increments.

- ✔ **Skew:** Drag a side handle.

- ✔ **Distort:** Drag a corner handle.

- ✔ **Perspective:** Drag a corner handle.

Book
***III***
Chapter
**3**

CONTINUED
▼ ▼ ▼ ▼

**Figure 3-12**

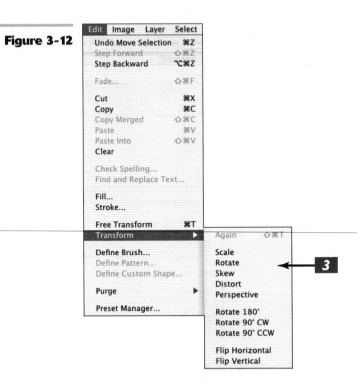

Choosing Rotate 180°, 90° CW, or 90° CCW or Flip Horizontal or Vertical will just execute the command. Handle dragging isn't necessary.

All the transformations are executed around a point called the *reference point.* The reference point appears in the center of the transform box by default.

 You can move the center point anywhere you want, even outside of the bounding box. In addition, you can set your own reference point for the transformation by clicking a square on the reference point locator in the Options bar. Each square corresponds with a point on the bounding box.

**5.** You can choose a second transformation type from the Edit➪Transform submenu, if desired.

If you're an ultraprecise type of person, you can also numerically transform the selection by entering values in the Options bar, shown in Figure 3-13.

In Figure 3-14, all the transformations were executed at the same time.

Be sure to execute all of your transformations in one fell swoop if possible. In other words, don't scale a selection now and then five minutes later rotate it and then five minutes later distort it, because every time you apply a transformation to an image you are putting it through an interpolation process. Interpolation recalculates the pixels. When you transform a selection, pixels are either added or deleted. You want to try to limit how many times an image is interpolated because it has a degrading effect — your image will start to appear soft and mushy.

**6.** **After you have distorted your selection to your liking, do one of the following: Double-click inside the bounding box; click the Commit button in the Options bar; or press Enter (Return on the Mac).**

To cancel the transformation, press Esc or click the Cancel button in the Options bar.

Your image is now magically transformed. Note that if your image isn't on a layer, you can leave a hole filled with the background color after your image is transformed. Check out Book V to avoid this snafu.

 To repeat a transformation, choose Edit⇨Transform⇨Again.

Book
*III*
Chapter
*3*

**Figure 3-13**

**Figure 3-14**

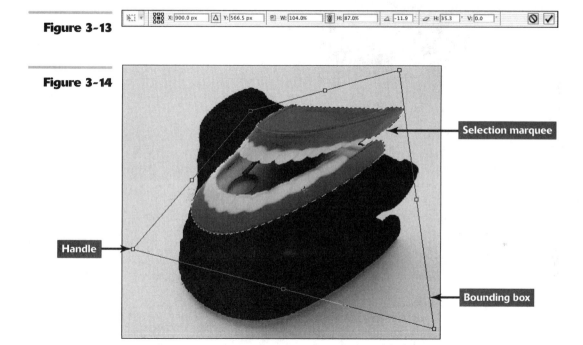

Selection marquee

Handle

Bounding box

# Transforming Selection Marquees

To transform just the selection marquee, without affecting the underlying pixels, make your desired selection and then choose Select⇨Transform Selection. There is no submenu with individual transformations to choose from. Instead, you must apply the transformations like you do with the Free Transform command: by using the keyboard shortcuts. You can also enter values in the Options bar to transform numerically, or you can access the context menu. To move the selection marquee and the bounding box, simply drag inside the marquee or nudge it by using the keyboard arrow keys. Transforming selections is particularly handy when you're trying to select elliptical objects. It is often hard to get the selection precise the first time around, as shown in Figure 3-15, so applying a transformation is often necessary.

**Figure 3-15**

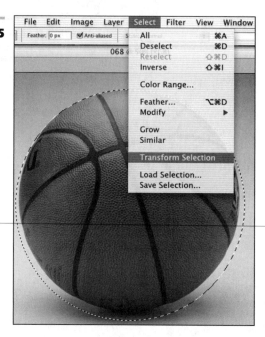

## Distorting selected pixels with Free Transform

The Transform menu isn't the only way to distort selected pixels. A much more efficient way is to use the Free Transform command, also found on the Edit menu.

Like the Transform command, the Free Transform command surrounds your selection with a bounding box. Within the bounding box, you can scale, rotate, skew, distort, or apply perspective without having to choose the individual distortions. You just have to use the right keyboard shortcuts. To scale and rotate, use the same method as the Transform commands. Here's the scoop on the rest:

✔ **Skew:** Ctrl+Shift+drag (⌘+Shift+drag) on a side handle.

✔ **Distort:** Ctrl+drag (⌘+drag on the Mac) on any handle.

✔ **Perspective:** Ctrl+Shift+Alt+drag (⌘+Shift+ Option+drag) on a corner handle.

Unfortunately, if you want to apply a flip or rotate by degree while free transforming, you need to use the Transform submenu.

While the bounding box is surrounding your selection, you can also access a context menu that offers all of the transform options. Right-click (Control+click on the Mac) on your canvas to access this handy shortcut.

# Transforming Paths

Once the bounding box is around the path, the transformation technique for paths is the same as it is for selections and selection marquees, except that the distort and perspective commands can be applied only to whole paths. The major difference between transforming paths and selections is in how you first select the path.

▼▼▼▼▼▼▼▼▼▼▼▼▼▼▼▼▼▼▼▼▼▼▼▼▼▼▼▼▼▼▼▼▼▼▼▼▼

## All paths

To select all paths:

1. Choose Window⇨Paths.

2. Click the pathname in the Paths palette.

3. Choose Edit⇨Transform Path and choose your desired transformation from the submenu.

   You can also choose Edit⇨Free Transform Path.

▼▼▼▼▼▼▼▼▼▼▼▼▼▼▼▼▼▼▼▼▼▼▼▼▼▼▼▼▼▼▼▼▼▼▼▼▼

## Single path

To select a single path:

1. Choose Window⇨Paths.

2. Click the pathname in the Paths palette.

3. Choose the Path Selection tool.

4. Click the path with the Path Selection tool.

5. Choose Edit⇨Transform Path and choose your desired transformation from the submenu, as shown in Figure 3-16.

   You can also choose Edit⇨Free Transform Path.

▼▼▼▼▼▼▼▼▼▼▼▼▼▼▼▼▼▼▼▼▼▼▼▼▼▼▼▼▼▼▼▼▼▼▼▼▼

## Part of a path

To select part of a path:

1. Choose Window⇨Paths.

2. Click the pathname in the Paths palette.

3. Choose the Direct Selection tool.

4. Select the points you want with the Direct Selection tool.

5. Choose Edit⇨Transform Points and choose your desired transformation from the submenu.

   You can also choose Edit⇨Free Transform Points.

CONTINUED
▼▼▼▼▼

**Figure 3-16**

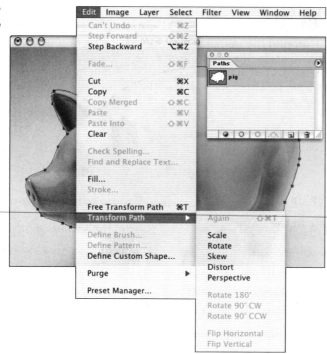

 **PUTTING IT TOGETHER**

### Removing a Person (Without Getting in Trouble with the Law)

Sometimes you may want to take an element out of a picture so that you can maintain the viewer's focus on something else. Or maybe you just don't want the element in the image. But remember, if you simply delete an unwanted element without cloning, you leave a huge space (colored with the background color) where the element was. Not smooth.

In the following steps, I show you how to seamlessly remove an unwanted element (in this case a person) from an image.

When you're first attempting this technique, I recommend that you start with an image that has an element that isn't physically attached to something that

you want to keep in the image. In this example, I use an image of a father and son at the beach. What I'm moving out of the picture (the son) isn't touching what I'm leaving in the picture (the father). Although in this example I'm removing a person, you can use the same technique to remove other objects as well: trees, dogs, an old wagon, and what have you.

1. Open an image that contains something that you want to remove.

2. Use the selection tool of your choice to select the element that you want to remove.

In this step, you're creating a selection marquee that you'll use to clone another area of the image. You'll then use the cloned portion — which is shaped like what you're removing — to cover up the element you're removing.

You don't have to be super precise, so feel free to grab the Lasso tool. If you need a Lasso refresher, see Chapter 1 of this book. (For more precise selecting, use the Pen tool, explained in Chapter 2 of this book.) When you make your selection, be careful not to cut off any portion of your element. Otherwise, you'll leave some stray pixels — a dead giveaway that something was once there. Using the Lasso tool, I made a rough outline around the little boy.

**3.** **Position your cursor inside the selection marquee, press the mouse button and then the Shift key, and drag your selection to move it horizontally (or vertically if the image warrants it) to an area of the photo that you want to clone.**

In the example, I moved the selection to the right of the little boy. Notice how the selection marquee is the only thing that I moved. The pixels were left untouched.

**4.** **With the Move tool selected, position your cursor inside the selection marquee, press Alt+Shift (Option+Shift on the Mac), and then drag to move the cloned area on top of the element that you're removing. Carefully match up the edges, release your mouse button, and then release the Alt and Shift keys (Option and Shift on the Mac).**

**5.** **Choose Select⇨Deselect.**

Selection marquee

▼ **CONTINUED**

The cloned area should now cover the element that you want to remove. In the example, the beach/ocean selection now covers the little boy.

 Depending on your image, you may want to choose Select➪Feather and enter 1 or 2 pixels before you move the cloned area. Doing this softens the edges and smoothes out the transition between the cloned area and the background. (See the section "Using the Select Menu" in this chapter for more on feathering.) I didn't feather my selection because it didn't really need it. Try it both ways to see which looks best. Use the History palette to undo your steps, if necessary (see Book II, Chapter 4, for more on the History palette).

The final step is to clean up any telltale signs that the element was there.

Area to be cloned

Cloned area covers boy

**6.** **Choose the Clone Stamp tool and select a medium-size feathered brush from the Brushes palette, press Alt (Option on the Mac), and click a good area next to a flaw; release Alt (Option) and then click the flaw.**

If the Clone Stamp is a mystery to you, be sure to check out Book VIII, Chapter 3.

Repeat this step until you've fixed all the flaws and the clone blends in seamlessly with the background. Don't get carried away with the Clone Stamp tool, or else you'll end up with a smudgy mess. Being light-handed is a good thing, as I was in the now retouched image in the following figure. Nobody can tell that only one man stands where once stood two people.

# Book IV

# Painting, Drawing, and Typing

The 5th Wave          By Rich Tennant

SINCE INSTALLING PHOTOSHOP 7, THE 4th PRECINCT BECAME NOTED FOR ITS CREATIVE WANTED POSTERS

"Ooo — look! Sgt. Rodriguez has the felon's head floating in a teacup!"

# Exploring with the Painting Tools

Y ou're definitely going to want to brush up on your painting techniques now that you don't have to worry about messing up your clothes. Painting is one of the basic skills you need to work in Photoshop, along with selecting, working with filters, and other key abilities. Once you master the art of painting strokes, working with brushes, and using the many options Photoshop offers with its painting tools, you'll be well on your way to Photoshop guru-hood.

This chapter introduces you to a plethora of tools and techniques; I also give you a guided tour of the Brush palette.

## Discovering the Brush Tool

I'm going to be honest with you: If you can get the Brush tool to work for you, you'll be well on your way to Photoshop success. That's because so many of Photoshop's tools require the use of brushes.

The Brush tool, and its hard-edged version the Pencil, use brush tips and painting strokes to apply color to your images; but that's just the beginning. Take a look at Table 1-1 to check out the versatility of these other functions, which operate in a way similar to the Brush, even if their results are completely different.

You can see that there are a dozen different functions that you can choose from and apply using the basic techniques discussed in this chapter.

TABLE 1-1: A SMATTERING OF BRUSHES AND THEIR FUNCTIONS

| Function | Tool | See |
|---|---|---|
| Selection | In Quick Mask mode, you can use the Brush (among other tools) to paint a selection with fuzzy or hard edges, or even the sputtering spray of the Airbrush. | Book VI, Chapter 2 |
| Healing and cloning | The Healing Brush and Rubber Stamp let you clone areas of the image by using brush strokes. | Book VIII, Chapter 3 |
| Erasing | The Eraser tool and its variations the Background Eraser and Magic Eraser work like a brush in reverse, removing parts of an image with brush strokes. | Book VI, Chapter 2 |
| Blurring/sharpening/smearing | The Blur, Sharpen, and Smudge tools change the contrast of your pixels or move them around by using brush strokes. | Book VIII, Chapter 2 |
| Toning | The Dodge and Burn tools lighten and darken pixels of your image under brush-stroke control. | Book VIII, Chapter 2 |
| Restoring | The History Brush selectively restores portions of your image that have been changed. | Book II, Chapter 4 |
| Stroking | The Art History Brush adds artistic brush strokes to an image from a saved copy. | Book II, Chapter 4 |

# Introducing the Pencil and the Brush

The Pencil and Brush tools are like peanut butter and chocolate. Not only do they work well together, but they also share many important traits. You can access these tools in the Tools palette. Press B, and the Brush appears by default. To access the Pencil, press Shift+B. You can toggle between the tools by pressing Shift+B again.

As you can imagine, the main difference between the tools is that one has a hard edge and the other has a softer impact. There are some other differences between the Pencil and the Brush. Find out more in the following sections.

## Finding out what the Pencil does

The Pencil and Brush are very much alike, except that the Pencil has hard edges by default (as shown in Figure 1-1) and the Brush can have soft, feathered edges. The Pencil also has the ability to erase itself!

**Figure 1-1**

You can do all of the following with the Pencil:

🖊 Drag the mouse to draw freehand lines.

🖊 Click at one point, release the mouse button, and then Shift+click at a second point to draw a straight line between the points.

 As long as you keep the Shift key depressed, you can keep clicking to draw straight lines between each of the points.

🖊 Click, hold down the Shift key, and then drag up or down to draw a perfectly straight vertical line. Drag left or right to draw a perfectly straight horizontal line instead.

🖊 Hold down the Alt key (the Option key on the Mac) and click in any area of your drawing to switch the foreground color to that hue.

🖊 Choose the Auto Erase option in the Options bar to activate the Auto Erase feature.

 Auto Erase is a handy feature that lets you remove portions of your pencil strokes without switching to the Eraser.

When Auto Erase is turned on, the operation of the Pencil tool is slightly different from the default. The effect of either of the following actions is that lines you've drawn are erased:

▶ When you click in any area of the drawing other than an area that is foreground colored (for example, the pencil lines you've already drawn), the Pencil begins drawing a line in the foreground color (this is the default mode).

▶ When you click in any area of the drawing that is foreground colored (such as the pencil lines you've drawn), the Pencil tool draws by using the background color.

 Because the Pencil tool doesn't use soft-edged lines to draw, anything other than straight vertical or horizontal lines has rough, jagged edges, as shown in the close-up image in Figure 1-2. *Jaggies* aren't objectionable in many cases, but if you zoom in on an area containing pencil lines, the jaggies will be readily apparent. I show you how to modify the characteristics of the lines drawn with the Pencil later in this chapter in "Working with the Brushes palette."

**Figure 1-2**

▼ ▼ ▼ ▼ ▼ ▼ ▼ ▼ ▼ ▼ ▼ ▼ ▼ ▼ ▼ ▼ ▼ ▼ ▼ ▼ ▼ ▼ ▼ ▼ ▼ ▼ ▼ ▼ ▼ ▼ ▼ ▼ ▼ ▼ ▼ ▼ ▼ ▼

## Using the Pencil

If you're ready to start using the Pencil, keep in mind that lines that aren't straight will look jagged up close. To try out the Pencil, work your way through these steps:

**1. Activate the Pencil tool by choosing it from the Tool palette. (It's grouped with the Brush tool.)**

You can press Shift+B to make it appear if it's hidden underneath the Brush.

The Pencil's current brush tip (usually the 1-pixel brush unless you select something else) is shown next to the Brush box in the Options bar.

Click the tool and hold down the mouse button to summon the Brush Preset picker palette if you want to choose a different-sized pencil tip.

**2. If you want to draw using anything other than the Normal drawing mode, choose a mode from the Mode options list.**

You find more about modes in Book V, Chapter 3.

**3. Choose an opacity for your pencil strokes.**

If you want whatever is in the background to show partially through your strokes, choose an opacity of less than 100 percent by using the slider or by typing an opacity percentage directly into the text box.

**4. Stroke with the mouse to create your pencil lines.**

## Painting with the Brush

The Brush tool is a basic tool used throughout Photoshop in various incarnations, so you'll want to master its use as quickly as possible.

The most important difference between the Brush and the Pencil is that, by default, the Brush produces soft-edged lines that are rendered smoother by a process known as *anti-aliasing*. This is a technique that substitutes partially filled pixels along the edges of lines to produce the illusion of gradual fading. Our eyes merge the transparent pixels together so the line looks smooth rather than hard edged.

Although jaggy edges are most apparent in diagonal lines, Photoshop applies anti-aliasing to brush stroke edges even in horizontal and vertical lines. The fuzzier the brush, the more semi-filled pixels used to produce the effect, as you can see in Figure 1-3.

The Brush shares most of the basic features found in the Pencil, except the Auto Erase feature is not available:

- ✔ Activate the Brush from the Tool palette or by pressing B (or Shift+B if the Pencil was used last).

- ✔ Choose a brush tip from the Brush Preset picker in the Options bar.

- ✔ Select a Mode and Opacity from the options in the Options bar.

- ✔ Drag to paint, click and Shift+click to paint straight lines, and hold down the Shift key while dragging to constrain the Brush to horizontal or vertical lines.

- ✔ Hold down the Alt key (the Option key on the Mac) and click in any area of color to switch the foreground color to that color.

**Figure 1-3**

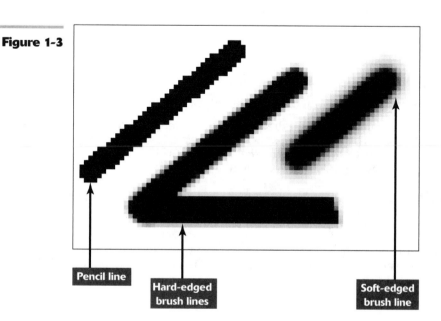

Pencil line

Hard-edged brush lines

Soft-edged brush line

The Brush tool has several other options to select from:

✔ **Flow:** *Flow* determines how quickly the Brush applies the paint. You can set a flow rate from 1 to 100 percent by using the Flow slider or by typing a percentage directly into the text box. You might think of it as controlling how wet or liquid the paint is. At low flow rates, the paint is applied slowly so the color is not as dark; at higher flow rates, the paint quickly reaches its full strength as you drag.

 You can set flow rates in 10-percent increments by pressing the number keys while the Brush tool is active. The 1 key equals 10 percent, the 2 key equals 20 percent flow rate, and so forth.

✔ **Airbrush:** Click the Airbrush icon in the Options bar to switch the Brush tool (as well as many of the other tools that use brush tips) to Airbrush mode. This produces the spray effect you get with a traditional airbrush. The longer you hold down the mouse button, the more paint that pumps out of the tool, and the wider the airbrush effect will spread, as shown in Figure 1-4.

✔ **Toggle Brushes Palette:** At the far right of the Options bar is an icon that shows or hides the Brushes palette. It's a quick way to access this value tool, and is also available with the Pencil and other tools that use brush tips. I show you how to use the Brushes palette later in this chapter.

## Working with the Brushes Palette

You'll find the Brushes palette extremely useful for changing the characteristics of preset brush tips and for creating your own. You can also access and select brush presets, as I discuss later in this chapter.

The Brushes palette normally resides in the Palette Well. You can view the Brushes palette in several ways:

✔ Click the Brushes palette tab in the Palette Well.

✔ Choose Window⇨Brushes from the menu bar.

✔ Click the Brushes palette button on the right side of the Options bar.

✔ Grab the Brushes palette's tab and drag it out of the Palette Well and onto your Photoshop desktop. This mode keeps the Brushes palette visible until you put it away by dragging it back to the Palette Well, clicking its close box, or rendering it hidden with the Window⇨Brushes command.

The Brushes palette displays a list of brush properties at the left side of the palette, and includes a brush stroke at the bottom of the palette, much like the one available when you select Stroke Thumbnail view from the Brush pop-up palette.

The largest pane in the dialog box is the upper-right area that shows various types of information, such as the size and type of brush tip, or the different controls offered for any of the 12 different properties you can set.

**Figure 1-4**

## Choosing a Brush Tip Shape

When Brush Tip Shape is selected in the left column of the Brushes palette, a scrolling box shows the available brush tips, as shown in Figure 1-5. You can use the palette options menu to choose any of the views available for the Brush pop-up palette, including text only, small and large thumbnails, small and large lists, and stroke thumbnail.

Twelve brush parameters that you can choose to apply and edit are arrayed in the column under the Brush Tip Shape entry. You can select any of these options to apply them to the currently selected brush.

**Figure 1-5**

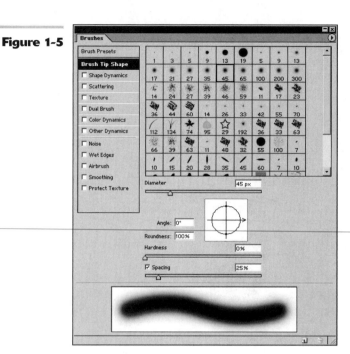

Select an option to edit its characteristics. Here are the characteristics:

✔ **Brush Tip Shape:** These controls let you choose the size and shape of the brush tip, including the diameter, angle, roundness, hardness, and spacing.

✔ **Shape Dynamics:** These controls include the amount of randomness or variation produced when a stroke is drawn, amount of fade, the size, the jitter angle, the roundness, and other options. The higher the value, the greater the amount of variance for each option. Some of these apply only when you are using a pressure-sensitive digital tablet. Check your digital tablet's instruction manual for more information on how to customize brushes for your tablet.

✔ **Scattering:** This parameter controls the amount and position of brush marks in a stroke. The higher the value, the higher the number of brush marks and the farther apart they are. When Both Axes is selected, the brush marks are distributed radially as if on a curve. The Count controls the number of brush marks at each spacing point. The higher the value, the greater the number of marks.

✔ **Texture:** This control allows you to impart a texture pattern to a brush stroke, either one of Photoshop's preset textures or one of your design. Select Invert to reverse the light and dark pixels in the pattern. Scale sizes the pattern in each stroke. Texture Each Tip renders each tip as it is stroked, giving a more saturated effect. Depth controls how prominent the pattern appears against the brush stroke. Minimum Depth specifies the minimum depth that the paint of each stroke shows through the pattern. Mode lets you choose one of Photoshop's blending modes, as described in Book V, Chapter 3. You can find more about creating and working with patterns in Chapter 3 of this book.

✔ **Dual Brush:** You can use two tips to draw with a single brush. This option lets you select the characteristics of the second tip by using the same type of attributes — such as diameter, spacing, and scatter — applied to the first tip. You can also specify a blending mode between the two tips.

✔ **Color Dynamics:** This control uses your foreground and background colors to adjust how the color varies during a stroke, allowing you to create a multicolored brush. Slight variations give the stroke a more natural, organic look. You can introduce slight (or major) "jitter" to the hue, saturation, brightness, and purity of the colors, as well as some randomness between the foreground and background colors as a stroke is drawn. Without color dynamics, the stroke color remains constant.

✔ **Other Dynamics:** These introduce randomness into the opacity and flow factors of a brush, again making the brush stroke look more natural and less machine-generated. You'll want to experiment with all the dynamics to see exactly how they can affect your image. Note that the Flow and Opacity settings in the Brushes palette do not override those in the Options bar.

Here's a list of tip characteristics:

✔ **Noise:** Adds random pixels to brush tips, giving them texture and an organic quality. This option is more apparent in feathered brushes.

✔ **Wet Edges:** Makes the brush tip leave a stroke that looks more like watercolor, with paint building up along the edges.

✔ **Airbrush:** Gives the brush tip an airbrush look.

✔ **Smoothing:** Smoothes out the curves when drawing arcs with the brush. Again, this option is more noticeable when using a pressure-sensitive drawing tablet.

✔ **Protect Texture:** Ensures that all brush tips that use a texture use the same texture. This allows you to switch back and forth between brush tips while painting and still achieve a consistent texture.

Book
*IV*
Chapter
*1*

### PUTTING IT TOGETHER

#### *Colorizing Black-and-White Images*

Just as there are valid artistic reasons for shooting a photo in black and white, there are equally reasonable rationales for changing a grayscale image into a color one. Perhaps the picture is an old one, taken before color film was widely used, and you'd like to colorize it. Or you may come across a monochrome image that would look even better in color. Photoshop lets you restore black-and-white pictures to their original colors or create whole new color schemes. If you can imagine an image in color, use Photoshop to add the hues you want to see.

In my example, I choose a black-and-white photo of a young girl. Instead of a full-color treatment that attempts to duplicate a color photograph, I want to apply a trendier transformation that adds a touch of color to the hair, face, and clothing. This approximates the hand-colored look of

▼ **CONTINUED**

### PUTTING IT TOGETHER

the venerable Marshall's Photo Coloring System of pigments, photo oils, spot colors, retouch pencils, and other products so popular in the '50s and '60s and enjoying a rebirth today. Although I've worked with a Marshall's kit myself, Photoshop is a lot faster, easier, and more versatile.

Similar techniques will work for just about any black-and-white image, so don't freak out if you're colorizing, say, a landscape.

1. **Open a grayscale image in Photoshop.**

2. **Choose Image➪Mode➪RGB Color to convert the grayscale image to a full color image (even though it presently still lacks any color).**

3. **Choose Layer➪New Layer.**

   This creates a new transparent layer to paint on. Although you can paint directly on an image layer or a copy of an image layer, using an empty layer is safer and gives you more flexibility in backtracking when you make a mistake. For more information on working with layers, consult Book V.

   The New Layer dialog box appears.

4. **Name the layer.**

   Although you can paint all your colors on a single layer, you'll find that using a separate layer for each component lets you fade that color in and out as required to blend smoothly with your other hues.

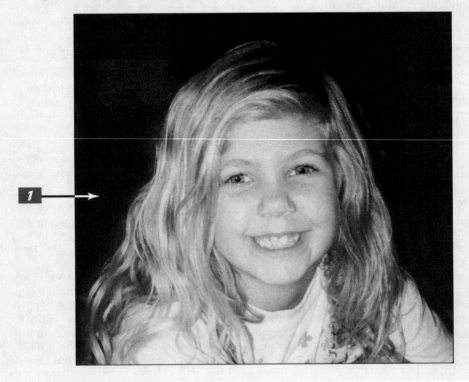

**5.** **Select the Color mode from the Modes drop-down list in the Layers palette.**

This blending mode is used by Photoshop to combine the painting layer with the image layer underneath, and will let you apply colors on top of the detail in the grayscale image without obscuring it entirely.

**6.** **Select a color you want to apply from the Swatches palette.**

If you don't find the exact color you want, you can also use the Color palette to mix your own. You'll find information on this tool in Book II, Chapter 3.

**7.** **Press B to activate the Brush tool.**

You may have to press Shift+B to cycle to the Brush tool if the Pencil was used last.

**8.** **Click the down arrow next to the Brush icon in the Options bar and choose a brush from the array.**

The top row shows hard-edged brushes; the soft-edged brushes start in the second row. You might want to start with a 9- or 13-pixel-wide brush.

If you're already comfortable with the Brush, you can choose the Airbrush option in the Options bar to get a very subtle and soft effect. Just be sure you pick the kind of brush that works best for the area of the picture you're colorizing. (Use a small, fuzzy brush for smaller areas, and use a bigger, sharper brush for more stark lines and wider areas.)

**9.** **Paint over all the parts of the image that contain that color.**

If you make a mistake, you can erase the mis-strokes without affecting the

Book
*IV*
Chapter
**1**

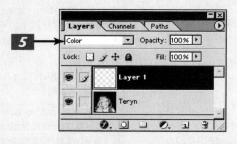

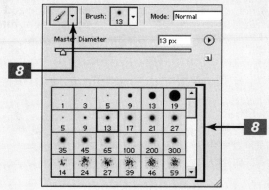

▼ CONTINUED

▼ **CONTINUED**

underlying grayscale image because you're painting on a separate transparent layer.

 In my example, I chose a nice, light blue color to change the color of the girl's eyes. A small fuzzy brush is perfect for a small area such as the eyes.

Change brushes as necessary by clicking the Brush icon in the Options bar and choosing a larger or smaller brush.

 You can also make your brush larger or smaller one size at a time by pressing the left and right bracket keys on your keyboard.

10. **When you've finished with that area of the image, create a new layer for each of the main components of the photograph and repeat Steps 4 through 8 with an additional color.**

I painted the eyes, lips, shirt, cheeks, hair, and hair highlights separately because creating natural, subtle effects with people's skin, hair, and eyes takes a special touch:

✔ **Eyes:** When painting the eyes, paint only the irises and leave the pupils their original black color. Don't paint over the catchlights in the eyes, either.

✔ **Lips:** Color the inner surface of the lips a darker, rosier pink than the outer surface. Lips look best when portrayed in at least two shades. Don't forget to color the gums with an even lighter pink.

✔ **Hair:** Hair looks best when the highlights and darker portions are slightly different colors.

 I applied an ash blonde to the darker tones of the girl's hair, and a more yellow color to the highlights.

✔ **Skin tone:** To put a little blush in the cheeks, choose the Airbrush option from the Options bar and work with a relatively large brush size. Apply a good dash of color to each cheek, and a lighter bit of color to the forehead and chin. (I used a 100-pixel brush for this picture.)

 Be sure to pick a color that's as close to real life as possible. If the subject has darker skin, you may need to move away from rosier blush tones.

Color Plate 4-3 shows the resulting image of the young girl.

11. **When you're finished coloring your layers, you can experiment with different opacity levels for each colorized layer to see if more transparent hues might look better.**

▼▼▼▼▼▼▼▼▼▼▼▼▼▼▼▼▼▼▼▼▼▼▼▼▼▼▼▼▼▼▼▼▼▼

# *Creating Your Own Brush*

Although you can apply any of the options listed in the preceding section to existing brushes, you'll find these parameters most useful when creating your own brush.

To create a brush, follow these steps:

**1.** **Click the Create New Brush icon at the bottom of the Brushes palette, or choose New Brush from the palette options menu.**

**2.** **Enter a name for the brush in the dialog box that opens.**

**3.** **With Brush Tip Shape selected, set the shape and angle of your brush in the Brushes palette, shown in Figure 1-6.**

   ✔ Use the slider to set a diameter for the brush, or enter a diameter in the text box.

   ✔ Adjust the roundness of the brush. You can use the Roundness text box to specify an exact ratio, or drag the handles in the preview box to custom-shape the brush.

   ✔ Specify an angle for the brush. Enter an angle in the text box, or drag the handles in the preview window to customize the brush angle.

**4.** **Use the Hardness slider to adjust the fuzziness of the brush, from 0 percent (pretty fuzzy) to 100 percent (hard-edged).**

**5.** **Use the Spacing slider to insert a gap between strokes as you draw (producing a dotted-line effect).**

   At 1 percent, the line is drawn solid; as you move the slider to the right,

you insert more space between short strokes, up to 1,000 percent (10X) of the diameter of the brush tip.

 You can activate/deactivate this feature by selecting the Spacing option box.

**6.** **Choose other brush characteristics by selecting one or more of the following:**

   ✔ Shape Dynamics

   ✔ Scattering

   ✔ Texture

   ✔ Dual Brush

   ✔ Color Dynamics

   ✔ Other Dynamics

   Figure 1-7 shows examples of these options.

**7.** **Finish up with some brush tip options. There are no controls for these parameters; you can toggle them on or off:**

   ✔ Noise

   ✔ Wet Edges

   ✔ Airbrush

   ✔ Smoothing

   ✔ Protect Texture

Book
*IV*
Chapter
**1**

CONTINUED
▼ ▼ ▼ ▼

**Figure 1-6**

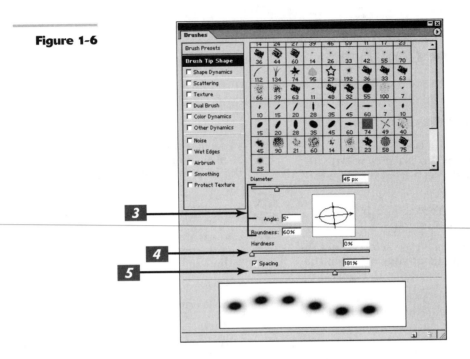

**Figure 1-7**

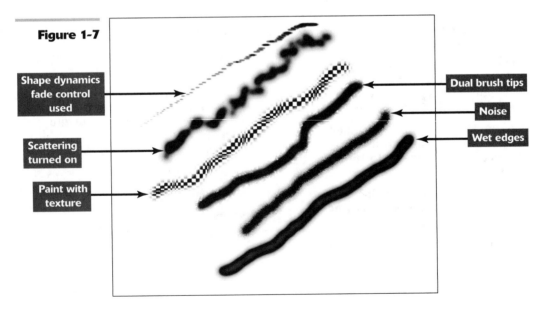

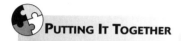

**PUTTING IT TOGETHER**

### A Fast Way to Colorize Skin

In the Putting-It-Together project earlier in the chapter, you find out how to colorize a black-and-white image. This project shows you how you can get a more realistic skin color by colorizing a person's skin. This technique works especially well with those who have naturally dark complexions.

Just follow these steps:

**1.** **Create a copy of the underlying black-and-white picture layer and then choose Image⇨Adjustments⇨ Hue/Saturation.**

The Hue/Saturation dialog box appears.

**2.** **Choose the Colorize option and move the Hue slider all the way to the left to produce a sepia tone. Set Saturation to 25 percent and click OK to colorize this layer.**

**3.** **Use the eraser to remove everything in the colorized layer that isn't face.**

In my example (see the picture of the young girl in the Putting-It-Together project earlier in this chapter), I removed the hair, background, eyes, lips, teeth, and shirt.

This gives the entire face a nice sepia tone.

## Saving a New Brush Tip

After you've created your new brush tip, you can save it with the currently active brush presets by choosing Save Brushes from the palette options menu. For more information on saving, loading, appending, and replacing libraries of presets, see the discussion of the Preset Manager in Book I, Chapter 6.

For some practice in using the brushes, try out the Putting-It-Together project that follows and find out how to eliminate the dreaded red-eye effect.

## Using the Preset Brushes

Photoshop has two brush palettes, in a sense. The Brush Preset picker, shown in Figure 1-8, is tucked away in the Options bar and appears when you click the down-pointing triangle next to the box that displays the currently active brush tip. I explain how to use the Preset picker in this section.

Photoshop is furnished with a large number of predesigned brush presets that you can use. The default set includes six round, hard-edged brushes (which still have softer edges than the Pencil) and a group of 12 round soft-edged brushes. There are also squarish, elliptical, and odd-shaped brush tip presets, as well as a group of brush tip patterns such as stars, leaves, and other shapes.

A preset brush's pixel diameters are shown as text below a thumbnail image of the brush shape when the palette's display is in default mode. (I show you how to change the default display of the preset picker shortly.)

**Figure 1-8**

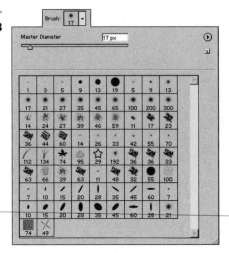

To use one of these brush tips, just click the Brush Preset picker arrow and choose the tip you want from the scrolling preset list. You can augment your choices with any of the following options:

- ✔ Move the Master Diameter slider to change the diameter of the selected brush. This is a quick way of getting a slightly larger or smaller brush when none of the presets meet your needs exactly. For example, the largest hard-edged brush preset is 19 pixels in diameter. You can click this brush tip and move the slider to the right to get a hard-edged brush in any size up to 2500 pixels.

 To change the brush size from the keyboard when a tool is active, press the right bracket to increase the size and the left bracket to decrease the size. The amount of change varies according to the initial size of the brush. To adjust the size more dramatically, hold down the bracket key.

- ✔ Choose any of the library of additional brush tip presets provided with Photoshop. Click the Brush Preset picker picker's option menu and choose one of the other brush tip libraries shown at the bottom. They have names like Assorted Brushes, Calligraphic Brushes, and Drop Shadow Brushes. Select one to append the brushes to your current set or to replace the current set with the library you select (a dialog box appears that offers a choice of either action).

 You can also manage brush tip libraries by using the Preset Manager. See Book I, Chapter 6, for information on using the Preset Manager.

- ✔ Select your own custom library of brush tips that you've created. Click Load Brushes to append new brushes to your current collection or to replace them with the new library.

In the next section, I show you how to manage and edit brush presets.

# *Managing Preset Brushes*

You can change the way brushes are shown in the pop-up palette by choosing a viewing mode from the pop-up palette's option menu:

- ✔ **Text Only:** This displays the names of the brush tips in several columns (depending on how wide you've made the pop-up palette), as shown in Figure 1-9.

**Figure 1-9**

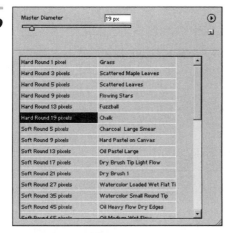

- ✔ **Small Thumbnail:** This is the default view, with a thumbnail image of the brush tip and its diameter in pixels.
- ✔ **Large Thumbnail:** This view provides a closer look at the brush tip, as shown Figure 1-10.
- ✔ **Small list:** This view shows a single-column list of the brush tips with their text names.

**Figure 1-10**

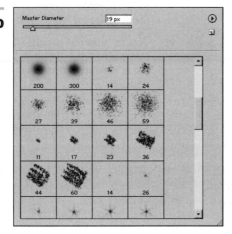

✔ **Large list:** The larger list adds thumbnails so you can see the brush shape.

✔ **Stroke thumbnail:** This view shows a typical ess stroke by using the selected brush so you can see how it looks when applied, as shown in Figure 1-11.

**Figure 1-11**

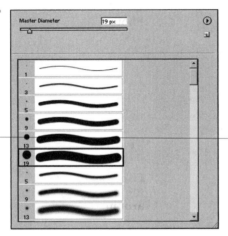

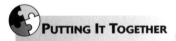

### Getting the Red Out without Eyedrops

*Red eye* occurs when the subject of a picture looks directly into the flash, and the unfortunate result is that eerie reddish luminescence in the eyes that says, "Not only didn't I get any sleep last night, but I'm also auditioning for the remake of Michael Jackson's *Thriller* video." Color Plate 4-1 shows an example of red eye.

The red-eye effect is caused by the flash bouncing off the blood vessels in the retina and right back into the camera's lens. You'll see red eye most often in pictures taken in dim light because the pupils are at their largest in low-light conditions. You may also see red eye if you're using a camera with a flash that's very close to the camera's lens (thereby making it easier for the light to bounce straight back into the lens). The best way to fix red eye is to avoid it completely. That usually means getting a flash camera that can work around it:

✔ Many cameras have a red-eye prevention mode. Usually, this mode triggers a quick, bright preflash just before the actual picture is taken. The preflash causes the subjects' irises to contract, making their pupils smaller when the second flash (that is, the *real* flash) goes off.

✔ Some cameras mount the flash high or to one side of the lens. This simple trick also minimizes the chance of red eye.

However, these preventive measures are of little solace when you've got a great picture that features bright red pupils as its most dominating feature.

Here's a quick way to paint out red eye and restore your image to a less zombielike look:

**1.** **Open the original photo with red eye showing.**

**2.** **Select the pupil of one of the eyes.**

An easy way to avoid changing the color of more than the red part of the eye is by *painting* the selection by using the Quick Mask tool.

**3.** **Double-click the Quick Mask icon in the Tool palette.**

The Quick Mask Options dialog box appears.

 Make sure that the Selected Areas option is selected. This tells Photoshop that the area you're painting should be considered a selection. See Book III, Chapter 1, for more on selections.

**4.** **Double-click the Color preview box to produce the Color Picker dialog box. Choose a bright green color as the mask color.**

Photoshop uses a red hue by default that would make it difficult to see what part of the image you've already painted, so using a contrasting color eliminates this problem.

**5.** **Click OK to dismiss the Color Picker dialog box, and then click OK to close the Quick Mask Options dialog box and begin painting a mask.**

**6.** **Choose a fuzzy-edged brush from the Brushes palette and paint around one iris.**

Book
*IV*
Chapter
**1**

▼ **CONTINUED**

▼ **CONTINUED**

**7.** **Press Q to exit Quick Mask mode.**

Only the pupil of the eye is selected, so you can paint without fear of covering up any other parts of the eye.

**8.** **Choose Select⇨Save Selection and store the pupil selection. Give it a name, such as "Last Iris."**

You can reuse the pupil selection later if you accidentally deselect the area while working.

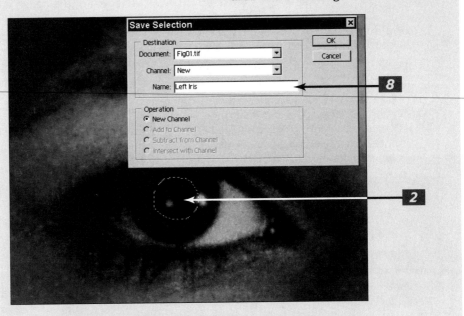

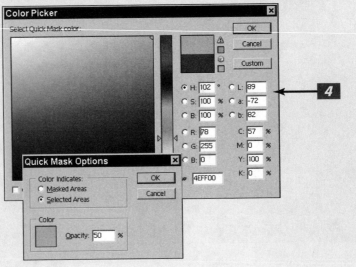

9. **Select the Brush tool and choose a small fuzzy-edged brush.**

10. **In the Options bar, choose Hard Light as the blending mode from the Mode drop-down list.**

11. **Choose a color that matches the iris color but is quite a bit darker.**

    Pupils are ordinarily much darker than the iris that surrounds them.

12. **Paint over the pupil.**

 You may notice that two *catchlights* (reflections of light sources such as windows or the flash that made the picture) on the eye, which is unnatural. Of course, having no catchlight at all is even more unnatural! Cover the extraneous left catchlight in each pupil, but try not to obscure the main, right catchlight.

If you must paint over one of the main catchlights to remove the red-eye effect, use some white paint to insert a new one.

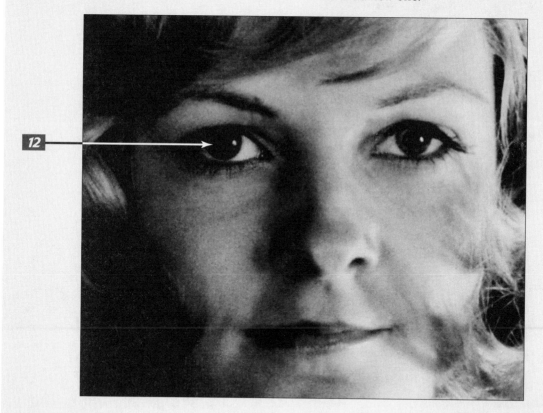

# Creating Vector Shapes

**2**

Photoshop's shape tools add an important dimension to your drawing and painting capabilities. Whereas many of the tools in the Tool palette are pixel oriented, creating shapes and outlines from swarms of pixels, the Shape tool, like the Pen and Type tools, initially creates scalable outlines by using vectors instead of pixels.

Working with vector shapes gives you the freedom to resize your objects at will, and convert them to pixels only when you need to merge them with the rest of your image. This chapter focuses on how you can create, resize, modify, and manipulate vector shapes with the Shape tool.

## Pixel and Vector Basics

Vectors describe a shape mathematically; pixel images, on the other hand, describe the same shape in terms of a map of pixels. An easy way of understanding this concept is to imagine how a square is measured by each of these graphical measurements:

✔ **Measured in pixels:** A square might be 200 pixels on a side with the corners at particular X and Y coordinates in the image file. The square contains a total of 40,000 different pixels, each of which must be created and stored with the image file.

✔ **Measured in vectors:** The same square might be simply defined as four points with equal-length lines connecting each of them at right angles. The length of the lines is determined by the scale of the square. It isn't necessary to store information about the area inside the square; the vector image file needs to contain only the position of the four points and the fact that they are each connected by lines at a 90-degree angle.

You can see that to enlarge a square created by vectors all you need to do is increase the distance between the points. To enlarge a pixel square, you need to create a lot more pixels. The difference between the way these measurements handle shapes becomes magnified (so to speak) if the shape's outlines aren't perfectly straight or if points don't connect at neat right angles.

Resizing any sort of object made of pixels causes a problem: As you enlarge the pixels, the object takes on a jaggy appearance in lines that aren't horizontal or vertical. To enlarge a vector object, on the other hand, you only need to rearrange the points that define the lines or curves; the lines and curves themselves don't grow and become jaggy.

## Making Basic Shapes

The Shape tool can create five different kinds of basic shapes. There is also a custom shape tool that lets you use preset shapes or create shapes of your own design. To access the Shape tool, press U on your keyboard to select the currently active shape, or press Shift+U to cycle through the available shapes. You can see the Shape tools in the Tool palette in Figure 2-1, and in the Options bar in Figure 2-2.

Simply press U once and then choose the shape you want from the icons that appear on the Options bar. These include rectangle, rounded rectangle, ellipse, polygon, and line tools.

**Figure 2-1**

**Figure 2-2**

The Options bar shows icons for the Pen tool, Freeform Pen tool, and Shape tool whenever any of these tools are active. You can switch back and forth between Shape and Pen tools by clicking the appropriate icon in the Options bar. You can find out more about the Pen tool in Book III, Chapter 2.

### Choosing a preset shape to create

When you create a shape, you can place the shape in its own layer, which is called a *shape layer*. The advantage of a shape layer is that, as with any layer, you can keep the elements residing in that layer separate from the rest of the image. You can put several shapes in a single shape layer, and you can control how the shapes interact with each other when they overlap. (Some options include making the shapes appear to have been added together, subtracted from, and so on.) Shapes in a shape layer are linked to a *vector mask,* which, like selections stored as alpha channels, can show or hide portions of an image. You find out more about shape layers and vector masks later in this chapter. Alpha channel selections are discussed in Book VI, Chapter 1.

Here's a list of shapes you can create:

- ✔ **Rectangle/ellipse:** The rectangle and ellipse have no special parameters on the Options bar; however, they both behave much like their counterparts among the selection tools. For example, you can hold down the Shift key while dragging a shape to produce a perfect square or circle; hold down the Shift key plus the Alt key (Option key on the Mac) to draw the shape outward from the center. You have other geometry options that let you determine how the shapes are drawn (unconstrained, fixed size, from center, and so forth). I give you a quick rundown of your geometry options later in this chapter.

- ✔ **Rounded rectangle:** This shape has the same options as the rectangle shape, with the addition of a box in which you can type the radius of the circle used to round off the corners of the rectangle.

- ✔ **Polygon:** This shape includes a box in which you can enter the number of sides you'd like for the polygon, in the range of 3 to 100, as well as geometry options.

- ✔ **Line:** You can give the line shape a width from 1 to 1000 pixels and assign a layer style and/or fill color. You can also enter parameters for an arrowhead at either or both ends. I explain that option in more detail later.

## Choosing a shape mode

Here's a list of ways in which you can create a shape:

- ✔ **Shape Layers:** Click this icon to create the shape in a new layer of its own. When you choose this mode, icons appear in the Options bar that let you choose a layer style and/or fill color.

> Shape Layers is a good choice if you want to keep your shapes in separate layers so you can manipulate them further. The shapes remain scalable until you change them into pixels by choosing Layer➪Rasterize➪Shape.

- ✔ **Path:** Click this icon to create the shape on an existing layer. It will appear as a path that you can edit by using the Pen tools and the Paths palette. For everything you need to know about paths, check out Book III, Chapter 2.

- ✔ **Fill Pixels:** Click this icon to create a shaped area filled with the foreground color. This option *doesn't* produce a vector shape, but instead fills the shape with pixels. It is similar to filling a selection created with the Rectangular or Elliptical Marquee or painting on your canvas with a painting tool. When you choose this mode, the Options bar includes choices that let you specify a blending mode, the transparency of the filled area, and whether you want the area anti-aliased. You cannot edit the shape created with this option.

▼▼▼▼▼▼▼▼▼▼▼▼▼▼▼▼▼▼▼▼▼▼▼▼▼▼▼▼▼▼▼▼▼▼▼▼▼▼

## Creating a preset shape

Follow these steps to draw a preset shape in your document:

1. **Access the Shape tool by pressing U.**

2. **Choose the mode of shape you want to draw from the three icons in the Options bar.**

   See the preceding section, "Choosing a shape mode."

3. **Choose the type of shape you want to create from the Options bar.**

   The Options bar changes to reflect each type of shape; each type has its own options. Your options are listed in "Choosing a preset shape to create," earlier in this chapter.

4. **Drag with the mouse in the document to produce the shape you've defined.**

   The shape appears in the image window, as well as in the Layers palette in its own layer. A generic shape icon appears in the image column, and the shape itself is shown in the mask column as a vector mask, as you can see in Figure 2-3.

**Figure 2-3**

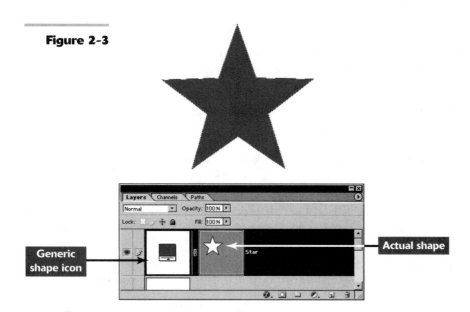

Generic shape icon

Actual shape

## Drawing multiple shapes in a shapes layer

After you've created a shape layer, you can draw additional shapes in the layer, adding to the vector mask associated with that layer. You can add, subtract, overlap, and intersect shapes in exactly the same way you do with selections, as described in Book III, Chapter 3.

You can combine and join two or more shapes, subtract one shape's outline from another shape, create a shape only from the areas that overlap, and so on.

Four buttons on the Options bar, similar to their counterparts when a selection tool is active, let you choose from these modes. These buttons are shown in Figure 2-4.

Hold down the Shift key to temporarily switch to Add to Shape Area while drawing a new shape. Hold down the Alt key (Option on the Mac) to temporarily switch to Subtract from Shape Area. This works just like adding or subtracting selections.

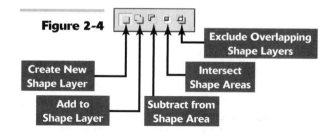

**Figure 2-4**

# Setting Geometry Options

Geometry options for your shapes (rectangle/rounded rectangle, ellipse, polygon, and line) help define how the shapes look. The following sections show you what you can do with these options.

## Rectangular shape geometry options

Here are the Geometry options for the rectangle shapes, as shown in Figure 2-5:

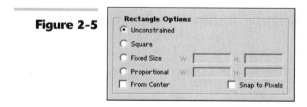

**Figure 2-5**

✔ **Unconstrained:** When this option (the default) is selected, the size and proportions of the rectangle are defined as you drag.

✔ **Square:** Select this button to constrain the shape to a perfect square. (You can also hold down the Shift key to do the same thing on the fly.)

✔ **Fixed Size:** This option lets you draw rectangles only in fixed sizes. Type in a width and height to specify the exact size.

✔ **Proportional:** This option lets you define an aspect ratio, or proportion, for the rectangle. Type *3* into the W box, and *4* into the H box, and you'll be constrained to drawing any size rectangle with fixed proportions in a 3:4 ratio.

✔ **From Center:** Mark this box to expand the shape from the center point you click.

✔ **Snap to Pixels:** This option aligns the shape to the pixels on your screen.

## Elliptical shape geometry options

The ellipse shape has the same options that are available for rectangles (as shown in Figure 2-6):

✔ Unconstrained

✔ Circle

✔ Fixed Size

✔ Proportional

✔ From Center

Of course, instead of being able to create a perfect square, you can restrain the shape to be a perfect circle. Also, the Snap to Pixels option (available for rectangles) doesn't exist for ellipses.

**Figure 2-6**

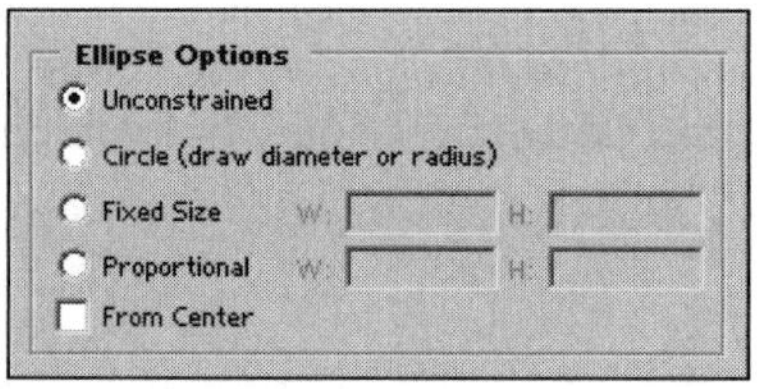

Ellipse Options
- ⦿ Unconstrained
- ○ Circle (draw diameter or radius)
- ○ Fixed Size    W:      H:
- ○ Proportional  W:      H:
- ☐ From Center

## Polygon shape geometry options

These are the geometry options for the polygon shape, as shown in Figure 2-7:

✔ **Radius:** You can enter the radius of a circle used to round off the corners of a polygon when the Smooth Corners option is selected.

✔ **Smooth Corners:** Choose this option to round off the corners.

✔ **Star:** Select this option to create a star shape — that is, a polygon where the sides indent inward rather than extend outward from the corner points.

✔ **Indent Sides By:** The value entered here determines the amount the sides are curved inward.

✔ **Smooth Indents:** This option rounds off the inner corners created by indenting the sides.

**Figure 2-7**

Polygon Options
Radius: 20
☑ Smooth Corners
☑ Star
Indent Sides By: 50%
☐ Smooth Indents

You can see the difference between an indented five-sided polygon (a star) at right in Figure 2-8, and an outdented five-sided polygon, at left.

**Figure 2-8**

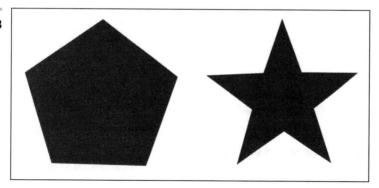

## Line geometry options

The line's geometry settings, shown in Figure 2-9, include whether to put arrowheads at the start or end of the line, or both; the width and length of the arrowhead in relation to the weight (width) of the line itself; and the amount of concavity in the arrowhead. Typical arrowhead shapes are shown in Figure 2-10. The arrowheads in the figure are as follows, from top to bottom:

- 4-pixel line, width 500%, length 1000%
- 4-pixel line, width 300%, length 600%
- 4-pixel line, width 600%, length 1200%, concavity 50%
- 4-pixel line, width 600%, length 1200%, concavity –50%

**Figure 2-9**

**Figure 2-10**

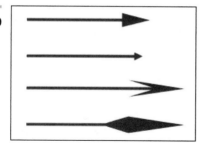

## Creating Custom Shapes

With the Custom Shape tool, you can choose from preset custom shapes, which Photoshop provides, as well as shapes that you define yourself.

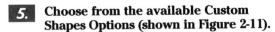

### Using preset custom shapes

Photoshop's preset custom shapes probably look familiar to you if you've been reading the earlier sections in this chapter (in particular "Choosing a preset shape to create"). But there are a couple of new additions:

✔ **Defined Proportions:** When you use this option, any shapes created using this new custom shape will be limited to the *proportions* you use when you create it now. That is, you can change the size of a new shape but only in proportion with the original custom shape you create.

✔ **Defined Size:** When you use this option, any shapes generated based on this new custom shape will be limited to the *size* you set now.

Choosing a preset custom shape couldn't be easier:

**1.** Choose the Custom Shape tool from the Tool palette or Options bar.

**2.** Choose Shape Layers, Paths, or Fill Pixels.

**3.** Click the pop-up shapes palette triangle.

**4.** Select a shape from the scrolling list and press Enter (Return on the Mac) to close the palette.

**5.** Choose from the available Custom Shapes Options (shown in Figure 2-11).

You can choose Defined Proportions and Defined Size in addition to the other preset shapes Photoshop offers.

**6.** Drag in your document to draw the shape.

 Many more custom shapes, like those shown in Figure 2-12, can be loaded into the Shapes palette by choosing a shape library from the palette options menu.

**Figure 2-11**

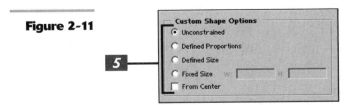

Custom Shape Options
- Unconstrained
- Defined Proportions
- Defined Size
- Fixed Size   W:          H:
- From Center

**Figure 2-12**

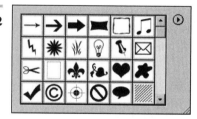

## Creating your own custom shape

You can create your own custom shape by defining the shape using a vector mask, work path, or saved path. You can find out more about creating work paths and saved paths in Book III, Chapter 2. To add the shape to your shape library, follow these steps:

**1.** **Choose the Pen tool from the Tool palette, or press Shift+P until the Pen tool is selected.**

**2.** **Use the Pen to draw the shape you want to create.**

The techniques for adding, removing, and adjusting the shapes of curves with the Pen are described in Book III, Chapter 2.

The shape you create is placed in its own shape layer as a vector mask automatically. Find out more about what you can do with a vector mask in the following section, "Using vector masks."

**3.** **In the Paths palette, select the path or vector mask you want to convert into a custom shape.**

**4.** **Choose Edit⇨Define Custom Shape from the menu bar.**

The Shape Name dialog box appears, as shown in Figure 2-13.

**5.** **Enter a descriptive name for your new shape in the dialog box and then click OK.**

The new shape appears in the custom shapes pop-up palette.

**6.** **Choose Save Shapes from the pop-up palette's menu to store your new library on your hard disk.**

Although you can't create a shape with the Presets Manager, you can use it to manage the shapes in your shape library.

**Figure 2-13**

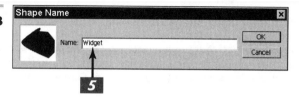

## Using vector masks

When you create a custom shape from scratch, the shape is automatically saved as a *vector mask* (which means that it can hide or show different portions of a shape). The vector mask, in turn, is placed in a shape layer.

You can edit a shape that's been saved as a vector mask at any time. Simply click the vector mask thumbnail to select it. Then use the shape and pen tools to edit the shape.

Here are some additional things you can do with a vector mask:

✔ To remove a vector mask, drag its thumbnail in the Layers palette to the trash icon at the bottom of the palette. You can also select the layer and choose Layer⇨Delete Vector.

✔ To enable or disable a vector mask, Shift+click its thumbnail in the Layers palette, or select the layer and choose Layer⇨Disable (or Enable) Vector Mask. The thumbnails of disabled vector masks are marked with an X.

✔ You can convert a vector mask to a layer mask by selecting the layer and choosing Layer⇨Rasterize⇨Vector Mask.

# Manipulating Shapes

You can manipulate shapes you've created by using a variety of tools. Here's a quick list of the things you can do:

✔ **Move:** Choose the Move tool (press V) to move shapes in their layer.

✔ **Delete:** Select a shape and press Delete to remove it.

✔ **Change anchor points:** Use the Direct Selection tool to manipulate anchor points, directional handles, lines, and curves.

✔ **Transform shapes:** Use the Edit⇨Transform Path command or select the Show Bounding Box option in the Options bar to transform shapes. For more information, see Book III, Chapter 3.

✔ **Align and distribute shapes:** Use active buttons in the Options bar when the Move tool is selected to change alignment and distribution along an imaginary line (which is shown on the button itself).

You'll find more information on manipulating shapes in Book III, Chapter 2.

 Like all vector objects, vector paths print at the full resolution of the printer and are resolution independent. To avoid having your vector shapes first converted into pixels when printing, you must select the Include Vector Data option in the Print Options dialog box.

# Filling and Stroking

**3**

Photoshop offers several different ways to create objects (shapes) out of pixels, and filling and stroking are two of the most venerable object-builders at your disposal. You can also paint objects on your canvas by hand, or convert vector shapes to pixels (see Chapter 2 of this book for more on that topic). But if you need pixels arranged into regular circles, ellipses, and polygons, the Fill and Stroke facilities of Photoshop should be your first stop.

Photoshop creates these pixel objects by filling selections or closed paths with color or patterns, or by tracing the outlines of the selections or paths. Those coming to Photoshop from some other image editors may be confused at first, looking for separate tools to create, say, rectangles and filled rectangles when they want to build a shape filled with pixels. The Shape tool, which creates vector outline objects rather than pixel shapes, isn't quite what they are looking for.

You can thank Adobe for not overloading the crowded Tool palette with separate tools you don't really need. When you realize that you can simply make a selection of any shape and then fill it or stroke it, you'll never miss separate pixel-object tools.

This chapter shows you how to create these objects by filling and stroking selections and paths, how to add smooth gradient blends, and the best ways to apply patterns. After reading this chapter, you will have your fill of different strokes.

Another way of filling is through the use of a fill layer, which you can use to fill a shape. Because fill layers work a little differently than the types of fills discussed in this chapter, I cover them in Book V, Chapter 1.

▼ ▼ ▼ ▼ ▼ ▼ ▼ ▼ ▼ ▼ ▼ ▼ ▼ ▼ ▼ ▼ ▼ ▼ ▼ ▼ ▼ ▼ ▼ ▼ ▼ ▼ ▼ ▼ ▼ ▼ ▼ ▼ ▼ ▼ ▼ ▼ ▼

# Filling a Selection with the Foreground or Background Color

The following steps show you the basics of filling a selection with either the foreground or background color (there are plenty of other filling options, which I discuss later in the chapter):

*1.* **Create your selection on a layer.**

*2.* **Choose a fill color as the foreground or background color.**

*3.* **Choose Edit⇨Fill.**

The Fill dialog box, shown in Figure 3-1, appears. Here, you can select whether to fill with the foreground or background colors. You also can choose black, 50 percent gray, or white.

*4.* **Click OK.**

The foreground (or background) color fills the selection.

 You can also choose a blend mode, the opacity of the fill, and whether or not to fill the entire selection or only portions of the selection that contain pixels (the nontransparent areas). I recommend not adjusting your blend mode and opacity in the Fill dialog box, but instead adjusting those settings in the Layers palette where you have more flexibility.

**Figure 3-1**

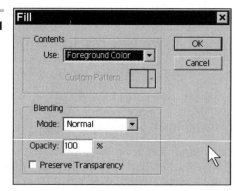

---

## Knowing your selection options

The first step to filling a selection is to make a selection. You can

✔ Draw a freehand selection with the Lasso, Polygonal Lasso, or Magnetic Lasso tool. (See Book III, Chapter 1.)

✔ Drag a selection with the Rectangular or Elliptical Marquee tools. (See Book III, Chapters 1 and 3, for more information about creating and modifying selections with these and other selection tools.)

✔ Select pixels by using the Magic Wand. (Check out Book III, Chapter 1.)

✔ Paint a selection by using Quick Mask mode. (See Book VI, Chapter 2.)

✔ Change a path into a selection. (Take a look at Book III, Chapter 2.)

✔ Use the Type Mask tools to create selections shaped like text (see Chapter 4 of this book).

# Filling Options and Tips

After you've made a selection, you're ready to use one of the filling options. You can use the Fill dialog box (as described in the preceding section) to fill the selection with the foreground or background color; you can also choose to fill the selection with black or gray. Photoshop is full of shortcuts and options. Here are just a few:

✔ Fill the selection with the foreground color by pressing Alt+Delete (Option+Delete on the Mac).

   With the selection active, press Alt+Delete (Option+Delete on the Mac) to fill it with the foreground color.

✔ Fill only the pixels in a selection with the foreground color, leaving any transparent pixels transparent, by pressing Alt+Shift+Backspace (or Option+Shift+Delete on the Mac).

✔ *Lock* the transparent pixels in a layer (and its selections) by clicking the Transparency icon in the Lock area of the Layers palette.

   I will describe some other choices available here, such as filling with a pattern or with information from the History palette, shortly.

✔ If you're working on the Background layer, you can also fill the selection with the background color by pressing the Delete key. (Pressing Delete on other layers creates a transparent area that shows the image in the layer underneath the selection.)

✔ Paint part or all of the interior of the selection by using any of the brush tools, as shown in Figure 3-2. This option lets you partially fill a selection by using a bit of flexibility and creativity. When you paint a selection with brush tools, the paint is confined inside the boundaries of your selection. For more on painting, see Chapter 1 of this book.

✔ Pour color from the Paint Bucket into the selection.

**Figure 3-2**

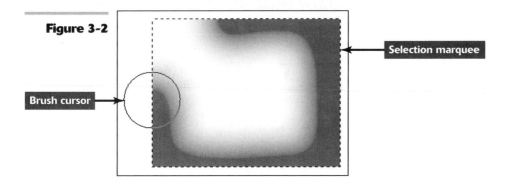

Selection marquee

Brush cursor

# Pouring with the Paint Bucket

The Paint Bucket tool, available from the Tool palette, operates much like a combination of the Brush and the Magic Wand, as you'll see from looking over its options. To use it, select the tool (press Shift+G until it's active) and click inside the selection you want to fill.

Here are your options:

- ✔ **Fill:** You can choose whether to fill with a solid color or a pattern.

- ✔ **Pattern:** When you've chosen Pattern from the Fill list in the Options bar, you can select a preset pattern, load patterns from your pattern libraries, or create a pattern of your own. You'll find more information on patterns later in this chapter.

- ✔ **Mode:** You can select a blending mode, too. You'll find more information on these modes in Book V, Chapter III.

- ✔ **Opacity:** Adjust this value to make your fill semitransparent.

- ✔ **Tolerance:** Like the Magic Wand, you can choose a tolerance level that specifies how similar in brightness a pixel must be before it is selected for painting. You can find more information on tolerance levels in Book III, Chapter 1.

- ✔ **Anti-aliased:** Choose this option to blend the paint in smoothly with the areas not filled.

- ✔ **Contiguous:** When selected, the paint fills only pixels that are touching. When deselected, paint fills all pixels within the brightness tolerance you specify.

- ✔ **All Layers:** This option applies paint to pixels in all layers that are within the selection and brightness/tolerance levels you specify.

 As with other tools that fill, you can protect the transparent pixels from being filled by the Paint Bucket. Just select the Transparency icon in the Lock area of the Layers palette.

▼▼▼▼▼▼▼▼▼▼▼▼▼▼▼▼▼▼▼▼▼▼▼▼▼▼▼▼▼▼▼▼▼▼▼▼▼▼▼▼

## Stroking a Selection

Stroking enables you to create outlines of selections, layers, or paths. Stroking a selection creates a border around the selection. It's up to you to decide whether to put the border inside, outside, or centered on the selection. (Photoshop doesn't care either way.)

To stroke a selection, follow these steps:

**1.** **Choose a foreground color and make a selection.**

(Stroke can't automatically use the background color, although you can select that color in the dialog box.)

**2.** **Choose Edit⇨Stroke.**

The Stroke dialog box opens.

**3.** **Adjust the settings and the options, as described in the following section.**

In the example shown in Figure 3-3, I specified a 22-pixel stroke, centered around the selection.

**4.** **Click the OK button to apply the stroke.**

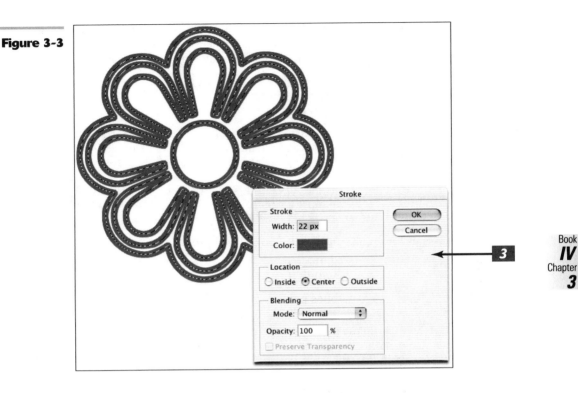

**Figure 3-3**

# *Knowing Your Stroking Options*

You can adjust the following settings in the Stroke dialog box:

- ✔ **Width:** Enter a width for the stroke in the Width box. You can select 1 to 250 pixels. You can also type in a value by using another measurement, such as inches, but Photoshop will convert it to pixel values before applying.

- ✔ **Color:** Choose a color if different from the foreground color, by clicking in the Color box. You can select the hue you want from the dialog box that appears.

- ✔ **Location:** Select whether the stroke should be applied outside the selection, inside the selection, or centered on the selection. (For example, a 3-pixel stroke would extend 1 pixel inside and 1 pixel outside the selection.)

- ✔ **Mode:** Choose a blend mode to determine how the stroke will merge with other colors.

- ✔ **Opacity:** The default value is 100 percent. If you want the stroke to be semitransparent, type another value.

- ✔ **Preserve Transparency:** Choose this option to apply the stroke only to pixels that already exist, leaving transparent areas alone.

I recommend leaving the blend mode and opacity setting options in the Stroke dialog box alone. Instead of adjusting these settings, create a new layer for your stroke and then choose a different blend mode and opacity setting in the Layers palette for maximum editability.

# Filling and Stroking Paths

Just as you can fill and stroke selections, you also can fill and stroke paths. These capabilities enable you to create pixel shapes that take advantage of the powerful vector-oriented features of the Path tools.

For example, you can use the Pen to create complex paths to form shapes and then rescale the shapes to your heart's content. Then, when you're ready, convert shapes to pixels or make an outline of the shape by using the fill and stroke features.

You'll find the basics for creating paths in Book III, Chapter 2.

▼▼▼▼▼▼▼▼▼▼▼▼▼▼▼▼▼▼▼▼▼▼▼▼▼▼▼▼▼▼▼▼▼▼▼▼▼▼▼▼▼▼

## Filling a path

To fill a path with a color, follow these steps:

1. **Select the image layer you want to fill.**

    You must choose a layer other than a type layer or layer clipping mask. For more information on type layers, see Chapter 4 of this book; you'll find information on clipping layers in Book V, Chapter 4.

2. **In the Paths palette, select the path you want to fill.**

3. **Choose the foreground color you want to fill the path with.**

4. **To fill the path by using the current setting, click the Fill Path button in the Paths palette. You then can skip the remaining step.**

   **To fill the path by using different settings, choose one the following methods:**

   ✔ Hold down the Alt key (Option key on the Mac) while clicking the Fill Path button.

   ✔ Drag the path to the Fill Path button while holding down the Alt key (Option key on the Mac).

   ✔ Choose Fill Path from the palette menu.

   Any of these methods opens the Fill Path dialog box (which looks similar to Figure 3-1).

5. **In the Fill Path dialog box, enter or change settings to meet your needs.**

   In addition to the regular Fill dialog box options (see "Filling Options and Tips," earlier in this chapter), there are a few bonus settings:

   ✔ **Use:** This option enables you to pick a fill color, pattern, or history state. You can select the current foreground or background colors, black, 50 percent gray, white, a pattern, or the area encompassed by the path in its currently selected state in the History palette. (For more on the History palette, see Book II, Chapter 4.) If you select Pattern, you can choose a pattern from the Custom Pattern menu.

✔ **Blending:** This option enables you to choose a blending mode and opacity; you can also decide whether to protect transparent pixels within the path while you're filling it with color.

✔ **Rendering:** With this option, you can choose a feathering radius to fade out the color of the fill at the edges of the path; you can also decide whether or not you want to smooth out the edges by using anti-aliasing options.

▼▼▼▼▼▼▼▼▼▼▼▼▼▼▼▼▼▼▼▼▼▼▼▼▼▼▼▼▼▼▼

## Stroking a path

Stroking a path produces quite a different result than stroking a selection — even if the selection is the same shape as the path. That's because when you stroke a selection, you always use a simple, solid line.

On the other hand, when you stroke a path, you can use any of the drawing or painting tools, such as the Pencil, Brush, Smudge, or any of the other tools that use a brush tip. If you want to add some flair to the outline of a shape, stroking a path is the way to go.

Book **IV** Chapter **3**

Aside from this visible difference, stroking a path outline is otherwise similar to filling a path. Just follow these steps:

1. **Select the image layer you want to contain the stroked path.**

    As with filling a path, you must choose a layer other than a type layer or layer clipping mask.

2. **In the Paths palette, select the path you want to stroke.**

3. **Choose the foreground color you want to use to stroke the path.**

4. **Choose the painting tool you'd like to use to stroke the path.**

5. **Select the brush size, mode, opacity, flow, or other parameters for that painting tool.**

   For more information on setting parameters for painting tools, see Chapter 1 of this book.

6. **Stroke the path by using any of these methods:**

   ✔ Click the Stroke Path button at the bottom of the Paths palette.

This strokes the path using the current settings of the Stroke Path dialog box. You can click more than once; each click reapplies the stroke, making a partially transparent stroke more opaque and thicker.

✔ Choose Stroke Path from the palette menu to enter changes in the Stroke Path dialog box. You can specify a different drawing/painting tool, and select the Simulate Pressure option, which varies the width of the stroke.

✔ Hold down the Alt key (Option key on the Mac) while clicking the Stroke Path button to access the Stroke Path dialog box.

✔ Drag the path to the Stroke Path button while holding down the Alt key (Option key on the Mac) to access the Stroke Path dialog box, shown in Figure 3-4.

CONTINUED
▼▼▼▼

**Figure 3-4**

## Working with Gradients

A *gradient* is a wonderful blend of colors that can be applied to a layer or selection, gradually fading from one hue to another. Gradients can involve more than two colors, producing a veritable rainbow of variations. You can apply gradients by using preset selections of colors, or you can create your own gradient.

You can create the following gradient effects:

- ✓ **Foreground to background:** The gradient is a transition from the current foreground color to the background color.

- ✓ **Foreground to transparent:** The gradient is a transition from the current foreground color to transparent, allowing whatever is under the transparent portion to show through.

- ✓ **Black to white:** The gradient is a transition from black to white.

- ✓ **An array of colorful selections:** This includes rainbows, coppery sheens, and other effects.

 Other sets of gradients can be loaded from the Gradient palette menu's libraries. They have names like Color Harmonies, Metals, and Pastels. For more information on managing preset libraries, see Book I, Chapter 6.

In addition to being able to control the appearance and application of a gradient, you also have the opportunity to adjust the Gradient tool's options:

- ✔ **Mode:** Select any of Photoshop's blending modes.

- ✔ **Opacity:** Choose how transparent the gradient is.

- ✔ **Reverse:** Reverse the order in which the colors are applied.

- ✔ **Dither:** Add *noise,* or random information, to produce a smoother gradient that will print with less banding (color stripes caused by the limitations of the printing process to reproduce a full range of colors).

- ✔ **Transparency:** This option determines whether or not the gradient's transparency settings are ignored when you apply a gradient. If you deselect this option, all portions of the gradient will be fully opaque. I show you how to add transparency to a gradient later in this chapter.

Book
**IV**
Chapter
**3**

### *Choosing a method for applying a gradient*

Five different kinds of gradient methods are available in Photoshop, as shown in the following figure:

- ✔ **Linear** gradient blends the colors of the gradient from start color to end color in a straight line.

- ✔ **Radial** gradient blends the colors from start to end in a circular arrangement.

- ✔ **Angle** gradient creates a counterclockwise sweep around the starting point, resembling a square radar screen.

- ✔ **Reflected** gradient blends the colors by using symmetrical linear gradients on either side of the starting point.

- ✔ **Diamond** gradient blends the colors outward in a diamond pattern.

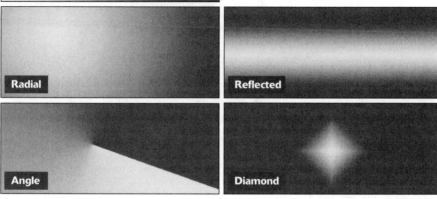

▼▼▼▼▼▼▼▼▼▼▼▼▼▼▼▼▼▼▼▼▼▼▼▼▼▼▼▼▼▼▼▼▼▼▼▼▼▼

### Applying a preset gradient to a selection

Here's how to apply a preset gradient:

**1.** Choose the layer or selection you want to apply the gradient to.

**2.** Select the Gradient tool from the Tool palette, or press G or Shift+G until the Gradient tool becomes active.

**3.** Choose one of the preset gradients from the Options bar list.

**4.** Choose the method for applying the gradient by clicking one of the icons in the Options bar.

You can select a linear, radial, angle, reflected, or diamond effect.

**5.** Choose any other options you want from the Options bar.

I introduce these options in "Working with Gradients," earlier in this chapter.

**6.** Place the cursor at the position in the layer or selection where you want to place the starting color of the gradient.

**7.** Drag in any direction to the point you want to place the end color.

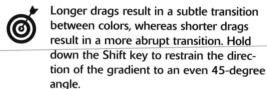 Longer drags result in a subtle transition between colors, whereas shorter drags result in a more abrupt transition. Hold down the Shift key to restrain the direction of the gradient to an even 45-degree angle.

**8.** Release the mouse button to apply the gradient.

The gradient I created is shown in Figure 3-5.

**Figure 3-5**

## Creating and editing gradients

Although Photoshop includes dozens of different gradient presets, you may want to create your own. Perhaps you'd like to create a gradient with your company colors or build one to match the predominant colors in an image. Or you might want to create a gradient that includes more than two colors. The Gradient Editor lets you create your own gradient preset, using two or as many colors as you want, which you can save and reuse at any time.

The Gradient editor has lots of options, but it's easy to use once you know what all the controls and options do. This next section leads you through the steps for creating your own new gradient preset.

▼ ▼ ▼ ▼ ▼ ▼ ▼ ▼ ▼ ▼ ▼ ▼ ▼ ▼ ▼ ▼ ▼ ▼ ▼ ▼ ▼ ▼ ▼ ▼ ▼ ▼ ▼ ▼ ▼ ▼ ▼ ▼ ▼ ▼ ▼ ▼ ▼ ▼ ▼ ▼

### *Creating a two-color smooth gradient*

Follow these steps to create a simple two-color smooth gradient:

*1.* **Select the Gradient tool from the Tool palette.**

*2.* **Click in the gradient sample window in the Options bar.**

The Gradient Editor dialog box opens, as shown in Figure 3-6.

*3.* **If you want to base your new gradient on an existing gradient preset, click that gradient in the Presets window.**

*4.* **Click the New button.**

A copy of the gradient you selected is appended to the end of the Presets. If you didn't select a preset, the default Foreground to Background gradient will be used as your model instead.

**5.** **In the Name box, type in a name for your new gradient.**

**6.** **Choose Solid or Noise from the Gradient Type pop-up menu.**

A Noise gradient is one containing random colors. You can choose which color model to use and how rough the gradient is and select a range of acceptable colors.

**7.** **Next, define the color of the starting point for your gradient by first clicking the left color stop button under the gradient bar.**

The triangle on top of the stop turns black to indicate you are working with the starting point of the gradient.

*8.* **Choose the starting color by using one of these methods:**

✔ Double-click the left color stop and select a color from the Color dialog box that appears.

✔ Double-click the Color box in the Stops area of the dialog box and choose a color from the dialog box.

✔ Choose Foreground, Background, or User Color from the Color pop-up menu in the Stops area of the dialog box.

✔ Position the cursor anywhere in the gradient bar to select a start color from the bar, or position the cursor anywhere within an image on your screen, and then click to select the color under the cursor.

CONTINUED
▼ ▼ ▼ ▼

**9.** Click the end point color stop at the right side of the gradient bar and use any of the methods described in Step 8 to choose the end color of the gradient.

**10.** Change the proportions of one color to the other by moving the starting or ending point's color stops to the left or right. Drag the midpoint slider (a diamond icon) to adjust where the colors mix 50-50.

You can also change the position of the midpoint by typing a value into the Location box.

Because the centerpoint of the gradient is halfway between the start and end points, the gradient will proceed smoothly from one color to the other, meeting to blend evenly in the middle. Moving the color stops and the midpoint changes the proportions.

**11.** Click OK to apply the settings to your new gradient.

**Figure 3-6**

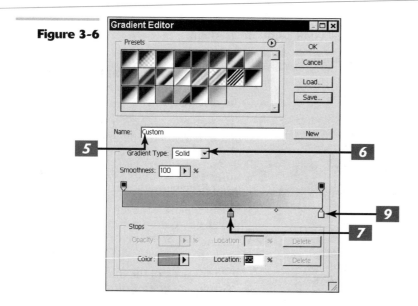

## Creating a multicolor gradient

You can also create a fancier gradient that includes more than two colors. Follow these steps to add a third color:

**1.** To add a third color, click below the gradient bar at the position you want to place the next color.

A new color stop appears.

**2.** Define a color for the new color.

**3.** Click again to add a fourth color.

You can keep going like this for hours.

**4.** Specify the color for any and all additional color stops.

**5.** Move the color stops to the left or right to assign proportions for the additional colors.

You can also type in a position for each stop by selecting it and typing a value in the Location box.

**6.** Adjust the midpoint sliders between the colors.

**7.** If you change your mind, you can redefine the color or click the Delete button.

 You can also remove a color stop by dragging it down from its position under the gradient bar.

**8.** Click OK to apply the settings to your new gradient.

▼ ▼ ▼ ▼ ▼ ▼ ▼ ▼ ▼ ▼ ▼ ▼ ▼ ▼ ▼ ▼ ▼ ▼ ▼ ▼ ▼ ▼ ▼ ▼ ▼ ▼ ▼ ▼ ▼ ▼ ▼ ▼ ▼ ▼

## Adding transparency to a gradient

By default, a gradient has 100 percent opacity in the start color and progresses to 100 percent opacity in the end color. If you like, you can have the gradient fade out to transparency so that the portion of the image under the gradient shows through. To add transparency to a gradient, follow these steps.

**1.** Create a single or multicolor gradient as described in the two previous sections.

**2.** Select the left Transparency stop.

This stop is located just above the gradient bar, as shown in Figure 3-7.

**3.** Use the Opacity slider to specify the amount of transparency for the gradient at its start point.

You can also type a value into the Opacity box.

**4.** Select the right transparency stop and use the Opacity slider or text box to specify transparency for the gradient at its end point.

**5.** Move the Opacity stops to the right or left to adjust the position where each stop's opacity setting is applied.

**6.** Click above the gradient bar to add more Opacity stops if you want to vary the transparency of the gradient at different points.

For example, you could fade transparency from 100 percent to 50 percent back to 100 percent to produce a particular effect.

 Gradients will ordinarily proceed smoothly from one color to another. If you'd like a less homogeneous appearance, adjust the Smoothness slider to a value of less than 100 percent.

C\ONTINUED
▼ ▼ ▼ ▼

**Figure 3-7**

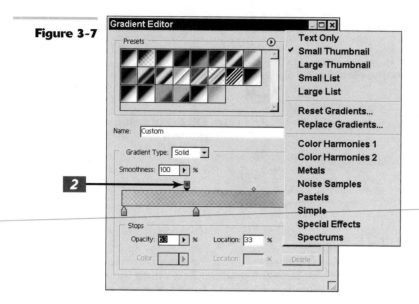

## Managing and Saving Gradients

If you're smart, you'll want to store the gradients you create so that you can use or edit them again later. Here are some tips for managing your gradients:

✔ To save a gradient, click the Save button in the Gradient Editor dialog box. The current presets, including your new gradient, can be saved under the current library's name or another one that you choose.

✔ To load gradient presets into the Gradient Editor, click the Load button and select the name of the gradient library you want to add to the Presets list.

✔ To add an additional set of presets to the current presets, choose the name of the presets from the Gradient Editor's pop-up menu.

For more information about managing gradient presets with the Preset Manager, see Book I, Chapter 6.

## Working with Patterns

*Patterns* are textures or repeating configurations of pixels that you can use to fill selections or layers, apply with painting tools, smear around your image with the Pattern Stamp, or use as a basis for the Healing Brush and Patch tools. Photoshop offers a large selection of patterns, and you can create your own in two different ways.

You select patterns from palettes that appear in the Options bar for many of the tools just mentioned, much like brush tips and gradients, and you manage them in much the same way, using the Preset Manager (see Book I, Chapter 6). The following sections show you how to apply a preset pattern and create your own.

▼ ▼ ▼ ▼ ▼ ▼ ▼ ▼ ▼ ▼ ▼ ▼ ▼ ▼ ▼ ▼ ▼ ▼ ▼ ▼ ▼ ▼ ▼ ▼ ▼ ▼ ▼ ▼ ▼ ▼ ▼ ▼ ▼ ▼ ▼

## Applying a preset pattern

Although you can apply patterns by using many different tools, this chapter sticks with applying patterns as fills. To fill a layer or selection with a preset pattern, follow these steps.

1. **Choose the layer or selection you want to fill with a pattern.**

2. **Choose Edit⇨File and select Pattern from the Contents pop-up list.**

3. **In the Custom Pattern palette, select the pattern you want to fill with.**

   ✔ Choose a pattern from the current palette, as shown in Figure 3-8.

   ✔ Replace the current patterns with new patterns by choosing Replace Patterns from the palette menu. Then choose the new pattern library from the dialog box that appears.

   ✔ Append new patterns to the current set by choosing Load Patterns from the palette menu (click the right-pointing triangle at the right side of the dialog box).

   ✔ Append one of the preset libraries furnished with Photoshop by choosing the pattern from the list at the bottom of the palette menu.

4. **Choose any other Fill options you want to apply, such as Mode, Opacity, or Preserve Transparency.**

5. **Click OK to fill the layer or selection with the chosen pattern.**

Book **IV**
Chapter **3**

**Figure 3-8**

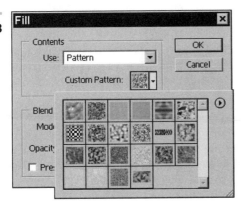

▼▼▼▼▼▼▼▼▼▼▼▼▼▼▼▼▼▼▼▼▼▼▼▼▼▼▼▼▼▼▼▼▼▼▼▼▼▼▼▼▼▼

## Creating a new pattern

You can create your own new pattern, basing it on an existing image or on one you create yourself. Select a small portion of an image to build an abstract pattern, or use a recognizable object to define that object as a pattern stamp. Anything from a logo to your signature can be used as a pattern.

To create your own pattern, follow these steps:

**1.** **Open the image that contains the area you want to use as a pattern, or create an image from scratch.**

**2.** **Make any modifications to the image to produce the exact pattern that you want.**

**3.** **Use the Rectangular Marquee to select the area you want converted into a pattern.**

 You have to use a rectangular selection.

**4.** **Choose Edit⇨Define Pattern.**

The Define Pattern dialog box opens.

**5.** **Enter a name for your pattern in the Define Pattern dialog box.**

Your new pattern appears in the Pattern palette for use.

## Using the Pattern Maker filter

The Pattern Maker filter is an advanced tool that provides even more ways to customize your patterns. An easy-to-use dialog box, shown in Figure 3-9, helps you build a pattern that will fill an entire layer of your choice. The cool part is that you can create a whole series of different patterns and review them to find the one you like best.

 As with creating a pattern from a selection, you must use a rectangular shape to build your new pattern.

The most valuable feature of the Pattern Maker is that it creates patterns that will tile smoothly. That is, you can repeat the pattern as many times as you need to fill an area, and the boundaries between sections will blend together smoothly.

The filter's dialog box has lots of features. Here's a quick description of them:

✔ **Tool palette:** In the upper-left corner is a small tool palette, containing a Rectangular Marquee tool you can use to select the area to derive the pattern from; a Zoom tool to magnify or reduce the image (you can also press the Shift+Alt [Shift+Option on the Mac] and Shift+Ctrl [Shift+⌘ on the Mac] shortcuts to zoom in and out); and a Hand tool to move the image around in the viewing window.

✔ **Status bar:** Along the bottom edge is a status bar that shows the following bits of information:

- ▶ Magnification of the preview

- ▶ Width and height of the whole image in pixels

- ▶ Tile grid, the number of copies of the image that will be needed to fill the entire selected layer

- ▶ Sample, the width and height in pixels of the current image area selected by the Marquee tool

- ▶ Preview, the number of different patterns you've generated so far from the current sample (more on this in a bit)

✔ **Tile Generation:** This area shows the size of the tiled image that will be created, the type of offset used (horizontal, vertical, or none); and the amount of smoothness and detail in the sample picture.

✔ **Preview:** This area governs whether the preview window shows the original image or the patterns you generate, and whether the patterns are separated by a boundary.

✔ **Tile History:** This area provides a slide show of all the patterns you generate.

Book
***IV***
Chapter
***3***

**Figure 3-9**

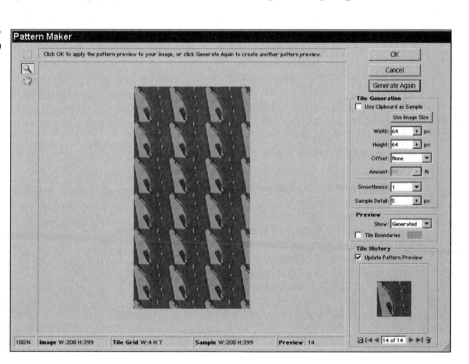

▼▼▼▼▼▼▼▼▼▼▼▼▼▼▼▼▼▼▼▼▼▼▼▼▼▼▼▼▼▼▼▼▼▼▼▼▼

## Generating a pattern

To create a pattern using this filter, just follow these steps:

*1.* **To apply a pattern to an existing image, first make a copy of the layer that contains the image area you want to convert to a pattern.**

To apply the pattern to a new image, select the area you want to use with the Rectangular Marquee tool and choose Edit⇨Copy. Then choose File⇨New, choose Custom from the New File dialog box, click OK to create the new file, and then paste the selection in the new image.

*2.* **Choose Filter⇨Pattern Maker.**

*3.* **Select the area to be used as the basis for the pattern.**

*4.* **If you're creating the pattern in the current layer, choose the Rectangular Marquee tool from the dialog box's Tool palette, and select the portion of the image you want to convert to a pattern.**

You can drag the selection marquee around the image, use the zoom features to change the magnification, or drag the image around by using the Hand tool.

*5.* **If you want to completely fill the layer with tiled versions of the pattern, specify the size of the tile by typing values into the Width and Height boxes in the Tile Generation area. You can also enter the offset to use and the amount of offset. If you'd rather have only a single, non-tiled image, click the Use Image Size button.**

*6.* **Set other options:**

   ✔ **Smoothness.** Set a value to determine how smooth the edges of the patterns are blended with the surrounding tiles.

   ✔ **Sample Detail.** This parameter controls the maximum size of details in the pattern.

   ✔ **Preview.** Choose whether to display the original image or the generated patterns in the preview window.

   ✔ **Tile Boundaries.** If you want, you can insert a line between tiled images to show their boundaries. Select the Tile Boundaries option and, if you like, choose a color for the boundary that will show up well against your sampled image.

*7.* **Click the Generate button to create a pattern from your selection. You can click the button multiple times to create multiple pattern variations.**

All the different patterns you generate are displayed in the Tile History panel in the lower-right corner of the dialog box.

You can review patterns in a slide-show manner by clicking the Previous, Next, First, and Last arrows.

**8.** If you see a pattern you want to save, click the floppy disk icon at the bottom-left edge of the Tile History panel.

**9.** You can get rid of patterns that you don't like by selecting them and then double-clicking the trash can icon in the lower-right edge.

Tile History can save up to 20 generated patterns.

**10.** Click OK when you've saved all the patterns you want to reuse.

A typical pattern is shown in Figure 3-10.

**Figure 3-10**

# Creating and Editing Type

Photoshop has morphed into a surprisingly good tool for creating type used in images. The last few releases have added features that let you create paragraphs of text or simple lines of text used as headlines or labels. You can change the spacing between characters, warp your type, check your spelling, or even create selections in the shape of text. Drop shadows, beveled type, and other special effects are yours quickly and easily.

So, if an old-timer tells you, "Photoshop is for photos; use Adobe Illustrator to create text," take that advice with a grain of salt. Use Adobe Illustrator to create professional layouts in which you can keep text and image files separate, combining images and text when the project is printed. But if what you're looking for is a great-looking image that includes great-looking text, Photoshop can do the job.

This chapter introduces you to Photoshop's Type tools. If you want to get fancy, check out Chapter 5 in this book, which explains some of our favorite image editor's more advanced capabilities.

## Selecting a Type Mode

The text you create in Photoshop can be categorized in several different ways, but ultimately, you're either adding just a little text (like a word or single line of text) or a lot (maybe a paragraph or two). Accordingly, Photoshop separates type into two modes:

➦ **Point type:** Use this mode to create a headline or label. You can create point type by clicking in your image and typing; the line appears as you type and grows to whatever length is needed (even if that length is wider or taller than your image). Point type never wraps around to a new line.

✔ **Paragraph type:** Use this mode to create long descriptions in an image. It's (unsurprisingly) similar to the kind of type you're accustomed to working with in word processing programs. In Paragraph mode, all the text goes into a resizable box, and if a line is too long, Photoshop automatically wraps it around to the next line.

The point type and paragraph type modes each operate a bit differently, although they share many features and options. I explain each of them separately later in this chapter.

## Understanding Different Kinds of Type

Whether you're using Point type mode or Paragraph type mode, you can choose several type options, each designed to help you work with, display, print, and edit text. These options determine how Photoshop expresses text in a file:

✔ **Vector type:** All text in Photoshop is initially created as *vector* type. Vector type provides scalable outlines that can be resized without producing jaggy edges in the diagonal strokes. You can also edit type in this mode, adding or subtracting characters and correcting typos.

✔ **Rasterized type:** When vector type is converted into pixels, it's *rasterized*. When text is rasterized, it is no longer editable, but is, rather, a frozen picture of what the text looks like. When you've finished editing vector type and are ready to merge the text with the other pixels in an image (or to perform some manipulations that can only be done with pixel text), you transform the vector type into pixels by rasterizing it. You can't resize rasterized type without losing some quality or risking a bad case of the jaggies. For more on rasterized type, see Chapter 5 of this book.

✔ **Pixel fonts:** Pixel fonts are tiny fonts designed for display at small sizes on computer screens. Unlike traditional fonts, which don't fit into the natural pixel grid of your screen (and thus look rough at small sizes, particularly when they're anti-aliased), pixel fonts are designed so every pixel corresponds to a pixel on your screen. These fonts, with names like MINI 7, MiniSerif, and Tenacity, are created in fixed sizes (say, 7 pixels high for MINI 7 or 10 pixels high for Tenacity and PixelDust). Diagonal lines are avoided as much as possible, with the font designs favoring horizontal and vertical strokes. As a result, pixel fonts look crisp and clear at small sizes without anti-aliasing. Indeed, you shouldn't use anti-aliasing with pixel fonts, nor should you attempt to resize or rescale them. You can buy or download pixel fonts, install them on your computer, and use them just as you would use other fonts, keeping in mind they look their best at their fixed size. You can see an example of a pixel font compared to a traditional font in Figure 4-1.

 Photoshop treats pixel fonts as if they were vector type, creating them on their own type layer that must be rasterized. However, pixel fonts look and behave more like bit-mapped raster fonts; you can't resize them easily. You'll find them easier to work with if you change your font measurement unit to pixels; choose Edit⇨Preferences⇨Units & Rulers (or Photoshop⇨ Preferences⇨Units & Rulers under Mac OS X) and choose Pixels from the Type menu.

**Figure 4-1**

this is pixeldust, a pixel font only 10
pixels high, designed to be readable
at very small sizes.

It's useful for web pages and other
applications calling for tiny fonts.

IN CONTRAST, A FONT LIKE THIS EXAMPLE
OF GARAMOND AT 10 POINTS, DOES NOT LOOK
NEARLY AS CLEAR AND CRISP.

## Exploring the Type Tools

Strictly speaking, Photoshop has four type tools (found in the Tools palette), but two of them are simply vertically oriented versions of the main two text implements. You can use either Paragraph or Point text mode with any of the type tools:

- ✔ **Horizontal Type tool:** Use this tool to enter point or paragraph type oriented horizontally on your screen. If you want text that is oriented at an angle other than vertical, you can rotate it by choosing Edit⇔Rotate after the text has been entered. This tool creates the type on its own Type layer, except when used in Bitmap, Multichannel, or Indexed Color modes, which don't support layers. (Book II, Chapter 2 covers these modes.)

- ✔ **Vertical Type tool:** Use this tool to enter point type oriented in a vertical column. You can also use the Vertical Type tool to create columns of paragraph text, but the results look a little strange. After you've entered your text columns, you can rotate the text to an orientation other than vertical by choosing Edit⇔Rotate. Like the Horizontal Type tool, this tool creates type in its own Type layer, except with file modes that don't support layers.

- ✔ **Horizontal Type Mask tool/Vertical Type Mask tool:** These tools operate identically to their siblings described in the two preceding bullets, with two exceptions. Instead of adding filled type, both the Horizontal and Vertical Type Mask tools create a selection border in the shape of the type you enter. Both tools add a selection mask to the current active layer. You can do anything with a type selection that you can do with any other selection, including saving it for reuse later. You'll find a longer discussion of the type mask tools in Chapter 5 in this book.

The Horizontal and Vertical Type tools have some interesting options, which I explore in the next section. There are also controls you can set by using the Paragraph and Character palettes, which are discussed later in this chapter.

▼▼▼▼▼▼▼▼▼▼▼▼▼▼▼▼▼▼▼▼▼▼▼▼▼▼▼▼▼▼▼▼▼▼▼▼▼▼▼▼▼▼▼▼▼▼

## Entering Text in Point Type Mode

If you're image oriented (and why wouldn't you be if you're using Photoshop?), you're probably not planning to include a novella with your graphics.

Point type is great for callouts, labels, and similar small amounts of text. You can also use it to create logos and headings for Web pages. The Web is one place that text that isn't tack-sharp can still do the job. Unlike paragraph text, however, you can't easily resize point type.

 Although a Photoshop image is generally not the place you'll want to insert a whole lot of text, you can add larger blocks of text that are professional and effective — read "Entering Text in Paragraph Type Mode," later in this chapter. You can modify how point type and paragraph type are displayed by using the Paragraph and Character palettes.

To enter point type, just follow these steps:

**1.** **Open a saved image or create a new Photoshop document.**

**2.** **Select either the Horizontal or Vertical Type tool from the Tool palette, or press T to select the type tool if the one you want is active.**

Hold down the Shift key and press T to cycle through the four available type tools until the one that you want is active.

Your cursor looks like an I-beam, similar to one you'd see in a word processing program. (See Figure 4-2.)

**3.** **Click the area of the image where you want to insert the text.**

This is called the insertion point.

A small horizontal line about one-third of the way up the I-beam shows where the baseline (on which the line of text rests) will be for horizontal type. If you've selected the Vertical Type tool, the cursor is rotated 90 degrees. The

baseline is centered in the I-beam and represents the center axis of the vertical column of text you type.

**4.** **Choose any of the type options from the Options bar, Character palette, or Paragraph palette.**

I describe these options later in the chapter.

**5.** **Type your text. Press Enter (or Return on the Mac) to begin a new line.**

Lines of point type don't wrap around. When you press Enter/Return, you're inserting a hard carriage return that doesn't move. You have to remove hard returns if you want to change the length of the lines you type.

**6.** **When you've finished entering the text, click the Commit button in the Options bar.**

A new type layer with your text is created.

## Committing type to a type layer

To commit your type to its type layer, you can also do any of the following in addition to clicking the Commit button:

✔ Press Enter on the numeric keypad (the main Enter/Return key starts a new line or paragraph, instead).

✔ Hold down the Ctrl key (or the ⌘ key on the Mac) and press the main Enter key (Return key on the Mac).

✔ Click any other tool in the Tool palette. You don't actually have to use the tool, but you must click the tool (as opposed to pressing the keyboard shortcut that's associated with the tool).

✔ Click in the Layers, Channels, Paths, Actions, History, or Styles palettes.

✔ Select any menu command.

**Figure 4-2**

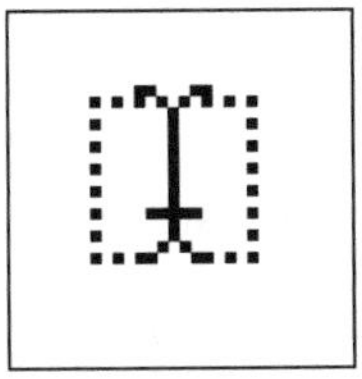

# Entering Text in Paragraph Type Mode

Paragraphs are best allocated to captions or text descriptions that accompany an image. Large amounts of text in an image don't look their best because when you rasterize the type, even the most carefully entered text may have a fuzzy look.

Paragraph type is similar to the text you're accustomed to entering within a word processing program, except that it's contained inside a border, called a text box or a *bounding box*. As you type into a text box, the lines of text wrap around to fit the dimensions of the box. If you resize the box, the wrapped ends are adjusted to account for the new size.

You can type multiple paragraphs, use typographical controls, and rotate or scale the type. Unlike point type, paragraph type can be easily resized by entering a new point size value in the Character dialog box without having to reselect all the text.

To enter paragraph type, follow these steps:

**1.** Open a saved image or create a new Photoshop document.

**2.** Select either the Horizontal or Vertical Type tool from the Tool palette, or press T to select the type tool if the one you want is active.

Hold down the Shift key and press T to cycle through the four available type tools until the one you want is active.

Your cursor looks like an I-beam, similar to one you'd see in a word processing program.

**3.** Insert and size the text box by using one of the following methods:

  ✔ Drag to create a text box of an arbitrary size. After you release the mouse button, you can drag any of the handles at the corners and sides of the box to customize the size.

  ✔ Hold down the Alt key (Option key on the Mac) and drag a box of any size. The Paragraph Text Size dialog box appears. You can enter the exact dimensions of the box you want to create. When you click OK, a bounding box of the size you specified appears, complete with handles for resizing the box later, if you choose.

**4.** Choose the type options you want from the Options bar, or Character or Paragraph palettes.

**5.** Enter your text. To start a new paragraph, press Enter (or Return on the Mac).

CONTINUED

Each line wraps around to fit inside the bounding box, as you can see in Figure 4-3.

If you type more text than fits in the text box, an overflow icon appears. You can resize the text box by gripping any of the eight handles and dragging.

**6.** **Click the Commit button.**

A new type layer is created.

You can also use any of the options in the "Committing type to a type layer" sidebar, earlier in this chapter.

**Figure 4-3**

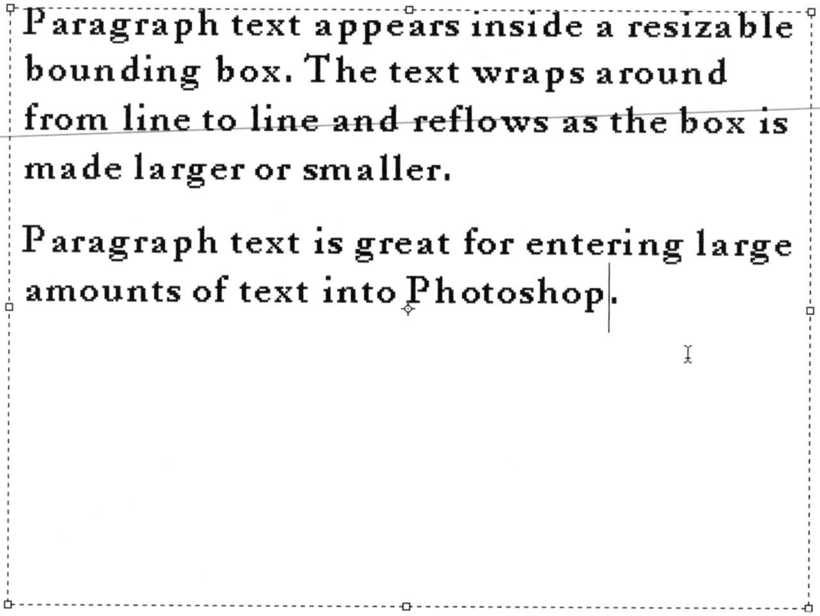

Paragraph text appears inside a resizable bounding box. The text wraps around from line to line and reflows as the box is made larger or smaller.

Paragraph text is great for entering large amounts of text into Photoshop.

## Using the Options Bar

The Options bar, shown in Figure 4-4, contains a group of options, some (but not all) of which are duplicated in the Character palette. Those options that appear in both places are the most frequently used options. Talk about convenience.

Your options, shown from left to right in Figure 4-4 (starting after the Text pop-up menu), include

**Figure 4-4**

✔ **Toggle Vertical/Horizontal Type tools:** Use this handy button to toggle between vertical and horizontal type orientations. Just select the type layer you'd like to transform and click. This option works with point type and paragraph type, although the results you get from switching the paragraph type to vertical orientation may not please you.

✔ **Font family:** Choose the font/typeface you want from the drop-down list. If more than one version of a particular font family is installed on your computer, you'll find one of these abbreviations after the font name: T1, Adobe Type 1 (PostScript) fonts; TT (TrueType); OT (OpenType); BM (Bit-Mapped).

✔ **Font weight:** The term *weight* is the traditional term for a particular font's style, but the options are familiar enough. While fonts can have additional weights, such as light or demi-bold, most other styles are assigned as separate typefaces. Only the weights available for a particular font appear in the list. Some are available only in regular and italic, for example.

> If a font you want to use doesn't offer bold or italic styles, you can simulate either or both by choosing a faux style in the Character palette.

✔ **Type size:** Choose the size of the type from this list, or type in a size in the text box. Generally, type sizes are shown in points because that's how type is most commonly measured, with 72 points equaling 1 inch. (A 36 point font is ½-inch in size at 72 ppi.)

Book *IV* Chapter **4**

> If you don't like points, you can switch to millimeters or pixels in the Units and Rulers Preferences dialog box. (You can find instructions for doing this in Book I, Chapter 6.) You might want to use, say, pixels instead of points when creating text for Web graphics. If you're creating a banner that is 100 pixels tall, you will know that text that is 25 pixels tall will fill 25 percent of that space, for example.

✔ **Anti-aliasing:** This list includes four different types of smoothing to use on your text, plus *none* (which leaves your text unsmoothed). Some kinds of anti-aliasing are better for type that will be displayed at smaller sizes.

✔ **Text alignment:** Three buttons specify whether your Horizontal Type tool text is aligned flush left, centered, or flush right. When you use the Vertical Type tool, the buttons rotate 90 degrees clockwise and are transformed into Flush Top, Centered (vertically), and Flush Bottom choices.

✔ **Text color:** Click in this box to select a color for your text from the Color Picker.

✔ **Warp text:** This option lets you warp and bend text by using 15 different types of distortion. You can find out about all of them in Chapter 2 of this book. When used with Paragraph type, the bounding box warps on-screen, too, so you can see how the paragraph is being changed.

✔ **Toggle Character/Paragraph palettes:** Click this button any time a type tool is active to show or hide the Character and Paragraph palettes.

✔ **Cancel text entry:** Click this button (or press the Esc key) to cancel the text entry you're making. (This button is not shown in Figure 4-4.)

✔ **Commit:** Click this button to apply the text to a type layer. (This button is not shown in Figure 4-4.)

## *Working with the Character Palette*

The Character palette, shown in Figure 4-5, is a tabbed palette, usually paired with the Paragraph palette, which lets you format the appearance of individual type characters. Five of the options in the Character palette are exactly the same as those found in the Options bar. The duplicated features include

✔ Font family

✔ Weight

✔ Type size

✔ Anti-aliasing

✔ Text color

The other menus, buttons, and text boxes provide additional functions. I discuss these options in the following sections.

**Figure 4-5**

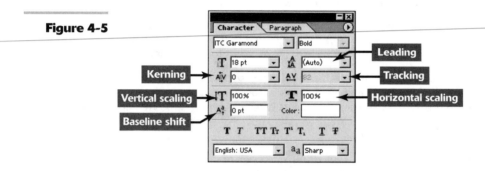

Leading

Tracking

Kerning

Vertical scaling

Horizontal scaling

Baseline shift

## Leading

*Leading* is the amount of space between the baselines of consecutive lines of type, usually measured in points. (The *baseline* is the imaginary line on which a line of type rests.) You can choose a specific amount of leading or allow Photoshop to determine the amount automatically by choosing Auto from the Leading menu.

Wider line spacing can make text easier to read (as long as you don't go overboard!) or be used for artistic effect. Tighter line spacing makes for more compact text but can decrease readability if you go too far.

When Auto leading is specified, Photoshop takes the type size and uses a value of 120 percent. So the baselines of 10 point type would be spaced 12 points apart. You can change this automatic value by clicking the Paragraph palette and choosing Justify from the palette's menu. A dialog box appears with several values. Type the amount you want in the Auto Leading box. If all this seems confusing, I recommend experimenting with leading to get a true idea of how various values affect the space between lines of text.

## Tracking

*Tracking* is the amount of space between letters in a string or line. You can specify tight tracking to squeeze all the letters together more closely, or loose tracking to let them spread out a bit.

 Don't confuse tracking with *kerning*, which deals with the space between two individual letters. Tracking sets a value to evenly space all the letters you select, and kerning helps you close or widen the gap between two individual letters.

One use for tracking is to help lines of text fit a specified horizontal space, and you can make this technique work if you use it judiciously. Beginners typically overdo tracking, squeezing letters together so tightly they touch, or spreading them apart so that wide gaps appear. You can see examples of tracking in Figure 4-6.

**Figure 4-6**

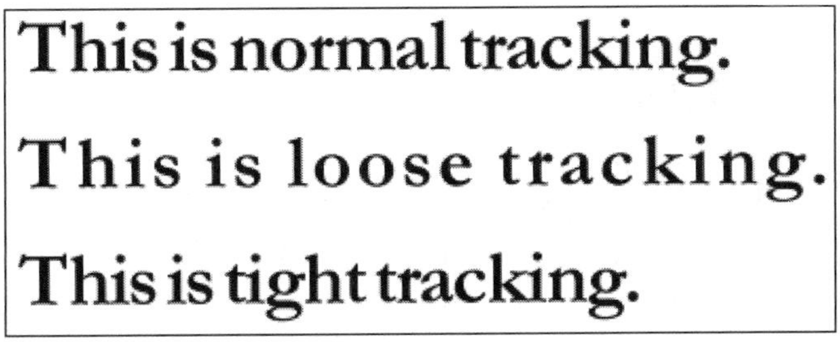

> This is normal tracking.
>
> This is loose tracking.
>
> This is tight tracking.

To track a set of characters or a line, select the text you want to squeeze or expand, and either choose a value from 0 to –100, or 0 to 200, from the Track menu, or type in a specific value in the Track text box. Each unit is equal to $\frac{1}{1,000}$ of an em (the width of an em dash in a particular typeface), so a setting of –100 would reduce the space between characters by $\frac{1}{10}$ the width of an em dash (quite a lot!).

## Kerning

*Kerning* is a technique for adding or removing space between pairs of letters to make them fit together more closely and aesthetically. For example, the letters A and V are a natural fit and often look better when kerned slightly. If you choose Metrics from the Kern menu, Photoshop automatically tries to kern the characters to provide an attractive look, like that shown in Figure 4-7.

**Figure 4-7**

> Unkerned
>
> Kerned

To manually kern letters, click at a point between the two characters and either choose a percentage from 0 to –100, or 0 to 200, from the Kern menu, or type in a specific value in the Kern text box. As with the Track menu, the values represent $\frac{1}{1,000}$ of an em.

## Vertical and Horizontal scale

The Vertical and Horizontal Scale options represent the relationship between the height and width of the text. By default, this relationship is 100 percent. If you wanted to make the width of the type proportionately 50 percent more than the height, you'd enter 150 percent into the Horizontal Scale box. You can see examples of scaling in Figure 4-8.

**Figure 4-8**

> # Text at 100% Scale
> ## Vertical Scale 50%
> ### Horizontal Scale 50%

## Baseline shift and text attributes

The Baseline option adjusts the height above or below a typeface's normal baseline that the text appears. This option is usually used to create superscripts and subscripts.

A bar with eight buttons in the Character palette lets you to turn on or off several type attributes with a single click. The text attributes are as follows, from left to right in Figure 4-9:

- **Faux Bold/Faux Italic:** Some fonts don't have true bold or italic options; Photoshop can fake either or both of these if you click the appropriate button. Faux fonts can look good, except at smaller sizes.

- **All Caps:** This button changes the case of the characters in selected text to all capitals, or back to their normal case when you turn it off.

- **Small Caps:** Small caps are uppercase letters about the size of lowercase letters in a font. They are most frequently used for acronyms and abbreviations, such as NASA or AM/PM because they are less obtrusive than full-size caps in text passages. Click this button, and Photoshop will either use the small caps characters built into many fonts or will create faux small caps for you.

- **Superscript:** Click this button to raise a character automatically to create a superscript, as in $E=MC^2$. You'll probably also want to reduce the size of the character.

- **Subscript:** Click this button to lower the character below the baseline, creating a subscript. Usually, subscripts are reduced in size, as in $H_2O$.

- **Underline:** Click this button to underline the selected characters, like <u>this</u>.

- **Strikethrough:** Click the button to provide a ~~strikethrough~~ effect to the selected characters. In legal applications, strikethrough is widely used to show sections that have been removed, but in their original context.

- **Character Set:** Use this option to select the language you want to use for Photoshop's spell checker. It includes variations, such as USA English or British English, and French or Canadian French.

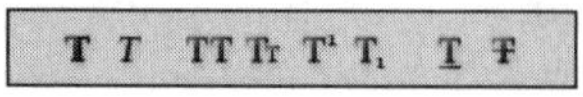

**Figure 4-9**

> **T** *T*  TT T̲t  T' T,   T̲ T̶

# *Working with the Paragraph Palette*

The Paragraph palette, shown in Figure 4-10, can be used to format any or all paragraphs in a type layer. Simply select the paragraph or paragraphs that you want to format by clicking in an individual paragraph. You can drag a selection to select multiple paragraphs; or click a type layer containing the paragraphs to format all of them at once.

 The Paragraph palette's options menu gives you access to Justification and Hyphenation dialog boxes. You can use these to customize the default settings Photoshop uses for these functions.

**Figure 4-10**

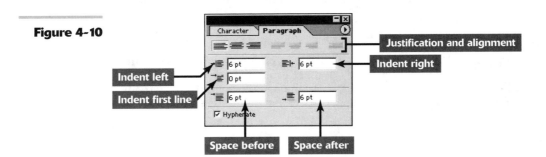

Justification and alignment

Indent right

Indent left

Indent first line

Space before    Space after

Book
**IV**
Chapter
**4**

## Changing paragraph alignment

At the top of the Paragraph palette, you see a set of five alignment buttons. Three are used to align nonjustified text. They include the following:

- **Flush left, ragged right:** All text is even with the left margin and allowed to be ragged on the right side of the column.
- **Centered:** Text is evenly centered in its column and ragged on both right and left edges.
- **Flush right, ragged left:** All text is even with the right margin and allowed to be ragged on the left side.

 With vertical type, these choices align the text to the top, a center axis, and the bottom of a column.

## Changing paragraph justification

The other four options produce justified text, in which Photoshop inserts spaces between characters as necessary so each line is flush on both left and right sides. The options apply only to the last line of text in each paragraph. You can choose to make this last line flush left, flush right, centered, or force justified on both sides with spaces inserted by Photoshop. This last option sometimes calls for some manual tweaking to avoid a final line that is squeezed or expanded too much.

 With vertical type, the justification choices are top aligns, center aligns, bottom aligns, or force justifies the last line of text.

### Changing paragraph indentation

The next three options let you enter an amount of indentation between the sides of the text bounding box and the actual text. You can specify the amount of indentation from the left, right, and for the first line of the paragraph (creating a first line that is indented more than the others in the paragraph). For vertical type, the indentations are rotated 90 degrees.

### Changing spacing between paragraphs

The next two options let you specify the amount of space between paragraphs. You can specify the amount of space before every paragraph, the amount after every paragraph, or both.

### Breaking long words across two lines

The final option in the Paragraph palette is the Hyphenation check box, which specifies whether Photoshop hyphenates words that are too long to fit on a line or leaves them intact. Turning hyphenation on can avoid awkward spacing, particularly with justified text that would otherwise contain a lot more spaces between characters to make a line fit.

▼▼▼▼▼▼▼▼▼▼▼▼▼▼▼▼▼▼▼▼▼▼▼▼▼▼▼▼▼▼▼▼▼▼▼▼▼

## Editing Text

You can apply all the options described in this chapter as you enter text, or later, when you're rearranging words or fixing typos and other errors.

To make changes to the text itself, just follow these steps:

1. Open a saved image or create a new Photoshop document.

2. Select the Type tool.

3. Select the type layer you want to modify, or click in the type in the document.

4. You can begin typing at the place you clicked, backspace to eliminate characters, or drag the mouse from the insertion point to select characters to copy, delete, or format.

5. When you're done entering your changes, click the Commit button.

▼▼▼▼▼▼▼▼▼▼▼▼▼▼▼▼▼▼▼▼▼▼▼▼▼▼▼▼▼▼▼▼▼▼▼▼▼

### Finding and replacing text

You can make global changes in a text layer, switching all occurrences of a set of characters to another string. For example, you might have typed **Ghandi** a few dozen times before remembering that the Mahatma's name is spelled Gandhi. To replace text, follow these steps:

1. Open a saved image or create a new Photoshop document.

2. Select the type layer you want to modify.

3. Choose Edit➪Find and Replace.

   The Find and Replace Text dialog box appears, as shown in Figure 4-11.

**4.** Type or paste the text you want to replace in the Find What box in the dialog box.

**5.** Enter the replacement text in the Change To box.

**6.** If you want the search to locate only text that exactly matches the case of the Find string (that is *FREEdom* but not *Freedom*), choose the Case Sensitive option.

**7.** To ignore the search word embedded in another word (say, to find *the* but not *there* or *they*), choose Whole Word Only.

**8.** Click Find Next.

**9.** As each string is found, select whether you want to

✔ **Change:** This changes only the string of text just located. Click this button if there was one particular occurrence you were looking for.

✔ **Change/Find:** This changes the found text and then looks for the next occurrence.

✔ **Change All:** This changes all occurrences of the search text with the replacement string in your text.

**Figure 4-11**

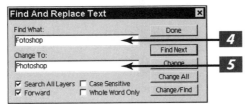

## Checking your spelling

Photoshop can check your spelling by using an internal dictionary that you can update with words of your own. Even though you're not likely to enter huge amounts of text in Photoshop, that's no excuse for misspelling the words that you *do* include. Indeed, because it's so difficult to change text after you've rasterized a text layer, the spell checker can save you a great deal of work. Here's how to use it:

**1.** Open a saved image or create a new Photoshop document.

**2.** Make sure that you've specified the correct language in the Character palette's language menu.

**3.** Select the text that you want to check, or select a type layer to check all the text on that layer.

**4.** Choose Edit⇨Check Spelling.

**5.** When Photoshop identifies a possible error in the Not in Dictionary box, click Change to substitute the recommended correction for the word that is spelled incorrectly.

Or you can choose from one of these options:

✔ **Ignore:** Leaves the word alone and continues to check the next text.

CONTINUED
▼ ▼ ▼ ▼ ▼

✔ **Ignore All:** Ignores all instances of the word for the rest of the spell-check session.

✔ **Suggestions:** Choose a different word from the Suggestions text box, or type in the correct spelling yourself.

✔ **Change All:** Corrects all occurrences of the misspelled word.

✔ **Add:** Adds the unfamiliar word to Photoshop's dictionary.

The Check Spelling dialog box is shown in Figure 4-12.

 Deselect the Check All Layers option to check only the currently selected layer.

6. **Click Done when you're finished.**

The Check Spelling dialog box closes.

**Figure 4-12**

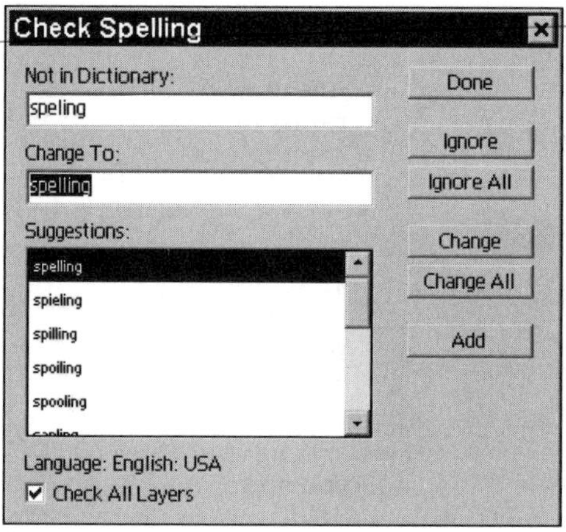

**Check Spelling** ☒

Not in Dictionary:

| speling |

Change To:

| spelling |

Suggestions:

| spelling |
| spieling |
| spilling |
| spoiling |
| spooling |

Language: English: USA
☑ Check All Layers

[Done]
[Ignore]
[Ignore All]
[Change]
[Change All]
[Add]

# Masking, Shaping, and Warping Type

You can do a lot more with type than create labels, captions, or paragraphs of text. Type can become an integral part of the decorative design, especially when you stylize, warp, or otherwise transform it in interesting ways.

Your Photoshop text can have character, too, communicating messages with more than just words. The text of a beach scene can appear to be wavy or watery and translucent. Halloween type can take on a ghostly or spooky appearance. Type can be romantic, otherworldly, cheerful, or comical. It all depends on how you create and apply it.

This chapter shows you some of the tricks you can perform by masking, warping, and shaping your type so your words come to life and add something special to your images.

## Playing with Type Layer Opacity

Layers, are the stacks of overlays on which each of the elements of your image reside. (Check out Book V, Chapter 1, for the lowdown on layers.) You can change the transparency of a type layer the same as you can with any other layer in Photoshop, reducing the opacity (transparency) of the type so it allows the underlying layer to show through. Take a look at the teaser business card I created for a new (imaginary) theatrical production, as shown in Figure 5-1. The main text is bold and black, but an underlying idea, "A Star Is Born!" is shown with a layer of text set to an opacity of 36 percent.

Changing the opacity of a type layer can convey an idea of gradual visibility of words onto an image. When working with opacity in multiple layers of type, you can create a sort of nonanimated fade in, especially when you experiment with several font types and styles, each with a greater opacity. Figure 5-2 shows an example of this effect.

Figure 5-1

Figure 5-2

One way to alter the transparency of type is to use a layer mask. (Check out Book VI, Chapter 3, for more information on layer masks.) Why would you want to use the layer mask instead of simply applying a gradient to the type itself? In practice, you can't apply a gradient to a type layer until the type has been rasterized (as described later in the chapter). By fading the type with a layer mask, you can customize your fading effect as much as you like and still edit the text to change the wording, type size, font, or anything else.

The first Putting-It-Together project in this chapter shows you another way to use type opacity to create a ghostly effect.

▼▼▼▼▼▼▼▼▼▼▼▼▼▼▼▼▼▼▼▼▼▼▼▼▼▼▼▼▼▼▼▼▼▼▼▼▼▼▼▼

# Creating Fade Effects

To create a "fade out" image, just follow these steps:

1. **Enter the words** Fading out slowly **(or other text of your choice) into a new type layer.**

   You find out how to enter text in Chapter 4 of this book.

2. **Choose Layer➪Add Layer Mask➪ Reveal All.**

   This creates a mask for the layer that can be used to show or hide some of the layer. With Reveal All selected, the

   layer defaults to showing everything on the layer without hiding any of it.

3. **Press D to make sure Photoshop's colors are the default black and white.**

4. **Choose the Gradient tool from the Tool palette.**

   Or press Shift+G until it is active.

5. **Select the Linear Gradient from the Options bar.**

**6.** Click the layer mask's icon in the Layers palette to make sure it is active.

**7.** Click the right side of the type layer and drag to the left side.

Photoshop creates a gradient in the layer mask that is black on the right and fades to white on the left, as

shown in Figure 5-3. That means the mask is most transparent on the left side (where it's white) and least transparent on the right side (where it's black). It reveals more of the original type on the left and fades it out on the right, as you can see in Figure 5-4 to the left of the words "Fading out slowly."

**Figure 5-3**

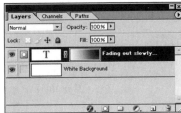

**Figure 5-4**

 **PUTTING IT TOGETHER**

### Ghosting Your Type

Need some ghostly, semitransparent type? You can twist, transmogrify, and transform your text by using Photoshop's arsenal of features.

You can create your type from scratch in an empty document or add the type to an existing picture or background. For the heck of it, these steps show you how to add ghostly writing to an existing image. Just follow these steps:

**1.** Open the background image you want to overlay with the ghost type.

The image I chose is already a little eerie because I reversed the colors

of the original picture like a negative by pressing Ctrl+I (⌘+I on the Mac) and then colorized the negative to its original orange hue. See Book VIII, Chapter 1, to find out how to colorize an image.

**2.** Choose the color you'd like to use for your text from the Swatches palette.

Black is a good Halloween complement to orange, but you can use any contrasting color.

**3.** Choose the Horizontal Type tool from the Tool palette and then click the area where you want to add the text.

▼ **CONTINUED**

▼ **CONTINUED**

The vertical cursor that appears is the same size that the text will be.

**4.** **Choose a type size from the drop-down list in the Options bar.**

**5.** **Choose a font and style for the font.**

You probably know the font *weight* as the style. Not every style (regular, italic, bold, or bold italic) is available for every font.

**6.** **Use anti-aliasing to select how you want Photoshop to smooth the edges of your type.**

Anti-aliasing, which I cover in Book IX, Chapter 1, softens a hard edge by adding partially-transparent pixels.

You can choose None (meaning you'll have jagged edges, also known as *jaggies*), Sharp, Crisp, Strong, or Smooth.

**7.** **Type your text.**

The text appears on top of the background.

**8.** **Click the check mark button on the Options bar to insert the text you've typed into a layer of its own.**

**9.** **Choose File⇨Save to save your finished image.**

You can make modifications to the type by using filters. You should save the project before moving forward. That way, if you don't like what you get, you don't have to keep it.

◎ To make additional changes to the text (such as to make it zig and zig, as I did in my example), use a filter. For example, if you want to make the text wavy, use the Wave filter in the Distort Type submenu.

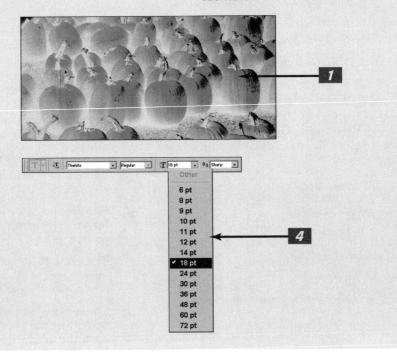

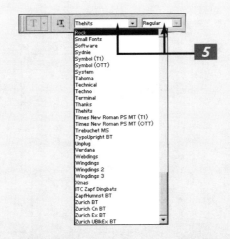

**_1._** **Choose Filter➪Distort➪ZigZag.**

The ZigZag dialog box opens.

Or you can choose other filters from the array discussed in Book VII.

A warning dialog box pops up informing you that the type layer must be *rasterized* (converted from editable text to pixels) before the filter can be used. Click OK.

**2.** **If you're using the ZigZag filter, choose an option from the Style drop-down list in the dialog box. Move the Amount slider to add as much distortion as you like.**

In my example, I chose Around Center from the Style drop-down list. I moved the Amount slider to 23 percent and adjusted the Ridges slider to increase waviness even more.

**3.** **Click OK to apply the distortion.**

**4.** **To change the opacity of the type (such as to make it semitranspar-ent), adjust the Opacity setting in the Layers palette.**

**_5._** **When you're satisfied with the look, save your image for additional editing later, or choose Layer➪Flatten Image to combine the text and background.**

▼ **CONTINUED**

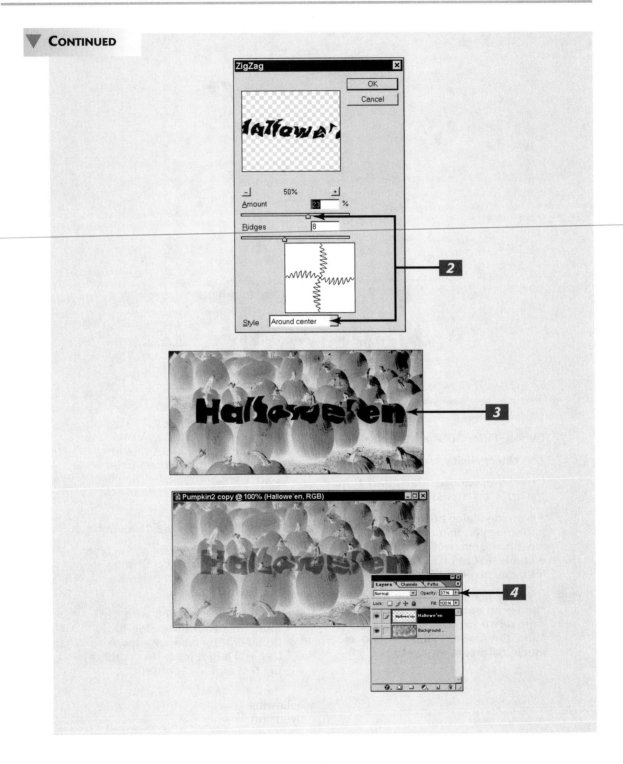

## Creating Type Outlines

In addition to its Vertical and Horizontal Type tools (discussed in Chapter 4 of this book), Photoshop includes Vertical and Horizontal Type Mask tools. These function almost identically to their conventional counterparts, with one important exception: Type mask tools don't create a new layer. Instead, they create a selection within the currently active layer, like the one shown in Figure 5-5.

**Figure 5-5**

You can treat the selections created with the type mask tools just as you can any other selection. Try the following:

- ✔ Move type mask selections around your document when any of the selection tools are active.

- ✔ Store type selections as alpha channels by using the Select⇨Save Selection command. I introduce selections in Book III, Chapter 3. You can find out how to save selections in Book VI, Chapter 1.

- ✔ Skew type selections (or change them in some other way) by using the Select⇨ Transform command. You can find more information on transforming selections in Book III, Chapter 3.

- ✔ Convert a selection into an editable path, as described in "Creating Vector-Based Type with Shapes," later in this chapter.

- ✔ Use the selection to cut or copy portions of an image in text-shaped chunks, as shown in Figure 5-6.

**Figure 5-6**

You can find out how this last suggestion works by following the steps in the Putting-It-Together project at the end of this chapter, in which you find out how to literally carve your words in stone.

# Rasterizing Your Type Layer

The Type tool creates editable type layers. You can change the wording, spacing, font, type size, and other factors as much as you want, as long as the type remains in a type layer. (For more information on editing type, see Chapter 4 in this book.)

However, after you've made all the changes you want, you need to convert your type layer to pixels in the form of rasterized type. After they're rasterized, you can apply filters, paint on the type, and apply gradients and patterns. Rasterizing type layers allows you to merge the type with other pixels in your image and, eventually, flatten the image to create a finished document suitable for use with other programs.

 **After you've converted your type to pixels, you can no longer edit the type. Nor can you resize the text without risking jaggies. You'll want to rasterize your type only when you're certain you won't need to edit or resize it. Better yet, save a copy of the document with type layers intact so you can return to that version if you need to.**

To rasterize your type, select the type layer that you want to convert to pixels. Then choose Layer➪Rasterize➪Type. The type is shown in the Layers palette on a transparent background.

# Creating Vector-Based Type with Shapes

By default, regular type created with the Type tool is vector-based type, not bitmapped type. You can also convert regular type (each character) to individual vector shapes. The individual characters then become shapes defined by vector masks. You can edit the shapes like any shapes created with the shape tools, by manipulating anchor points and straight and curved segments. And regular type can also be converted to work paths where each character becomes a path, editable like any other path with the selection arrows and pen tools. Type is usually converted into a path in order to create a clipping path based on the type (see Book III, Chapter 2).

 **In order to retain the vector properties of regular text, you must select the Include Vector Data option in the Save dialog box. Otherwise, Photoshop will rasterize the text upon saving.**

*Vector type* is type that has been converted to Photoshop line/curve-oriented shapes in the form of a vector mask or work path. You can find more information on vector type in Chapter 4 of this book, and more on working with paths in Book III, Chapter 2. You'd convert type to vectors in order to edit it with the Pen tools. Here are the ways to do that:

- ✔ To convert type to an editable work path, choose Layer➪Type➪Create Work Path. (You can also choose Make Work Path in the Paths palette option menu.)

- ✔ To convert type to shapes, choose Layer➪Type➪Convert to Shapes.

Here are the chief things to know about vector type:

- ✔ Like type layers, you can resize vector type without producing jagged diagonal lines.

✔ Unlike type layers, vector type has been transformed into pure shapes. You can edit the shape of the characters, but you cannot edit the text, as shown in Figure 5-7.

✔ You must rasterize vector type before you can merge it with pixel-based layers or apply special effects with filters. You can apply layer styles to vector type, however. Be sure to check out Book V, Chapter 4, for all you need to know about layer styles.

✔ Vector type becomes a vector mask exactly like other vector masks in Photoshop, and you can edit the shape of the characters by using the pen tools. You can find detailed information on editing vector masks in Book VI, Chapter 3.

**Figure 5-7**

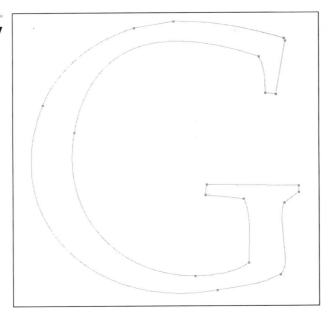

## Rasterizing type the other way

In addition to rasterizing a type layer in the usual way, you can also rasterize it by merging it with a non-type layer. For example, if your type layer appears immediately above a text layer that has already been rasterized, you can merge the layers by pressing Ctrl+E (⌘+E on the Mac).

You may also come across the opportunity to rasterize a type layer because Photoshop reminds you to. Some commands, for example, particularly filters, operate only on pixels. When you try to use them, you may see a warning dialog box. Often, the dialog box will include an option for immediately converting the type layer to raster form.

# Wreaking Havoc on Your Type

Photoshop's great automated Warp feature can twist your type in predictable ways that are not only repeatable but, thanks to the controls in their dialog boxes, customizable as well. The cool part is that even though type has been warped, it remains fully editable until you rasterize it. All you need to do to warp your text is click the Warp icon in the Options bar. This opens the multifaceted Warp Text dialog box, shown in Figure 5-8.

 Web developers take note: You cannot warp text that has Faux styles applied (found in the Character palette).

Figure 5-8

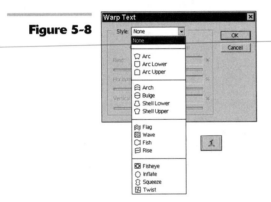

You'll find a whole list of special effects, such as Arc, Arch, Bulge, Flag, Wave, Fish, Fisheye, and Twist. Each of these effects provides a special look to your type, as shown in Figure 5-9.

Figure 5-9

Each effect has a dialog box of its own that allows you to set the parameters for the amount, direction, degree of distortion, amount of bend, and so forth. For example, the dialog box for the Shell Lower style is shown in Figure 5-10.

You can watch your type warp right on your display screen and tailor the distortion as you like. Most asymmetrical warp effects can be applied to type in either horizontal or vertical directions. Fisheye, Inflate, and Twist are among those that can't be rotated, because their effects are already oriented in horizontal and vertical directions that you can control with sliders.

**Figure 5-10**

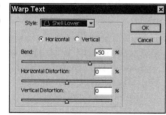

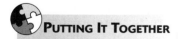

PUTTING IT TOGETHER

### *Carving Your Type in Stone*

You can use the Type tool to create selections shaped like text and then use images themselves as textures for the type. For example, if you were creating a floral-themed Web page, you could use pictures of flowers as the fill for your text (shown in the following example). A Type selection can cut out any part of a picture for use any way you want.

Follow these steps to carve letters into a stone texture image:

**1.** Open the stone texture image you'd like to use.

 I'm using a photo of a weathered brick wall in this example, but you can use other kinds of stone, wood, or any texture that interests you. Best of all, the embossed look that results is only one of many different looks you can achieve simply by making small changes in the Layer style that you apply to the text.

**2.** Choose the Horizontal Type Mask tool from the Tool palette and then click in the area where you want to enter your text.

**3.** Choose the font, type style, type size, and other text parameters from the drop-down lists in the Options bar.

**4.** Enter the text you want to use into the texture you've chosen (the center of the brick wall, in my example), and then click the Commit button (the check mark icon) in the Options bar to set your text.

▼ **CONTINUED**

▼ **CONTINUED**

The selection in the shape of the text appears where you typed the text.

5. **Press Ctrl+C to copy the selected area of your chosen texture (the brick in the shape of the text in my example), and then press Ctrl+V to paste a text-shaped section of that texture in a layer of its own.**

The text blends in with what's in the background layer (in my example, the brick) and is invisible (for now).

6. **Choose Layer➪Layer Style➪Bevel and Emboss to open the Layer Style dialog box.**

In the Layer Style dialog box, you'll find dozens of different effects that you can create.

7. **Experiment with the settings in the Layer Style dialog box to try out different looks and to achieve various effects.**

✔ **Choose the kind of beveling or embossing you want from the Style and Technique drop-down lists in the Structure area of the dialog box.**

I chose Inner Bevel and Chisel Hard to produce a dramatic, hard-edged embossing effect.

✔ **Move the Depth slider to the right to increase the depth of the bevel.**

I set the value at 411% for a raised effect. A lower value produces a less 3-D effect, while a higher value produces a more drastic 3-D effect.

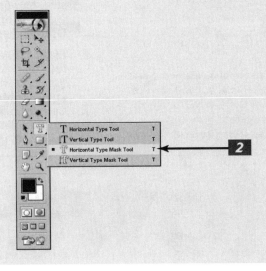

✔ Select the Contour check box on the left side of the dialog box for an even more pronounced 3-D look.

✔ In the Shading area of the dialog box, you can adjust controls that allow you to change the apparent angle of the illumination that produces the bevel's shadow.

I moved the angle to 95 degrees (roughly straight overhead), but I left the other controls alone.

You can find out how to use the other options in the Layer Style dialog box in Book V, Chapter 4.

**8.** Click OK to apply the effects that you've chosen.

**9.** As a finishing touch, choose Image⇨Adjustments⇨Brightness/ Contrast to darken the text layer to make it stand out even more distinctly from the background.

Book
*IV*
Chapter
**5**

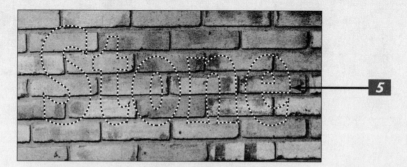

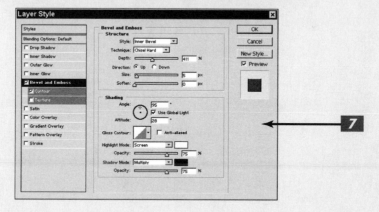

▼ **CONTINUED**

▼ **CONTINUED**

# Book V

# Working with Layers

**Color Plate 2-1:** Resampling your images (right) can cause quality degradation (Book II, Chapter 1).

RGB

Grayscale

Monotone

Duotone

Tritone

Quadtone

Indexed Color

Bitmap

Multichannel

**Color Plate 2-2:** Photoshop offers several image modes that define the color values used to display an image (Book II, Chapter 2).

**Color Plate 4-1:**
The dreaded red-eye effect is caused by the camera's flash bouncing off the retina of the eye and back into the camera's lens (Book IV, Chapter 1).

**Color Plate 4-2:**
Red eye can be fixed easily with a few swipes of the Brush tool using either the Hard Light or Color blend modes (Book IV, Chapter 1).

**Color Plate 4-3:**
Create the look of a hand-tinted photograph by using the Brush tool, with the Color blend mode, on a grayscale image (Book IV, Chapter 1).

**Color Plate 5-1:** Levels and Hue/ Saturation adjustment layers add the lighting and color adjustments (bottom) necessary for a realistic composite of two different images (Book V, Chapter 1).

**Color Plate 5-2:** Lowering the opacity of a layer allows for soft transitions between multiple images (Book V, Chapter 1).

Normal

Darken

Color Dodge

Hard Light

Difference

Luminosity

**Color Plate 5-3:**
Applying blend modes to layers allows the colors to interact in interesting ways
(Book V, Chapter 3).

Drop Shadow

Inner Shadow

Outer Glow

Inner Glow

Inner Bevel

Pillow Emboss

Satin and Gradient Overlay

Color Overlay, Pattern Overlay,
and Drop Shadow

**Color Plate 5-4:**
Layer styles allow you to easily enhance both images and
type (Book V, Chapter 4).

**Color Plate 5-5:**
You have the option of applying blend modes (bottom) to your interior layer effects, such as glows, or leaving them unaffected by blend modes (top) (Book V, Chapter 3).

**Color Plate 5-6:**
Clipping groups allow you to mask a group of layers, creating effects such as this type, which is filled with images (Book V, Chapter 4).

**Color Plate 6-1:**
When you split and merge channels, you can create botanical
specimens from another world (right) (Book VI, Chapter 1).

**Color Plate 6-2:**
By editing individual color channels, you can selectively and
subtly apply filters (left) or adjust color (right) (Book VI,
Chapter 1).

**Color Plate 6-3:**
Masking an element using Color Range can create clean selections that result in realistic composite images (Book VI, Chapter 2).

**Color Plate 6-4:**
Make a photo fade from color to grayscale by using a layer mask (Book VI, Chapter 3).

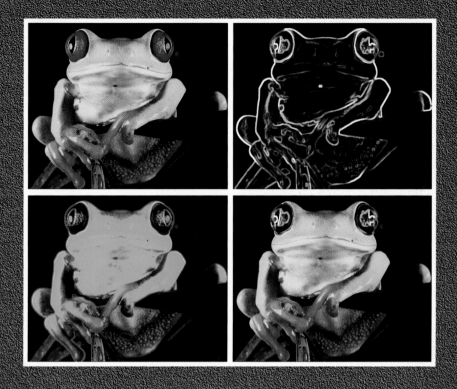

**Color Plate 7-1:**
You can apply a filter to an entire image (top right), to a color channel (bottom left), or to a selection (bottom right) (Book VII, Chapter 1).

**Color Plate 8-1:**
Apply the automatic color correctors — Auto Levels and Auto Color — for quick-and-dirty retouching (Book VIII, Chapter 1).

**Color Plate 8-4:**
Get that vintage feel by making a new photo look old with the Hue/Saturation adjustment and the Dust & Scratches filter (Book VIII, Chapter 1).

**Color Plate 8-5:**
Repairing flaws while retaining tonal values is the job of the Healing Brush and Patch tools (Book VIII, Chapter 3).

**TIFF**
Millions of colors
628K

**JPEG**
75 Quality
75.8K

**JPEG**
10 Quality
14.2K

**PNG-24**
Millions of colors
389.8K

**PNG-8**
128 colors
Selective Palette
Diffusion Dither
706.5K

**GIF**
256 colors
Selective Palette
Diffusion Dither
126K

**GIF**
64 colors
Perceptual Palette
Diffusion Dither
81K

**WBMP**
Diffusion Dither
26.4K

**Color Plate 9-1:**
The Save for Web command allows you to optimize, preview, and save your image in a variety of Web-friendly formats (Book IX, Chapter 2).

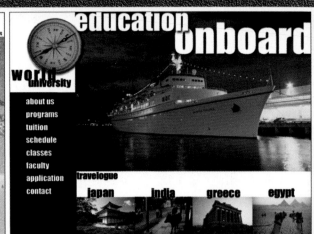

**Color Plate 9-2:**
Creating composite Web pages in Photoshop allows you access to powerful tools and features and gives you creative freedom (Book IX, Chapter 3).

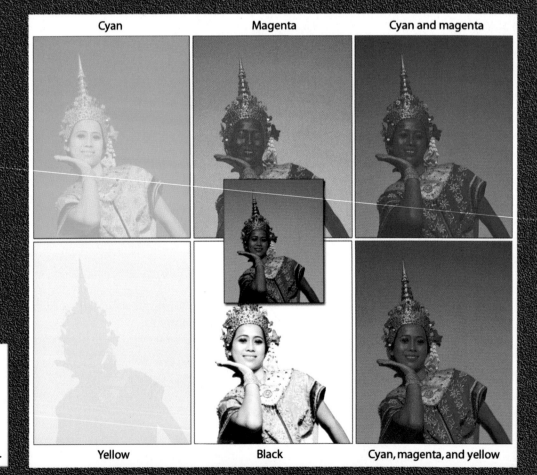

**Color Plate 10-1:**
Offset print jobs require your file to be color separated into the four process colors (Book X, Chapter 2).

# Creating Layers

1

People are often surprised and even downright shocked when I tell them that everything they can do with layers they can also do without them. Not using layers would be more technically challenging and a heck of a lot more tedious, but you could still get the job done. The benefit to using layers is that you have tremendous flexibility. The changes you make to the pixels on the individual layers are permanent, but the interaction between the pixels on different layers is dynamic. You can make endless edits as long as those layers exist. Layers make working in Photoshop a lot more forgiving, allowing you to make changes quickly and productively.

But hey, it's not just the technical and practical aspects that make layers so wonderful. Layers also make it easier for you to express your creative side, allowing you to composite several images into one, with just a drag of the mouse. The only downside to layers is that each one makes your file size grow and therefore can start to slow your system performance. And you can only save layers in a few file formats. But the downsides are a small price to pay for something that makes your image-editing life so much easier.

## Getting to Know the Layers Palette

In terms of a real-world analogy, think of layers as sheets of acetate, similar to those clear plastic sheets used in the old days of overhead projectors. You draw different elements on the various sheets. What you draw on one sheet doesn't affect the other sheets. You can show just one sheet, or you can stack several on top of one another to create a combination image. You can reshuffle the order of the sheets, add new sheets, or delete old sheets. Any space on the sheet that doesn't have a mark on it is clear, or transparent.

That's how layers work in Photoshop. You can place elements on separate layers, yet show them together to create a combination image, or *composite*. You can also add, delete, or rearrange layers. And unlike sheets of acetate, you can also adjust how opaque or transparent the element on the layer is, as well as change the way the colors between layers interact (blend modes).

Just like every other important aspect of Photoshop, layers are housed in a single location, called a palette. It's time to formally meet the powerful palette that controls the operations of layers. To display the palette, shown in Figure 1-1, choose Window⊃Layers or, easier yet, press F7.

**Figure 1-1**

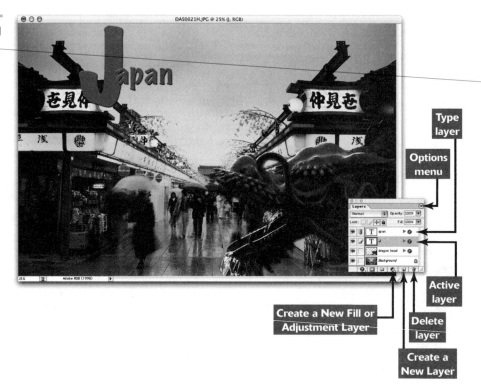

The order of the layers in the Layers palette represents the order in the image. The top layer in the palette is the top layer in your image, and so on.

You can edit only one layer at a time, and that layer is the active layer.

Here's the lowdown on how to work with the Layers palette:

- ✔ **Select a layer:** Simply click its name or thumbnail. The *active layer* then becomes highlighted in the palette and has a little paintbrush icon to the left of the layer name.

- ✔ **Select the actual element (the non-transparent pixels) on the layer:** Ctrl+click (⌘+click on the Mac) on the layer's name in the palette. If you forget this handy shortcut, you can also choose Select➪Load Selection. Make sure that the layer name that appears in the Channel pop-up menu is [layer name] Transparency and click OK.

- ✔ **Create a new blank layer:** Click the Create a New Layer icon at the bottom of the palette. See the next section for more on creating layers.

- ✔ **Create an adjustment or fill layer:** Click the Create a New Fill or Adjustment Layer icon at the bottom of the palette. See "Introducing Different Types of Layers," later in this chapter, for more on these layers.

- ✔ **Duplicate an existing layer:** Drag the layer to the Create a New Layer icon at the bottom of the palette. See the next section for more on creating layers.

- ✔ **Rename a layer:** When you create a new layer, Photoshop provides default layer names (Layer 1, Layer 2, and so on). If you want to rename a layer, simply double-click the layer name (the name not the thumbnail) in the Layers palette and enter the name directly in the Layers palette. This renaming shortcut works throughout Photoshop (the Channels palette, the Paths palette, and so on). You can also select the layer and choose Layer Properties from the Layers palette options menu or choose Layer➪Layer Properties.

- ✔ **Determine what layer holds the element you want to edit:** Select the Move tool and Ctrl+click (⌘+click on the Mac) on the element. Photoshop automatically activates the appropriate layer. Or you can right-click (Control+click on the Mac) on the element. A context menu appears telling you what layer the element resides on and then enables you to select that layer.

  🎯 You can use the keyboard shortcut Alt+] (right bracket) (Option+] on the Mac) to move up one layer; Alt+[ (left bracket) (Option+[ on the Mac) to activate the next layer down. Press Shift+Alt+] (Shift+Option+] on the Mac) to move to the top layer; press Shift+Alt+[ (Shift+Option+[ on the Mac) to move to the background or bottom layer.

- ✔ **Adjust the interaction between colors on layers and adjust the transparency of layers:** You can use the blend modes and the opacity and fill options at the top of the palette to mix the colors between layers and adjust the transparency of the layers. For details, see Chapter 3 of this book.

- ✔ **Delete a layer:** Drag it to the trash icon at the bottom of the Layers palette. You can also choose Layer➪Delete➪Layer or choose Delete Layer from the palette options menu.

- ✔ **Change the size of the layer thumbnails:** Choose Palette Options from the palette options menu and select a thumbnail size.

The remaining icons at the bottom of the Layers palette allow you to create layer styles, layer masks, and layers sets, all of which warrant sections of their own. See Chapter 4 of this book for more on layer styles and Chapter 2 for more on layer sets. Check out Book VI, Chapter 3, for more on layer masks.

The preceding list represents just the tip of the iceberg. You can also view and hide layers, link, lock, color-code, rearrange, merge, and flatten layers. Again, these topics are covered in detail in Chapter 2 of this book.

▼ ▼ ▼ ▼ ▼ ▼ ▼ ▼ ▼ ▼ ▼ ▼ ▼ ▼ ▼ ▼ ▼ ▼ ▼ ▼ ▼ ▼ ▼ ▼ ▼ ▼ ▼ ▼ ▼ ▼ ▼ ▼ ▼ ▼ ▼ ▼ ▼ ▼ ▼

## Looking at the Background and Layers

When you create a new image with white or background colored contents, scan an image into Photoshop, or open a file from a stock photography CD, Photo CD, or your own digital camera, you basically have a file with just a *background*.

An image contains only one background, and you can't do much to it. You can't rearrange the background in the stack of layers — it's always on the very bottom of the Layers palette. You can't change the opacity, fill, or blend mode of a background either. What you can do is convert a background to a layer, and then the world's at your feet. It's no surprise that converting the background of an image into a layer is a common Photoshop activity.

To convert a background into a layer, follow these steps:

**1.** **Double-click Background in the Layers palette.**

In addition, you can choose Layer⇨New⇨Layer from Background. Note that the name Background is italicized in the Layers palette, as shown in Figure 1-2.

**2.** **Name the layer.**

You can also color-code your layer by choosing a color from the pop-up menu. All this does is make your layer stand out more noticeably in the Layers palette. In addition, you can group the layer with the previous layer or change the blend mode, opacity, or fill settings. For now, leave all of these options at

the default settings. You find out more about these options in Chapter 3 of this book.

**3.** **Click OK.**

Your background is now converted into a layer as indicated in the Layers palette. Note that the layer name is in boldface type and no longer italicized, as shown in Figure 1-3.

 When you create a new image with transparent contents, the image doesn't contain a background but instead is created with a single layer. You can also convert a layer back into a background by selecting it and then choosing Layer⇨New⇨Background from Layer.

**Figure 1-2**

**Figure 1-3**

# Introducing Different Types of Layers

Although turning the background into a layer (discussed in the previous section) is a popular activity, there's a reason Photoshop refers to *layers* in the plural. Image editing would be no fun if you didn't have a variety of different layers to mess around with.

Photoshop offers five types of layers. Four of the five have very specific purposes in the life of your image. Some you may never use, and some you'll use only occasionally. But the vanilla-flavored type, which you'll use the most, is simply called a layer. Pretty generic, huh? Read on to find out more.

## Using plain vanilla layers

The regular layer is the one that most closely matches the acetate analogy discussed in the preceding section. You put various elements on separate layers to create a composite image. You can create blank layers and add images to them, or you can create layers from images themselves. You can create as many layers as your computer's RAM will let you. And sometimes layers are created automatically by a specific action that you execute in Photoshop.

Because each layer in an image is a separate entity, you can edit, paint, transform, mask, or apply a filter on a layer without affecting the other layers. And once an element is on a layer, you no longer have to make a selection (get the selection outline) to select it — you simply drag the element with the Move tool. The element freely floats in a sea of transparency. Because it's impossible to show "clear" areas or transparency on a computer monitor, Photoshop uses a gray and white checkerboard, by default, to represent the transparent areas of a layer.

Because regular layers are the ones you'll be working with on a daily basis, I spend the majority of the sections in this chapter and this book discussing them.

▼ ▼ ▼ ▼ ▼ ▼ ▼ ▼ ▼ ▼ ▼ ▼ ▼ ▼ ▼ ▼ ▼ ▼ ▼ ▼ ▼ ▼ ▼ ▼ ▼ ▼ ▼ ▼ ▼ ▼ ▼ ▼ ▼ ▼ ▼ ▼ ▼ ▼ ▼ ▼

## Using adjustment layers

An adjustment layer is a special kind of layer that is used expressly for color correction. What's great about adjustment layers is that you can apply that color correction without permanently affecting any of your layers. Adjustment layers apply the correction to all of the layers below them (in the stacking order in the Layers palette), without affecting any of the layers above them.

Because the color correction actually resides on a layer, you can edit, delete, duplicate, merge, or rearrange the adjustment layer at any time. This gives you more flexibility in your image-editing chores and more freedom for experimentation.

## Playing around with layer masks

A *layer mask* is like a second sheet of acetate that hovers over a layer. Layer masks are used with regular layers, adjustment layers, and fill layers. For example, you may paint on a layer mask (typically with black, white, and various shades of gray) to selectively hide or display an adjustment.

Any black areas on the mask hide the adjustment, any white areas show the adjustment, and anything in between (gray) partially shows the adjustment. I cover layer masks in detail in Book VI, Chapter 3.

Photoshop has 11 kinds of adjustment layers, and you can use as many as your heart desires. The adjustments offered are the same adjustments you find under the Image⇨Adjust submenu. For specifics on each adjustment and what it corrects, see Book VIII, Chapter 1.

Here's how to create an adjustment layer:

1. **Open an image of your choice.**

   Because you're applying an adjustment layer, you may want to use an image that is in need of some color correction. In the case of adjustment layers, you don't need to convert your background into a layer. I chose an image that was way oversaturated.

2. **Choose Layer⇨New Adjustment Layer. From the submenu, choose your desired adjustment. Name the layer if you want, leave the other options at their defaults, and click OK.**

   For my example, I chose Hue/Saturation.

   You can also just click the Create a New Fill or Adjustment Layer icon (the black and white circle icon) at the bottom of the Layers palette and choose an adjustment from the pop-up menu.

   The dialog box pertaining to your adjustment appears.

3. **Make the necessary corrections and click OK.**

After you close the dialog box, the adjustment layer appears in the Layers palette. Two thumbnails appear on the adjustment layer. The thumbnail on the left represents the actual adjustment. The thumbnail on the right represents a layer mask, as shown in Figure 1-4. For more on layer masks, check out the "Playing around with layer masks" sidebar.

In my example, the layer mask is all white, as shown in Figure 1-4, so my adjustment shows up full strength over my image. Like regular layers, you can adjust the opacity, fill, and blend modes of an adjustment layer. For more on these options, see Chapter 3 of this book.

 If you want to view your image without the adjustment, click the eye icon in the far-left column of the Layers palette to hide the adjustment layer. You can find more on viewing layers in Chapter 2 of this book. If you want to delete the adjustment layer, simply drag it to the trash icon in the Layers palette or choose Delete from the Layer menu or Layers palette options menu.

Book
**V**
Chapter
**1**

CONTINUED
▼ ▼ ▼ ▼ ▼

**Figure 1-4**

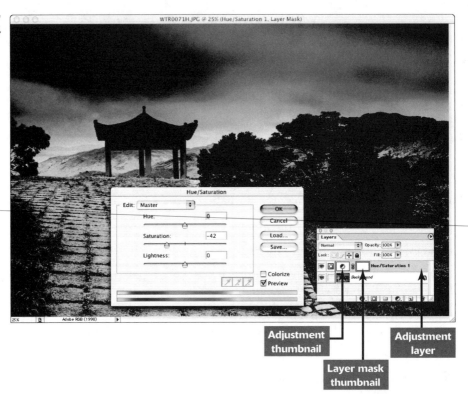

Adjustment
thumbnail

Layer mask
thumbnail

Adjustment
layer

### Editing adjustment layers

Once created, an adjustment layer can be easily edited. Simply double-click the adjustment layer thumbnail in the Layers palette or choose Layer⇨Layer Content Options. In the dialog box that appears, make any edits and then click OK. The only adjustment layer that cannot be edited is the Invert adjustment. It is either totally on or totally off.

To change the content of an adjustment layer, choose Layer⇨Change Layer Content and select a different adjustment layer from the submenu. Editing and changing the content works the exact same way for fill layers (which are discussed in the next section).

### Isolating your adjustments

If you don't use an adjustment layer when you make color corrections, the correction you apply affects only the *active* layer (the layer highlighted in the Layers palette). This may be the way to go if you want to just tweak the color on a single layer.

Here are some tips for using and isolating adjustment layers:

✔ **Correct part (but not all) of a layer:** To enable the adjustment layer to correct only a portion of a layer, make a selection before you create the adjustment layer. Only the pixels within the selection outline are affected by the adjustment.

This is referring to the pixels within the selection outline *on each layer that resides below the adjustment layer.* In addition to making a selection, you can also create and select a closed path (see Book III, Chapter 2, for more on paths).

✔ **Create a clipping group:** When you create a *clipping group* of the layers you want to adjust, you can place the adjustment layer in or at the bottom of the clipping group, and it will only affect those clipped layers. In a clipping group, the bottommost layer acts as a mask for the layers in the group. For more on clipping groups, see Chapter 4 of this book.

✔ **Create a layer set:** You can create a *layer set* (a grouping of layers, as described in Chapter 2 of this book) and place the layers you want adjusted in that set. Then make sure that the blend mode is set to any mode except Pass Through. For more on modes, see Chapter 3 of this book.

▼ ▼ ▼ ▼ ▼ ▼ ▼ ▼ ▼ ▼ ▼ ▼ ▼ ▼ ▼ ▼ ▼ ▼ ▼ ▼ ▼ ▼ ▼ ▼ ▼ ▼ ▼ ▼ ▼ ▼ ▼ ▼ ▼ ▼ ▼ ▼ ▼ ▼ ▼ ▼

## Taking advantage of fill layers

A *fill layer* lets you add a layer of solid color, a gradient, or a pattern. Like adjustment layers, fill layers also have layer masks, as indicated by the mask icon thumbnail in the Layers palette.

You can create as many fill layers as you like, just as you can with regular layers and adjustment layers. You can also edit, rearrange, duplicate, delete, and merge fill layers. And you can blend fill layers with other layers by using the opacity, fill, and blend mode options (described in Chapter 3 of this book) in the Layers palette.

 Fill layers can also be confined in the same ways I mention in the preceding section, "Isolating your adjustments."

 Like an adjustment layer, to confine the effects of a fill layer to a portion of the image, make a selection or create and select a closed path before you create the fill layer (see Book III, Chapter 2, for more on paths). And editing or changing the contents of a fill layer is similar to editing or changing the contents of an adjustment layer (see the preceding section for details).

Book
**V**
Chapter
**1**

Here's how to create a fill layer:

**1. Open an image of your choice.**

In this case, open an image that would look good with a cool border or cool type. For my example, I created the word *fujiyama* by using the Horizontal Type Mask tool (for details, see Book IV, Chapter 4). If you want to create a simple border, you can just create a rectangle along one of the sides of your image. If you don't have an active selection, the fill layer will encompass your entire canvas.

**2. Choose Layer➪New Fill Layer. From the submenu, choose your desired adjustment. Name the layer, leave the other options at their defaults, and click OK.**

For my example, I chose Pattern from the submenu.

You can also just click the Create a New Fill or Adjustment Layer icon (the black and white circle icon) at the bottom of the Layers palette and choose a fill from the pop-up menu.

CONTINUED
▼ ▼ ▼ ▼ ▼

The dialog box pertaining to your fill appears.

**3.** **Follow the steps that correspond with the option you chose in Step 2:**

✔ **Solid Color:** Choose your desired color from the Photoshop Color Picker. (For more on color, see Book II, Chapter 3.)

✔ **Gradient:** Choose a preset gradient from the pop-up palette or click the gradient preview to display the Gradient Editor to create your own gradient. Set additional gradient options as desired. (For gradient details, see Book IV, Chapter 3.)

✔ **Pattern:** Select a pattern from the pop-up palette. Click Scale and enter a value or drag the scale slider. I scaled my bubble pattern 250%. Click Snap to Origin to position the origin of the pattern with the document window. Finally, select the Link with Layer option to specify that the pattern moves with the fill layer if you move it. I chose Pattern in my example in Figure 1-5.

**4.** **Click OK.**

After you close the dialog box, the fill layer appears in the Layers palette, as shown in Figure 1-6. Similar to adjustment layers, you'll notice the layer mask that was created on the fill layer. In my example, the word *fujiyama* appears white on the layer mask, thereby allowing my pattern to show through. The remaining areas are black, hiding my pattern. Again, if you want to know more about layer masks, see Book VI, Chapter 3. I added a couple of Layer Styles (Drop Shadow and Inner Bevel) to my type to jazz it up a bit. If you want to do the same, jump ahead to Chapter 4 of this book.

If you want to delete the fill layer, do one of three things: Drag it to the trash icon in the Layers palette; choose Delete from the Layer menu; or choose Delete Layer from the Layers palette options menu.

**Figure 1-5**

**Figure 1-6**

**4**

## Making use of shape layers

In Version 6, Photoshop expanded its repertoire from just painting and added a whole slew of shape drawing tools, six to be exact. Shapes can be filled with solid color, gradients, or patterns. When you create a shape, it resides on its own unique shape layer. A shape layer contains a *vector mask,* similar in concept to the adjustment layer mask described earlier.

If you look at the Layers palette, you can see that the Shape layer has two thumbnails: One is entirely filled with color, and the other contains the path of the shape, as shown in Figure 1-7. To state it simply, the color is peeking through the path of the shape, and the rest of the layer is hidden or masked. The paths that comprise a shape are *vector paths,* which means that, when printed, they retain their smooth curves without the jagged edges you often see from bitmap editing programs. Although you can edit, move, and transform shapes, shape layers have limited editability. To apply filters and other special effects, you must first *rasterize* the shape layers — that is, convert the vector paths to pixels. For more details on shapes, see Book IV, Chapter II.

 You can also create shape layers with the Pen tool. For more on the Pen tool, see Book III, Chapter 2.

## Using type layers

To create type, click your canvas with the Type tool (horizontal or vertical) and type your desired text. After you commit your text by pressing Enter on the numeric keypad or clicking the Commit button on the Options bar, you've created a type layer. In the Layers palette, you see a layer with a T icon, indicating that it's a type layer. The name of the type layer corresponds to the text you typed. Like shapes, the text in Photoshop is true vector type so, if left in that format, will always print smooth and without the *jaggies.*

**Figure 1-7**

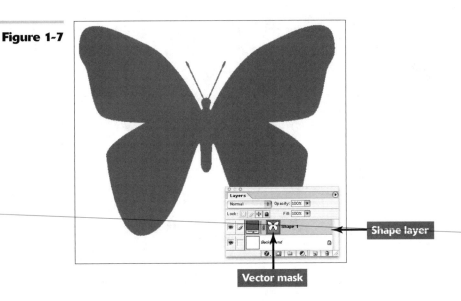

Another great thing about type in Photoshop is that it is live; the text can be edited at any time. You can also change the orientation, apply anti-aliasing (softening of the edges), create paths from the type, and even warp it into various distortions, as in my example in Figure 1-8. The type can also be converted to a shape. And like regular layers, you can move, rearrange, copy, and change the layer options (opacity, fill, and mode) of a type layer. If, however, you want to apply certain special effects, such as filters, you must first *rasterize* (convert into pixels) the text. For everything you need to know about type, see Book IV, Chapters 4 and 5.

**Figure 1-8**

# Making Layers

As I mention earlier in the chapter, good, old-fashioned, regular layers are the backbone of the world of layers. The next few sections take a look at the various ways to create these layers.

## Creating a new layer

If you want to create a new blank layer, click the Create a New Layer icon at the bottom of the Layers palette. You can also create a new layer by choosing New Layer from the palette options menu or by choosing Layer⇨New⇨Layer. The latter method prompts you with a dialog box to name your layer and includes other options for grouping, color-coding, blending, and opacity (all of which are explained in other chapters in this book). Provide a name for your layer and click OK. If you chose one of the first two methods, a layer with the default name of Layer 1 appears in the Layers palette.

You can also create an entirely new document with a layer by choosing File⇨New. In the New dialog box, select the Transparent for the Contents option. Your new file then appears with Layer 0 instead of a background.

 When you click the Create a New Layer icon, the layer is added above your active layer. By holding down the Ctrl key (⌘ on the Mac) when you click, the new layer is added below the active layer.

Book **V**
Chapter **1**

Your new transparent layer is now ready for content. Remember, because it isn't possible to show transparency on your screen, Photoshop uses a gray and white checkerboard to represent the transparent areas of a layer. You can put content on the new layer several ways:

- ✔ Use one of the painting tools and paint directly on the layer.

- ✔ Make a selection on another layer or the background (for the difference between the two, see the previous sections in this chapter) within the same document or from another image entirely and then choose Edit⇨Copy. Select your new blank layer in the Layers palette and then choose Edit⇨Paste, as shown in Figure 1-9.

- ✔ Make a selection on another layer (or the background) within the same document or from another image and then choose Edit⇨Cut. Select your new blank layer and then choose Edit⇨Paste. Just remember that the selection is deleted from the source and added to your new layer.

- ✔ Transfer an entire image to your new layer by choosing Select⇨All and then either Edit⇨Copy or Edit⇨Cut. Select your new blank layer and then choose Edit⇨Paste.

## Using Layer via Copy and Layer via Cut

Another way to create a layer is to use the Layer via Copy command found on the Layer menu. Make a selection on a layer or background and choose Layer⇨New⇨Layer via Copy. The copied selection is placed on a new layer with the default name of Layer 1. You can do the same with the Layer via Cut command, but in this case, the selected area is deleted from the source layer or background and relocated on the new layer. The source layer is left with a gaping transparent hole. If you used the background for the source, the space is filled with your background color, as shown in Figure 1-10. Remember that you can only use these two commands within the same image. You cannot use them between multiple images.

**Figure 1-9**

**Figure 1-10**

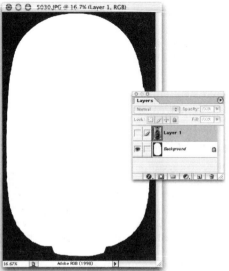

## Duplicating layers

If you want to duplicate an existing layer, first select it in the Layers palette. Then drag the layer to the Create a New Layer icon at the bottom of the palette. You can also duplicate a layer by choosing Duplicate Layer from the palette options menu or by choosing Layer⇨Duplicate Layer. Like with creating a new layer, the latter method prompts you with a dialog box to name your layer and includes other options. Provide a name for your layer and click OK. If you chose either of the first two methods, Photoshop provides the default name of the original layer with Copy appended to the name. Duplicating layers can be especially handy when you want to experiment with a special effect but don't want to harm your original image.

# Compositing with Multiple Images

Often when working with layers, you are not confined to using a single image. I mean, there's only so much you can do to that family portrait taken down at the local photo studio. But take your family and put them in front of the ruins at Machu Picchu or the summit at Mount Everest (you can even add faux snow with a technique shown in Book VII), and we're talking about endless hours of fun. When you get the hang of working with several images, you'll find that it opens a whole new door of creative possibilities. And you're not limited to just plain old snapshots. You can incorporate type, vector illustrations, and scans of just about anything you can place on a scanning bed. Apply some layer styles, maybe a filter of two (see Book VII), and you've got an image worthy of some major wall space.

## Copying and pasting images

Earlier in the "Making layers" section, I explain how to use the copy, cut, and paste commands within the same image or between two different images when you want to fill a new blank layer with content. You can also use the copy and paste commands without having a blank layer first. When you copy and paste a selection without a blank layer, Photoshop automatically creates a new layer from the pasted selection. You can go about your merry way and perform all of your layer creation by using only those commands. However, I rarely use them when working with multiple images. I prefer the drag and drop method described next.

 The Copy Merged command under the Edit menu creates a merged copy of *all* the visible layers within the selection.

## Dragging and dropping layers

To copy an entire layer from one document to another, simply select the layer in the Layers palette, grab the Move tool, press your mouse button down, and drag and drop that image onto your destination document. Photoshop automatically introduces the dropped layer as a *new* layer above the active layer in the image. You don't need to have a selection outline to copy the entire layer. However, if you want to copy just a portion of the layer, make your desired selection, as shown in Figure 1-11, before you drag and drop with the Move tool. If you want the selected element to be centered on the destination image, hold down the Shift key as you drag and drop. See the sidebar, "Bypassing the clipboard" for more on dragging and dropping.

**Figure 1-11**

## Using the Paste Into command

You may occasionally want to place an image on a separate layer, yet have it fill a selection. That's where the Edit⇨Paste Into command comes into play. This command enables you to insert a copied or cut selected image into a selection outline.

For example, if you want to make it appear as if a snake is poking its head out of the opening of a cave, or a possum is emerging from a trash can, this is your command. It's hard to visualize this description unless you actually do it, so be sure to check out the Putting-It-Together project in this chapter.

Follow these steps to insert a copied or cut selected image into a selection outline:

*1.* **Make the selection on the layer that you want the image to fill.**

I'll call this the destination layer.

*2.* **Select the image that will fill that selection.**

I'll call this the source image.

*Note:* The source image can be within the same image or from another image.

*3.* **Choose Edit⇨Copy.**

*4.* **Return to the destination layer and choose Edit⇨Paste Into.**

The selection outline on the destination layer is then converted into a layer mask. The pasted selection is only visible inside the selection outline, like it is peeking out of a hole. For a brief description of layer masks, see the "Using adjustment layers" section, earlier in this chapter. For a detailed explanation, see Book VI, Chapter 3.

# Transforming Layers

When compositing multiple images, you will no doubt have to scale some of your image to fit into your layout. Fortunately, Photoshop makes this an easy chore by providing you with the Transform and Free Transform commands found on the Edit menu. Transforming layers is almost identical to transforming selections except that you don't need to make a selection first. Once an element is on a layer, you can just choose the appropriate transformation command and off you go. In addition, you can apply a transformation to multiple layers simultaneously if you link the layers first. For more on linking layers, see Chapter 2 of this book. Because I explain each transformation in excruciating detail in Book III, Chapter 3, check that out if you need more detail.

 In addition to transforming individual layers and selections, you can also transform the entire image. You find these commands — Image Size (for scaling) and Rotate Canvas — on the Image menu. For details on these commands, see Book II, Chapter 1.

 Try to perform all of your transformations in one execution. Don't go back numerous times and apply various transformations. Each time you transform pixels, you are putting your image through the interpolation process (manufacturing pixels). Done repeatedly, your image may start to turn into mush. And if not mush, it will not be as pristine and crisp as it was before.

If your image looks jagged after you transform it, you may have your preferences set incorrectly for your interpolation method. Choose Edit➪Preferences➪General (Photoshop➪Preferences➪General on Mac OS X) and select the Bicubic (Better) option from the Interpolation pop-up menu. This enables a smoother appearance to your interpolated pixels.

 When the Move tool is active, you can transform a layer without choosing a command. Simply select the Show Bounding Box option in the Options bar. This option surrounds the contents (or an active selection) of the layer with a bounding box with handles, as shown in Figure 1-12. Drag these handles to transform the contents.

Book
**V**
Chapter
**1**

## Bypassing the clipboard

Yes, you can always cut and paste or copy and paste a layer from one image to another, but I prefer to drag and drop rather than copying and pasting between two images because by dragging and dropping you bypass the temporary storage area for copied and stored data, the *clipboard*. (Whenever you copy or cut a selection, the selection is stored on the clipboard until you are ready to paste it to its new home.) So what's wrong with that? Well, nothing, unless you're working with high-resolution images. Storing images on the clipboard, even on a temporary basis, can slow down your system. Keeping your clipboard clear of data ensures that Photoshop is running lean and mean so that you can drag and drop more images, selections, and layers, quicker and more efficiently. Take my advice and try the drag-and-drop method. I guarantee that, like me, you'll be flexing your trigger finger — all the better to drag and drop even faster.

**Figure 1-12**

Transform box

![Putting It Together icon] **PUTTING IT TOGETHER**

### Creating Layers and Using the Paste Into Command to Make a Collage

If you remember your elementary-school days, you probably remember cutting out a bunch of pictures from magazines and pasting them on a piece of construction paper. Well, with Photoshop, the idea of a collage isn't much different, but the activity is a little more refined.

Maybe you want to let loose your artistic side. Or maybe you need to combine several images into one as part of a job. Or you may just want to get a better handle on how layers work. Whatever your reason, you can use the steps you find here to get started on your first collage. And by the way, if *collage* is too froufrou a word for you, you can substitute it with *composite* — as in the definition of "derived from many components." I usually do.

Creating a collage takes many steps. Throughout Book V, you find several ongoing Putting-It-Together projects, all of which lead you to a finished collage. Be sure to save your collage file so that you can work on it as you make your way through this book.

If you're short on photos, you can go to www.gettyimages.com. Be sure to register so that you can have access to a huge gallery of free *comping images*. Comping images are small, low-resolution images that are used for internal corporate or personal noncommercial use only.

What makes a collage a collage is the fact that you layer a variety of images over each other. So it makes sense that you need to understand how layers work in order to get started. I discuss layers throughout Book V. To create the first layer of your collage, follow these steps:

**1.** **Decide on two images you want to use in your collage and open them by choosing File⇨Open.**

I recommend picking an image to use as your main canvas and then opening up a supporting image that you can select and then drag onto that main image. However, if you want, you can also start with just a blank document. For my example, I decided on a travel theme and opened an image of the Grand Canyon and another image of a passport.

**2.** **Choose Window⇨Layers to open the Layers palette.**

Always be sure that the Layers palette is visible whenever you're creating a composite from multiple images. You need to see what is happening as you drag and drop, and you need to be aware of what layer you are working on at all times.

**3.** **Select the desired element in the supporting image.**

Feel free to use whatever selection method suits your fancy, but remember, the finished collage will look only as good as its individual selections. For more on making selections, see Book III.

Because the contrast between my passport and the background behind it was very good, I grabbed the Magic Wand, set the Tolerance to 50, and clicked the passport. I then held down the Shift key and, with the Lasso tool, circled the remaining pixels in the gold type that the Magic Wand didn't pick up.

To add a selection, you must press and hold down the Shift key.

**4.** **Choose Select⇨Modify⇨Contract and enter a value. Then choose Select⇨Feather and enter a value.**

Contract the selections lightly (I chose a value of 1 pixel) before you apply a feather (I chose a 0.5 pixel value) to avoid picking

Book
**V**
Chapter
**1**

▼ **CONTINUED**

**CONTINUED**

up some of the background during the feathering process.

Using a small feather helps to avoid the harsh, looks-like-I cut-it-out-with-a-pair-of-pinking-shears look.

**5.** **With the Move tool, drag and drop the selection onto the background.**

The Layers palette shows that you've produced a layer. You'll notice that your main image remains as the background below the layer.

Don't worry if your element isn't the right size. You can find a Putting-It-Together project in Chapter 2 of this book that shows you how to scale the layer.

**6.** **Choose File➪Save. Name the file collage and make sure the format is Photoshop.**

Keep the file in a handy spot on your hard drive so that you can find it when you're ready to do more with your collage.

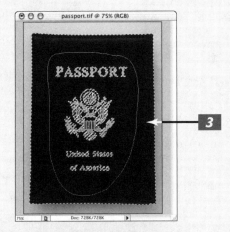

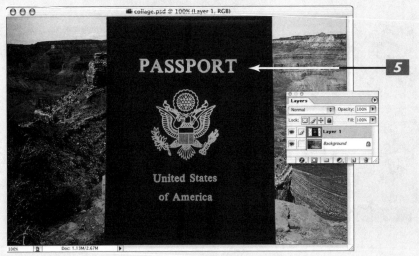

I've already shown you how to create a layer by dragging and dropping a passport onto a background image of the Grand Canyon. The process I'm demonstrating here is a little different. It entails pasting one selection into another.

Sticking with my travel theme, I opted to take the image of a compass and paste it into the background so that the compass looks like it's peaking out from the side of the canyon.

To paste one selection into another on your collage, follow these steps:

1. **Choose File⇨Open. Select the file you saved from the last exercise. Also open a new supporting image.**

2. **Choose Window⇨Layers to open the Layers palette.**

   The Layers palette should always be visible whenever you are creating a composite from multiple images.

3. **Select the part of the supporting image that you want to use.**

   Feel free to use whatever selection method you desire, but try and get as accurate a selection as you can.

   For the compass, I used the Elliptical Marquee tool, while pressing the Alt key (Option on the Mac),

to draw from the center out to select the bottom portion of the compass. With the same tool, I pressed the Shift key and then the mouse button and then the Alt key (Option) to add the top portion of the compass.

   If the Alt (Option) and Shift keyboard commands are fuzzy to you, check out Book III, Chapter 3.

4. **Contract and feather the selection (as described in Step 4 in the previous set of steps).**

   Unless you're going for some special effect, be consistent with the treatment of the edges of each of your elements in your composite. See Book III for more on selections.

5. **Choose Edit⇨Copy.**

6. **In your saved collage file, move the first supporting image (the image you added in the previous set of steps) to the side with the Move tool. Then use the Lasso tool (or any other selection tool) to create a selection in which to paste your new supporting image.**

   I want the compass image to look as if it is peeking up from behind the side of the canyon, so I made a selection in the cliffs of the Grand Canyon.

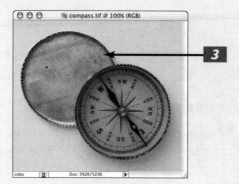

▼ **CONTINUED**

▼ **CONTINUED**

**7.** **Choose Edit⇨Paste Into.**

If you use the Move tool to move the pasted image around the canvas, you see that the pasted image is invisible outside the boundaries of the selection outline.

Don't be concerned if your element isn't the right size. I show you how to scale your layer in Chapter 2.

The Layers palette shows a second thumbnail next to the compass thumbnail. This thumbnail represents the layer mask that was

created automatically when you pasted into a selection. A layer mask allows portions of the layer to show and be hidden. In my example, the white areas on the layer mask are where my compass shows through. Those white areas happen to correspond to the selection I made in Step 6. The black areas represent where my compass would be hidden if I were to move it into those areas. For more on layer masks, see Book VI, Chapter 3.

**8.** **Choose File⇨Save.**

# Managing Layers

Hopefully, you had the time and inclination to check out the first chapter of this book. That's where you get all the basic information on creating layers. In this chapter, you get the scoop on how to manage the layers you've created. And unlike some coworkers, clients, or family members, layers are downright agreeable to being managed, even micromanaged for that matter. The beauty of layers is that they're so darn easy to get along with. You can hide them, shuffle them around, link and lock them, herd them into sets, and even smush them together into one loving, collective layer. Yes, Photoshop has a whole slew of ways to get your layers in the orderly and organized fashion you deserve.

## Viewing and Hiding Layers

Often, it's useful to hide all the layers in your image except for the one you want to edit. You can focus on the element at hand without the distraction of all the other components of the image. You can do this with a single quick click of the mouse, as described in the following list:

- **Hide all the layers but one:** Select the layer you want to display. Alt+click (Option+click on the Mac) on the eye icon, for that layer, in the far-left column of the Layers palette. To redisplay all the layers, Alt+click (Option+click on the Mac) on the eye icon again.

- **Hide an individual layer:** Click the eye icon for that layer, as shown in Figure 2-1. To redisplay the layer, click the blank space in the eye column.

You can also hide layer styles or entire layer sets by using the same method as with layers. You can find out more about layer sets later in this chapter. For the lowdown on layer styles, see Chapter 4 of this book.

Only layers that are visible will print. This can be useful if you want to have several versions (each on a separate layer) of an image for a project within the same document. You can view selective layers, print them, get approval from the powers that be, and then delete the layers with the scrapped versions. Only one file to manage — even I can handle that.

 If clicking the mouse is just too strenuous for you, try this neat trick. *Drag* your mouse through the eye column to hide or display multiple layers in one fell swoop. Now that's technology.

**Figure 2-1**

Visible layer

Hidden layer

# Rearranging Layers

If you read my analogy in Chapter 1 of this book, comparing layers to sheets of acetate used with old overhead projectors, it will make sense to you when I say that you can shuffle the order of layers like, well, sheets of acetate. The *stacking order* of the layers in the Layers palette corresponds to the order of the layers in the document. If you want to move a layer to another position in the stacking order, drag the layer (or layer set) up or down in the Layers palette. As you drag, you will see a fist icon. Release your mouse button when a highlighted line appears where you want to insert the layer.

Alternatively, you can also change the order by selecting the layer (or layer set) and then choosing Layer⇨Arrange. Then select one of the following commands from the submenu:

✔ **Bring to Front** and **Send to Back** send the layer to the very top or very bottom of the stacking order.

✔ **Bring Forward** and **Send Backward** move the layer one level up or down.

 If there is a background in your image, it always remains the bottommost layer. If you need to move the background, first convert it to a layer by double-clicking the name in the Layers palette. Enter a name for the layer and click OK.

# Moving Layer Elements

Rearranging layers is different from moving the content on the layer. Because the elements on a layer are free floating on a bed of transparency, it's a piece of cake to move the element whenever necessary. Moving the element has no effect on any of the other layers, and it doesn't harm the image one iota.

To move an image on a layer, just drag it with the Move tool, the four-headed arrow tool located in the Toolbox; it doesn't get any simpler than that. Here are a few more handy tips when moving an image and using the Move tool:

✔ **Move the layer in 1-pixel increments:** Press an arrow key with the Move tool selected. To move the layer in 10-pixel increments, press Shift as you press the arrow key.

✔ **Find out what layer holds the element you want to move (or edit in some other way):** Select the Move tool and Ctrl+click (⌘+click on the Mac) on the element. Photoshop automatically activates the layer the element resides on. Or you can right-click (Control+click on the Mac) on the element. A context menu appears telling you what layer the element resides on and then enables you to select that layer from the context menu.

Book
**V**
Chapter
**2**

 This technique only works on pixels that have an opacity of 50% or more. If you click pixels with opacities of 50% or less, Photoshop burrows down into successive layers and selects the first layer below on which it encounters a pixel with an opacity of 50% or more.

✔ **Switch to a layer when you click with the Move tool on any part of a layer:** Select the Auto Select Layer option on the Options bar. But be careful if you use this option; you may inadvertently select a layer when you don't want to.

✔ **Display a bounding box around the elements on your layer:** Select the Show Bounding Box check box on the Options bar. This can be useful if all your elements are melting into one another in an indistinguishable conglomeration.

 To temporarily access the Move tool, Ctrl+drag (⌘+drag on the Mac) with any other tool except the Pen tools, the Hand tool, the Slice and Slice Select tools, the Path Selection tool, the Direct Selection tool, and any of the Shape tools. Release the Ctrl (⌘) key to return to your original tool.

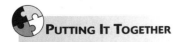 **PUTTING IT TOGETHER**

### Transforming and Moving Layers in a Collage

When you have a couple of images in your collage (see the Putting-It-Together projects in Chapter 1 of this book), you can start transforming them to your liking. Moving and scaling are the manipulations you'll probably do the most. Photoshop enables you to transform layers without affecting any of the other layers within the image, (For more on transformations, see Chapter 1 of this book and Book III, Chapter 3.)

Here's how to tweak images:

**1.** Choose File⇨Open. Select your saved collage file.

**2.** Choose Window⇨Layers to open the Layers palette.

**3.** In the Layers palette, select the layer you want to transform.

In my example, I chose the layer that has the passport on it.

**4.** Choose Edit⇨Free Transform.

Because you're going to adjust the scale and rotate the image at the same time, choose Free Transform rather than Transform. Then choose a transformation type from the submenu. This way you are only interpolating the image once, rather than twice. For more on interpolation, see Book II, Chapter 1.

**5.** Shift+drag a corner transformation handle to scale the image to the desired size.

Using the Shift key when you drag maintains the relative proportions of the image and reduces the amount of distortion.

I reduced the passport in my example to about half its original size.

**6.** **Position the cursor just outside the handle until a curved arrow appears. Rotate the image the desired amount.**

In my example, I rotated the passport approximately 45 degrees.

**7.** **When you've transformed the selection to your liking, double-click inside the transform box or press Enter (Return on the Mac).**

The transform box disappears.

 Avoid as much interpolation as possible to ensure less quality degradation.

**8.** **To transform a selection that is on a layer mask, in the Layers palette choose the selection's layer and follow Steps 4 through 7.**

In my example, that's the compass layer.

 Be sure to click the selection's thumbnail and not the layer mask thumbnail. Otherwise, you'll transform the layer mask thumbnail instead of the selection.

**9.** **When you've transformed the selection to your liking, double-click inside the transform box.**

I scaled the compass slightly so that the top portion of the compass became visible. Then I rotated the compass to show more of the compass face rather than the cover.

**10.** **Choose File⇨Save.**

Book
**V**
Chapter
**2**

▼ **CONTINUED**

▼ CONTINUED

You probably already have a pretty good sense of the possibilities (which are infinite) available to you when you create and change collages. Of course, you can always add more stuff to a collage, and you can also rearrange the layers as needed. Just follow these steps:

**1.** **Choose File⇨Open and then select your collage file. Also open another supporting image.**

I chose a boarding pass image.

**2.** **Choose Window⇨Layers to open the Layers palette if it isn't already visible.**

**3.** **Select the desired element in the supporting image.**

It goes without saying that making the selection accurate can only enhance your composite. I selected the boarding pass with the Polygon Lasso tool.

**4.** **Contract and feather the image's edges and use the Move tool to drag the selection into the background.**

For the most professional appearance possible, make sure that the values you use are consistent with the values you chose when you modified and feathered all the other selections in this composite.

**5.** **Position and transform the selection as needed.**

Follow the directions provided in the preceding steps list.

In my example, I scaled the boarding pass to the same size as the passport, rotated it clockwise, and positioned it a little lower than the passport.

**6.** **In the Layers palette, select a layer and drag it above another layer.**

I dragged Layer 1 above Layer 3, for example.

Because they are independent entities, the layers can be shuffled indefinitely like a deck of cards.

**7.** **Choose File⇨Save.**

Book
**V**
Chapter
**2**

▼ ▼ ▼ ▼ ▼ ▼ ▼ ▼ ▼ ▼ ▼ ▼ ▼ ▼ ▼ ▼ ▼ ▼ ▼ ▼ ▼ ▼ ▼ ▼ ▼ ▼ ▼ ▼ ▼ ▼ ▼ ▼ ▼ ▼

# Aligning and Distributing Layers

If you are as precise as I am, you'll appreciate Photoshop's ability to align and distribute your layers. These commands can be especially useful when you need to align items such as navigation buttons on a Web page or a row of headshots for a corporate publication.

Here are the steps to align and distribute your layers:

1. **In the Layers palette, select the anchor layer that you want all of the other layers to align to.**

   The selected anchor layer will remain stationary, and the other layers will align to the anchor.

2. **Link the layers you want to align.**

   In the Layers palette, click the second column from the left (next to the eye column) to display the link icon, as shown in Figure 2-2. (For more on linking, see the next section.)

3. **Choose Layer⇨Align Linked and select one of the alignment commands.**

   Photoshop provides you with handy little icons that illustrate the various alignment types. You will also find these icons as buttons in the Options bar when the Move tool is selected, as shown in Figure 2-2. Feel free to use either method.

4. **In the Layers palette, link three or more layers that you want to distribute.**

This command evenly spaces the layers between the first and last elements in either the row or column.

5. **Choose Layer⇨Distribute Linked and select one of the distribute commands, as shown in Figure 2-3.**

Again for the word challenged, there is an icon illustrating the distribution types. And like alignment, you will also find the distribute icons as buttons in the Options bar when the Move tool is selected.

You can also align a layer (or linked layers) to a selection outline. First, make your desired selection in the image. Then select a layer or linked layers in the Layers palette. Choose Layer⇨Align to Selection and choose a command from the submenu. Note that the Align to Selection command doesn't appear in the Layer menu until you have both linked layers and an active selection outline.

 The alignment and distribution commands only work on layers with an opacity greater than 50%. For more on opacity, see Chapter 3 of this book.

**Figure 2-2**

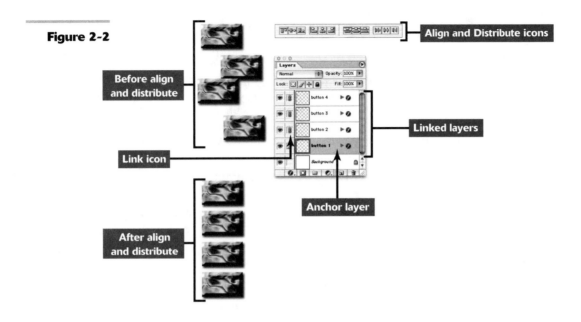

Before align and distribute

Link icon

After align and distribute

Align and Distribute icons

Linked layers

Anchor layer

**Figure 2-3**

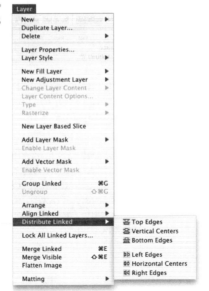

▼▼▼▼▼▼▼▼▼▼▼▼▼▼▼▼▼▼▼▼▼▼▼▼▼▼▼▼▼▼▼▼▼▼▼▼▼

## Linking Layers

In the preceding section, you find out how to link layers to align and distribute them. Linking layers temporarily groups two or more layers and allows you to perform a multitude of commands to those layers as a unit, as described in the following list:

- ✔ **Move linked layers:** Just drag with the Move tool, and elements on the linked layers move together.

- ✔ **Drag linked layers into another document:** See Chapter 1 of this book for more on dragging.

- ✔ **Merge linked layers:** See "Flattening and Merging Layers," later in this chapter, for more on merging.

- ✔ **Apply transformations:** See Chapter 1 of this book and Book III, Chapter 3, for details on transformations.

- ✔ **Create a new layer set:** See "Creating Layer Sets," later in this chapter.

- ✔ **Create clipping groups:** See Chapter 4 of this book for info on clipping groups.

- ✔ **Delete linked layers:** Select any one of the layers in the group and Ctrl+click (⌘+click on the Mac) the trash icon in the Layers palette. Or choose Layer⇨Delete⇨Linked Layers.

- ✔ **Delete hidden layers:** Choose Layer⇨Delete⇨Hidden Layers.

To link layers, follow these short steps:

**1.** **Select a layer or layer set in the Layers palette.**

This is your active layer. Next, you link the other layers to it.

**2.** **Click in the second column from the left (next to the eye column) on the layer you want to link.**

A link icon appears in the column. Repeat this step for any other layers you want to link.

To remove a link, click the link icon.

 To link and unlink multiple layers in a single flick of the wrist, drag your mouse up and down the link column. To unlink all the layers at once, Alt+click (Option+ click on the Mac) the paintbrush icon in the link column.

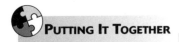 **Putting It Together**

### Linking Layers in a Collage and Adjusting Their Size

When you're working on composites, you may find the need to adjust the size or angle of more than one layer. You can link the layers you want to scale or rotate and transform all the layers at the same time.

This strategy enables you to adjust all the layers the same amount at the same time — thus ensuring that they stay proportional in size. In addition, linking layers can come in handy when you want to align and distribute layers evenly or if you want to merge several layers into one to save file space (both techniques are described in this chapter).

1. **Open your saved collage file.**

   Make sure that the Layers palette is visible.

2. **Select a layer.**

   In my example, I selected Layer 1.

3. **In the Layers palette, click in the second column (just to the right of the eye) next to a *different* layer.**

   I clicked the middle column for Layer 3.

A chain link icon appears. You've just linked two layers (such as Layers 1 and 3).

 **Choose Edit⊃Free Transform and Shift+click to move the corner transformation handle. When you're satisfied, double-click inside the transform box or press Enter (Return on the Mac).**

Because the images are linked, any transformation you apply, including moving and scaling, affects all the linked layers.

5. **Save the file when you're done.**

   To unlink layers, click the link icon. In my example, the link icon appears on Layer 3.

Book
**V**
Chapter
**2**

# Locking Layers

After you get your layers the way you want them, you may want to lock them to prevent them from being changed. To lock a layer, select it in the Layers palette and select one or more of the lock options at the top of the Layers palette, as shown from left to right in Figure 2-4:

✓ **Lock Transparent Pixels:** Prevents you from painting or editing any transparent areas on your layer. To quickly select or deselect the Lock Transparent Pixels check box, press the forward slash key (/).

**Figure 2-4**

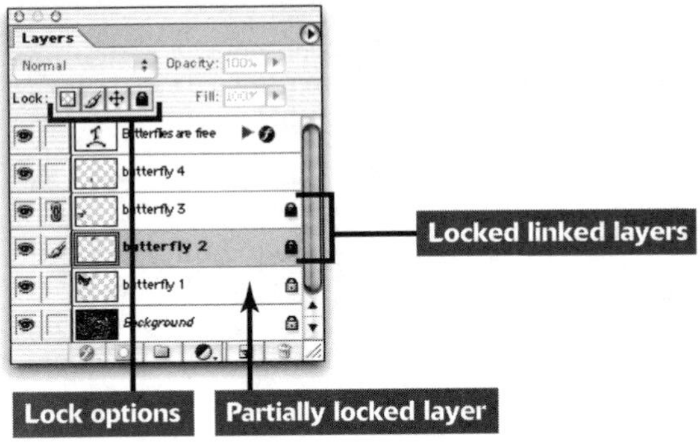

Locked linked layers

Lock options   Partially locked layer

✔ **Lock Image Pixels:** Prevents you from painting or editing your layer. You can still select, move, or transform items on the layer.

✔ **Lock Position:** Prevents you from moving and transforming the layer but gives you free rein on everything else.

✔ **Lock All:** Prevents you from painting, editing, moving, or transforming your layer. (But you can still make selections.)

When you select the Lock All option, a solid lock icon appears on the layer, indicating the layer is fully locked. When you select any of the other lock options, the lock appears hollow, indicating the layer is partially locked.

By default, type layers have the Lock Transparent Pixels and Lock Image Pixels options selected. These options are grayed out and cannot be deselected. However if you need to paint on the type layer, you can always rasterize it, thereby removing all locking options. For more on type, see Book IV, Chapter 4.

In addition, you can lock layer sets. Choose Lock All Layers in Set from the Layers palette options menu or choose Layer➪Lock All Layers in Set. For more on sets, see "Creating Layer Sets," later in this chapter.

You can also lock your linked layers. Select the linked layers (or linked set) and then either choose Lock All Linked Layers from the Layers palette options menu or choose Layer➪Lock All Linked Layers. In the dialog box that appears, select which items you want to lock.

## Color-Coding Layers

To visually distinguish your layers in the Layers palette, Photoshop lets you color-code your layers or layer sets, as shown in Figure 2-5. Choose Layer➪Layer Properties or choose Layer Properties from the Layers palette options menu. Choose a color from the pop-up menu and click OK. I find that color-coding works especially well with layer sets. First, organize your layers into sets, such as navigation buttons, type, images, border, background, and so on. Then assign a color to each set. By using the same color-coding system from one project to the next, you can get a little productivity boost by instinctively knowing where to find your elements.

**Figure 2-5**

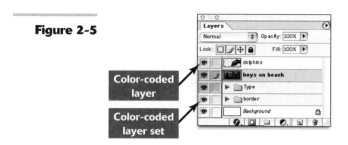

Color-coded layer

Color-coded layer set

# Creating Layer Sets

I don't know about you, but there's something very satisfying about having a file cabinet full of neatly labeled manila folders containing all of your vital paperwork. It's compact. It's organized. It's "at the ready" as they say in the military. Okay, so I need to get a life. But fellow geeks will revel in Photoshop's digital answer to the physical world's manila folder. You can group your layers into *layer sets* that can be expanded to see their contents or collapsed to hide their contents. In their collapsed state, layer sets are a great antidote for the annoying scrolling one must do to locate layers in an abundantly layered file.

To create a layer set, click the Create a New Set icon (the folder icon) at the bottom of the Layers palette, shown in Figure 2-6. You can also choose New Layer Set from the Layers palette options menu or choose Layer➪New➪Layer Set. The latter two methods prompt you for a set name in addition to a few other options (similar to regular layers). You can color-code your set and specify a blend mode and opacity setting. Note that the default mode is Pass Through, which lets the blend modes applied to the individual layers to remain intact. If you choose any other mode, it overrides all the layers in the set.

Book
**V**
Chapter
**2**

**Figure 2-6**

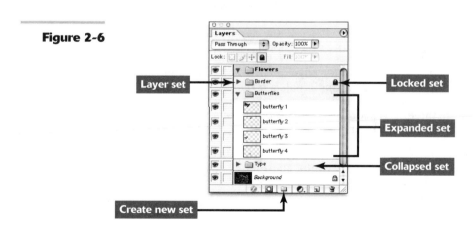

Layer set

Create new set

Locked set

Expanded set

Collapsed set

After you have created your set, drag your layers into the set folder in the Layers palette. If the set is collapsed when you drag or if you drag a layer on top of the layer set icon itself, the layer is placed at the bottom of the layer set. If the set is expanded, you can drag the layer to a specific location within the set. To collapse or expand the set, click the triangle icon to the left of the folder icon.

Although layer sets are pretty straightforward, here are few points to keep in mind:

- ✔ As with regular layers, you can select, duplicate, show, hide, lock, and rearrange layer sets. See other sections in this chapter for more on these commands.

- ✔ You can't move one layer set into another, nor can you create a new set within an existing set.

- ✔ You can create a layer set from linked layers. Link the layers you want in a set and choose New Set from Linked from the Layers palette options menu or choose Layer➪ New➪Layer Set from Linked. Name the set and click OK.

- ✔ If you select a layer within a set and then choose Layer➪Arrange, the command applies to the stacking order only within the layer set.

- ✔ You can merge layer sets. Select the set and choose Merge Layer Set from the Layers palette options menu or choose Layer➪Merge Layer Set. For more on merging, see the next section.

- ✔ You can rename your set by double-clicking the set name in the Layers palette. Or choose Layer➪Layer Set Properties or choose Layer Set Properties from the Layers palette options menu.

## Flattening and Merging Layers

Being the true layers evangelist that I am, I have spent the last two chapters touting the glories of layers. And they are wonderful. But they do have a dark side. They can make your file go from slim and trim to bulky and bloated. A consequence of a larger file size is that it slows your computer system performance. And you are limited in the types of file formats that allow you to save layers. You can only preserve layers in Photoshop's native format (.psd), TIFF (.tif), and PDF (.pdf). If you save your file in any other format, your layers are smashed down into a background. This file limitation often forces users to save two versions of every layered file — one as a native Photoshop file and one as something else, such as EPS or JPEG, to import into another program. For more on file formats, see Book II, Chapter 2.

Merging layers combines visible, linked, or adjacent layers into a single layer (not a background). The intersection of all transparent areas is retained. You can merge layers or layer sets. You can also merge adjustment or fill layers (see Chapter 1 of this book for details), but they cannot act as the target layer for the merge. Merging layers can help to decrease your file size and make your document more manageable.

Flattening an image combines all visible layers into a background. Hidden layers are deleted and any transparent areas are filled with white. Flattening is usually reserved for when you're completely finished editing your image.

When you convert an image from one color mode to another, it may cause the file to flatten. Look out for the warning dialog box that prompts you of this result and go back and save a copy of your file as a native Photoshop file, thereby preserving your layers.

▼ ▼ ▼ ▼ ▼ ▼ ▼ ▼ ▼ ▼ ▼ ▼ ▼ ▼ ▼ ▼ ▼ ▼ ▼ ▼ ▼ ▼ ▼ ▼ ▼ ▼ ▼ ▼ ▼ ▼ ▼ ▼ ▼ ▼ ▼ ▼ ▼ ▼ ▼

## Merging layers

You can merge your layers several ways. Here's the first option:

**1. Ensure that all the layers (and layer sets) you want to merge are visible.**

Note that you will be prompted with a dialog box informing you that all hidden layers will be discarded. Click OK.

**2. Choose Merge Visible from the Layers palette options menu or the Layer menu.**

All visible layers are combined into a single layer, as shown in Figure 2-7. The newly merged layer takes on the name of the topmost layer.

To merge visible layers without discarding your hidden layers, press Alt (Option on the Mac) when choosing Layer⇨Merge Visible.

You may also want to check out the "Alternative methods for merging layers" sidebar.

**Figure 2-7**

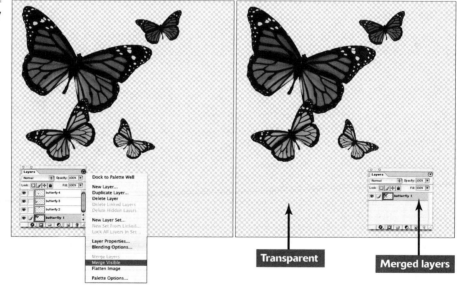

Transparent

Merged layers

### Alternative methods for merging layers

Because merging layers is such an important aspect of your Photoshop experience, I thought you'd want to know that (as with other Photoshop options and tools) there's more than one way to merge layers. In fact, here are two sets of steps to help you get the job done. I know, I know, I'm such a giver. Try this method to merge layers:

**1. Link all the layers and layer sets you want to merge.**

**2. Choose Merge Linked from the Layers palette options menu or the Layer menu.**

All linked layers are combined into a single layer. The newly merged layer takes on the name of the topmost layer.

Or you can try this method:

**1. Position the layer or layer sets you want to merge adjacent to each other in the Layers palette.**

**2. Select the top layer of those you want merged.**

**3. Choose Merge Down from the Layers palette options menu or the Layer menu. If the top layer is a layer set, the command is called Merge Layer Set.**

Note that Merge Down merges your active layer with *all* layers below it, so make sure that every layer underneath your active layer should be merged.

## Stamping layers

Photoshop also allows you to *stamp* your layers. Stamping merges layers onto a target (or active) layer while leaving the other layers untouched, similar to Merge Visible while holding down the Alt (Option on the Mac) key.

To stamp layers, follow these steps:

**1. Move the layer you want to stamp to above the layer you want to stamp from. Both layers must be visible.**

**2. Select the top layer and press Ctrl+Alt+E (⌘+Option+E on the Mac).**

You can also stamp linked layers by selecting one of the linked layers and choosing the same command.

If you want to stamp all visible layers, select the layers (or layer sets) and press Shift+Ctrl+Alt+E (Shift+⌘+ Option+E on the Mac). You may need to borrow a friend's fingers for that keyboard combo.

## Flattening layers

To flatten an image, follow these steps:

**1. Ensure that all the layers you want to retain are visible.**

Remember that all hidden layers will be discarded.

**2.** **Choose Layer⟹Flatten Image, or choose Flatten Image from the Layers palette options menu, shown in Figure 2-8.**

Note that Photoshop doesn't prompt you with a warning like, "Are you sure you really want to do this?" But if you mistakenly flatten your image, you can undo the command by immediately choosing Edit⟹Undo. If you've gone ahead and performed another action, then undo your mistake by using the History palette (see Book II, Chapter 4).

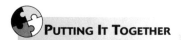

**Figure 2-8**

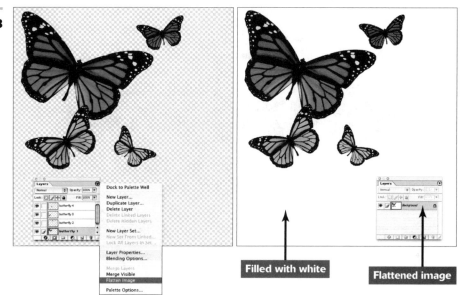 

Filled with white

Flattened image

Book
**V**
Chapter
**2**

 **PUTTING IT TOGETHER**

### Checking Your Collage for Flaws and Consolidating Layers

When you begin a project, you may think you know what you want the final result to look like. But as your creative juices start flowing, you may decide that something doesn't look right. For example, as I was working on my collage, I discovered that the sky behind and above the canyon was a little on the ordinary side.

**1.** **Open the saved collage file and open a new image that you want to incorporate into the collage.**

In my example, I thought the sky needed some kick, so I opened an image that contained a sky I liked.

**2.** **In the Layers palette, select the part of the image that you want to add to your collage.**

I chose the Rectangular Marquee tool and selected a strip of sky.

Most of the time, consistency is key. In my example, however, I didn't

▼ **CONTINUED**

▼ **CONTINUED**

need to feather the image. Because it's going to be pasted into the old sky, the edges of the element won't be seen.

**3.** **Using the Move tool, drag the selection into the collage.**

Because I'm pasting the image into the background image, I first needed to make the selection I wanted to paste into. I used the Magic Wand tool. After a couple of additional

Shift+clicks, I selected the entire sky behind the canyon. Then I copied and pasted the image (using the Edit⇨Paste Into command) into its new location.

When you're close to finalizing your collage, you might want to consolidate layers. Minimizing the number of layers makes projects easier to manage, which is great when you get ready to add the finishing touches to your collage.

Be sure that before you merge your layers, you will never have to manipulate them separately, especially if the elements on the layer overlap each other as mine do.

To consolidate two layers, follow these steps:

**1.** **Select a layer in the Layers palette and click in the second column**

next to the layer you want to consolidate it with.

**2.** **Choose Merge Linked from the Layers palette options menu.**

The two layers merge and become one.

**3.** **Choose File⇨Save.**

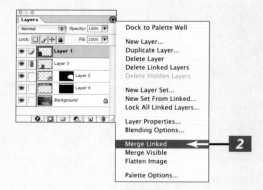

# Playing with Opacity and Blend Modes

3

If you've read Chapters 1 and 2 of this book, you have a pretty good handle on the methods of layer creation and management. (If not, what are you waiting for? Take a look at them and come on back when you're ready.) In this chapter, I show you how to let down your hair and get those creative juices flowing. Yes, I'm about to say the "F" word: Fun.

This chapter, along with Chapter 4 of this book, focuses on how to tweak the layers you've made. Maybe you want to make one of your layers semi-transparent so that you can see the layer beneath it; or say you want to try blending the colors between a couple layers in a way that is slightly offbeat. Look no further.

Although some of the techniques in this chapter may start to reek of being too complex or technical, keep in mind that it's not mandatory to totally understand them. Take these techniques as far as you want to. And remember there's no substitute for good old experimentation.

 If you want to play around with blend modes and opacity but you're not ready to commit just yet, make a back-up copy of an image (it helps to use an image that contains layers, of course). You can play around without permanently hurting the image. If the results of your activities offend you, you can always choose File➪Revert. And try, try again.

## Adjusting Layer Opacity

By far one of the easiest ways to make your image look oh so sophisticated is to have one image ghosted over another, as shown in Figure 3-1 (and in full, living color in the color insert). This is a snap with the Opacity option in the Layers palette. To adjust the opacity, select your desired layer in the Layers palette. Then either access the slider by clicking the right-pointing arrow or enter a percentage value in the Opacity text box. You can also double-click a layer thumbnail, choose Layer⇨Layer Style⇨Blending Options, or choose Blending Options from the Layers palette options menu. All three methods bring up the Layer Style dialog box, where you can enter a value or drag the slider for opacity.

The Opacity setting allows you to mix the active layer with the layers below it in varying percentages from 100% (completely opaque) to 0% (completely transparent). Remember that you can only adjust the opacity on a layer, not a background. That's because there's nothing behind the background to mix with.

You can also change the Opacity percentage by using keyboard shortcuts. With any tool active, except a painting or editing tool, press a number key. Press 5 for 50 percent, 25 for 25 percent. You get the picture. Note that for the default of 100 percent, you must press 0.

**Figure 3-1**

Images combined with an opacity of 30%

## Adjusting the Fill Opacity

In addition to adjusting the regular opacity for a layer, you can also adjust the fill opacity. Fill opacity works a little differently from regular opacity. The regular Opacity setting affects layer styles (see Chapter 4 of this book) and blend modes (see the following section, "Creating Effects with Blend Modes"), which have been applied to the layer.

Fill opacity, however, only affects the pixels or shapes that reside on the layer. It doesn't affect the styles or blends. As you can see in Figure 3-2, the drop shadow and emboss styles in the bottom example show through full strength. To adjust the Fill Opacity setting, select your desired layer in the Layers palette and enter a value in the Fill Opacity text box or drag the pop-up slider. The other methods for adjusting fill opacity are similar to the regular opacity option.

**Figure 3-2**

## Creating Effects with Blend Modes

You'll see them called blend modes, painting modes, brush modes, layer modes, calculations, or just plain modes. They are usually referred to as blend modes or layer modes when working with layers and painting modes, and brush modes when using them in conjunction with a painting or editing tool. But whatever you call them, the 24 blend modes determine how the colors in different layers interact with each other. Blend modes can produce a multitude of interesting, sometimes even bizarre, effects. And what's more, blend modes can be easily applied, easily changed, and easily discarded with no permanent damage to your layers.

The options in the Blend Mode pop-up menu in the Layers palette are the same as those found under the Mode drop-down list in the Options bar, with the exception of two modes. Behind and Clear are only found in the Options bar because they are only available for use with painting and editing tools.

I urge you to pick an image with a few layers and apply each blend mode to get a good handle on what the various blend modes do. In fact, try a few different images, because the effects may be subtle or intense depending on the colors in the image. Throw in some different opacity percentages, and you're on your way to endless hours of creative fun.

## General blend modes

You're probably very familiar with the Normal blend mode by now. It is the default and lets each pixel appear in its very own unadulterated state. The other three can only be used in certain circumstances. Behind and Clear can only be used when you have a painting or editing tool in hand. And Dissolve can only be used with a layer that has an opacity setting of less than 100% — the lower the opacity, the more intense the effect. The general blend modes are shown in action in Figure 3-3 and described in Table 3-1.

**Figure 3-3**

**TABLE 3-1: GENERAL BLEND MODES**

| Blend Mode | Description |
| --- | --- |
| Normal | Default mode. Each pixel appears in its original, normal state. |
| Dissolve | Only affects images that have Opacity settings of less than 100%. Allows some pixels from lower layers, which are randomized, to show through the target layer. |

| Blend Mode | Description |
|---|---|
| Behind | Only available with a painting or editing tool active. Type must be rasterized, and Lock Transparency must be deselected. Allows you to edit or paint only on the transparent areas of the layer, giving the illusion that the strokes are behind the layer. |
| Clear | Only available with a painting or editing tool active. Type must be rasterized, and Lock Transparency must be deselected. Allows you to edit or paint with transparency, giving the appearance that holes are being punched into your image. |

## Blend modes that darken

Overall, the blend modes in this category all produce effects that darken your image, as shown in Figure 3-4. However, one of my favorite uses for the Darken blend mode is a little different. Scan a handwritten letter or sheet of music and layer it over an image. Apply the Darken blend mode to the letter or sheet music layer. The white areas of the paper will become transparent, and only the letters or musical notes will display, creating a nice composite image. Table 3-2 describes these modes.

**Figure 3-4**

Book
**V**
Chapter
**3**

### TABLE 3-2: BLEND MODES THAT DARKEN

| Blend Mode | Description |
|---|---|
| Darken | If the pixels on the layer are lighter than those below, they turn transparent. If the pixels on the layer are darker, they display unchanged. A great mode for superimposing scanned text or line art because it allows the white color of the paper to essentially drop out leaving only the dark letters or lines. |

*continued*

**TABLE 3-2:** *(CONTINUED)*

| Blend Mode | Description |
|---|---|
| Multiply | Burns the layer into the layers underneath. The Multiply mode darkens all colors where they mix. With layers, it is comparable to sticking two slides in the same slot in a slide projector. If painting, each successive stroke creates a darker color, as if drawing with markers. |
| Color Burn | Darkens the layers underneath and burns them with color. Increases contrast. Blending with white pixels has no effect. Like applying a dark dye to your image. |
| Linear Burn | Darkens the layers underneath by decreasing the brightness. Similar to Multiply but tends to make portions of your image pure black. Blending with white pixels has no effect. |

## Blend modes that lighten

If you have blend mode that darken, well, it just makes good sense to have those that lighten. So if you have the need to throw some digital bleach on your brightly colored pixels, try out a couple of these blend modes, described in Table 3-3. Figure 3-5 shows examples of these effects.

**Figure 3-5**

**TABLE 3-3: BLEND MODES THAT LIGHTEN**

| Blend Mode | Description |
|---|---|
| Lighten | If the pixels on the layer are darker than those below, they turn transparent. If the pixels on the layer are lighter, they display unchanged. The opposite of Darken. |

| Blend Mode | Description |
|---|---|
| Screen | Lightens the layer where it mixes with the layer underneath. Blending with black pixels has no effect. Like putting two slides in two different projectors and pointing them at the same screen. The opposite of Multiply. |
| Color Dodge | Lightens the pixels in the layers underneath and infuses them with colors from the top layer. Like bleaching your layer. Blending with black pixels has no effect. |
| Linear Dodge | Lightens the layers underneath by increasing the brightness. Similar to Screen but tends to makes parts of your image pure white. Blending with black pixels has no effect. |

## Lighting blend modes

Three of these blend modes — Vivid Light, Linear Light, and Pin Light — are newcomers, courtesy of Version 7. Some of these blend modes, like Overlay and Pin Light, are reserved for the occasional wacky special effect. Figure 3-6 shows examples of these effects. Table 3-4 describes the modes.

**Figure 3-6**

Overlay

Soft Light

Hard Light

Vivid Light

Linear Light

Pin Light

**TABLE 3-4: LIGHTING BLEND MODES**

| Blend Mode | Description |
|---|---|
| Overlay | Multiplies the dark pixels in the top layer and screens the light pixels in the underlying layers. Enhances the contrast and saturation of colors. |
| Soft Light | Darkens the dark pixels and lightens the light pixels. If the pixels on the top layer are lighter than 50% gray, they are lightened. If the pixels on the top layer are darker than 50% gray, the pixels are darkened. Blending with black or white results in darker or lighter pixels but doesn't make parts of your image pure black or pure white. Similar to Overlay, but softer and more subtle. Like shining a soft spotlight on the image. |
| Hard Light | Multiplies the dark pixels and screens the light pixels. Like shining a bright, hard spotlight on the image. If the pixels on the top layer are lighter than 50% gray, they are screened. If the pixels on the top layer are darker than 50% gray, the pixels are multiplied. Can be used to add highlights and shadows to an image. Blending with black or white gives you black and white. |
| Vivid Light | If the pixels on the top layer are darker than 50% gray, it burns, or darkens, the colors by increasing the contrast. If the pixels on the top layer are lighter than 50% gray, it dodges, or lightens, the colors by decreasing the contrast. A combination of Color Burn and Color Dodge. |
| Linear Light | If the pixels on the top layer are darker than 50% gray, it burns, or darkens, the colors by decreasing the brightness. If the pixels on the top layer are lighter than 50% gray, it dodges, or lightens, the colors by increasing the brightness. A combination of Linear Burn and Linear Dodge. |
| Pin Light | Replaces the colors of pixels, depending on the colors in the top layer. If the pixels on the top layer are darker than 50% gray, pixels darker than those on the top layer are replaced, and lighter pixels don't change. If the pixels on the top layer are lighter than 50% gray, lighter pixels than those on the top layer are replaced, and pixels that are darker don't change. A combination of Darken and Lighten and useful for special effects. |

## Blend modes that invert

If the preceding blend modes are a tad too tame for you, you may want to check out the "Inverters" — Difference and Exclusion (described in Table 3-5). These blend modes invert your colors and can produce some interesting special effects, as shown in Figure 3-7.

**Figure 3-7**

Difference

Exclusion

**TABLE 3-5: BLEND MODES THAT INVERT**

| Blend Mode | Description |
|---|---|
| Difference | Produces a negative or inverted effect according to the brightness values on the top layers. If the pixels on the top layer are black, the colors of the underlying layers are unchanged. If the pixels on the top layer are white, the colors of the underlying layers are inverted. Can produce bizarre results. |
| Exclusion | Similar to Difference but with less contrast and saturation. If the pixels on the top layer are black, the colors of the underlying layers are unchanged. If the pixels on the top layer are white, the colors of the underlying layers are inverted. Medium colors blend to create gray. |

## HSL color model blend modes

These blend modes use the HSL (Hue Saturation Lightness) color model to mix colors. My favorite blend mode in this group is Color, which allows you to apply color to images without obscuring the tonality. Table 3-6 lists these modes, and Figure 3-8 shows their effects.

**Figure 3-8**

Hue

Saturation

Color

Luminosity

**TABLE 3-6: HSL COLOR MODEL BLEND MODES**

| Blend Mode | Description |
|---|---|
| Hue | Takes the luminance (brightness) and saturation (intensity of the color) of the underlying layers and blends them with the hue (color) of the top layer. |
| Saturation | Takes the luminance and hue of the underlying layers and blends them with the saturation of the top layer. |

*continued*

**TABLE 3-6:** *(CONTINUED)*

| Blend Mode | Description |
| --- | --- |
| Color | Takes the luminance of the underlying layers and blends them with the saturation and hue of the top layer. This mode is great for colorizing grayscale (with a color mode set to RGB) images because it preserves the shadows, highlights, and details of the underlying layers. |
| Luminosity | Takes the hue and saturation of the underlying layers and blends them with the luminance of the top layer. Preserves the shadows, highlights, and details from the top layer and mixes them with the colors of the underlying layers. The opposite of Color. |

## Working with the Advanced Blending Options

If you want to get serious about layers, then you need to know about the Advanced Blending Options, found in the Layer Style dialog box. These options allow you to tailor the way your layer styles and blend modes interact with your layers. Getting to the advanced options is just like accessing opacity and blend modes: You can double-click a layer thumbnail, choose Layer➪Layer Style➪Blending Options, or choose Blending Options from the Layers palette options menu. The massive Layer Style dialog box rears its multipaneled head, as shown in Figure 3-9.

(By the way, if you're ready to know about more blending features, skip to Chapter 4 of this book, where I cover layer styles.)

The advanced options are not for the faint of heart. To be frank, the options are, well, advanced, so you might find them a tad too eggheady for your taste, but if not here you go:

**Figure 3-9**

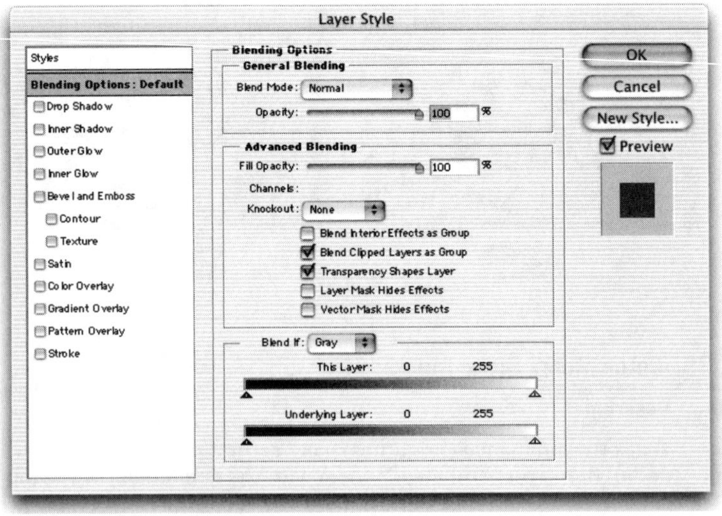

## Advanced options to blend with

✔ **Fill Opacity:** I cover this in "Adjusting the Fill Opacity," earlier in this chapter.

✔ **Channels:** This option allows you to restrict your blending options to specific channels only. For all you need to know about working with channels, check out Book VI.

✔ **Knockout:** This option allows you to specify which layers have holes in them so that you can view the layers underneath. You first have to use the Fill Opacity option to set the opacity of the knockout. The lower the opacity, the more the hole will show; therefore, set it to 0% (as in my example in Figure 3-10) to see all the way through. Set the Knockout to Shallow to create a hole through one layer set (see Chapter 2 of this book) or a clipping group (see Chapter 4 of this book). Set the Knockout to Deep to create a hole all the way through to the background. If you're just working with layers, and not sets or clipping groups, the knockout cuts through to the background. If there is no background, it cuts through to transparency.

**Figure 3-10**

✓ **Blend Interior Effects as Group:** This option applies the blend mode of the layer to interior layer effects, such as inner glows, satin and color overlay, and so on. Uncheck this option, and the blend mode does not affect the layer effects. (See Figure 3-11. Check out the color insert, as well.)

✓ **Blend Clipped Layers as Group:** The blend mode of the bottom layer in the clipping group affects all the other layers in the group. Uncheck this option, and each layer retains its own blend mode and appearance. (See Figure 3-12.)

✓ **Transparency Shapes Layer:** Confines layer effects and knockouts to opaque areas of a layer. Uncheck this option, and layer effects and knockouts are applied to the entire layer.

**Figure 3-11**

Blend Interior Effects as Group unchecked

Checked

**Figure 3-12**

**Blend Clipped Layers as Group checked** →

**Unchecked** →

✔ **Layer Mask Hides Effects:** Confines layer effects to the area designated by the layer mask. (For more on layer masks, see Book VI, Chapter 3.)

✔ **Vector Mask Hides Effects:** Confines layer effects to the area designated by a vector mask. (For more on vector masks, see Book VI, Chapter 3.)

## Blend If options

By using the slider bars, you can specify which colors are visible in the active layer and which colors show through from the underlying layers. You can choose a specific channel from the Blend If pop-up menu to apply the option to a single channel. The default channel of Gray affects all channels in the image.

✔ The slider bar under **This Layer** allows you to set a blending range. In other words, you can hide certain colors according to the brightness values in the active layer. By dragging the black triangle to the right, you exclude darker colors. By dragging the white triangle to the left, you exclude lighter colors.

✔ The slider bar under **Underlying Layers** forces the colors from the underlying layers to show through the active layer. Again dragging the black and white triangles excludes ranges of colors.

 Excluding and forcing colors can result in some harsh color transitions. You can provide for a smoother transition between blended and unblended areas by splitting the slider into two parts. This allows the pixels to gradually fade to transparency. Alt+drag (Option+drag on the Mac) on either the black or white triangle in either slider bar to split the triangle into two halves. The left and right triangles mark the beginning and end of the blending range, where pixels will fade into or out of view.

### Fine-tuning and Adjusting Opacity Settings in Your Collage

If you've followed along with the Putting-It-Together project I discuss in Chapters 1 and 2 of this book, you may have a collage that you're pretty satisfied with. You just need to make the final tweaks and finally go to sleep (or get home to your spouse and children). But not before running around the room congratulating yourself on a project well done. Not so fast, Bucko. You still haven't made those tweaks I mentioned.

One of the most important tweaks you can make is to opacity. Here's how to adjust the opacity settings on some of the layers:

**1.** **Open your saved collage file.**

   If the Layers palette isn't already visible, open it.

**2.** **Select a layer in your collage and move the opacity slider to the left or to the right.**

If you want the layer to be more opaque, move the slider to the right. If you're interested in making the layer more transparent, move the slider to the left.

I chose Layer 4 and adjusted the opacity to 75%. I like the blue sky in my collage, but it's a tad too vibrant in comparison to the rest of the image. Adjusting the opacity tones down allows the blue to blend in more naturally.

**3.** **When you're done adjusting opacity for a layer, save the file and move on to the next layer you want to adjust.**

If you have more complicated opacity settings to adjust, keep reading.

**4.** **Select the background layer and then choose Duplicate Layer from the Layers palette pop-up menu.**

Click OK to close the Duplicate Layer dialog box.

Making a copy of the background is great because it allows you to add a blend mode, as you'll do in the next step, and then adjust it to get just the right amount of the effect.

For example, if you want to define an element in your collage, but applying it directly on the layer produces too intense of an effect, make a copy of the layer. I wanted to pump up the definition of the canyon in my collage, but when I used the blend mode directly on the

background, the result looked too harsh.

By the way, I couldn't resist the urge to include a pair of hiking boots in my collage.

**5.** **Select the background copy layer and choose a mode (such as Vivid Light) from the Mode pop-up menu in the Layers palette.**

It's likely that now the definition looks great but the contrast is over the top.

**6.** **Adjust the opacity to tone it down.**

I changed the opacity in mine to 35%.

**7.** **When you're satisfied with the opacity and contrast, save the collage file.**

Book
**V**
Chapter
**3**

▼ **CONTINUED**

**CONTINUED**

# Getting Jazzy with Layer Styles and Clipping Groups

I f you've already read the first three chapters of Book V, you're reaching the end of your guided tour on layers. And like most tours, I wanted to leave some of the more interesting items for last. You know, go out with a bang and all that. (If you haven't already checked out the other chapters on layers, what are you waiting for? This chapter assumes that you're using layers, so you're free to excuse yourself and come back later.)

After you have all the basic elements in your layered composite image, you may want to give it a little pizzazz and finesse. Maybe a headline would pop out a little more if you beveled the edge, or maybe that silhouetted image would take on a little more dimension if you placed a drop shadow behind it. This is the chapter where you find out how to do that and more. But remember the old adage, less is more. Just because you can do something doesn't necessarily mean you should. I mean, if you bevel and shadow *everything*, your image may go from well done to overdone.

## Layer Styles Basics

In the old days, creating a drop shadow in Photoshop took a concerted effort. And beveled or embossed type? Well, let's just say you really had to have the inside scoop on some Photoshop tricks. Now, however, Photoshop makes creating these kinds of effects as easy as selecting an option box.

 You may see the terms *effect* and *style* used interchangeably. Technically, Adobe says that after layer effects have been applied to a layer, they become part of a layer's *style*. As far as I'm concerned, effects create a style, so, for the purposes of this chapter, the terms are one and the same.

Layer effects can be applied to regular layers, shape layers, fill layers, and type layers, but not to backgrounds, locked layers, or layer sets. For more on backgrounds, see Chapter 1 in this book. For details on locking layers and creating layer sets, see Chapter 2 in this book.

Layer effects are *dynamically linked* to the contents of a layer. If you move or edit the contents of the layers (even just to change the letters of your type), the effects are updated.

When you apply effects, they become part of the layer's style. A styled layer has a florin symbol (which looks like a fancy letter *f*) next to the layer's name in the Layers palette. You can expand (to view the individual effects) or collapse the layer style by clicking the triangle icon next to the florin. If you create a style so fantastic that you want to save it for later use, you can do that by saving a custom style as a preset and storing it in the Styles palette (see "Creating your own style," later in this chapter).

## Introducing Layer Styles

Layer effects fall into a few categories. You can add shadows, glow effects, beveled and embossed edges, overlay colors and patterns, and, of course, tweak to your heart's content. The following sections give you the basics. I go into detail on each layer style later in this chapter, and I show you the effects in full-color glory in the color insert.

### Shadows

Shadows add a soft drop or inner shadow to a selection or the contents of a layer. You can adjust the blend mode, color, opacity, angle, size, and contour of the shadow to suit your needs. Figure 4-1 shows examples of both types of shadows.

- **Drop Shadow:** Applies a shadow behind the elements.
- **Inner Shadow:** Adds a shadow that falls inside the edges of the elements making them look recessed.

**Figure 4-1**

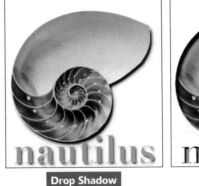
Drop Shadow

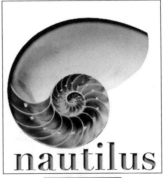
Inner Shadow

## Glow effects

Glows add a soft highlight that appears either on the outside or inside edges of a selection or the contents of a layer, as shown in Figure 4-2. Like shadows, you can fine-tune the appearance of the glow by adjusting numerous options.

- ✔ **Outer Glow:** Applies a glow around the outside edges of the elements.
- ✔ **Inner Glow:** Adds a glow around the inside edges of the elements.

**Figure 4-2**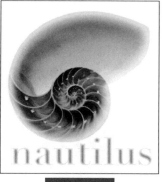

Outer Glow        Inner Glow

## Beveled, embossed, and satiny looks

Bevels create a 3-D edge on either the outside or inside edges of a selection of the contents of a layer, giving the element some dimension. Similarly, emboss effects make elements appear as though they are raising off or are punched into the page. Satin is intended to create a satiny or draped fabric effect over your element. All of these effects (shown in Figure 4-3) offer numerous options to adjust their appearances.

- ✔ **Outer Bevel:** Creates a 3-D raised edge around the outer edges of the elements.
- ✔ **Inner Bevel:** Makes a 3-D edge on the inside edge of the elements.
- ✔ **Emboss:** Combines the inner and outer bevels' effects to give the illusion that the elements are raised off the page.
- ✔ **Pillow Emboss:** Reverses an inner bevel making it seem that the elements are stamped or punched in along the edges and raised in the center.
- ✔ **Stroke Emboss:** Applies an emboss to a stroke that has been applied via the Stroke layer style.
- ✔ **Satin:** Applies a shading to the inside shape of the elements, creating a satiny appearance.

Figure 4-3

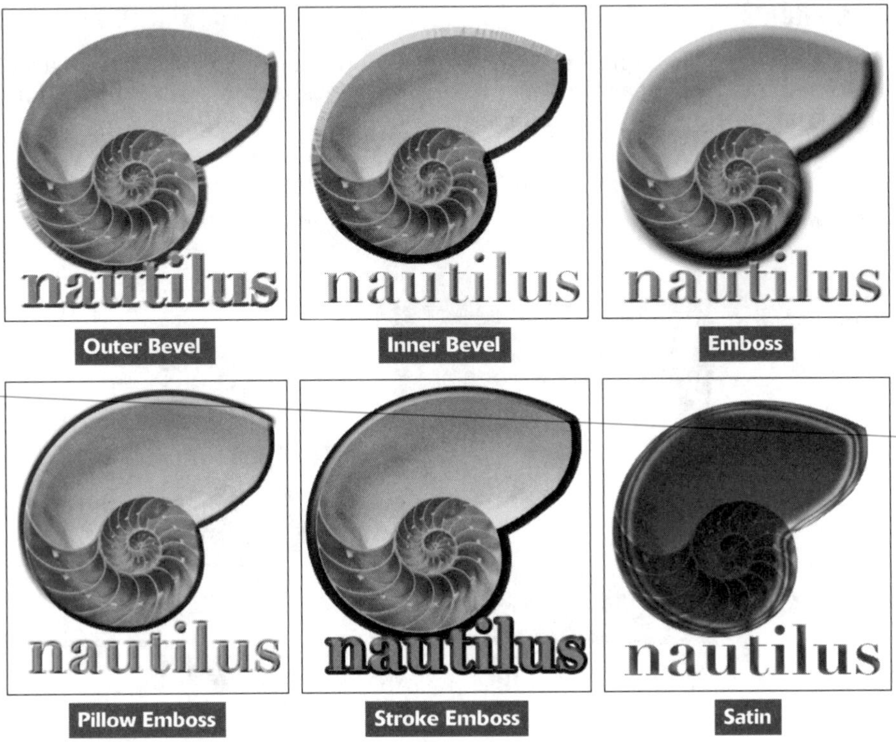
nautilus
Outer Bevel
nautilus
Inner Bevel
nautilus
Emboss
nautilus
Pillow Emboss
nautilus
Stroke Emboss
nautilus
Satin

## Overlays and Stroke

Overlays apply a fill of color, a gradient, or a pattern over your selection or the contents of your layer, as shown in Figure 4-4. You can adjust the opacity of the overlay, among other options, to allow your original element to show through more clearly. You can also surround your element with a stroke consisting of color, gradient, or pattern.

- **Color Overlay:** Covers the elements with a color.
- **Gradient Overlay:** Covers the elements with a gradient.
- **Pattern Overlay:** Covers the elements with a pattern.
- **Stroke:** Outlines the elements with a color, gradient, or pattern.

**Figure 4-4**

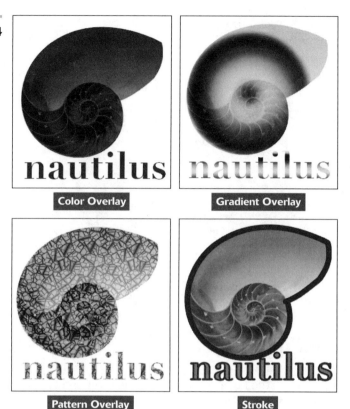

Color Overlay

Gradient Overlay

Pattern Overlay

Stroke

## Applying a Layer Effect

Follow these steps to apply a layer effect:

**1.** Select your desired layer in the Layers palette.

**2.** Choose Layer⇨Layer Style and choose an effect from the submenu.

You can also use a shortcut by clicking the Layer Style icon in the Layers palette and choosing an effect from the pop-up menu.

An intimidating dialog box with a ton of options rears its head, as shown in Figure 4-5.

**3.** Select the Preview check box so you can see your effects as you apply them.

**4.** To accept the default settings, just click OK. Or you can experiment with the settings.

You can use sliders, or you can enter values in the text boxes. The upcoming sections in this chapter describe the options and settings in detail.

CONTINUED

**5.** **When you're done refining your effect settings, click OK.**

Your effect is applied to your layer as indicated by the florin.

 The Layer Style dialog box also has options for Styles and Blending Options (default). See Chapter 3 of this book for blending options and this chapter for styles.

**Figure 4-5**

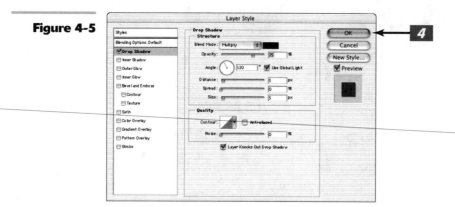

# Managing and Editing Layer Styles

You can always just apply the layer effect with Photoshop's default settings, but what fun is that? To edit a style, double-click the layer thumbnail or the layer style icon in the Layers palette and make your desired adjustments in the Layer Style dialog box.

The following sections give you the details on each of the options. But a picture is worth a thousand words. Experiment to really see these effects come alive.

## Managing layer styles

Here are a few pointers to keep in mind when working with and editing layer styles:

- ✔ **Choose several effects at one time:** Simply select the check box for the effect on the left side of the Layer Style dialog box. To access the options for each effect, you must select the effect name so that it is highlighted.

- ✔ **Remove an effect:** Deselect the check box associated with it.

- ✔ **Move a style onto a separate layer:** By default, layer styles are attached to a layer. To put a style on a separate layer, select the styled layer and choose Layer⇨Layer Style⇨Create Layer. You see a new layer in the Layers palette with a name, such as *Layer 0's Drop Shadow,* as shown in Figure 4-6.

 Although separating a style onto its own layer may give you more manual editing capability and allow you to apply filters, you lose all editing ability with the Layer Style dialog box. Also, the style won't dynamically update when you change the layer itself. Your style basically becomes just a generic mass of colored pixels.

**Figure 4-6**

✔ **Copy and paste effects onto other layers:** Select the layer containing the effect and choose Layer⇨Layer Style⇨Copy Layer Style. Select the layer on which you want to apply the effect and choose Layer⇨Layer Style⇨Paste Layer Style. Even easier, you can also just drag and drop an effect from one layer to another.

✔ **Copy an effect onto multiple layers in one fell swoop:** Link the layers and choose Layer⇨Layer Style⇨Paste Layer Style to Linked.

✔ **Hide effects:** Choose Layer⇨Layer Style⇨Hide All Effects.

   **Display hidden effects:** Choose Layer⇨Layer Style⇨Show All Effects. You can also Alt+double-click (Option+double-click on the Mac) the style in the Layers palette.

✔ **Remove all the effects on a layer:** Choose Layer⇨Layer Style⇨Clear Layer Style.

   You can also drag the *Effects bar* (what Adobe calls the name Effects) to the trash icon in the Layers palette.

✔ **Remove a single effect:** Double-click the effect in the Layers palette and deselect it in the Layer Style dialog box. You can just drag and drop the single effect to the trash icon in the Layers palette.

✔ **Resize a layer effect:** Choose Layer⇨Layer Style⇨Scale Effects. Select Preview and enter a value between 1 and 1,000 percent. This command allows you to scale the effect without scaling the element.

### Editing drop shadow or inner shadow effects

If you used the default settings to apply your drop shadow or inner shadow and now want to do some tweaking, feel free to edit at will by following these steps:

*1.* **Double-click the layer thumbnail or the layer style icon (florin).**

   The Layer Style dialog box opens.

*2.* **Change the Blend Mode setting to adjust how the colors of the shadow mix with the colors of your elements.**

   Usually the default mode works best.

**3.** **Adjust the Opacity setting to change how transparent the shadow appears.**

*4.* **Choose a shadow color by clicking the swatch to go to the Color Picker.**

**5.** **Establish the angle of your light source.**

CONTINUED
▼ ▼ ▼ ▼ ▼

**6.** **Select the Use Global Light option to ensure that all the shadows and highlights of all your elements are consistent.**

You don't want one layer to look like it's 6 a.m., and another to look like it's 2 p.m.

The neat thing is that if you change the angle on one layer style, all the styles that have been applied to your layers adjust to that new angle dynamically.

**7.** **Specify how far the shadow is offset from your element with the Distance setting.**

**8.** **Adjust the Spread or Choke and Size settings to specify the boundary, intensity, and size of the shadow.**

**9.** **Select the Layer Knocks Out Drop Shadow option if you have a transparent object on top of the shadow.**

This prevents the shadow from showing through the object.

**10.** **When you're done refining your effect settings, click OK.**

Your effect is edited and ready to go, as shown in Figure 4-7.

You can also choose to apply various contours and noise to your shadow. See "Playing with Contours," later in this chapter, for details.

**Figure 4-7**

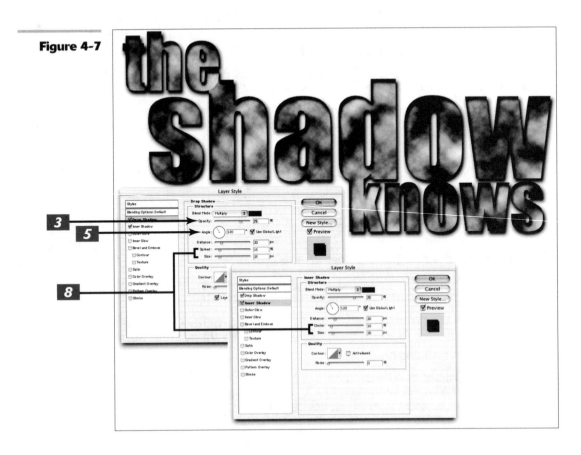

▼ ▼ ▼ ▼ ▼ ▼ ▼ ▼ ▼ ▼ ▼ ▼ ▼ ▼ ▼ ▼ ▼ ▼ ▼ ▼ ▼ ▼ ▼ ▼ ▼ ▼ ▼ ▼ ▼ ▼ ▼ ▼ ▼ ▼ ▼ ▼ ▼ ▼ ▼ ▼ ▼ ▼ ▼

## Changing default inner and outer glow effects

The inner and outer glow effects possess many of the same settings as the shadows. But unlike shadows, with glows you also have the option of using a gradient for your glow. This can produce an interesting custom halo effect, as shown in Figure 4-8.

Follow these steps to edit your own glow:

***1.*** **Double-click the layer thumbnail or the layer style icon (florin).**

The Layer Style dialog box opens.

***2.*** **Specify Blend Mode, Opacity, Color, Spread, and Size settings.**

If you are editing an inner glow effect, you see the options of Source (Center or Edge) and Choke instead of Spread.

The Center option applies the glow over the entire image except the edge, whereas the Edge option applies only to the element's edge. The Choke option behaves similarly to Spread.

***3.*** **Choose a preset gradient from the Gradient drop-down palette or click the Gradient Editor button to edit or create your own gradient.**

**Figure 4-8**

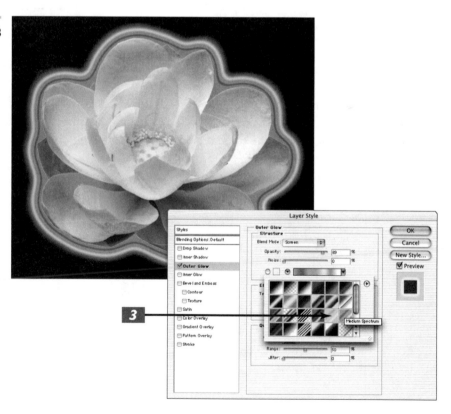

CONTINUED
▼ ▼ ▼ ▼ ▼

**4.** **In the Technique option, choose either the Softer or Precise setting.**

Choose Softer to apply a blurred glow. This option doesn't preserve detailed edges of the element.

Choose Precise to create a glow that is good for hard-edge elements such as type. This option does preserve the details.

**5.** **Use the Range and Jitter options for the Contour setting.**

For more on contours, see the "Playing with Contours" section.

**6.** **When you're done refining your effect settings, click OK.**

Your effect is edited and ready to rock.

## Editing Bevel and Emboss Effects

Because Photoshop offers five bevel and emboss styles, there are, of course, a ton of options. Some are similar to those found with the shadow and glow effects, whereas others are unique. The dialog box is divided into four panels.

### Structure

This panel contains the most relevant options, as shown in Figure 4-9:

- ✔ The **Technique** settings of Smooth, Chisel Hard, or Chisel Soft determine how soft or hard the edge of the bevel is. Chisel Hard works well with type and harder-edged elements.

- ✔ **Depth** affects how raised or sunken the edge of the bevel or the pattern appears.

- ✔ For the **Direction** settings, Up positions the highlight along the edge, closest to the light source, and the shadow on the opposite edge. Down does the opposite and positions the shadow near the light source.

- ✔ **Size** controls the size of the bevel or emboss effect.

**Figure 4-9**

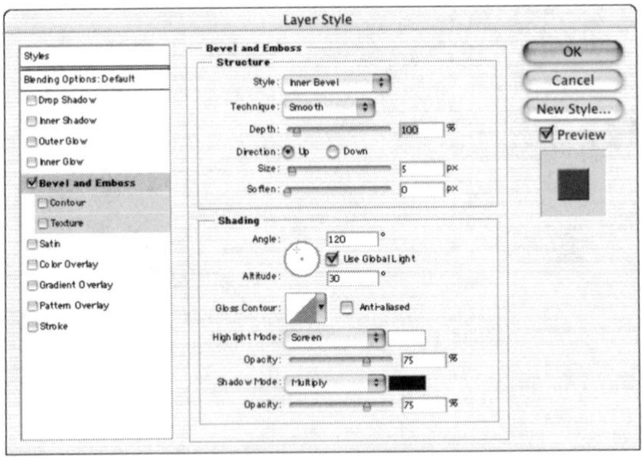

- ✔ **Soften** blurs the shading of the effect.
- ✔ **Angle** is the same as with Drop Shadow.

## Shading

Because of the 3-D nature of bevel and emboss effects, there are settings for Highlight and Shadow (each with separate Blend Modes and Opacity options) and Depth. Because bevel and embosses are more dimensional, an additional setting of Altitude affects the light source.

## Texture

In the Texture panel (click Texture on the left side of the dialog box), shown in Figure 4-10, you can apply a pattern onto your layer that creates a texture. Adjust the scale and depth of the pattern, and link the pattern to the layer if desired. If the pattern and layer are linked, the pattern will move if the layer is moved. The Snap to Origin command aligns the pattern origin with the document if the Link with Layer option is selected. If the option is not selected, the Snap to Origin command aligns the pattern to the top-left corner of the layer.

**Figure 4-10**

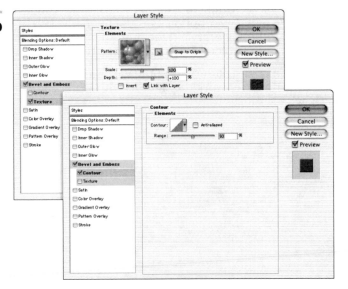

Book
**V**
Chapter
**4**

## Contour

Contours change the distribution of the colors in the effect. You can use the various presets offered to create interesting, and sometimes bizarre, shadows, glows, bevels, and other effects. For details on contour and its various iterations, see the upcoming section, "Playing with Contours."

## Editing Satin Effects

You can adjust the blend modes, opacity, angle, distance, and size — all of which have been explained in the preceding sections. You can also adjust the contour, which is discussed later in "Playing with Contours."

## Changing Overlay Effects

Shadows, being based in reality, are the kind of effects you will find yourself using frequently. On the other hand, you will probably find yourself only occasionally, if at all, using overlay effects. In most cases, overlays are reserved for the realm of the special effect. But in case you need to apply an overlay, here are the options:

- ✔ **Color Overlay:** Adjust the Blend Mode, Opacity, and Color settings of the overlay. This effect, along with the Gradient Overlay and Pattern Overlay, is best used with an opacity setting of less than 100% or a Blend Mode other than Normal. That way, the elements underneath aren't totally obliterated.

- ✔ **Gradient Overlay:** Choose a preset gradient from the drop-down Gradient picker, shown in Figure 4-11, or click the Gradient swatch to access the Gradient Editor to create your own. The Align with Layer option uses the bounding box of the layer to calculate the gradient. Specify the angle, style (Linear or Radial), and scale of the gradient. Reverse flips the gradient. Adjust Blend Modes and Opacity settings.

- ✔ **Pattern Overlay:** Choose a preset pattern from the Pattern picker drop-down palette. Snap to Origin and Link with Layer work the same as with Bevel and Emboss. Choose Blend Modes and Opacity settings.

**Figure 4-11**

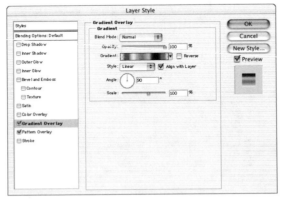

## Changing Stroke Effects

As shown in Figure 4-12, specify the size of your stroke in pixels and whether you want it to ride the outside, center, or inside of the edge of the element. Determine the Blend Mode and Opacity settings. And finally, specify whether to fill your stroke with a color, gradient, or pattern. Choose your desired color, gradient, or pattern from the corresponding options.

**Figure 4-12**

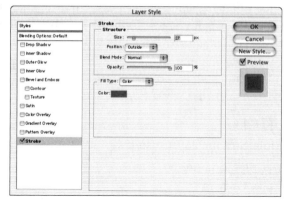

# Playing with Contours

Several of the layer effects have various options for contours. *Contours* change the distribution of the colors in the effect. The default setting for all the effects, except satin, is *linear contour*. In an effect with a linear contour, the opacity drops off in a straight line.

But you're not limited to the linear contour option. Click the arrow of the Contour option, and you'll find a variety of preset contours, as shown in Figure 4-13. Click the palette arrow, and you can load yet another contour preset library.

**Figure 4-13**

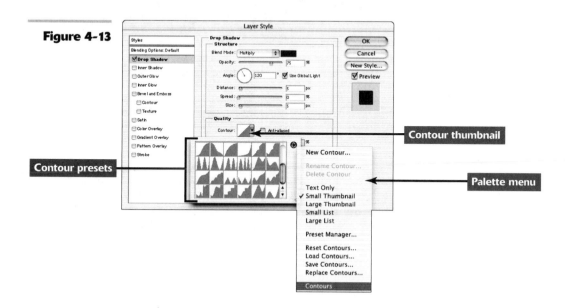

Contour thumbnail

Contour presets

Palette menu

The presets offer contours like ring, rolling, sawtooth, and steps, all of which create rings of transparency within the shadows and glows. If you use contours with bevel and emboss effects, you can create nooks, crannies, bumps, and lumps that are highlighted and shaded.

You can also find options for naming and deleting contours as well as saving, loading, resetting, and replacing contour libraries. Choosing different contours can create fun and funky shadows and glow. These are the effects in Figure 4-14 from top to bottom:

- ✔ Drop Shadow with Linear contour
- ✔ Drop Shadow with Ring-Triple contour, 25% Noise
- ✔ Drop Shadow with Gaussian Inverse contour
- ✔ Drop Shadow with Valley-High

**Figure 4-14**

## Adjusting contour settings

Of course, you're using Photoshop, the Swiss Army Knife of the graphics-editing world, so you can do a whole lot more than choose a preset contour and apply it to a layer. Depending on the effect you're working with, you can change the appearance of the contour in a variety of ways:

- **Noise:** Randomizes the colors of selected pixels in the drop shadow to give a gritty effect.

- **Anti-aliasing:** Slightly softens the edge pixels of a contour.

- **Range:** Controls how much of the glow is targeted for the contour, as shown in Figure 4-15. Reduce the Range setting to get a less feathered, tighter, and larger glow.

**Figure 4-15**

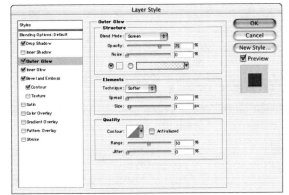

- **Jitter:** Doesn't affect the appearance of the default glow, but with other gradients, the Jitter setting varies the color and opacity of selected pixels to give a roughened effect.

- **Invert:** Turns the colors of the satin effect inside out.

- **Gloss Contour:** Changes the distribution of color in the effect over the layer. It creates a metallic effect when used with the Bevel and Emboss styles. The indented Contour, which appears below the Bevel and Emboss style in the Styles list, does the same for the edges of the layer. It creates shaded and highlighted nooks and crannies when used with the Bevel and Emboss styles.

## Modifying contours with the Contour Editor

If the preset contours just don't do it for you, feel free to create your own by using the Contour Editor dialog box, accessed by clicking the Contour thumbnail. Click the line on the mapping line to add points and drag the line to adjust the slope. You can also select a point on the mapping line and enter values for Input and Output.

To create a sharp corner instead of a curve, select a point and click Corner. When you have the contour to your liking, click the New button, give it a name, as shown in Figure 4-16, and click OK. Your custom contour has now been saved as a preset and will be available from the Contour palette.

You can save custom contours for reloading later or for trading with friends and neighbors. (Try giving them away on Halloween.) Photoshop saves contours as a .shc file in the Contours folder in the Presets folder in the Photoshop application folder.

**Figure 4-16**

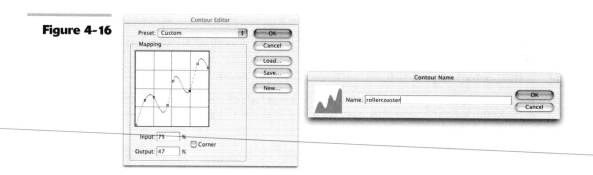

## Applying and Modifying Preset Styles

In addition to layer effects, Photoshop also offers you a multitude of preset layer styles that you can access via the Styles palette, shown in Figure 4-17.

You can also access these styles by using the Style Picker pop-up palette in the Options bar, when the Pen or Shape tools are active and the Shape layer option is selected. And you'll find the Styles palette nestled in the Layer Style dialog box as well, as shown in Figure 4-18.

**Figure 4-17**

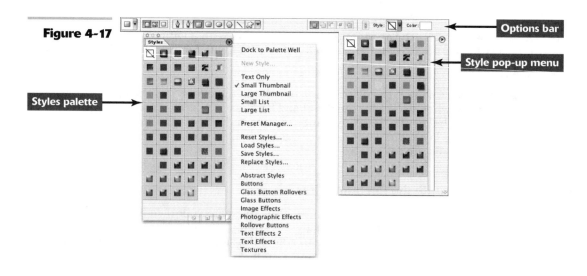

**Figure 4-18**

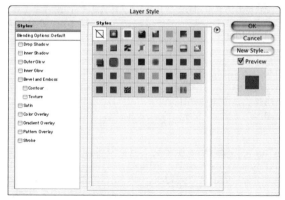

Here are the many splendid ways to apply a preset style:

- ✔ Select the layer and click a style in the Styles palette.

- ✔ Drag and drop a style from the Styles palette onto a layer in the Layers palette.

- ✔ Drag and drop a style directly onto the image window. When your cursor is over the element to which you want to apply the style, release your mouse button.

- ✔ Double-click the layer thumbnail in the Layers palette. Select Styles in the top-left side of the Layer Style dialog box. Choose a style from the palette. Click OK to close the Layer Style dialog box.

- ✔ If you're using the Pen or one of the shape tools, select the Shape Layer option. Then select a style from the pop-up Styles palette in the Options bar before drawing the shape.

 By default, applying a style over another style replaces it. To add a style along with another, press the Shift key while clicking or dragging the style.

## Managing preset styles

Here are some additional points to remember when using the Styles palette. You can do any of the following:

- ✔ **Load another Style preset library:** Click the triangle at the top right of the Styles palette, Styles pop-up palette, or the palette in the Layer Style dialog box. From that menu, choose Load Styles to add a library to your current preset list. Select the library and click Load. You can also choose Replace Styles. Even easier, just choose a preset library from the bottom of the menu and click OK to replace or append your current list.

- ✔ **Use the Preset Manager to load preset style libraries:** You can also rename, delete and save whole libraries of presets. See Book I, Chapter 6.

- ✔ **Return to the default library of presets:** Choose Reset Styles.

Book
**V**
Chapter
**4**

✔ **Choose a viewing option for your palette:** You can choose Small or Large Thumbnail or Small or Large List. And, of course, there's also Text Only, but what fun is it if you can't see the presets?

✔ **Rename a preset style:** Double-click the style in the Styles palette. If you're in Thumbnail view, enter a new name in the dialog box and click OK. If the view is set to list, simply type a new name directly and press Enter (Return on the Mac). You can also choose Rename Style from the palette options menu, from the Styles palette pop-up menu in the Layer Style dialog box, or from the Styles pop-up palette menu in the Options bar.

✔ **Save a set of preset styles as a library:** Choose Save Styles from the Styles palette options menu, from the Styles palette pop-up menu in the Layer Style dialog box, or from the Styles pop-up palette menu in the Options bar. Name the library, navigate to the Styles folder in the Presets folder in the Photoshop folder, and click Save.

✔ **Delete a preset style:** Drag the style to the trash icon in the Styles palette or Alt+click (Option+click on the Mac) on the style. You can also choose Delete Style from the palette options menu, from the Styles palette pop-up menu in the Layer Style dialog box, or from the Styles pop-up palette in the Options bar.

✔ **To clear a style (that is, remove it from the layer):** Click the Clear Style button in the Styles palette. You can also click the No Style swatch in the stand-alone Styles palette or the ones located in the Layer Style dialog box or Options bar.

✔ **Change the style or color of the currently active shape layer:** Click the link icon in the Options bar and select a different style or color. This option allows you to experiment with different styles for that shape. Also, the color swatch in the Options bar changes as the foreground color changes.

Conversely, deselect the link, and Photoshop won't change the style of the active shape layer when you select a different style. This option allows you to choose a different style or color for a new shape layer without affecting the previous shape layer. If deselected, the color swatch in the Options bar is determined by the active shape layer.

▼▼▼▼▼▼▼▼▼▼▼▼▼▼▼▼▼▼▼▼▼▼▼▼▼▼▼▼▼▼▼▼▼▼▼▼▼▼▼▼

## Creating your own style

If you get bored using the preset style libraries or if you really went to town and created a custom style that you think is so fabulous that you'll want to use it again and again, you can easily save it to the Styles palette. Here's all you need to know about saving custom styles:

**1.** **Create your own custom style by applying layer effects and/or styles to your layer.**

**2.** **After you complete your style, click the Create New Style button in the Styles palette or choose New Style from the palette options menu.**

You can also drag your selected layer from the Layers palette onto the Styles

palette or simply click in an empty space in the Styles palette. Or you can double-click the layer thumbnail to open the Layer Style dialog box where you can click the New Style button.

**3.** **In the New Style dialog box, shown in Figure 4-19, name your style and select your desired options.**

Include Layer Effects will include any effects you applied via the Effects section of the Layer Style dialog box — drop shadows, bevels, and so on.

Include Layer Blending Options will include any blending you did using the Blending Options section of the Layer Styles palette. For more on blending options, see Chapter 3 in this book.

Your new style is added to the end of the Styles palette. Unfortunately, unlike effects, after you create custom styles, you can't edit them. So make sure you like it before you make it a custom style, or you'll end up redoing it.

 Press Alt+click (Option+click on the Mac) to create a new style and bypass the dialog box. Your style gets the default name of Style 1.

**Figure 4-19**

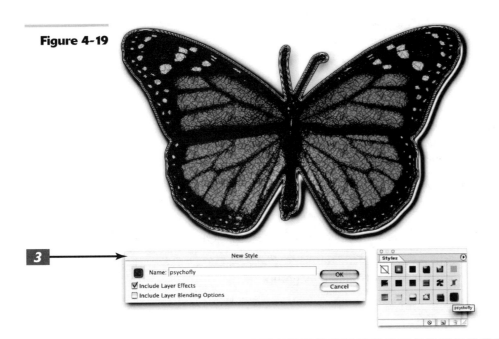

## Clipping Layers into Groups

In a *clipping group,* the bottommost layer, also known as the base layer, acts as a mask for the layers in the group. The layers in the group clip to the opaque areas of the base layer and do not show over the transparent areas of the base layer.

At this point, you might be saying, "Huh?" Rather than trying to decipher the definition, a better way to understand a clipping group is to just create one. Follow the steps listed here and I know that instead of "Huh," you'll be saying "Yeah, baby," just like Austin Powers.

Creating a clipping group works well if you want to fill type with different images on multiple layers.

### Managing clipping groups

Here is some clipping group trivia:

✔ You can also select a layer in the Layers palette and choose Layer⇨Group with Previous. You've probably seen the Group with Previous option before — it appears in the New Layer dialog box.

✔ To remove a single layer from the clipping group, you can simply Alt+click (Option+click) the line between the two layers in the Layers palette. Or you can select the layer and choose Layer⇨Ungroup. Both commands remove the selected layer and any layers above it from the clipping group.

✔ To ungroup all the layers in the clipping group, select the base layer and choose Layer⇨Ungroup.

✔ Clipping groups can also be applied to adjustment and fill layers. If you clip between a regular layer and an adjustment layer, or a regular layer and a fill layer, the adjustment or fill layer only affects the pixels of the adjacent underlying layer, instead of all the underlying layers. For more on adjustment and fill layers, see Chapter 1 in this book.

Using the steps that follow, I created a new document with a white background. I took the shape tool and, choosing the Fill Region option (see Book IV, Chapter 2, for more on shapes), drew a fish on my second layer.

I then opened an image of some fish and dragged and dropped that image onto my composite. I opened an image of some dolphins, selected a dolphin, and dragged and dropped it onto my composite.

And, finally, I created some type and applied a drop shadow and inner bevel layer effect to the type.

Follow these steps to create your own clipping group:

1. **Open or create an image that has several layers.**

2. **Press Alt (Option on the Mac) and position your mouse cursor over the line dividing the two layers in the Layers palette.**

   Your cursor changes to two overlapping circles with a small arrow icon.

3. **Click your mouse button.**

   I did this three times, in between my type and the dolphin layer, in between the dolphin and the fish layer, and in between the fish layer and my fish shape. Notice how all of my images and

my type clip to the base layer (the fish shape).

Nothing outside the boundaries of the fish shape is visible on any of the layers in the clipping group, as shown in Figure 4-20. The down-pointing arrow icon indicates that the layers are clipped.

You can also link layers and choose Layer⇨Group Linked. With either command, Group with Previous or Group with Linked, the clipping group takes on the opacity and blend mode of the base layer.

**Figure 4-20**

Before clipping group

After clipping group

## PUTTING IT TOGETHER

### Adding Text and Layer Styles to a Collage

If you've been reading Book V faithfully, then you may have a nearly complete collage on your hands. If you're at all interested in using words with your images, then now (at the end of the project, not the beginning) is the time to add them in. Adding type can take a good composite and turn it into a dynamite and cohesive image that conveys exactly what you want it to. I'm no Shakespeare and can't help you create the perfect tag line, but I can show you how to add some text and incorporate it into your collage. Adding layer styles gives you a lot of versatility in the kinds of effects you can apply to styles, so I show you how to apply those to a collage.

 If you need a type refresher, check out Book IV, Chapter 4.

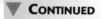 **CONTINUED**

▼ **CONTINUED**

To add and adjust type, follow these steps:

**1.** **Open the saved collage file.**

Make sure that the Layers palette is open.

**2.** **Select the Eyedropper from the Toolbox. Click a color in the collage that you like.**

The color you sampled is now the foreground color.

**3.** **Select the Type tool. In the Options bar, select a font, style, and point size, and other formatting options.**

I recommend choosing an easy-to-read serif font and applying a bold style to it. I'm using Times Bold, and I set the point size to 100.

I set the anti-aliasing to Crisp and the Alignment to Left, but you can explore your options until you're dizzy (or your deadline passes).

**4.** **Click inside your image and type some text.**

I typed "Go Outside" for my travel collage.

**5.** **Select the Move tool from the Toolbox and position the type in the collage.**

I put my text in the upper-left corner.

**6.** **Adjust your settings as you desire.**

If you want to add a second, smaller, line of text, grab the Type tool again, and, in the Options bar, reduce the point size. You can change other settings, as well.

**7.** **When you're satisfied with your changes, click under the first line of text and type your next line.**

Under Go Outside, I typed "and Play."

With the Move tool, fine-tune the position of the type.

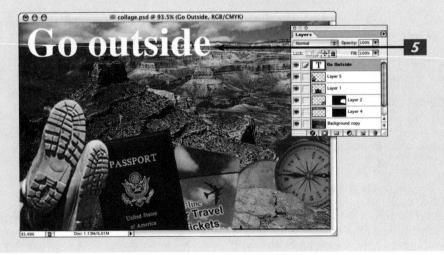

When you're satisfied with the size, style, color, and appearance of the type in your collage, you can make some more large-scale changes by creating layer styles. Follow these steps:

**1.** **Add a drop shadow and make sure that Global Light is selected so that all the layers will use the same angle.**

In the Layers palette, first select the layer that includes the first line of text. Then choose Layer⇨Layer Style⇨Drop Shadow. Make sure the Drop Shadow box is selected in the left column.

You can change the angle so that the light source is coming from one direction or another (mine's set at 120% so that the light's coming from the left).

**2.** **Add bevels and embossing.**

Click the Bevel and Emboss style in the left column.

Make sure that you actually select the style and not just check the box; otherwise, the right panel with all the options won't appear.

In my example, I selected Inner Bevel from the Style pop-up menu in the right panel. Then I selected Chisel Soft from the Technique pop-up menu. My idea was to give the type a carved-in-stone look.

**3.** **Click OK when you're satisfied with the styles you've created in the layer so far.**

**4.** **Apply the same styles to the layer where the second line of text is.**

To get the exact same settings without having to go through every adjustment again, right-click (Control+click on the Mac) on the florin (the f symbol) on the first layer you worked on and choose Copy Layer Style from the menu that appears. Select the second type layer and right-click (Control+click on the Mac) on the layer name and choose Paste Layer Style from the context menu.

Book
**V**
Chapter
**4**

▼ **CONTINUED**

▼ **CONTINUED**

**5.** **Make any last adjustments and choose File⇨Save.**

You're all done. If you feel like it, keep adding or refining the collage as you learn new tricks.

# Book VI

# Channels and Masks

The 5th Wave · By Rich Tennant

"I'm going to assume that most of you — but not all of you — understand that this session on 'masking' has to do with Photoshop 7."

# Using Channels

If you're reading this, it probably means that you didn't quickly thumb through this chapter, say "Yuck, boorrrrringgg!" and move on to sexier topics like blending, filtering, and retouching. You knew that would be a huge mistake.

The wonderful thing about channels is that they offer you greater control and selectivity when doing those very things — blending, filtering, and retouching. Channels bring one more level of control when editing your images. You can use individual channels for layer blending options, filters, and as starting points for masks.

Channels also come into play when saving selections for later use or for adding spot (custom) colors to your image. You can also use channels to turn color images into nicely contrasted grayscale images. And finally, you can play around with the colors in an image by mixing up the channels. So bear with me. The topic of channels may be a bit dry and technical, but in the end, they'll enable you to hold the envious title of Master Editor.

It would also be helpful in understanding how channels work to know a few things about colors — specifically the various color modes, which I cover in Book II, Chapter 2.

## Understanding Channels

When you look at a color image, you see one big 24-bit composite collection of colored pixels. Technically speaking, however, Photoshop doesn't see that at all. Photoshop perceives a color image as individual bands of 8-bit, grayscale images. RGB images have three bands; CMYK images have four bands.

I know it's strange to think of a color image as being composed of several grayscale images, but it's true. Each one of these bands, or grayscale images, is a *channel*. Specifically, they're color channels.

 If you just can't get past the fact that a color image is the sum of several grayscale channels, as shown in Figure 1-1, then just think of channels as holding tanks of color data.

Another way of relating channels to the real world is in terms of hardware. Here's how the most common hardware handles color:

- ✔ When you offset print a CMYK image, the colors are separated (see Book X, Chapter 2) into four colors — cyan, magenta, yellow, and black. Paper is fed through four individual rollers on the printing press, each roller containing one of those four colored inks.

- ✔ Scanners scan in RGB via a pass of red, green, and blue sensors over your image.

- ✔ Screens display images via red, green, and blue tubes.

**Figure 1-1**

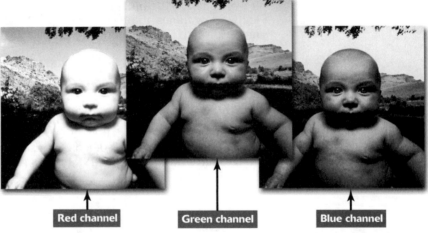

Red channel    Green channel    Blue channel

## A little bit about bit depth

When you're standing around the water cooler, or the color printer, and you hear people talking about a 1-bit or an 8-bit image, they're referring to something called *bit depth*. Bit depth measures how much color information is available to display and print each pixel. A higher bit depth means the image can display more information — specifically, more colors. For example, a 1-bit image can display two color values — black and white. That's why a purely black-and-white image is called a bitmap image. Likewise,

- ✔ An 8-bit image has 256 grayscale levels ($2^8$). Grayscale images are 8 bit (1 channel x 8 bits).

- ✔ A 24-bit image has about 16 million colors ($2^{24}$). RGB images are 24 bit (3 channels x 8 bits).

- ✔ CMYK images are 32 bit (4 channels x 8 bits). CMYK images, however, are limited to the number of colors that are physically reproducible on paper, which is around 55,000.

Bit depths typically range from 1 to 64 bits. Scanners often allow you to scan an image at 64 bits. At 64 bits, each channel contains 16 bits, for a total of 4,096 levels of gray. This added color information gives you more data to work with when you adjust levels, curves, hue/saturation, and color balance, and when you apply filters such as Unsharp Mask.

Note, however, that the tools and commands available for 16-bit images are somewhat limited. When your adjustments are made, you can then convert your 16-bit image to an 8-bit image. Make sure your images are flattened if you have any layers. Then choose Image⇨Mode⇨8 bits/Channel. You'll find this necessary because you cannot print 16-bit images.

---

In addition to color channels, there are channels called *alpha channels* (covered later in this chapter); others are called *spot channels* (discussed in Book X, Chapter 2).

Briefly, alpha channels are used to create, store, and edit selections. These selections are defined not by a selection outline, but by black, white, and varying shades of gray pixels, in other words, a grayscale image. Black pixels represent unselected areas of the image, while white represents selected areas and gray represents partially selected pixels.

Spot channels are created when you want to add a spot, or custom, color to your image. Spot colors are premixed inks that are often used in addition to or in lieu of CMYK colors.

All images, no matter what their color mode, have at least one channel. Grayscale, Duotone, and Indexed Color modes (Indexed Color is used for Web images) have only one channel. RGB and CMYK images have three and four channels respectively. They also contain a composite channel, which reflects the combination of the individual color channels and gives you the full color display.

Book
**VI**
Chapter
**1**

# Working with Channels

As with layers, channels have their own palette that acts as command central for viewing, creating, and managing tasks. The first step is accessing channels by choosing Window⇨Channels. The Channels palette appears, as shown in Figure 1-2.

**Figure 1-2**

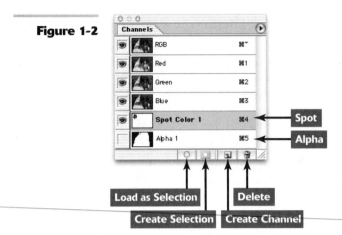

## Viewing channels without a remote

To select a channel, click the channel thumbnail or name in the palette. To select more than one channel, Shift+click. To show or hide a channel, click in the eye column in the far left of the palette. Selecting a channel automatically makes it show. You can also drag through the column to hide or show the channels quickly.

CMYK, RGB, and Lab images have a *composite* channel in addition to their individual channels. This composite channel is the combination of all of the channels in the image and is named after the color mode. For example, the composite channel in Figure 1-2 is the first one, called RGB.

## Changing the default channel view

The default setting is to view your channels in grayscale. You can, however, view them in color. To do so, choose Edit⇨Preferences⇨Display & Cursors (Photoshop⇨Preferences⇨Display & Cursors on Mac OS X) and select Color Channels in Color.

Although this option *graphically* exemplifies the way an image is comprised into separate color channels, it really does you no good if you want to work with your channels for editing. That's because the color view obscures details and makes measuring the impact of adjustments and filters more difficult. You need to see the channels in their true grayscale form for that.

 If you select or show more than one channel, even in the default grayscale view, the channels always appear in color.

To change the size of the thumbnail that appears, choose Palette Options from the Channels palette options menu. Select your desired thumbnail size. If you're working with a lot of channels and you have a dinosaur of a computer, you can also choose None to turn off the thumbnails. This should help performance.

## Duplicating and deleting channels

Duplicating channels is something you may do quite often. I know I do. And of course, deleting channels isn't something you do only if you're a neat freak. Channels take up a lot of memory, so it's always good to get rid of the ones you no longer need.

Here are some instances when duplicating channels is a good idea:

- **When you want to create a channel mask:** First, you find a suitable channel and then make a duplicate. (For more on this technique, see Chapter 3 in this book.) Channel masks are often created to select difficult elements involving fine details, such as hair, fur, smoke, and so on.
- **When you want to make a backup copy of the channel before doing some editing:** It's always a good idea to have a backup just to be on the safe side. For example, you may want to apply an Unsharp Mask filter to one or two channels to improve the focus of the image. For more on the Unsharp Mask filter, see Book VII, Chapter 1.
- **To insert a copy of an alpha channel into another image:** For example, maybe you spent an hour creating elaborate alpha channels for shadows and highlights on a product that was photographed in flat lighting.

  You may have 12 products, all the same shape, but different colors that you need to apply those highlights and shadows to. Rather than re-creating the wheel each time, you could simply duplicate the alpha channels into each file.

## Duplicating channels

To duplicate a channel, follow these short steps:

1. **Select your desired channel in the Channels palette.**
2. **Choose Duplicate Channel from the palette options menu.**

   The Duplicate Channel dialog box appears, as shown in Figure 1-3.
3. **In the Duplicate section, name the channel.**

   You can also drag the channel to the New Channel icon at the bottom of the palette. If you do this, Photoshop provides a default name and bypasses Steps 4, 5, and 6.
4. **In the Destination section, select a file from the Document drop-down menu. Or choose New to create a new image.**

   You can choose your current image or any open image with the same pixel dimensions (size and resolution) as your current image. (For more on pixel dimensions, see Book II, Chapter 1.)

   If you choose New, a new image with a single channel is created. Provide a name for the file.
5. **Select Invert if you want to reverse the selected and unselected areas of the duplicate channel.**

   The Invert option is primarily used when you are duplicating an existing alpha channel. For more on alpha channels, see the upcoming section.
6. **Click OK.**

   The dialog box closes. Your duplicate channel appears in the Channels palette.

Continued

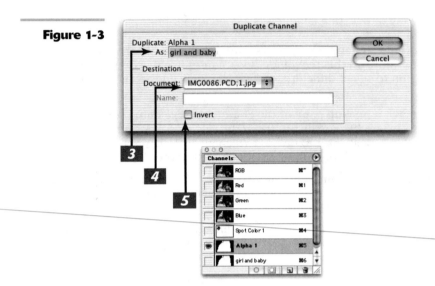

**Figure 1-3**

### Replacing one channel over another

To replace one channel over another, you can use the copy and paste method. In your current image, select your desired channel. Choose Select⇨All and then Edit⇨Copy. Select the channel in the destination image that you want to replace and choose Edit⇨Paste. The pasted channel replaces the original one.

### Deleting unwanted channels

To delete an unwanted channel — something you definitely want to do because channels can eat up a lot of space — select it in the Channels palette and do one of the following:

- ✔ Drag the channel to the trash icon at the bottom of the palette.
- ✔ Choose Delete Channel from the palette options menu.
- ✔ Click the trash icon and then click Yes.
- ✔ Alt+click (Option+click on the Mac) on the trash icon.

### Rearranging and renaming channels

Although color channels can't be shuffled or renamed, you can do so with spot and alpha channels. To move a spot or alpha channel, simply drag it up or down in the Channels palette. When you see a dark line appear where you want the channel to go, release your mouse button. You can only move a spot or alpha channel above a color channel in a multichannel image. In short, in a multichannel image, each channel becomes an independent spot channel, and the channels no longer have a relationship with each other. Multichannel images also do not support layers. The only file formats that support this mode are Photoshop and Raw. For more details, see Book II, Chapter 2.

To rename a spot or alpha channel, double-click the name in the Channel palette and type a new name. You can also choose Channel Options from the palette options menu.

## Splitting channels

You can split the channels of your image into separate images in separate files, as shown in Figure 1-4. Choose Split Channels from the palette options menu. When you do so, your original image is closed. The channel files have the name of your original image plus the channel name. You can only split channels on a flattened image, in other words, an image with no individual layers.

You might want to split channels if you need to save your original file in a format that doesn't preserve channels — such as EPS, which doesn't support alpha channels — or you may want to split channels to merge them later on.

 Make sure that you save all changes in your original image before you split it because it will be closed.

**Figure 1-4**

## The quick and dirty method for duplicating channels

You can also duplicate a channel to another image by dragging the channel. Open your destination image and drag the desired channel from your current image into the destination image window. The duplicated channel appears in the Channels palette.

▼▼▼▼▼▼▼▼▼▼▼▼▼▼▼▼▼▼▼▼▼▼▼▼▼▼▼▼▼▼▼▼▼▼▼▼

## Merging channels

You can merge channels into a single image. The channels must be open, in grayscale mode, and have the same pixel dimensions. You can only merge channels with flattened images and no layers. You may find a need to merge channels because you have a DCS (Desktop Color Separation) file that has lost its link (the original image) and it's unusable. You can open the individual channel files and merge them into a single image. Then resave it as a DCS EPS once more. For more on DCS and other file formats, see Book II, Chapter 2.

You can also merge color channels to create some unique special effects. For example, by mismatching your channels when you merge them, you can create some really bizarre, and sometimes beautiful, color shifts.

To merge channels, follow these steps:

1.  **Open you channel files and activate any one of them.**

2.  **Choose Merge Channels from the palette options menu.**

3.  **Choose your desired color mode.**

    Any modes that are unavailable are grayed out. That's because you may not have enough channels for that mode.

4.  **Enter the number of channels you want.**

    When you choose your mode in Step 3, Photoshop automatically fills in the number of channels for the mode. If you deviate and enter something different, the file becomes a multichannel file.

5.  **Click OK.**

6.  **Select your channels.**

    If you want to merge the channels normally, make sure that each channel matches (Red for Red and so on). If you want to rearrange the channels, you can mix them as I did in Figure 1-5.

7.  **If you are merging into a multichannel image, click Next. Repeat Step 6 for each channel.**

8.  **Click OK.**

    Your files are now merged into a single image, which appears in your Photoshop window.

    Individual channel files are closed. Any spot channels will be merged as alpha channels.

    Check out Color Plate 6-1 to see how my sunflower went from yellow to magenta just by merging the layers a little differently.

**Figure 1-5**

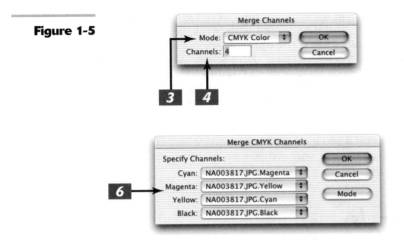

# Using Painting and Editing Tools with Channels

Sometimes it's better to edit individual channels rather than the composite image. Mediocre flatbed scanners often reproduce an image that is slightly soft or out of focus. You may want to counteract that effect by applying an Unsharp Mask filter. Before you do, you should examine each channel separately. You may find that the Blue channel contains a lot of garbage — artifacts, dithering, and other nasty crud.

 Blue channels are notorious for acquiring this junk, so try to avoid applying an Unsharp Mask filter on this channel unless you *really* want to accentuate what's already ugly.

Instead of applying the Unsharp Mask filter on Blue channels, select the Red and Green channels and then choose Filter⇨Sharpen⇨Unsharp Mask. Similarly, you can apply a Gaussian Blur filter to a channel to soften the unsightly pattern (called a *moiré* pattern) caused by scanning a halftone. (See Book VII, Chapter 1, for more on moiré patterns.)

While Unsharp Mask and Gaussian Blur are a couple of your corrective filters that you'll use frequently, I also find it useful to apply a special-effect filter to individual channels as well. Sometimes applying a filter to the composite image produces an effect that's, well, overdone. Applying the filter to one or two channels can produce an effect that is more subtle and less in-your-face, as shown in Color Plate 6-2.

You can select a color channel and then edit that channel by using a painting or editing tool to paint in the image. Keep these facts in mind:

- ✔ Painting with white adds the color channel's color at full intensity in the composite image.
- ✔ Painting with black removes the color in the composite image.
- ✔ Painting with a value of gray adds color at varying levels of intensity in the composite image.

For example, if you paint with white on the Blue channel in an existing image, more blue is added to the color composite image. But if you paint with black, yellow is added to the image because when you remove blue, what's left is the opposite, or complementary, color — yellow. To perform this channel magic, select the Brush tool and then choose your desired brush size from the Options bar. Choose your desired color in the Color palette. Select the channel you want to edit in the Channels palette. You can see the results by selecting the composite channel in the Channels palette. Take a look at Color Plate 6-1 to see how I gave a flower a channel color makeover.

 The results are a little different if you try this technique on a blank CMYK canvas. If you paint with black on the Cyan channel, your composite color image will display cyan. If you paint with white you will get nothing.

## Using Alpha Channels

You use alpha channels to make and store selections that you make with the selection tools, such as the Lasso or Magic Wand. You can also use alpha channels to edit selections.

An alpha channel is a type of mask. Masks, which you find out more about in Chapters 2 and 3 in this book, can be thought of as selections using some or all of the 256 available levels of gray, instead of a selection outline. Alpha channels define a selection in black, white, and varying shades of gray pixels. In other words, alpha channels store selections as 8-bit grayscale images.

In alpha channels, selected pixels are white, black pixels are unselected, and anything in between is partially selected or partially unselected depending on whether you think the glass is half full or half empty.

You can create a mask by duplicating a color channel and then editing the channel by using painting and editing tools and filters. Most graphics geeks refer to this as a *channel mask*. See Chapter 3 in this book for more on channel masks.

If you create an alpha channel from a saved selection, the channel most likely consists of just black or white pixels. If you have a feathered or even an anti-aliased selection, you may have a few gray pixels. If you create an alpha channel by duplicating and editing a color channel, your alpha channel most likely contains varying shades of gray pixels as well.

▼▼▼▼▼▼▼▼▼▼▼▼▼▼▼▼▼▼▼▼▼▼▼▼▼▼▼▼▼▼▼▼▼▼▼▼▼▼▼▼▼

### Modifying an alpha channel's options

To modify the options for an alpha channel, follow these steps:

1. Select the channel and then choose **Channel Options** from the palette options menu.

2. Enter a name for the alpha channel.

3. Specify the color and opacity of the overlay.

4. Specify whether you want the masked area (what the overlay will cover) to include the Masked Area (the unselected area), Selected Area, or Spot Color.

5. Click OK to close the Channel Options dialog box.

You can also simply double-click the channel thumbnail to bring up the Channel Options dialog box. Then follow Steps 2 through 5.

▼▼▼▼▼▼▼▼▼▼▼▼▼▼▼▼▼▼▼▼▼▼▼▼▼▼▼▼▼▼▼▼▼▼▼

## Saving a selection as an alpha channel

One of the great things about alpha channels is that you can save them and then retrieve them time and time again. This can be especially handy if you've taken a lot of time and effort to create the selection. Why reinvent the wheel if you want to select the element again in the future? Sure, you can create a mask using Quick Mask Mode and Color Range (see Chapter 2 in this book), but those masks are only temporary.

The hardest part about creating an alpha channel is making the initial selection. After that, it's a piece of cake. Follow these steps to create an alpha channel:

1. **Make a selection in your image.**

2. **Choose Select⇨Save Selection.**

   You can also click the Save Selection as Channel button (a circle on a square icon) at the bottom of the Channels palette. A new channel appears with the default name of Alpha 1 and bypasses Steps 3 through 6.

3. **Choose a destination image in the Document pop-up menu.**

   You can choose your current image or any other open image with the same pixel dimensions.

4. **Choose a destination channel from the Channel pop-up menu.**

   You can choose a new channel or any existing channel or layer mask. (See Chapter 3 in this book for more on layer masks.)

5. **If you choose New, name the channel.**

6. **If you choose an existing channel or layer mask, select your desired combination.**

   Replace, Add To, Subtract From, or Intersect With are the self-explanatory options.

7. **Click OK.**

   Your alpha channel is complete and appears in the Channels palette, as shown in Figure 1-6.

Book
**VI**
Chapter
**1**

**Figure 1-6**

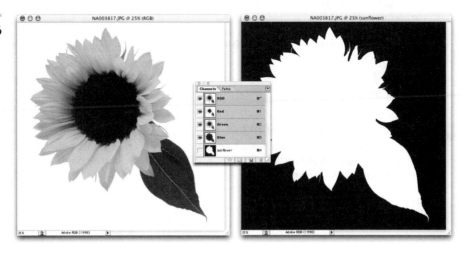

## Alpha channel tips and tricks

Here are a few closing alpha channel tidbits:

✔ Try showing the alpha channel along with the composite channel. That way you can see how clean your mask is.

 Note that when you display them both, the alpha channel appears as a semitransparent color overlay.

✔ You cannot add channels to images that are in Bitmap mode. That's because all pixels in a Bitmap mode file are either black or white. No intermediary shades are supported.

✔ You can convert alpha channels to spot channels. For more on spot channels, see Book X, Chapter 2.

## Loading an alpha channel

No doubt if you've gone through the trouble of creating an alpha channel, it's because you want to be able to easily load, or access, the selection again and again. To load an alpha channel, use any one of these many methods:

✔ Choose Select➪Load Selection. Select your document and channel. Click Invert to swap selected and unselected areas. If your image has an active selection, choose how you want to combine the selections.

✔ Select the alpha channel in the Channels palette, click the Load Channel as Selection button at the bottom of the palette, and then click the composite channel.

✔ Drag the channel to the Load Channel as Selection icon.

✔ Ctrl+click (⌘+click on the Mac) the alpha channel in the Channels palette.

✔ Ctrl+Shift+click (⌘+Shift+click on the Mac) to add the alpha channel to an active selection.

✔ Ctrl+Alt+click (⌘+Option+click on the Mac) to subtract the alpha channel from an active selection.

✔ Ctrl+Alt+Shift+click (⌘+Option+Shift+click on the Mac) to intersect the alpha channel with an active selection.

 Adding channels can start to bloat your file size, so use them, but use them judiciously. The Photoshop native format and TIFF format compress channel information and therefore are good file formats to use when working with a lot of channels. The only formats that preserve alpha channels are Photoshop, TIFF, PDF, PICT, Pixar, or Raw. A single image can have a maximum of 24 channels.

▼▼▼▼▼▼▼▼▼▼▼▼▼▼▼▼▼▼▼▼▼▼▼▼▼▼▼▼▼▼▼▼▼▼▼▼▼▼▼▼

# Using the Channel Mixer

The Channel Mixer actually does what its name implies — it mixes color channels. This feature lets you repair bad channels and produce grayscale images from color images. It also allows you to create tinted images and more intense special effects. Finally, it allows you to do the more mundane tasks of swapping or duplicating channels.

While Photoshop elitists worldwide tout this as an advanced feature not to be mucked with by amateurs, I say, "Give it a whirl." Intimidation is a nasty roadblock to creative fun. Just make a backup copy of an image before diving into the mix:

**1.** **Select the composite channel in the Channels palette.**

If you have an RGB image, it will be the RGB channel. For CMYK images, it will be the CMYK channel.

**2.** **Choose Image⇨Adjustments⇨Channel Mixer.**

The Channel Mixer dialog box appears, as shown in Figure 1-7.

**3.** **For Output Channel, choose the channel in which to blend one or more source (existing) channels.**

For example, if your Blue channel is lousy, select it from the Output Channel pop-up menu.

**4.** **Drag any source channel's slider to the left to decrease the channel's effect on the Output channel. Or drag to the right to increase the effect.**

Because my Blue channel contains artifacts and dithering picked up by the scanner, I am raising the Red and Green values from 0% to 25% and lowering the Blue value from 100% to 50%. To retain good contrast, try to use a combo of Red, Green, and Blue values that add up to close to 100%.

You can also enter a value from –200 to +200%. Using a negative value inverts the color data of the source channel.

**5.** **Tinker with the Constant option to add a black or white channel of varying opacity.**

Drag the slider to a negative value to get a black channel. Positive values give a white channel.

This option brightens or darkens the overall image. I recommend leaving it at 0 most of the time. But try it. It may help.

**6.** **Select Monochrome to apply the same settings to all output channels producing a color image that has only values of gray.**

Adjust the individual sliders to mix the values until you are satisfied with the contrast.

This option is one of the best ways to produce grayscale images from color images because it preserves detail and provides better contrast control.

**7.** **Click OK to exit the Channel Mixer.**

After you exit the Channel Mixer, choose Image⇨Mode⇨Grayscale to complete the conversion.

Continued
▼ ▼ ▼ ▼ ▼

If you select and then deselect the Monochrome option, you can modify the blend of each channel separately. By doing so, you can create color images that appear to be hand tinted with color inks. Go for the subtle treatment or a more intensely colored look.

 Swapping color channels can produce some bizarre color effects. For example, try selecting the Red channel from the Output Channel pop-up menu. Set the Red source channel to 0 and then set the Green source channel to 100. Try other combinations, Green for Blue, Blue for Red, and so on. Sometimes they can be downright freakish, but occasionally you may stumble on one that's worthy.

**Figure 1-7**

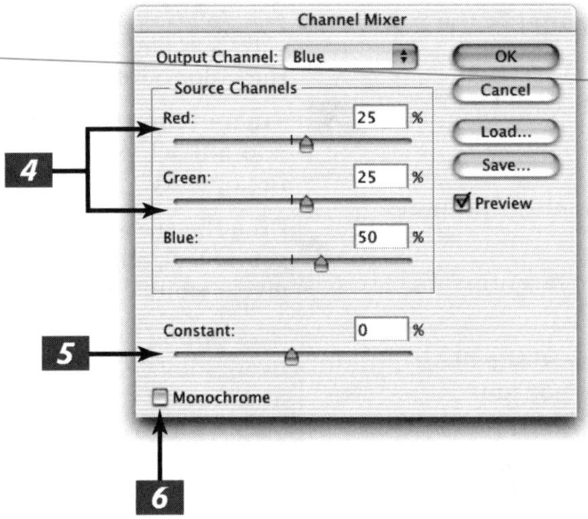

Channel Mixer

Output Channel: Blue

**Source Channels**

Red: 25 %

Green: 25 %

Blue: 50 %

Constant: 0 %

☐ Monochrome

OK
Cancel
Load...
Save...
☑ Preview

**4**

**5**

**6**

 **PUTTING IT TOGETHER**

## Giving Flat Art Highlights and Shadows

Sometimes you need to give your art — whether it's a photo or another type of image — a little shine and shadow to bring it to life.

You can do this by creating and saving your selections as alpha channels and filling them with translucent color.

The great thing about alpha channels is that because you save them with your document, you can use them time and time again.

Just follow these steps:

**1.** **Create a simple piece of artwork to use as a basis for your shadows and highlights.**

I created a pool ball by creating two layers.

✔ On each layer, I used the Elliptical Marquee tool to create different-sized circles.

✔ I filled each of the circles with a separate color.

**2.** **Choose Window⇨Channels.**

The Channels palette appears.

Be sure to keep this palette visible because you will be creating some new channels for the highlights.

**3.** **Choose the Pen tool from the Toolbox and create a path for the highlight.**

I created a path for the highlight on the top-left portion of the ball in my example, assuming that the light source is coming from the upper-left corner.

If the Pen tool seems like a foreign object to you, you may need to check out Book III, Chapter 2.

**4.** **Choose Window⇨Paths.**

The Paths palette appears.

**5.** **Click the third icon from the left at the bottom of the Paths palette.**

You see your work path disappear and a selection marquee appear.

**6.** **Choose Select⇨Save Selection.**

The Save Selection dialog box appears.

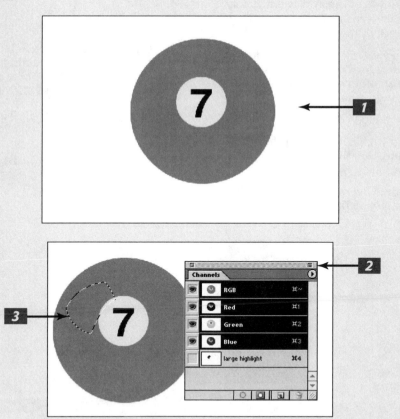

Book
**VI**
Chapter
**1**

▼ **CONTINUED**

▼ **CONTINUED**

**7.** **Name the channel. Make sure the channel is new and click OK.**

An additional channel appears in the Channels palette. This new channel is the alpha channel — your saved selection.

**8.** **Click the New Layer icon in the Layers palette. Double-click the layer name and rename it.**

I named mine "Large Highlight."

It's important to put your highlights and shadows on a separate layer so that you can apply different opacity settings and also retain the ability to tweak them later if needed.

**9.** **Choose Edit⇨Fill, choose the White option for Contents, and leave all of the other options at their default settings. Click OK.**

The dialog box closes.

Your highlight is now filled with white. Don't worry; it won't stay this opaque.

**10.** **In the Layers palette, adjust the Opacity setting to 50%.**

The highlight should now appear translucent.

**11.** **Choose the Pen tool and create a path for the highlight on the bottom of the object.**

Make sure the path matches up to the edge of the object. Use the Direct Selection tool if you need to adjust the anchor points or curve segments of the path.

**12.** **In the Paths palette, click the third icon from the left at the bottom of the palette.**

The work path disappears, and a selection marquee appears.

**13.** **Choose Select⇨Save Selection. In the Save Selection dialog box, name the channel. Make sure the channel is new and click OK.**

Mine is called "Bottom Highlight." Another alpha channel appears in the Channels palette.

**14.** **Repeat Steps 8, 9, and 10, but only adjust the Opacity to 30%.**

**15.** **Use the Pen tool to create a path for the smaller shadow.**

For example, I created a path on the bottom right of the ball.

**16.** **Load the path as a selection in the Paths palette and choose Select➪ Feather. Enter 3 pixels and click OK.**

The idea is to give the shadow a softer edge.

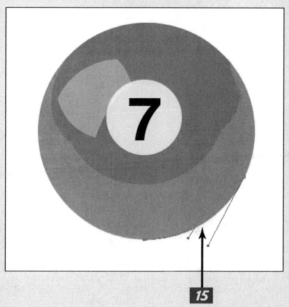

Book
*VI*
Chapter
*1*

▼ **CONTINUED**

▼ **CONTINUED**

**17** Repeat Steps 6 through 10, but fill the selection with black instead of white and adjust the opacity to 20%.

**18.** Use a selection tool to add a cast shadow.

In my example, I used the Ellipse tool, pressed Alt (Option on the Mac), and created an ellipse at the base of the ball.

Then I feathered the selection 25 pixels before I saved the selection.

 The cast shadow needs to have really fuzzy edges, thus the large number of pixels for the feather.

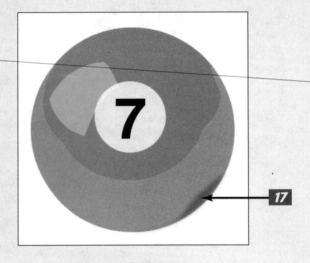

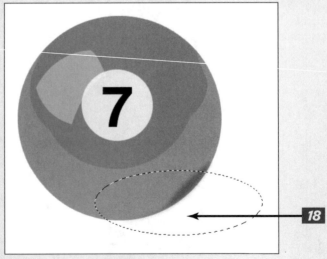

**19.** **Repeat Steps 8 and 9, filling the selection with black.**

My highlighted and shadowed pool ball is ready to roll.

If your cast shadow layer is above your object, you will have to change the stacking order and move your shadow layer so that it's below your object.

Now that you've spent all this time on the front end creating your alpha channels, you can then save time on the back end by using those alpha channels to apply highlights and shadows to similar artwork.

**20.** **To load alpha channels, choose Select⇨Load Selection and select your alpha channels from the Channel pop-up menu. Then repeat these steps.**

In my example, I took the highlights and shadows I created with lucky pool ball number 7 and loaded them as alpha channels in lucky pool ball number 5.

# Quick and Dirty Masking

2

If you checked out the last chapter on channels you've been at least briefly introduced to masks via the world of alpha channels. Alpha channels, a type of mask, are used to create, store, and edit selections. But just in case you skipped right to this chapter, allow me to give you a brief introduction. Masking is essentially just another way of making a selection. Instead of defining your selection with a selection outline, masks define your selection with 256 levels of gray, which allows you to have varying levels of selection. Unselected pixels are masked or protected from any commands you execute. Selected pixels are not masked and are fair game to any executed commands.

There are different types of masks for different purposes — channel masks, layer masks, and vector masks. You can use them to temporarily make a selection, save and load selections, define vector shapes, selectively apply an adjustment layer or filter, blend one layer into another, and so on. This chapter covers using masks for selection purposes.

Although selecting with the Marquee, Lasso, and Magic Wand tool can be fine, you'll soon find that these tools have a limited repertoire and can't be used with much accuracy on more complex images. Sure, you could break out the Pen tools and for some difficult images they do a superb job — that is, if you can get the hang of drawing Bézier curves.

But when you need to play with the big boys, that's when you turn to masking. Most things that pack a powerful punch are either expensive or hard to master or both. Well, you already forked out a pretty penny for Photoshop. And yes, masking isn't for those who get their selections via a drive-thru window.

In this chapter, I ease you into masking by using Photoshop's automated masking tools. They make it easier on you, but the downside is they aren't as accurate as the hard-core masking I cover in Book V, Chapter 3. But with certain images (or a serious time crunch), the quick-and-dirty masking tools get the job done.

▼ ▼ ▼ ▼ ▼ ▼ ▼ ▼ ▼ ▼ ▼ ▼ ▼ ▼ ▼ ▼ ▼ ▼ ▼ ▼ ▼ ▼ ▼ ▼ ▼ ▼ ▼ ▼ ▼ ▼ ▼ ▼ ▼ ▼ ▼ ▼ ▼ ▼ ▼ ▼ ▼ ▼

## Working with Quick Masks

As you can probably guess from the name, Quick Masks allow you to create and edit selections quickly without having to bother with the Channels palette. They are also user friendly in that they allow you to see your image while you're working (typically masking with channels doesn't). You can begin your Quick Mask by using a selection tool or by using a painting tool. Once you have your Quick Mask, you can edit it using any painting or editing tool.

Quick Masks are temporary, so if you create one you really like, be sure and choose Select➪Save Selection at the end of the following steps. That way you can save the mask as an alpha channel. For more on alpha channels, see Chapter 1 in this book.

Follow these steps to create your very own Quick Mask:

**1. Open a new document and using any selection tool, select the element you want in your image.**

Don't worry about getting the selection perfect. You'll be able to fine-tune your selection once you have the Quick Mask in place. Note that you can also just paint your mask from scratch. But I think starting with a selection is easier.

**2. Click the Quick Mask mode button in the Toolbox.**

The Quick Mask mode button is the white circle on a gray square icon shown in Figure 2-1. A color overlay covers and protects the area outside the selection. The selected pixels are unprotected.

**3. Refine the mask by selecting a painting or editing tool.**

Paint with black to add to the mask, thereby making the selection smaller. Paint with white to delete from the mask, making the selection larger. Paint with a shade of gray to partially select the pixels. Partially selected pixels take on a semitransparent look, perfect for feathered edges.

You can also apply a filter or adjustment (Image➪Adjustment) to the Quick Mask. See this technique in action in Book VII, Chapter 2.

Even though the Quick Mask displays a red overlay, you are still working with a grayscale image. If you don't believe me, pull up the Channels palette and look at the Quick Mask channel.

## Changing Quick Mask options

You can change Quick Mask options by double-clicking the Quick Mask mode button in the Toolbox.

When you add a Quick Mask to a selection, by default a red overlay covers the selected area. The overlay has an opacity setting of 50%.

In addition to changing the color and opacity of the overlay, you can also choose whether you want the overlay to represent the masked (unselected, protected) areas or the selected (unprotected) areas.

---

**4.** **Once your mask is fully edited, click the Standard mode button in the Toolbox to exit the Quick Mask.**

The Standard mode button is just to the left of the Quick Mask mode button, as shown in Figure 2-2.

The overlay disappears and a selection outline appears, as shown in Figure 2-3.

The selection outline correlates with the unmasked or selected areas of the Quick Mask.

Your selection is ready and waiting for your next command.

**Figure 2-1**

Book
**VI**
Chapter
**2**

CONTINUED

**Figure 2-2**

**Figure 2-3**

# *Using the Color Range Command*

The Color Range command allows you to select similarly colored pixels in a selection or within an entire image. You can think of it as a smarter Magic Wand tool. Unlike the Magic Wand, however, Color Range lets you adjust your selection before you ultimately get the selection outline. It does this by using Fuzziness (a cousin of Tolerance), which allows you to select colors relative to how closely they resemble the sampled colors. Identical colors are totally selected, similar colors are partially selected and dissimilar colors are unselected. You adjust the Fuzziness and Photoshop adjusts the selection.

## Color Range basics

Here are some Color Range command tips before you get started:

✔ You can save and load color range settings by clicking the appropriate buttons in the dialog box. But heck, once you have a selection you can also choose Select⇨Save Selection to save it as an alpha channel.

✔ You can select a color range based on preset colors or tones that you choose from the Select pop-up menu. For example, choosing red will automatically choose all the red in the image. Choosing midtones will choose all the medium range tones in the image. And Out-of-Gamut (only available for RGB and Lab modes) will choose all colors that cannot be printed using CMYK colors. For more on modes, see Book II, Chapter 2.

 If you choose the Color Range command when you have an active selection, Photoshop selects only colors within the selection outline. The rest of your image is ignored.

Book
***VI***
Chapter
***2***

▼ ▼ ▼ ▼ ▼ ▼ ▼ ▼ ▼ ▼ ▼ ▼ ▼ ▼ ▼ ▼ ▼ ▼ ▼ ▼ ▼ ▼ ▼ ▼ ▼ ▼ ▼ ▼ ▼ ▼ ▼ ▼ ▼ ▼ ▼ ▼ ▼ ▼ ▼ ▼ ▼ ▼ ▼

## Executing the Color Range command

Here's all you need to know about working with the Color Range command:

*1.* **Choose Select⇨Color Range.**

The Color Range dialog box appears in full glory.

**2.** **Choose Sampled Colors from the Select menu and then choose the Eyedropper (or Sampled Colors) tool in the dialog box.**

*3.* **Select a display option — Selection or Image.**

I recommend leaving the setting at the default of Selection so that you can see the mask as you build it. You can toggle between the two views by pressing Ctrl (⌘ on the Mac).

*4.* **Either in the image itself or in the image preview in the Color Range dialog box, click to sample your desired colors.**

The image preview changes to a mask. Black areas show unselected pixels, white areas show selected pixels, and gray areas show pixels that are partially selected.

 Your goal is to try and make what you want all white and what you don't want all black. And if you want some things partially selected, they can remain gray.

CONTINUED
▼ ▼ ▼ ▼ ▼

**5.** **Adjust the selection by adding or deleting colors.**

You can select or delete as many base colors as you desire.

Use the plus eyedropper to add, and use the minus eyedropper to delete.

You can be lazy like me and just stick with the regular eyedropper. Simply use Shift and Alt (Option on the Mac) to add and delete.

**6.** **Fine-tune the range of colors by dragging the Fuzziness slider.**

The Fuzziness ranges extend from 0 to 200. A higher value selects more colors, and a lower value selects less colors. As you adjust the Fuzziness, the mask dynamically updates.

The Invert option selects what is currently unselected and deselects what is currently selected. And if you totally muck things up, you can reset the dialog box by pressing Alt (Option on the Mac) and clicking Reset.

**7.** **Choose a Selection Preview from the pop-up menu to preview the selection in the image window.**

✔ **None** displays the image normally, as shown in Figure 2-4.

✔ **Grayscale** displays just the grayscale mask.

✔ **Black Matte** and **White Matte** display the selection against a black or white background.

✔ **Quick Mask** shows the mask, using your Quick Mask settings, over your image.

**8.** **Click OK.**

Your image appears with a selection outline based on the Color Range mask.

Now do what you will with your nice, clean selection.

I decided my Thai dancer needed to be in a more exotic locale so I transported her (by dragging and dropping with the Move tool onto another image) to a mystical Shangri La, shown in Figure 2-5.

**Figure 2-4**

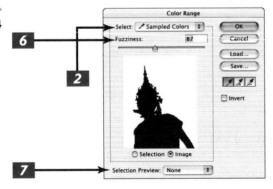

**Figure 2-5**

# Selective Erasing with the Eraser Tools

The Eraser tools let you erase portions of an image to the background color, to transparency, or even to the way your image looked earlier in your editing session. There are three Erasers — the regular Eraser, the Magic Eraser, and the Background Eraser. All three share a tool flyout menu.

The Eraser tools look like real erasers so you can't miss them. But just in case you do, press E and then Shift E to toggle through the three tools.

 When you erase pixels (which is basically what the Eraser tools do), those pixels are gone. Gone. For good. Before using the Eraser tools or the Extract command (coming up in the next section) it might be wise to make a backup of your image. You can save the image either as a separate file or as another layer. That way, if things run amuck, you have some insurance.

## The Eraser

The Eraser tool allows you to erase areas on your image to either the background color or to transparency. Select it, drag through the desired area on your image, and you're done.

If the image isn't layered and has just a background, you erase to the background color, as shown in Figure 2-6. If the image is on a layer, you erase to transparency.

**Figure 2-6**

I rate this tool in the same category as the Lasso tool. It's quick, it's easy, but it has limited applications. Use it only for minor touchups. The Eraser definitely isn't a tool to use for making accurate selections.

 The most useful function I find for the Eraser tool is to clean up my channel masks. Set the mode to Block, zoom into your mask, and clean up those black and white pixels.

Here are the options found in the Options bar that control the Eraser:

✔ **Mode:** Select from Brush, Pencil, and Block. When you select Brush or Pencil you have access to the Brush Picker palette on the far left of the Options bar.

   Use the Brush Picker palette to select from a variety of brush sizes and styles. Block only has one size, a square of 16 by 16 pixels.

✔ **Opacity:** Specify a percentage of transparency for the erasure. Opacity settings less than 100 percent only partially erase the pixels. The lower the opacity setting, the less it erases. This option isn't available for the Block mode.

✔ **Flow:** Set a flow rate percentage when using Brush mode. Flow specifies how fast the erasure is applied and is especially handy when using the Airbrush option.

✔ **Airbrush:** Click the button when using Brush mode to turn your Brush into an Airbrush. With this option, the longer you hold your mouse down, the more it will erase.

✔ **Erase to History:** This option allows you to erase back to a selected source state or snapshot in the History palette. You can also press Alt (Option on the Mac) to temporarily access the Erase to History option. See Book II, Chapter 4, for more information.

✔ **Brush Palette toggle:** Click the toggle button to bring up the full Brushes palette.

## The Magic Eraser

The Magic Eraser tool works like a combination Eraser and Magic Wand tool. It both selects and erases similarly colored pixels:

- ✔ **When you click a layer:** The Magic Eraser erases pixels of a similar color based on a specified range and leaves the area transparent, as shown in Figure 2-7.

- ✔ **When you click an image that has just a background:** The Magic Eraser automatically converts the background to a layer and then does the same thing.

- ✔ **When you click a layer with locked transparency:** The Magic Eraser tool erases the pixels and replaces the area with the background color.

**Figure 2-7**

Book
*VI*
Chapter
*2*

The range of colors that is erased is defined by the Tolerance value, just like it is with the Magic Wand. The value determines how similar a neighboring color has to be to the color that you click. A higher value picks up more colors while a lower value picks up fewer colors. In my example, I set my Tolerance to 8 and clicked in the upper left of my image. Only a limited shade of black was selected and erased due to my lower Tolerance setting.

Here are the other options:

- ✔ **Anti-aliased:** Creates a slightly soft edge around the transparent area.

- ✔ **Contiguous:** Only selects similar colors that are adjacent to each other. Uncheck this option to delete similar colored pixels wherever they appear in your image.

- ✔ **Use All Layers:** Samples colors using data from *all* visible layers, but erases pixels on the *active* layer only.

- ✔ **Opacity:** Works like it does for the regular Eraser.

## The Background Eraser

The Background Eraser tool is probably the most sophisticated of the Eraser lot. It erases away the background from an image and leaves the foreground untouched, in theory anyway.

 If you're not careful, it will erase the foreground and anything else in its path.

Like the Magic Eraser, the Background Eraser erases to transparency on a layer. If you drag an image with only a background, it converts the background into a layer.

To use the Magic Eraser tool, you need to carefully keep the crosshair in the center of the cursor, also known as the *hot spot,* on the background pixels as you drag. Then all background pixels under the brush circumference are deleted. But, if you touch a foreground pixel with the hot spot, it's gobbled up as well. As you can see from my example in Figure 2-8, I got a little too close to his face in some spots and it left him a little chewed up.

**Figure 2-8**

Here's the run down on the options for the Background Eraser:

- ✔ **Brush Presets picker:** Provides various settings to customize the size and appearance of your eraser tip. The size and tolerance settings at the bottom are for those using pressure-sensitive drawing tablets. You can base the size and tolerance on the pen pressure or position of the thumbwheel.

- ✔ **Limits:** Only erases similar colors that are adjacent to one another. Discontiguous erases all similarly colored pixels wherever they appear in the image. Find Edges erases contiguous pixels while retaining the sharpness of the edges.

- ✔ **Tolerance:** Works just like the Magic Eraser Tolerance setting.

- ✔ **Protect Foreground Color:** Prevents the erasing of areas that match the foreground color.

✔ **Sampling:** Determines what area should and shouldn't be erased. The default Continuous setting allows you to sample colors continuously as you drag through the image. Once erases only areas that contain the color that you first clicked. If the background is pretty much one color, you can try this option. Background Swatch erases only the areas containing the background color.

▼ ▼ ▼ ▼ ▼ ▼ ▼ ▼ ▼ ▼ ▼ ▼ ▼ ▼ ▼ ▼ ▼ ▼ ▼ ▼ ▼ ▼ ▼ ▼ ▼ ▼ ▼ ▼ ▼ ▼ ▼ ▼ ▼ ▼ ▼

# Extracting an Image

The last of Photoshop's automated masking tools is the Extract command. The name sounds great. You expect that it plucks your desired element right out of the image, cleanly, neatly, and without pain. But to be honest with you, I find the Extract command to be overly complex for the results it provides. Sometimes you can get lucky and pick an image that works well with the command. But frequently, it does a marginal job. Once you learn the art of true, manual masking you may never visit the Extract command again.

Here's how it works:

*1.* **Choose Filter➪Extract.**

Photoshop brings up the Extract window, shown in Figure 2-9.

*2.* **Select the Edge Highlighter tool, located at the top of the Toolbox.**

You can also press the B key to access the tool.

Photoshop offers a Smart Highlighting option, under the Tool Options on the right side of the dialog box.

If your image has a well-defined edge, but the foreground and background colors are similar or the image is highly textured, this option helps the Edge Highlighter to cling to the edge as you use the tool. You can toggle the option on and off by pressing Ctrl (⌘ on the Mac) when using the tool.

*3.* **Trace around the edges of the element you want to select. As you trace, feel free to change the Brush size, again under the Tool Options.**

Use a small brush for well defined, sharp edges. Use a larger brush for wispier detailed edges such as hair, fur, leaves, and the like. To change the brush size using keyboard shortcuts, click the left (smaller) and right (larger) bracket keys. Hold the bracket key down and the brush size will change more dramatically.

Be sure that the highlighted edge overlaps both the element and the background.

You can change the colors of the highlight and fill in the Tool Options as well.

I traced around the man in Figure 2-9. Make a complete path around the element. If one or more sides of your element is cropped off the edge, you don't have to highlight that side:

✔ Use the Hand tool to move your image if needed. You can temporarily access the Hand tool by pressing the spacebar.

✔ Use the Zoom tool to zoom in. Press Alt (Option on the Mac) to zoom out. You can also Zoom by using keyboard shortcuts by pressing Ctrl++ and Ctrl+- (⌘+= and ⌘+-) on the Mac.

CONTINUED
▼ ▼ ▼ ▼ ▼

✔ The Channel option allows you to load an alpha channel as a starting point for the extraction. You can then modify the highlighted area using the Edge Highlighter and Eraser tools.

 Beware. For some reason when loading the alpha channel into the Extract dialog box, the black areas in the mask are converted into the highlighted area, while the white areas are not highlighted. This is the opposite of what you would expect, but it works out just the same. After you complete the highlighted area, fill the unlighted area with the Fill bucket (see Step 7).

**4.** If you make a mistake as you create your highlighted outline, press Ctrl+Z (⌘+Z on the Mac) to undo your error.

**5.** Once you have made your outline, use the Eraser tool to clean up any hiccups in the outline.

 Press the E key to select the Eraser from the keyboard. You can have the best of both tools and toggle between the Edge Highlighter and the Eraser tool by pressing Alt (Option on the Mac).

**6.** To erase an entire highlight, press Alt+Backspace (Option+Delete on the Mac).

**7.** Select the Fill tool, the second tool in the Toolbox (or press the G key) and click inside the highlighted outline.

The outline fills with color, shown in Figure 2-10.

**Figure 2-9**

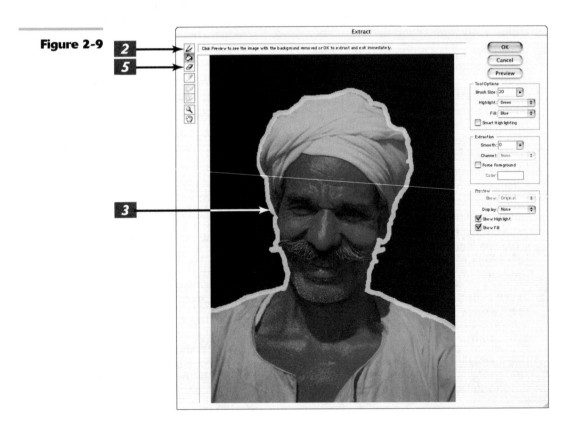

If, by chance, the color leaks outside of the highlighted edge, you may have a small hole somewhere along the outline. Locate the offending hole and patch it with the Edge Highlighter tool. Click it again with the Fill tool. To unfill an area, click inside with the Fill tool.

As an alternative to using the Fill tool, you can select the Force Foreground option. This option can be useful if the element you want to select is mostly tones of one color. Use the Eyedropper to sample the color in the area you want to select. Then use the Edge Highlighter to highlight those areas containing your desired color.

**8.** **Click the Preview button and take a gander at your extracted element (or click OK to skip the preview and get your extraction).**

If your background is solid and uncluttered, your foreground element has a simple, uncomplicated edge, and there is quite a bit of contrast between the foreground and background elements (and if the planets are aligned just so), your results are likely to be pretty good. In my example, there is only a minor bit of background fringe around the moustache and the top of the turban.

If you need to clean up a bit of fringe, give the Smooth option a shot. This option removes stray pixels or artifacts from the selection. A high value smoothes out the edges around the selection, but can cause some undesirable blurring as well. Start with 0 or a small value first, before increasing the Smooth amount.

**9.** **If you're happy with the results, click the OK button.**

The masked areas are deleted. If your image was a background, Photoshop converts it to a layer, so the selected element will be against transparency.

**10.** **If you would rather preview your image against something other than the transparent checkerboard, choose another option from the Display pop-up menu.**

You can view the image against a white, gray, black, or other colored background. Or you can view it as a mask (if you view it as a mask, the white areas represent the selected areas and the black areas represent the transparent areas).

**11.** **If you're not happy, use the editing tools in the Extract dialog box to fix your mask, using the various view options.**

**12.** **You can choose between the Original and Extracted view from the Show pop-up menu.**

**13.** **You can also check Show Highlight and Show Fill. Drag with the Cleanup Tool (press C on the keyboard) to erase background pixels around your extraction by subtracting opacity. Alt+drag (Option+drag on the Mac) to bring the opacity back.**

This tool is useful for creating feathered edges.

**14.** **The Edge Touchup tool (T is the keyboard shortcut) sharpens the edges of the selection by adding opacity to your selection or subtracting opacity from the background.**

**15.** **You can adjust the Brush Size of these editing tools as well.**

**16.** **When you're done editing, click OK to exit the dialog box. If you still have some areas that need some cleanup, use Photoshop regular editing tools, such as the Background Eraser and the History Brush.**

Book
**VI**
Chapter
**2**

CONTINUED
▼ ▼ ▼ ▼ ▼

**Figure 2-10**

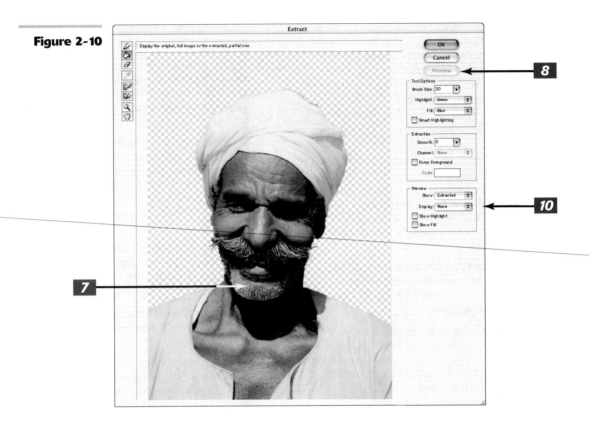

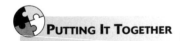

![Puzzle piece icon] **PUTTING IT TOGETHER**

### Framing a Photo with Quick Mask

Sometimes you may want to add a decorative border or edge to your image. Maybe you're creating a postcard or greeting card and the standard rectangular shape image just doesn't provide enough pizzazz. While it looks like it would be difficult, it is a snap with the Quick Mask command.

**1.** Using any selection tool, create a selection on your image.

I started with a rectangle in my image and then chose Select⇨Inverse to turn the selection inside out.

**2.** Click the Quick Mask mode button in the Toolbox.

A color overlay covers and protects the area outside the selection.

Your selected area is open for you to edit as you so desire.

**3.** Grab the Brush tool, choose the Heavy Stipple brush, and set the brush diameter to 168 pixels.

You can find the Heavy Stipple brush in the Wet Media brush library of the Brushes palette.

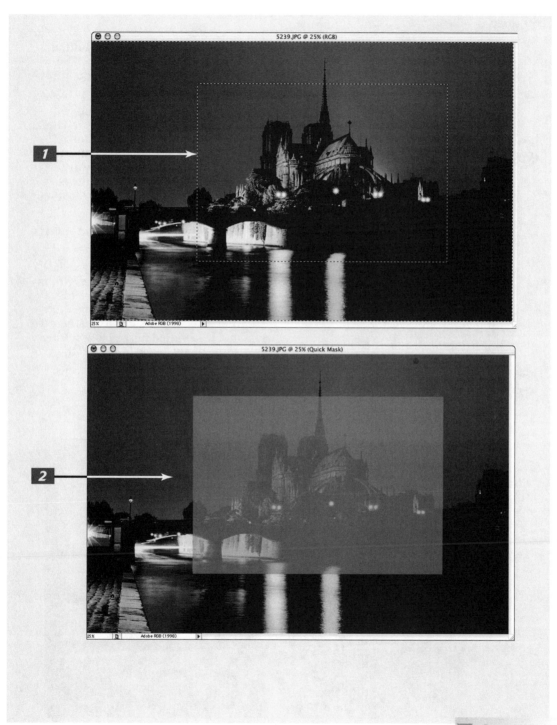

▼ **CONTINUED**

Book
*VI*
Chapter
*2*

▼ **CONTINUED**

**4.** Paint around the edges of the mask with black to add to the masked area.

**5.** Adjust the Flow setting to 35% to get a semitransparent area, and then click a few more times.

🎯 You could also paint with gray to get the same effect.

**6.** Again, adjust your brush diameter, this time to 80 pixels, and add a few random clicks here and there.

**7.** Switch your color to white and repeat the steps, clicking around the image and also in the interior of the mask.

Because white adds to the selected area, your image will start to show through.

I ended up with a mottled mess.

🎯 You can also apply a filter or adjustment (Image⇨Adjustment) to the Quick Mask. See this technique in action in Book VII, Chapter 2.

**8.** Click the Standard mode button to exit the Quick Mask mode. The overlay disappears and you are left with a selection outline.

The selection outline correlates with the unmasked or selected areas of the Quick Mask. If you had a feathered mask, such as mine, the selection outline runs halfway between the selected and unselected areas of the mask indicating a soft transition.

**9.** Your selection is ready and waiting for your next command.

In my example I deleted my selection, thereby filling the hole with my background color of white and leaving me with a stippled image. Note that since my brush was feathered and also varied in the Flow settings, some of my image is also feathered and semitransparent.

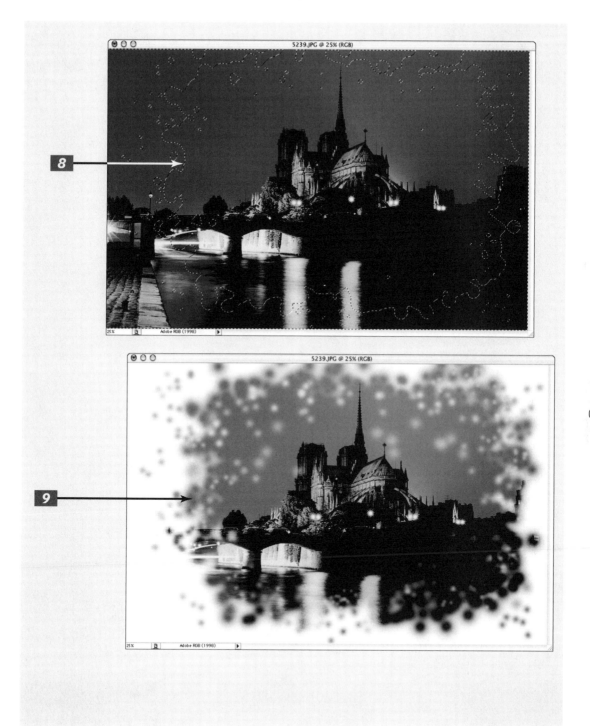

# Getting Exact with Advanced Masking Techniques

If you haven't already checked out Chapter 2 of this book, which covers Photoshop's quick and easy masking tools, you might want to breeze through that chapter first, especially if the word mask brings to mind an image from Halloween instead of a selection technique. In this chapter, I dive into some manual masking techniques.

Layer masks are tremendously useful, and if you're like me, you'll find yourself addicted to them. They can be fantastic for blending layers and making multiple images dissolve into one another. Vector masks create shapes defined by vector paths and produce clean, smooth-edged graphic elements.

Channel masks are probably the most time consuming of the masking lot, but they're powerful and accurate. Like anything in life, the more you practice using them, the faster and better you get.

After you get through this final chapter of Book VI, you'll be familiar with every masking technique Photoshop has to offer. By then, you'll be prepared to use masks to select a very hairy orangutan, dyed green, perched in a tree in a lush rainforest. And how many people can say that?

## Working with Layer Masks

Like any other mask, a *layer mask* is a grayscale image that can be edited to your heart's content. Layer masks are excellent for blending layers of images together and creating soft transitions between elements.

For versatility, layer masks are unparalleled. They allow you to gradually brush in transparency and opacity on a selective pixel basis. Paint with black to hide portions of the layer; paint with white to display portions; and paint in varying shades of gray to partially show elements. You can even apply gradients, image adjustments, and filters to your layer masks to create interesting special effects.

After you get the concept of layer masks, you'll never use the Eraser tools (covered in Chapter 2 of this book) again. You won't have to because one of the great things about layer masks is that they can forever be edited, or even deleted, with no permanent harm whatsoever to the image.

### Creating layer masks

To create a layer mask, select your desired layer and choose Layer➪Add Layer Mask➪Reveal All or Hide All.

- ✔ **Reveal All** creates a mask filled with white, which shows the layer.

- ✔ **Hide All** creates a mask filled with black, which hides, or *masks*, the layer and shows nothing but transparency.

You can also click the Add layer mask icon at the bottom of Layers palette (which by default selects Reveal All).

You can't add a layer mask to a background layer. You must convert the background layer to a regular layer if you want to use a layer mask on the background of an image.

You can also apply a layer mask only to a certain portion of a layer by first making a selection using one of the selection tools before choosing the Add Layer Mask command.

After you create the layer mask, you can grab the painting tool of your choice and apply color. *Remember:* Add white to the mask to display the image. Add black to hide the image. Add gray to make the image semi-transparent.

### Using the Gradient and Brush tools on a Layer Mask

I must confess: I use two of the layer masking tools more than the others:

- ✔ The Gradient tool, set to a linear gradient of black to white or white to black is truly awesome. Simply drag the layer mask to create the gradient. The darker areas of the gradient gradually hide the image, while the lighter areas gradually show the image.

- ✔ The Brush tool, with a large, feathered tip, using the Airbrush option and the Flow set to around 10% is amazing. With these settings in place, you can create feathered edges that blend one layer into another without any harsh lines.

In Figure 3-1, which is an image with two layers, the flag on the bottom and the girl on top, I used a combination of both these tools. I started with the black-to-white linear gradient, which I dragged from the left edge of my image through to the right edge. I then took the Brush tool with a large feathered tip (265 pixels), clicked the Airbrush option, set the Flow to 10%, and worked my way around the profile of the girl's face to get rid of some more of the background behind her (see Figure 3-2).

**Figure 3-1**

Before

**Figure 3-2**

After

Image thumbnail

Link

Layer Mask thumbnail

To edit a layer mask, click the layer mask thumbnail in the Layers palette. Select your desired painting or editing tool, and paint or edit the mask to perfection. Just be sure that you're working on the layer mask, instead of editing the image itself. Otherwise, you'll apply paint directly to your image. You can tell because you'll see a layer mask icon next to the eye icon in the Layers palette.

## Managing layer masks

Here are some tips to help you work with your layer masks. You can do the following:

✔ **Load a layer mask:** *Loading* a layer mask means getting a selection outline based on the layer mask. Simply Ctrl+click (⌘+click on the Mac) the layer mask thumbnail.

✔ **View the mask without viewing the image:** Sometimes when you're editing a layer mask you may find it helpful to see the mask itself without having to view the image, too, as shown in Figure 3-3. Simply Alt+click (Option+click on the Mac) the layer mask thumbnail to view the mask and hide the image on the layer.

To redisplay the image, Alt+click (Option+click on the Mac) again or click the eye icon in the far left column.

✔ **View the layer mask as a red overlay:** If you prefer to see your layer mask as a red overlay (called a *rubylith*), Alt+Shift+click (Option+Shift+click on the Mac) the layer mask thumbnail.

Click again with the same keys to remove the overlay. You can change the opacity and color of the overlay in the Layer Mask Display Options dialog box, which you access by double-clicking the layer mask channel in the Channels palette.

A rubylith is similar to the red overlay used with Quick Masks, covered in Chapter 2 of this book.

✔ **Paste a copied selection into a layer mask:** Simply Alt+click (Option+click on the Mac) the layer mask thumbnail. Choose Edit⇨Paste and then Select⇨Deselect. Click the image thumbnail in the Layers palette to return to the image.

The copied selection can consist of anything, but this technique comes in particularly handy when you're copying one layer mask into another.

✔ **Disable (temporarily hide) or enable a layer mask:** Just Shift+click the layer mask thumbnail or choose Layer⇨Disable Layer Mask or Enable Layer Mask.

✔ **Unlink a layer from its layer mask:** By default, a layer mask is linked to the contents of the layer. This allows them to move together. To unlink a layer from its layer mask, click the link icon in the Layers palette. Click again to re-establish the link.

✔ **Discard a layer mask:** Just drag the layer mask thumbnail to the trash icon in the Layers palette. Click Discard in the dialog box. Or you can choose Layer⇨Remove Layer Mask⇨Discard.

✔ **Apply a layer mask:** When you apply a layer mask, you fuse the mask to the image. All black areas in the mask are replaced with transparent pixels; all gray areas are replaced with partially transparent pixels; and all white areas are image pixels. Drag the thumbnail to the trash icon in the Layers palette. Click Apply in the dialog box. Or you can choose Layer⇨Remove Layer Mask⇨Apply.

**Figure 3-3**

Girl's layer mask

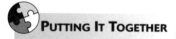PUTTING IT TOGETHER

### Making a Photo Gradually Fade from Color to Grayscale

Layer masks are extremely powerful when it comes to blending multiple images so that one seems to dissolve into the others. I'm not going to show you how to use a layer mask to blend different images, but rather the same image — one in color and one in grayscale.

**1.** **Open a copy of your favorite color image.**

The subject matter isn't critical here, so feel free to whip out that old prom picture.

**2.** **Choose Image⇨Duplicate.**

Accept the default name and click OK in the dialog box.

**3.** **With the duplicate image active, choose Window⇨Channels.**

**4.** **View each of the channels to find the one that gives you the best grayscale image.**

If you need a refresher on channels, see Chapter 1 of this book. The Red channel gives the best contrast for the portrait in my example. Skin tones tend to have a lot of red in them, and the Red channel usually provides the best grayscale image.

**5.** **Choose Image⇨Mode⇨Grayscale and click OK in the Adobe Photoshop dialog box.**

▼ CONTINUED

▼ **CONTINUED**

The color has now been stripped from the image.

This is only one way to convert a color image to grayscale. There are others, usually yielding better results — converting to Lab mode, using the Channel Mixer. Check them out in Book II, Chapter 2. Feel free to choose your own method.

**6.** **Choose Window⇨Layers. With the Move tool and holding the Shift key down, drag and drop your grayscale image onto your color image.**

This action automatically creates a new layer from the grayscale image. (See Book V for more information.)

By holding down the Shift key you keep the two images perfectly aligned.

**7.** **Close your duplicate image.**

**8.** **Press D for default colors.**

This gives you a black foreground swatch and a white background swatch in your Toolbox.

I'm going to show you now how to use one of my favorite techniques, a black-to-white gradient, on the layer mask.

**9.** **Make sure that Layer 1 is the active layer in the Layers palette. Click the Add Layer Mask icon at the bottom of the palette.**

It's the icon that looks like a dark square with a white circle on top. Photoshop adds a second thumbnail on your layer, indicating that a layer mask has been applied.

 A layer mask acts like a piece of clear acetate over your layer.

**10.** **Select your Gradient tool. Then select the default gradient of Foreground to Background.**

To get the default gradient, click the Gradient picker in the Options bar and select the first gradient.

It should be a gradient of white to black because it's based on the current foreground and background colors, which reverse when you select the Layer Mask thumbnail. For a gradient refresher, see Book IV, Chapter 3.

**11.** **Drag the gradient from the top of your image to the bottom.**

Or from left to right. Or at a diagonal. It's your call.

**12.** **Experiment with long drags and short drags. The angle and length**

of your mouse movement determines how the layer mask reveals the underlying image.

In my example, I dragged from the top of the image to the bottom and stopped about two-thirds of the way down.

 Where black appears on the layer mask, the grayscale image is hidden. Where white appears on the mask, the grayscale image shows through and everything in between allows the grayscale image to partially show.

Although I used a linear gradient in my example, you can experiment with the other types as well. Radial gradients can provide some interesting effects.

**13.** **When you've completed your mask, save and close the file.**

Book
**VI**
Chapter
**3**

▼ **CONTINUED**

▼ **CONTINUED**

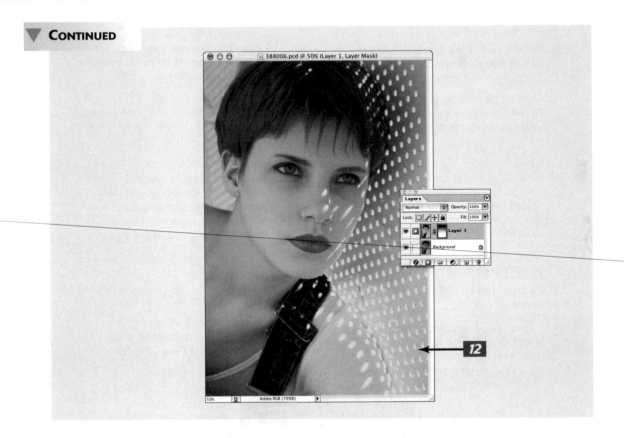

# Creating and Editing Vector Masks

Whereas layer masks let you create soft-edged masks, vector masks create hard-edged masks defined by shape created by a vector path on a layer. Vector-based shapes produce clean, smooth, and well-defined edges that are never jagged. And you can size and transform vector shapes without ever degrading the appearance of the element.

You create a vector mask when you create a shape with any one of the Shape tools. You can also create a vector mask when you convert type to a shape (Layer⇨Type⇨Convert to Shape). See Book IV, Chapter 5.

▼▼▼▼▼▼▼▼▼▼▼▼▼▼▼▼▼▼▼▼▼▼▼▼▼▼▼▼▼▼▼▼▼▼▼▼▼▼▼▼

### Adding a vector mask to a layer

To add a vector mask to layer, follow these steps:

1. **Select the layer in the Layers palette and choose Layer⇨Add Vector Mask⇨Reveal All or Hide All.**

   I describe Reveal All and Hide All in the Layer Mask section.

2. **On the vector mask, create a path with the Pen tool or grab any Shape tool and create a shape.**

See Book III, Chapter 2 for more on paths and Book IV, Chapter 2 for more on shapes.

I selected the Custom Shape tool and dragged a sunburst shape on my vector mask. Notice how everything outside of the path is hidden, or masked, as shown in Figure 3-4.

 Like layer masks, you can add vector masks only to layers, not backgrounds.

If necessary, simply convert your background to a layer by double-clicking background in the Layers palette.

**3.** **If your vector mask is satisfactory, save your file and then close it.**

 Another way to add a vector mask is to select your desired layer, draw a work path with the Pen tool or one of the Shape tools and then select Layer⏎Add Vector Mask⏎Current Path.

 ## Getting wild with Ocean Ripple and Twirl filters

Not only can you apply gradients and use the painting and editing tools on the layer mask, but you can also apply filters. Filters are sets of instructions that tell Photoshop what to do with a particular pixel in an image or selection, using a process called convolution. They can be used for tasks as mundane as sharpening an image to the more creative use of special effects. In the following figure, I started with a striped radial gradient and then applied an Ocean Ripple and Twirl filter. I mean, I know it's a little out there, but keep these filters in mind for those off-the-wall party invitations. For the low-down on filters, see Book VII, Chapters 1 and 2.

**Figure 3-4**

## Managing vector masks

Here are a few more vector mask tips. You can perform the following tasks:

- ✔ **Edit a vector mask path:** Use the Freeform Pen and Pen tools, as described in Book III, Chapter 2.

- ✔ **Add multiple shapes or paths to the existing vector mask:** All you need to do is just drag another shape with any of the Shape tools. Or add another path with the Pen tool.

- ✔ **Remove a vector mask from a layer:** Drag the thumbnail to the Trash icon in the Layers palette or choose Layer➪Delete Vector Mask.

- ✔ **Disable (temporarily hide) or enable a vector mask:** Shift-click the vector mask thumbnail or choose Layer➪Enable (or Disable) Vector Mask.

- ✔ **Rasterize a vector mask:** Rasterizing (or turning the mask into a pixel-based image) converts the vector mask into a layer mask. Choose Layer➪Rasterize➪Vector Mask.

- ✔ **Apply layer styles to vector shapes:** This is a quick and easy way to create buttons for a Web page or a custom logo, as shown in Figure 3-5. Just select the layer, not the vector mask, and choose Layer➪Layer Style. Select your style of choice. For details on layer styles see Book V, Chapter 4.

**Figure 3-5**

Book
**VI**
Chapter
**3**

▼▼▼▼▼▼▼▼▼▼▼▼▼▼▼▼▼▼▼▼▼▼▼▼▼▼▼▼▼▼▼▼▼▼▼▼▼▼▼▼▼▼

# *Creating Channel Masks*

Photoshop's channel masks are probably the most time-consuming masks to use because they require a lot of manual labor. Not heavy lifting, mind you, but work with Photoshop's tools and commands.

But, don't get me wrong, it's time well spent. Channel masks can usually accurately select what the other Photoshop tools can only dream about — wisps of hair, tufts of fur, a ficus benjamina tree with 9,574 leaves.

There are lots of ways to create a channel mask, but I'm here to offer you one that works most of the time. To create a channel mask, follow these steps:

**1. Analyze your existing channels to find a suitable candidate to use to create a duplicate channel.**

This is usually the channel with the most contrast between what you want and don't want. For instance, in my example, the Red channel provided the most contrast between the tree and lanterns, which I wanted to mask, and the background, which I didn't.

After you duplicate the channel, it then becomes an alpha channel.

**2. Choose Image➪Adjustments➪Levels.**

Using the Histogram and the sliders in the Levels dialog box, increase the contrast between the element(s) you want and don't want selected.

**3. Choose a tool, such as the Brush, and paint and edit the alpha channel to refine the mask.**

See Figure 3-6. My mask was pretty clean to start with, so it didn't require much editing.

**4. When you complete the mask, click the Load Channel as Selection icon (the dotted circle icon on the far left) at the bottom of the Channels palette. Then click your composite channel at the top of the list of channels.**

**Figure 3-6**

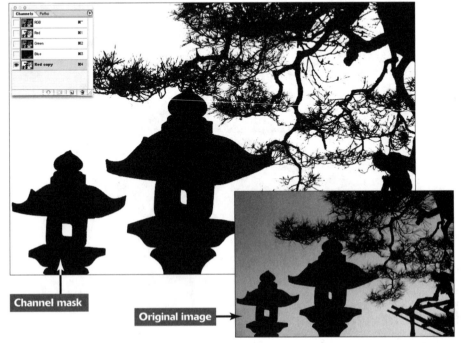

Channel mask

Original image

This will load your mask as a selection, giving you that familiar selection outline. You can also use one of my favorite keyboard shortcuts: Ctrl+click (⌘+click on the Mac) directly on the alpha channel to load the mask as a selection.

Your selection is now ready to go.

**5.** **You can leave it within the original image or drag and drop it onto another image, as I did in Figure 3-7.**

If you've done a good job, nobody will be the wiser that the two images never met in real life.

**Figure 3-7**

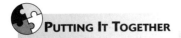 **PUTTING IT TOGETHER**

### Masking Hair, Fur, and Other Wispy Things

Hair, fur, fuzz, and other objects with complex or loosely defined edges can prove difficult to select with the run of the mill selection techniques. But that's where asking can save the day. Because a mask allows for a 256 level selection, it does a great job in picking up those illusive strands of hair and such that would otherwise probably be cut off in the selecting process.

Perhaps you've seen those photos where everyone in a composite image appears to have helmet hair? Here are the steps to avoid the Aqua Net look and select even the smallest wisp of hair:

**1.** **Choose File⇨Open.**

Select an image that contains something hairy, furry, or fuzzy. A portrait is an ideal choice (unless it's a portrait of Telly Savalas).

 **CONTINUED**

▼ **CONTINUED**

 For your first attempt at this technique, it is best to start with an image that has a pretty simple and uncluttered background.

In my example, I used an image of a pensive, young urban professional.

**2.** **Choose View⇨Channels. View each channel by clicking the channel name.**

Each channel is an independent grayscale image. Each of the channels in the document is a potential starting point for a mask.

It is best to start with the channel that contains the most contrast between what you want to select and what you don't. If it is a toss up, go with the channel that will make it easiest to select the difficult part of the image (in my example, that's the hair).

In my example, I'm using the Blue channel.

**3.** **Choose Duplicate channel from the Channels pop-up menu. Name the channel *mask* and click OK.**

You've created an alpha channel for the mask. Now you can edit the mask without harming the original channel.

**4.** **Choose Image⇨Adjustments⇨ Levels and boost the contrast in the image by adjusting the Input sliders for Shadows, Midtones, and Highlights.**

If you need help using the Levels adjustment, see Book VIII, Chapter 1.

**5.** **Select the person and his or her hair.**

You can do that one of two ways:

✔ By selecting the person.

✔ By selecting the background first and then inverting the selection.

In a mask, traditionally white represents a selected area, black represents an unselected area, and gray represents a partially selected area.

**6.** **Adjust the Levels settings such that the element you want to select is either all white or all black with a little gray in the wispy areas. In other words, you want to change**

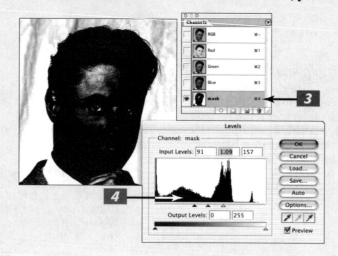

most of the pixels in the image to either black or white.

In my example, because my guy is darker than the background, I adjusted the contrast to make the subject as black as I could while making the background lighter.

**7.** **If you feel the edges of your image need to be accentuated, you can apply a High Pass filter (Filter⇨Other⇨High Pass) before you apply the Level adjustment.**

High Pass turns your overall image gray while leaving the edges white.

Don't use too low a radius value (start with a setting between 8 and 10) or completing the mask will be too time consuming.

**8.** **Refine the mask by selecting the Eraser tool and choosing Block Mode from the Options bar.**

 The Block Eraser is a great tool for cleaning up masks. It allows you to paint inside the mask without creating any feathered edges.

**9.** **Press D for default colors.**

Remember the Eraser paints with the background color, so be sure you have the color you want before you drag. Press X to switch the foreground and background colors.

**10.** **Clean up your mask by painting with black and white.**

Make sure to use short strokes so you can undo any mistakes you make.

**11.** **Use the Zoom tool if you need to touch up the details.**

The Block Eraser cursor has only one size, so you have to zoom in to paint thinner strokes and zoom out to erase a larger area.

Remember to leave some gray around the wispy areas; otherwise, they may look chopped off.

Take your time and be as accurate as you can. This is where patience makes a big difference.

Book
**VI**
Chapter
**3**

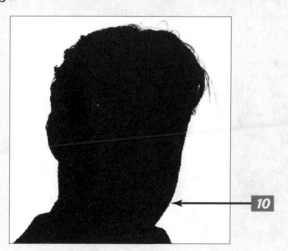

▼ **Continued**

▼ CONTINUED

 If you're not sure what you need to paint on the mask and you want to refer to the color image, simply click the composite channel (either RGB or CMYK depending on your image) at the top of the Channels palette. Then click on the mask channel again to return to your mask. Or better yet, you can view both the mask and the composite simultaneously. Your mask appears as a red overlay.

Your mask is refined and ready to go.

**12.** **Click the first icon on the left at the bottom of the Channels palette to load the mask as a selection (or Ctrl+click [⌘+click on the Mac] the channel mask).**

A selection marquee appears around your mask.

 If you want to soften the edge a little, you can choose Select⇨Feather and enter a value somewhere between .5 pixel (for a low-resolution image) to 2 pixels (for a high-resolution image). Feathering allows for a softer, natural looking transition between your masked element and the background. I used a one-pixel feather for my image.

**13.** **Return to the composite image by clicking on the RGB channel (or CMYK if warranted).**

**14.** **If you need to invert your selection, choose Select⇨Inverse.**

In my example, I just filled my background with a solid color, so I left the background selected.

**15.** **Choose Window⇨Color and mix a color of your choice. Choose Edit⇨Fill, choose Foreground Color for your Contents, and click OK.**

The background is now replaced with a solid color. Check the edges to see how clean your mask is.

**16.** **Make any final edits you need to make.**

My guy looked like he spent too much time at the local tanning booth, so I toned the redness in his skin by using the Variation commands (see Book VIII, Chapter 1).

**17.** **When you're happy with your channel mask, save and close the file.**

It takes practice to get masking down to a science, but believe me,

14

15

it's worth your time. Nine times out of ten, a channel mask lends a much better selection than any of the easier, quicker selection tools and techniques.

 Inside of filling the background with a color, you can also open a second image and, with the Move tool, drag and drop your masked element into the second image. A couple of things to keep in mind when compositing with two images: First try and use two images whose lighting isn't so dissimilar that it looks artificial. Take into account the time of day, the angle of the light, and so on. Secondly, try and select two images whose levels of focus make sense. If you need to soften one of the images, apply the Gaussian Blur filter. If your mask is good, your person should look right at home in his or her new digs.

# Book VII

# Filters and Distortions

The 5th Wave     By Rich Tennant

"I THINK YOU'VE MADE A MISTAKE. WE DO PHOTO RETOUCHING, NOT FAMILY PORTRAI... OOOH, WAIT A MINUTE-I THINK I GET IT!"

# Making Corrections with Daily Filters

Filters have a long and glorious history, ranging from performing essential tasks like removing abrasive particles from the oil in your car's crankcase to even more important chores involving the pixels in your Photoshop images. In both cases, filters seize tiny, almost invisible bits of stuff and rearrange them in useful ways. The results are something you'd never want to do without.

Within Photoshop, filters (also called *plug-ins* because they can be installed or removed from Photoshop independently) can help you in many ways. They correct imperfect images, improve our best photos, or transform an object from one thing into another. Filters can mimic artistic painting styles, blur things that are too sharp, sharpen things that are too blurry, or create brand new objects (like clouds) that didn't exist before. This chapter introduces you to the basics of Photoshop's filter facilities and starts you on the road to plug-in proficiency.

 Just because all filters are plug-ins doesn't mean that all plug-ins are filters. You'll find plenty of plug-ins out there that have nothing to do with filters — or image editing, for that matter.

## You Say You Want a Convolution?

All filters do one simple thing in a seemingly complicated way: They make Photoshop do your bidding. Deep within a filter's innards is a set of instructions that tells Photoshop what to do with a particular pixel in an image or selection. Photoshop applies these instructions to each and every pixel in the relevant area by using a process the techies call *convolution* (creating a form or shape that's folded or curved in tortuous windings), but which we normal folk simply refer to as *applying a filter*.

### Corrective and destructive filters

Filters fall into two basic categories, *corrective* and *destructive:*

✔ Corrective filters are used to fix problems in an image. They fine-tune color, add blur, improve sharpness, or remove nastiness like dust and scratches. Although corrective plug-ins can be fairly destructive to certain pixels, in general, they don't change the basic look of an image. You might not even notice that a corrective filter has been applied unless you compare the new version of the image with the original.

✔ Destructive filters tend to obliterate at least some of an image's original detail (some to a greater extent than others) as they add special effects. They may overlay an image with an interesting texture, move pixels around to create brush strokes, simulate light and shadow to create 3-D illusions, or distort an image with twists, waves, or zigzags. You'll often be able to tell at a glance that a destructive filter has been applied to an image: The special effect often looks like nothing that exists in real life.

An unaltered image (such as the image on the left in Figure 1-1) can be improved by using a corrective filter like Unsharp Mask (center) or changed dramatically with a destructive filter like Find Edges (right).

**Figure 1-1**

### Filter basics

Whether or not a filter is corrective or destructive, it is one of a couple of flavors — boring or super cool. (I made these names up myself. Can you tell?) Seriously, here's the scoop:

✔ **Single-step filters:** The easiest filters to use, single-step filters have no options and use no dialog boxes. Just choose the filter from the menu and watch it do its stuff on your image or selection. The basic Blur and Sharpen filters are single-step filters. So is the Invert filter, which I describe a bit later in this chapter.

✔ **Mini-application filters:** Most filters come complete with at least one dialog box, perhaps a few lists, buttons, and check boxes. And almost every mini-app filter has sliders you can use to adjust the intensity of an effect or parameter (see Figure 1-2). These filters are marked in the menus with an ellipsis (series of dots) following their names so that, like other menu commands with those dots, you'll know that there's more to come.

**Figure 1-2**

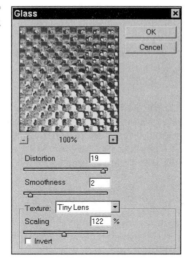

The controls themselves are easy to master. The tricky part is learning what the various parameters you're using actually do. How does changing brush size affect your image when using a brush stroke filter? What happens when you select a particular pattern with a texturizing filter? You can read descriptions of how various filter controls affect your image, but your best bet is to simply experiment until you discover the effects and parameters that work best for you. Just be sure that you save a copy of the original image; filters do permanent damage to files — modifying, adding, and deleting pixels.

 Most filters include a preview window, but some, particularly those from third-party vendors, may require you to select a Preview option to activate the display. Others can be set to preview the effect in the entire image, rather than just in the filter dialog box's preview window. That's because those particular filters use enough computer resources that constant updates take some time. The filter operates more quickly with the full preview turned off.

## Using Filters

There are tons of different types of filters to choose from. Photoshop has 13 different categories and roughly 100 filters that do things like sharpening and blurring your image, adding brush strokes, distorting, creating textures, and creating other effects. You'll find a complete description of all the categories and what they do in Chapter 2 of this book.

The simplest filter to understand and use is one that's not even found in the Filter menu: the Invert filter, a single-step filter. Invert isn't in the Filter menu because, technically, it really isn't a filter, but it illustrates nicely what filters do to your images. (Find it at Image⇨Adjustments⇨ Invert.)

When you apply Invert to an image, Photoshop examines each pixel and immediately flips it to its exact opposite in tone and color. A black pixel becomes a white pixel, a dark gray pixel becomes a light gray pixel, and a dark red pixel becomes a light cyan pixel. (For more information on the relationship between colors, see Book II, Chapter 2.) Why, pray tell, would you want to invert all the colors in an image? Why not? Seriously, this filter allows you to change negatives into positives.

Actually, you can use many other filters to do much the same thing. Based on the information in your image, pixels are lightened, darkened, changed in color, or moved around from place to place as the filter changes contrast, blurs, sharpens, corrects color, or distorts your image. Some other filters (such as the Clouds filter, which I discuss in Chapter 2 of this book) ignore image information, but they change pixels in similar ways based on their own internal rules.

## *Sharpening What's Soft*

Sometimes your images aren't as sharp as you'd like. Or, perhaps, you want only a particular part to be sharper so that it stands out from its surroundings.

All sharpening tools operate by increasing the contrast between adjacent pixels. If you look at a sharpened image side by side with the original version (as shown in Figure 1-3), you'll see that no new information has been provided. Instead, the contrast is boosted so that edges are more distinct. The dark parts of the edges are darker, and the light parts at their boundaries are lighter.

**Figure 1-3**

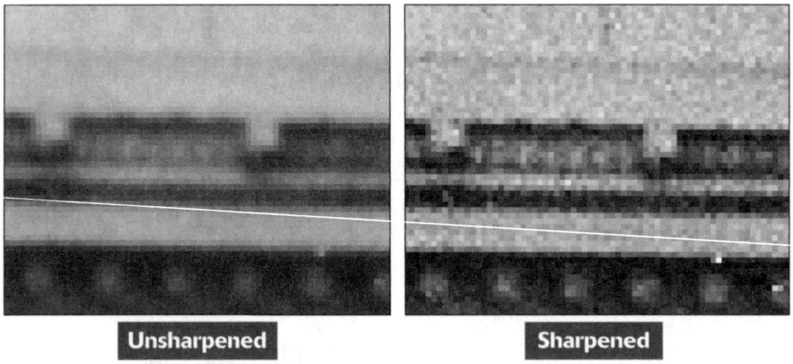

Unsharpened    Sharpened

Photoshop has five main sharpening tools, only four of which are actually filters. I discuss the four that are filters in the following sections. The fifth, the Sharpen tool, isn't a filter, strictly speaking. It's more like a paintbrush that lets you sharpen areas selectively by using strokes.

 The sharpening filters give you more control because they can be easily applied to selections that you carefully craft. Three of the four sharpen filters are single-step filters that you can apply quickly without resorting to dialog boxes.

## Sharpen

The Sharpen filter is best used for minimal touchups in small areas. Enable this filter by choosing Filter⇨Sharpen⇨Sharpen.

This single-step filter increases the contrast between all the pixels in the image or selection. While this makes the image look sharper, it can add a grainy look to solid areas that aren't part of the edges.

## Sharpen More

Choose Filter⇨Sharpen⇨Sharpen More to use the Sharpen More filter, a single-step filter that increases the contrast between all the pixels even more than the regular Sharpen filter. Like the Sharpen filter, Sharpen More is best relegated to non-critical sharpening because it doesn't do a very good job of sharpening large areas. Also, it doesn't provide the control you need for more intense projects.

## Sharpen Edges

The Sharpen Edges filter (choose Filter⇨Sharpen⇨Sharpen Edges) is a single-step filter that's superior to the Sharpen and Sharpen More filters because it concentrates its efforts on the edges of images, adding sharpness without making the image grainy or noisy. Still, it, too, is best used for quickie fixes.

## Unsharp Mask

Don't feel bad. Everyone is confused by the Unsharp Mask filter's name the first time they encounter it. (Find this filter by choosing Filter⇨Sharpen⇨Unsharp Mask.) This filter provides a sophisticated attempt to duplicate a sophisticated photographic effect called *unsharp masking*, in which two sheets of film are sandwiched together to create a final image. One sheet is the original film negative (or a duplicate), and the second is a positive image (the "normal" photograph) that's blurred slightly.

When the two are mated together, the light and dark areas cancel each other out, except at the edges — because of the blurring of the positive mask, which causes the edges to spread at those points.

Unsharp masking is a tricky procedure in the darkroom. It's much more precise in the digital realm because Photoshop can easily control the width of the areas to be masked, as well as a relative brightness level to use before beginning to apply the masking effect. The filter's dialog box is shown in Figure 1-4. After looking at the top image in Figure 1-5, don't you feel like you need glasses when you see the bottom image?

Scanned images almost always benefit from a little unsharp masking, but you should be conservative and not overdo things. That's especially true because two out of three of the Unsharp Mask controls are not the sort you can apply intuitively. The Radius and Threshold sliders work best when you've had some experience using Unsharp Mask. However, the Amount slider is a bit easier to work with. Here's how to use each of these controls:

Book
*VII*
Chapter
*1*

**Figure 1-4**

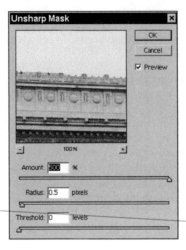

**Figure 1-5**

 **Amount:** Use this control to vary the amount of edge sharpening. Your choices range from 1 percent to 500 percent. For subtle amounts of sharpening, anything around 100 percent or less provides the effect you're looking for without making the image appear overly contrasty (yes, that is a technical term) or unrealistic.

Sharpening always increases contrast, so you should use any of the Sharpening tools before trying other contrast-adjusting tools. When you've sharpened your image to your satisfaction, you can then use the other contrast controls to fine-tune the image with additional contrast (if it's still required).

✔ **Radius:** This slider controls the width of the edges, in pixels, that the Unsharp Mask filter will modify. Your range varies from .1 pixel (for fine control) to 250 pixels (for broader sharpening effects). Your use of this control will vary chiefly on the resolution of your original image. Low-resolution images (100 pixels per inch and lower) look best when only a small radius value is used, from a fraction of a pixel up to three or four pixels.

A small amount of sharpening may produce no visible effect on high-resolution images, especially those with 300 ppi resolution or more. You may need to move the slider to the 5 pixel range before you see any effects. Regardless of the resolution of your image, setting the radius too high emphasizes the edges of your image unrealistically, and boosts the contrast too much.

A good rule to consider when you select a radius is to divide your image's ppi resolution by 150 and then adjust from there. For example, if you have a 150 ppi image, set the radius at 1 and then tweak from there.

✔ **Threshold:** This slider controls the difference in brightness between adjacent pixels that must be present before the edge is sharpened. That is, you need to have a distinct contrast between adjacent pixels along an edge in order to sharpen the edge. Your choices range from brightness values of 0 to 255. Selecting a low value causes edges with very little contrast difference to be emphasized (which is usually what you want). You'll usually be better off leaving this control at 0 unless there is a lot of noise. Higher values force Photoshop to provide edge sharpening only when adjacent pixels are dramatically different in brightness. Increasing the threshold too much can cause some harsh transitions between sharpened and unsharpened pixels.

In most cases, the Amount and Radius sliders will be the only controls you need to use. Threshold is most useful when the first two controls create excessive noise in the image. You can sometimes reduce this noise by increasing the Threshold level a little.

# Blurring What's Sharp

What, me blurry? The answer is yes, if you have an image that contains unwanted grain (the roughness or noise added by the photographic film) or, perhaps, an objectionable pattern of halftone dots used in a printed image.

You might need to blur a background to make the foreground seem sharper, or blur a portion of an image to create an angelic glow. Here are your blurring options (all found in the Filter⇨Blur menu):

✔ **Blur:** This single-step filter provides overall blurring of an image.

✔ **Blur More:** This filter provides a significantly increased amount of blurring than the regular, old-fashioned Blur filter.

✔ **Gaussian Blur:** This filter offers a radius control to let you adjust the amount of blurring more precisely. It's also got a really cool name.

The Gaussian Blur filter is an excellent tool because it gives you a great deal of control over the amount and type of blurring you get. That's especially true when compared to the single-step filters Blur and Blur More, which apply a fixed amount of blur. Use these latter two filters when you simply want to desharpen an image a tad, and turn to Gaussian Blur when you're looking for a specific effect.

✔ **Motion Blur:** This filter simulates the blur you see in objects that are moving.

✔ **Radial Blur:** This filter produces the kind of blur you might get when photographing a revolving automobile tire.

✔ **Smart Blur:** This filter lets you control how the blur is applied to edges and other details of the image.

# Smoothing with the Facet and Median Filters

One application for blurring an image is to reduce dust and scratches, or to smooth away sharp edges. For an example of the Dust & Scratches filter, see Chapter 2 of this book. You'll also find information on Photoshop's Despeckle filter there. Here, I show you how to use the versatile Facet and Median filters to soften an image.

 Although the Facet and Median filters smooth images by eliminating some detail, you can compensate for the blurring effect by applying Unsharp Mask with a low radius setting to sharpen things up a little.

## The Facet filter

Facet breaks up an image using a posterizing effect. It gathers up blocks of pixels that are similar in brightness and converts them to a single value using geometric shapes. (When you *posterize* an image, you reduce it to a very small number of tones.)

The geometric shapes make the image look more randomly produced, while eliminating much of the banding effect you get with conventional posterizing filters.

The effects of the Facet filter are subtle, and best viewed close up. The original image in Figure 1-6 contains some dust, scratches, and a few other defects. Instead of retouching them one by one, I used Facet.

Facet is a single-step filter, so you don't need to adjust any controls. Just choose Filter⇨ Pixelate⇨Facet and evaluate your results. You can apply the filter multiple times. However, even one application smoothes out the picture and eliminates the worst of the artifacts, as shown in Figure 1-7.

If you apply the Facet filter multiple times, your image will take on a pointillist, stroked look that becomes obvious. Maybe you wouldn't frame Figure 1-8, but using the filter again and again can yield quite interesting special effects. For more on creating painterly looks with filters, see Chapter 2 of this book.

**Figure 1-6**

**Figure 1-7**

**Figure 1-8**

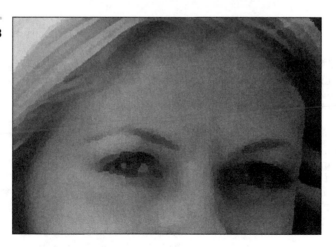

## The Median filter

The Median filter (look for it in the Filter⇨Noise menu) operates similarly to the Facet filter in that it reduces the difference between adjacent pixels by changing the values of some of them. In this case, it assigns the median values of a group of pixels to the center pixel in the group.

Unlike the Facet filter, the Median filter gives you a bit of control. You can choose the radius of the group that Photoshop will use to calculate the median value.

As you can see in Figure 1-9, Median tends to make an image look a bit blurrier because it reduces the contrast of adjacent pixels. However, it does a good job of smoothing the image and removing artifacts.

**Figure 1-9**

 **PUTTING IT TOGETHER**

### Creating an Angelic Glow

Sometimes, a little blur can add a soft, romantic mood or angelic glow that can improve glamour photos, pictures of kids, or even something as mundane as a flower. The secret is to apply only enough blurring to provide the soft effect you want without completely obliterating your original subject. This assumes, of course, that your subject doesn't *deserve* obliteration, that the kids are your own (or those of a close friend or relative), and are, in fact, of that rare angelic variety.

You won't want to use this affect on other subjects, like men, who generally like a rugged, masculine appearance (minus any hint of an angelic glow), and many senior citizens regard the age lines on their faces as badges of distinction earned over a long, rewarding life. Don't try softening them up with glowing effects, either.

This Putting-It-Together project combines Gaussian Blur with the Photoshop Opacity feature (which enables you to easily make one layer partially transparent so that the one underneath shows through) and the Merge Layers mode. I use an image of a young girl. The original photo isn't bad, but I can make the girl's face glow with an inner life of its own.

To add an angelic glow to your little angel, just follow these steps:

**1.** Open the image in Photoshop.

**2.** Choose Layer⇨Duplicate Layer to create a copy of the image layer.

**3.** Select Image⇨Filter⇨Blur⇨ Gaussian Blur.

Gaussian blur softens the upper layer, producing an airy glow.

**4.** Move the Radius slider to the right to produce a moderate amount of blur, and then click OK to apply the blurring effect.

I used a value of 9.

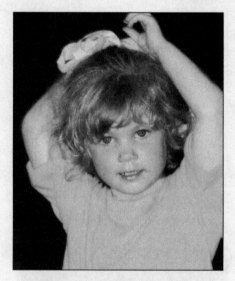

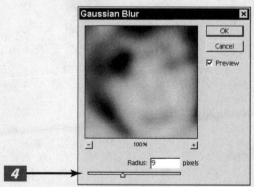

▼ **CONTINUED**

▼ CONTINUED

**5.** In the Layers palette, choose Lighten from the Modes pop-up menu.

**6.** Use the Opacity slider to reduce the amount of glow (if it's too much for your tastes).

**7.** Choose Layer⇨Flatten Image to combine all the layers.

Experiment with different amounts of Gaussian Blur until you find the perfect glowing effect.

When Photoshop applies the Lighten mode as it merges two layers, it looks at each pixel in the top layer and its corresponding pixel in the layer below it. That pixel in the final merged layer is always the *lighter* of the two. The result is an image in which darker pixels are replaced with lighter ones, but light pixels don't change at all.

5

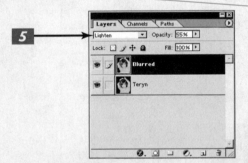

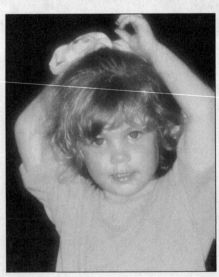

# Applying a Filter Again

You can reapply the last filter you worked with, using the same settings, by pressing Ctrl+F (Cmd+F on the Mac). (It's also the first command in the Filter menu.) You might want to do this to strengthen the effect of a filter on a particular image, layer, or selection. Or, you simply may want to apply the same filter to a succession of images or selections.

To bring up the dialog box for the last filter you applied, press Ctrl+Alt+F (Windows) or ⌘+Option+F (Mac). This shortcut can be very useful when you apply a filter and then decide you want to go back and use different settings. After applying the filter, press Ctrl+Z (⌘+Z on a Mac) to undo, and then press Ctrl+Alt+F (⌘+Option+F on a Mac) to bring up the filter's dialog box. The dialog box opens up with the settings you used last time, allowing you to make adjustments and then reapply.

# Fading a Filter

There are times when you may not want the full effects of a filter applied to your image or selection. Photoshop has a handy Fade Filter facility that lets you control the intensity of the filter's effects. You can access this feature by choosing Edit⇨Fade, or by pressing Shift+Ctrl+F (Shift+⌘+F on the Mac). The dialog box in Figure 1-10 appears.

The Fade Filter facility also has a Preview option so that you can preview the changes you're making to the original image.

 You must fade your filter *immediately after* you use the filter. If you use a painting or editing tool after the filter, for example, you won't find Fade Filter in the Edit menu anymore. It will be replaced by Fade Brush or something else.

**Figure 1-10**

You can also add a fade effect in the following ways:

✔ **Adjust opacity settings:** Just about every filter allows you to adjust opacity, so most of the time the Opacity slider will be all you need to adjust the strength of the filter applied to your image.

✔ **Use a blending mode:** Use one of Photoshop's blend modes to merge the filter effect with the original image. For more on blend modes, see Book V, Chapter 3.

✔ **Apply a filter to a duplicate layer or a selection on that layer:** Then adjust the opacity of the filtered layer so that it merges with the unfiltered layer below it.

One of the advantages to this method is that you can selectively erase portions of the filtered image to allow the unaltered portion to show through. For example, you might apply a blur filter to a face to smooth out a complexion, and then erase the blurred portion that covers the eyes.

You could just select the face (minus the eyes) and blur only that with the filter, but using multiple layers gives you more flexibility. You can also fade a filter by using a layer mask to selectively hide or show the filtered area. Find out more about layer masks in Book VI, Chapter 3.

## Selectively Applying a Filter

Filters don't need to be applied to an entire image or entire layer. Some of the best effects are achieved when a filter is applied only to a portion of an image, say to an object in the foreground, but not on the background. Your choices include

✔ **Selections:** Make a selection and apply the filter only to that selection. You can use Quick Mask mode (see Book VI, Chapter 2 for more information on Quick Mask) to paint a selection. This technique can give you a high degree of control; it even lets you feather the edges of the selection so that the filter effect fades out.

✔ **Channels:** Selections can be stored as alpha channels, visible in the Channels palette, of course. But you can also choose to apply a filter only to one of the other channels, such as the Red, Green, or Blue channels in an RGB image. This is a good way to create a filter effect that's applied only to one color in an image. (Check out Book VI, Chapter 1 for information about channels.)

### That's a moiré

Moiré is caused when two patterns with different frequencies are overlaid on each other. The original halftone screen pattern used a series of repeating lines, probably somewhere between 85 and 133 lines per inch. When you scan a halftone, a second pattern results when the image is displayed on your computer screen (at, say, 72 to 120 "lines" per inch) or printed again (at 300 to 600 dots per inch). The two patterns interfere with each other at regular intervals, producing the unpleasant moiré look.

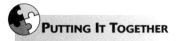

**PUTTING IT TOGETHER**

### *Sprucing Up a Scanned Halftone*

Publications such as newspapers and magazines use only a limited number of ink colors to reproduce a photograph. Every tone you see in a black-and-white image must be reproduced by using pure black ink and the white (okay, dirty beige) of the paper. Full-color images are represented by combining CMYK (cyan, magenta, and yellow, and black). Printers (both the commercial kind and the kind that sits on your desktop) can't use various shades of gray ink to create grayscale photos. They also can't use different strengths of color inks to generate the rainbow of hues you see in an image on-screen. Instead, photographs have to be converted to a series of dots in order to be printed.

Our eyes blend the dots together to produce the illusion of a grayscale or color image with smooth gradations of tone.

However, a problem arises if you want to reuse a photograph and don't have access to the original. Scanners can capture the halftone dots, but the resulting image usually has an unpleasant pattern, called moiré.

You have several ways of reducing the moiré effect, usually by blurring the image so that the dots merge and the underlying pattern vanishes. Many scanners have a *descreen* setting that partially eliminates the effect, but that setting may actually blur your image more than you'd like. Fortunately, you can usually do better in Photoshop.

In the following steps, I demonstrate an easier way. Over the years I managed to lose the original negative and print. You can see the dreadful moiré pattern that results when I scanned the clip.

▼ **CONTINUED**

▼ **CONTINUED**

To rid your scanned halftone print of bothersome moiré, follow these steps:

**1.** **Open the image in Photoshop.**

**2.** **Zoom in so that you can see the halftone pattern clearly as you work.**

**3.** **Choose Filter⇨Blur⇨Gaussian Blur.**

The Gaussian Blur dialog box appears.

**4.** **Move the Radius slider to the right until the halftone pattern**

is blurred, and then click OK to apply the blur.

I used a value of 1.7 pixels.

**5.** **Choose Filter⇨Sharpen⇨Unsharp Mask to restore some of the image's sharpness now that you've eliminated the pattern.**

As long as the Radius value for the Unsharp Mask filter doesn't exceed the radius of the Gaussian blur that you first applied, the two filters won't cancel each other out. You want the sharpening to make the details of

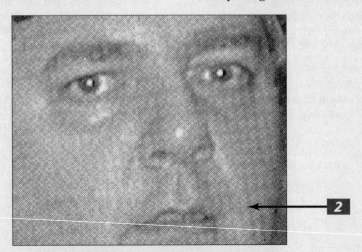

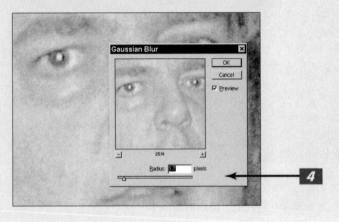

the image crisper without bringing back those blurred halftone dots.

**6.** **Move the Amount slider to the right to sharpen the image.**

A setting of roughly 166 percent will do the job without making the image appear unnaturally sharp or have too much contrast.

When working with your own photos, you may need to use different Radius and Threshold values. In most cases, leaving the Threshold at 0 is fine. Calculate a starting Radius value by dividing the ppi (pixels per inch) of the scanned image by 150. If a moiré pattern reappears, reduce the Radius value.

**7.** **Click OK to apply the sharpness.**

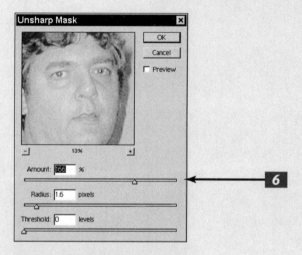

# Applying Filters for Special Occasions

**2**

Photoshop has dozens of filters that let you enhance your image in unusual ways. You can create Old Masters portraits from common snapshots, shatter your image into a thousand sparkling pieces, create clouds in a cloudless sky, add textures, or perform hundreds of other tricks.

The big challenge in using these filters is learning what each filter can do and how to apply it to the best effect. This chapter introduces you to some more of those fabulous Photoshop plug-ins and shows you some typical applications for them. There are several Putting-It-Together projects with step-by-step instructions. For the first few examples, I provide you with the settings I used to achieve a particular look. However, filter effects vary greatly when applied to different images, so you will have to play with the filter controls yourself when you use these techniques with your own images.

## Getting Artsy

Quite a few of Photoshop's filters produce artistic effects. You'll find a large collection of them in the Sketch and Stylize submenus. However, the Artistic menu contains 15 versatile filters that you can use to add brush strokes to your images, wrap them in plastic, create poster-like effects, and manufacture other interesting looks.

Many Photoshop veterans use these filters to create images that look like they were painted. What they might not tell you, unless pressed, is that artsy filters can make terrible photos look okay, or even great. These filters can disguise a multitude of photographic sins, turning shoebox rejects into prize-winning digital transformations.

This photo of a duck (see Figure 2-1) has several problems, but the worst of them is that it's blurry because the camera moved while I was trying to follow the fast-paced duck. (That's why both the duck and the background are blurry.) On the surface, there appears to be no way to salvage this image.

You can fix that. Really, I mean it. Just try the following filters:

✔ **Poster Edges filter:** A quick application of this filter (choose Filter➪Artistic➪Poster Edges) improves the photo 100 percent. (See Figure 2-2.) The filter not only gives the picture an arty poster-like look, but the enhanced edges made the duck's outline appear to be sharper.

I set the Poster Edges filter's Edge Thickness to 4, bumped the Edge Intensity up to a value of 6 to create dramatic-looking edges, and set the Posterization level to 6 to allow more tones for a bit more realism.

**Figure 2-1**

**Figure 2-2**

✔ **The Dry Brush filter:** This filter (choose Filter⇨Artistic⇨Dry Brush) can add an even more stylistic effect, reducing the duck's shape to a series of broad brush strokes, as shown in Figure 2-3. I used a large brush size (9), set the amount of Brush Detail almost to the maximum (9), and used the most Texture possible (3).

Some of the other useful artsy filters you'll find in Photoshop's repertoire are located in the Artistic submenu. Just choose Filter⇨Artistic to find them.

✔ **Colored Pencil:** This filter crosshatches the edges of your image to create a pencil-like effect.

You can also get a cross-hatching effect when you use the Colored Pencil in areas of flat color.

✔ **Cutout:** This effect assembles an image from what looks like cut out paper shapes. This effect looks kind of like a kid's art project.

✔ **Film Grain:** This photographic effect diffuses an image with thousands of tiny dots that simulate clumps of film grain. Think old home movies.

✔ **Fresco:** This effect looks (supposedly) like pigments applied to fresh, wet plaster. I guess . . . if you squint.

**Figure 2-3**

- ✔ **Paint Daubs:** This effect uses smears of color from your choice of a half-dozen different brush types. Very Jackson Pollock.

- ✔ **Plastic Wrap:** This filter can produce a wet look, particularly when you apply it to a selection and then fade the filter so that it doesn't overpower the detail in your image.

- ✔ **Watercolor:** This is a nice pastel effect that diffuses an image while adding an interesting, watery texture.

## Stroking Your Image with Filters

More stroking filters are found in the Brush Strokes submenu, with some interesting texturizing filters that can spruce up less-than-perfect photos, and add a new look to even your best shots.

Choose Filter⇨Brush Strokes to find the stroking filters that you'll enjoy messing around with, including

- ✔ **Ink Outlines:** Adobe describes this filter as producing the look of a corroded ink drawing.

- ✔ **Spatter:** This filter generates the look you might get from a sputtering airbrush.

- ✔ **Accented Edges:** Use this filter to make a subject jump out from its background by emphasizing the edges of all the objects in the picture, as I did with the photo of a sleeping flamingo (see Figure 2-4).

**Figure 2-4**

I set the Edge Width to a narrow value of 2, but moved the Edge Brightness all the way up to the maximum value of 50 so that the edges would seem to glow. I kept the Smoothness slider at a minimum (3) so that the edges would be clearly delineated. Then, I did a simple thing: I applied the filter twice to produce the soft, pastel look shown here.

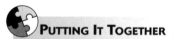

### PUTTING IT TOGETHER

### *Creating Exotic Edges for Your Images*

An attractive border can give your image an edge. If you want an edgy look or want to take your work right to the edge, you can apply this next technique faster than you can say, "Overworked metaphor!" Photoshop lets you apply deckled looks and other effects to the borders of your image by using any of several plug-ins built right into your trusty Filters menu.

Follow these easy steps to the edge of image immortality:

*1.* **Choose a photo that you think could use a fancy border, and open it in Photoshop.**

In these steps, I show you how to apply an interesting edge, using the crouching tiger in this photograph.

▼ **CONTINUED**

▼ **CONTINUED**

**2.** With the Rectangular Marquee tool, select the object you're framing.

**3.** Double-click the Quick Mask mode icon in the Tool palette, and make sure that the Selected Areas radio button is marked in the Color Indicates area.

**4.** Click OK to enter Quick Mask mode.

The rectangle you selected will be highlighted in color.

**5.** Choose Select➪Deselect, and then choose Filter➪Blur➪Gaussian Blur and set the Radius.

To give a softer edge when the selection is deckled, I've set the Radius to 20.

**6.** Choose Filter➪Brush Strokes➪ Sprayed Strokes.

**7.** Adjust the Stroke Length and Spray Radius sliders to acquire the desired effect.

In this case, I moved the sliders all the way to the right. I needed the maximum amount of stroking because this picture is a high resolution digital snapshot (2048 x 1536 pixels). If you're working with a photo with less detail, say 1024 x 768, move the slider only about two-thirds of the way to the right.

**8.** **Choose Horizontal from the drop-down Stroke Direction list.**

You can also select Diagonal or other directions to create different effects.

**9.** **Click OK to apply the effect to the Quick Mask selection.**

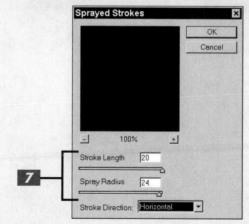

Book
**VII**
Chapter
**2**

▼ **CONTINUED**

▼ **CONTINUED**

The edges of the highlighted area will appear frayed.

**10.** **Press Q to exit Quick Mask mode.**

A selection border with stroked edges appears around the object.

**11.** **Press Ctrl+C to copy the selected area, and then press Ctrl+V to paste it in a new layer.**

🎯 Be sure that your background color is what you want. (Usually, white is a good choice.)

**12.** **Click the Eyeball icon for the background (bottom) layer in the Layers palette to render it invisible.**

**13.** **Choose Layer⇨Flatten Image to create your final image with deckled edges.**

# Distorting for Fun

With one startling exception, Photoshop's Distortion filters twist, turn, and bend your images in surprising ways, turning ordinary objects into wavy images, pinched shapes, and bloated spheres.

The single exception? The Diffuse Glow filter (which you access by choosing Filter⇨Distort⇨ Diffuse Glow) distorts images only to the extent that it imbues them with a soft, romantic fuzzy look that can make the sharpest image look positively ethereal.

I've never figured out why this useful filter was dumped in the Distort submenu, but there it is. (And here it is applied to a doll in Figure 2-5.)

Other filters of this ilk can produce wavy images, add pond ripples, pinch images, or transform them into spheres. Check out Figure 2-6 of a videogame console.

**Figure 2-5**

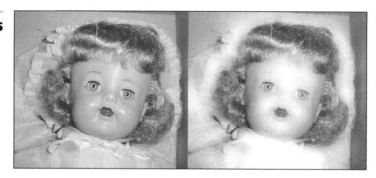

Choose Filter⇨Distort⇨Glass to play with the Glass filter, which can do the following to your images:

- ✔ Add a glass block texture
- ✔ Add a canvas texture
- ✔ Create a frosted glass fuzziness
- ✔ Break up your image with tiny lenses

  Take a look at the image on the right in Figure 2-7, which is nothing more than the tiny lenses variation of the Glass filter applied to an image of the data side of a CD-ROM.

**Figure 2-6**

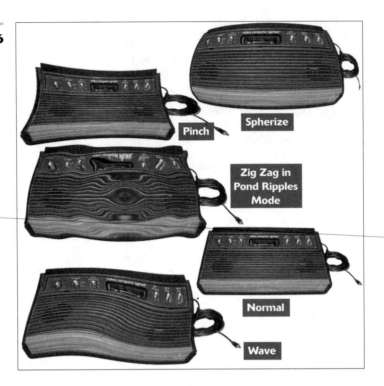

Pinch

Spherize

Zig Zag in Pond Ripples Mode

Normal

Wave

**Figure 2-7**

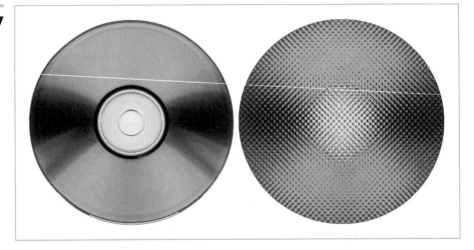

# Pumping Up the Noise

*Noise* in images consists of any graininess or texture that occurs, either because of the inherent quality of the image or through the editing process. Noise filters, like Photoshop's Add Noise plug-in, produce random texture and grain in an image. If you're new to image editing, you might wonder why you'd want to add noise to an image in the first place. Wouldn't it be smarter to remove it? In practice, though, you'll find lots of applications that call for a little noise here and there:

✔ **To add texture:** Objects that become too smooth, either because of blurring or other image editing you may have done, often look better when you add some noise to give them a texture. This technique is particularly useful if one object in an image has been edited, smoothed, or blurred more than the other objects in the image.

✔ **To blend foreign objects into a scene:** When you drop a new object into the middle of an existing scene, you'll often find that the amount of grain or noise in the new object is quite different from the other objects it's being combined with.

For example, say you've decided to take a photo of your house and want to insert a certain luxury car in your driveway. Unfortunately, your digital photo of your brother-in-law's luxo-mobile is a lot sharper than the picture of your house. Adding a little noise can help the two objects blend more realistically. You may even forget that the car isn't yours.

✔ **To improve image quality:** Images that contain smooth gradients often don't print well because many printers (especially older ones) are unable to reproduce the subtle blend of colors from one hue to another. The result is *objectionable banding* in your printed image: You can see distinct stripes as the colors progress from one to another in the top image of Figure 2-8. Adding a little noise (as shown in the bottom image in Figure 2-8) can break up the gradient enough that your printer can reproduce the blend of colors, and the noise/grain itself is virtually invisible on the printed sheet.

**Figure 2-8**

# Pumping Down the Noise

Although many Noise filters add grain, other filters in the Noise submenu don't add noise at all; instead, they make noise and artifacts like dust and scratches less noticeable. Choose Filter➪Noise to find your tools, which include

✔ **Despeckle:** This filter makes dust spots in your image less noticeable by decreasing the contrast of your entire image — except at the edges. That translates into a slightly blurry image (which masks the spots) that still retains sharpness in the edges of image components. You end up with a little blur to soften the image, but enough detail in the edges that the picture still looks good.

✔ **Dust & Scratches:** This filter concentrates its blurring effect only on those areas of your image that contain scratches and other artifacts, as shown in Figure 2-9. Photoshop performs this magic by looking at each pixel in an image, moving out in a radial direction until it encounters an abrupt transition in tone. (That's a signal that a spot or scratch has been found.) You can specify the radius Photoshop searches for the little culprits, from 1 to 16 pixels.

While working with any of the Noise filters, it's best to be very conservative at first. All the Noise filters involve destruction of image data. A little bit can help and be just the effect you're looking for. Just a little bit more, however, may completely wreck things.

✔ **Median:** This filter reduces contrast around dust motes, thus hiding them, in a slightly different way. This filter looks at the pixels surrounding each pixel in the image and replaces the center one with a new pixel that has the median brightness level of that group. The process is a little hard to describe succinctly, but, basically, bright spots are darkened while leaving the rest of the image alone.

**Figure 2-9**

PUTTING IT TOGETHER

### *Making Your Own Background Textures*

Whether you need a background texture for a portrait or to give your Web page a bit of personality, Photoshop has all the tools you need. While Photoshop features dozens of different ways to create these textures, here I show you a quick technique that employs the Noise filter. You'll see

that in Photoshop — like at concerts — noise can sometimes be a very good thing, indeed.

In these steps, I show you how to create the texture, make it fade into the background, and fill up a large Web page with a small background image. You don't need a starter image; you can create this texture from scratch.

**1.** **Choose File⇨New and create a new, empty RGB document.**

In this exercise, I show you how to create a fairly large background texture (400 x 400 pixels). For Web pages, however, you can use much smaller sizes (typically 128 x 128 pixels) because the background repeats or *tiles* to fill the screen.

**2.** **Because you need an existing tone in the image to noisify, choose Edit⇨Fill to access the Fill dialog box, and then choose from the Use drop-down list.**

In this case, I'm choosing 50% gray.

**3.** **Choose Filter⇨Noise⇨Add Noise to access the Add Noise dialog box, where you'll make some choices:**

- ✔ **Amount:** I recommend choosing a significant amount of pixel "dirt," roughly 60 percent.

- ✔ **Distribution:** Select the Gaussian option to create an interesting random pattern (rather than a bland, uniform pattern).

- ✔ **Monochromatic:** Selecting this option eliminates random color specks.

Your image now looks a bit like one of those "Magic Eye" graphics, except you can squint all you like and probably not see the image of an elephant.

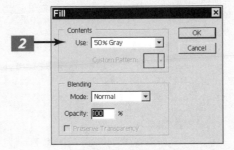

Book
***VII***
Chapter
**2**

▼ **CONTINUED**

▼ **CONTINUED**

**4.** To produce a 3-D texture, choose Filter⇨Stylize⇨Emboss, and then adjust the following settings:

✔ **Angle:** An Angle setting of 135 degrees gives the texture the appearance that it's being illuminated from a light source coming above and to the right of the texture. Using other angles produces slightly different texture looks.

✔ **Height** and **Amount:** A Height setting of 3 pixels and an Amount of 100% creates a moderate 3-D

look. Increasing these values offers additional looks, but also can create an intrusive effect for a background that's supposed to reside in, well, the background.

**5.** Click OK to apply the texture.

**6.** To add a little color, choose Image⇨Adjustments⇨Hue/Saturation, and then adjust these settings:

✔ **Colorize:** Be sure to select this check box.

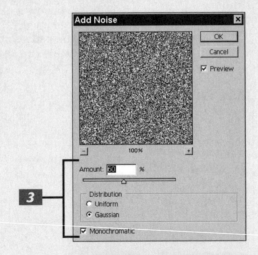

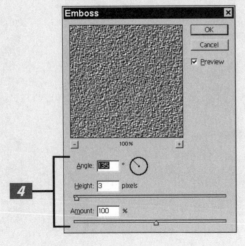

✔ **Hue:** Move the Hue slider until you find a color you like.

✔ **Saturation:** Use the Saturation slider to create a light, pastel version of your chosen hue.

**7.** **Click OK to apply the color.**

To enable a Web browser to repeat a background texture over and over, you need to make the edges blend together. Some Photoshop filters produce random patterns that will automatically tile. Others, particularly those you create from your own images, you have to offset so

that the center portions become the edges.

**8.** **Choose Filter➪Other➪Offset, and then enter values for Horizontal and Vertical.**

Type in a value that's half the height/width of your image. With this 400 x 400 pixel background, that value is 200. If you're making a 128 x 128 pixel background texture, use a value of 64.

**9.** **Select the Wrap Around button to have continuous texture, and then click OK.**

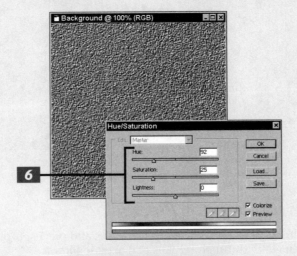

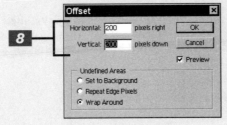

Book
*VII*
Chapter
*2*

▼ **CONTINUED**

▼ **CONTINUED**

**10.** To tone down your background texture a bit, choose Image⇨ Adjustments⇨Levels, and then move the gray center triangle to the left (approximately three-quarters of the way) until the background takes on a less contrasty appearance.

**11.** To use this background on a Web page, you have to save it as a JPEG image by selecting File⇨Save As and then choosing JPEG from the Format drop-down list.

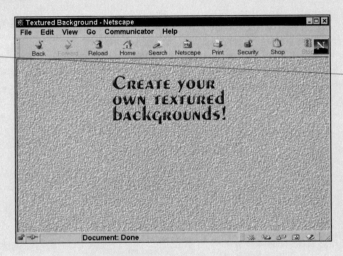

# Breaking Your Image into Pieces

Photoshop's Pixelate filters break up your images into bits and pieces, providing more of those painterly effects you can get with brush strokes and artistic filters.

The Pixelate submenu (found at Filter⇨Pixelate) includes the Crystallize filter applied to the ancient castle wall shown in Figure 2-10, as well as plug-ins that produce color halftone effects, fragmented images, and the Pointillism effect used in the "Creating Snow and Rain" Putting-It-Together project later in this chapter.

# Rendering

In computerese, *rendering* means creating something from nothing, in a way. That's why Photoshop's rendering filters all produce special effects by creating a look, object, or lighting effect that's melded with your original image.

## Using the Clouds filter

Photoshop's Clouds filter, for example, can muster a skyful of clouds from scratch with a few clicks of the mouse, as in the now cloudy picture shown in Figure 2-11. Indeed, this filter is used so much that most Photoshop veterans have a surprising number of clouds in their images. Find it at Filter⇨Render⇨Clouds.

## Using other rendering filters

Other useful filters in the Render submenu (found at Filter⇨Render) include

- ✔ **3D Transform:** Use this filter to wrap objects around three-dimensional shapes, producing say, a mock-up of your favorite championship breakfast cereal with *your* photo on the front.

- ✔ **Difference Clouds:** Use this filter to create puffy objects in the sky (or foggy clouds at lower levels). Instead of performing this magical feat the way the Cloud filter does, the Difference Clouds filter uses image information to figure the difference in pixel values between the new clouds and the image they will be merged with. The result is a unique cloud effect.

- ✔ **Lens Flare:** This filter creates the reflection effect that plagues photographers when they point their cameras towards a strong light source, such as the sun. Photoshop mimics several different kinds of photographic lenses, giving you useful flares that can spice up concert photos, add a sunset where none existed, and create other kinds of lighting bursts.

- ✔ **Lighting Effects:** A sort of photo studio lighting setup, this filter uses pixels to do its work. You can set up 16 different lights and manipulate how they illuminate your photo.

**Figure 2-10**

Book
**VII**
Chapter
**2**

**Figure 2-11**

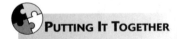  PUTTING IT TOGETHER

### Creating Snow and Rain

Sometimes you may come across that photo that needs a little bit of atmosphere thrown in to give it extra punch. And by atmosphere I mean that literally. By using a couple of filters and a blend mode you can add some rain or snow to any image.

Just follow these steps to create either rain or snow:

*1.* **Open a color image. It if isn't currently in RGB Mode, then choose Image⇨Mode⇨RGB Color.**

You need to be in RGB mode because the blend mode used in these steps doesn't work correctly with CMYK images.

**2.** **Drag the background layer to the Create a New Layer icon at the bottom of the Layers palette.**

You now see a layer that says Background copy in the Layers palette.

**3.** **Double-click the name Background copy and type** Snow.

This isn't a mandatory step. I'm just being ultra organized.

**4.** **With the Snow layer active, choose Filter⇨Pixelate⇨Pointillize. In the dialog box, set your cell size to 7 or a value you prefer. Click OK.**

The bigger the cell size, the bigger the snowflakes or raindrops.

For rain, you might try a cell size of 3, which is the minimum, or 4. For snow, try a larger cell size, between 6 and 9. I used a value of 7.

**5.** **On the Snow layer, choose Image⇨Adjustments⇨Threshold. Move the slider all the way to the right to a max value of 255.**

This adjustment takes the colored cells and first turns them to either black or white.

By using a value of 255, all brightness values less than 255 turn black and the remaining value turns white.

▼ **CONTINUED**

▼ CONTINUED

**6.** **On the Snow layer, choose Screen from the Mode pop-up menu in the Layers palette.**

The Screen blend mode lightens the Snow layer, where it mixes with the Background underneath. Blending with black pixels has no effect, therefore they drop out.

**7.** **Choose Filter⇨Blur⇨Motion Blur. In the dialog box, specify the Angle and Distance values.**

 If you want it to appear that the wind is blowing hard, set the angle more diagonally, around 45°. If you want it

to appear that the weather is coming straight down, set it to 90°. Setting the distance elongates the pointillized cells that you created in Step 4, making them look a little more realistic. For snow, start with a range of about 8 to 12 pixels. For rain, start a little higher, 15 to 25 pixels. I used a value of 12 pixels.

If you're creating rain, proceed to Step 8. If you are a snow person, you're done.

**8.** **Choose Filter⇨Sharpen⇨Unsharp Mask.**

The Unsharp Mask dialog box appears.

**9.** **Specify the Amount, the Radius, and the Threshold values.**

The Unsharp Mask filter gives the illusion of sharpening the focus of the image by increasing the contrast between the pixels. (For more about this filter, see Chapter 1 of this book.)

I used an amount of 500%, a Radius of 1, and kept the Threshold at 0. This gives the raindrops a little more definition.

**10.** **Choose Filter⇨Blur⇨Motion Blur. In the dialog box, specify the Angle and Distance values.**

Again, the angle is up to you, but make it consistent with the value that you used in Step 7. Set the distance according to how you want your rain to appear, a moderate spring rain or a torrential, close-to-hurricane type of downpour. I used 45° and 25 pixels.

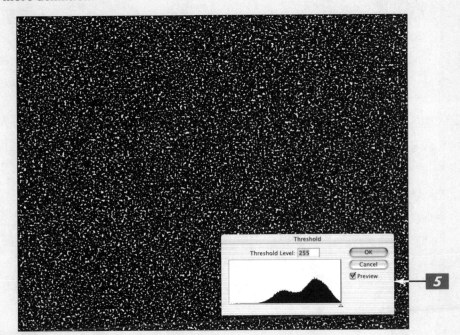

Book
**VII**
Chapter
**2**

▼ CONTINUED

▼ **CONTINUED**

## Getting Organic with the Sketch Filters

In true Adobe fashion, the Sketch filter submenu contains a few filters that don't really belong there, almost as if the programmers were trying to supply you with a bonus or surprise when you opened the submenu.

If you were to encounter a picture of Rodin's *Thinker* (upper-left image in Figure 2-12), you might be tempted to sketch the famous sculpture, using one of the following filters (all found by choosing Filter➪Sketch).

Perhaps a Conte Crayon effect or a Graphic Pen and Ink look would be nice. But the Sketch submenu also includes other artistic effects, such as the Note Paper look, a halftone screen, chalk and charcoal, and even a bas relief effect that turns flat images into Rodin-like sculpture.

You'll also want to experiment with these other Sketch filters (again, find them at Filter➪Sketch):

- **Photocopy** gives that infamous, anachronistic look (dating back from the days when photocopiers didn't do a very good job of reproducing halftone images).

- **Plaster** creates a look that resembles molten plastic more than it looks like plaster.

- **Stamp** mimics a rubber stamp (not very sketch-like, indeed!).

✔ **Reticulation** adds texture by reproducing a veritable photographic disaster: the wrinkling of film emulsion that occurs when film is moved from one developing chemical to another that has an extreme difference in temperature (think hot developer followed by a bath in cold water!).

Even if the Sketch filters don't all produce sketchy effects, they do have one thing in common: They give your images an organic look that's decidedly non-computerish.

**Figure 2-12**

Normal

Conté Crayon

Pen and Ink

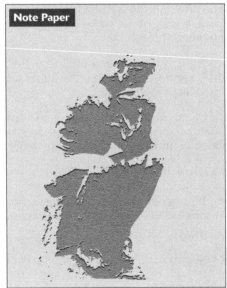

Note Paper

**PUTTING IT TOGETHER**

## Adding Water Droplets and Other Wet Effects

You'll find lots of techniques for creating nice, neat round drops of water by using Photoshop. Unless you've just waxed your car and expect a rain shower within moments, however, perfectly beaded water droplets can be fairly rare in real life. Instead, you're likely to encounter some sloppy drops and driblets any time liquid splashes onto a formerly dry surface.

This technique simulates that look. You could use it to add sparkling water drops to a flower, create a wet-look texture for artistic effect, or add a three-dimensional *trompe l'oeil* ("fools the eye") optical illusion.

After you create water drops by using this Putting-It-Together project, experiment with different ways of applying them to images.

*1.* **Open a plain, old, dry-looking photograph in Photoshop.**

I'm using a flower photograph, which will look great wet.

*2.* **Press D to make sure Photoshop's foreground and background colors are set to the default values of black and white.**

*3.* **Choose Window➪Channels, click the palette menu, and then choose Create New Channel.**

Book
**VII**
Chapter
**2**

▼ **CONTINUED**

▼ **CONTINUED**

This creates a new alpha channel for the water droplets. (For more on channels, see Book VI.)

**4.** In the New Channel dialog box, check the Color Indicates Selected Areas button, and set Opacity to 100%.

**5.** Select Filter⇨Render⇨Clouds to create a motley cloud effect to use as the basis for your random water droplets.

**6.** Choose Image⇨Adjustments⇨ Threshold, and then move the slider to create black blotches that will become water droplets.

I used a value of 83, but, because the Clouds filter produces random results, you may find that a different value works better for you.

**7.** Choose Filter⇨Blur⇨Gaussian Blur, and move the Radius slider enough to blur the jagged edges of the droplets.

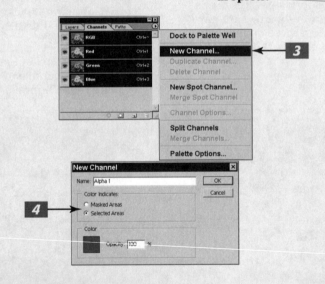

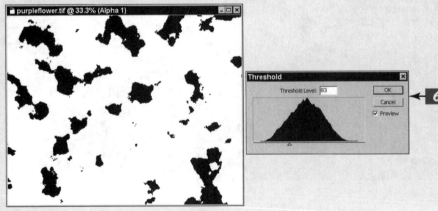

I used a value of 3.8 pixels.

**8.** **Choose Filter➪Sharpen➪ Unsharp Mask and adjust the Amount and Radius sliders to firm up the edges of the droplets.**

I found that an Amount of 85% and a Radius of about 46 creates soft-edged, but distinct water droplets.

**9.** **Control+click (⌘+click on the Mac) on the new channel in the Channels palette to load the selection that you've created.**

**10.** **Click the RGB Channel in the Channels palette to return to your full-color picture.**

The droplets appear as selections.

**11.** **Choose Layer➪New➪Layer via Copy to create a new layer for the droplets to reside in.**

**12.** **Choose Layer➪Layer Style and select Bevel and Emboss.**

The bevel/embossing effect adds a third dimension to the drops. You can experiment with the depth and size controls to get the exact effect you want. I used the Inner Bevel style, set to the Smooth Technique in the Structure area of the dialog box. I used the sliders to increase the size of the bevel to 27 pixels, and softened the edges by 11 pixels.

**13.** **If you like, you can choose Image➪ Adjustments➪Brightness/Contrast and move the brightness slider to the left to darken the droplets against their background.**

The final image looks like a print that has been drenched with liquid.

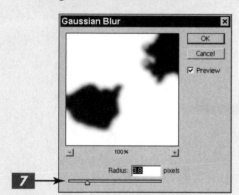

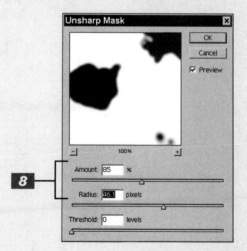

Book
*VII*
Chapter
**2**

▼ **CONTINUED**

▼ **CONTINUED**

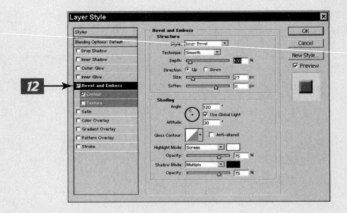

## Adding Texture

Photoshop lets you add lots of interesting textures to your images, such as the cracked canvas effect generated by the Craquelure filter (see Figure 2-13), or the pixel effect produced by the Patchwork filter (see Figure 2-14). Find these filters at Filter➪Texture.

You'll find other filters in this menu to help you create mosaic effects, add yet another kind of film grain, and create stained glass effects in your images.

## Introducing the Texturizer

The most versatile filter in this set is the Texturizer.

Choose Filter➪Texture➪Texturizer to bring up the Texturizer dialog box, shown in Figure 2-15. The Texture filter enables you to apply various kinds of textures to your images or selections, including Canvas, Sandstone, Burlap, or Brick.

You can choose the relative size of the texture compared to the rest of your image by using the Scaling slider, and govern the 3-D relief effect. You can even select the direction of the light source that produces the 3-D look, choosing from top, bottom, either side, or any of the four corners of the image. If those variations aren't enough for you, create your own texture, save it as a Photoshop PSD file, and use that to texturize your image.

 You'll find a handful of other filters that allow you to load your own (or someone else's) textures, including Rough Pastels, Underpainting, and Conte Crayon.

**Figure 2-13**

**Figure 2-14**

**Figure 2-15**

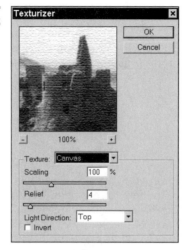

## Looking at the Other Filters

The Video and Other categories are where you might expect to find oddball filters that don't fit very well anywhere else. However, given that Adobe tends to sprinkle oddball filters anywhere it likes anyway, it's no surprise that the Other category is the home of the oddest of the odd.

For example, the Other submenu is home to the Custom filter, shown in Figure 2-16, which is no filter at all but rather a dialog box with a matrix in which you can type numbers that Photoshop uses to process the pixels in your image in unexpected ways.

 **The results will be surprising, especially if you don't have a fairly intimate knowledge of how Photoshop filters work.**

**Figure 2-16**

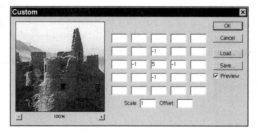

The center box in the matrix represents a pixel in your image; the surrounding boxes represent the pixels that surround that pixel. The numbers you type tell Photoshop whether to darken or lighten pixels. You can experiment to see what will happen, and if you like the effect, tell all your friends that you *meant* to do that.

The Video menu contains its own share of strange filters, including the NTSC Colors filter, which performs the rather obscure function of converting all the colors in your image to match the colors used for television reproduction. (NTSC stands for National Television Systems Committee.) You'd use this filter to process digital presentations or slides that will be shown on television, if you were really, really particular about how the colors are portrayed.

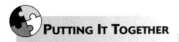 **PUTTING IT TOGETHER**

### Getting Rid of Video Scan Lines

Do you wish you had a "motor drive" camera that could capture multiple still images in rapid succession, letting you analyze your golf stroke or provide a selection of images to choose from? While many digital still cameras and some film cameras have multi-shot modes, your video camera can also do the job. All video cameras capture the equivalent of 30 still frames per second. All you need to do is extract the individual pictures you want, with a video card in your computer that includes a frame grabber. You can also pause a video image on your television and shoot a still picture with your camera on a tripod or other sturdy support.

Unfortunately, you'll also probably capture a set of dark horizontal lines known as *video scan lines*. They're produced as the television or monitor display "paints" an image on your screen line by line, one full screen each ⅟₃₀ of a second.

Actually, that description is not quite true. Most video displays provide an *interlaced* picture, drawing odd-numbered lines in one pass and even-numbered lines in a second pass. Our eyes merge these two interlaced images into one, and combine successive frames to produce the illusion of motion.

Photoshop allows you to take advantage of the interlacing phenomenon to remove those pesky scan lines. It can create a new, line-free picture by ignoring either the odd-numbered or even-numbered scans. One set is often enough to create a smooth image.

In the steps that follow, I use a Photoshop De-Interlace filter to create such an image. Just follow these easy steps:

**1.** **With a photograph in need of de-interlacing open in Photoshop, choose Filter⇨Other⇨De-Interlace.**

**2.** **Mark the Odd Fields button in the Eliminate area of the De-Interlace dialog box.**

You can use either button in most cases. The exception is when your original image happens to already be non-interlaced, as was the case with older video monitors. You'll know when that happens — if you choose the "wrong" field, you end up with a totally black image because that set of scan lines didn't exist.

**3.** **Mark the Interpolation button in the Create New Fields area.**

With interpolation, Photoshop looks at the odd-numbered (or even-numbered, if you chose that option) scan lines on either side of a line being processed, and creates a new line of pixels that are an average of the three lines examined. This usually produces better results and smoother transitions than simply duplicating each line.

**4.** **Click OK to apply the filter.**

**5.** **You may have to adjust the brightness and contrast of the photo to produce the best image.**

For some hints about adjusting the brightness and contrast, see Book VIII.

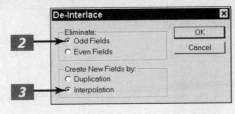

▼ **CONTINUED**

Book
**VII**
Chapter
**2**

▼ **CONTINUED**

# Distorting with the Liquify Command

L iquify is the only Photoshop filter that gets a chapter of its own. But then again, Liquify is no ordinary filter; it's the ultimate in image distortion tools, and therefore a good deal more complex than most of its kin in the Filter menu. What other filter has its own hefty tool palette, eight buttons, several different modes, and more than a dozen option categories with what amounts to dozens more variations?

The Liquify command lets you push and pull on parts of your image, twist, turn, and pinch other parts, bloat sections, freeze portions in place so that they remain immune to the transformations going around them and, if you don't like everything you've done, perform selective reconstructions. You can perform this magic with a remarkable degree of control, too. Liquify isn't one of those "Ooops! I meant to do that!" tools.

This chapter explores all the features of the Liquify command, and shows you how to use them to create sensational images.

## Exploring the Liquify Window

At first glance, the Liquify window is a little daunting. It's a little daunting on second, third, and fourth glances, too. However, once you quit glancing and dive into this versatile filter, you'll find that the tools and options make a lot of sense.

The Liquify tool palette resides at the left side of the Liquify window shown in Figure 3-1. The other options available with Liquify (which I describe later in the section appropriately named "The Options Areas") appear at the right side of the window. The tool palette includes a baker's dozen tools that you can use to paint and distort your image. Like Photoshop's main tool palette, you can activate each tool by pressing a letter associated with its name.

**Figure 3-1**

## The painting tools

The first group of tools is those used to paint distortions on your image. Shown in this list with their keyboard shortcuts in parentheses, the painting tools are (from top to bottom; refer to Figure 3-1):

✔ **Warp (W):** This tool is faintly reminiscent of the Smudge tool, but it doesn't blur the pixels quite as much as it pushes them along, creating a stretched effect. Use Warp to push pixels where you want them to go, using short strokes or long pushes.

> When compared to a tool like the Smudge tool, which tends to destroy detail, the Warp tool can preserve detail within distortions.

✔ **Turbulence (A):** This tool adds a random jumbling effect to your pixels. You can use Turbulence to recreate maelstroms of air, fire, and water with clouds, flames, and waves.

✔ **Twirl Clockwise (R)** and **Twirl Counterclockwise (L):** Place the cursor in one spot, hold down the mouse button, and watch the pixels under your brush rotate like a satellite photo of a tropical storm. Or drag the cursor to create a moving twirl effect. Pixels move faster along the edges of the brush than in the placid center, just like a real hurricane.

> Try this technique with the other tools I describe here (with some tools the effect is more obvious than with others). Simply click and hold the mouse. The longer you hold down the mouse the more prominent the effect becomes.

✔ **Pucker (P):** This tool is the equivalent of the Pinch filter, squishing pixels toward the center of the area covered by the brush.

✔ **Bloat (B):** Here we have an analog to the Spherize filter, pushing pixels toward the edge of the brush area.

✔ **Shift Pixels (S):** This odd tool moves pixels at a 90-degree angle to the motion of the brush. Hold down the Alt key (Option key on the Mac) to reverse the direction.

✔ **Reflect (M):** The Reflect tool drags a reversed image of your pixels at a 90-degree angle to the motion of the brush. Hold down the Alt key (Option key on the Mac) to force the reflection in the direction opposite the motion of the brush (for example, to the left of a brush moving right, or above a brush moving down). This tool is a good choice for producing shimmery reflections.

You can see the effects of each of these tools in Figure 3-2.

**Figure 3-2**

Undistorted    Warp    Turbulence

Twirl    Pucker    Reflect

Shift pixels    Bloat

Book
**VII**
Chapter
**3**

## The other tools

The remaining tools on the palette perform different functions. Continuing down the tool palette (refer to Figure 3-1), these tools are (shown here with their keyboard shortcuts):

- ✔ **Reconstruct (E):** This tool lets you completely or partially cancel the distortions you've made, letting you retrace your steps if you went overboard in your warping activities.

- ✔ **Freeze (F):** Use this tool to protect areas from changes. It paints the frozen area with a red overlay, just like the Quick Mask mode (which, in a sense, the Freeze tool is, as you can find out later in this chapter in the section "Mastering Freezing and Thawing").

- ✔ **Thaw (T):** This tool unprotects areas by erasing the red protective "freeze" tone. This is a lot like erasing areas you've painted in Quick Mask mode.

- ✔ **Zoom (Z):** The Zoom tool works exactly like the standard Photoshop Zoom tool. Indeed, you can also zoom in and out by using the Spacebar+Alt+click (Spacebar+Option+click on the Mac) and Spacebar+Ctrl+click (Spacebar+⌘+click on the Mac) shortcuts to zoom in and out. See Book I, Chapter 5 for more on using the regulation Zoom tool.

- ✔ **Hand (H):** The Hand tool works exactly like the standard Photoshop Hand tool. Click and push the image to move it around within the preview window. You'll find more about the Hand tool in Book I, Chapter 5.

Separate from the tool palette at the bottom-left corner of the Liquify window is a magnification box with an option list that you can use to select magnifications from 6.5 percent to 1600 percent. You can also type in a specific value to zoom the image to that size.

## *The Options Areas*

At the right side of the Liquify window (refer to Figure 3-1) are some menus and buttons that let you specify options for the tools, for reconstructing and freezing, and for viewing. I point them all out to you now, and cover exactly how to use them later in this chapter.

- ✔ **Load/Save Mesh:** Liquify lets you show or hide a criss-cross area called a *mesh,* shown in Figure 3-3. The mesh provides a visual map of the distortions you've applied. The mesh starts out as a checkerboard-like set of squares and changes as you apply distortions. The mesh lets you clearly see exactly what you've done to the image, and, even better, provides a way to save those distortions on your hard disk so that you can reapply them to the same or a different image later.

- ✔ **Tool Options:** The Tool Options area is used to apply parameters to the painting tools. You can specify brush size, brush pressure and, for some tools, the amount of random turbulent jitter applied (which gives the stroke a more natural, organic look). If you have a stylus, you can also choose to use the amount of pressure you apply to control the width of your brush stroke.

- ✔ **Reconstruction:** Here, you can select one of several reconstruction modes, such as Stiff, Smooth, and Loose. I explain exactly what these modes do later in this chapter. There are also Reconstruct and Revert buttons that let you cancel all changes made on unfrozen areas (a little at a time) or revert to your last set of distortions. I show you how to use these, too.

**Figure 3-3**

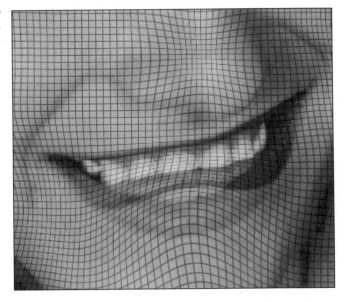

✔ **Freeze Area:** These options let you apply freeze areas from alpha channels, invert the frozen area (thawing frozen portions of the image, and freezing the areas that were previously thawed), and thaw all the areas that were frozen with one click.

✔ **View Options:** You can show or hide frozen areas, the mesh, or the image. I'll show you why you'd want to do each of these shortly. You can also choose the mesh size and color, and select the color that indicates frozen areas (for example, when your image contains lots of the default red color). You can also apply a backdrop that makes it easier to see how the image being liquified will appear when merged with other layers.

 To view your distorted image along with other layers, mark the Backdrop option and then choose the layers you want to view (or All Layers) from the option list. You can select an opacity level for the displayed layers so that they won't overpower the selection being liquified.

▼ ▼ ▼ ▼ ▼ ▼ ▼ ▼ ▼ ▼ ▼ ▼ ▼ ▼ ▼ ▼ ▼ ▼ ▼ ▼ ▼ ▼ ▼ ▼ ▼ ▼ ▼ ▼ ▼ ▼ ▼ ▼ ▼ ▼

# *Transforming an Image*

Liquify seems impossibly complex on the surface, but it's easy to apply as fingerpaint once you've played with it a little. Here's a step-by-step scenario of the things you might do to apply some distortion to your own image:

1. Select and open an image, layer, or selection that you want to transmogrify with Liquify.

2. Choose Filter⇨Liquify or press Shift+Ctrl+X (Shift+⌘+X on the Mac).

   The Liquify dialog box appears.

3. In the View Options area, make sure that the Frozen Areas, Mesh, and Image options are all marked.

   You can hide any or all of these at any time to get a different view of your image. For example, you might want to hide the frozen areas and mesh to view only your image with the distortions you've applied so far. Or, perhaps, you might want to look only at the mesh, as shown in Figure 3-4, to get a stylized look at the distortions by themselves. The ability to see the liquification process in several different ways is one of the reasons why Liquify is so controllable.

4. If you're having trouble seeing the mesh, or think the freeze color will blend in with a dominant color in your image, use the View Options controls to change the size and color of the mesh, and the hue of the freeze.

**Figure 3-4**

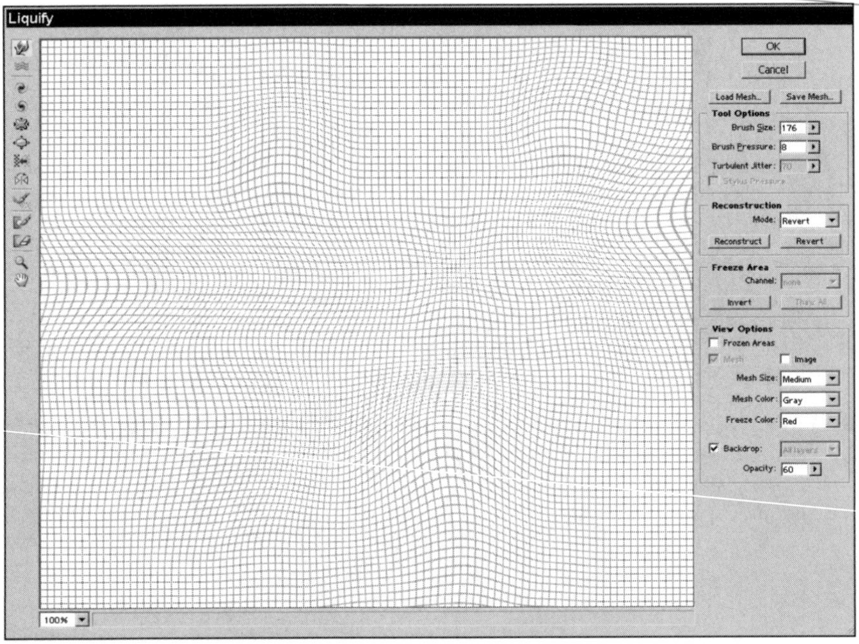

5. **Use the painting tools to apply various effects to your image, as shown in Figure 3-5.**

   Remember to adjust the brush size and pressure to get the exact coverage you want.

   At various points while you work, you may decide that you want to protect parts of the image from further changes (either temporarily or permanently).

6. **Click the Freeze tool and paint over the areas that you want to protect.**

   After you've frozen an area, you may want to get rid of the freeze highlighting for a while. Click the Frozen Areas choice in View Options to turn the display on or off.

7. **If you decide you want to work on an area again, turn on the display of frozen areas again (if necessary). Then select the Thaw tool and erase all or part of the freeze.**

8. **When you're finished, save the mesh you created by clicking Save Mesh. Give the mesh a name and store it on your hard disk.**

   This step is totally optional, but it's a good idea if you really like what you've done.

9. **Apply the distortion to your image by clicking OK.**

**Figure 3-5**

Book
***VII***
Chapter
***3***

# Mastering Freezing and Thawing

Liquify's ability to protect areas by freezing, and unprotect areas by thawing, deserves a closer look. Here's a summary of the things you need to know:

✔ **The easiest way to freeze/unfreeze is to use the Freeze and Thaw tools to paint the areas you want to protect or unprotect, as shown in Figure 3-6.** Use the brush controls to modify how either tool paints or erases. When brush pressure is set to less than 100 percent, the opacity of the mask you're painting determines how frozen that area is. For example, if an area is only 25 percent frozen, using a tool on that area will produce only one-quarter the distortion you'll get in an area that's completely thawed.

**Figure 3-6**

✔ **You can use selections that you have saved in Photoshop to define a frozen area.** This is a great capability; you can use all the selection tools in Photoshop to define frozen/unfrozen areas before you invoke Liquify. You could, for example, select a portion of your image by using the Magic Wand, another portion using selection marquees or Quick Mask mode, and then save all these (choose Selection⇨Save Selection) as alpha channels. Then, when you use Liquify, choose any of these selections to freeze an area.

 To use an alpha channel, select the channel from the Channel menu in the Freeze Area selection of the dialog box. When you click the Border pop-up list, you'll find all your stored selections there to choose from.

✔ **To thaw all frozen areas, click the Thaw All button in the Freeze Area.**

✔ **To reverse your frozen/unfrozen areas, click the Invert button.** That which was frozen will be thawed, and that which was unfrozen will be frozen. Amen!

# Reconstructing an Image

One of the most powerful capabilities of Liquify is the ability to fully or partially reconstruct your image, restoring some or all of it to its pre-Liquify state. This ability gives you a great deal of control over exactly how your image is transformed because you can backtrack any particular part of the transformation exactly as you want to. Here are some of your options:

✔ **To cancel all the changes made on your image (say, you really, really messed up), click the Revert button in the Reconstruction area.** The image returns to its original state when you first opened the Liquify window.

✔ **To change only unfrozen areas of your image to their original state, select the Revert mode in the Reconstruction area of the dialog box, and then click the Reconstruct button.** The frozen areas remain distorted, but everything else returns to normal.

 Use this option when you're displeased with some sections but like the distortions in others. Freeze the stuff you like, and let Liquify cancel the changes elsewhere.

✔ **To paint portions of your image back to normalcy, choose Revert mode, then select the Reconstruct tool from the tool palette.** You can use the Reconstruct brush to restore the areas that you paint. The image reverts more quickly at the center of the brush, so you have an extremely fine degree of control in how you revert your image. The mesh may help you see exactly what portions are being restored, too.

# Extending Distortions

Liquify allows you to extend distortions you've made in frozen areas into parts of the image that are unfrozen. If you have an image that has the requisite frozen and unfrozen portions, you should first choose a mode, which determines how the image from the frozen areas are extended into the unfrozen area.

## Distortion modes

The Distortion modes include the following four:

✔ **Rigid:** This mode keeps rigid (natch) right angles in the mesh's grid, which can generate some mismatches (Adobe calls them *discontinuities*) at the edges where the frozen and unfrozen portions meet.

✔ **Stiff:** Adobe describes this as a *weak magnetic field,* attracting the edges between the frozen and unfrozen areas strongly where they meet, and producing less distortion the farther away from the edges the unfrozen areas are.

✔ **Smooth:** This mode smoothly spreads the frozen areas' distortions through the unfrozen areas. It produces a smooth blending effect.

✔ **Loose:** This generates an even smoother blending effect between the frozen and unfrozen areas.

Use the Reconstruct tool to expand the frozen-area distortions into the unfrozen area, using the mode you've selected to blend the pixels as you paint. You can drag to paint, or click and Shift-click to paint in straight lines (much as you do with Photoshop's regular Brush tools).

You can also apply this reconstruction to all the unfrozen areas in an automated way. Click the Reconstruct button in the Reconstruction area, and then watch carefully as Liquify extends the distortion to all the unfrozen areas. You can stop the process at any time by pressing the Esc key (⌘+period on the Mac) when you've achieved the results you want.

### More Distortion modes

There are three more reconstruction modes that work slightly differently from the previous four. These modes more or less clone distortions you've already applied elsewhere in the image:

- ✔ **Displace:** Displace copies the amount of displacement at the starting point of the distortion to unfrozen parts of your image. You can use this mode to displace parts of your image to a different position in the image.

- ✔ **Amplitwist:** Amplitwist applies the displacement, scaling (sizing up or down) and rotation of the distortion to unfrozen areas.

- ✔ **Affine:** Affine does much the same thing as Amplitwist, using displacement, scaling, rotation, and skew in the distortion to modify unfrozen areas.

▼ ▼ ▼ ▼ ▼ ▼ ▼ ▼ ▼ ▼ ▼ ▼ ▼ ▼ ▼ ▼ ▼ ▼ ▼ ▼ ▼ ▼ ▼ ▼ ▼ ▼ ▼ ▼ ▼ ▼ ▼ ▼ ▼ ▼ ▼ ▼ ▼ ▼ ▼ ▼

### Using Displace, Amplitwist, and Affine

All three of these modes use a different combination of distortion factors, such as displacement, scaling, rotation, or skew. Unlike the modes listed previously, the Reconstruct button isn't available for these three.

To use Displace, Amplitwist, or Affine, follow these steps:

**1.** Open an image to work on, and choose Filter⇨Liquify.

**2.** Choose one of the three special modes: Displace, Amplitwist, or Affine.

**3.** Choose the Reconstruct tool.

**4.** Click somewhere in the image where you want to mimic the distortion present.

**5.** Drag with the mouse in the unfrozen areas to apply the distortion.

**6.** To change the origin of the distortions being copied, click again anywhere in a distorted area to choose a new sampling point. Then resume dragging in unfrozen areas. Your image will take on a distorted appearance, like the one shown in Figure 3-7.

**7.** When you're finished, click OK to apply the distortion.

**Figure 3-7**

# Book VIII

# Retouching and Restoration

The 5th Wave    By Rich Tennant

"...AND THROUGH IMAGE EDITING TECHNOLOGY, WE'RE ABLE TO RE-CREATE THE AWESOME SPECTACLE KNOWN AS TYRANNOSAURUS GWEN."

# Enhancing Images with Adjustments

Photoshop can provide magical transformations to images, making them unrecognizable from the original, but sometimes what you really want is simply to make an image look the same as the original — only better. Perhaps the colors are a little too warm, or the shadows a bit inky. Whatever's wrong with the image, the last thing you want is to change it so much that it looks like it's been processed more than a freeze-dried floral arrangement. You'd be happy to have everyone admire your image without a clue that you'd made major corrections in Photoshop.

Welcome to the world of image enhancements. This chapter concentrates on the things you can do to correct color, contrast, hue, and color saturation. After you've mastered the basic tools, you'll want to explore some even more sophisticated things you can do by using features like Photoshop's Adjustment Layers (in Book V, Chapter 1), which let you dynamically apply your changes in remarkably flexible ways.

## Choosing Automatic Color Correctors

Photoshop has three automatic correction tools that can, in many cases, provide an improved appearance with a simple click of a menu command. However, none of the automatic controls is likely to do as good a job as you can do manually, and sometimes, automatic controls even do more harm than good. If you have an average image (one that doesn't require a great deal of correction), you can try them out to see if they help. If not, you'll want to apply the manual tools explained later in this chapter to produce the exact look you want.

Here's an introduction to the three tools:

- ✔ **Auto Levels:** Adjusts the highlights (brightest portions of an image that contain detail) and shadows (the darkest portions of an image that contain detail).

- ✔ **Auto Color:** Adjusts the color balance of an image.

- ✔ **Auto Contrast:** Controls the relationship between the balance of bright and dark tones.

You don't need to know much about levels, color balance, or contrast to use the automatic correctors (that's why they're automatic), but you'll learn more about each of them later in this chapter when I show you how to take over the controls and make adjustments manually.

## Auto Levels

The Auto Levels command uses a bit of built-in Photoshop intelligence to automatically apply the Levels command (discussed later in the chapter) to your image.

 Auto Levels works best with average images that have lots of detail in the highlights, shadows, and mid-tones, but which could use a bit of tweaking.

Auto Levels defines the very lightest and darkest pixels of each of the three colors as white and black, respectively, and then arranges the mid-tone pixels in between. Along the way, as it balances the tones in your image the command may reduce color casts or even introduce some. You can fine-tune the color manually after Auto Levels has done its work, using the tools described later.

To try out the Auto Levels command, just choose Image➪Adjustments➪Auto Levels, or press Shift+Ctrl+L (Shift+⌘+L on the Mac).

## Auto Color

The Auto Color command adjusts both the color and contrast of an image, based on the shadows, midtones, and highlights it finds in the image. You can access it by choosing Image➪ Adjustments➪Auto Color, or by pressing Shift+Ctrl+B (Shift+⌘+B on the Mac).

Although Auto Color can do a good job on its own, you can customize the parameters it uses to make its color corrections in the Auto Color Corrections Options dialog box, which I discuss in "Setting Auto Color Correction Options," later in this chapter. Check out the color insert to see an image that was corrected using Auto Levels and Auto Color.

## Auto Contrast

Like its manually-operated cousin, the Brightness/Contrast command, the Auto Contrast command fiddles with the overall contrast and colors (if you're working with a color image) in an image, rather than making adjustments to each color individually. It converts the lightest and darkest pixels to white and black, respectively, making all highlights in the image lighter and all shadows darker. No changes are made to the color values.

To use Auto Contrast, choose Image➪Adjustments➪Auto Contrast, or by pressing Alt+Shift+ Ctrl+L (Option+Shift+⌘+L on the Mac).

# *Setting Auto Color Correction Options*

The options available in the Auto Color Correction dialog box are on the advanced side, and this set of tools is best used if you already understand manual color and contrast corrections. You'll want to brush up on your color theory, too, in Book II, Chapter 3.

You can use the Auto Color Correction Options dialog box to tweak exactly how Photoshop applies its Auto Levels, Auto Color, and Auto Contrast controls, as well as for the manually operated Levels and Curves commands.

▼ ▼ ▼ ▼ ▼ ▼ ▼ ▼ ▼ ▼ ▼ ▼ ▼ ▼ ▼ ▼ ▼ ▼ ▼ ▼ ▼ ▼ ▼ ▼ ▼ ▼ ▼ ▼ ▼ ▼ ▼ ▼ ▼ ▼ ▼ ▼ ▼ ▼ ▼ ▼ ▼

## Understanding your Auto Correction options

Photoshop uses algorithms to make adjustments to images. When you use the Auto Correction Options dialog box, you have to decide which algorithms to use. Here are your options:

- **Enhance Monochromatic Contrast:** This option applies the same changes to the red, green, and blue channels, making brighter areas appear lighter, and shadow areas appear darker, with no changes made to the colors. (This is the method used by the Auto Contrast command.)

- **Enhance Per Channel Contrast:** This option individually adjusts the red, green, and blue colors so that each has its own best balance of light and dark tones, even if the color balance is changed a bit. (This is the algorithm used by the Auto Levels command.)

- **Find Dark & Light Colors:** This option locates the average lightest and darkest pixels, and uses their values to maximize the contrast of the image. (This is the algorithm used by the Auto Color command.)

When you understand these commands, feel free to customize the automatic options, following these steps. You can apply the settings only to a particular image-editing session, or save the settings as defaults for all your Photoshop work.

*1.* **Open an image and choose Image⊃ Adjustments⊃Levels or Ctrl+L (or ⌘+L on the Mac).**

You can also use the Curves command by pressing Ctrl+M (or ⌘+M on the Mac).

*2.* **Click the Options button in the dialog box to access the Auto Color Correction Options dialog box.**

See Figure 1-1.

**3.** **In the algorithm area, click the method you want Photoshop to use**

**to adjust the tones. Your choices include**

- Enhance Monochromatic Contrast
- Enhance Per Channel Contrast
- Find Dark & Light Colors

**4.** **Click to add a check mark in the Snap Neutral Midtones if you want Photoshop to base its gamma correction values around a neutral color located in the image.**

This option is used by the Auto Color command. You can find more about gamma correction in Appendix A.

Book
**VIII**
Chapter
*1*

CONTINUED
▼ ▼ ▼ ▼ ▼

**5.** In the Target Colors & Clipping area, enter a value in each of the clip text entry boxes.

 Setting clipping values between 0.5 and 1 percent eliminates the too-dark and too-light pixels.

These values adjust the amount of black and white pixels that Photoshop removes from the darkest and lightest areas of the image.

This option is useful because every image includes some very dark pixels that contain no real image information, as well as some very light pixels that are completely washed out.

Factoring in these two kinds of pixels when you adjust tonal values is a waste.

**6.** Click the Shadows, Midtones, or Highlights patch.

The Color Picker appears, allowing you to set a preferred value for the darkest, medium, and lightest areas.

You can click one, two, or all three of the patches.

**7.** Select the Eyedropper tool and choose 3 x 3 Sample in the Options bar.

**8.** Move your mouse over the image and locate the dark, middle, or light tone you want to use. Click it when you find it.

As you move the mouse over the image, the values in the Info palette change, helping you pick the shadow, midtone, or highlight area you want.

**9.** Mark the Save As Defaults option to store the settings you just made for subsequent use in any Photoshop session. If you don't mark the option, the changes you made will apply only to the current session.

**Figure 1-1**

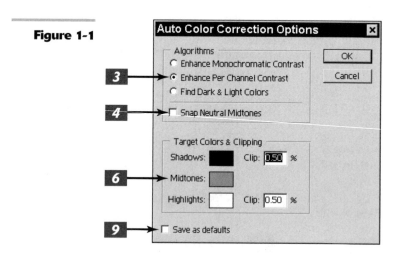

## Using Simple Color Correctors

Photoshop has several simple manual tools you can use to fix color in ways that are different from the Auto Levels, Auto Contrast, and Auto Color commands. They are the Brightness/Contrast control, Color Balance, Desaturate command, and the ever-popular Variations tool. You should learn when to use (and when not to use) each of them, as described in the following sections.

## Avoiding Brightness/Contrast

Beginners gravitate to the Brightness/Contrast control because it seems so simple to use. If your image is too dark, move a slider to make it lighter; if it's too light, move the same slider to make it darker. Right? You can fix an image that's overly contrasty or overly flat looking the same way. Right?

Nope.

In practice, the Brightness/Contrast control is a bad choice for making an image darker or lighter, and for adding or reducing contrast. Its chief failing is that it applies all its changes equally to all areas of your image. For example, you may have a photo that has some shadows that need brightening up but all the middle tones and highlights are just fine. The Brightness slider doesn't take that into account.

Move the slider to the right, and sure enough, your shadows become brighter. But so do your midtones and highlights, which you probably *don't* want. (See Figure 1-2.)

 The impulse is to try and fix the bright spots you create with the Brightness slider by fiddling with the Contrast slider. Before you know it, your image is a mess. Be careful.

Although there are some kinds of pictures that can be helped a little with the Brightness/ Contrast control, you're better off learning to use Levels and Curves, which can tailor your image enhancements to the exact portions of the image you want to work with.

**Figure 1-2**

▼▼▼▼▼▼▼▼▼▼▼▼▼▼▼▼▼▼▼▼▼▼▼▼▼▼▼▼▼▼▼▼▼

## Tweaking Color Balance

If you remember your color theory (review it in Book II, Chapter 3, if you like), you can probably use the Color Balance controls to make some simple changes to the color in your image. The difficult part is in recognizing exactly which color you need to add or subtract from your image in the first place.

Colors are subtler than you might think. For example, a slight *color cast* (or bias) toward cyan can look a lot like a slightly green or blue color cast. Is your image too red, or does it have too much magenta?

 Use the Variations command, described in the following section, to learn to tell the various color casts apart. Variations displays each of the different types of color casts in an array so you can compare them.

To use the Color Balance controls, follow these steps:

**1.** Choose Image⇨Adjustments⇨Color Balance, or press Ctrl+B (⌘+B on the Mac) to access the Color balance dialog box.

**2.** Choose the Shadows, Midtones, or Highlights option to select the tones of an image you want to work on.

Usually, Midtones is the best choice, unless your image has a color cast in the shadows or highlights that doesn't affect the overall image.

That can sometimes happen when a subject is close to a colored wall or other object that reflects light onto, say, the shadowed side of a subject.

**3.** Make sure the Preserve Luminosity option is chosen. That way, the colors of the image will be modified, but the brightness and contrast of the tones will stay the same.

**4.** Move the Cyan/Red, Magenta/Green, or Yellow/Blue sliders to add or subtract color, watching the effects of your adjustments on the original image.

The amount of each color that is added and subtracted is shown in the Color Levels boxes. For example, in Figure 1-3 a value of –22 is shown, indicating that red has been subtracted from the image.

The colors are arranged by their opposites on the color wheel. Dragging the slider towards Cyan adds cyan to the image and subtracts its complement, red. Dragging towards Green adds green to the image and subtracts magenta.

**Figure 1-3**

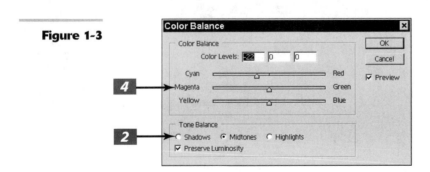

## Resisting the urge to go nuts with sliders

If you're like me, you like clicking options, adjusting values, and sliding sliders back and forth. Thankfully, Photoshop is happy to oblige you with options to make you feel so powerful that you can take on any project.

Was that a sinister laugh I heard? Easy there, partner. I'm about to tell you something that will break your heart at first, but which you'll thank me for later: Always pick a single slider and stick with it when you're trying to compensate for any color cast. Moving two sliders is a waste because you can accomplish anything you want with just one.

For example, if you move both the Cyan/Red and Magenta/Green sliders an equal amount to the left (adding cyan and magenta), you're actually just adding blue. Moving three sliders is even worse because, depending on the amount and direction of movement, the three are likely to at least partially cancel each other out or multiply the effects. However, if there is a cast just in one area, such as the shadows, and a different color cast in another area, it may be useful to do more than one adjustment.

## Correcting Color Cast with Variations

Photoshop's Variations feature is a variation (so to speak) on the professional photographer's *ring around* (a set of color prints, each made with slightly different color balance) or *test strip* (a single print of an image made so that each section is shown using a different color balance). Both tools let you view several renditions of an image and choose the best one visually by comparing them. You might want to use Variations when you're unsure about exactly how the color is biased, and would like to compare several versions of an image to see exactly what the color cast is.

Although not as sophisticated as some color correction techniques, the Variations feature has the advantage of being quick and simple, and it doesn't require a lot of training to use. The color insert shows an example of an image that was greatly improved by using the Variations adjustment.

Here are the components of the Variations dialog box (shown in the Putting-It-Together project that follows):

- ✔ In the upper-left corner is a pair of images — the original image and the image as it will appear when the corrections are applied.

- ✔ Below these thumbnails is a set of six variations on the original image, each with a fixed amount of correction applied using (clockwise from upper-left) green, yellow, red, magenta, blue, and cyan. In the center of this ring is the current version of the image.

- ✔ At the right edge of the dialog box is a stack of three thumbnails showing a lighter version of the image (at top), the current version (in the middle), and a darker rendition (at bottom).

- ✔ In the upper-right corner of the dialog box is a control area that includes radio buttons that let you choose shadows, midtones, or highlights for your correction, as well as saturation. Beneath the buttons is a slider that controls whether your correction will be subtle (Fine) or dramatic (Coarse).

- ✔ Four buttons also let you save the corrections you've made for use with the same or another photo, load settings you've already stored, apply the current corrections (by clicking OK), or forget about the whole thing (by clicking Cancel).

### PUTTING IT TOGETHER

## *Correcting Tinted, Faded Photos*

In the Putting-It-Together project that follows, I employ the Variations feature to restore the color in a scan of a color print originally made in April 1973. Unfortunately, the years have not been kind to this photo; it has a slight, but annoying, greenish tinge that's a result of the magenta dye layer of the print fading. As the magenta fades, the other two color layers, cyan and yellow, appear proportionately stronger when compared to the magenta that remains and, as you may recall, cyan and yellow make green.

I plan to use the Variations feature of Photoshop to restore the magenta layer in this photo that's green with age, putting the ruddy glow back into the subject's cheeks.

To correct color cast in an old photograph by using the Photoshop Variations feature, follow these steps:

**1.** **Open an old, fading photo that needs color correction in Photoshop.**

In this case, I'm using an old, greenish-looking picture.

**2.** **Choose Image⇨Adjustments⇨ Variations from the menu bar.**

The Variations dialog box appears.

**3.** **Check the Show Clipping box to tell Photoshop to show any areas of the image that will be "overwhelmed" by the correction you're contemplating. That is, no new information is added.**

**4.** **Save the corrections you've made for use with the same or another photo, load settings you've already stored, apply the current corrections (by clicking OK) or forgetting**

about the whole thing (by clicking Cancel).

**5.** **Make adjustments with the Fine/ Coarse slider.**

In my example, the greenish picture needs some magenta, so I dragged the Fine/Coarse slider to the left (the default midpoint is waaay too much).

You can also click one of the tick marks to move the slider to that position. Photoshop doesn't allow setting the control to any of the intermediate positions between the marks.

**6.** **Make sure that the Midtones radio button is selected, and then click the preview window containing the amount of color you want to add.**

Watch the Current Pick image to reflect the correction.

In my case, I need to click the More Magenta image.

Click several times if your initial application isn't enough or click other preview windows to add other, additional colors.

Your corrections are applied only to the middle tones of the image. In many cases, that's sufficient. However, sometimes shadows take on a particular hue, or the highlights may gain a color cast of their own.

**7.** **Click the Highlights and/or Shadows radio buttons to add colors only to those parts of the photo.**

Variations isn't the best tool to make complex color corrections, so be careful.

You might be able to see a highlight color in the shadows under the

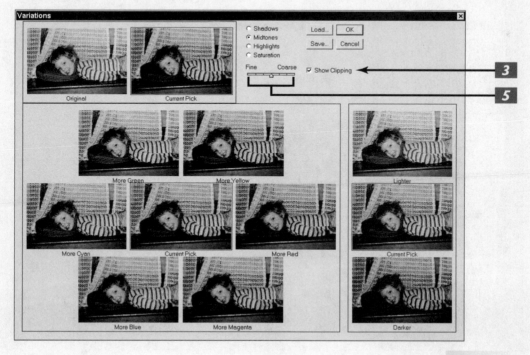

▼ **CONTINUED**

▼ **CONTINUED**

pillow, most noticeable in the More Magenta preview. The highlight is the Clipping indicator showing that the change made by that preview window is too much for that particular area of the picture. That is, Photoshop can't add any more magenta to the highlighted area without losing detail in the image.

**8.** **Click the Darker preview (in the lower-right corner of the dialog box) to make the photo a little darker.**

The Fine/Coarse slider has no effect on the amount of change applied. Instead, you can click the Lighter or Darker previews several times to achieve the look you want.

In my case, only one click is necessary.

**9.** **Click the Saturation radio button to brighten the colors, and use the Fine/Coarse slider to control how much saturation you add or remove.**

The Variations feature also lets you adjust the richness, or *saturation*, of the colors in an image. Now only three previews appear: a less saturated version, the current choice, and a more saturated version.

**10.** **To save your settings, click the Save button, apply a name to the settings, and store them in the folder of your choice.**

I recommend saving your settings, especially if you're working on a copy of the original image and want to apply the same corrections later, or if you plan on correcting several photos that have the same color defects.

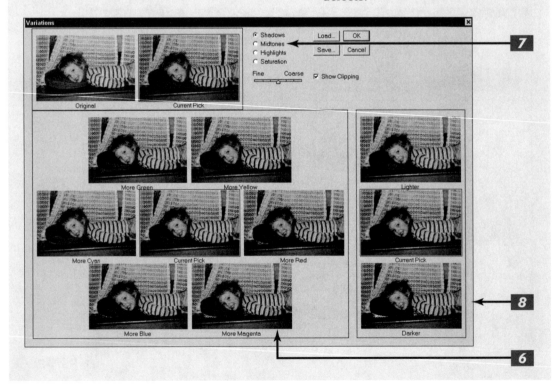

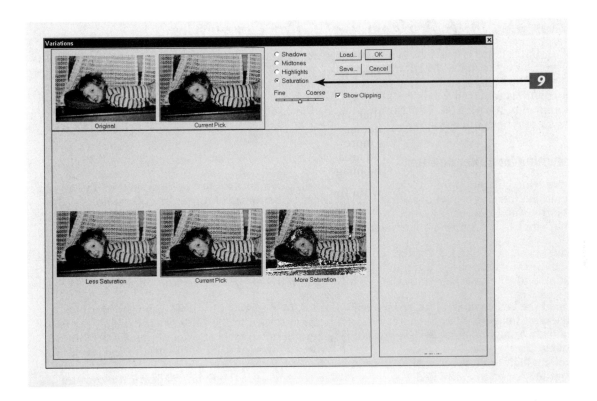

# *Washing Out Color with Desaturate*

Sometimes, you don't want any color at all. Photoshop's Desaturate command can wash all the color out of a layer or selection, giving you a plain grayscale image.

 Just because you can do something doesn't mean you should. Use this command with caution because neither the Desaturate command nor Photoshop's Image⇨Mode⇨Grayscale command is the best technique for converting a color image to monochrome. (See Book II, Chapter 2, for a better method.)

What people perceive as contrast, or differentiation, between tones in an image is determined in a color picture by more than the tonal values of the grays. Differences in color and saturation are also perceived as contrast by our eyes. Simply removing the color can produce an image that appears to be too low in contrast, which is another kettle of fish altogether.

However, if you simply want to eliminate the color from a layer or selection image quickly, the Desaturate command will do the job. To apply it, select the area you want to operate on and choose Image⇨Adjustments⇨Desaturate, or press Shift+Ctrl+U (Shift+⌘+U on the Mac).

I show you how to play with saturation using the Hue/Saturation controls later in this chapter.

Book
**VIII**
Chapter
**1**

# Working with Professional Color Correctors

The simple color correctors I've shown you so far in this chapter usually aren't enough to provide thorough color correction if you've got a really problematic image on your hands. Fortunately, Photoshop has the kind of professional tools needed to make sophisticated color corrections required for reproduction. You don't have to be a pro to use the Levels or Curves commands, nor to work with the Hue/Saturation controls. But you'll feel like one after you've mastered these powerful tools.

## Leveling for better contrast

I described the automatic variation of the Levels command earlier in this chapter. If you want to adjust tonal values of images (the brightness or darkness of tones) or correct colors (the relationship between the colors), this is the tool for you. The color insert includes an image that came to life after an adjustment with the Levels command.

The Levels command is a much more sophisticated tool than the Brightness/Contrast control because you can work with individual tones, brightening or darkening individual tones as you want, and you have a great deal more information to help you make your choices.

Open the Levels dialog box, shown in Figure 1-4, by pressing Ctrl+L (⌘+L on the Mac) or selecting Image⇨Adjustments⇨Levels. The graph shown in the center of the dialog box is called a *histogram*. It is used to measure the numbers of pixels at each of the 256 brightness levels. Each vertical line represents the number of tones at each of the brightness levels. The default histogram displays information for the entire image, but you can view separate histograms for each of the Red, Green, and Blue channels (or the Cyan, Magenta, Yellow, and Black channels if you happen to be working with a CMYK image).

The horizontal axis displays the range of these pixel values, with 0 (black) on the left and 255 (white) on the right. The vertical axis measures the number of pixels at each level. The pattern of lines in the histogram shows you when an image has a preponderance of one kind of pixels (say, bright or dark ones), as well as gaps in the distribution that represent tones that are not represented at all.

There are three triangles at the bottom of the histogram, in black, gray, and white, representing the shadow on the left, midtone in the middle, and highlight on the right. Even though they're located where they are, many images have no black tones at the far left side of the scale, or no white tones at the far right side. (In Figure 1-4, for example, the shadow tone triangle is set at the point where the image begins to have dark tones.)

**Figure 1-4**

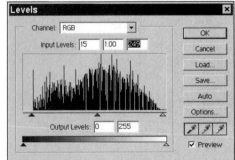

One of the simplest corrections you can do is to move the black and white sliders so that they actually correspond to the pixels containing dark and light tones. Simply slide the black triangle so that it corresponds to the first true black pixels in the image (the beginning of the histogram), and then move the white triangle so it is aligned with the lightest pixels (the end of the histogram). That ensures that there are no wasted tones allocated to areas of the image that actually have no image detail.

The Levels dialog box has an Auto button, which operates similarly to the Auto Levels command, except that you can see exactly what happens. When you click the Auto button, Photoshop applies its own suggested changes, resetting the white point and the black point, and redistributing the gray values of the pixels in between. Afterward, the histogram shows that the pixels fill the complete range from white to black.

▼▼▼▼▼▼▼▼▼▼▼▼▼▼▼▼▼▼▼▼▼▼▼▼▼▼▼▼▼▼▼▼▼▼▼▼▼▼▼▼▼

## Setting black and white points manually

For more control, you can use the Eyedroppers in the Levels dialog box to set the black and white points. Just follow these steps:

**1.** **Open an image and choose Image⇨Adjustments⇨Levels.**

Make sure the Info palette is open and that the HSB and RGB color models are displayed.

**2.** **Select the White Eyedropper tool and drag it around the image while watching the Info palette.**

**3.** **Look for the lightest white in the image, which may be anywhere from 90 to 100 percent. Select that point by clicking.**

**4.** **Use the Black Eyedropper tool to select the darkest black in the image. The combination of these two choices redistributes the pixels from pure white to pure black.**

You can also reset the white and black points by moving the position of the white and black triangles on the input sliders (upper scale). Or, you can enter numbers in the Input Levels boxes. The three boxes represent the black, gray, and white triangles, respectively. Use the numbers 0 to 255 in the white and black boxes.

**5.** **Use the Gray Eyedropper to remove color casts. Select a neutral gray portion of your image, one in which the Info palette shows equal values of red, green, and blue.**

Although you will generally make changes to the entire document by using the RGB channel, you can apply changes to any one of an image's component color channels by selecting the specific channel with the Channel pop-up menu.

**6.** **Adjust the output sliders.**

Moving the black triangle to the right reduces the contrast in the shadows and lightens the image. Moving the white triangle to the left reduces the contrast in the highlights and darkens the image.

**7.** **Adjust the midtones with the gray triangle slider.**

The values you're adjusting are called the *gamma* values.

Dragging this triangle to the left lightens the midtones. Dragging it to the right darkens the midtones while leaving the highlights and shadows alone.

Book
*VIII*
Chapter
*1*

CONTINUED
▼ ▼ ▼ ▼ ▼

You can also move the gray triangle by entering numbers from 9.99 to 0.1 in the center option box. The default value, 1.0, lies exactly in the middle of the range.

If you're working with a series of similar images (such as a bunch of video captures), you can save the settings to reuse them later.

**8.** **Click the Save button to store your settings.**

(Just click the Load button to retrieve them.) This saves the settings, but doesn't apply them.

### Adjusting curves for hard-to-correct photos

The Curves command is one of the most advanced Photoshop correction tools available, offering sophisticated control over the brightness, contrast, and gamma levels in an image; I'm talking about control that is far beyond that offered by the Levels and Brightness/Contrast dialog boxes. This section introduces you to the functions of the Curves command, but you'll want to practice using it a great deal to gain the kind of experience you need to work with it effectively.

Whereas the Brightness/Contrast dialog box lets you change an image globally, and the Levels command allows you to change the shadows, highlights, and midtones, separately, Curves goes far beyond that. It lets you change pixel values at any point along the brightness level, giving you 256 locations at which you can make corrections. You can work with the combined Red, Green, and Blue color channels (or CMYK channels) or apply your changes to the individual colors.

Here are some tips for using Curves:

✔ Access the Curves dialog box, shown in Figure 1-5, by choosing Image⇔Adjustment⇔ Curves or by pressing Ctrl+M (⌘+M on the Mac).

✔ The horizontal axis maps the brightness values as they are before image correction.

✔ The vertical axis maps the brightness values after correction.

Each axis represents a continuum of 256 levels, divided into four parts by finely dotted lines. In the default mode, the lower-left-hand corner represents 0,0 (pure black) and the upper-right-hand corner is 255,255 (pure white). By default, the dialog box shows a 4 x 4 grid; Alt+click (Option+click on the Mac) inside the grid to toggle it to a 10 x 10 grid, as shown in the figure.

**Figure 1-5**

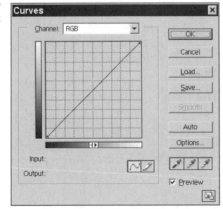

✔ Whenever you open the Curves dialog box, the graph begins as a straight line. Unless changes are made, the input is exactly the same as the output, a direct 1:1 correlation.

✔ When you use the Eyedropper tool from the toolbox to click in the image, a circle appears on the graph to show you the value of the pixel being sampled. At the bottom of the Curves dialog box, you can read the pixel's input and output values.

✔ When you click the Auto button, the darkest pixels in the image (the deep shadows) are reset to black and the lightest areas are set to white. As with in the Levels dialog box, this is the easiest way to make a correction.

✔ The Curves dialog box has black, white, and gray eyedroppers you can use to set the black, white, and midtone points, just as you can with Levels.

### Adjusting curves

If you click at any point on the curve other than the endpoints, a control point will be added that shows your position. You can remove a control point by dragging it downward until it is completely off the graph.

Experiment with the curves to see how they affect the image. For example:

✔ Flattening a curve lowers contrast.

✔ An S-shaped curve increases contrast, especially in the highlight and shadow areas. Using a curve like this also helps to define the midtones.

✔ For ultimate control, Photoshop lets you draw a curve with the precise shape you'd like, creating an arbitrary curve or map. Click the Pencil tool in the dialog box, and then draw peaks and valleys in the Curves dialog box. Watch the changes in your original image.

 Arbitrary maps, like the one shown in Figure 1-6, create distinctive solarization color effects as the colors of your image are warped.

### Getting colorful with Hue/Saturation

Photoshop's Hue/Saturation controls let you adjust colors based on their hue, saturation, and lightness. The Hue/Saturation dialog box doesn't work with the red, green, and blue (or cyan, magenta, yellow, and black) channels of an image. Instead, it operates on the different colors, or hues. You can select all of the colors (Master) in the Edit menu, or choose one color to modify.

There are three sliders in the Hue/Saturation dialog box. (See Figure 1-7.)

✔ **Hue:** Shifts all the colors clockwise or counter-clockwise around the color wheel, depending on the direction you move it.

✔ **Saturation:** Increases or decreases the richness of the colors in an image.

✔ **Lightness:** Modifies the brightness values.

You can adjust any of these values by moving the sliders and watching the results in the image window. The top color bar at the bottom of the dialog box represent the colors in their order on the color wheel before you've made any adjustment. The lower color bar shows how the modifications you make affect the colors.

**Figure 1-6**

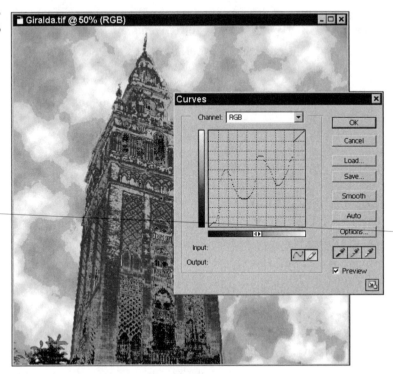

**Figure 1-7**

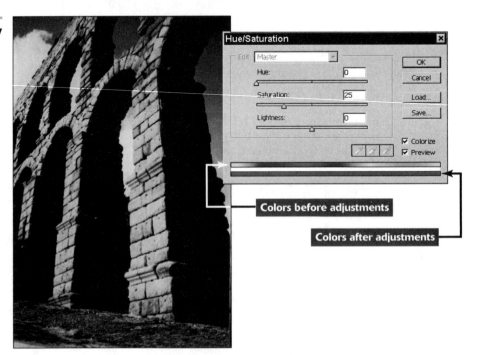

Colors before adjustments

Colors after adjustments

When you select an individual color to adjust, sliders appear between the color bars so that you can define the range of color to be adjusted. You can select colors, add colors, or subtract colors from the range by choosing one of the eyedropper tools and clicking in the image.

The Hue/Saturation dialog box also lets you colorize images, a useful option for creating sepia colored images, as in the Putting-It-Together project that follows.

▼ ▼ ▼ ▼ ▼ ▼ ▼ ▼ ▼ ▼ ▼ ▼ ▼ ▼ ▼ ▼ ▼ ▼ ▼ ▼ ▼ ▼ ▼ ▼ ▼ ▼ ▼ ▼ ▼ ▼ ▼ ▼ ▼ ▼ ▼ ▼ ▼

## Using the Colorize option

Use the Colorize option in the Hue/Saturation dialog box to change the color of any selected area to a new, solid color. This is unlike the Hue slider, which changes only individual pixels based on their present color values. Just follow these steps:

**1.** Open an image and access the Hue/Saturation dialog box by pressing Ctrl+U (or ⌘+U on the Mac).

**2.** Click the Colorize button.

**3.** Drag the Hue slider in either direction to change a color.

Pure white pixels and pure black pixels are not colorized. This is because colorization only affects gray pixels (from value 1 to 254).

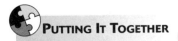 **PUTTING IT TOGETHER**

### *Making a New Photo Look Old*

Black-and-white photography is a newer phenomenon than you might think. Daguerreotypes and other early photographs frequently had a brownish or bluish tone to them. These photos were often hand colored with paints, too. A great deal of research went into producing the neutral black-and-white photos you associate with early- to mid-20th century photography.

You can create sepia-toned masterpieces of your own. Or, if you like, you can create a tint in green, blue, or another shade. Toned pictures can create a mood or otherwise transform a mundane photo into something interesting.

In this Putting-It-Together project, I chose a recent photo of a 2000-year-old Roman aqueduct that has no nasty anachronisms such as automobiles or satellite dishes in

it, which just makes it that much easier to age. To get the full effect of this technique, check out the color insert.

The Photoshop Hue/Saturation feature is all you need to perform this time-traveling magic. Just follow these easy steps:

**1.** Open the image in Photoshop and convert it to black and white by choosing Image⇨Adjustments⇨Desaturate.

You choose Image⇨Adjustments⇨Desaturate (instead of Image⇨Mode⇨Grayscale) to convert the photo to black and white because you're going to continue to work with it as a color image — only one with no colors until you add them.

Book
**VIII**
Chapter
**1**

▼ **CONTINUED**

▼ **CONTINUED**

**2.** **Choose Image⇨Adjustments⇨Hue/Saturation.**

The Hue/Saturation dialog box appears.

**3.** **Select the Colorize check box so that you can add color to the image.**

**4.** **Adjust the Hue slider to produce the tone you're looking for.**

To produce a rich sepia tone, move the Hue slider all the way to the left. If you'd prefer green or blue or some other shade, you can experiment with this slider to get the exact color you want.

**5.** **Adjust the Saturation slider to modify the richness of the color.**

I used a setting of 25. As you move the slider to the right, the color becomes more pure, until you end

up with a striking red at the far-right position.

**6.** **Adjust the Lightness slider to lighten or darken the photo, depending on your mood.**

Generally, you'll want to leave the Lightness slider at the default middle position. To create a darker, moodier picture, move it to the left; to produce a more faded look, move it to the right.

**7.** **When you're satisfied with your changes, click OK.**

Now my photo looks as old as the aqueduct.

You can create similar effects by using the Photoshop Duotones, Tritones, and Quadtones feature. See Book II, Chapter 2, for more information on these tools.

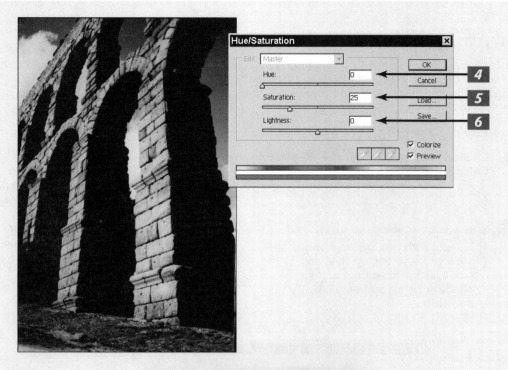

▼▼▼▼▼▼▼▼▼▼▼▼▼▼▼▼▼▼▼▼▼▼▼▼▼▼▼▼▼▼▼▼▼▼▼▼▼

# *Switching Colors with Replace Color*

The Replace Color command creates interesting creative effects by allowing you to substitute one set of colors for another. It does this by building a mask using colors you select, then replacing the selected colors with others that you specify. You can adjust hue, saturation, and lightness of the masked colors.

Just follow these steps:

**1. Choose Image➪Adjustments➪Replace Color.**

The Replace Color dialog box appears, as shown in Figure 1-8.

**2. Choose either Selection or Image.**

✔ Selection shows the mask in the preview window. The masked area is black, semitransparent areas are shades of gray, and unmasked areas are white.

For details on masks, see Book VI, Chapter 2.

✔ Image shows the full image itself in the preview window. Use this option if you zoomed in on the original image to select colors more easily, but you still want to be able to see the full image in the preview.

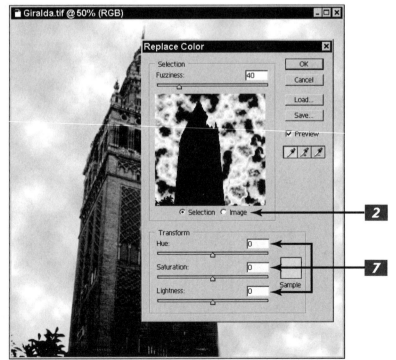

**Figure 1-8**

**3.** **Click the colors you want to select.**

You can click either the image or the preview box.

**4.** **Hold down the Shift key and click or use the +Eyedropper to add more colors.**

**5.** **Hold down the Alt key (Option key on the Mac) or use the -Eyedropper to remove colors.**

**6.** **To add colors that are similar to the ones you select, use the Fuzziness slider to refine your selection, adding or subtracting from the selection based on the tolerance value.**

**7.** **Move the Hue, Saturation, and Lightness sliders to change them to new values.**

# *Increasing and Decreasing Color*

Increasing and decreasing color is a popular Photoshop activity, so it's no surprise that there's more than one way to do it. In addition to the Selective Color command, which I describe in the following section, there are several other commands that are a lot easier to understand — and a lot easier to use.

This is the place to start reading if you want to know all about the Gradient Maps command, and the various color mapper tools, all of which are designed to change the arrangement of the colors in your photos in ways that *don't* produce realistic-looking images. Images that have been color mapped are certainly interesting to look at.

## Using the Selective Color command

The Selective Color command is chiefly of use for manipulating the amount of process colors (that is, cyan, magenta, yellow, and black) used when an image is printed. In the Selective Color dialog box, choose the color you want to edit from the Colors pop-up menu. Adjust the CMYK sliders to modify the selected color.

When the Relative method is selected, you can add or subtract color. For example, if a pixel is 30 percent cyan and you add 20 percent cyan, 6 percent cyan is added to the pixel (20 percent of 30 percent is 6 percent).

When the Absolute method is selected, the amount of change is based on the exact value you enter. For example, if a pixel is 30 percent cyan and you add 20 percent cyan, the pixel changes to a total of 50 percent cyan.

Book
**VIII**
Chapter
**1**

▼ ▼ ▼ ▼ ▼ ▼ ▼ ▼ ▼ ▼ ▼ ▼ ▼ ▼ ▼ ▼ ▼ ▼ ▼ ▼ ▼ ▼ ▼ ▼ ▼ ▼ ▼ ▼ ▼ ▼ ▼ ▼ ▼ ▼ ▼ ▼

## Using gradient maps

Gradient maps convert your image to grayscale, then replace the range of black, gray, and white tones with a gradient of your choice, in effect colorizing your image — often in startling ways.

The lightest tones of your image are mapped to one color in the gradient, while the darkest tones are changed to the other color of the gradient (assuming you're using just two colors for the gradient). All the formerly gray tones are changed to an intermediate color between the two. When you use multiple colors or fancy gradients, the image really gets interesting. Just follow these steps to try out this feature:

*1.* **Open an image and access the Gradient Map, shown in Figure 1-9, by choosing Image⇨Adjustments⇨ Gradient Map.**

*2.* **Choose the gradient you want from the gradient list.**

 This list is exactly like the one offered with the Gradient tool. You can edit the gradient used for your map exactly as you do for the Gradient tool. For more information on choosing gradients, see Book IV, Chapter 3.

*3.* **Choose either or both of these options:**

✔ Dither adds random noise to smooth out the gradient and reduces banding.

✔ Reverse changes the direction of the gradient.

 Use the Reverse option to reverse the image (creating a negative) quickly.

*4.* **Click OK to apply the gradient map.**

**Figure 1-9**

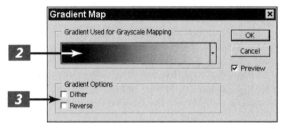

## Playing with the color mappers

Photoshop also includes some fun-filled color mapping commands, so-called because they change the colors of your image in specific ways. Two of them, Invert and Equalize, don't even have any options. They're akin to single-step filters that you apply and forget. (I cover filters in Book VII.) I show all the color mappers in Figure 1-10.

### *Invert*

Invert simply reverses all the colors and tones in your image, creating a negative image. Black tones are changed to white; white tones are changed to black; dark grays are changed to light grays; and colors are flipped to their complements. For example, a light yellow color would become a dark blue, and so forth.

 Some folks mistakenly think they can use this command to create a positive (or color correct) version of a scanned color negative. It ain't so simple because color negatives have an orange mask overlaying the color information. To really do that correctly requires a lot of color correcting and tweaking. Don't try this at home!

**Figure 1-10**

| Invert | Equalize | Threshold | Posterize |

## Equalize

This command locates the lightest and darkest pixels in an image, defines them as white and black, respectively, and then changes all the other pixels in between so the grayscale values are evenly divided. Depending on your image, this process may increase contrast or otherwise alter the color and tones as the values are evenly distributed.

## Threshold

Threshold converts your image to black and white, with all pixels that are brighter than a value you specify represented as white, and all pixels that are darker than that value as black. You can change the threshold level to achieve different high-contrast effects.

## Posterize

This color mapper creates an interesting graphic effect by reducing the number of colors in your image to a value you specify, from 4 to 255. Low values provide distinct poster-like effects. As you increase the number of color levels the image begins to look either more normal, or a bit like a bad conversion to Indexed Color.

Book
**VIII**
Chapter
**1**

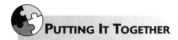

**PUTTING IT TOGETHER**

### Cleaning Up a Line Art Scan

Line art consists of (you guessed it!) lines, rather than the continuous tones of a photograph or painting. Line art can consist of outlines, shapes (like you'd find in a bar chart), patterns (like the fills in the bar chart), or freehand drawings like those produced in pen or pencil. Often, line art consists of just one color, plus white, such as black lines on a white background, or colored lines on a plain background. Line art can also include several distinct colors: Your bar chart may have bars in a variety of different hues.

What you don't want to see when you scan line art is an extra color: the background color of the paper, which should be nominally white, but often doesn't scan that way. Often the paper will appear as a dull gray, and you may see other artifacts you don't want, such as wrinkles or spots in the paper.

Luckily, Photoshop has a handy Threshold command that you can use to determine which tones appear as black and which are dropped altogether. When you set a threshold for your image, anything darker than the brightness you choose is rendered as black, and anything lighter is converted to white. You end up with a nice black-and-white line art image with all the intermediate tones removed.

Follow these instructions to clean up a piece of line art:

**1.** **Open a line drawing in Photoshop.**

**2.** **Choose Image⇨Adjustments⇨ Threshold from the menu bar.**

The Threshold dialog box includes a chart called a histogram. The histogram includes a series of vertical lines showing how many of an image's tones are represented by a certain brightness level. You can see that a relatively small number of tones are represented by a brightness value of 93, marked by the gray triangle at the bottom of the histogram. Many more tones are used at the other levels, forming a sloping mountain in the chart.

**3.** **Move the slider to the right until the tones you want to appear in the image are shown.**

The more you move the slider to the right, the darker the image gets. A threshold of about 129 seems about right for this image.

**4.** **Click OK to apply the modification.**

Some small artifacts may remain in your image. These will be spots and parts of wrinkles that were darker than the page background, approaching the darkness of the line art itself.

**5.** **To clean up these slight defects, use the Eraser.**

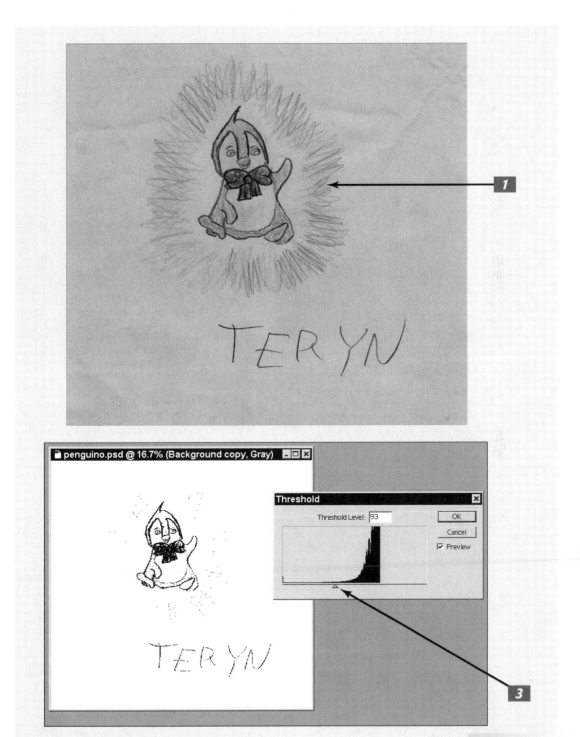

▼ **CONTINUED**

**CONTINUED**

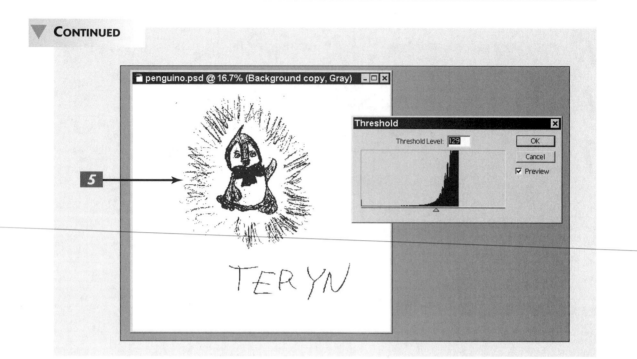

# Repairing with the Focus and Toning Tools

2

One of the coolest things about Photoshop is the way it lets you choose one of several tools to accomplish similar end results, but with distinctly individualized looks. Photoshop's focus and toning tools are an example of this. The focus tools blur, sharpen, and smudge your image in much the same way as the Blur, Sharpen, and Liquify filters. The toning tools lighten, darken, and change the richness of the color in your image a bit like commands such as Levels, Curves, and Hue/Saturation.

But where their counterparts operate only on layers or selections, the focus and toning tools let you *paint* the effects you want directly onto your image. Using these tools, you can create much more subtle, natural looks that are tailored to meet your exact needs.

This chapter introduces you to the wonderful world of applying focus and toning effects to your image. As you work through the sections that follow, keep in mind all the tips I give you in Book IV, Chapter 1 about using brushes. Most of that information applies to the brush-like focus and toning tools, as well.

## Lighten and Darken with Dodge and Burn

*Dodging* and *burning* originated in the darkroom when photographers discovered that negatives that contained areas that were too dark or too light could be salvaged by adding or subtracting a bit of exposure as prints were made with an enlarger.

An enlarger makes a print by projecting an image of a negative onto a piece of photosensitive paper. During the exposure, the darkroom worker can reduce the amount of light falling onto the paper by placing some object (often a disk shape of cardboard or metal impaled on a piece of wire) in the light-path to *dodge* part of the image. Other parts of an image can be *burned in* by shielding the entire image from the light except for a small portion exposed through an opening, such as the fingers in a cupped pair of hands. Photoshop's Dodge and Burn tools adopt their icons from the most popular real-world tools used to achieve these effects in the darkroom.

However, Photoshop's counterparts are a great deal more flexible than the versions used in the darkroom. For example, in a darkroom the size of the dodging or burning tool is varied by moving it up or down in the light path. Unfortunately, the closer the real-world tool gets to the paper the sharper it appears, forcing the darkroom worker to move the tool more rapidly and frequently to blur the edges of the lighten or darken effects. With Photoshop's Dodge and Burn tools, you can set the size of the tool and its softness independently simply by selecting a brush of the size and hardness/softness you require.

Photoshop's tools can also be set to operate primarily on shadows, midtones, and highlights. You can adjust the degree of lightening and darkening applied by specifying an exposure, too.

▼▼▼▼▼▼▼▼▼▼▼▼▼▼▼▼▼▼▼▼▼▼▼▼▼▼▼▼▼▼▼▼▼▼▼▼▼▼▼▼▼▼

## Using Dodging and Burning

The Dodge and Burn tools can be very effective tools, but remember that you can't add detail that isn't there. Keep the following in mind:

✔ If you lighten very dark shadows that contain little detail, you'll end up with grayish shadows.

✔ Darkening very light areas that are completely washed out won't look very good either.

In either case, you'll want to use Dodge and Burn in moderation, and work only with small areas. To dodge or burn a portion of an image, just follow these steps:

*1.* **Open an image with under- or over-exposed areas and choose the Dodge or Burn tool from the Tool palette.**

Press the O key to choose the active toning tool, or press Shift+O to cycle through the available toning tools until the one you want is active.

*2.* **Select a brush from the Brush palette.**

Larger, softer brushes spread the dodging and burning effect over a larger area, making it easier to blend with the surrounding area.

You can choose the same brushes available with any of the painting tools, including preset brushes from your library. For more information on choosing brushes, see Book IV, Chapter 1.

*3.* **From the Range options, select Shadows, Midtones, or Highlights.**

Use Shadows to lighten or darken detail in the darker areas of your image, Midtones to adjust the tones of average darkness, and Highlights to make the brightest areas even lighter or, more frequently, darker.

**Figure 2-1**

In Figure 2-1, the original image (left) had both dark and light areas, so I dodged the shadows and burned in the darker stones.

**4.** **Choose the amount of the effect to apply with each stroke using the Exposure slider/text box.**

**5.** **Paint over the areas you want to lighten or darken with the toning brush, gradually building up the desired effect.**

The Exposure control is similar to the Opacity control offered by other painting tools, but it's especially important with dodging and burning.

 It's best to use a low value (I often work with 10 percent exposure or less) so you can carefully paint in the lightening or darkening you want.

High exposure values work too quickly and produce unnatural-looking, obviously dodged/burned areas in your images.

 For an even softer, more gradual effect, click the Airbrush option in the Options bar.

**6.** **If you go too far, press Ctrl+Z (⌘+Z on the Mac) to reverse the stroke.**

**7.** **When you're finished, choose File⇨Save to store the image.**

# Turning Down the Color with the Sponge

The Sponge, which soaks up color like, well, a sponge, reduces the richness (or saturation) of a color in the areas you paint. It can also perform the reverse, imbuing a specific area with richer, more vibrant colors.

Surprisingly, the Sponge tool also works in grayscale mode, pushing light and dark pixels towards a middle gray, providing a darkening or lightening effect to those pixels. Unlike the Hue/Saturation or Desaturate commands (Image⇨Adjustments), which work only on layers or selections, you can use the Sponge on any area you can paint with a brush.

You can use the Sponge on an image in subtle ways to reduce the saturation in selected areas for an interesting effect. For example, you may have an object that is the center of attention in your picture simply because the colors are so bright (or even garish). The Sponge lets you reduce the color saturation of that area (only) to allow the other sections of your image to come to the forefront. The Sponge also can be used to make an artistic statement: You could reduce or increase the saturation of a single person in a group shot to make that person stand out (perhaps as being more colorful than the rest).

▼ ▼ ▼ ▼ ▼ ▼ ▼ ▼ ▼ ▼ ▼ ▼ ▼ ▼ ▼ ▼ ▼ ▼ ▼ ▼ ▼ ▼ ▼ ▼ ▼ ▼ ▼ ▼ ▼ ▼ ▼ ▼ ▼ ▼ ▼ ▼

## Applying the Sponge

To use the Sponge tool, just follow these steps:

**1.** **Open an image and choose the Sponge tool from the Tool palette.**

Press the O key to choose the Sponge if it is the active toning tool, or press Shift+O to cycle through the Sponge, Dodge, and Burn tools until the Sponge is active.

**2.** **Select a brush from the Brush palette.**

Use large, soft brushes to saturate/desaturate a larger area.

Smaller brushes are useful mostly when you need to change the saturation of a specific small object in an image.

**3.** **Select either Desaturate (reduce color richness) or Saturate (increase color richness) from the Mode pop-up menu.**

**4.** **Choose a flow rate (the speed with which the saturation/desaturation effect builds up as you apply the brush) with the Flow slider/text box.**

**5.** **If you want an even softer effect, choose the Airbrush option.**

The only special thing you need to do to use the Sponge in Grayscale mode is to work with a grayscale image!

**6.** **Paint carefully over the areas you want to saturate or desaturate with color.**

You can't see the effects of the Sponge tool in black and white as shown on the right in Figure 2-2, but you should see the effects on-screen.

**Figure 2-2**

## Smoothing with the Smudge Tool

Although grouped among the Focus tools, the Smudge tool performs more of a warping effect, something like the Warp brush in the Liquify filter (see Book VII, Chapter 3 for information on this command).

Smudge pushes your pixels around on the screen as if they consisted of wet paint, using the color that's under the cursor when you start to stroke.

However, don't view Smudge as a simple distortion tool that produces only comical effects. I use it on tiny areas of an image to soften the edges of objects in a way that often looks more natural than blurring tools. It can come in handy when retouching images to create a soft, almost painted look, as you can see on the right in Figure 2-3, in which the wrinkles around the neck have been softened.

**Figure 2-3**

## Applying a Smudge

Smudged areas may stand out because of their smooth appearance. It's often a good idea to add some texture using the Noise filter after you've smudged, to help blend a smudged section in with its surroundings. You'll find tips on applying Noise in Book VII, Chapter 2.

To apply the Smudge tool, just follow these steps:

**1. Open the image and choose the Smudge tool from the Tool palette.**

Press the R key to select it, or press Shift+R to cycle through the available focus tools (including Blur and Sharpen) until the one you want is active.

**2. Choose the settings you want from the Options bar.**

**3. Select a brush from the Brush palette.**

Use a small brush for smudging tiny areas, such as edges. Larger brushes produce drastic effects, so use them with care.

**4. Choose a blending mode from the Mode pop-up menu.**

**5. Choose the strength of the smudging effect with the Strength slider/text box.**

Low values produce a lighter smudging effect; high values really push your pixels around.

**6. If your image has multiple layers, you can select the Use All Layers option to tell Photoshop to use the color information from all the visible layers to produce the smudge effect.**

The smudge still appears only on the active layer, but the look is a bit different, depending on the contents of the underlying layers.

**7. Use the Finger Painting option to begin the smudge using the foreground color.**

You can get some interesting effects with this option, such as the one shown in Figure 2-4.

 You can switch the Smudge tool into Finger Painting mode temporarily by holding down the Alt key (the Option key on the Mac) as you drag.

**8. Paint over the areas you want to smudge.**

**9. Watch the screen carefully as you smudge so that you can redirect your daubs to achieve the look you want.**

This tool can be a little on the destructive side. If you're looking to preserve reality, use it with restraint. If you want to get wild, go crazy.

**10. When you're finished, choose File⇨Save to store your image.**

▼▼▼▼▼▼▼▼▼▼▼▼▼▼▼▼▼▼▼▼▼▼▼▼▼▼▼▼▼▼▼▼▼▼▼▼▼▼▼

## Softening with the Blur Tool

Adding a little blur here and there can save an image with a few defects. Blurring can also be used for artistic effect — say to add a little motion to a soccer ball frozen in time by too-fast a shutter speed. Photoshop's Blur tool makes it easy to paint your blur effects exactly where you want them.

The Blur tool doesn't push pixels around like the Smudge tool. Instead, it decreases the contrast among adjacent pixels in the area painted.

**Figure 2-4**

Blur is a good choice for softening edges or removing small defects. However the mechanics of using Blur and several of its options are similar to Smudge. Just follow these steps:

**1.** **Open an image and choose the Blur tool from the Tool palette.**

Press the R key to select it if it happens to be the active focus tool, or press Shift+R to cycle through the Sharpen and Smudge tools until Blur is active.

**2.** **Select a brush from the Brush palette.**

Use a small brush for applying small areas of blur.

 Use larger brushes with caution, say, to blur the entire backgrounds to make a foreground object appear sharper in comparison.

**3.** **Choose a blending mode from the Mode pop-up menu.**

**4.** **Choose the strength of the blurring effect with the Strength slider/ text box.**

**5.** **If your image has multiple layers, you can select the Use All Layers option to blur based on the pixel information in all visible layers in your image.**

This can produce a smoother blur when the layers are later merged.

**6.** **Paint over the areas you want to blur, as shown in Figure 2-5.**

**7.** **When you're finished, use File⇨Save to store your image.**

Book
**VIII**
Chapter
**2**

CONTINUED
▼ ▼ ▼ ▼ ▼

**Figure 2-5**

# Cranking Up the Focus with the Sharpen Tool

In theory, the Sharpen tool is nothing more than the Blur tool in reverse — instead of decreasing contrast among pixels, Sharpen increases the contrast. In practice, however, you'll need to use this tool with a bit more care. Where blurred areas tend to fade from a viewer's notice (at least in terms of how our eyes perceive them), sharpened areas of an image jump out at people.

If you blur an area a little too much, you may not even notice. But even a small area that has been oversharpened can change the entire appearance of an image — and not flatteringly.

▼▼▼▼▼▼▼▼▼▼▼▼▼▼▼▼▼▼▼▼▼▼▼▼▼▼▼▼▼▼▼▼▼▼▼▼▼▼▼▼▼▼▼

# Sharpening an Image (With Care)

You *can* often successfully sharpen up small areas with the Sharpen tool. Sometimes the eyes in a portrait can benefit from a little sharpening. Or, you might want to sharpen an area to make it stand out more distinctly against a slightly blurred background.

Here are the simple steps to follow to use the Sharpen tool:

*1.* **Choose the Sharpen tool from the Tool palette.**

Press the R key to select it directly if it's the last focus tool used. If not, press Shift+R to cycle through the Blur and Smudge tools to activate the Sharpen tool.

*2.* **Select the brush of your choice from the Brush palette.**

*3.* **Choose a blending mode from the Mode pop-up menu.**

4. **Choose the strength of the sharpening effect with the Strength slider/text box.**

Using a fairly low value (say, 25 percent or less) is a good idea because you can build up sharpness slowly, being careful not to overdo it.

You'll know when you have gone too far with the sharpness when the pixels start to look noisy and grainy.

5. **Use the information on all your layers for Photoshop's contrast-increasing algorithms by checking the Use All Layers option.**

6. **Paint over the areas you want to sharpen.**

7. **When you're finished, use File⇨Save to store your image, which might look something like Figure 2-6.**

Sharpening increases contrast, so you should be careful when using the Sharpen tool if you plan to also adjust the Levels or Curves controls. Any change that increases contrast in the whole image will also boost the contrast of an area you've sharpened.

The Unsharp Mask filter offers more options and better overall control, so unless you really need to paint the sharpening effect, you're usually better off using the filter instead. If you really want to apply the effect with brushstrokes, you could always apply the Unsharp Mask filter to a whole layer, take a snapshot, undo the filter operation, and then use the snapshot as a source to paint from using the History palette. See Book II, Chapter 4 for information on how to paint from the History palette.

**Figure 2-6**

Book **VIII** Chapter **2**

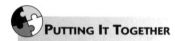 **PUTTING IT TOGETHER**

### *Fixing an Underexposed Foreground*

Sometimes editing tools just don't cut the mustard when it comes to fixing large areas of an underexposed image. Instead, you have to use three tools together to repair the damage: a filter, a fill, and a blend mode.

If you're like me, you've taken at least a couple of photos where your subject was lit from behind, thereby underexposing the foreground and burying the subject in the shadows. Here's how to bring your subject back into the light:

*1.* **Open the image in need of repair.**

*2.* **Choose Image⇨Duplicate.**

   Name the file "Repair" and click OK in the dialog box.

*3.* **Select Image⇨Mode⇨Grayscale.**

   The color has now been stripped from the image.

   Don't worry; this is just an intermediary step.

**4.** **On the duplicate image, choose Filter⇨Blur⇨Gaussian Blur. Enter a radius value and click OK.**

For a low resolution image (72 ppi) 5 pixels should be enough. For higher resolution images (300 ppi) use 20 pixels.

 Your goal is to get rid of the detail in the image. My image was 170 ppi so I used 12 pixels to do the job.

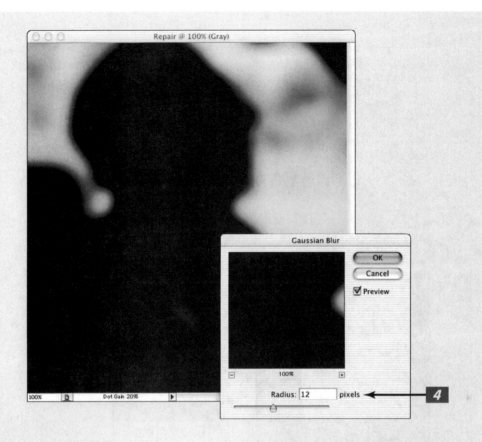

5. **Return to the original image. Choose Select⇨Load Selection.**

   Under Document make sure it says
   `Repair`.

6. **Choose Gray for the Channel. Check the Invert box. Leave the Operation as New Selection. Click OK to load the Load Selection dialog box.**

You're loading the only available channel in the duplicate grayscale image as a selection.

A selection outline appears, which corresponds to the blurry gray areas in your duplicate image.

7. **Choose Edit⇨Fill. Select 50% Gray from the Use pop-up menu under Contents. Select Color Dodge from the Mode pop-up menu. Leave the Opacity at 100%. Click OK.**

▼ **CONTINUED**

▼ **CONTINUED**

Although the selection is filled with 50 percent gray, the Color Dodge mode *lightens* the pixels in the image, creating a kind of bleaching effect.

**8.** **You can now see the subject of your image in a better light.**

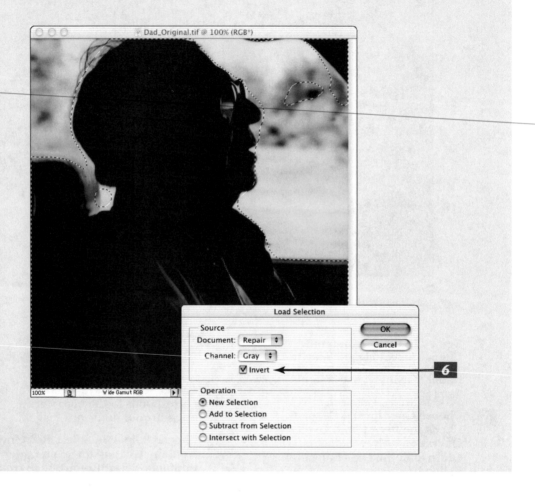

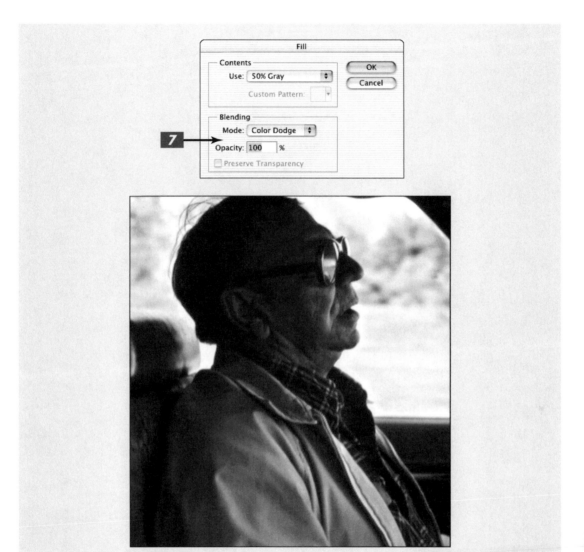

# Fixing Flaws and Imperfections

3

Say you want to duplicate an element in your image. That's easy enough, right? Make a selection and copy and paste it into the new location. Presto. That works fine most of the time. But what if the element has a shadow behind it, next to it, over it, or under it?

You face the dilemma of having a hard edge on the copied element because the shadow (called a *cast shadow*) is cut off by the selection outline. You could feather the selection, but then you have to make sure that the copied element blends in realistically with the background. What a pain. The better method is to *clone* the element using the Clone Stamp tool. It's quick, easy, and no one will know there was really only one element there originally.

Here's another hypothetical situation: What if you already have the right number of elements but some unsightly flaw mars your otherwise perfect image? Or maybe the corporate executive, whose head shot you took last week, has requested a little digital Botox around the eyes and mouth. No problem. Wrinkles, scars, blemishes, scratches, spots, and any other nasty imperfections can be taken care of in a matter of minutes in Photoshop with the healing tools.

In this chapter, I reveal secrets of cloning that won't make medical ethicists scream. And I show you how to heal scars, scratches, and other imperfections without calling a plastic surgeon.

# Cloning with the Clone Stamp Tool

Tell Dolly the sheep to move over and make room. The Clone Stamp tool, also known as the Rubber Stamp, one of Photoshop's more popular tools, always arouses a "Wow," "Cool," or similar remark of approval when demonstrated.

The Clone Stamp tool takes sampled pixels from one area and *clones* (or copies) them onto another area.

Believe it or not, you can also reach for this tool when retouching imperfections, such as scratches, scars, bruises, and other minor flaws. In fact, that used to be one of its major functions. In some retouching instances it does a great job, although the advent of the new Healing Brush and Patch tools have relegated the Clone Stamp tool more to the pure cloning functions and less to the hard-core retouching jobs.

▼ ▼ ▼ ▼ ▼ ▼ ▼ ▼ ▼ ▼ ▼ ▼ ▼ ▼ ▼ ▼ ▼ ▼ ▼ ▼ ▼ ▼ ▼ ▼ ▼ ▼ ▼ ▼ ▼ ▼ ▼ ▼ ▼ ▼ ▼ ▼ ▼ ▼ ▼ ▼ ▼ ▼ ▼ ▼

## Using the Clone Stamp tool

Cloning is often better than making a selection, copying, and pasting it because cloning allows you to retain soft edges on details such as shadows, giving you a more realistic duplicate image.

Follow these steps to clone an element without any genetic engineering:

**1.** **Open an image and select the Clone Stamp tool from the Toolbox.**

Press the S key on the keyboard.

You have several options to choose from on the Options bar.

**2.** **Select a brush and change its size or shape in the Brush pop-up palette.**

For more information on brushes, see Book IV, Chapter 1.

**3.** **You can specify the Clone tool's brush size to control the area that you're cloning.**

I recommend having your Clone Stamp tool cursor display your Brush Size so you can judge the amount of the area you are cloning. To do so, choose Edit⇨Preferences⇨Display & Cursors (Photoshop⇨Preferences⇨Display & Cursors on Mac OS X). Select the Brush

Size radio button from the Painting Cursors area of the dialog box. I used a 65 pixel feathered brush.

**4.** **Choose the blend mode of your choice.**

Selecting a mode such as Difference, Multiply, or Color can produce some interesting special effects. For more on modes, see Book V, Chapter 3. I left my setting at Normal.

**5.** **To make the clone more or less opaque, use the Opacity slider or text box on the Options bar.**

I left the opacity at 100 percent.

**6.** **Specify how fast the clone is applied by the Clone Stamp tool.**

Again I left my option at 100 percent.

**7.** **Activate the Airbrush option for Airbrushing capabilities.**

**8.** **Activate the Aligned option.**

With Aligned activated, when you move your cursor to a different location, the clone source moves as well. If you want to clone multiple times from the same location, leave the Aligned option unchecked. I left mine checked.

**9.** **Check the Use All Layers option to clone part of an image with multiple layers.**

This tool samples pixels in all of the visible layers for the clone. If you leave it unchecked, the Clone Stamp tool clones only from the active layer.

**10.** **Alt+click (Option+click on the Mac) the area of your image that you want to clone. By doing this you are defining the *source*.**

See Figure 3-1.

**11.** **Click or drag along the area where you want the clone to appear.**

As you drag, Photoshop displays a cross hair icon along with your Clone Stamp icon. The cross hair represents the source you are cloning from while the Clone Stamp icon shows where the clone is being painted. As you move the mouse, the cross hair moves as well. This provides a continuous reference to the area of your image that you're cloning. Make sure and keep an eye on the cross hair, otherwise you may clone something you don't want. Try to clone your entire object in one fell swoop so it doesn't get fragmented.

When you've successfully completed the cloning process, you have two identical objects. Figure 3-2 shows my identical twin Siberian tigers.

**12.** **Save the image and close it.**

Figure 3-1

CONTINUED
▼ ▼ ▼ ▼ ▼

**Figure 3-2**

### Tips for excellent cloning results

Here are a few useful tidbits regarding the Clone Stamp tool:

- ✔ **Use the Clone Stamp for fixing simple flaws:** To clean up a flaw that is pretty straight, such as a stray hair or scratch, Alt+click (Option+click on the Mac) with the tool to define the source. Then click at one end of the straight flaw and Shift+click at the other end. The cloned source pixels will then cover up the flaw.

- ✔ **Clone a selection and put it in a separate image:** To clone between two images, Alt+click (Option+click on the Mac) inside one image to define the source in image number one and drag inside image number two where you want the object to appear.

- ✔ **Clone patterns:** To use the Pattern Stamp tool, which shares the flyout menu with the Clone Stamp, select a custom pattern from the Pattern Picker palette in the Options bar. Drag with the Pattern Stamp tool, and you see the pattern appear.

## Digital Bandaging with the Healing Brush Tool

The Healing Brush and Patch tools are similar to the Clone Stamp. They let you clone pixels from one area and apply them to another area. But that's where the healing tools leave the Clone Stamp eating their dust.

The Clone Stamp used to be one of the main tools for retouching flawed or blemished areas. But the problem was that if you weren't careful, you could end up with telltale blotches and smudged areas that were a sure giveaway that some retouching had occurred. That's because the Clone Stamp tool just takes the pixels from the sampled area and copies them over the flaw. There is no consideration for the tonality of the flawed area — the shadows, midtones, and highlights. So if the pixels you are sampling from aren't shaded and lit exactly like the ones your covering, you have a mismatch in color. This makes it hard to create repairs that are seamless and indecipherable to the eye.

That is, until the Healing Brush arrived. This very intelligent tool clones by using the *texture* from the sampled area (the source) and then using the *colors* around the brush stroke as you paint over the flawed area (the destination). The highlights, midtones, and shadows remain intact and the result of the repair is more realistic and natural — not retouched and phony.

To use the Healing Brush, select the tool that looks like a bandage. Choose your options, such as brush size. Specify your Source option — Sampled or Pattern. For most retouching jobs, Sampled will be the option of choice. Check the Aligned option. This allows your sampling point to move in relation to your mouse movement. Establish the sampling point by Alt+clicking (Option+clicking on the Mac) the part of your image you want to clone from. Release the Alt (Option on the Mac) key and click or drag on the flawed area.

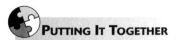 **PUTTING IT TOGETHER**

### Resurfacing Wrinkles and Sags

While wrinkles, scars, bags, sags, and other less than desirable facial imperfections were once the domain of the Airbrush and Clone Stamp tool, they are now fair game for the awesome Healing Brush tool. The Healing Brush, as you've learned, is a much more effective flaw fixing tool due to its ability to preserve the various tones of an image. Here are the steps to heal your favorite, but imperfect photo:

**1.** **Open your image and select the Healing Brush tool.**

Use the J key to select it from the keyboard. Note that you can also heal between two images. Just make sure that they have the same color mode.

**2.** **In the Options bar, click the Brush Picker.**

In the palette, select your desired diameter and hardness for your brush tip. You will do this several times while retouching your image. It is important to use the appropriate brush size for the flaw you are repairing.

**3.** **Leave the blend mode set to Normal.**

You can change your blend mode if necessary. For most simple retouching jobs, such as this one, you'll probably leave it at Normal.

**4.** **Choose a Source option.**

You have a choice between Sampled and Pattern.

✔ Sampled, which you will probably use 99 percent of the time, uses the pixels from the image.

✔ Regarding Pattern, well, you can probably infer that it uses pixels from a pattern you have selected from the Pattern picker palette.

For my example, I am sticking with Sampled because I don't think my guy would look that good with a Tie-Dye or Nebula pattern across his face. He's just way too corporate for that.

**5.** **Select how you want to align the sampled pixels.**

Book
**VIII**
Chapter
**3**

▼ **CONTINUED**

▼ **CONTINUED**

When you click or drag with the Healing Brush, Photoshop displays a crosshair along with the Healing Brush cursor. The crosshair represents the sampling point, also known as the source. As you move the Healing Brush, the crosshair also moves, providing a constant reference to the area that you are sampling from. However, if you deselect the Aligned option in the Options bar, the source pixels are applied *only* from your *initial* sampling point, despite how many times you stop and start dragging. I left Aligned checked in my example.

**6.** **Establish the sampling point by Alt+clicking (Option+clicking on the Mac). Make sure and click the area of your image you want to clone *from*.**

In my example, I clicked the smooth area on the chin and portions of the forehead.

**7.** **Release the Alt (Option on the Mac) key and click or drag over the area of your image that contained the flaw.**

Pay attention to where the crosshair is located because that's the area you are sampling from.

In my example, I brushed over the wrinkles under and around the eyes and on the forehead. I also zapped some dark spots here and there. In just five or ten minutes this gentleman lost about ten years. Save the file, close it, and send in your invoice for your digital dermabrasion.

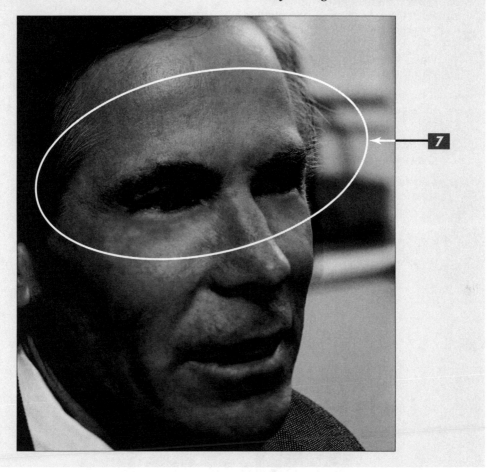

Book
**VIII**
Chapter
**3**

# Patching without Seams

While the Patch tool is similar to the Healing Brush in theory, its application method is slightly different. Instead of painting over the flaws with a brush, you select your flawed area and apply a patch to that selection. The Patch tool does a good job in fixing larger flawed areas or isolated imperfections rather than a few wrinkles or scars here and there. What's more, it's a breeze to use. To apply a patch, grab the tool that looks like, well, a patch of material. Specify either Source or Destination in the Options bar — Source if you want to select the flaw, Destination if you want to select the good pixels. Drag around the flaw to select it and then drag the selection to the portion of the image from which you want to fix.

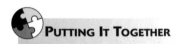

**PUTTING IT TOGETHER**

### Repairing Scratches and Cracks

The companion tool to the Healing Brush, the Patch tool also creates seamless repairs, but uses a slightly different approach. Here are steps to patching an area in need of repair:

**1.** **Open your image and select the Patch tool.**

It looks like a patch of material. Use the J (or Shift+J) key to select it from the keyboard.

**2.** **Choose Source or Destination in the Options bar.**

Choose Source if you want to select the flawed area. Select Destination if you want to select the good area you want to clone from. You can also choose a Pattern if so desired.

**3.** **Drag around the flawed area of your image.**

Think of the Patch tool as a kind of super cloning Lasso tool. Drag completely around the flawed area as you would when selecting with the Lasso tool. If you need to, you can apply a slight feather of .5 to 2 pixels, depending on the resolution, to soften the edge of the selection. I selected my area without a feather.

You can actually select your flawed area with any selection tool you'd like. After you have your selection, then select the Patch tool and proceed to Step 4.

**4.** **Drag to the area on your image that you want to clone (or sample) from.**

When you release the mouse, Photoshop patches your flawed selection with the cloned pixels.

**5.** **Repeat the process if needed.**

Book
***VIII***
Chapter
***3***

▼ **CONTINUED**

▼ **CONTINUED**

# Book IX

# Photoshop and the Web

## The 5th Wave    By Rich Tennant

"If I'm not gaining weight, then why does this image take up 3MB more space on my Web page than a comparable one from six months ago?"

# Prepping
# Web Graphics

Preparing an image for display on a Web page can be as just important as creating it. That razor-sharp, 6-megapixel image you carefully composed through the viewfinder of your digital camera may end up cropped, sliced, and transformed into a miniature 128-x-128-pixel graphic perched in a corner of your Web page. Visitors to your site are likely to be more concerned with how quickly the image downloads and how clearly they can view its content than its glorious digital genesis.

Although Photoshop has some marvelous tools for optimizing an image for the Web (see Chapters 2 and 3 in this book), you can (and should) prepare your images ahead of time. This chapter introduces you to some of the tools and concepts you should be familiar with before you start optimizing in earnest.

## Understanding Resolution

When it comes to resolution, size matters. Resolution is always expressed in units per length:

✔ Dots per inch (dpi) for printed output

✔ Samples per inch (spi) for scanned input

✔ Pixels per inch (ppi) for images viewed on a computer display

So what do you need to know about resolution if you're planning on putting images on the Web? Here are two golden rules to follow:

- ✔ **Start out by creating the image at the resolution you'll use to display it.** Images lose detail when you change the resolution settings after editing.

- ✔ **Choose the resolution based on what will look good on a 17-inch screen with resolution settings of 800 x 600.** This is the standard display that most Web sites use. You don't need a high resolution if you're going to display the image on a Web site.

Different applications call for different resolutions. You'll find more information on choosing the right resolution and how to change resolution, if you absolutely must, in Book II, Chapter 1.

### Picking a resolution (and sticking with it)

Changing resolution is often bad because you'll always lose some image detail when you convert from one resolution to another while resizing images. Therefore, it's a good idea to create a graphic destined for the Web at the resolution that you'll use to display it. If possible, do not create the image at a different size and then change the resolution later.

So, when choosing the resolution and size of your images, keep in mind the final destination of the image — that is, Web or print — and how large you want it to appear on the screen or printed page.

Smaller monitors display images at 72 ppi. Larger monitors use 96 ppi or 120 ppi. You can use these figures to visualize the size your images will appear on the displays of other users' computers. For example, a graphic that measures 150 pixels x 150 pixels appears to be about 1.25 x 1.25 inches on a monitor with 120 ppi resolution (rather tiny), but a little more than 2 x 2 inches (relatively large) on a smaller monitor with 72 ppi resolution.

Resolution values always translate into sizes. For example, a Photoshop image measuring 600 x 600 pixels created at 600 dpi will print as a 1-x-1-inch square on a 600 dpi printer because each pixel is translated into one printer dot, or as a 2-x-2-inch square on a 300 dpi printer (unless you tell the printer to scale the image to a different size) because each pixel will translate into two printer dots.

### Dealing with differences in monitors

You can't control what size monitor and which resolution settings viewers use when they look at your images online, but if you've read the previous section, you probably have had the point driven home that you *can* control your images' resolution. And at least that's somewhere to start.

A Photoshop image measuring 600 x 600 pixels created at 600 dpi will appear as a 6.25-x-6.25-inch square on a monitor with 96 ppi resolution or as a 5-x-5-inch square on a monitor with 120 ppi resolution.

The resolution issue of monitors can be confusing because the pixels per inch being displayed varies depending on the resolution setting you've used. For example, consider a 19-inch monitor that has a viewable width of 14.6 inches. You can set it to 800 x 600, 1024 x 768, or, like me, 1920 x 1440 pixels. The following mini-table shows the pixels per inch displayed:

| Resolution | Viewable Width | Pixels Per Inch |
|---|---|---|
| 800 x 600 | 14.6 | 54 |
| 1024 x 768 | 14.6 | 70 |
| 1920 x 1440 | 14.6 | 133 |

Obviously, the monitor doesn't have a higher physical resolution at a higher screen resolution setting. It just uses fewer of its dots to represent a screen pixel. When you get to a roughly 1:1 ratio, you've reached the maximum displayable resolution of the monitor. For example, the top horizontal resolution of my 19-inch monitor is 2048 pixels, or 140 ppi.

The resolution settings you make in Windows are designed to approximate the physical pixels per inch displayed so that objects appear at roughly the proper size on the screen. For example, my 19-inch screen that can display 133 ppi at 1920 x 1440 resolution is set to 120 ppi, so an object that measures 120 pixels wide appears to be 90 percent of 1 inch wide (120/133), which is close enough. If I used 1024 x 768 on that same monitor, I'd set Windows to 72 ppi so that a 72 pixel wide object would be almost exactly 1 inch wide on the screen.

# Understanding Color Modes

In Web graphics terms, *color mode* refers to the number of colors or grays that appear in an image. Common modes include

- **Grayscale:** 256 different gray levels
- **Indexed color:** 256 or fewer colors
- **RGB color:** 16.8 million different colors created from red, green, and blue values

 Unfortunately, CMYK (approximately 55,000 printable colors created from cyan, magenta, yellow, and black values) is not an option for Web display.

In practical terms, only grayscale, indexed color, and RGB color are used for the Web because they're the only modes supported by the two most popular Web-capable file formats, GIF and JPEG (described later in this chapter). (Actually, JPEG does support CMYK color, but it must be converted back to RGB for display in a browser, so the option is of little value.)

The mode you choose affects how your image is displayed. Modes of 256 (or fewer) colors are great for images that contain a limited number of hues, but not for the display of images that call for full color. But if you use RGB color with full-color images, they frequently (but not always) produce larger files that take a long time to download. For reasons like these, you have to make tradeoffs when selecting the right mode. Fortunately, the Save for Web feature (discussed in Chapter 2 of this book) enables you to compare the different modes and make a wise decision.

However, you can still work with colors manually, as you find out later in this chapter.

Book

*IX*

Chapter

*1*

# Understanding File Formats

Web browsers can display images in several ways. The fastest, easiest, and most compatible solution is to use graphics that the majority of browsers can display natively, in-line (that is, consecutively with text). Except for some browsers that display only text, the most commonly used browsers can handle only files saved in GIF (Graphics Interchange Format), JPEG (Joint Photographic Experts Group), and, in many cases, PNG (Portable Network Graphics) formats.

Browsers can display other types of images if users have installed the appropriate *helper applications* or *plug-ins.* For example, if you're browsing and click a link that leads to a PDF (Portable Document Format) file, your browser can display the file if you've installed the Adobe Acrobat Reader plug-in and the Adobe Acrobat Reader application. (Most people have; if not, most sites that include PDF documents also include a link to Adobe to download the plug-in or the stand-alone free Acrobat Reader software.)

Flash animations are another kind of image that requires a plug-in to view. However, formats other than GIF, JPEG, and PNG are beyond the scope of this book. All you really need to know is how to choose between these three file formats. (The Save for Web feature can help you make that decision, too; see Chapter 2 of this book for details.)

The following sections discuss each of the major formats and run down all the advantages and disadvantages to using them.

## Introducing GIF

The GIF format was one of the earliest image file formats developed for online display. It was created back in the 1980s, even before the government-supported predecessor of the Internet (called ARPANet) was transformed into the public information highway we have today.

The GIF format's earliest use was at CompuServe, back in the days when dial-up modems moved information at a sluggish 300 baud (roughly 100 times slower than the average dial-up connection today). As you might guess, the impetus to speed up image downloads was intense.

GIFs produce smaller files by discarding some colors, if necessary, to produce a file that has a maximum of 256 different colors. Similar colors are combined into fewer hues, or represented by a pattern of similar colors (called *dithering*) that the eye merges into an approximation of the original range of colors.

If an image already has 256 or fewer colors, it may not be necessary to discard any colors. Or you can choose to reduce the number of colors anyway to produce an even smaller file size. Although reducing the number of colors in a full-color image can produce an artistic effect, like the one in the bottom image in Figure 1-1, in most cases you must reduce colors with care.

The GIF format's 256-color palette is called indexed color. You can find more information on indexed color in Book II, Chapter 2.

The kind of compression used for GIF files is called *lossless* compression because the image can be uncompressed and reconstructed exactly as it was before compression. Of course, information is lost when colors are discarded *prior* to compression (when you optimize the number of colors); indeed, Adobe includes a GIF option called lossy, but that's another story. (For more about reducing the number of colors before data compression, see the later section "Using a Web-Safe Palette and Hexadecimal Colors.")

### A short snippet on compression

Each file format has its own file compression pros and cons, so continue reading if you're looking for the whole scoop. For now, keep in mind that the amount of compression you get out of a file format can be a big advantage because the more you compress, the smaller the file size becomes. That's a good thing when you're thinking about displaying a file on the Web or transporting it electronically.

In a nutshell, compression reduces file size by replacing long strings of numbers (representing the data) in a file with shorter codes that signify the same information. Compression is not a technique that's unique to image files; just about any file that contains redundant information can be compressed by using programs such as WinZip (under Windows) or StuffIt (originally a Mac program, but now available for both platforms).

The advantages and disadvantages to using the GIF format are summarized in the following two sections.

**Figure 1-1**

### GIF advantages

These are the advantages to using GIF files:

- **GIF files can be very small in size.** If you start with an image that has few colors in it, GIFs can be positively tiny. I've converted some logos with three or four colors into files that are smaller than 1K in size. You can use a full 256 colors, slim down to a trim 128 colors, or try to get away with 64 or 32 hues if your subject matter lends itself to serious reduction.

  *Bottom line:* GIFs are great for images with 256 or fewer colors and can be useful with many images with more colors, too.

- **GIFs preserve the sharpness in your original image.** Because no pixels are discarded (only colors), sharp images remain sharp.

  *Bottom line:* GIFs are excellent for line art, charts, graphs, cartoons, logos, and most other images that emphasize solid areas instead of continuous tones.

- **GIFs can be interlaced.** In this process, every eighth line is displayed as the file begins to be downloaded, providing a rough image that can be viewed immediately. The other lines are filled in until the full image is available.

  *Bottom line:* Interlacing is mostly useful to visitors who have slow connections. Virtually all graphics-capable browsers can display interlaced GIFs, but not all can display interlaced JPEG or PNG images.

- **GIFS can be made transparent.** You can make a single color transparent to the browser so that the underlying background shows through.

  *Bottom line:* This is a great feature for creating "floating" images.

- **GIFs can be animated.** Browsers display multiple GIF images consecutively as animations.

  *Bottom line:* This is a great feature if you don't overdo it by creating animations that are huge and take a long time to download or that are annoying to visitors.

### GIF disadvantages

Here are a few disadvantages to using GIF files:

- **Other file formats may produce smaller file sizes.** Depending on the content of the image, a well-optimized JPEG or PNG file can be smaller. Whether a GIF file is smaller than a JPEG or PNG file depends on the number of colors in the original and how well those colors can be combined in a JPEG or PNG file without losing too much information.

 Of course, when you compare the file size, you should also compare the image quality. After all, the proof is in the pudding.

  *Bottom line:* Always compare the file size of GIF and JPEG images by using the Save for Web feature to see which format provides the smallest file.

✔ **GIFs don't preserve the colors in your images.** Continuous-tone images, particularly those with fine gradations of color (even something as simple as a drop shadow), may display with objectionable bands of color in GIF format.

*Bottom line:* Use GIFs for graphics, especially those with broad areas of color, and use other formats for photographs, in which a wide range of colors is important.

## Introducing JPEG

The JPEG format was developed somewhat later than GIF in response to the need for a file format that provides smaller images without sacrificing all the colors found in true photographic images.

The JPEG format reduces file sizes by using a somewhat different scheme than GIF, a type of *lossy* compression that discards some image information as the image is squeezed down. Each image is divided into 8-x-8-pixel blocks, the pixels in those blocks are analyzed, and the pixels that are similar in color are combined. The color information for the pixels that are merged is discarded, producing an image that has less detail than the original, but is still a good representation of all the colors it contained.

As a result of this process, JPEG images have that distinctive blocky look when you zoom in on them in Photoshop, as shown in Figure 1-2.

**Figure 1-2**

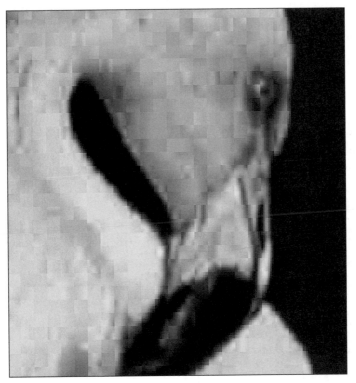

Book
***IX***
Chapter
***1***

### Choosing between GIF and JPEG file formats

Knowing the differences between GIFs and JPEGs helps you make your images more suitable for one format or the other. Here are some tips for getting the most from these file formats:

✔ **Make a better GIF.** Modify your image so that it contains larger areas of a single color; reduce unneeded colors manually (you know what they are better than the Save for Web tool); convert anti-aliased lines to solid lines where possible.

✔ **Make a better JPEG.** Decrease the color saturation of your image. Lower the contrast. Blur unimportant areas if feasible. The JPEG algorithms do a better job on low-saturation, low-contrast, blurry images than on vivid-color, high-contrast, or sharp images.

You can choose the amount of compression the JPEG uses and, therefore, the tradeoff between file size and sharpness. Photoshop uses a sliding scale from 0 (small file size/maximum compression) to 12 (larger file size/minimum compression). The Save for Web command helps you decide how to make the tradeoff for individual images.

You can also save JPEG files by choosing File➪Save. If you save from the File menu, you can choose from these options:

✔ **Matte:** Use this option to choose a color to represent any transparency in the image.

✔ **Image Options:** Specify the amount of compression/quality level by using the slider (from 0 to 13), or by typing a value into the Quality text box, or by choosing a quality level from the menu.

✔ **Format Options:** Select *Baseline ("Standard"),* a format compatible with virtually all graphics-capable Web browsers; *Baseline Optimized* to create a file with optimized color and a more compact file size; or *Progressive* to show a series of scans that increase in resolution as the download proceeds (similar to GIF's interlacing). You can choose between three and five scans. Baseline ("Standard") is the only option supported by all Web browsers.

✔ **Size:** If the Preview option is chosen in the Save dialog box, the Size area displays the file size and approximate download time at a particular connection speed. You can change the connection speed in the range 14.4 Kbps to 2 Mbps.

## JPEG advantages

The advantages of the JPEG format are in many cases nearly identical to those of the GIF format:

✔ **The file sizes can be very small.** In some cases, JPEGs are even smaller in size than their GIF equivalents. The amount of compression you can use varies with the particular image. Compression works best when you have images with lots of low-contrast areas that have only subtle variations that won't be missed when pixels are combined.

*Bottom line:* The JPEG format works best with images that can be squeezed without the process becoming obvious to the unaided eye.

✔ **JPEGs preserve the colors of your original image.** Gradations in tone are preserved well, so your gradients and soft edges look good.

*Bottom line:* JPEGs are great for continuous-tone color photographs.

✔ **You can save JPEGs in *progressive* format.** Progressive format is similar to the interlacing process most commonly used in GIFs, in which alternate lines are displayed as the file downloads.

*Bottom line:* Use this capability when you really need a full-color rendition and want to provide interlacing for visitors with slow dial-up connections. If their browsers don't support interlaced JPEGs, they'll still see the image.

### JPEG disadvantages

The following list details the disadvantages of JPEG files:

✔ **Files saved in other formats may be smaller.** Broad areas of a single color won't be compressed at all, so the equivalent GIF may be a lot smaller in size.

*Bottom line:* Compare the file size of JPEG and GIF images by using the Save for Web feature to see which provides the smallest file.

✔ **JPEGs don't preserve the detail in your image.** At high compression ratios, JPEGs can take on an objectionable, blocky appearance.

*Bottom line:* Review the final appearance of your JPEG before using it. Some images can take high compression and still look good, but others can't.

✔ **JPEGs don't support transparency.** Often, you'll end up using a GIF instead, even when JPEG would do a much better job.

*Bottom line:* Choose your images carefully so that they don't require transparency if using JPEG is really important.

 Editing JPEGs isn't a good idea because each time you save a JPEG file, additional information is lost. Work with an original TIFF or PSD file and save it as a JPEG when you're finished editing it. If you need to make additional changes, return to the TIFF or PSD file.

### Understanding PNG

Is this the Year of PNG? I've been writing about the PNG (often pronounced *ping*) format seemingly forever (actually, only since 1995 when the PNG standard was frozen). Every year, support for the PNG format grows, but its actual usage remains pitifully small.

The chief roadblock has been a lack of browsers that support PNG fully, but that roadblock has largely vanished. (The vast majority of browsers in use today, including Netscape 4.*x* and later versions, as well as Internet Explorer 5.*x* and later, support at least some PNG features.)

However, only later versions of Internet Explorer and Netscape Navigator support PNG natively; other versions require a plug-in, which can be irritating to viewers of your Web page. In the Mac realm, support is good. Although Web developers are a cautious lot and want the largest group of people possible to be able to view their efforts, the main reason today that so few people use the PNG format is that so few other people use it.

That's a pity, because the PNG format is a potential GIF-killer. (It can give JPEG a run for the money, too, but it's not specifically designed to reproduce photographic-quality images.) The features built into the PNG format (the letters of which are sometimes said to represent *PNG's Not GIF*) counter most of the objections to GIF. Because of that, the advantages greatly out-weigh the disadvantages. So, I focus on the advantages to the PNG format only, as listed here:

- ✔ **It's free.** Unisys holds the patent on the compression algorithm used in GIF and charges a royalty to any software vendor who wants to support GIF. The PNG specification is a potential advantage because software developers can incorporate it into their products without paying for the privilege.

- ✔ **It offers better compression.** The PNG format produces files that are up to 20 percent smaller than the equivalent GIF, but they sometimes can be larger. In fact, one disadvan-tage is that they can sometimes be larger than the equivalent JPEG file.

- ✔ **It isn't limited to 8-bit, 256-color images.** In fact, the PNG format isn't limited to 24-bit, 16.8 million color images. It can support a selected range of bit depths from 1 to 64 bits, for zillions and zillions of colors. The bottom line is that the PNG format supports Grayscale, Indexed Color, and RGB modes.

- ✔ **It uses a smarter interlacing scheme.** The PNG format provide images that fade in faster and better than interlaced GIFs.

- ✔ **It offers four different types of transparency.** The PNG format allows 64 to 254 (not 256) different levels of transparency, so even full-color images can float over a back-ground, as shown in Figure 1-3.

**Figure 1-3**

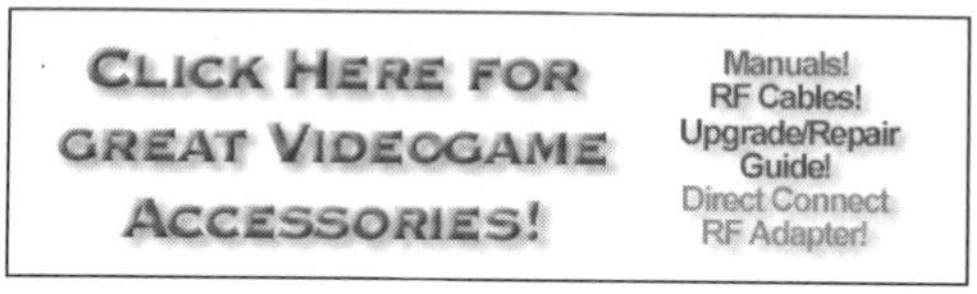

CLICK HERE FOR GREAT VIDEOGAME ACCESSORIES!

Manuals!
RF Cables!
Upgrade/Repair Guide!
Direct Connect RF Adapter!

The PNG format also offers some technical advantages that aren't readily visible to the user, such as the ability to adjust for variations in the display of images by certain devices (called *gamma correction*) and an error-correction routine that patches images that have lost a bit or two in transmission to your computer.

 The PNG format does not support animation. A related file format, MNG does, but it's used even less widely than PNG.

## Using a Web-Safe Palette and Hexadecimal Colors

If you've tinkered with HTML, then you've probably at least heard of hexadecimal colors. Photoshop's Web-safe palette is a set of 216 colors that should, theoretically, be displayed by any browser regardless of whether the user's video card displays 256 hues, 16.8 million, or something in between. Using only these Web-safe colors is a way to ensure that your image will be represented without dithering in any browser.

Of course, who views Web pages on a display using only 256 colors these days? Haven't all computers been furnished with video cards offering a minimum of full 24-bit, 16.8-million-color images for ages and ages and ages? Well, not exactly.

Here are some instances when you might be working with 256-color images:

- ✔ You're using GIFs. Oops! GIFs always have 256 or fewer colors, even when you're displaying them on a full-color monitor.

- ✔ A visitor is using a computer on which resolution is more important than the number of colors. Users who don't edit graphics may need 1600-x-1200-pixel resolution on their large-screen displays and not care that their older video cards offer only 256 colors at that resolution.

- ✔ Your visitor is using a PDA, Web-capable cell phone or some other device that has an LCD display that doesn't support more than 256 different shades. If your Web page needs to reach these people, you may need to consider a Web-safe palette for at least some of your images.

In all of these cases, you may need to use the Web-safe palette features to optimize your colors. If you're going to make a wholesale conversion of the colors in an image to a Web-safe palette, you're better off using the Save for Web feature, which is automated and provides visual feedback of your results.

## Selecting individual Web-safe colors

Photoshop lets you select individual colors based on their Web-safeness. You can do that two ways:

- ✔ Access the Adobe Color Picker by double-clicking the Foreground or Background color boxes in the Tool palette. Select the Only Web Colors check box, as shown in Figure 1-4. Now, only Web-safe colors are displayed in the Color Picker, and you can choose any of them.

**Figure 1-4**

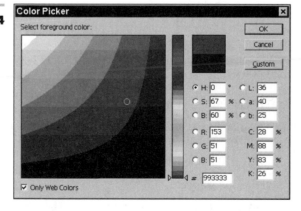

Book
*IX*
Chapter
*1*

If you don't select the Only Web Colors box, the Adobe Color Picker still lets you know when you've selected a nonsafe color. A small cube appears above the selected color patch in the dialog box (to the left of the Custom button).

✔ In the Color palette, choose Make Ramp Web Safe from the palette options menu. You can also select Web Color Sliders from the same menu. When either option is selected, the colors shown in the color bar and/or selected by the color sliders are Web safe. In the case of the sliders, the sliders automatically snap to a value that is Web safe and do not allow the selecting of intermediate values.

## So what are hexadecimal colors?

Hexadecimal colors are simply a way of representing hues in the notation used by computer programmers. Hexadecimal values are calculated by using the digits 0 to 9 and the letters A through D. Fortunately, you don't need to bother with the math. You just need to know that the 256 shades of red, green, and blue are each represented by a hex value from 00 (no color) to FF (maximum color).

For example, a deep rose color might be represented by a value of F0306F. This cryptic value can be broken into three parts: Red — F0 (240 in decimal); Green — 30 (240 in decimal); and Blue — 6F (111 in decimal). The hex numbers are handy because you can enter them into HTML text to reproduce the color.

You can read the hexadecimal values of a selected color in the Info palette and use the same values to specify that color in any dialog box (such as the Adobe Color Picker) that accepts them. You are also likely to use these values when you use HTML or another markup language to specify the text and background colors on your Web page or Web site.

# Making Type Look Good On-Screen

The last thing you may want to consider when prepping your images for the Web is how your type looks. You can make changes as you prepare or edit the image that will affect how well your type shows up on-screen. Here are some of your options.

## Anti-aliasing

For most non-Web applications, you'll generally want to use one of the Photoshop anti-aliasing schemes. (You can find more on anti-aliasing type in Book IV, Chapter 4.) Photoshop offers five different anti-aliasing methods (which are shown in Figure 1-5):

✔ **None** uses no anti-aliasing. This is often a good choice for small type.

✔ **Sharp** applies only enough anti-aliasing to soften the edges of diagonal strokes, keeping the type quite sharp. This is another sensible choice for smaller type.

✔ **Crisp** increases the amount of anti-aliasing a bit, but the type still looks fairly sharp.

✔ **Strong** gives the type a heavier appearance.

✔ **Smooth** provides the maximum amount of anti-aliasing but can slightly affect the sharpness of the type.

**Figure 1-5**

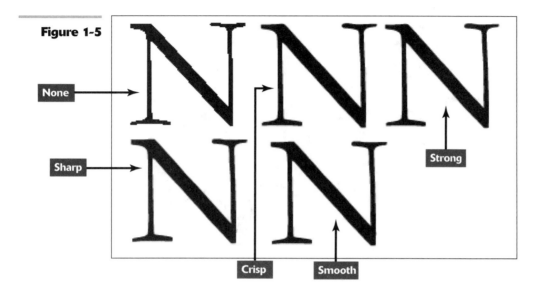

None

Sharp

Strong

Crisp

Smooth

 While these recommendations usually hold true, your results may vary depending on specific typeface and size; you may want to experiment in some cases.

## Fractional width/system layout

At small sizes and low resolutions, such as those typical of Web display, type can be rendered inconsistently with the default Photoshop type setting of Fractional Width. In this mode, Photoshop varies the distance between characters by using fractions of whole pixels. At sizes smaller than 20 points, such type may either have too much space between characters, or not enough space, causing the characters to run together.

To prevent this, choose System Layout from the Character palette options menu. System Layout displays text as the operating system would by using a program like WordPad or SimpleText. Photoshop switches to whole pixel increments and removes all anti-aliasing. The type won't look quite as neat, but the spacing problems will be prevented. It can also be a good choice for smaller text.

## Faux styles

Photoshop cobbles together imitations of italic or bold typefaces for fonts that don't have them. The program normally does a pretty good job of slanting the Roman (upright, or normal) version of the type, or making the type thicker to simulate bold. However, at smaller type sizes and for type displayed online, the results are often less than pleasing. So when creating type for online display, try to avoid using the Faux styles.

To apply these styles, choose Faux Bold or Faux Italic from the Character palette options menu or click the Faux Bold or Faux Italic buttons that appear near the bottom of the Character palette, as shown in Figure 1-6.

**Figure 1-6**

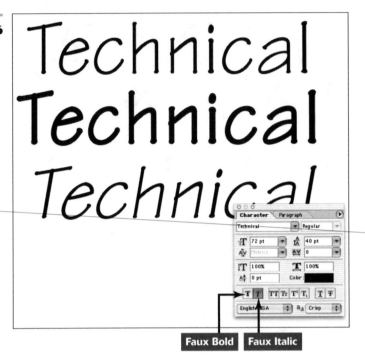

Faux Bold    Faux Italic

# Optimizing Images with Save for Web

2

After you've done all your prep work for images destined for Web display (as described in Chapter 1 of this book), it's time to optimize them so that they'll look their best, download their fastest, or some combination of the two. *Save for Web* is one of three methods available to you in Photoshop to create those optimized images. You can manually tinker with your graphics by using some of the tips offered in Book IX, Chapter 1, and then save the images in a Web-friendly file format. Or you may elect to jump to ImageReady and use some of the tools built into that stand-alone program (including the powerful animation tools described in Chapter 5 of this book).

In most cases, however, Save for Web provides the kind of automation and preview capabilities you need right inside Photoshop itself. This chapter introduces you to this multi-layered tool and its multilayered capabilities.

## Quality or Loading Time

One thing to keep in mind as you work with Save for Web is that optimization always involves trading off between two goals that conflict with each other to a certain extent:

✔ **Image quality:** With a few exceptions confined to the artistic realm, you'll generally want your image to appear on a Web page as sharp as it possibly can be, with the full range of colors shown in the original. The best quality image should also be sized to fit in well with your Web page design no matter what size browser window users are viewing a page through.

✔ **Download speed:** Short download times are desirable, with *no* exceptions. The ideal Web page image should appear on-screen as quickly as possible, regardless of the user's connection speed. Although fast loading times are essential when users have pokey 14.4K to 33.3K connections, you'll also want fast download speeds for those using 56K dial-up links, 128K ISDN connections, or 256K and faster cable modem/DSL broadband links.

Unfortunately, you can't fully meet either of these two goals at all times. The best quality images and the largest and flashiest photos also take the longest to download. Conversely, the images that download the fastest can potentially look the worst.

But don't panic yet. You can make tradeoffs to ensure that your images have the quality you expect and the fast download times users demand. By choosing the best file format for your image, making some choices about how much quality you're willing to give up, and tweaking your image with Photoshop, you can frequently get the best of both worlds. Chapter 1 of this book offers some advice on some of the manual prep you can do. Save for Web provides the automated half of that equation.

In fact, Save for Web has the simplest automation tool of all: Optimize to File Size, shown in Figure 2-1. This option is tucked away in the Save for Web dialog box's palette menu (see the next section for more on this dialog box). Select the file size you want, click a few other settings, and Photoshop gives you a file that meets that file size requirement.

**Figure 2-1**

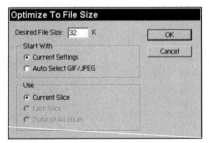

## Exploring the Save for Web Dialog Box

You can access the Save for Web dialog box by choosing File⇨Save for Web from the menu bar. The dialog box, shown in Figure 2-2, has four tabbed pages, a tool palette, a clutch of options and menus, and a generous preview window that you can use to evaluate your results.

The following sections briefly describe each of the dialog box's key components.

### Tool palette and image preview

At the left edge of the dialog box is the Tool palette, which includes four tools and a preview box that closely resemble their counterparts in the main Photoshop program. Here's a quick rundown, from top to bottom, of the tool palette options:

✔ **Hand tool (H):** Select this tool and then drag in the preview window to move the image.

✔ **Slice tool (K):** Use this tool to divide an image into slices. For more information on creating slices, see Chapter 3 of this book.

✔ **Zoom tool (Z):** Use this tool or press down the spacebar and press Ctrl in Windows (or press down the spacebar and press ⌘ on the Mac) to zoom in. To zoom out, press the spacebar and press Alt in Windows. On the Mac, press the spacebar and then press Option.

> If you're using the Hand tool and you want to zoom in and out, you don't have to press the spacebar when you zoom in or out. If the Zoom tool is selected, hold down Alt or Option to zoom in and out, respectively.

✔ **Eyedropper (I):** Use the Eyedropper to sample colors in the preview image. If you're sampling in a GIF or PNG image, the Color Table is available and, if shown, highlights the color you sample in the table. For more information on GIF, PNG, and JPEG file formats, see Chapter 1 of this book.

✔ **Eyedropper color:** This patch shows the color most recently sampled by the Eyedropper. Click the patch to access the Color Picker and select a color of your choice.

✔ **Toggle Slices Visibility (Q):** Click this icon to turn the display of slices on or off.

**Figure 2-2**

**Tool palette**

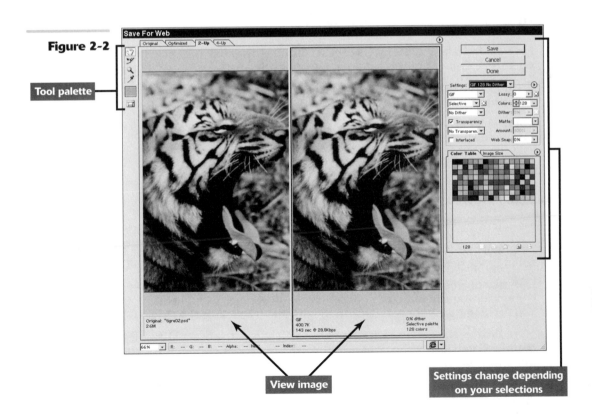

**View image**

**Settings change depending on your selections**

Book
**IX**
Chapter
**2**

The Save for Web dialog box also lets you control your view of images. Along the bottom of the window, you see these options:

- ✔ **Zoom text box:** Type in a zoom value here, or choose zoom levels from 12.5 percent to 1,600 percent, or select Fit on Screen.

- ✔ **Status bar:** This bar shows the RGB values of the color under the cursor, the value of any alpha channel, and the Hex values and Index.

- ✔ **Browser preview:** Click to preview the image in the browser selected from the pop-up menu.

The majority of the Save for Web dialog box shows you a preview of the image you're working with:

- ✔ **Preview windows:** The tabs at the top of the window show the original image, or one of three other optional views. See "Introducing Preview options," later in this chapter.

- ✔ **Preview status:** This area shows the size of the original image, as well as various parameters of optimized images, such as download speed and number of colors.

## Change settings

Along the right side of the window, you can make adjustments to the various color, file, and size settings for your image. Here's a rundown of what you see:

- ✔ **Save/Cancel/Done buttons:** Use these buttons to save an optimized image, cancel the operation, or indicate that you're done optimizing.

- ✔ **Settings:** You can choose settings, including the type of file. These settings are described in detail later in this chapter.

- ✔ **Color Table:** Shown only when a GIF or PNG image is selected in the Preview window, this tab displays the color table for the optimized image.

- ✔ **Image Size:** Click this tab to resize your image.

## Introducing Preview options

You have four Preview options:

- ✔ **Original:** Fills the preview with the original image, giving you a chance to review it, zoom to the desired size, or divide the image into slices to be optimized separately.

- ✔ **Optimized:** Fills the preview window with the optimized version of the original image. If you like, you can make all your optimization settings with only this view available. You can compare your results with the original by clicking the Original tab.

- ✔ **2-Up:** Divides the preview window in two and shows the original on the left and the optimized version on the right, with information about each in the status box below the previews.

- ✔ **4-Up:** Divides the preview window into four panes. The original image is shown in the upper-left corner, and three different optimized versions are shown in the other three panes, as shown in Figure 2-3.

**Figure 2-3**

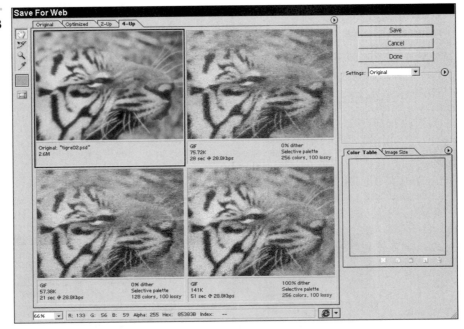

---

# Optimizing Your Image

Before getting into the nitty gritty of working with the tools and options described in the preceding sections, I'm going to give you a quick overview of the procedures for using the Save for Web dialog box. To optimize an image, you follow these steps:

**1.** Open the image in Photoshop.

**2.** Choose File⇨Save for Web.

**3.** Select the kind of preview you want to use by clicking one of these four tabs:

 ✔ Original

 ✔ Optimized

 ✔ 2-Up

 ✔ 4-Up

 Although the upper-left pane displays the original image by default, you can select this pane and change into a fourth optimized preview.

**4.** Click in any of the four panes and, in the Settings area of the dialog box, choose the kind of optimization you'd like to apply to that version.

These options are explained in detail throughout the rest of this chapter.

**5.** After you have fine-tuned the optimization settings and are satisfied with the results, select one of the previews and click Save.

Your image is stored on your hard disk with those optimization settings.

**6.** Repeat Step 5 to create as many different versions as you like, using a different optimization method for each.

## JPEG Options

To optimize an image as a JPEG, choose the file format by doing one of the following:

✔ Choose one of the preset JPEG optimization settings from the Settings pop-up menu:

> ▸ **JPEG High:** High quality (low compression)
>
> ▸ **JPEG Medium:** Medium quality (medium compression)
>
> ▸ **JPEG Low:** Low quality (high compression)

 If you save your own presets for optimization settings, they'll appear in the same list.

✔ Choose the JPEG file format and Maximum, High, Medium, or Low directly from the File Format and Compression pop-up menus, shown in Figure 2-4.

**Figure 2-4**

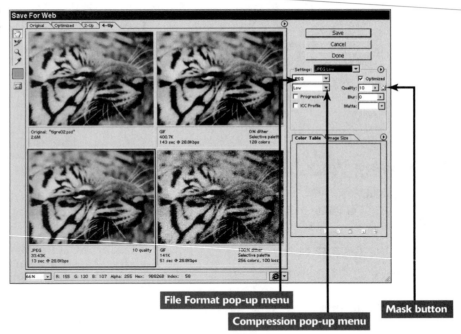

File Format pop-up menu

Compression pop-up menu

Mask button

Then select any or all of these options:

✔ **Progressive:** This option creates a low-resolution version of the image that downloads quickly (much like an interlaced GIF) and that is followed by progressively detailed overlays until the full image is seen. Again, not all browsers can benefit from this setting. You can find out more about interlacing in Chapter 1 of this book.

✔ **ICC Profile:** Choose this option to embed the ICC color profile of the image in the JPEG file. Very few browsers can correct the colors they display based on this information, and because it adds about 3K to your file size, you're better off leaving it deselected for now. For more on color management, see Book II, Chapter 3.

✔ **Optimized:** This option creates a JPEG file that is occasionally a little smaller at any quality setting (and often doesn't change the size at all), but not all browsers can display images with this type of optimization. If you feel your page will be viewed by many users with older browsers, you might want to forego the small additional size reduction.

✔ **Quality:** You can specify an exact quality/compression level by using a slider or by typing a value into the text box.

✔ **Blur:** Images that are slightly blurred can be squeezed more thoroughly by using the JPEG compression scheme. If your image still looks good with a tiny bit of blur applied, you can use a setting of 0.1 to 0.5 to gain a smaller file size. However, most likely you won't want to sacrifice image detail, in which case it is better to go with a higher rate of compression and leave the blur setting at 0.

✔ **Matte:** This setting lets you specify a color to use to fill in pixels that were completely or partially transparent in the original. Partially transparent pixels are blended with the color you choose. Select a color from the pop-up menu, or click in the color swatch to select a color from the Color Picker.

You can save any customized JPEG settings you make by choosing Save Settings from the dialog box's palette menu. Your stored settings then appear in the Settings menu for reuse.

---

### Selectively changing quality levels in an image

You can use the Mask button next to the Quality box to selectively apply different quality levels to different areas of your image. This is called Weighted Optimization. To use this option, follow these steps:

*1.* **Click the Mask button.**

*2.* **Select whether you want to use all text layers, all vector shape layers, or both. You can also select one of the alpha channels.**

For more on vector shapes, see Book IV, Chapter 2. For more on alpha channels, see Book VI, Chapter 1.

*3.* **Adjust the minimum and maximum quality sliders in the Quality bar to the levels you want.**

For example, you can specify a minimum quality level of 19 percent and a maximum quality level of 62 percent. Photoshop will use the grayscale values found in the masks and/ or alpha channels you've selected to apply those quality levels. The lightest areas of the mask will be optimized at the highest quality level you've specified, whereas the darkest areas of the mask will be optimized at the lowest quality level you've specified.

See the GIF optimization options later in this chapter for more ways to weight optimization by using masks.

*4.* **Click OK to apply the weighted optimization.**

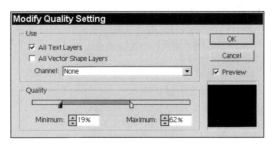

You have some additional options in the Palette menu, including a choice of browser dither schemes, whether or not you want to hide slices created automatically (see Chapter 3 in this book for more on slices), whether to include the color compensation option, and the display of the estimated time for downloading.

## GIF Options

The GIF options, shown in Figure 2-5, are generally different from those available for JPEG, as befits the very different nature of the GIF image.

**Figure 2-5**

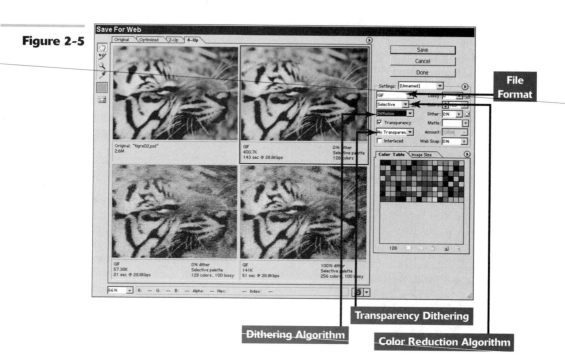

## File Format

To optimize an image as a GIF, choose the file format by doing one of the following:

✔ Choose one of the preset optimization settings from the Settings pop-up menu. You'll find presets for GIF 128, GIF 64, and GIF 32 (both dithered and undithered), plus GIF Web Palette. The figures represent the number of colors in the GIF image.

✔ Choose the GIF file format directly from the File Format menu.

## Color Reduction Algorithm

This menu includes three categories of options for creating a palette for the color table:

✔ **Dynamic:** The options in this category include

▶ **Perceptual:** Favors colors the human eye is most sensitive to

▶ **Selective:** Weights the colors toward those considered to be Web safe

▶ **Adaptive:** Builds a color table emphasizing the portion of the spectrum containing the colors that are most commonly found in the image — for example, greens in scenic photos or flesh tones in portraits

With the dynamic options, a new palette of colors is collected every time you change or optimize the image.

✔ **Fixed:** These options include Web (only browser-safe colors), Mac OS and Windows (the palettes used by the Mac and Windows operating systems, respectively), and Black and White. The colors available are fixed, but the actual colors used vary with the image they are applied to.

✔ **Custom:** This option uses a fixed color palette created by the user, but which is not updated automatically when the image is modified.

### Dithering Algorithm

Choose the dithering scheme used to simulate colors that can't be represented by the hues in the color table. Your choices are *Diffusion* (a random type of dithering), *Pattern* (a regular, halftone screenlike pattern), *Noise* (a random pattern that doesn't spread across pixels), and *None*. You can also choose the amount of dithering to allow in the Dither slider/box.

You can apply weighted optimization to dithering by clicking the Mask button next to the Dither box, and selecting the mask and amount of dithering as described in the sidebar "Selectively changing quality levels in an image."

### Transparency and Matte

Choose Transparency and Matte options to control how transparent pixels are handled during optimization. Select a matte color from the menu, or click the matte color patch and choose a hue from the Color Picker. You'll want the matte color to match the background color of the Web page as closely as possible.

✔ **Select transparency and a matte color.** This option keeps transparent pixels in the original image transparent, and blends partially transparent pixels with a matte color you choose.

✔ **Select transparency and no matte color.** Choosing None from the Matte menu makes transparent pixels and those that are more than 50 percent transparent fully transparent, while rendering pixels that are 50 percent or less transparent as fully opaque.

✔ **Select no transparency and a matte color.** Deselecting transparency and choosing a matte color fills pixels that are completely transparent with the matte color you select, and blends them.

Book
**IX**
Chapter
**2**

Consult an HTML manual to find out how to determine the hexadecimal values of the background colors of the page. Hexadecimal colors are described in Chapter 1 of this book.

### Transparency Dithering

Set the options for Transparency Dithering. This option determines how Photoshop will dither pixels that are partially transparent:

- ✔ **No Transparency Dither:** Leaves partially transparent pixels in the image alone.

- ✔ **Diffusion Transparency Dither:** Adds a random pattern to partially transparent pixels. Like diffusion dither, the pattern is spread across adjacent pixels. You can specify the degree of dithering with the Amount box/slider.

- ✔ **Pattern Transparency Dither:** Applies a halftonelike pattern to the pixels that are partially transparent.

- ✔ **Noise Transparency Dither:** Applies a random, nondiffused pattern to the semi-transparent pixels.

### Interlaced

Choose whether you want the image *interlaced* (to appear gradually in the browser when it downloads) or not interlaced.

### Lossy

Select the amount of lossy file compression allowed in the Lossy slider/text box. Lossy compression can also be given weight from masks by clicking the Mask button and applying the mask settings as described earlier in the chapter.

### Colors

Choose the number of colors in the image from the Colors list. Select a specific number of colors from 2 to 256, or choose Auto to let Photoshop choose the number of colors automatically based on the colors in the color table.

### Web Snap

Use the Web Snap slider/box to specify a tolerance level that will automatically change pixels that are within that tolerance level of a Web-safe color to that Web-safe hue. The higher the value, the more Web-safe colors there are in the image.

### PNG Options

If you elect to create a PNG file, two sets of options are available for the two types of PNG files: PNG-8 (256 colors) and PNG-24 (16.8 million colors).

The PNG-8 options, shown in Figure 2-6, are similar to the GIF options (described earlier in the chapter), with the following exceptions:

✔ Lossy compression is not available for PNG-8.

✔ Weighted optimization can be applied to the color reduction algorithms, which are otherwise similar to those used with GIF.

**Figure 2-6**

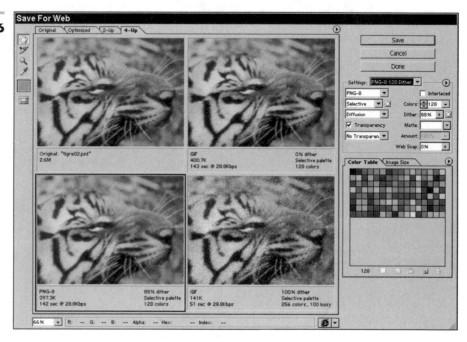

The PNG-24 options include only interlacing and the transparency/matte options described under GIF options, as shown in Figure 2-7.

## Image Size

The Save for Web dialog box includes its own version of the Image Size dialog box, which resides on a separate tab, next to the Color Table tab, as shown in Figure 2-8. Although slightly different in appearance, it operates the same as the Image Size dialog box. You can specify a new width and height for the image or change the size by a percentage. You also can select the type of resampling performed when resizing the image, although you'll almost always want to use the default Bicubic algorithm. For more information on changing image size, see Book II, Chapter 1.

Figure 2-7

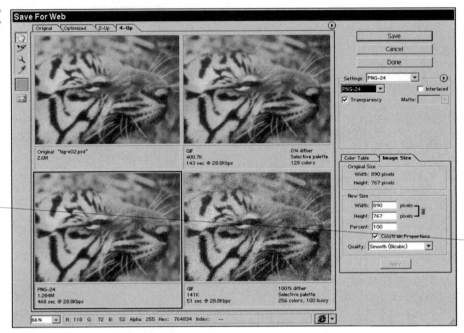

Figure 2-8

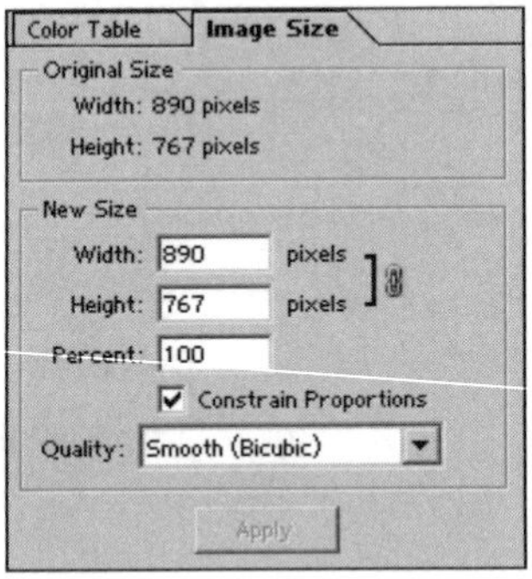

## Optimizing Colors

You can manually shift one or more colors toward Web-safety (discussed in more detail in Chapter 1 of this book). You can also change specific colors in an image that has already been converted to 256 colors (see Book II, Chapter 2, for details) to make them Web safe. Just follow these steps:

**1.** **With the color table visible, choose the colors you want to convert.**

These are your options:

✔ Click an individual color in the color table to select only that color.

✔ Hold down the Ctrl key (or ⌘ key on the Mac) to add additional colors to your selection.

✔ Hold down the Shift key and click in an additional color to select all the colors between the last color selected and the additional color.

✔ To choose all colors in the color table that are already Web Safe

(or all those that are not Web safe), choose All Web Safe Colors or All Non-Web Safe Colors from the color table's palette menu.

**2.** **Choose either Web Shift or Shift Selected Colors to Web Palette from the color table palette menu.**

 You can also select colors in the color table and convert them to transparency by clicking the Transparency button in the color table, or lock them to keep them from being removed by clicking the Lock Color button. To remove colors from the color table, select the colors and click the trash button.

# Slicing Your Image

3

Are the images on your Web page an attraction or a distraction? Do they invite visitors to explore your page, or send them fleeing to the Back button? Attractive images that load quickly are the key to captivating those who visit your site. Unfortunately, even the most gorgeous images will never be seen at all if they take forever to download.

Slicing images is a great tool for improving the download speed of your Web pages. Instead of loading up your page with huge pictures that download slowly, you can slice up your images into byte-sized pieces optimized for speed, appearance, and special functions such as links. Photoshop creates the HTML (the language used to create Web pages) needed to reconstruct your images on your page.

This chapter introduces you to the Slice tool found in Photoshop. ImageReady has a similar tool and expanded slicing capabilities, but Photoshop's built-in slicer-dicer has more than enough versatility to get you started.

## Why Slice?

Although speedy broadband connections are becoming more common, a huge number of Internet cruisers are still using dial-up connections with top speeds of 56 Kbps or slower. For these users, nothing is more painful than clicking a link and watching a blank page laboriously download a few pixels at a time. When confronted with a page like this, users are likely to click their Back buttons and move on.

Your solutions, as Webmaster, fall into several categories:

✔ **Use images with very small dimensions.** Buttons and graphic rules download quickly. However, they are usually ornamental or functional rather than centerpieces of your page design.

✔ **Select the best format for your image.** Choosing the JPEG or GIF format when appropriate can make a significant difference in how quickly your image downloads. You find out about these formats and how to make this determination in Chapter 1 of this book.

✔ **Optimize the heck out of the image.** One image in a particular format can be five or ten times as large as the same image in the same format, depending on how you've optimized it. You find out how to optimize your images in Chapter 2 of this book.

✔ **Slice your image into pieces.** Individually optimize each piece for its intended purpose: appearance, download speed, or a combination of the two. With a little care, you can take a complicated image and divide it into slices that look as good or better than the original, and download much faster, too.

Another point to keep in mind is that visitors will be using different screen resolutions. If you're happily cruising the Internet at 1024 x 768 resolution, that doesn't mean you should include really large images on your pages (even if sliced and optimized). Other users with the same screen resolution you use may have set their browser windows to a smaller size or may be using displays with a maximum of 800 x 600 pixels or smaller. The ability to slice images doesn't mean you can fill your screen with gigantic graphics.

Slices also let you treat different parts of an image in different ways, associating some with Web links to other images or pages, just as you can do with image maps. (Image maps are discussed briefly in Chapter 5 of this book.)

 Design your Web pages to fit your audience. If your site is geared toward the masses, make the pages a maximum of 800 x 600 pixels. If it is aimed at a specialized high-end audience, then you can go as large as 1024 x 768 pixels.

## Slicing Up Images

You can create slices from many different kinds of images. Figure 3-1 shows a fanciful fictitious Web page, but with the kinds of images you might want to slice.

For example, you might be interested in slicing the menu of choices on the left side of the figure so that you can include links to the individual pages referenced. The lower image of the four foreign lands offers even more motivation for slicing. It's fairly huge and would load much more quickly if you sliced it up into four sections. Each slice is also a candidate for a link that would take visitors to a page devoted to that particular country.

**Figure 3-1**

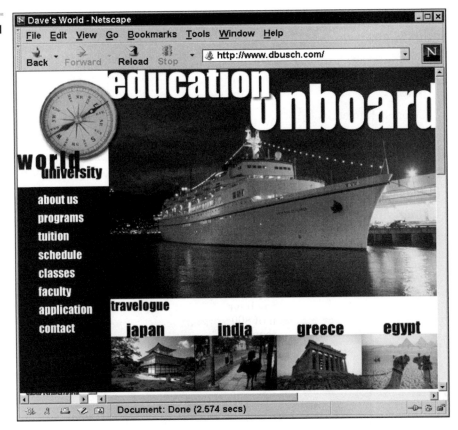

## Types of slices

Photoshop enables you to create several different types of slices:

- ✔ **User slices:** You create these slices by defining areas of the image.
- ✔ **Layer slices:** These slices are created from layers of an image.
- ✔ **Auto slices:** Photoshop creates these slices automatically to account for the rest of the image when you've sliced a bit out of it.

You find out more about the differences between these kinds of slices throughout the rest of this chapter.

Book
**IX**
Chapter
**3**

▼ ▼ ▼ ▼ ▼ ▼ ▼ ▼ ▼ ▼ ▼ ▼ ▼ ▼ ▼ ▼ ▼ ▼ ▼ ▼ ▼ ▼ ▼ ▼ ▼ ▼ ▼ ▼ ▼ ▼ ▼ ▼ ▼ ▼ ▼ ▼ ▼ ▼

## Creating slices

To slice up an image into user slices, just follow these steps:

1. **Select the Slice tool from the Tool palette.**

   Or press K to activate it.

   When you choose the Slice tool, an indicator graphic appears in the upper-left corner of the image, marking the whole image as Slice 01, even before you've selected a new slice.

2. **Drag with the Slice tool to select the part of the image you want to slice.**

   For example, select the entire Japan area in the lower edge.

   A solid slice selection box appears around the new slice, with handles at each corner and at the sides, top, and bottom. The slice is assigned a number and icon in its upper-left corner.

3. **Repeat Step 2 to slice the image into as many individual portions as you want.**

   For example, continue to select the other countries to slice the image into individual portions.

   Each of your user slices is assigned its own slice number and icon, as shown in Figure 3-2.

Figure 3-2

## Slicing options

The steps in the preceding section show the slicing operation in its simplest form. You do have some additional options, however, as described in the following list:

✔ **Use a fixed size or fixed aspect ratio (proportion).** Choose *Fixed Size* from the Style pop-up menu in the Options bar and type a width and height in pixels in the Width and Height boxes. Or choose *Fixed Aspect Ratio* and type the relative proportions you want to use (that is, 1:2, 3:4, and so forth) in the Width and Height boxes. The Slice tool is constrained to the size or proportions you specify.

You might want to use Fixed Size to create equal-size slices in an image, especially an image composed of similar-sized elements, and Fixed Aspect Ratio to create slices that have similar proportions.

 If you've already created a slice that's the right size to apply to another portion of your image, you can duplicate the slice by dragging the slice while holding down the Alt key (Option key on the Mac). Drag the new slice to the location where you want to apply it.

✔ **Create a square slice.** Hold down the Shift key as you drag a slice's boundaries to create a slice in a perfect square when the Slice or Slice Selection tool is active.

✔ **Create guides.** If your slices will make up a grid of horizontal and vertical lines, you can create guides that mark their boundaries. Click the Slices from Guides button in the Options bar to automatically slice the image by using these guides.

✔ **Put each slice in its own layer.** You can put each portion of the image you want to define as a slice in its own layer. Then just select the layer and choose Layer⊅ New Layer Based Slice. This is how you create a *rollover state* (an action taken on a Web page when the mouse passes over, clicks on, or leaves a defined area). You can find more information on rollovers in Chapter 5 of this book.

*Auto slices* are slices created by Photoshop to account for the area you haven't defined as a user slice or layer slice. They're shown on-screen as dotted lines to differentiate them from the solid lines that define user slices and layer slices. Auto slices also have gray slice numbers and icons, as opposed to the blue numbers and icons used to represent their nonautomatic siblings. If you want to change an auto slice to a user slice (say, it encompasses an area you were going to slice anyway), select the slice and choose Promote to User Slice from the Options bar.

# Selecting and Modifying Slices

Each slice is assigned a dynamic number, starting with the slice at the top-left corner of the image, and going from left to right and top to bottom. As you rearrange slices, the numbers are updated. Each slice also receives an icon that reflects its type, as shown in Figure 3-3. You can have user slices with and without content, layer slices, slices that contain rollovers, and slices that have links associated with them.

**Figure 3-3**

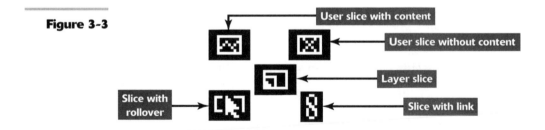

## Showing/hiding slices and slice numbers

You can show or hide slices and show or hide the slice numbers:

✔ **Show or hide slices:** Choose View⊅Show⊅Slices.

✔ **Show or hide slice numbers:** Choose Edit⊅Preferences⊅Grid, Guides, & Slices (or Photoshop⊅Preferences⊅Grid, Guides, & Slices under Mac OS X) and select or deselect the Show Slice Numbers option.

Book
**IX**
Chapter
**3**

### Changing the color of the lines

To change the color used to represent slices, choose Edit⊏>Preferences⊏>Grid, Guides, & Slices (or Photoshop⊏>Preferences⊏>Grid, Guides, & Slices under Mac OS X) and select a color from the Line Color pop-up menu under Slices.

### Selecting slices

To make any changes to a slice, you must first select it. You can select a slice by clicking any visible portion of the slice with the Slice Select tool. Here are a few tips for using this tool:

✔ **Switch from the Slice tool to the Slice Select tool:** Hold down the Shift key and press K when the Slice tool is active. The Slice Select tool becomes the default tool.

✔ **Alternate between the Slice tool and the Slice Select tool:** Hold down the Ctrl key (⌘ key on the Mac) to temporarily activate the other tool. For example, if you're busy slicing images and want to quickly select a slice, hold down the Ctrl (or ⌘ key) and click the slice you want to select. When you release the key, the Slice tool becomes the default tool again.

To remove a slice, select the slice and press the Delete or Backspace keys (Delete on the Mac). To remove all slices from an image and start over, choose View⊏>Clear Slices. To protect slices from accidental modifications, choose View⊏>Lock Slices.

### Resizing and moving slices

You can easily resize a user slice or move it to a new location. If you want to resize or move a layer slice, first select it and then click the Promote to User Slice button in the Options bar to change it into a user slice.

✔ **Move a user slice:** Select the slice and position the cursor inside the slice's borders. Then drag to its new position. To help keep slices aligned evenly, you can hold down the Shift key to restrict movement horizontally, vertically, or to 45-degree angles.

✔ **Place a slice at specific coordinates in your image:** Click the Slice Options button on the Options bar or use the Slice Select tool to double-click inside the slice you want to position. The Slice Options dialog box, as it appears with an image slice, is shown in Figure 3-4. In the X box, type the number of pixels you want between the left side of the slice and the left border of the image. In the Y box, type the number of pixels you want between the top edge of the slice and the top border of the image.

✔ **Resize a user slice in any direction:** Grab one of the corner or side handles of a selected slice and drag.

✔ **Use pixel dimensions to resize a user slice:** Use the Slice Select tool to double-click inside the slice you want to resize. Then type the width and height, in pixels, in the W and H boxes.

To simplify positioning slices, choose View⊏>Snap To and select Guides and/or Slices to tell Photoshop you want to snap slices to guides or other slices. Then choose View⊏>Snap to turn on the snapping feature.

✔ **Duplicate a slice:** Select the slice with the Slice Select tool and then Alt+drag (Option+drag on the Mac).

**Figure 3-4**

Slice Options

Slice Type: Image

Name: Japan

URL:

Target:

Message Text:

Alt Tag:

OK

Cancel

Dimensions

X: 177     W: 155

Y: 471     H: 129

Slice Background Type: None    Background Color:

▼▼▼▼▼▼▼▼▼▼▼▼▼▼▼▼▼▼▼▼▼▼▼▼▼▼▼▼▼▼▼▼▼▼▼▼

## Dividing a slice

You can further divide a slice you've made by following these steps:

1. **Using the Slice Select tool, select the user slice or auto slice you want to divide.**

2. **Select the Divide Slice check box in the Options bar.**

   The Divide Slice dialog box appears, as shown in Figure 3-5.

3. **Select the appropriate check box(es) to divide the slice horizontally, vertically, or both.**

4. **Enter a number in the Slices Down, Evenly Spaced or the Slices Across, Evenly Spaced text boxes to split up your slice into that number of equal slices. Alternatively, specify a size per slice in the Pixels Per Slice box.**

5. **Select the Preview option if you want to view the new slices in the document window.**

6. **Click OK to divide the slice.**

**Figure 3-5**

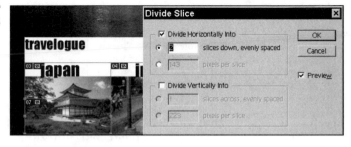

Divide Slice

☑ Divide Horizontally Into
○ 2    slices down, evenly spaced
○ 143  pixels per slice

☐ Divide Vertically Into
○ 1    slices across, evenly spaced
○ 229  pixels per slice

OK

Cancel

☑ Preview

Book
**IX**
Chapter
**3**

## Stacking slices

Slices can overlap, but the top slice in a stack of overlapping slices defines the area allocated to them. You can usually resize slices so that they closely fit the areas you want to define, but overlapping allows you to create custom-shaped slices. You might want to change the stacking order of slices so that the slice encompasses the exact area you want to define.

To do so, select the slice you want to reorder. Then in the Options bar, shown in Figure 3-6, click one of the following icons (left to right):

✔ **Bring to Front** to move the selected slice to the top of the stack

✔ **Bring Forward** to move the selected slice up one layer in the stack

✔ **Send Backward** to move the selected slice down one layer in the stack

✔ **Send to Back** to move the selected slice to the bottom of the stack

**Figure 3-6**

## Setting Slice Options

Okay, here's the part you've been waiting for: What do you *do* with these slices, anyway? In the Slice Options dialog box (discussed briefly earlier in this chapter), you can control how the slices are used in a Web browser.

You can set or view the options for any slice by double-clicking the slice with the Slice Select tool or by clicking the Slice Options button in the Options bar. Either command opens the Slice Options dialog box, shown in Figure 3-7. Here are the parameters you can set in this dialog box:

**Figure 3-7**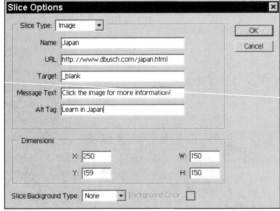

✔ **Slice Type:** You can choose Image (the usual choice) or No Image. Select No Image if you have a slice that contains only a solid background color or text because a nonimage slice downloads *very* quickly. If the slice is part of a larger image and contains no actual image content, you can speed up the download of that portion considerably.

 If you choose No Image, the Slice Options dialog box changes, providing space for you to enter the HTML tags or text you want to appear in the slice, as shown in Figure 3-8.

**Figure 3-8**

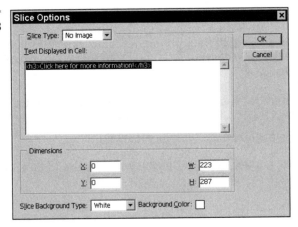

✔ **Name:** In this text box, you can enter a custom name for your image slice (unless you chose No Image as the Slice Type), usually based on its content. You can name slices automatically by using the Slice Output Options, described in the next section.

✔ **URL:** If you enter a Web address in this text box, clicking anywhere in the slice links to this address. The slice behaves like a defined portion of an image map. (See Chapter 5 of this book for more on image maps.)

✔ **Target:** Briefly, the *target* is the default frame (if your Web page has frames) that will be accessed in the URL you specified in the URL text box. Describing how to write HTML tags (the language used by Web browsers) is beyond the scope of this book, but if you're interested in more information, check out *HTML 4 For Dummies*, 3rd Edition, by Ed Tittel, Natanya Pitts, and Chelsea Valentine (Wiley Publishing, Inc.).

✔ **Message Text:** In this text box, type a message you'd like to appear in the browser's status bar when the mouse passes over the slice. If you enter nothing, the URL is displayed.

✔ **Alt Tag:** This is important text that's too often neglected. Alt text appears in non-graphical browsers (that is, browsers that show only text and not images) and also pops up as sort of a *tool tip* when the mouse passes over the slice. Many people still use nongraphical browsers, particularly users who are visually impaired and rely on text-to-speech software to translate Web pages to sound. Alt text allows these folks to "see" a description of your image and serves as a handy explanation for users who have graphical browsers. The Alt text also shows up if users suffer a lengthy wait while images download.

✔ **Dimensions:** These text boxes show the width and height of the slice and its coordinate location in the image. You generally won't want to change these settings at this time.

✔ **Slice Background Type:** Choose a color for the transparent portion of an image slice (for example, when you're using a transparent GIF) or the full area of a No Image slice. Your choices include None, Matte, Black, White, or Other. Click the Background Color patch to select a specific hue.

Book
**IX**
Chapter
**3**

## Saving Your Slices

After you've defined your slices and set all the options, you can save your image with its slices. Use the Save for Web feature (discussed in Chapter 2 of this book) to optimize your slices. Photoshop then lets you

 Choose the best parameters for each slice. For example, you can save a slice containing line graphics or graphical text as a GIF, or a slice containing many colors as a JPEG.

 Optimize each slice for appearance and download speed.

Photoshop also saves the HTML code needed to display your slices and link them to the URLs you specified.

 **PUTTING IT TOGETHER**

### Creating a Splash Page Mockup

Many designers conceptualize and mock up their Web pages in Photoshop before they compile the components in an HTML editor such as GoLive, Dreamweaver, or FrontPage.

If you plan on really getting into preparing graphics for Web design purposes, I highly recommend getting a book solely devoted to the topic, where you'll find tons of great tips targeting your specific needs.

While the exact steps for designing and mocking up a Web page vary widely according to the style and nature of the page, this example will at least give you some idea of the process. For example, you might want to create a logo, button, or other standard element that appears on your page, identifying it as yours and yours alone.

Follow these steps to create a splash page with great images, buttons, and logos:

*1.* **Open all the images you want to use in the page.**

For example, you can create a splash page (also called a home page in some circles) for a pseudo company called *adventuretrekker.com*.

Before you sit down in front of the computer, have an idea of what you are going to create. I always do some rough sketches of any page I design. That way, I'm not staring at the monitor waiting for my page to magically take form.

For the lowdown on prepping your images for the Web, check out Chapter 1 of this book.

 Rather than give you a million cross-references in this exercise, let me just provide a blanket caveat that there are lots of techniques, such as selecting, masking, blending, applying effects, and using layers, that are covered in detail elsewhere in the book.

**2.** **Choose File⇨New to create the canvas you will use to composite your Web page.**

The New dialog box appears.

**3.** **Specify your dimensions, mode, resolution, and contents.**

The mode should always be RGB. You can set your contents to any color or to transparent. The resolution is really irrelevant because it's the pixel dimensions that count for on-screen viewing. However, people often use 72 ppi to make it easy.

The dimensions depend on the demographics of your audience. If you want to design a page that anyone in the world can view, even those in less-developed countries who are still cruising on old 486 PCs, you may want to stick with 640 x 480 pixels. The page can be even smaller if you want to take into account the browser menu bar and controls. If you're designing for the middle of the road, 800 x 600 pixels may be the ticket, again a little less to account for the browser controls. If your audience is made up of sophisticated and high-end users only, you

can get away with 1024 x 768 pixels. I'm sticking with 800 x 600, 72 ppi, and white contents for my splash page. You can also give your file a name in the Name text box.

 You don't have to create a new blank canvas to composite your multiple images. Instead, you can use an image as your canvas and then drag your supporting images onto it. Just be sure that the base image is the correct mode and dimensions.

**4.** **Make your first selection. Then with the Move tool, drag and drop the image onto your blank canvas.**

For my page, I'm using the image on which I created a snowstorm in Book VII, Chapter 2. I made a rectangular selection with the Rectangular Marquee tool and dragged the image onto my white canvas. I left an open area at the top where my navigation bar will go.

 Be sure to name all of your layers (double-click the name in the Layers palette). Creating a splash page can require a lot of layers, so layer management is essential.

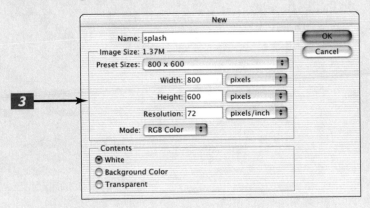

**5.** **Make your second selection and again drag and drop the image onto your splash page.**

For my page, I am using an image of a polar bear sticking his head out of a hole in the ice.

**6.** **Apply any layer masks you need for your images to blend in with the canvas or the other images.**

Click the Add Layer Mask icon at the bottom of the Layers palette. Use the painting tools to create your desired mask.

My polar bear doesn't quite look like he actually is part of the snowy landscape background, so I applied a layer mask and blended him in

accordingly. I then used the Brush tool, with a feathered tip, set to Airbrush mode with a Flow Rate of 10%, to paint around the edges of my polar bear. I also added a layer mask on my snow layer because I wanted to mask out some of the snow over my polar bear so that he would stand out a little better.

**7.** **If you have prepared a logo, drag it onto the splash page.**

If you're using a vector art logo, such as one created in Illustrator, just choose File➪Open. Specify your rasterization settings. If the logo is at least 100% of its intended size, rasterize it as RGB, 72 ppi, and leave the dimensions at the default setting.

**8.** **Create the type and/or buttons for your navigation bar.**

I'm not a big fan of buttons unless they are simple and understated. I prefer to use type only for my navigation bars. But hey, it's a free world; if you like buttons, go for it.

 Be sure that your type looks legible on-screen. Check out Chapter 1 of this book for tips on making your type look its best on-screen. I used the font Verdana for both my logo and navigation bar, using 24 points and 12 points respectively. I set my anti-aliasing to Crisp.

 You can create buttons quickly and easily in Photoshop. Using the Marquee or Shape tools, draw a shape such as a rectangle, an ellipse, or even a custom shape on a separate layer. Open the Styles palette and, with that layer active, simply click a preset style. Several preset libraries are dedicated to buttons. You'll find them at the bottom of the palette options menu.

**9.** **Apply any layer effects or styles to your images or type.**

I kept it simple and just applied a drop shadow and inner bevel to my logo type and a drop shadow to my logo. Be sure to keep Use Global Light selected so that your light source for effects is consistent among all your elements.

**10.** **Add title text to your page and apply any layer effects or styles desired.**

I added my title type in the font Impact by using two sizes. Because my type overlapped and was offset, I put it on two different layers. I then applied layer effects — drop shadow, inner glow, and inner bevel. Of course, you can do this step concurrently with Steps 7 and 8, if you want. Then again, you can do any of the steps in whatever order you desire. There are no hard and fast rules, so just let your creative juices take over.

▼ **CONTINUED**

▼ **CONTINUED**

**11.** If you want to, you can now slice your image into chunks, which can then be optimized separately.

Although not mandatory, sometimes slicing your image can help your page download more quickly. And a Web page with slices loads as pieces, so users don't have to wait for the entire page to load at once.

Slicing also allows you to take chunks of your page and apply separate optimization settings to them in the Save for Web dialog box.

**12.** Use the Save for Web dialog box to compress the slices at different rates according to the quality needed.

You can also apply image maps and rollovers to slices in Image Ready. If it makes more sense to apply your slices to individual *layers*, rather than the image as a whole, you can do that as well.

To preview how your image would look in a browser without HTML coding it, save a copy in the JPEG file format. Launch your browser and choose File⇨Open. Your image appears in the browser window.

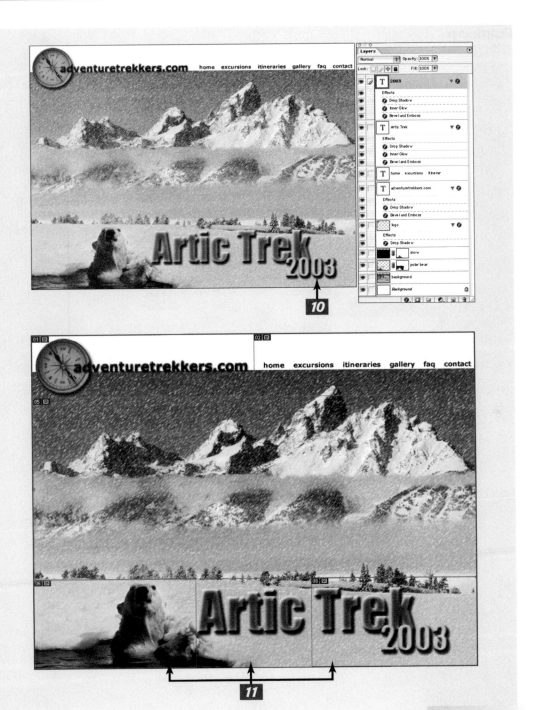

▼ **CONTINUED**

▼ **CONTINUED**

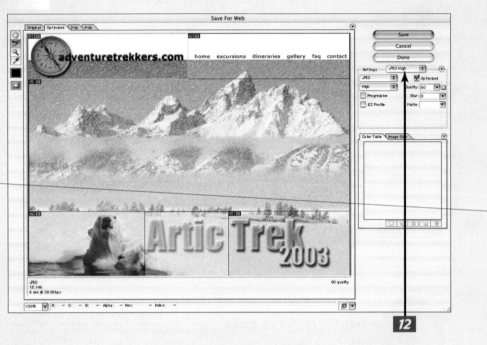

# Creating a Web Photo Gallery

**B**y now, you may be so proud of your Photoshop artistry that you want to show it off to the world on a Web page. Photoshop has a crafty Web page construction tool built right in, so even if you don't know anything about HTML — except that it's an acronym you hear a lot — you can create a Web-based display page for your images with very little trouble.

All you need to do is show Photoshop the location of the images you want to include on your Web page, select a style, enter a little information, and sit back and watch while your favorite image editor does the rest. Of course, you still need to upload the resulting Web page and images to a hosting service on the Internet and tell all your friends and colleagues where to find it. But that's not too difficult.

If you want to know more about creating Web pages and posting them for anyone and everyone with a browser to see, check out *Creating Web Pages All-in-One Desk Reference For Dummies* by Emily A. Vander Veer (Wiley Publishing, Inc.).

 A Web gallery is a Web page that includes small *thumbnails* — miniature versions of your main images — and links that enable visitors to view those images in a larger size. But using thumbnails isn't your only option. The gallery can also showcase one image at a time in large form and change the view at intervals, just like a slide show.

## Planning Your Page

Creating a gallery requires using the Web Gallery dialog box, which isn't all that tough to use — after you know what your choices are. Here's a rundown:

✔ **Styles:** Your style options include a variety of horizontal and vertical layouts in several different color schemes.

✔ **Folders:** Choosing a folder path is as simple as remembering where you saved the files you want to share online.

✔ **Options:** Your options run the gamut:

▸ **Banner:** The optional banner displays certain information about your page. Enter a name for your site, the name of the photographer, contact information, the date, and the font style and type for the banner.

▸ **Large Images:** With this option, you're able to control how the full-size images appear when displayed. You can have them displayed in their normal size or resize them to small, medium, large, or custom-specified pixel widths. You can even specify JPEG compression/quality, add a border, and show or hide the filename, caption, credit, title, or copyright information.

 You must enter the information for captions, credit, title, copyrights, and so forth for each image separately by choosing File➪File Info. In the File Info dialog box that appears, you'll find boxes to enter all this information. Photoshop then saves that information with the image file and uses it with the Web Photo Gallery tool and some other specialized functions.

▸ **Thumbnails:** This option enables you to control the size of the thumbnails, the number of rows and columns used to display them, the size of any border you want to put around the thumbnails, and whether the filename, caption, credits, title, and copyright information you've entered is displayed. *Note:* You can't set rows and columns if you select the Vertical or Horizontal Frame styles.

▸ **Custom Colors:** Using this option, you can select colors for the background, the text that describes the images, and any links displayed in the background, as well as the color of the banner, the active links in the banner, and any links in the banner that your visitor has clicked.

▸ **Security:** This option lets you specify any copyright and security notices that you want displayed with your images.

▼▼▼▼▼▼▼▼▼▼▼▼▼▼▼▼▼▼▼▼▼▼▼▼▼▼▼▼▼▼▼▼▼▼▼▼▼▼

# Cooking Up a Web Gallery

The advantage of displaying your images in a Web gallery (compared to simply constructing one humongous page that shows all the images at their full file size) is that viewers with slower Internet connections don't have to wait for all the images to download. Even visitors with fast Internet connections will appreciate not being inundated with a flood of images.

To create your Web gallery, follow these steps:

*1.* **Collect the images you want to display in a single folder on your hard disk.**

You may want to deposit copies of your images, leaving the originals untouched.

**2.** **Open the first image in Photoshop and make any changes that you want.**

For example, you may want to correct the colors or crop the images. You'll find more about correcting colors in Book VIII, Chapter 1.

**3.** **Save the image.**

Save your images in a size that will display well on the Web (not too big, not too small) and in a Web-friendly file format, such as JPEG or GIF. Check out Chapter 2 of this book for more information.

**4.** **Repeats Steps 2 and 3 for each image.**

**5.** **Open the Web Photo Gallery tool by choosing File⇨Automate⇨Web Photo Gallery.**

The Web Photo Gallery dialog box, shown in Figure 4-1, opens.

**6.** **From the Styles drop-down list, choose one of the standard styles, such as Vertical Slide Show (which arranges the images as a slide show) or Horizontal Frame (which arrays them in a horizontal format).**

A preview of the Web Gallery style you select is shown in the window on the right side of the dialog box. Some styles show thumbnail previews of your images, which visitors can click to view the larger originals. Others present a slide show that cycles through the available images at intervals.

**7.** **If you want your e-mail address to appear on your Web page, enter it in the E-Mail text box (refer to Figure 4-1).**

**8.** **From the Extension drop-down list, choose either .htm or .html as the file extension for your Web page.**

 The Web server that hosts your page may be fussy about the extension you choose for your Web page. Servers running Windows-based software may insist that pages have an .htm extension. Those running under UNIX or a similar operating system may prefer .html. Most of the time, the server software doesn't care, and .htm does just fine.

**9.** **Click the Browse button (or the Choose button on the Mac) and navigate to the folder containing your images. Click OK (or Choose on the Mac) to select it.**

**10.** **Click the Destination button and choose a folder for Photoshop to deposit the files it creates for your Web Photo Gallery.**

The destination folder must be different from the source folder.

**11.** **From the Options drop-down list, select an option and enter the information required.**

The dialog box changes as you move from option to option. See the section "Planning Your Page" for details about the options you find here.

**12.** **Click OK to tell Photoshop to create your Web page(s).**

Photoshop creates your Web page and loads it into your browser. Figure 4-2 shows how a Web page would look with a vertical frame style, while Figure 4-3 shows the horizontal slide show style.

**13.** **Upload your Web gallery to your Internet Web page hosting service by following your usual procedures.**

Check with your ISP for details on how to do this.

Book
***IX***
Chapter
**4**

CONTINUED
▼ ▼ ▼ ▼ ▼

**Figure 4-1**

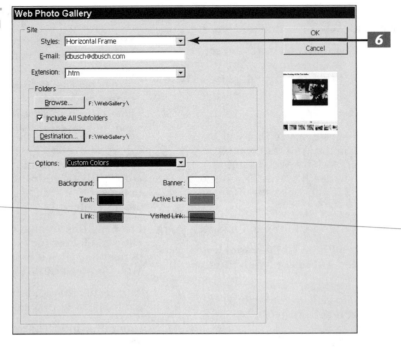

**Figure 4-2**

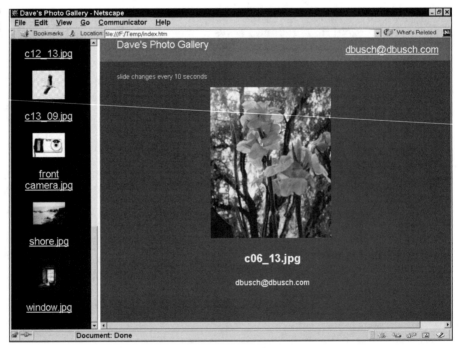

**Figure 4-3**

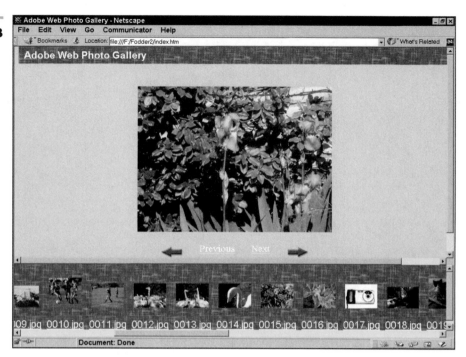

# Looking to
# ImageReady

**5**

Adobe ImageReady is a stand-alone program bundled with Photoshop that serves as your one-stop-shopping source for a variety of Web-based tricks, such as image maps (which let you link portions of an image to a Web address), rollovers (which tell your browser to do certain things when the mouse passes over a portion of the Web page), and animations (those often annoying rotating logos and dancing bunnies that you see on some Web pages).

You can even combine two or more of these effects. For example, you can create an image with separate areas that change their appearance when the mouse cursor passes over or clicks them. This change can be an animated glowing effect that vanishes when the visitor clicks to jump to a new page on your Web site.

There's a lot of overlap between the programs, and many functions you can carry out in both. Photoshop has more features related to creating and editing content, whereas ImageReady has more extensive options for optimizing and configuring images for the Web. If your Web needs are modest, you can probably do all you need within Photoshop itself and may rarely need to call on ImageReady.

This chapter provides an overview of what you can do in ImageReady rather than step-by-step instructions for each of the functions, so you can decide when you're ready for ImageReady, so to speak.

## Firing Up ImageReady

Adobe provides an easy link between Photoshop and ImageReady. If you're working on an image in Photoshop and want to create one of the ImageReady effects, just choose File⇨Jump To⇨Adobe ImageReady 7.0, or press Shift+Ctrl+M (Shift+⌘+M on the Mac). ImageReady then opens with the same image. When you're finished in ImageReady, you can jump back to Photoshop by using the same menu choice or shortcut keystrokes; Photoshop displays an updated version of the image file, so any changes you've made in ImageReady are reflected in Photoshop.

When you're manipulating an image in ImageReady, the image is dark in Photoshop to indicate that the file is inactive. When you jump back to Photoshop, the image becomes darkened in ImageReady.

## Mapping Your Images

*Image maps* associate certain areas of an image with a Web address, or URL, so that when the user clicks those areas, the browser loads the image or Web page that the URL points to. These linked image areas act much like image slices, which you can prepare in Photoshop itself (see Chapter 3 of this book).

The main difference between image maps and slices is that slices are always rectangular in shape, whereas areas in image maps can be virtually any shape, even irregular polygons. If you want to associate each square in a checkerboard with a URL, you could do that just fine with slices. But if you want to create clickable links to the 50 U.S. states, you need an image map to handle the uniquely shaped states. Figure 5-1 shows an image with callouts that lend themselves to links that provide more information.

**Figure 5-1**

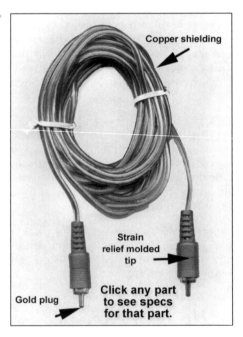

The easiest way to create an image map is with the Image Map tool, available in ImageReady's Tool palette or by pressing P. There are three variations of the tool: rectangle, circle, and polygon. You use the tools in much the same way as the rectangular, elliptical, and polygonal lasso selection tools: Drag to create an image-map selection in the desired shape. After you create an area, selection handles appear at each of the corners and sides (in the case of rectangular and circular areas) or at each of the defining points for a polygonal area, as shown in Figure 5-2. You can drag these handles to resize and reshape the area.

**Figure 5-2**

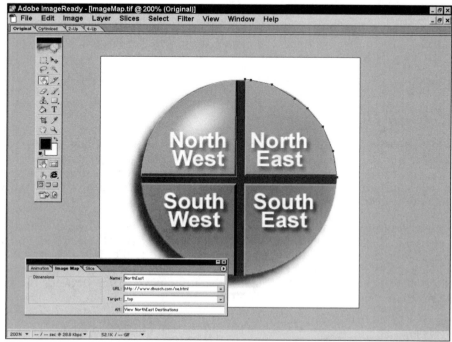

Each of the map selections you choose is given a generic name, which you can change to something more descriptive in the Image Map palette. You also need to enter the following information:

- ✔ The URL that the browser should jump to when that area of the image is clicked.

- ✔ The Target area in the destination page (such as the top of the page or another location you define).

- ✔ The alternate text that should appear when the mouse passes over that area of the image map. The ALT text helps the visitor understand what a particular area of the image map represents. For example, if you're creating an image map from a map of the United States, you might use the name of each state as alternate text for that state's image-map area. This can be an aid to people with vision problems who are using a screen reader to navigate your site.

If you create a rectangular or circular image-map area, the dimensions of the area appear at the left side of the Image Map palette.

Book

*IX*

Chapter

**5**

You can also create image maps from layers. Select the areas you want to transform into image-map areas and copy and paste them into their own layers. Then choose Layer↷ New Layer Based on Image Map Area. ImageReady creates an area from each layer's contents. This is often a better choice when you want to add a rollover effect to an area because the image-map area automatically adjusts to any changes in the area produced by the rollover effect (such as a glow).

After you've defined your image-map areas, ImageReady creates and stores an HTML file you can use with your Web-authoring software to activate the image maps on your pages.

▼ ▼ ▼ ▼ ▼ ▼ ▼ ▼ ▼ ▼ ▼ ▼ ▼ ▼ ▼ ▼ ▼ ▼ ▼ ▼ ▼ ▼ ▼ ▼ ▼ ▼ ▼ ▼ ▼ ▼ ▼ ▼ ▼

## Rolling Over

A *rollover* is an effect on a Web page that causes an image to change appearance when the mouse performs some action, such as passing over or clicking the image. For example, an image might reverse to show its negative version, pulsate with an eerie glow, or change appearance entirely (for example, a button's text might change from OFF to ON when clicked). Rollovers are an excellent way to provide interactivity on a Web page.

To create a rollover, you need to decide what you want your image to do in response to a particular mouse action: change color, size, texture, or even the text that appears in the image when the mouse cursor passes over the image or the visitor clicks it. You simply need to create versions of the image in the different states and have ImageReady provide the JavaScript instructions that tell the Web browser to switch between them at the appropriate time.

You can create a rollover effect in ImageReady by following these steps:

**1.** **Choose an image to be used with a particular rollover effect.**

If you want to use only part of the image, define an area by using slices or image maps.

**2.** **Create the different appearances, or** *states*, **for your image in individual layers.**

For example, if you want a button to flip between OFF and ON, you need to create two layers, one for the normal, ON state and one for the OFF state. You'll find more information on creating layers in Book V, Chapter 1.

**3.** **Click each layer and choose New Rollover State from the Rollover Palette's flyout options menu.**

**4.** **Right-click the new state layer and choose Set State.**

This lets you specify what mouse action activates that particular state or appearance, as shown in Figure 5-3. For example, you can choose Over (the mouse cursor passes over the image), Down (the mouse button is pressed down), Up (the mouse button is released), Click (the visitor clicks the area with the mouse), Out (the mouse cursor leaves the image area), and other actions.

ImageReady creates JavaScript instructions for you that you can incorporate into your Web pages to use these rollover effects with your images.

**Figure 5-3**

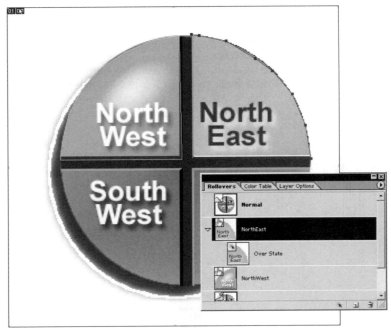

# Getting Animated

ImageReady can also take your multilayered images and create animated GIF files that provide motion effects when displayed on your Web pages. Unfortunately, animations are often poorly used and overused. Few Web page visitors admire wildly rotating logos, backgrounds that induce vertigo, or banners that flash and swirl.

However, motion can be effective if you don't overdo it. One or two (max) objects that, say, call attention to a special area of a page or a helpful link might be okay if well done. And keep in mind that some browsers allow the user to disable animations, so using animations for something critical may not be a good idea. You might even find other applications for animations, such as within PowerPoint presentations. ImageReady has all the tools you need to create these animations and can even streamline the job for you.

Animations are nothing more than successive images, or frames, that are displayed one after another to create the illusion of motion. For example, you might have an image in which an object moves from left to right, one tiny increment at a time. Or you might have four views of an object, each from a different angle, which, when viewed consecutively, produce the illusion of rotation. The GIF format enables you to store each version in a separate layer within the GIF file. A Web browser (or other program, such as PowerPoint) that displays the GIF file automatically shows each of the different image layers in turn. All you need to do to create an animated GIF is to produce the individual layers and find a way to combine them into a GIF file. That's where ImageReady comes in.

Here are some of the ways ImageReady can help you create animations:

- ✔ **Build animations from layers.** Create each of the individual frames needed for an animation in a separate layer in Photoshop (or ImageReady). Then open the image in ImageReady and choose Create from Layers from the Animation palette. ImageReady will create a set of frames that you can edit, change the order of, and then save as an animated GIF, as shown in Figure 5-4.

**Figure 5-4**

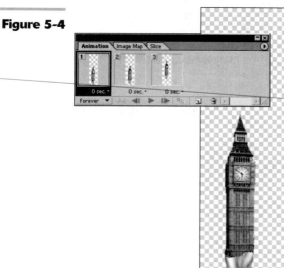

- ✔ **Create *tweened* images for you.** If you want to move an object in your image from Point A to Point B, you don't need to create each layer manually. You can specify the frames that show the start and end positions of your object and ask ImageReady to create new, intermediate frames.

The term tweening comes from the process used to automatically create and insert the frames "in be*tween*" the start and ending frames.

- ✔ **Specify the time interval between frames.** ImageReady can add a Delay value between two or more frames, determining how long each frame is shown before the next is displayed. Shorter display times and faster frame rates produce smoother animations, but also dramatically increase the size of your animated GIF. You can play around with time intervals in ImageReady until you get the best compromise.

- ✔ **Optimize animations.** ImageReady can squeeze your animated GIFs down to a manageable size by discarding pixels that don't change from frame to frame, leaving you with only the pixels required to generate the animated effect you want.

# Book X

# Photoshop and Print

The 5th Wave          By Rich Tennant

@RICHTENNANT

"FRANKLY, I'M NOT SURE THIS IS THE WAY TO ENHANCE OUR COLOR GRAPHICS."

# Working with Other Programs

Photoshop is an application with such breadth and depth that you may never find a need to integrate your images with any other application. But just in case you need to, you'll be happy to know that working between Photoshop and other programs is easier than ever, especially if you're working within the latest versions of Adobe's companion programs. I obviously can't cover every program you may want to partner with Photoshop, but I'll hit a few of them. You'll find that similar types of programs also share similarities in the kinds of Photoshop files they will accept and so on. So if I don't cover the specific program you have in mind, read up on one that's similar. It may give you the information that you need. But if all else fails, you may have to break open the dreaded application user manual.

## Illustrator

Illustrator, Adobe's vector graphics drawing program, is probably the friendliest program to work with Photoshop. Maybe it's just that it's natural that a drawing program and an image-editing/painting program go hand in hand. Or it may be because the two applications share a lot of common elements — paths, filters, layers, colors, and so on. Whatever the reason, feel free to move files between Photoshop and Illustrator. Layers, masks, transparency, and shapes are all preserved.

Why would you want to bring your images into Illustrator when Photoshop now has vector capabilities? Well, even though Photoshop can now create vector shapes and type, it's still an image editor at heart and doesn't quite have the same drawing capabilities of Illustrator. Illustrator is superior when it comes to creating complex, compound paths and handling large chunks of text here and there. For example, say you want to create a large poster that includes photographs and vector graphics and type. The best course of action is to prepare your photos in Photoshop and save them as EPS or TIFF files. Then you open a new file in Illustrator by using your poster's dimensions. Place your photos in the Illustrator file, add your vector graphics and type, and save your file as a native Illustrator or Illustrator EPS file.

 Illustrator accepts TIFF, EPS, PSD, PDF, JPEG, GIF, PNG, BMP, FLM, PCX, and PICT files from Photoshop.

▼ ▼ ▼ ▼ ▼ ▼ ▼ ▼ ▼ ▼ ▼ ▼ ▼ ▼ ▼ ▼ ▼ ▼ ▼ ▼ ▼ ▼ ▼ ▼ ▼ ▼ ▼ ▼ ▼ ▼ ▼ ▼ ▼ ▼ ▼ ▼ ▼ ▼ ▼ ▼ ▼ ▼ ▼ ▼

## Moving images into Illustrator

Photoshop lets you drag and drop images directly into Illustrator. You can also choose File⇨Open in Illustrator to bring in a Photoshop file. Choosing this command creates a new Illustrator file with the same name as the Photoshop file and also automatically embeds the file.

 If you're importing ImageReady files, any image maps, slices, rollovers, and animations are preserved when you import the files into Illustrator.

But the best way to move images into Illustrator is to follow these steps:

1. **Save the Photoshop file you want to move into Illustrator.**

2. **In Illustrator, choose File⇨Place to import the file. Be sure to deselect the Link option in the Place dialog box.**

   If you select the Link option, Illustrator brings your Photoshop file in as a link. This means that it will refer to the external Photoshop file where it resides on the hard drive or media and not embed the image data within the Illustrator file.

   The Photoshop Import dialog box (shown in Figure 1-1) appears.

3. **Select an option for how you want to deal with Photoshop's layers (if you have any).**

You can choose to convert Photoshop's layers to objects, which will maintain all the Photoshop layers, along with their associated transparency. Or you can flatten Photoshop layers to a single image, which merges all the layers but leaves any remaining open areas transparent after the merge.

Any type layers or layer styles are rasterized into pixels and become uneditable. Any layer masks are converted into Illustrator's opacity masks (similar to layer masks).

Your Photoshop image is now embedded in the Illustrator file.

**Figure 1-1**

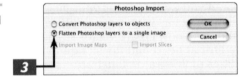

## Cutting and pasting

You can use the clipboard to copy and paste between Photoshop and Illustrator. In Photoshop, select your desired image and choose Edit⇨Copy. Then in Illustrator, choose Edit⇨Paste.

To go the other way, select your artwork in Illustrator. Then choose Edit⇨Paste in Photoshop. In the dialog box that appears, choose one of these options:

✔ **Paste as Pixels** to rasterize the artwork

✔ **Paste as Paths** to paste the artwork as a path

✔ **Paste as Shape Layer** to create a shape layer

 I don't recommend the clipboard method for large or high-resolution selections. Storing a big file on your clipboard can eat up precious RAM and slow your computer's performance.

## Exporting Photoshop paths

You can also export Photoshop paths as Illustrator files. For example, you may have an image with a clipping path that you want to import into Illustrator in order to combine it with vector graphics and type. (For more on clipping paths, see Book III, Chapter 2.) Choose File⇨ Export⇨Paths to Illustrator. Choose a location for the path, give it a name, and click Save. Open the path in Illustrator as a new file. The path is fully editable in Illustrator.

## Placing an Illustrator file into Photoshop

You can *place* an Adobe Illustrator file into Photoshop, along with a PDF or EPS file, by using the File⇨Place command. When you place a file, it is rasterized at the resolution of the file into which it's being placed. You can't edit text or vector paths.

The placed artwork appears inside a bounding box in your Photoshop image window. If it is larger than the window, it is resized to fit. You can move or transform the artwork by dragging inside or on the handles of the bounding box, respectively. You can also apply anti-aliasing by choosing the option in the Options bar. To commit the artwork, click the Commit icon (the check mark icon) in the Options bar or press Enter (Return on the Mac).

 To maintain consistent color control between Photoshop and Illustrator, and also between InDesign and Acrobat, be sure to check out the chapter on color, Book III, Chapter 2.

# *InDesign*

InDesign is Adobe's professional page layout program. You can paste, drag and drop, or place Photoshop files into InDesign. Any paths, masks, alpha channels, and transparency are retained, depending on your file format. You can even use the Photoshop paths to create special effects such as text wraps in InDesign.

Photoshop allows you to specify your image width in columns. Using columns is handy when you plan to import an image into a page layout program like InDesign (or even PageMaker or QuarkXPress) and you want the image to fit exactly within a certain number of columns, based on the established grid of your layout page. You can specify columns in the New, Image Size, and Canvas Size dialog boxes. To set the specific values for the width of the column and *gutter* (the space between the columns), go to the Units and Ruler panel of your Preferences (under Edit in Windows and Mac OS 9, and Photoshop in Mac OS X).

InDesign has a nice feature called Edit Original, which allows you to double-click a linked image to launch the native application, such as Photoshop. Make your edits and save and close the file, and it appears edited in your page layout.

InDesign accepts PSD, TIFF, EPS, JPEG, GIF, PCX, BMP, DCS, and PICT file formats. Stick with TIFF or EPS. If you have layers and transparency, you can also use the native Photoshop format. For proper color modes and resolution settings for image files to be printed, see Book II, Chapter 1 (resolution); Book II, Chapter 2 (modes); and Chapter 2 of this book (prepping graphics for print).

## PageMaker

PageMaker is Adobe's business- and consumer-level page layout program. Like InDesign, PageMaker allows you to import a number of file formats — including the native Photoshop format — and to retain layers.

Unfortunately, unlike InDesign, PageMaker doesn't support transparency. That means that if your image contains transparent areas and you place it over a background containing a color or image, you see a white box around your image. All transparent areas are filled with white pixels, as shown in Figure 1-2. Your workaround is one of two methods:

- ✔ **Save your image with a clipping path.** (See Book III, Chapter 2, for more on clipping paths.) Any pixels outside of the path will be hidden, allowing your image to be silhouetted and not boxed in.

- ✔ **Composite your desired background with your image in Photoshop.** Save and place it into PageMaker as a single file.

For bringing in images, PageMaker supports the OLE method (described in the "Microsoft Word" section, later in this chapter), dragging and dropping, the clipboard copy-and-paste method, and my preferred method, the good old File⇨Place command. PageMaker accepts PSD, TIFF, EPS, JPEG, GIF, PDF, PICT, and BMP file formats.

 I would stay with TIFF or EPS. If you save your file in a PSD format, however, when you update the file in Photoshop, it is automatically updated in PageMaker. As with InDesign, for proper color modes and resolution settings for image files to be printed, see Book II, Chapter 1 (resolution); Book II, Chapter 2 (modes); and Chapter 2 of this book (prepping graphics for print).

 Page layout programs, such as PageMaker, InDesign, and QuarkXPress, make it a snap to transform your placed images within those programs. It isn't a disaster to do it within those programs, but it is really best to do any kind of image manipulation (outside of moving) in Photoshop. Your image quality will be better retained, and the page layout file prints much faster and has less potential for errors.

**Figure 1-2**

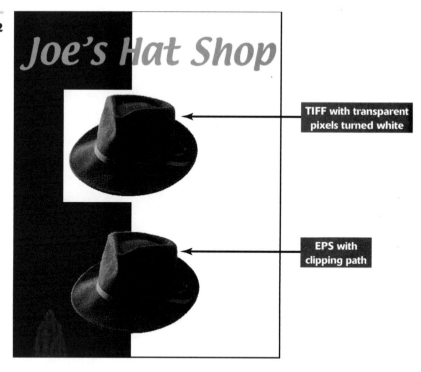

# *Acrobat*

Photoshop can open both generic PDF (Portable Document Format) files and Photoshop PDF files. Generic PDFs are created in applications like Acrobat, Illustrator, InDesign, and PageMaker. These PDFs can be single or multipage documents. When opening a multipage PDF, Photoshop asks you what pages you want to open. Each page opens in a separate image window.

## Placing a PDF into Photoshop

As I mention in the "Illustrator" section, earlier in this chapter, you can also place a PDF file into Photoshop by using the File⇨Place command.

If you are placing a multipage PDF, select the page you want to place in the PDF Page Selector dialog box. Then select your desired dimensions, resolution, and color mode in the Rasterize Generic PDF Format dialog box, shown in Figure 1-3. If the file was saved with an embedded color profile, you can choose it from the Mode pop-up menu.

 Be sure to select the Constrain Proportions check box to maintain the aspect ratio, and the Anti-aliased check box to smooth the edges of any rasterized artwork. Generic PDFs are rasterized in total when they're opened in Photoshop.

**Figure 1-3**

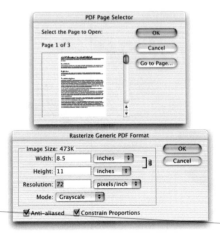

## Opening PDF files

To quickly and efficiently open a multipage PDF, choose File⇨Automate⇨Multi-page PDF to PSD. Choose your source PDF, page range, resolution, color mode, and anti-aliasing options. Then choose your base name for the files. Photoshop will add a number after the base name that corresponds with the page number. Choose a location for the saved files and click OK.

If you want to open an image, rather than a page, from a PDF, you can use the File⇨ Import⇨PDF Image command. If it is a multi-image PDF, you can scroll through and select a single image. To open all images, click Import All Images. Each image opens as a separate Photoshop file. Note that if there are other vector graphics along with the image, only the image portion is imported. You can also bring in PDFs by using the copy and paste method and by dragging and dropping.

## Saving files as Photoshop PDFs

You can save Photoshop files as Photoshop PDFs. When you save the files, all transparency is preserved. You can add password protection to secure your PDFs and use the Include Vector Data option to preserve text and vector graphics as resolution-independent vector elements. Photoshop PDFs support all the same color modes and features that the native Photoshop format supports.

Saving a copy of your Photoshop file as a Photoshop PDF file is especially beneficial in a workflow environment where approval is necessary. PDF is a cross-platform and cross-application file format. All fonts and graphics are preserved and displayed exactly as they were intended. Send your PDF to a manager, colleagues, or clients, and the only equipment they need to view your image, and view it *exactly* like you do, is a computer and Acrobat Reader, downloadable for free at www.adobe.com. And if they happen to have the full version of Acrobat, they can even make notes and annotations within the electronic document.

# LiveMotion

LiveMotion is Adobe's Web program that enables you to create Flash animations and other interactive Web content. You import your Photoshop files to use in LiveMotion animations. The Photoshop image data remains editable as you animate and code — layers, layer sets, blend modes, layer masks, and layer effects are preserved.

In Live Motion, choose File⇨Place and open the Photoshop file. You can also drag and drop the Photoshop file into your Live Motion file. If you bring in a native Photoshop file with layers, you can choose to convert the layers into individual objects, a group of individual objects, or into a keyframe sequence. When your Photoshop data is animated, you can use LiveMotion's Edit Original command to edit the placed native Photoshop file. Choose Edit⇨Edit Original. Photoshop launches. Make any necessary changes and then save and close the file. All edits are automatically updated in the animation.

 LiveMotion offers the same filters that you find in Photoshop, so you don't have to apply them in advance before importing a file into LiveMotion.

Live Motion accepts GIF, JPEG, PNG, and native PSD files. Keep your images in RGB color mode and at a low resolution (72 to 96 ppi). For more on resolution, see Book II, Chapter 1.

# GoLive

GoLive is Adobe's WYSIWYG Web authoring application. If you're like me and like to design your Web pages in Photoshop before you write the markup, GoLive is the perfect companion program for you.

## Importing Web pages with GoLive

You can design your entire Web page in Photoshop and then import the layered file into GoLive. Each layer is imported into the Save for Web dialog box, where you can optimize the layer as a separate Web image. The optimized image is then saved as a floating box that can be moved, stacked, and animated on the GoLive Web page.

Of course, you can import flattened, nonlayered images as well. You can then select each floating box and drag a Smart Photoshop icon into the box. When you tag it as a Smart Photoshop Object, you can then edit the original Photoshop image by simply double-clicking any of the Smart Photoshop images on the page.

## Using sliced images with GoLive

GoLive also recognizes sliced Photoshop images. Slices are sections of your image, shown in Figure 1-4, which can then be optimized individually for speed, appearance, and special functions such as links. (For more on slices, see Book IX, Chapter 3.) Save your sliced image as a native Photoshop file in your site folder (the folder containing all your Web page images). Drag the Photoshop image from the site folder onto a new GoLive page. GoLive converts the sliced image into a Smart Photoshop Object, assembles the slices in a table, and opens the Save for Web dialog box to optimize the individual slices. You can then use the slices for links, rollovers, and so on. Because they're Smart Objects, image slices are updated automatically in GoLive when you edit the original Photoshop image.

Book
**X**
Chapter
**1**

**Figure 1-4**

GoLive recognizes native Photoshop, GIF, JPEG, and PNG formats. Again, keep your images in RGB color mode and at a low resolution (72 to 96 ppi). For more on resolution, see Book II, Chapter 1.

## Microsoft Word

Photoshop supports Object Linking and Embedding (OLE) on Windows platforms. This means that you can either link or embed a Photoshop file in what's called an OLE container application. Microsoft Word and Adobe PageMaker are OLE applications.

If you *link* the Photoshop file in the OLE application, it links, or refers, to the file on the hard drive or other media; it doesn't save the Photoshop file with the OLE application file. If you *embed* the file, it inserts and saves the file in the OLE application file.

To link or embed an image, you can copy a selection in Photoshop and then use the Paste Special command to paste it in your Word document. The selection is embedded, not linked. Or you can choose the Insert Object command to insert a Photoshop file as an OLE-embedded or OLE-linked object. The useful thing about using the OLE method is that if you double-click the linked or embedded image in your Word document, Photoshop automatically launches and opens the image for editing purposes. After you complete the editing, just close the file if it's embedded, or save and close the file if it is linked. Your file is updated in the Word document. Note that you can also modify the linked file directly in Photoshop without going through Word. The linked image will be updated the next time you open the document in Word.

If you don't want to mess around with all this OLE business, you can just save the Photoshop file in a file format that Word will accept and choose Insert➪Picture➪From File. Word accepts the following Photoshop file formats: TIFF, EPS, JPEG, GIF, PNG, PCX, and BMP file formats. I would keep it simple and use TIFF. It's a good overall format for printing images.

▼ ▼ ▼ ▼ ▼ ▼ ▼ ▼ ▼ ▼ ▼ ▼ ▼ ▼ ▼ ▼ ▼ ▼ ▼ ▼ ▼ ▼ ▼ ▼ ▼ ▼ ▼ ▼ ▼ ▼ ▼ ▼ ▼ ▼ ▼ ▼ ▼ ▼

# Microsoft PowerPoint

PowerPoint, Microsoft's presentation program, is fine when it comes to creating quick and easy on-screen and slide presentations. However, it's a real lame duck when it comes to creating any kind of graphics that are engaging and even remotely original and creative. That's why I repeatedly turn to Photoshop to create all of my background slides, shown in Figure 1-5, and to refine any other images I plan to incorporate into my presentation. You can easily create great backgrounds by employing filters, layer masks, varying opacity settings, creative brush-strokes, patterns, and so on.

**Figure 1-5**

Follow these steps to create a slide in Photoshop to use in PowerPoint:

**1. In Photoshop, create an image that is 10 inches in width and 7.5 inches in height at 96 ppi (72 ppi on the Mac).**

If that size doesn't seem to work, you can experiment with other sizes.

**2. Use an RGB color mode.**

**3. Save your Photoshop image in a file format that PowerPoint accepts.**

PowerPoint accepts EPS, TIFF, JPEG, GIF, PICT, PNG, or BMP.

**4. In PowerPoint, choose Insert⇨Picture⇨From File.**

Or you can apply the Photoshop image on your master slide if you want to use it throughout your presentation. In that case, choose View⇨Master⇨Slide Master and then insert the picture.

You can also get Photoshop images into PowerPoint by using the Clipboard method. Select the image in Photoshop and choose Edit⇨Copy. Go into PowerPoint and choose Edit⇨Paste. However, if you want to print the presentation on a PostScript printer (for handouts, for example), don't use the Clipboard method. Instead, import your images as TIFFs or EPSs.

## Premiere

Premiere is Adobe's digital-video-editing program. You can import still images from Photoshop into Premiere and incorporate them with video sequences, sounds, and titles to create QuickTime, MPEG, AVI, RealMedia, or Windows Media movies. Save your images in RGB color mode and in the native Photoshop, PICT, GIF, JPEG, TIFF, Filmstrip, TGA, PCX, or BMP file format. Premiere doesn't accept any 16-bit TIFF files.

By default, Premiere alters the size and aspect ratio of the image to match that of the video frame you specify for your video project. This can vary from 320 x 240 pixels, to 720 x 480, to 720 x 576, and so on, depending on whether your intended output is for NTSC, PAL, or multimedia. I recommend setting up your video project in Premiere first and then sizing your still images in Photoshop to fit the exact aspect ratio of your video frame. That way, Premiere doesn't have to do any sizing, your image quality remains the best possible, and you don't have files that are larger than they need to be, as illustrated in Figure 1-6.

**Figure 1-6**

If your Photoshop file has layers, you can import the file as a merged file, or you can import just a single layer. After the image is in Premiere, you can select it and choose Edit↔Edit Original. Photoshop launches, where you can make your necessary edits. Save and close the file, and it is automatically updated in Premiere. If you have problems importing a Photoshop file with multiple layers or layer masks, you may have to flatten the image before importing.

You can edit individual frames in Premiere movies with Photoshop. Export a premiere movie as a Filmstrip file format. In Photoshop, you can then apply filters or paint on the individual frames. Open the edited filmstrip in Premiere and convert it back into a QuickTime movie. Just make sure that you don't resize, resample, change the color mode, or remove alpha channels in the Filmstrip file, or you won't be able to save it back in a Filmstrip file format.

# Third-Party Plug-Ins

There are more third-party Photoshop plug-ins than you can shake a big stick at. So don't be surprised if you come across quite a few that aren't listed here. To list them all would require another *All-in-One Desk Reference For Dummies.* Table 1-1 lists some of the better-known plug-ins, along with their suggested retail price at the time this book went to press. Some have demos available so you check them out before you plunk down your hard-earned cash.

TABLE 1-1: THIRD-PARTY PLUG-INS

| Plug-In | Description | Vendor | Price |
|---|---|---|---|
| 3D HotTEXT | Creates 3-D text with bevels, lighting, and textures. Flows text on a 3-D path. | Vertigo Technology at www.vertigo3D.com | $80 |
| AutoEye | Reclaims color and detail lost in the transition from film/prints to digital format. Also contains filters simulating creative photographic techniques. | Auto F/X at www.autofx.com | $130 |
| AV Bros. Puzzle Pro 7.2 | Creates realistic jigsaw-puzzle effects. | AV Bros. at www.avbros.com | $40 |
| AV Bros. Page Curl 7.2 | Creates a page-turning effect. | AV Bros. at www.avbros.com | $30 |
| Color Darkroom 1.0 | Similar to Photoshop's Curves Adjustment but more powerful (Windows only). | Antelligent at www.antelligent.com | $99 |
| CSI PhotoOptics | Eighteen filters to adjust color, contrast, and exposure. Simulate film and lens filter effects. | Cytopia Software at www.cytopia.com | $100 |
| Cutline Filter 1.1 | Applies engraving and woodcut effects to grayscale images. | Andromeda Software at www.andromeda.com | $74 |

*continued*

**TABLE 1-1:** *(CONTINUED)*

| Plug-In | Description | Vendor | Price |
|---------|-------------|--------|-------|
| Deep Paint | Creates lighting and texture effects to mimic oil, acrylic, and watercolor mediums (Windows only). | Right Hemisphere at www.us.righthemisphere.com | $250 |
| Eye Candy 4000 | Twenty-three filters that create 3-D bevels, shadows, glows, and special effects such as fire, fur, wood, and smoke. (See Figure 1-7.) | Alien Skin at www.alienskin.com | $170 |
| Flaming Pear Filters | Lumped under the heading of the developer of a ton of filters such as SuperBladePro (surface and texture generator), Melancholytron (makes photos moody), Flexify (bends into strange shapes), Flood (submerges your image underwater), Mr. Contrast (adds dramatic contrast and hyper detail), and much more. (See Figure 1-7.) | Flaming Pear at www.flamingpear.com | $15 to $49 |
| Genuine Fractals | Creates resolution-independent images from any size file and lets you print enlargements without any quality degradation. | Lizard Tech at www.lizardtech.com | $159 |
| Genuine Fractals Print Pro | Encodes images as scalable, reusable assets. Generates any size output from a single file. | Lizard Tech at www.lizardtech.com | $299 |
| Intellihance Pro | Color corrects and enhances images (contrast, dust and scratches, casts, and so on) | Extensis at www.extensis.com | $200 |
| KnockOut 2 | Plug-in for precise and detailed masking of complex objects such as hair, water, shadow, glass, and smoke. | procreate at www.procreate.com | $329 |
| KPT Effects | Nine filters that create effects such as liquid, fractals, gradients, tiling, paint, ink drops, lightning, and particles. | procreate at www.procreate.com | $199 |
| LensDoc 1.1 | Corrects zoom and wide-angle lens distortions such as barreling and pin-cushioning. | Andromeda Software at www.andromeda.com | $99 |
| Mask Pro | Plug-in for precise and detailed masking of complex objects such as hair, water, shadow, glass, and smoke. (See Figure 1-7.) | Extensis at www.extensis.com | $200 |

| Plug-In | Description | Vendor | Price |
| --- | --- | --- | --- |
| Paint Alchemy 2 | Creates painterly effects and special effects. | XaosTools at www.xaostools.com | $99 |
| PhotoFrame | Creates interesting borders and frames with edge effects, textures, bevels, shadows, and more. | Extensis at www.extensis.com | $200 |
| PhotoTools | Creates realistic shadows, textures, animated GIFs, custom bevels, and more. (See Figure 1-7.) | Extensis at www.extensis.com | $150 |
| Photo/Graphic Edges 5.0 | Creates a variety of artistic edge effects, such as torn, film frames, painted edges. | Auto F/X at www.autofx.com | $200 |
| Powertone 1.5 | Enhances duotone images. | CreoScitex at www.creo.com | $250 |
| Scatter Light Lenses | Creates scattering highlights such as mist, fog, glitter, sparks, flares, and glows. | Andromeda Software at www.andromeda.com | $98 |
| Series 3 Screens 1.6 | Converts grayscale images into special-effect line art, mezzotints, and engravings. | Andromeda Software at www.andromeda.com | $110 |
| Shadow Filter | Creates realistic 3-D shadows. Also includes a perspective filter. | Andromeda Software at www.andromeda.com | $110 |
| Splat! | Filter set including textures, edges, borders, mosaics, and frames. | Alien Skin at www.alienskin.com | $69 |
| Studio Bundle Pro 2.0 | Eleven-product set of filters, rich media, and utilities including frames, patterns, textures, edges, rasterization, and animation software. | Auto F/X at www.autofx.com | $200 |
| Terrazzo 2 | Creates symmetrical tiled backgrounds. | Xaos Tools at www.xaostools.com | $69 |
| VariFocus Filter | Creates smart Gaussian blurs and selective focus that mimics photographic techniques. | Andromeda Software at www.andromeda.com | $48 |
| Xenofex 1.0 | Sixteen special effects featuring realistic textures and natural distortions, with intriguing names such as baked earth, origami, and shower door. | Alien Skin at www.alienskin.com | $130 |

Book
**X**
Chapter

**1**

Figure 1-7 shows you how just a few of these effects look.

**Figure 1-7**

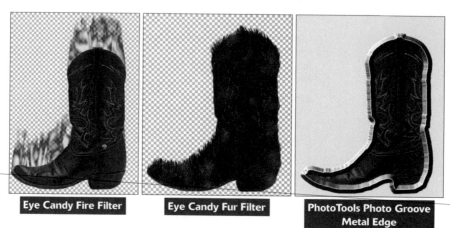

Eye Candy Fire Filter    Eye Candy Fur Filter    PhotoTools Photo Groove Metal Edge

Flaming Pear SuperBlade Pro Filter    Flaming Pear ChromaSolarize Filter

MaskPro

# Prepping Graphics for Print

*2*

Preparing images for the screen is a snap compared to what you have to go through to get images ripe for the printing process. If all you ever want to do is print your images to a desktop laser or inkjet printer, the task is a little easier, but you still must take some guidelines into account. And prepping your images for offset printing? Well, throw in an additional set of guidelines. It's not rocket science, mind you. If you stick to the basic rules and, more importantly, spend some time developing a good working relationship with your service bureau and printer, you'll be good to go.

## Getting the Right Resolution, Mode, and Format

If you're not familiar with the concept of resolution, I suggest taking a look at Book II, Chapter 1. That's where I cover all the basics on resolution, pixel dimension, re-sampling, and other related topics. For full descriptions on color modes and file formats, see Book II, Chapter 2. That said, the next few sections give you the lowdown on the proper settings for an image that will ultimately go to print.

### Resolution and modes

Table 2-1 provides some guidelines on what resolution settings to use for specific output. Remember these are just *guidelines*. They aren't chiseled into stone to withstand the sands of time or anything lofty like that. You need to communicate with your service bureau, printer, or client and get their specifications and/or recommendations. (See "Working with a Service Bureau," later in this chapter.)

TABLE 2-1: RECOMMENDED RESOLUTIONS AND IMAGE MODES

| Device | Notes | Recommended Resolution | Mode |
|--------|-------|------------------------|------|
| Fuji Frontier Photo Printer | Wallets to 10 x 15 inches. Great for printing digital photos. Service bureaus accept flash cards, or you can burn your images to CD. | 300 dpi | RGB |
| Digital presses | Brands include, Xeikon, Xerox, IBM, Indigo,* Scitex, Heidelberg, and so on. | 255 dpi | CMYK |
| ColorSpan Displaymaker large format printer | 16 x 20 inches to 60 x 100 inches; Encad engine; employs a software dithering process. | 150 dpi | RGB |
| Epson color inkjets | Resolution depends on the print setting. Epson recommends ⅓ of the horizontal resolution, but do test prints; settings may be higher than you need. | 720 dpi x ⅓ = 240 dpi; 1440 dpi x ⅓ = 480 dpi; 2880 dpi x ⅓ = 960 dpi | RGB or CMYK |
| Epson large format printer | Various models such as the 7000 and 9000 series | 300 dpi | RGB or CMYK |
| IRIS printer | Continuous-tone printer. Doesn't use screen frequencies. | 300 dpi | CMYK |
| Imagesetter color separations | Film separations or direct to plate for offset printing. | 2 x lines per inch (lpi); 2 x 133 lpi = 266 dpi; 2 x 150 lpi = 300 dpi; 2 x 175 lpi = 350 dpi** | CMYK and spot colors |
| Imagesetter composite printer | RC paper output for negatives and camera ready art. | 2 x 100 lpi = 200 dpi max for negatives; 2 x 150 lpi = 300 dpi for camera ready art | Grayscale or RGB |
| Laser printers | Color or B&W printouts. | 2 x lpi = 170 dpi | Grayscale or RGB |
| Film recorders | Output to 35mm slides (2 x 3 aspect ratio) or 4 x 5 transparencies. | 2K slides = 2048 x 1366 px; 4K slides = 4096 x 2732 px; 8K slides = 8192 x 5464 px; 16K slides = 16,384 x 10,928 px; 4K transp = 3072 x 4096 px; 8K transp = 6144 x 8192 px; 16K transp = 12,288 x 16,384 px | RGB*** |

| Device | Notes | Recommended Resolution | Mode |
|--------|-------|------------------------|------|
| Screen images | For Web and multimedia. | Actually based on pixel dimension of final product (for example, 800 x 600 px for a Web page, 320 x 240 px for a multimedia show, to 720 x 480 px for a Premiere video). But use 72–96 ppi as a general rule. | RGB |

*Indigo presses can handle a fifth spot color if necessary.
**See the following section "Screen frequencies."
***Warning: CMYK files print only in black.

## Screen frequencies

For the appropriate resolution for color separations in Table 2-1, I list the amount of 2 x the lines per inch. The lines per inch, or lpi, pertains to the screen frequency of the output device. Screen frequencies are measured in lines per inch in a halftone screen. You will also hear the terms *screen ruling* or *line screen*. When images are digitized, they are converted into a series of dots called *halftones*. When you print your halftone, you print it by using a halftone screen of a certain value. The average screen frequency for printing four-color images is 133 to 175 lpi. Therefore, when you multiply that by 2, you need to create your images by using a resolution setting of 266 to 350 dots per inch, dpi.

## File formats

As far as file formats go, what you choose depends on a couple of issues:

- What you intend to do with the image. Print it from Photoshop? Post it on the Web? Import it into InDesign?

- What your service bureau, printer, client, supervisor, or other interested parties prefer.

Table 2-2 lists some of the more popular recommended formats for specific jobs, but again communicate with the parties involved to see what is ultimately the best format to use.

**TABLE 2-2: RECOMMENDED FILE FORMATS**

| Job | Formats |
|-----|---------|
| Color inkjet printouts | EPS, TIFF, PDF, PSD |
| Color separations | PSD, PDF, EPS, TIFF, DCS 2.0 |
| Spot color separations | PSD, PDF, DCS 2.0 if importing into another application |
| Magazines | EPS, TIFF |

Book
**X**
Chapter
**2**

*continued*

**TABLE 2-2:** *(CONTINUED)*

| Job | Formats |
| --- | --- |
| Newspapers | TIFF |
| Importing to page layout programs | TIFF, EPS, PSD |
| Importing to illustration programs | EPS, TIFF, DCS, PSD |
| Slides | TIFF, PowerPoint, PICT, PCX, EPS (some bureaus can't do EPS) |
| Photo prints | JPEG, TIFF |
| Web graphics | JPEG for continuous-tone images like photographs; GIF for spot illustrations, buttons, and type; PNG for continuous-tone images such as photographs (but be aware that most browsers still require a plug-in to view PNGs) |
| Digital video (Premiere) | PSD, JPEG, TIFF, GIF, PICT |
| Web authoring (GoLive) | PSD, JPEG, GIF, PNG |
| Flash animation (LiveMotion) | PSD, JPEG, GIF, PNG |
| PowerPoint presentations | TIFF, EPS, JPEG, PICT |
| Word documents | TIFF, EPS |
| For e-mailing for workflow review | PDF (cross-platform, cross-applications, embeds fonts, great workflow review, compression) |
| For posting on the Web as a downloadable file | PDF |

# Working with a Service Bureau

Service bureaus provide a wide variety of services, depending on their size. Some handle photo processing and various photographic output options such as prints (of varying sizes) and slides. Mounting and lamination services may also be provided. Many service bureaus provide scanning services, including high-end drum scanning. A common service is taking scans or digital photos and burning them onto Photo CDs. Many provide output to color separations to film and RC Paper. Larger bureaus may even have a digital press to handle a short run (500 or less), on demand printing needs.

## Getting the ball rolling

Developing a good working relationship with your service bureau and/or printer will save you a lot of time, money, and frustration. These folks are the experts and know their equipment and processes. And believe me, they're only too willing to help. The fewer problems they have with your files, the better they like it. Here are some things you can do to keep the relationship on solid footing:

✔ **Get a dialogue going about the specs:** If your file is going directly to a newspaper, magazine, or other publication, talk with the art director, graphics production coordinator, or other knowledgeable person about the graphic specifications required. Different service bureaus and printers will accept files from different applications and files of various formats.

 Find out which file types they can handle and/or recommend *before* you prepare your files. Larger bureaus should be able to handle anything you can throw at them.

✔ **Build a lasting relationship:** Consistency is also key. When you find a good bureau or printer, stick with it for all your jobs. Jumping from one company to another because a quote came in a little cheaper doesn't always pay off in the long run. If you're a faithful customer, often your service bureau or printer will match that lower quote if it can. You don't want to have to relearn what a new company can and can't do and vice versa. And if possible, try to let one company handle your entire job. That way, one company controls the quality from beginning to end, and there's no finger pointing if things go bad.

✔ **Get on the Web:** Many service bureaus have Web sites where you can find a listing of services they offer, price lists, file specs, and even downloadable order forms, as shown in Figure 2-1. Larger printers also have Web sites offering general information and online requests for quote applications. Larger printers may provide services such as scanning and film separation output, so be sure to check the Web site for details.

## Using a prepress checklist

In addition to communicating with your printer and service bureau, you need to do some additional work to prepare your file for print. Here is a handy checklist that you can use whenever you're prepping a file for print. Use it to ensure your file is ready and rarin' for problem-free output. Note that this list isn't all inclusive when it comes to prepress; I include tips that pertain to Photoshop only.

✔ **Always transform your images in their native application.** Therefore size, crop, rotate, shear, and reflect art in Photoshop. Transforming images in an illustration or page layout program is very complex and calculation intensive and will cause the RIP (raster image processing, which converts objects to a series of dots/pixels for printing) to take a long time to process the file.

✔ **Ensure that images can first print from Photoshop.** Do this before importing the images into an illustration or page layout program.

✔ **If you're placing Photoshop EPS images into a page layout or illustration program, set the halftone screen frequency in the destination program instead of embedding it in each image in Photoshop.** Or better yet, don't set any halftone screen frequencies in your images and let your service bureau or printer handle setting them in the other program.

✔ **When saving Photoshop images for print purposes, stick to TIFF, EPS, native PSD, or PDF file formats.** If you're unsure of the proper format to use for a specific job, ask your printer or service bureau for recommendations.

✔ **Make sure that you have used the proper color mode.** For example, use CMYK for color separations and RGB for slide output. Again, if you're not sure, ask your printer or service bureau for recommendations.

Book
**X**

Chapter
**2**

**Figure 2-1**

✔ **Create vector shapes and paths efficiently.** Printing vector art involves using intense calculations for every anchor point, and overly complex paths can cause problems during the RIP process. Here are some suggestions:

▶ Use the fewest number of anchor points possible to draw the shape or create the path.

▶ Delete any unnecessary objects or points, even those that are invisible.

▶ Simplify the complexity and number of vector masks and clipping paths.

▶ Set optimum flatness levels for paths, dependent on complexity of the path and output resolution. Use 1–3 for low-resolution printing (300–600 dpi as with laser printers) and 7–10 for complex paths on high-resolution printing devices (1,200 and up as with imagesetters). Or you can leave the flatness setting text box blank. In that case, the default setting for the output device is used, which is usually a safe bet.

✔ **Limit the number of typefaces.** Downloading takes time. Limiting the number of typefaces will also make your document look more sophisticated and polished.

✔ **Make sure that all scans have been scanned at the appropriate dpi.** As a general rule, 2 x line screen (lines per inch or lpi) equals the dpi to use in scanning the images. If you need to resize your image, be sure to scan it at a higher resolution accordingly. For example, if you need it twice as big, scan it at twice the final resolution needed.

✔ **If your image will bleed (extend to the edge of the printed page), take that into account when creating your image.** Note that you need to allow for ⅛ to ¼ of an inch on any side that will bleed to allow for slippages when the paper is cut.

✔ **Always specify colors from a Pantone color swatch chart and then select the color, whether process or spot, in Photoshop.** *Never* trust the way colors look on-screen because of calibration deficiencies and differences between RGB and CMYK color models.

## How to keep your service bureau happy

In addition to the tips provided in the previous sections, I have some additional things you can do to keep the people at your service bureau or printer happy. Be sure to provide your service bureau or printer the following:

✔ Your media for transfer of the files (for example, Zip, CD, and so on) with files and fonts.

✔ A directory of everything on that media (optional but considerate).

✔ Laser proofs (both separations and composite).

✔ Any reflective art that must be digitally or traditionally stripped in (rare these days, but a possibility).

✔ Any order forms required by the service bureau/printer, include any instructions and be specific. It is good to have a written record for your sake and theirs.

---

✔ **Make spot color names consistent.** Make sure that the Photoshop spot color names match those of any programs to which you are importing your image, such as an illustration or page layout program. Otherwise, you may get an additional color separation.

✔ **Print and provide laser prints of your file, both separations (if warranted), and a composite print.** Print all with printer marks — crop marks, registration marks, labels, and so on.

✔ **Provide all fonts used in your file.** Provide both screen and PostScript printer fonts. (***Note:*** Avoid cheapie fonts; you usually get what you pay for. If you want to use them, consider rasterizing them.)

✔ **Choose File⇨Save As for your final save to squeeze down to the smallest file size.** Doing a Save As compresses your file as small as possible.

✔ **Organize your files into folders.** For example, put the image files together in one folder, all the fonts in another, and so on. Practice good file management and organization.

✔ **Communicate any trapping needs to your service bureau or printer.** For color separations, indicate whether you have created the trapping yourself or if you want the service bureau/printer to do it.

## Saving and Printing Vector Data in a Raster File

Photoshop allows you to create vector shapes and vector type with the Pen tools, Shape tools, and Type tools. Technically, the vector shapes are clipping paths that have been applied to a bitmap, or raster, layer. But the clipping path is *still* a vector path, thereby retaining vector qualities. This vector data is resolution independent, which means that it will print at the resolution of the PostScript output device. Photoshop sends the printer separate images for each type and shape layer, which are printed on top of the raster image and clipped by using their vector paths. The edges of the vector path print at the full resolution of the PostScript printer, but the contents, such as the colored pixels or the image pixels within the vector path, print at the resolution of the Photoshop file (all portions of the type are resolution independent). Therefore, type and shapes will always have crisp, hard edges, with curves appearing smooth and never jagged.

### Some file format warnings

If you save your file as an EPS or DCS and reopen the file in Photoshop, Photoshop rasterizes the vector data to pixels. Save the original in the native PSD format.

If you save your layered file as an EPS, Photoshop converts your vector type to clipping paths. Extensive and small type creates complex clipping paths, which can be time consuming and sometimes difficult to print. You can either flatten your file or deselect the Include Vector Data option in the Save as EPS Options dialog box. Either choice rasterizes the type into pixels at the resolution of your image. You may want to consider eliminating the type in your image file and applying it either in a drawing or page layout program where vector type can be retained.

But in order to retain vector designation, make sure that you select the Include Vector Data option in the Print with Preview dialog box when saving the image. Also, the only file formats that will allow you to retain vector data are PSD, PDF, DCS, and EPS. When saving to PDF, DCS, or EPS, be sure to select the Include Vector Data option in their respective Options dialog boxes. All other file formats will rasterize the vector data.

When you print the file, be sure to choose File⇨Print with Preview. Then in the Print with Preview dialog box, select the Show More Options check box, select Choose Output from the pop-up menu, and select the Include Vector Data option.

## Using Photoshop to Rasterize and Print Unruly Vector Art

Now that I have touted the merits of preserving vector art whenever possible, let me also give raster art an attaboy. If you are a user of drawing programs, such as Illustrator, FreeHand, or CorelDraw, you may occasionally run across a complex drawing with a multitude of anchor points that won't print. As a fail-safe, you can rasterize the drawing in Photoshop and print it from there. Sure you lose the crisp, clean vector lines, but at least you get some output. And if you rasterize it at a high enough resolution, you'll probably be okay.

You can rasterize your vector art several ways in Photoshop:

✔ **Choose File⇨Open.** Select your file and click Open. In the Rasterize Generic EPS Format dialog box, shown in Figure 2-2, specify your dimensions, resolution, and color mode. Deselect Constrain Proportions to maintain your aspect ratio. Select Anti-aliased to slightly soften the edges of the artwork and minimize jaggies.

**Figure 2-2**

| Rasterize Generic EPS Format | | |
|---|---|---|
| Image Size: 910K | | OK |
| Width: 1.986 | inches | Cancel |
| Height: 1.736 | inches | |
| Resolution: 300 | pixels/inch | |
| Mode: RGB Color | | |
| ☑ Anti-aliased  ☑ Constrain Proportions | | |

✔ **Create a new Photoshop file at your desired dimension, resolution, and color mode.**
Choose File➪Place, select the vector file (EPS or the latest native Illustrator, FreeHand, or CorelDraw formats), and click OK. The vector artwork comes into the Photoshop image window. If you need to size the image, hold down the Shift key and grab a handle on the corner. When you're finished, press Enter (Return on the Mac). The vector art is rasterized at the resolution of the Photoshop file and resides on a separate layer.

✔ **Drag and drop the vector artwork from the drawing program into Photoshop.** Just drag from one window to the other. The artwork automatically becomes rasterized at the resolution of the Photoshop document. To drag the artwork as paths, press the Ctrl key (⌘ on the Mac) when dragging. You can also use the clipboard method by using the Edit➪Copy and Edit➪Paste commands. For more on the clipboard method, see Chapter 1 in this book.

## Choosing Color Management Print Options

I highly recommend checking out the color management section in Book II, Chapter 3. There I go into great detail on the concept of color spaces, ICC profiles, and so on. Here, I cover the color management options you'll find in the Print with Preview dialog box.

Different output devices operate in different color spaces. Monitors, desktop printers, large format printers, film recorders, offset printers, and so on all have their own unique color space. The color management options enable you to convert the color space of your image while printing. So, for example, if the ICC (color) profile of your image is sRGB, you can choose to have your image's color space converted to the color space of your Epson printer when you print.

Choose File➪Print with Preview to open the Print dialog box, shown in Figure 2-3. Select the Show More Options check box and choose Color Management from the pop-up menu below it.

**Figure 2-3**

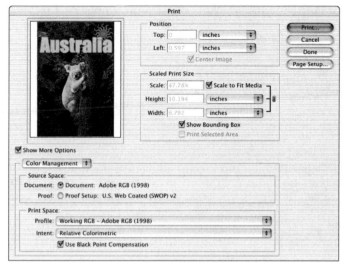

In the Source Space area, choose from these options:

- ✔ **Document:** Uses the color profile of your image.

- ✔ **Proof Setup:** Uses the color profile of the proof you selected in the ViewProof Setup menu. For details on proofs, see Book II, Chapter 3.

In the Print Space area, you have these options:

- ✔ **Profile:** Choose Same as Source to print using the color profile you specified for your Source Space. If you want to print by using the color profile of an output device — for example, an HP or Epson printer — choose that profile from the list.

  Choose PostScript Color Management to print to a PostScript printer (PS level 2 or higher). Photoshop will then instruct the *printer* to manage the color conversion instead of Photoshop.

- ✔ **Intent:** I recommend leaving this at the default setting of Relative Colorimetric and also leaving the Use Black Point Compensation check box deselected — unless, of course, you're a color guru and have a better reason not to.

When you finish making your selections, click Print.

That's all there is to it. If you want more information on printing, check out Book II, Chapter 3.

If all you want to do is print color prints on your desktop printer, I recommend choosing Document for your Source Space and choosing Same as Source for your Print Space. If you have a little time and paper to burn, then print another copy by using your printer's color profile for your Print Space. Do a side-by-side comparison to see which one looks superior. You can also crack the seal on the documentation that came with your printer for any recommendations.

When it comes to color management and printing, experimentation can really pay off. Try different color spaces for both Source and Print Spaces and compare the printouts. You'll even get different results from different types of paper. When you have some free time, get to know your printer and its strengths, shortcomings, and quirks.

## Getting Four-Color Separations

It is necessary to *color separate* your image whenever you plan on printing your image to an offset press. Your image must first be in CMYK color mode (choose Image⇨Mode⇨CMYK Color). Then the composite color image gets digitally separated into the four-color channels — cyan, magenta, yellow, and black — and is output. (These colors are also known as *process colors.*) Sometimes the separation output is onto film, and sometimes, it is output directly to aluminum printing plates. The plates are put on an offset press, paper runs through each of the four inked rollers (cyan first, then magenta, yellow, and finally black), and out comes your composite image.

▼ ▼ ▼ ▼ ▼ ▼ ▼ ▼ ▼ ▼ ▼ ▼ ▼ ▼ ▼ ▼ ▼ ▼ ▼ ▼ ▼ ▼ ▼ ▼ ▼ ▼ ▼ ▼ ▼ ▼ ▼ ▼ ▼ ▼ ▼ ▼ ▼ ▼ ▼ ▼ ▼ ▼ ▼

## Getting laser separations

Before you take your image to a service bureau or printer to get color separations, it is wise to get what are called *laser separations.* Basically, you are color separating your image, not to film or plates, but to paper. If it doesn't separate to paper, most likely it won't to film or plates either. This allows you to then go back and troubleshoot the problem and correct it, rather than paying upwards of $80 to $150 an hour to have the bureau or printer correct it for you. Consider it a cheap insurance policy.

Check out Color Plate 10-1, which illustrates the separations as they would appear in the actual printing process. Here are the steps to print laser separations:

**1.** **Be sure your image mode is CMYK. If it isn't, choose Image⇨Mode⇨CMYK Color.**

I'm assuming your image is a four-color image. But it may also be a grayscale, duotone, tritone, or quadtone image, in which case no conversion to CMYK is necessary. (See Book II, Chapter 2 for more on modes.)

If you're new to converting RGB images to CMYK, don't be surprised if your vibrant colors turn muddy and flat. This is because the *gamut,* a fancy word for range of color, for CMYK is much smaller than it is for RGB, and colors that are out of the CMYK gamut get converted to their closest match. It's a cold, harsh fact that we all have to live with. After the conversion, you have an image with four channels — cyan, magenta, yellow, and black.

**2.** **Choose File⇨Print with Preview. In the Print dialog box, shown in Figure 2-4, select the Show More Options check box and select Color Management from the pop-up menu below it.**

**3.** **Under Source Space, select Document.**

It should say U.S. Web Coated (SWOP) v2.

**4.** **Under Print Space, select Separations from the Profile pop-up menu.**

This option prints each of the channels from the image to a separate plate, or in the case of laser separations, paper.

**5.** **Select Output from the Show More Options pop-up menu. Then select additional options as desired.**

For general print options, see Book I, Chapter 4. For additional options, check out the next section in this chapter.

**6.** **Click the Print button.**

If all goes well, four pieces of paper, one for each of the four CMYK channels, should print, as shown in Figure 2-5. If you're printing a grayscale, duotone, tritone, or quadtone image, you get one to four pieces of paper, one for each color used. If that doesn't happen, something's amiss, and it's time for troubleshooting. Be sure to take these laser separations with you when you hand over your file to the service bureau or printer. They'll be appreciative knowing you took the time to ensure that your file separates are okay.

CONTINUED
▼ ▼ ▼ ▼ ▼

Book
**X**
Chapter
**2**

**Figure 2-4**

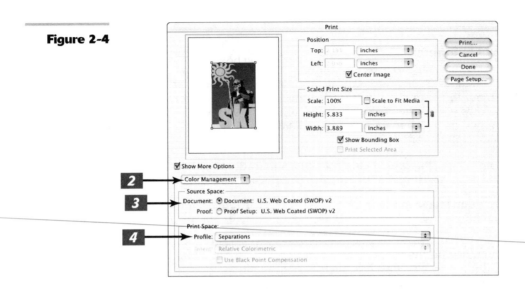

**Figure 2-5**

## Output options in the Print dialog box

The following list details many of the options that are available when you choose Output from the Show More Options pop-up menu in the Print dialog box, as shown in Figure 2-6. This list covers the options that pertain to separations and options that are not covered in Book I, Chapter 4.

- ✔ **Screen:** Click the Screen button to create a custom halftone screen by changing the size, angle, and shape of the halftone dots. I would leave this set to Use Printer's Default Screen. Let the service bureau or printer change it if necessary.

- ✔ **Transfer:** This option allows you to redistribute brightness levels in your image. Again, I wouldn't mess with this setting unless you're a prepress professional.

- ✔ **Interpolation:** This option is available for PostScript Level 2 or later printers to anti-alias low-resolution images by re-sampling. Leave it deselected.

- ✔ **Calibration Bars:** Select this option. It prints an 11-step grayscale bar outside the image area to gauge how accurately the shades are being printed. When printing separations, this option prints a gradient tint bar and color bar.

- ✔ **Registration Marks:** Select this option, which prints crosshair and target marks outside the image area allowing you to line up the four plates or pages.

- ✔ **Corner Crop Marks:** Select this option. It adds crops marks at the corners of the image to indicate where the image should be trimmed.

- ✔ **Center Crop Marks:** Select this option. It adds crop marks at the center of each side of the image to indicate where the image should be trimmed.

- ✔ **Labels:** Select this option to print the filename and channel name on each plate or page.

**Figure 2-6**

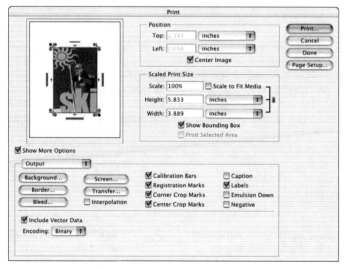

✔ **Emulsion Down:** Leave this option deselected for laser separations. *Emulsion* is the side of the film that is light sensitive. When the service bureau or printer prints the separations to film or plates, it may select this option, which allows the film to be printed with the emulsion side down.

✔ **Negative:** Leave this option deselected for laser separations. When the service bureau or printer prints the separations to film or plates, it may select this option, which prints black as white and white as black, and every other color inverts accordingly.

✔ **Include Vector Data:** Leave this option selected if you have type or vector paths. See the "Saving and Printing Vector Data in a Raster File" section, earlier in this chapter.

✔ **Encoding:** This option specifies the method of encoding used to send the image to the printer. Leave this option at the default of Binary.

Note that if you're printing to a non-PostScript printer, some of these options may not be available. You see a preview of most of these options as you apply them to your file.

# Creating Spot Color Separations

Photoshop allows you to add separate channels for spot colors (see Book 6, Chapter 1, for more on channels), which can then be color separated. Spot, or *custom*, colors are premixed inks manufactured by various ink companies, the most popular in the U.S. being Pantone. Others popular companies include Toyo and Focoltone. A spot color is often used for a logo, type, or small illustration. Spot colors are also used when you need to apply metallic inks or varnishes to your print job. Spot colors can be used instead of, or in addition to, the four process CMYK colors. Usually, it's easier and more convenient to add the spot color graphic — especially if it is type or a vector shape — in another program, such as a drawing program like Illustrator or a page layout program like InDesign. But if the spot color graphic has a Photoshop special effect applied to it or is an integral part of the Photoshop image, then create your spot channel(s) in Photoshop.

If you are delving in to the world of spot colors, I highly recommend that you choose your color from a printed Pantone swatch book, available from www.pantone.com. Because your screen is an RGB device and you're setting up your file for a CMYK output device, the colors you see on-screen do not match the colors that will ultimately be printed on paper and at best are a ballpark match. For accuracy, you must select the colors from the printed swatch book. For more on working with color and output, see Book II, Chapter 3.

▼▼▼▼▼▼▼▼▼▼▼▼▼▼▼▼▼▼▼▼▼▼▼▼▼▼▼▼▼▼▼▼▼▼▼▼▼▼▼▼▼

## Creating a spot channel

Follow these steps to create a spot channel:

*1.* **Create the graphic or type to which you want to apply the spot color on a separate layer.**

*2.* **Press Ctrl+click (⌘+click on the Mac) to select the graphic and then fill it with any solid color and an opacity of 100%.**

**3.** **With your selection active, choose Window⇨Channels, and choose New Spot Channel from the Channels palette pop-up menu.**

A spot color can only be applied to an active selection. It can't just be applied to a layer.

The New Spot Channel dialog box appears, as shown in Figure 2-7.

**4.** **In the Name text box, enter a name for your spot color. In the Ink Characteristics area, click the color swatch.**

I recommend naming it according to the spot color you want to use, such as Pantone 3405 C or PMS 3405 C. PMS stands for Pantone Matching System.

When you click the color swatch, the Color Picker appears.

**Click the Custom button in the Color Picker and select your Pantone color from the Custom Colors dialog box that appears (see Figure 2-7). Then click OK.**

**6.** **In the New Spot Channel dialog box, select a Solidity value between 0% to 100%.**

A value of 100% represents an ink that is completely opaque, such as a metallic ink, which completely covers the inks beneath it. A value of 0% represents a transparent ink, such as a clear varnish. But the solidity value only affects the *screen* view and *composite* prints; it doesn't affect the separations. It can be helpful to see where a "clear" varnish will print.

**Click OK to close the dialog box.**

Your spot channel appears in the Channels palette and is filled in the image as well. I created a spot channel

for my sun graphic and for the Australia type, as shown in Figure 2-8.

In the printing process, spot colors are overprinted on top of the four-color image. That means that the spot color is applied at the end of the printing process and is printed over the other inks. This can sometimes cause lighter spot colors to darken somewhat.

If you need your spot color graphic to *knock out* the underlying image, you should create it in an illustration or page layout program. A knock out is when a hole is left in the four-color image, and the spot ink then fills that hole. It does not print over the other inks.

**8.** **Save the image in the native Photoshop, Photoshop PDF, or Photoshop DCS 2.0 (Desktop Color Separations) formats.**

If the image is being separated directly out of Photoshop, leave it as a PSD or PDF file. If you want to import it into a different program, such as PageMaker, InDesign, or QuarkXPress, you must save it as a DCS file. You also have to go through a few more hoops:

✔ If your image is a duotone, tritone, or quadtone image, you must first convert it to multichannel mode with the Image⇨Mode command.

✔ In the DCS 2.0 Format dialog box, make sure that the Include Halftone Screen and Include Transfer options are not selected.

✔ Import the image into your destination application and set your screen angles (or have your service bureau or printer do it). Let the printer know what spot colors you want for each spot separation.

CONTINUED
▼ ▼▼▼▼▼

Book
**X**
Chapter
**2**

**Figure 2-7**

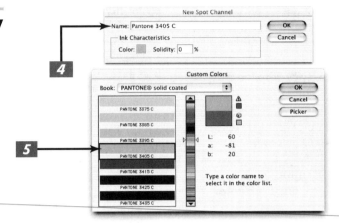

**Figure 2-8**

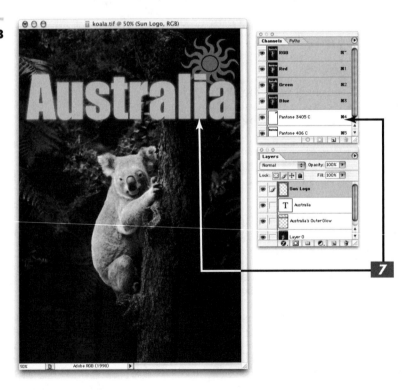

## Converting an alpha channel to a spot channel

If you want to convert an alpha channel to a spot channel, select the alpha channel in the Channels palette and choose Channel Options from the palette options menu. Rename the channel and select Spot Color. Choose a color from the Custom section of the Color Picker. Click OK. Note that all areas containing nonwhite pixels (unselected to partially selected areas) are converted to the spot color. Choose Image➪ Adjustments➪Invert to apply the spot color to the white pixels or selected areas of the alpha channel. For details on alpha channels, see Book VI, Chapter 1.

### Editing a spot channel

After a spot channel is created, you can edit it. Select the channel in the Channels palette and use a painting or editing tool to paint with black, white, or any shade of gray, just as you would with an alpha channel. To change any of the options of the spot channel, double-click the spot channel thumbnail, or select it and choose Channel Options from the palette options menu. Choose a different color or solidity.

You probably won't ever need to do this but to merge a spot channel, select it and choose Merge Spot Channel from the palette options menu. This converts the spot color and divides it among the four process color channels. The spot channel is then deleted, and all layers are flattened in your image. Also the spot color will now print according to the closest match it can reproduce by using process colors. And sometimes this isn't a very good match because CMYK inks can't reproduce the range of colors offered by spot inks.

# Creating Contact Sheets and Picture Packages

The Contact Sheet II and Picture Package features two common tasks that are tedious to perform manually. You can use these features to create documents of *thumbnail* images of groups of files and print multiple copies of a single image on one sheet, much like the picture packages of 5 x 7s and wallet prints you order from school or sports team photographers.

Both facilities make use of the same Photoshop scripting/macro facility called *actions,* as I describe in Book II, Chapter 6. Indeed, if you wanted to take the time, you could create a Photoshop action that performs much the same function as the contact sheet and picture package features. However, creating these actions is a bit tricky, and why would you bother? The programming wizards at Adobe have done all the work for you, while adding some convenient features.

This chapter leads you through creating contact sheets and picture packages.

## Cataloging with Contact Sheets

If you're not steeped in photographic darkroom lore (and fewer of us are, in these digital days), the origin of the term *contact sheet* might be fuzzy to you. A traditional photographic contact sheet is made by placing one or more negatives on a piece of photographic paper and held in tight contact with the paper while a light exposes the light-sensitive surface of the paper. A special frame, or, often, simply a piece of glass is used to mate the negatives and paper for the exposure.

The original purpose of contact sheets, like the one shown in Figure 3-1, was to show the photographer a small image of each picture in a set of negatives so they could be compared, perhaps cropped with a grease pencil right on the contact sheet, and the images to be printed selected. They also made a convenient way of filing away images as a sort of hardcopy catalog.

### Understanding the benefits of Contact Sheet II

Today, we have more sophisticated ways of previewing and cataloging digital images, including many different image cataloging programs, such as Ulead's Album application, which is included with PhotoImpact. One of these is furnished with virtually every digital camera. Even so, Photoshop's Contact Sheet II automated tool has some significant useful features. For one thing, it's free. (Well, almost. It's included with Photoshop.) Also, Contact Sheet II does the following:

- ✔ Prepares Photoshop documents so that you can store them, share them with others in digital form, or print them out for distribution.

- ✔ Works faster than database-type catalog programs that require you to enter keywords to sort and locate images.

- ✔ Creates ad-hoc catalogs adeptly. Just copy the files you want to include to a folder and fire up the Contact Sheet II tool.

- ✔ Allows you to specify the number of rows and columns in your contact sheet, filling a sheet with only a few images (if that's what you want) or packing dozens of them on a single contact sheet.

- ✔ Automatically creates multiple sheets if all the images selected won't fit on a single sheet.

**Figure 3-1**

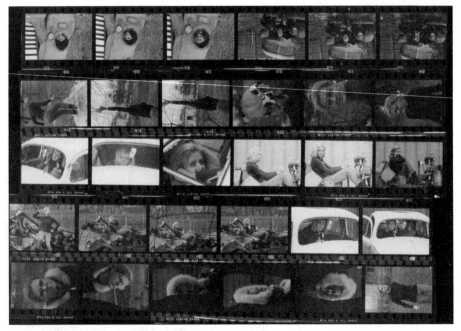

▼▼▼▼▼▼▼▼▼▼▼▼▼▼▼▼▼▼▼▼▼▼▼▼▼▼▼▼▼▼▼▼▼▼▼▼

## Using Contact Sheet II

With Contact Sheet II, you can create contact sheets that have several thumbnail images — small versions of pictures — on a single page. You can print the contact sheets or quickly browse through them paperlessly. To create a contact sheet catalog of your own images, follow these steps:

**1.** Copy all the files you want to include in your contact sheet into a folder on your hard drive.

**2.** Choose File⊅Automate⊅Contact Sheet II from the menu bar.

The Contact Sheet II dialog box appears, shown in Figure 3-2.

**3.** In the Source Folder area, click the Browse button (or the Choose button on the Mac) and navigate to the folder containing the images you want to include.

**4.** Choose the Include All Subfolders option if you want to include images contained inside folders nested within the main folder you select.

In the Document Area, you have several settings that you can use to control the size and type of thumbnail images you create.

**5.** In the Width and Height boxes, enter the dimensions of the contact sheet document.

Choose the default setting of 8 x 10 inches if you plan to print contact sheets on standard-sized paper.

**6.** Adjust the resolutions settings.

A setting of 72 pixels/inch for sheets works well for displaying contact sheets that you plan to print if all you want is a quick-and-dirty look at them. Use a higher resolution if you want a sharper contact sheet.

If you need the thumbnails to have a higher resolution (for example, you want to extract the thumbnails from the contact sheet and paste them into another document; or maybe you're showing the contact sheets to a client and want the individual images to look crisp and clear), you can choose a higher resolution. Also, if you want the thumbnails to be larger (with fewer per page), choose a higher resolution and adjust the number of columns and rows in Step 10.

Check out Book II, Chapter 1; Book X, Chapter 2, for more recommendations on resolution settings.

**7.** Choose a color mode.

RGB works best in most cases. However, if your images happen to be black-and-white photos, you can create smaller, more compact contact sheet files by selecting the Grayscale option.

Check your printer documentation to see which color mode is recommended for printing color images. You'll find more information on color modes in Book II, Chapter 2.

**8.** Click to activate the Flatten All Layers option if you want to create a contact sheet with a single layer in which all images and their captions (if any) are merged.

This option significantly reduces the contact sheet's file size — which is a very good thing if you have several images in the contact sheet. Otherwise, the file can be huge!

CONTINUED
▼ ▼ ▼ ▼ ▼

Book
**X**
Chapter
**3**

If you do not select this option, you'll end up with larger contact sheet files, but you have the additional flexibility of flattening the thumbnails yourself later both with and without captions. Or, you can make certain layers invisible or visible to show or hide some of the images.

You can now start adjusting the layout. A preview window at the right side of the dialog box shows roughly how the contact sheet will be laid out.

**9.** **Select the Across First option to orient the thumbnails in rows. Select the Down First option to orient the layout in columns.**

**10.** **In the Columns and Rows text boxes, enter the number of columns and rows you want the contact sheet to have.**

The more rows and columns you include, the smaller each thumbnail image will be. The maximum size each image can be is shown next to the columns and rows boxes.

If you choose a small number of rows and columns to produce fairly large thumbnails (see Figure 3-3), you

produce an effect much like Picture Package (described later). For example, if you choose 1 Column and 2 Rows, Photoshop creates a contact sheet with only two images, each roughly 4.6 x 5 inches in size.

 If you plan to print such a maxi-thumbnail contact sheet, you'll probably want to choose a higher resolution (such as 144 pixels/inch) to allow sharper thumbnails.

**11.** **Choose the Use Filename as Caption option if you want to be able to identify each image easily.**

You can also select the Font and Font Size from the option lists.

**12.** **Click OK to start Photoshop on its merry way creating your contact sheet.**

Figure 3-4 shows a contact sheet with six rows and five columns.

Photoshop creates as many pages as necessary to include all the selected images according to your specifications. This can take a few minutes, depending on how many images are included.

**Figure 3-2**

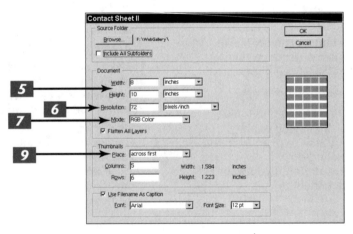

**Figure 3-3**

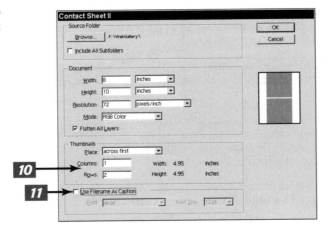

**Figure 3-4**

▼▼▼▼▼▼▼▼▼▼▼▼▼▼▼▼▼▼▼▼▼▼▼▼▼▼▼▼▼▼▼▼▼▼▼▼▼▼▼▼▼▼▼▼

# Pretty as a Picture Package

If you remember having your class pictures taken as a child, or have ever gone to a retailer or professional photographer's studio, then you have probably seen the contact sheets that come from these photo sessions. You purchase one of those special deals and wind up with, say, an 8-x-10-inch print, two 5 x 7s, four 4 x 5s, and eight wallet-sized shots.

The number of pictures you get at each of these dimensions isn't pulled out of a hat. That's the number of images at a given size that can be fit on a single 8-x-10-inch sheet of photographic paper.

Photofinishers have automated printers that can expose those duplicates onto a standard-sized section of a roll of photographic paper, which is then processed and cut apart by mechanized equipment.

Photoshop can perform much the same magic with your own photos, creating image documents that you can then print as your own picture packages. This is much easier and faster than cropping and pasting multiple copies of images onto a single document yourself. Just follow these steps to create your own picture package.

*1.* **Open the picture you want to use for your picture package in Photoshop.**

If you want to create multiple picture packages of different images using the same parameters, copy the images to a single folder.

🎯 You have your choice of using files in a folder, an opened file, or a specific file.

*2.* **Choose File⇨Automate⇨Picture Package from the menu bar.**

The Picture Package dialog box, shown in Figure 3-5, appears.

**3.** **In the Source area, select Frontmost Document to create the picture package from the image that is currently selected in Photoshop, or choose File and then select a single file from your hard disk.**

If you select Folder to create picture packages from all the files in a folder, all the picture packages must use the same parameters that you enter in the Picture Package dialog box.

*4.* **If you'd like to include more than one picture in a picture package, click a sample thumbnail in the preview area of the dialog box.**

A Select an Image File dialog box appears.

*5.* **Find the image you want to substitute and click it.**

The image appears in the thumbnail you chose in Step 4. See Figure 3-6.

*6.* **Repeat to insert other images in the picture package.**

**7.** **Choose a Page Size from the list.**

🎯 In most cases, you'll want to use 8 x 10 inches. You can also select 10 x 16 inches or 11 x 17 inches if you have a printer that can handle larger sheets of paper.

*8.* **Choose a layout.**

You can fill an entire sheet with only one size photo, if you like, such as two 5-x-7-inch pictures or eight 2.5-x-3.5-inch pictures. Or, you can select one of the other combinations, such as two 4 x 5s, two 2.5 x 3.5s, or four 2-x-2.5-inch photos.

*9.* **Adjust the resolution settings.**

The default value is 72 pixels/inch. You'll probably want a higher resolution, such as 288 pixels/inch, if you plan to print the picture package.

Check your printer documentation to see the recommended resolution. Also check out Book II, Chapter 1; Book X, Chapter 2, for more on recommended resolution settings.

**10.** **Choose a color mode.**

RGB is the best choice in most cases. However, if your images happen to be black and white, you can create smaller, more compact picture package files by selecting the Grayscale option. Check your printer documentation.

**11.** Activate the Flatten All Layers option to create a picture package with a single layer in which all images and their labels (if you choose to apply them) are merged.

**12.** If you want to apply some text, you can do it in the Label area of the dialog box.

Most picture packages don't require any sort of text descriptions, but the option is available if you want it.

**13.** If you do want text, select Custom Text and type what you want.

**14.** Adjust the font settings, position the text, and rotate the text to your heart's content. Use the Opacity drop-down list to adjust the type's opacity.

 You can also use text already associated with the file, such as file-name, caption, or copyright information, but you can't add that information in this dialog box. You have to add it directly to the image file itself using File➪File Info.

**15.** Click OK to create the picture package, ready for printing.

**Figure 3-5**

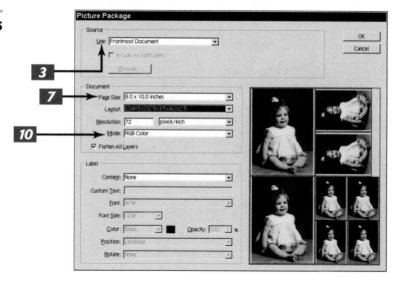

CONTINUED
▼ ▼ ▼ ▼ ▼

Book
**X**
Chapter
**3**

**Figure 3-6**

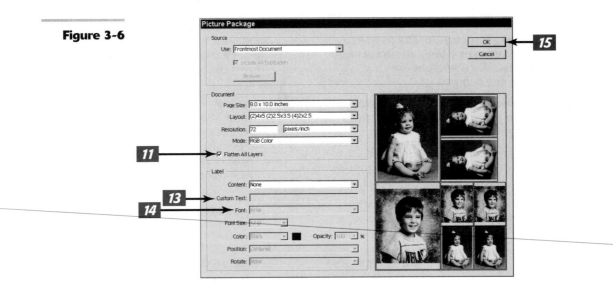

# Working with Digital Cameras and Scanners

Scanners and digital cameras are great tools for Photoshop users, providing basic fodder for your image-editing exploits. Scanners and digital cameras are also great resources that let you grab images quickly when you need them most (say when you're under a deadline and you need to drop that last object into your image or project). This appendix helps you transport images from digital sensor to Photoshop.

## Opening an Image from Your Digital Camera

Although importing digital camera images into Photoshop isn't an open-and-shut case, it needn't be a trial. In fact, it's likely that you have two or three different ways to transport your digital pictures from the camera to your computer's hard disk storage. You can choose whichever method is easiest for you. The following sections list the most common methods.

### Wires and cables: USB, FireWire, and IEEE-1394

Most new cameras are furnished with USB or FireWire connections (or ports) that allow linking directly to a Windows or Mac OS computer. All newer computers are equipped with matching USB ports (either the older USB 1.$x$ or the newer, faster USB 2.0), and some, particularly Macs, also have FireWire connections. If your computer lacks either or both of these ports, you can usually purchase a peripheral card that will add the missing connection. Some combo cards have both USB and FireWire ports, as shown in Figure A-1.

**Figure A-1**

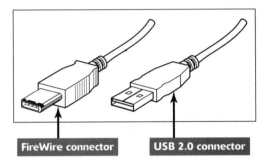

FireWire connector    USB 2.0 connector

## Direct wireless connections

A few digital cameras have included infrared capabilities, which allow wireless transfer of images to printers, laptops, or desktop computers equipped with an IrDA-compatible port. (IrDA stands for Infrared Data Association.) Any growth of IrDA applications is likely to be stunted by the coming availability of Bluetooth technology, which will allow rapid wireless transfer of information between many different devices, ranging from cell phones to remote controls to digital cameras. Although no Bluetooth digital cameras are available as I write this, you can expect to see them on shelves in the near future.

## Removable storage media

Only the least expensive digital cameras use ports and cables as their only means of transferring images. Other cameras use storage media that you can remove from the camera and read directly by using a card reader or some other device in your computer.

Here are the most common removable storage media options:

✔ **SmartMedia or CompactFlash cards:** These solid-state memory cards are thin, convenient, and can save between 8MB and 512MB of data (some cards can hold even more data) at attractive prices (considering the fact that you can use them over and over). Figure A-2 shows a CompactFlash card.

Most digital cameras have a slot for one of these two media; some accept both. To read them with your computer, you'll need a card reader accessory, which is usually a small USB device (often with slots for both types of cards), or an adapter (like a PC card slot found in most laptops and many desktop computers). Some scanners and printers also have memory card slots, which you can use to transfer photos to your computer.

---

### Serial or parallel port cables

Some older cameras used a computer's conventional serial port (such as the one used with a modem, mouse, or serial printer) or the computer's parallel port (used with printers and, sometimes, other devices such as CD-ROM drives). Because such connections are slower and can be more difficult to set up, they have fallen from favor. However, your digital camera may offer this option.

**Figure A-2**

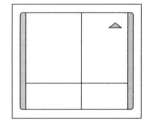

▰ **Memory Sticks:** Sony, which has also offered floppy disks and recordable CDs (CD-Rs) as storage in its digital cameras, uses these memory devices, which are about the size of a stick of chewing gum, for cameras, audio devices, and laptop PCs. The same type of card readers offered for SmartMedia and CompactFlash are available for Memory Sticks.

▰ **Mini–hard disks:** IBM has been a leader in offering Microdrives, tiny hard disks that have storage capacities as high as 1GB or more. Microdrives fit in a CompactFlash slot.

 Because these drives are powered by the device that's using them, not all digital cameras support them. Any laptop or desktop computer that can accept CompactFlash cards can read mini-drives.

▰ **Recordable/rewritable CDs:** Sony's nomadic search for the best digital camera media has led it to this novel solution, which uses 3-inch-diameter recordable CD (CD-R) and rewritable CD (CD-RW) media that can store 158MB of information. While cameras using this option are a little bulkier, mini-CDs are a convenient, permanent (or semi-permanent) storage medium that any computer with a CD-ROM drive can read.

▰ **Floppy disks:** Chalk up another option for Sony, which has offered floppy disk storage for several of its cameras. Floppies are best suited for low-resolution cameras because they only hold 1.44MB — not a whole lot of pictures. On the plus side, you can access these digital photos with any computer equipped with a floppy drive, which includes virtually all Windows PCs (but a dwindling number of Macs, which are no longer furnished with a floppy drive right out of the box).

▰ **PC cards:** Some older cameras used PC cards (formerly PCMCIA cards). If you have one of these, you'll need a laptop with a PC card slot, a desktop computer that has had a PC card slot added, or a PC card reader.

## Other media

A few other types of media have been tried with digital cameras, but have fallen by the way-side as less expensive and more convenient options have become available. These include the Imation SuperDisk (a sort of Iomega Zip disk wannabe) and the Iomega Clik disk. Iomega is constantly coming up with new storage products and new names for their old products (the latest being PocketZip and HipZip), so expect to see at least a few digital cameras with some of these non-standard storage media in the future.

# Transferring Images from Camera to Computer

The following sections summarize what you need to do to transfer images from your camera to your computer.

 You may need to consult your camera's manual to account for any differences from these general instructions.

▼▼▼▼▼▼▼▼▼▼▼▼▼▼▼▼▼▼▼▼▼▼▼▼▼▼▼▼▼▼▼▼

## Making a direct connection

Most digital cameras allow you to transfer images using connectors such as USB, FireWire (IEEE-1394), or a wireless connection. To transfer images by using your camera's direct connection cable, follow these steps:

1. **Make sure that you've installed the software furnished with your camera and then turn the camera off.**

   Some cameras come with stand-alone image transfer programs. Others use miniprograms that run within Photoshop, which you access from the Photoshop Import menu.

2. **Attach the cable to the camera's connector, and then plug the other end into the USB, FireWire, or other port on your computer.**

    If you're taking a lot of digital photographs, you may consider leaving your camera's cord plugged into the computer at all times.

3. **Turn on the camera.**

   Your computer's operating system detects the camera and loads *drivers* (support software) that are needed to connect to the camera. Many cameras also leave a permanent "overseer" program running in the background that detects the presence of the camera and loads the image transfer program automatically.

4. **If necessary, launch the image transfer program.**

   See Figure A-3.

   If your camera uses a stand-alone program, you may find it in your Windows PC Start menu (under Programs), the Mac OS Apple menu, or somewhere in the Mac OS X toolbar. It may also be listed under Photoshop's Import menu.

5. **Use the transfer program's options to copy the images to your hard disk and to delete images from your camera's built-in storage.**

6. **Close the transfer program.**

   You can now load the images directly into Photoshop from your hard disk drive.

    Some digital models place a Camera option in Photoshop's File⇨Open dialog box. If your camera makes itself accessible from Windows Explorer or the Mac Finder, the camera may appear to your operating system as if it were just another device. In that case, you can simply drag and drop files from your camera to your hard disk.

**Figure A-3**

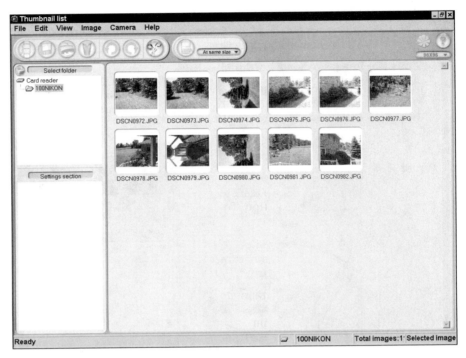

## Transferring from removable storage

The most common removable storage options are cards like SmartMedia and CompactFlash. You may also use Memory Sticks. Whichever removable option you choose to transfer images, just follow these steps:

**1.** **Make sure that you've installed the software your computer needs to support the card reader or other device.**

Newer versions of the Windows and Mac operating systems detect a new device the first time it is plugged in. Your OS may install the support software automatically, or ask for a disk supplied by the device vendor that contains the necessary drivers.

Although you can often access removable storage as if it were another disk drive on your computer (see Figure A-4), many cameras are furnished with transfer programs that streamline the process of copying the files from the media and removing old files.

**2.** **If necessary, install the transfer program separately the first time you use the card reader or other device.**

There may also be a program that runs within Photoshop, which you access from the Photoshop Import menu.

Miniprograms that run within Photoshop are called *plug-ins*.

**3.** **Insert the media into the reader device.**

Your computer detects the media automatically and launches a file transfer program provided by your camera vendor.

CONTINUED

You can also simply open the media from Windows Explorer or the Macintosh Finder just as you do any other storage device.

**4.** **Copy the images to your hard disk.**

Either use the transfer program's options to copy the images to your hard disk and to delete images from

your storage media, or use your operating system's file copying procedures to drag the images to the folders where you want to store them.

**5.** **Send the original copies on the removable media to the Recycle Bin or Trash.**

**Figure A-4**

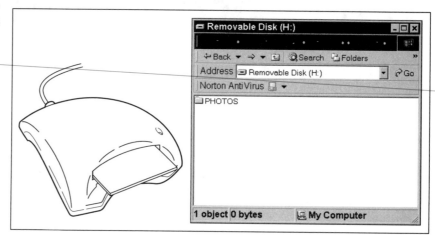

# Preparing to Scan

Sometimes the best way to use Photoshop is not to use it at all! When it comes to using your scanner, you may discover that you can do lots of things when you prepare a scan that will save you hours of work later in Photoshop. To make sure that you're on the right track before you ever slap down an original on the scanner bed, heed the following tips:

✔ **Start with good originals:** A scanner can't capture information that isn't there, so make sure that you're using the best, sharpest original available. If you have a choice between a 4-x-6-inch print and an 8-x-10-inch print, choose the larger size. While there's a point of diminishing returns (a really big print may only show really big grain or dye clumps), a larger original often contains more information.

 Scanning large images (especially at high resolutions) makes the scanning process take longer. Also, bigger image files take up a lot of space. Bigger is better, but only up to a point.

 Always use the sharpest, clearest original. Avoid using faxed or photocopied versions of photos or text.

✔ **Familiarize yourself with your scanner's software:** Many corrections that you can make in Photoshop you can make in the scanner instead. Your scanner can often better perform some tasks (such as adjusting for brightness/contrast, some color correction, and scaling) because the scanner is working with the "original" information.

Make your major adjustments with the scanner, and then use Photoshop to fine-tune your results.

✔ **Set up your scanner properly:** If this is the first time you're using your scanner, you need to make sure that you've set it up properly. Installation usually involves two steps:

▸ Adding the support software or drivers needed to let your computer talk to the scanner

▸ Installing the acquisition software that performs the actual image capture

✔ **Follow the vendor's instructions carefully:** Some vendors ask you to install the scanner's software before plugging in the scanner. Others use a setup procedure that installs the scanner files after the computer has already recognized the scanner and configured its support software. Doing these steps in the wrong order won't hurt anything, but may waste some of your time when you have to do them over.

✔ **Perform some maintenance:** Make sure that your scanner glass is clean. You'd be surprised how sharp almost invisible dust spots on the glass can be when scanned. Follow the scanner vendor's instructions for cleaning the glass, and dry it thoroughly before positioning an original. Color prints, in particular, contain dyes that can be harmed by wetness or the chemicals in glass cleaners.

# Image Scanning Essentials

After you've properly prepared your scanner, set up the software, and so on (see the preceding section), you're ready to scan your image.

## Image scanning options

As with digital cameras, you may have some choices in your method for acquiring an image. Indeed, some scanners have three or four different options for grabbing pixels. Here are some of the most common:

✔ **One-touch panel:** Most scanners these days have one-touch keys that you can use to automatically scan an image to a particular destination, such as an image editor (like Photoshop), a fax or e-mail program, or directly to your printer (in "photocopier" mode). Press the right button, and you're off. Frequently, this action simultaneously launches a one-touch panel program on your computer, with limited options that save you the trouble of manually making choices. Use this stand-alone mode when you're in a hurry and don't need a lot of control over your scan.

✔ **Simplified interface:** Many scanners offer a simplified interface with only a few controls, such as scan area selection, scaling, resolution, and perhaps some brightness/ contrast controls. These interfaces are great for beginners, and often are available both as a stand-alone program and as a choice within the Photoshop Import menu.

✔ **All-business interface:** A more advanced interface is often available with lots of controls, zoomed previews, complex brightness/contrast features, color correction features, and other options. Available as stand-alone programs, these interfaces make good day-to-day choices for use within Photoshop and are accessible from the Import menu.

✔ **Graphics pro interface:** (See Figure A-5.) A few more-expensive scanners have an interface that graphics professionals will love, including niceties such as mini-*densitometer* features, extensive correction of color and tonal curves, and other sophisticated options. If you need this choice, you'll know it, and you won't want to live without it.

**Figure A-5**

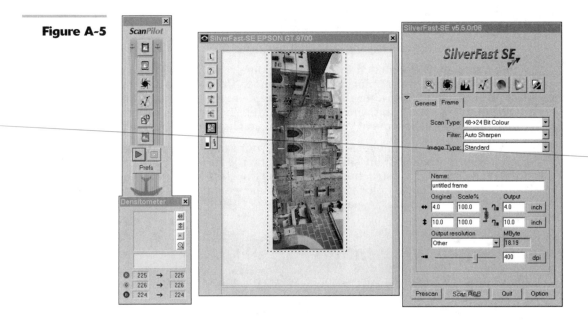

## Scanning an image

To grab your image, follow these steps:

1. **Launch your scanner's acquisition software, either as a stand-alone program or, preferably, from within Photoshop by choosing File⇨Import.**

   Under File⇨Import, you can usually find one or more scanner interface choices.

2. **Place the original face down on the scanner glass.**

   Make sure that the image is oriented square with the guide marks at the top, bottom, or sides of the scanner.

   If the original is small, place it in the center of the scanner where the light tends to be more even, taking extra care to make sure it's lined up square.

3. **Click the Prescan or Preview button in the software to grab a preview look at the original.**

   You may need to choose whether your original is line art, grayscale, or full color, or the scanner may identify the type for you automatically.

4. **Set the scan boundaries.**

   Your software may preselect the area for the final scan, or you may want to use its selection tools to set the scan boundaries yourself.

**5.** **Apply any of the correction, sizing, or scaling controls you want to use.**

Follow the vendor's instructions carefully.

**6.** **Choose a destination for the scan (printer, e-mail, image editor) if appropriate and/or select a resolution.**

Resolution is the number of samples per inch, often referred to as *pixels per inch* (ppi) or *dots per inch* (dpi) with less-than-perfect accuracy.

**7.** **Click the Scan button to acquire the image.**

**8.** **Save the image under an appropriate name.**

# Mastering the Controls

Even the most simple scanner interfaces may have a bewildering array of controls for the beginner. Your first step should be to read the manual furnished with your scanner, whether it's a printed booklet or a glorified Help system copied to your hard disk. Scan the text until you understand the following controls:

- **Brightness/Contrast:** An adjustment for the relative darkness of an image and the number of tones available. (See also Book VIII, Chapter 1.)

- **Gamma:** A control that allows you to compensate for the tendency of devices like computer displays and scanners to represent tones in a non-linear way. You can even out bumps with the gamma control.

- **Color Correction:** Controls that let you keep your color accurate. (See also Book VIII, Chapter 1.)

- **Bit Depth Selection:** An adjustment for the number of colors or tones captured by a scan. Black-and-white images may be captured using 8 bits of information (256 different gray tones), while color images are captured using at least 24 bits of data (16.8 million colors).

- **White Point and Black Point Adjustments:** These controls let you tell the scanner which parts of your subject are the brightest and darkest areas, respectively, that contain detail.

- **Histograms:** These are charts that show you how many tones at each brightness level appear in an image. You can use them as tools for adjusting brightness and contrast. (See also Book VIII, Chapter 1.)

- **Sharpening:** Scanners can presharpen images for you, although in most cases it's more productive to carry out this step in Photoshop. (See also Book VII, Chapter 1.)

- **Descreening:** Scanners can remove halftone screens with some success, but you gain flexibility when you do this in Photoshop. (See also Book VII, Chapter 1.)

- **ICC Profile Management:** This control lets you specify the color characteristics of your devices. (See also Book II, Chapter 3.)

- **Resolution:** This is one of the most important controls, as well as the one that is most often mishandled by scanning neophytes. *Resolution* is the amount of image detail captured by the scanner, measured in *samples per inch* (spi), but usually (and inaccurately) referred to as *pixels per inch* (ppi) or *dots per inch* (dpi).

Surprisingly, with resolution more is not always better. Use too high a setting, and you end up with needlessly large file sizes. Use too low a setting, and you wind up with not enough detail. Although Photoshop allows you to reduce the size of large images (through a process called *resampling*), you'll always lose a little (or a lot) of quality when you do this. Using the correct resolution for your applications, from Web display to desktop printing to professional color reproduction, is essential to Photoshop success. Check out Book II, Chapter 1; Book IX, Chapter 2; and Book X, Chapter 2, for more information.

## Cleaning Up Your Digital Image

After you import your digital photo and load it into Photoshop, you'll probably want to perform some simple clean-up tasks. In Table A-1, I show you what you need to do and where in this book you'll find instructions on how to perform these tasks.

 Making even your initial changes on a *copy* of the original is always a good idea so that you can return to the original photo if you change your mind or decide to make some different changes.

Digital-camera photos are subject to variations in lighting conditions, whereas scanners always use the same light source that changes only very slowly as the scanner ages. Digital-camera pictures are sometimes high in contrast or lack sharpness, two defects attributable to their sensors. Scanners, on the other hand, are subject to the vagaries of your original (bad high-contrast, off-color originals produce bad scans) but are flexible in terms of how much contrast is applied or resolution brought to bear for a given scan.

 You can also soften grain and minimize dust and scratches with several of the Photoshop blurring effects, including the amazing Dust & Scratches filter that looks specifically for anomalous shapes that may be photo dust bunnies in disguise. Read about filters and restoration in Books VII and VIII.

**TABLE A-1: SIMPLE IMAGE CLEAN-UP TASKS**

| Image Flaw | Solution | Cross-Reference |
| --- | --- | --- |
| Color looks funny because the picture was taken using a bad light source or under less-than-optimal conditions (indoors or late in the day). | Balance your color. | Book VIII, Chapter 1 |
| The image looks too bright, too dark, or has too much contrast. | Adjust tones. | Book VIII, Chapters 1 and 2 |
| There are dust or scratches on your image. | Use blurring or Dust & Scratches filter. | Book VII, Chapter 1 |
| Your image has too much extraneous picture around one or more edges. | Crop the image. | Book II, Chapter 1 |
| Image is too blurry, or objectionably sharp in some areas. | Use sharpening and blurring filters and tools. | Book VIII, Chapter 2 and Book VII, Chapter 1 |
| Subjects have bright red eyes. | Work with red-eye reducing techniques. | Book IV, Chapter 1 |

# A Visual Reference of Photoshop Tools

If you've already accessed the Tool palette, or, as most Photoshop users call it, the Toolbox, then you know how daunting it seems. If you haven't had a chance to open up the Tool palette, all you need to do is choose Window⇨Tools.

The Toolbox is divided into three basic sections — the tools, the color swatches, and the icons for masking modes and viewing options, which I cover in Book I. In this appendix, I created a visual reference that divides the tools logically by activity.

As you maneuver through Photoshop (and this book), you can always flip to Appendix B and get information at a glance. You can find

✔ The button that works with each tool

✔ An example of how each tool works

✔ The keyboard shortcut for each tool

✔ A cross-reference to the book and chapter that covers the tool in detail

To select a tool, simply point and click. Or use keyboard shortcuts. For example, to select the Move tool, press V. To select the Brush tool, press B. And to select the Pencil tool, which shares the flyout menu with the Brush tool, press Shift+B.

As a general rule, you can access a hidden tool by pressing Shift along with the keyboard letter of the visible tool. You can also (usually) Alt+click (Option+click on the Mac) a tool to cycle through all the tools hidden beneath it. Some of the tools on the Marquee and Pen flyout menus aren't accessible using this method.

## Selection Tools

**Left:** *Rectangular Marquee tool* (M) makes a rectangular selection. Book III, Chapter 1.
**Right:** *Elliptical Marquee tool* (Shift+M) makes an elliptical selection. Book III, Chapter 1.

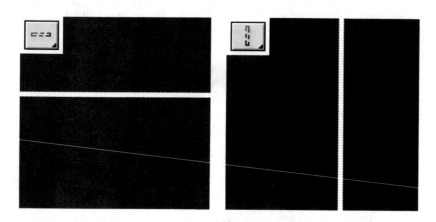

**Left:** *Single Row Marquee tool* (None) makes a selection of a single row of pixels. Book III, Chapter 1. **Right:** *Single Column Marquee tool* (None) makes a selection of a single column of pixels. Book III, Chapter 1.

**Left:** *Lasso tool* (L) makes a freeform selection. Book III, Chapter 1. **Right:** *Polygon Lasso tool* (Shift+L) makes a straight-sided selection. Book III, Chapter 1.

**Left:** *Magnetic Lasso tool* (Shift+L) makes a selection by magnetically snapping to the edge of an element. Book III, Chapter 1. **Right:** *Magic Wand tool* (W) makes a selection by selecting similarly colored pixels within a specified range. Book III, Chapter 1.

**Left:** *Move tool* (V) moves selections, layers, and guides. Book III, Chapter 3 (selections); Book V, Chapter 1 (layers); Book I, Chapter 5 (guides). **Right:** *Crop tool* (C) trims images. Book II, Chapter 1.

## Path Tools

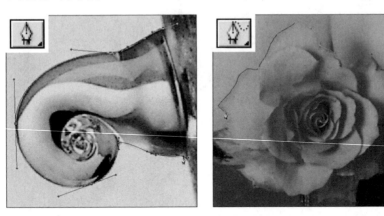

**Left:** *Pen tool* (P) makes a path consisting of anchor points and curved and straight segments. Book III, Chapter 2. **Right:** *Freeform Pen tool* (Shift+P) makes a path consisting of anchor points and curved and straight segments. It's more automated than the Pen tool. Book III, Chapter 2.

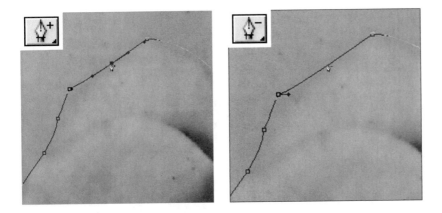

**Left:** *Add Anchor Point tool* (None) adds anchor points to a path. Book III, Chapter 2.
**Right:** *Delete Anchor Point tool* (None) deletes anchor points to a path. Book III, Chapter 2.

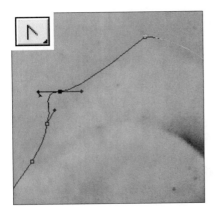

*Convert Point tool* (None) converts a smooth point to a corner point and vice versa. Book III, Chapter 2.

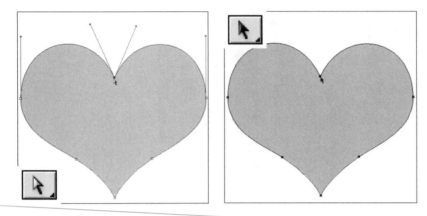

**Left:** *Direct Selection tool* (Shift+A) selects the various components of paths, including those comprising shapes. Book III, Chapter 2 (paths); Book IV, Chapter 2 (shapes). **Right:** *Path Selection tool* (A) selects paths, including those comprising shapes. Book III, Chapter 2 (paths); Book IV, Chapter 2 (shapes).

## Painting Tools

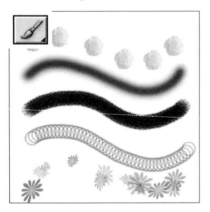
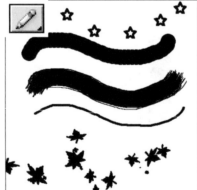

**Left:** *Brush tool* (B) paints with strokes by using a variety of attributes. Book IV, Chapter 1. **Right:** *Pencil tool* (Shift+B) paints with a hard-edged stroke. Book IV, Chapter 1.

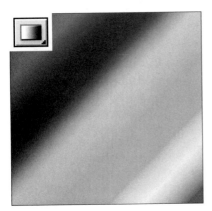 

**Left:** *Gradient tool* (G) creates a blend between two or more colors in a linear, radial, angled, reflected, or diamond pattern. Book IV, Chapter 3. **Right:** *Paint Bucket tool* (Shift+G) fills similarly colored pixels with color. Book IV, Chapter 3.

**Left:** *Art History Brush tool* (Shift+Y) paints with artistic strokes that create a water-color-like effect, using a selected state or snapshot from the History palette. Book II, Chapter 4. **Right:** *Eraser tool* (E) erases pixels. Or with the Erase to History option selected, restores the image to a source state in the History palette. Book VI, Chapter 2 (eraser); Book II, Chapter 4 (history).

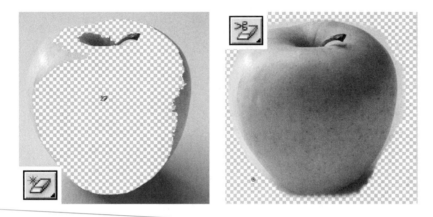

**Left:** *Magic Eraser tool* (Shift+E) erases similarly colored pixels. Book VI, Chapter 2.
**Right:** *Background Eraser tool* (Shift+E) erases the background pixels by detecting the edge between the foreground element and the background. Book VI, Chapter 2.

## Cloning and Retouching Tools

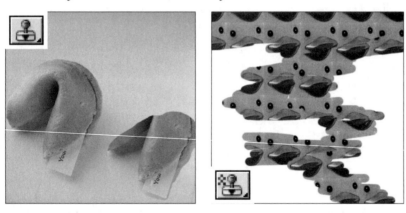

**Left:** *Clone Stamp tool* (S) paints with sampled pixels. Book VIII, Chapter 3. **Right:** *Pattern Stamp tool* (Shift+S) paints with a preset or custom pattern. Book VIII, Chapter 3.

**Left:** *History Brush tool* (Y) allows you to restore the image to a source state in the History palette by painting with a brush. Book II, Chapter 4. **Right:** *Healing Brush tool* (J) paints with sampled pixels to repair flaws in an image. Book VIII, Chapter 3.

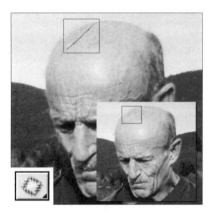

*Patch tool* (Shift+J) repairs flaws on a selected portion of an image by covering the area with sampled pixels. Book VIII, Chapter 3.

## Type Tools

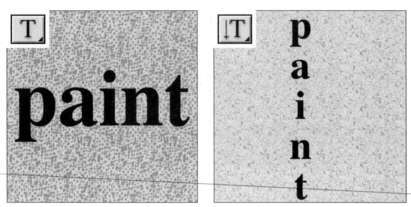

**Left:** *Horizontal Type tool* (T) creates type horizontally across the canvas. Book IV, Chapter 4.
**Right:** *Vertical Type tool* (Shift+T) creates type vertically across the canvas. Book IV, Chapter 4.

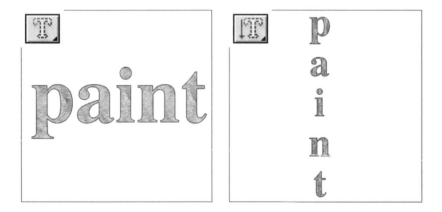

**Left:** *Horizontal Type Mask tool* (Shift+T) creates a horizontal selection marquee from the type. Book IV, Chapter 5. **Right:** *Vertical Type Mask tool* (Shift+T) creates a vertical selection marquee from the type. Book IV, Chapter 5.

## *Focus and Toning Tools*

**Left:** *Blur tool* (R) blurs pixels by decreasing the contrast between pixels. Book VIII, Chapter 2.
**Right:** *Sharpen tool* (Shift+R) sharpens pixels by increasing the contrast between pixels. Book VIII, Chapter 2.

**Left:** *Smudge tool* (Shift+R) smudges (smears) pixels in an image. Book VIII, Chapter 2.
**Right:** *Dodge tool* (O) lightens pixels in an image. Book VIII, Chapter 2.

**Left:** *Burn tool* (Shift+O) darkens pixels in an image. Book VIII, Chapter 2. **Right:** *Sponge tool* (Shift+O) saturates or desaturates color in an image. Book VIII, Chapter 2.

## Shape Tools

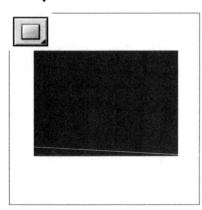

**Left:** *Rectangle tool* (U) creates a vector rectangle filled with the foreground color. Book IV, Chapter 2. **Right:** *Rounded Rectangle tool* (Shift+U) creates a vector, rounded rectangle filled with the foreground color. Book IV, Chapter 2.

**Left:** *Ellipse tool* (Shift+U) creates a vector ellipse filled with the foreground color. Book IV, Chapter 2. **Right:** *Polygon tool* (Shift+U) creates a vector polygon filled with the foreground color. Book IV, Chapter 2.

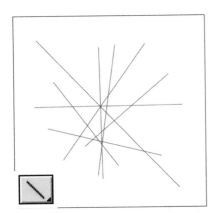 

**Left:** *Line tool* (Shift+U) creates a foreground colored line of specified thickness. Book IV, Chapter 2. **Right:** *Custom Shape tool* (Shift+U) creates a vector shape selected from a custom shape library and fills it with the foreground color. Book IV, Chapter 2.

# Viewing, Navigating, Sampling, and Annotating Tools

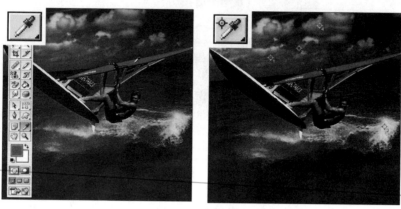

**Left:** *Eyedropper tool* (I) samples a color in your image and makes it the foreground color. Book II, Chapter 3. **Right:** *Color Sampler tool* (Shift+I) samples and evaluates up to four colors in your image. Book II, Chapter 3.

**Left:** *Measure tool* (Shift+I) measures distances and angles on your canvas. Book I, Chapter 5. **Right:** *Zoom tool* (Z) zooms you into or out of your image. Book I, Chapter 5.

**Left:** *Hand tool* (H) moves your image within the window. Book I, Chapter 5. **Right:** *Note tool* (N) creates a digital note that can be attached to your canvas. Book II, Chapter 5.

*Audio Annotation tool* (Shift+N) creates an audio annotation that is attached to your canvas and can be played back. Book II, Chapter 5.

## Web Tools

**Left:** *Slice tool* (K) creates slices (rectangular sections of an image used for display on the Web). Book IX, Chapter 3. **Right:** *Slice Select tool* (Shift+K) selects slices. Book IX, Chapter 3.

# *Index*

## Numbers

## G

# H

## S

# W

# FOR DUMMIES®

## The easy way to get more done and have more fun

## PERSONAL FINANCE

0-7645-5231-7

0-7645-2431-3

0-7645-5331-3

**Also available:**

Estate Planning For Dummies
(0-7645-5501-4)
401(k)s For Dummies
(0-7645-5468-9)
Frugal Living For Dummies
(0-7645-5403-4)
Microsoft Money "X" For Dummies
(0-7645-1689-2)
Mutual Funds For Dummies
(0-7645-5329-1)

Personal Bankruptcy For Dummies
(0-7645-5498-0)
Quicken "X" For Dummies
(0-7645-1666-3)
Stock Investing For Dummies
(0-7645-5411-5)
Taxes For Dummies 2003
(0-7645-5475-1)

## BUSINESS & CAREERS

0-7645-5314-3

0-7645-5307-0

0-7645-5471-9

**Also available:**

Business Plans Kit For Dummies
(0-7645-5365-8)
Consulting For Dummies
(0-7645-5034-9)
Cool Careers For Dummies
(0-7645-5345-3)
Human Resources Kit For Dummies
(0-7645-5131-0)
Managing For Dummies
(1-5688-4858-7)

QuickBooks All-in-One Desk Reference For Dummies
(0-7645-1963-8)
Selling For Dummies
(0-7645-5363-1)
Small Business Kit For Dummies
(0-7645-5093-4)
Starting an eBay Business For Dummies
(0-7645-1547-0)

## HEALTH, SPORTS & FITNESS

0-7645-5167-1

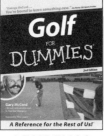

0-7645-5146-9

0-7645-5154-X

**Also available:**

Controlling Cholesterol For Dummies
(0-7645-5440-9)
Dieting For Dummies
(0-7645-5126-4)
High Blood Pressure For Dummies
(0-7645-5424-7)
Martial Arts For Dummies
(0-7645-5358-5)
Menopause For Dummies
(0-7645-5458-1)

Nutrition For Dummies
(0-7645-5180-9)
Power Yoga For Dummies
(0-7645-5342-9)
Thyroid For Dummies
(0-7645-5385-2)
Weight Training For Dummies
(0-7645-5168-X)
Yoga For Dummies
(0-7645-5117-5)

**Available wherever books are sold.**
Go to www.dummies.com or call 1-877-762-2974 to order direct.

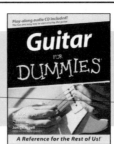

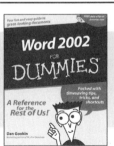

FOR
# DUMMIES®

**Helping you expand your horizons and realize your potentia**

## INTERNET

**0-7645-0894-6**

**0-7645-1659-0**

**0-7645-1642-6**

**Also available:**

America Online 7.0 For Dummies
(0-7645-1624-8)

Genealogy Online For Dummies
(0-7645-0807-5)

The Internet All-in-One Desk Reference For Dummies
(0-7645-1659-0)

Internet Explorer 6 For Dummies
(0-7645-1344-3)

The Internet For Dummie Quick Reference
(0-7645-1645-0)

Internet Privacy For Dum
(0-7645-0846-6)

Researching Online For Dummies
(0-7645-0546-7)

Starting an Online Busine For Dummies
(0-7645-1655-8)

## DIGITAL MEDIA

**0-7645-1664-7**

**0-7645-1675-2**

**0-7645-0806-7**

**Also available:**

CD and DVD Recording For Dummies
(0-7645-1627-2)

Digital Photography All-in-One Desk Reference For Dummies
(0-7645-1800-3)

Digital Photography For Dummies Quick Reference
(0-7645-0750-8)

Home Recording for Musicians For Dummies
(0-7645-1634-5)

MP3 For Dummies
(0-7645-0858-X)

Paint Shop Pro "X" For Dummies
(0-7645-2440-2)

Photo Retouching & Restoration For Dummies
(0-7645-1662-0)

Scanners For Dummies
(0-7645-0783-4)

## GRAPHICS

**0-7645-0817-2**

**0-7645-1651-5**

**0-7645-0895-4**

**Also available:**

Adobe Acrobat 5 PDF For Dummies
(0-7645-1652-3)

Fireworks 4 For Dummies
(0-7645-0804-0)

Illustrator 10 For Dummies
(0-7645-3636-2)

QuarkXPress 5 For Dumn
(0-7645-0643-9)

Visio 2000 For Dummies
(0-7645-0635-8)

**Available wherever books are sold. Go to www.dummies.com or call 1-877-762-2974 to order direct.**

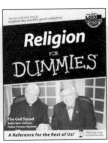

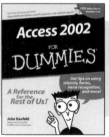